T0350831

REAL ESTATE DEVELOPMENT

PRINCIPLES AND PROCESS

FIFTH EDITION

Mike E. Miles
Laurence M. Netherton
Adrienne Schmitz

ABOUT THE URBAN LAND INSTITUTE

The mission of the Urban Land Institute is to provide leadership in the responsible use of land and in creating and sustaining thriving communities worldwide. ULI is committed to

- Bringing together leaders from across the fields of real estate and land use policy to exchange best practices and serve community needs;
- Fostering collaboration within and beyond ULI's membership through mentoring, dialogue, and problem solving;
- Exploring issues of urbanization, conservation, regeneration, land use, capital formation, and sustainable development;
- Advancing land use policies and design practices that respect the uniqueness of both built and natural environments;

- Sharing knowledge through education, applied research, publishing, and electronic media; and
- Sustaining a diverse global network of local practice and advisory efforts that address current and future challenges.

Established in 1936, the Institute today has more than 34,000 members representing the entire spectrum of the land use and development disciplines. ULI relies heavily on the experience of its members. It is through member involvement and information resources that ULI has been able to set standards of excellence in development practice. The Institute has long been recognized as one of the world's most respected and widely quoted sources of objective information on urban planning, growth, and development.

Library of Congress Control Number: 2015940940

ISBN: 978-0-87420-343-1

ABOUT THE AUTHORS

Mike E. Miles, PhD, is the PLUS portfolio manager for Guggenheim Real Estate. Before forming Guggenheim Real Estate, Miles served as portfolio manager for the Fidelity Real Estate Asset Manager, a series of institutional investment vehicles combining public securities with direct real estate ownership. Before joining Fidelity, he was executive vice president of the Prudential Realty Group and managing director of Prudential Real Estate Advisors. Miles also served as vice president of finance for Albert Investment Corporation, a real estate development firm. He was Foundation Professor of real estate at the University of North Carolina at Chapel Hill. Miles is a past president of the National Council of Real Estate Investment Fiduciaries and the American Real Estate and Urban Economics Association. He has received two of the real estate investment industry's most prestigious awards: the Robert Toigo Award for leadership in real estate portfolio management from *Institutional Real Estate* and the Graaskamp Award for contributions to real estate research from the Pension Real Estate Association. He was also editor of Institutional Investor's *Real Estate Finance* for ten years. He is a graduate of Washington & Lee University and holds an MBA from Stanford University and a PhD from the University of Texas.

Laurence M. Netherton is a 40-year real estate investment and development veteran based in Newport Beach, California. Since 1981, he has been engaged in the acquisition, entitlement, and development of infill and mixed-use land projects and master-planned communities. In the 1970s, Netherton worked in underwriting, syndication, and asset management for limited partnerships holding tax-sheltered, government-assisted multifamily housing projects, and later in financial restructuring, condominium conversions, and single-family development for a broad portfolio of properties throughout the Midwest and East Coast. Netherton is a graduate of the University of Washington in Seattle, where he received his BA in urban planning, an MA in urban planning, and an MBA. For six years he taught land planning in a certificate program at the University of California, Irvine. He is past chair of ULI Orange County and a member of the Community Development Council, and has served on a variety of ULI national committees.

Adrienne Schmitz is senior director of publications at the Urban Land Institute and has written, edited, and served as project manager for many publications. Schmitz was the primary author of *Resort Development* (2008), *Creating Walkable Places* (2005), *The Residential Development Handbook* (2004), *The New Shape of Suburbia* (2003), *Real Estate Market Analysis* (2001), and *Multifamily Housing Development Handbook* (2000). She was coauthor of *Real Estate Market Analysis: Methods and Case Studies* (2009) and editor of *Urban Real Estate Investment: A New Era of Opportunity* (2015), *Pedestrian- and Transit-Oriented Design* (2013), *Professional Real Estate Development: The ULI Guide to the Business* (2012), *Finance for Real Estate Development* (2011), and *Regenerating Older Suburbs* (2007). Before joining ULI, Schmitz was a market analyst, consulting with real estate developers and homebuilders. She holds an MA in urban planning from the University of Virginia.

Contributors

PREVIOUS EDITION

Content from previous editions of this text formed the foundation for the fifth edition. The authors thank previous authors for their significant contributions to this endeavor.

Gayle L. Berens
Senior Vice President, Education and
Advisory Group
Urban Land Institute
Washington, D.C.

Mark J. Eppli
Interim Dean of Business Administration
Marquette University
Milwaukee, Wisconsin

Marc A. Weiss
Chairman and CEO
Global Urban Development
Washington, D.C.

CONTRIBUTING AUTHORS (FIFTH EDITION)

John Brady
Guggenheim Real Estate (retired)
San Francisco, California

Roger S. Pratt
Prudential Real Estate (retired)
Newark, New Jersey

Alison Johnson
Program Manager
Urban Land Institute
Washington, D.C.

Tom Heffner, Garrett Jacobs, Tyler Jones, Ed Miles, Robert Speir, and Justin Trowbridge
University of North Carolina
Chapel Hill, North Carolina

REVIEWERS

John W. Gibb
Managing Director
Jones Lang LaSalle Americas Inc.
Washington, D.C.

David L. Leininger
Executive Vice President, CFO
DART
Dallas, Texas

Margaret McFarland
Director
Colvin Institute of Real Estate Development
University of Maryland
College Park, Maryland

Nelson Migdal
Greenburg Traurig LLP
Washington, D.C.

Ed Paska
Managing Partner
Eden Development LLC
Chantilly, Virginia

R. Matthew Shannon
Managing Director
Urbanus LLC
Irvine, California

PROJECT STAFF

Kathleen B. Carey
Executive Vice President/Chief Content Officer

Dean Schwanke
Senior Vice President, Case Studies and Publications

James Mulligan
Senior Editor

Lise Lingo, Publications Professionals LLC
Manuscript Editor

Betsy Van Buskirk
Creative Director

Deanna Pineda, Muse Advertising Design
Graphic Designer

Craig Chapman
Senior Director, Publishing Operations

Camille Galdes
Senior Research Associate

Joan Campbell
Manager, Information Center

Mark Federman
Researcher

Project Manager

Adrienne Schmitz
Senior Director, Publications

This book was funded in part by Nancy Voorhees in memory of her father, Alan M. Voorhees, a pioneer in the field of urban transportation planning who recognized the important link between land use and transportation. Mr. Voorhees is profiled in chapter 6 of this text.

This book is dedicated to the memory of Jim Graaskamp—dynamic, insightful, slightly opinionated, and one helluva guy.

Preface

The impetus for publishing this new edition remains the same as it was for the first edition: to provide future decision makers a complete look at the complex decision-making environment surrounding real estate development. The inherently interdisciplinary character of the real estate development process and its entrepreneurial nature give development a special status and create a decision-making environment best suited to a well-rounded, disciplined, thick-skinned person. Though many activities related to development now take place under the corporate or institutional umbrella, the activities themselves still bear a distinctive entrepreneurial stamp.

Real estate development is a dynamic discipline, with rapid changes occurring in construction, marketing, finance, and the regulatory environment. The ever-changing, multidisciplinary nature of the field makes development an exciting and challenging endeavor. Collectively, development decisions have an enormous effect on society. Development creates the built environment; produces shelter and places of work and commerce; contributes a significant portion of global investment; and helps determine how we will live in the future. Increasingly, development

designs and building materials aim to minimize humankind's footprint on the environment.

This text is intended to be useful to present and future developers, city planners, legislators, regulators, corporate real estate officers, land planners, lawyers specializing in real estate or municipal law, architects, engineers, building contractors, lenders, market analysts, leasing agents and brokers, and property owners.

The first edition was published in 1991. In the next three editions, we expanded, corrected, and updated the material. In doing so, the book gained nearly 200 pages. In this fifth edition, we rewrote significant portions, deleting redundancies and consolidating and streamlining as we updated content to reflect changes and trends in the real estate development industry. This new edition is therefore slimmer, more concise, and—we believe—easier to read. We have retained the basic framework of the first edition: the eight-stage model of real estate development, first elaborated by Dr. Miles. With an understanding of this process firmly in hand, the reader can proceed to do the additional detailed study of product types, local markets, finance, and the regulatory processes necessary to be a successful developer.

The book is divided into seven parts. Part 1, Introduction, lays out the general framework of the eight stages of the development process. Anticipating the future is important, and learning from the past is one aspect of projecting how the future will unfold. Thus, part 2, History, begins with the Colonial era in the United States, detailing the interplay of economics and politics and their influence on real estate development, with many of the themes that emerge still being relevant today. Part 3, The Public Interest, lays out the public's role in zoning, land use policy, impact fees, and infrastructure. New material examines how grass-roots mobilization has affected development. In part 4, Ideas, the book moves from this background to explain how ideas are generated for development projects. Part 5, Financing the Project, is core to the book and integral to decision making in real estate development. Part 6, Proving the Concept, explains how the initial concept is refined through rigorous feasibility analysis. Finally, Part 7, Making It Happen, looks at decision making once construction is initiated. It then moves through the related marketing and property and asset management. The book concludes with a chapter on the future of real estate development in the context of a rapidly changing world.

Two case studies are woven through the chapters to provide real-world examples of the academic concepts discussed. Shortbread Lofts is a student housing development in Chapel Hill, North Carolina, and Irvine Tech Center is a mixed-use business complex in Irvine, California. The two developments could not be more different, but both base their success on developers who understand the fundamental principles outlined here.

Many people had a hand in producing this book, especially those who researched and wrote the previous editions. Authors and reviewers include academics from several disciplines, practitioners from across the country, and members of ULI's staff. The authors would like to thank everyone listed on the preceding pages for their contributions.

Mike E. Miles
Laurence M. Netherton
Adrienne Schmitz

Contents

CONTENTS

PART 2: THE HISTORY OF REAL ESTATE DEVELOPMENT IN THE UNITED STATES

Chapter 4: The Colonial Period to the Late 1800s

Chapter 5: The Late 1800s to World War II

PART 4: IDEAS 173

PART 5: FINANCING THE PROJECT 187

PART 1

Introduction

The principles and process of real estate development should be studied by looking at both the people who are involved in the process and the people who are the end users of the product. Although this book focuses on the role of the developer and the development firm, a great many people affect and are affected by real estate development. Everyone consumes the end product. Individuals form the lending institutions and investment firms that provide financing for a project. Individuals make up the *public sector* that both allows development and provides *infrastructure* to a development. Individuals in many allied professions produce the *built environment* that is used by people of different backgrounds and income levels.

Although the private entrepreneurial developer is often considered the most typical type of developer, it is important to note that developers can also be financial institutions, corporations, universities, medical centers, cities, municipalities, and other entities. Regardless of the kind of developer or real estate sector, the process laid out in this book remains essentially the same. Market decisions must be made, pro formas should be sound, the *development team* must be retained, and all of the stakeholders should be consulted. The process may be layered with various institutional procedures, committees, and boards of trustees, but the product is achieved by going through the same steps.

Profiles of developers and the diverse set of professionals who work with developers are interspersed throughout the text. Their career paths are interesting and often surprising. Their perspectives on development are especially valuable because these individuals have lived the process this book describes.

In addition to the profiles, the book features two case studies depicting two developers and their respective projects. The first is Larry Short, who is developing high-end student housing in Chapel Hill, North Carolina. His development, Shortbread Lofts, consists of a 271-bedroom community in six stories of apartments above ground-level amenities. The second is Wil Smith, a developer working in southern California. His project, Irvine Tech Center, is a large, multi-building, mixed-use development in Newport Beach, California. These case studies tell stories of unexpected complications and their resolution in the developers' own words.

Part I looks at the people who make a development possible: the developer as prime mover, the future users, and the many participants who work with the developer to produce what society will want. Part II presents a historical overview of real estate development in the United States and the roles of regulatory and political actors. Part III builds on that history with a contemporary view of the public sector's role. Part IV introduces the eight-stage development process with the first stage, inception of an idea. It also covers the financial decision-making mechanics that support development and are used at each stage of the process. In parts V, VI, and VII, the book proceeds through the eight-stage model, looking in detail at decision making in the real estate development process.

Chapter 1

Introduction to the Real Estate Development Process

Real estate development is the continual recon-figuration of the *built environment* to meet society's needs. The creation of roads, sewer systems, housing, office buildings, and shopping centers requires much work. Someone must initiate and then manage the creation, maintenance, and eventual re-creation of the spaces in which we live, work, and play. The need for development is constant as population increases, technologies evolve, and tastes continue to change.

Both public and private participants have compelling reasons to understand the development process. The goal of *private sector* participants is to minimize risk while maximizing personal or institutional objectives—typically profit, but often nonmonetary objectives as well. Fortunes have been made and lost in real estate development. Few business ventures are as heavily *leveraged* as traditional real estate development projects, magnifying the risk of ruin but also the potential for high returns to investors. The *public sector*'s goals are to ensure public safety, to manage the impacts of real estate development on the community and the environment, and to promote smart development that is consistent with community's interests. These goals require balancing the market's need for constructed space against the public sector's responsibility to provide services, improve the quality of life, and limit environmental harm. A key tenet of this book is that all participants enjoy a higher probability of achieving their goals if they understand the nuances of how the development process works, who the key players are, how their objectives are interwoven, and why it is important to achieve consensus.

DEFINING REAL ESTATE DEVELOPMENT

Real estate development is the process of bringing built space to fruition. It starts with an idea and ends when consumers—tenants or owner-occupants—occupy the physical space put in place by the *development team*. Each real estate project is in essence a separate business entity employing the three factors of production—land, labor, and capital—to create a product. To transform an idea into reality, these factors are coordinated by entrepreneurial management and delivered by teams. *Value* is created by providing space to meet the needs of society. Although the definition of real estate development remains simple, the process grows more and more complex as municipalities, financial markets, and consumer tastes evolve.

Developments do not happen without financial backing, which often requires multiple agreements negotiated by multiple players. The developer works with public sector officials on approvals, zoning changes, exactions, building codes, and the provision of *infrastructure*. Community and special-interest groups play increasingly important roles. The time needed to conduct public outreach, negotiate with the public sector, and obtain financing must thus be factored into the equation when evaluating a potential project. Only after these functions are organized can the team of designers, engineers, and construction workers begin the physical development. The project is completed with the leasing or selling of the space to users. This final phase requires the expertise of marketing professionals, graphic artists, salespeople, website developers, and other specialists. The developer tries to ensure that every element in the process is properly executed on schedule and within budget.

Today, development requires more knowledge than ever about the specifics of prospective markets, patterns of urban growth, neighborhood associations, traffic patterns, legal requirements, local regulations, contracts, building design, site development, construction techniques, environmental issues, infrastructure, financing, *risk control*, and time management. Ever-increasing complexities in each arena have led to increased specialization within the development team. As more affiliated professionals work with developers, the size of the team has expanded and the roles of some members have changed. As development has become more complex, it has generated the need for better-educated developers.

THE EIGHT-STAGE MODEL OF REAL ESTATE DEVELOPMENT

Despite the growing complexity, developers still follow a standard sequence of steps from the moment they conceive a project through the time they begin ongoing *asset management* and/or sell the finished product. Although some may delineate the sequence of steps slightly differently, the essence does not vary significantly from the eight-stage model shown in figure 1-1.

The eight-stage model also applies to the redevelopment of projects, which requires most of the same steps as new development. In very large development projects, individual components can be nested within a larger development plan and may each be at different stages at a given time.

Before proceeding further with the model, a few points should be emphasized. First, the development process is neither straightforward nor linear. The flow chart shown in figure 1-1 can identify the discrete steps and guide an understanding of development, but no chart can capture the constant repositioning that occurs in the developer's mind or the nearly constant renegotiation that occurs between the developer and the other participants.

Second, real estate development is an art. It is creative and complex, partly logical and partly intuitive. Studying the components of development can help all players make the most of their chances for success. What cannot be taught are two personal qualities essential to success: creativity and drive.

Third, at each stage of the process, developers should consider all the remaining stages. Developers should make current decisions fully aware of their implications not only for the immediate next step, but also for the life of the project. The development process requires managing the interaction among the functions (design, construction, finance, management, marketing, and government relations) in each of the eight stages as well as over time.

The developer should recognize the importance of asset management and property management after the project is built by providing for those functions during design and construction. For example, operating a sophisticated building with advanced technological systems may require skills beyond those of most property managers in a particular market. Or, maintaining a particular material may require greater expense than would a different product.

Figure 1-1   **The Eight-Stage Model of Real Estate Development**

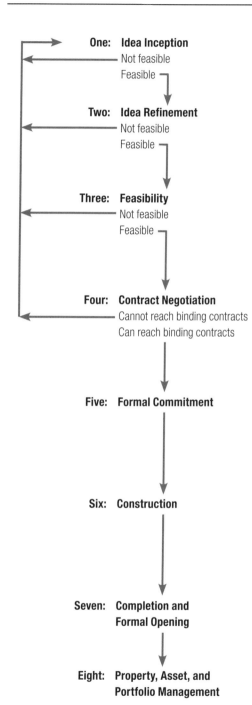

One: Idea Inception
— Not feasible
Feasible ⌐

Developer with extensive background knowledge and a great deal of current market data looks for needs to fill, sees possibilities, has a dozen ideas, does quick feasibility tests in his head.

Two: Idea Refinement
— Not feasible
Feasible ⌐

Developer finds a specific site for the idea; looks at physical feasibility; talks with prospective tenants, owners, lenders, partners, professionals; settles on a tentative design; options the land if the idea looks good.

Three: Feasibility
— Not feasible
Feasible ⌐

Developer conducts or commissions a more formal market study to estimate market absorption and capture rates, conducts or commissions feasibility study comparing estimated value of project with cost, processes plans through government agencies. Demonstrates legal, physical, and financial feasibility for all participants.

Four: Contract Negotiation
— Cannot reach binding contracts
Can reach binding contracts

Developer decides on final design based on what market study says users want and will pay for. Contracts are negotiated. Developer gets loan commitment in writing, decides on general contractor, determines general rent or sales requirements, obtains permits from local government.

Five: Formal Commitment

Contracts, often contingent on each other, are signed. Developer may have all contracts signed at once: joint venture agreement, construction loan agreement and permanent loan commitment, construction contract, exercise of land purchase option, purchase of insurance, and prelease agreements.

Six: Construction

Developer switches to formal accounting system, seeking to keep all costs within budget. Developer approves changes suggested by marketing professionals and development team, resolves construction disputes, signs checks, keeps work on schedule, brings in operating staff as needed.

Seven: Completion and Formal Opening

Developer brings in full-time operating staff, increases advertising. City approves occupancy, utilities are connected, tenants move in. Construction loan is paid off, and permanent loan is closed.

Eight: Property, Asset, and Portfolio Management

Owner (either developer or new owner) oversees property management (including re-leasing), reconfiguring, remodeling, and remarketing space as necessary to extend economic life and enhance performance of asset; corporate management of fixed assets and considerations regarding investors' portfolios come into play.

Furthermore, to keep a space competitive in an ever-evolving market, asset managers need to remarket it continually and to upgrade or remodel it periodically. *Institutional investors* and corporate owners are keenly aware of the periodic need for and cost of major remodeling to prolong a building's economic life. Careful planning during stages one through seven should enable developers to find ways to minimize the frequency and cost of retrofitting, while respecting the original concepts. Whether or not developers manage a property for the long term, they are responsible for considerations that affect asset management during the first seven stages. Given that developers' decisions help determine future *operating costs* and that such costs represent a significant part of the project's value (i.e., what it will sell for), developers typically focus sharply on making building operations cost-efficient.

Fourth, although the model for development is grounded in reality, it represents an ideal version of the process. The model assumes a well-informed developer, a thorough analysis of the market, accurate assessments of the construction costs, and so on. Real estate development is full of stories of people whose intuition has led them to success. The stages described here do not account for the lucky, intuitive person who had a gut feeling and used unconventional means to get a project built. Still, it is better to be skilled and lucky than just lucky.

Fifth, the development process is inherently *interdisciplinary* and dynamic. It is a complex process that demands attention to all aspects of creating the built environment. The developer must be conversant in many disciplines, in order to make informed decisions and balance competing goals. Furthermore, many of the components of this interdisciplinary world are changing rapidly, and the interfaces between disciplines are constantly in flux.

Finally, real estate development is a global industry. Financing sources are sometimes global, major tenants have international connections, and real estate service companies operate and compete globally. Most important, global factors are spurring changes in lifestyle preferences that are changing what people want in the built environment.

CHARACTERIZING DEVELOPERS

Developers are like movie producers; they promote and finance a project, assemble a team of specialists, and then manage that team to make sure that the project is realized. Developers are proactive; they make things happen. As discussed in later chapters, a great deal of uncertainty is associated with the development process, just as with the introduction of any new product. However, unlike many other industries that make new products which have limited lives, real estate development involves long-term commitments because buildings last for decades. Thus, the cost of making a mistake is extraordinarily high. The amount of related risk the developer assumes personally is an important issue that commands significant attention throughout this book. Regardless of which risk control devices the developer finds appropriate for a particular project, the developer ultimately is responsible for managing all aspects of that project. Clearly, successful developers must be able to handle (and thrive under) intense pressure and considerable uncertainty.

Developers are not all alike. Some develop only one type of property such as single-family homes; others develop a wide range of product types. Some carve out a niche in one city; others work regionally, nationally, or internationally. Some run extremely lean organizations, hiring outside expertise for every function from design to leasing; others maintain needed expertise in house. Some operate as publicly traded companies, such as real estate investment trusts (REITs), while others stay private, forgoing certain capital market advantages to avoid the short-term pressure of quarterly earnings. In between are many gradations. As in most professions, developers range from those who put reputation above profit to those who fail to respect even the letter of the law. Likewise, in ego and visibility, they vary enormously. Some name buildings for themselves, while others cherish anonymity.

Private developers must balance an extraordinary number of requirements for completing a project against the needs of diverse consumers of the product. First, as figure 1-2 shows, developers need

CASE STUDY Shortbread Lofts Summary

THE DEVELOPER

Larry Short/Shortbread Lofts LLC

PROJECT LOCATION

Shortbread Lofts is located in downtown Chapel Hill, North Carolina, within a short walk of the University of North Carolina. It sits along a bus route that runs throughout the town. Prime development sites such as this one are scarce, and approvals are painstakingly difficult to obtain, making this site a rare development opportunity in a market with limited competition.

LAND

The total land area is 1.28 acres on two sites. The primary site is 1.08 acres, level, and rectangular, with 313 feet of frontage on W. Rosemary Street, a commercial corridor. The secondary site, across the street, is 0.2 acre and is used for additional surface parking. The property was rezoned TC-3 (Town Center 3) for the development of Shortbread Lofts.

BUILDING

A seven-story podium construction building contains 85 units (271 bedrooms) of student housing. The six stories of residential units sit above a ground level that contains a leasing office, 6,459 square feet of retail space, and a parking garage. The residential units are two-, three-, and four-bedroom units, with a bath for each bedroom. The garage has 121 parking spaces that are leased to residents.

INITIAL CHRONOLOGY

Rezoning approved	February 2012
Construction began	January 2013
Leasing began	December 2013
Project completed	August 2014

DEVELOPER BACKGROUND

Larry Short moved to Chapel Hill in 1979, when the prime rate hit 18 percent. He had been in Chicago, earning an MBA at Northwestern University, working first as a CPA at Arthur Anderson, then doing real estate makeovers. He started developing single-family units while in school and eventually moved to developing small apartments full-time. His deals were usually owner-financed. When he hit Chapel Hill he couldn't write a $10,000 check.

Short avoids publicity. He hires the right people to work on his developments, people who have the right local connections. Before his first major development, the Warehouse, and the Shortbread project, he had rehabbed several small condominiums in Chapel Hill; he acquired the units, upgraded them, and resold them to new users. *Case study begins on page 176.*

CASE STUDY Irvine Tech Center Summary

THE DEVELOPER

Greenlaw Partners in single-purpose partnership with Guggenheim Plus Leveraged LLC

PROJECT LOCATION

Irvine Tech Center (ITC) is located in the Irvine Business Complex, a 2,700-acre planning area rapidly transitioning from relatively low-density industrial and office properties to mixed-use and residential development. The transformation is driven by proximity to Orange County's principal airport and to the University of California at Irvine, and by underlying shifts in the county's economy. The site sits at the intersection of two major arterials. One connects the airport to the university campus, and the other connects Orange County coastal cities to two major interstate highways and to inland job and residential areas.

LAND

The site was acquired in three phases:
ITC I, 10 acres and five buildings
ITC II, 8.9 acres and seven buildings
ITC III, 4.2 acres and one building
The project is divided by a collector street that separates ITC I from ITC II and ITC III. The existing tilt-up buildings provided interim income during the entitlement period.

DEVELOPMENT STRATEGY

Acquisition of vehicle trip allocations from other parcels in the IBC to support the density proposed for the ITC site.

INITIAL CHRONOLOGY

Acquisition of ITC I and II	2005
Initial entitlement application	2006
Acquisition of trip allocation units	2005–09
First purchase offer	2006
Entitlement application withdrawn and project reconceived	2009
Entitlements reinitiated under Irvine Vision Plan	2010
Acquisition of ITC III	2012
Sale of ITC I closed	2013
ITC II and III under contract for 2015 close	2014

DEVELOPER BACKGROUND

Wilbur (Wil) Smith came to Los Angeles to attend the graduate program in real estate development at the University of Southern California. Having an extensive family background in real estate, Smith had worked construction, leased and managed properties, and made acquisitions. After graduating, he joined Maker

Continued on page 8

This case study was written by John Brady, (retired) Guggenheim Real Estate, San Francisco.

Irvine Tech Center *Continued from page 7*

Properties, a private firm in Orange County engaged in residential, mixed-use, hospitality, and commercial developments.

In 2003, Smith formed Greenlaw Partners and began an acquisition program focused on office, industrial, and other income properties. He joins with institutional financing sources to identify opportunities where the highest risk-adjusted returns can be obtained "on the buy" by purchasing properties at or below replacement cost. He then creates and implements a business plan to increase cash flow or base asset value and to optimize the equity multiple and the internal rate of return (IRR).

Case study begins on page 132.

the blessing of local government and often of neighbors around the site. In many cases, to obtain public approval, developers must redesign a project. Thus, appropriate flexibility is one of a developer's most crucial traits. Second, developers need to be able to find tenants or buyers (users) who will pay for space and associated services over time. Third, developers must lead an internal team of specialists who depend on the developer for their livelihoods and recruit external players whose businesses contract with developers. Fourth, developers need to demonstrate the project's feasibility to the *capital markets* and pay interest or offer *equity* positions in return for funding. In each of these areas, developers use various forms of risk management, initiating and managing a complex web of relationships from day one through the completion of the development process.

This book refers many times to the "development team" that assists the developer in the design and construction of an idea. It is worth noting that only a small proportion of the people in real estate development are developers—the *entrepreneurs* who initiate and execute a project. The bulk of the players come from a wide range of professionals, support staff, and building tradespeople who are indispensable to the process. Clearly, challenging work abounds in real estate development for many participants, not just for the developer. In fact, most developers start their real estate careers in one of the supporting professional trades.

The developer's job description includes shifting roles as visionary, promoter, negotiator, manager, leader, risk manager, and investor—a much more complex job than merely buying low to sell high. Developers are more akin to entrepreneurial innovators (like Bill Gates or Elon Musk)—people who realize an idea in the marketplace—than to pure traders skilled primarily at arbitrage.

Balancing these roles is an art that is mastered through experience. Equally important as that mastery is a goal-oriented disposition to overcome problems and obstacles. Developers must be highly focused on success with the ability to negotiate, compromise, and shape a project to meet the demands of stakeholders. Without the drive of a developer, few developments would occur because the potential roadblocks are numerous.

REPUTATION OF THE INDUSTRY

By definition, developers are agents of change. As in any profession, some are models of ethical behavior, making innovative and attractive contributions to the community, while others exhibit little sensitivity to community standards. But unlike other consumer goods that can remain in a showroom, the developer's product is clearly manifested in the built environment. It is there for everyone to see and judge. It is extremely difficult to communicate the qualities of a project before it is completed. Thus the developer's public persona can be as much a part of a project as the product itself, making developers easy scapegoats for everything from more traffic to higher taxes or crime rates.

As growth infringes on communities, the appearance of NIMBYism ("not in my backyard") is inevitable. Without even knowing the individual or the firm, many people are wary of a developer's involvement in a project in their neighborhood. Neighbors await bulldozers with trepidation. In the face of growing animosity, developers, city planners, elected officials, and others involved in community growth have learned the hard way about the necessity of involving the broader community in guiding development. Chapter 8 discusses how a developer

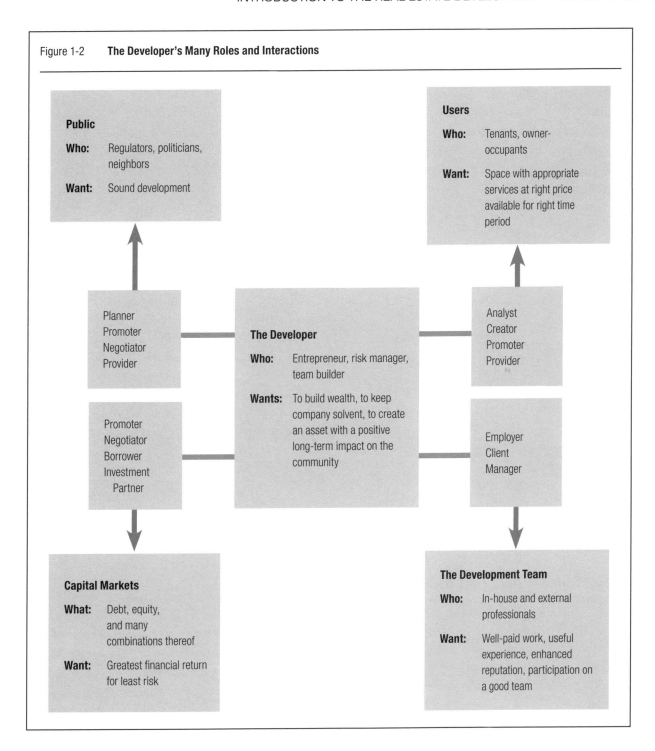

Figure 1-2   **The Developer's Many Roles and Interactions**

Public

Who: Regulators, politicians, neighbors

Want: Sound development

Users

Who: Tenants, owner-occupants

Want: Space with appropriate services at right price available for right time period

Planner
Promoter
Negotiator
Provider

The Developer

Who: Entrepreneur, risk manager, team builder

Wants: To build wealth, to keep company solvent, to create an asset with a positive long-term impact on the community

Analyst
Creator
Promoter
Provider

Promoter
Negotiator
Borrower
Investment
Partner

Employer
Client
Manager

Capital Markets

What: Debt, equity, and many combinations thereof

Want: Greatest financial return for least risk

The Development Team

Who: In-house and external professionals

Want: Well-paid work, useful experience, enhanced reputation, participation on a good team

can address these challenges. Communities will always change, with or without developers. A good developer can manage change with vision and sensitivity, and thus have a positive effect on a community.

THE DEVELOPMENT TEAM

The developer is the leader of a development team. He coordinates people and helps realize a vision. That vision may be his own, that of the community, one that is shaped by the team, or a blend of all of these. Developers seldom work in isolation. To design, finance, build, lease or sell their products, developers must engage the services of many other experts—public and private—some of them specialized professionals, others entrepreneurs like themselves. Chapter 3 describes the typical array of team members in detail.

With each project, developers must shape and sell an idea to secure commitments from others. Thus, they are first and foremost promoters. Like any team leader, they must also motivate players, often with incentives beyond money—with pride in the project, with the hope of future work, and with fear of the consequences of nonperformance. Knowing when and with whom to use different incentives is a key leadership skill for developers.

THE PUBLIC SECTOR: ALWAYS A PARTNER

The public sector is involved—as a stakeholder or a partner—in every real estate project. Real estate development is highly regulated, and the legal and regulatory environment surrounds the entire development process. Developers usually work hand in hand with local governments and the community, giving them the same respect and attention they would give any other partner. Chapters 7 and 8 discuss the public sector's involvement in depth.

MARKET AND FEASIBILITY STUDIES

Developers rely on *market research* to make decisions throughout the development process. Textbooks on marketing and market research seldom cover real estate in great detail. Likewise, real estate textbooks often fail to connect market research to broader marketing principles. Yet the connection is critical. Developers, planners, public officials, lenders, and investors need to apply the fundamental concepts of marketing to make better-informed decisions and control risks. That means they must gather information—and information carries a cost. The cost of a market study depends on what the level of detail is, who performs the analysis, and how much rigor a developer wants (or is required) to pay for. As with

all risk control techniques, the developer must weigh the cost in relation to the magnitude of the risk.

Developers look for indications of the kind of space that will satisfy the market's needs over a project's long expected life. The future is not just the one year or five years that it takes to develop a project; it is the entire useful life of the project, which may last 50 or 100 years. Although the market analyst scrupulously examines past performance and is exacting in determining current market conditions, it is what the analyst has to say about the future that matters most. No one can fully anticipate the future, but the developer's challenge is to be at least a few steps ahead of the pack.

A feasibility study completes the analysis (see chapter 13 for details). Simply put, the project is feasible if its estimated value exceeds its estimated costs. Value is a function of projected cash flow and a market-derived capitalization or discount rate (defined in chapter 11).

DESIGN: NEVER AN AFTERTHOUGHT

Good design has never been more important than it is today. Serious attention to the market—the people who will use the project—can show developers and their architects and planners how to capture market share from competitors or how to build for a new niche.

Design is a tool for connecting with and discriminating between specific market segments. Building designs convey direct messages, and architects have had to become proficient in creating appropriate ones. It is important to remember that for some uses and certain tenants, the appropriate message is pure functionality—that is, the most functional bay sizes and core elements, covered with a skin whose operating costs are low.

Each player in the development process brings some expectation of how a completed project will look and function. For example, stakeholders who want to maintain a town's character are concerned about continuity, context, preservation of a way of life, and interactions with surrounding areas. The developer brings her own aesthetic preferences and

In Portland, Oregon, the Brewery Blocks is a mixed-use urban community encompassing seven buildings on five contiguous blocks. The project transformed a deteriorated warehouse district into a thriving neighborhood.

her vision for the project. Financial sources may be reluctant to depart from proven designs—and market successes—of analogous projects. The developer charges the architect and design team with resolving the diversity of expectations into a single, coherent image. Still, the ultimate responsibility for a suitable design rests with the developer.

Design is about far more than aesthetics. Architect Louis Sullivan coined the phrase "form follows function" in the late 1800s, and today it is truer than ever. Sustainable design that is softer on the environment and more energy-efficient and cost-effective to manage over time wins out over beautiful but less functional design. Today's architects, landscape architects, and other designers take a holistic approach, considering a host of factors when designing a new project or redevelopment. Their goals include making the most of the site and

location, minimizing energy consumption, using the most environmentally friendly materials, conserving water, enhancing indoor air quality, and optimizing long-term operational practices.[1]

EVOLUTIONARY CHANGES IN THE DEVELOPMENT PROCESS

Evolutionary changes in the process in recent years have required adjustments to the time-honored eight-stage model. These changes are noted here and illustrated in later chapters.

Availability of Data

Good developers have always relied on a great deal of background information gleaned over a lifetime of conversation, observation, and reading—newsletters, newspapers, academic journals, websites, and the like. Data are fundamental to sophisticated players in the marketplace. More accurately, the ability to turn raw data into useful information often makes the difference between profit and loss.

Throughout the discussion of the eight-stage model, this book refers to a host of traditional information sources. What is new is the extent and delivery capacity of the information available today. Technology now makes vast databases easily accessible to the development community through the internet. Companies such as SNL Financial provide real-time information on the financial condition of publicly traded real estate companies. CoStar provides a sophisticated online commercial-property equivalent of a residential multiple-listing service. Websites such as GlobeSt.com and crenews.com send out daily market summaries that focus on national and regional news in commercial real estate. Most cities have local business journals that maintain websites that contain real estate sections. Moreover, it is easier than ever to find property listings and potential prices through websites such as LoopNet.com, Zillow.com, Trulia.com, and many others. And many more websites and resources continue to come online. The result is that the internet continues to make more local, national, and international market information ever more accessible, leading to better educated investors, developers, owners, tenants, and residents.

Technology and Social Media

The rise of technology and social media has had a profound impact on the evolution of real estate. As technology continues to improve, so do construction practices. New building techniques accelerate the pace of construction as well as boost its safety. The way that property owners and tenants interact with real estate is changing drastically from just a few years ago. People can now monitor their utility consumption and set certain preferences through online portals and smartphone applications. Rent can be paid online, and expense tracking systems can provide minute-by-minute analysis. These continuing technological advancements change the way people live in and use their built environment. "Smart" homes and office buildings are becoming the norm.

Social media, in particular, have grown in importance. Most property management firms have websites that include a messaging component or Facebook groups for their properties through which residents can communicate about upcoming events and happenings at a development. Twitter provides almost instantaneous news on transactions and other activities. Websites and smartphone applications such as Flickr and Instagram enable users to share pictures of their apartments or the hotels they visit. These changes in the way people interact provide a convenient medium for reaching a larger audience with more information. There is no doubt that advances in technology and the spread of social media will affect the evolution of how people select and interact with real estate. Most important, the new technological possibilities will influence what consumers want in their built environment.

Sustainability

A few years ago, sustainability and green building methods were interesting buzzwords. Now sustainable and green development is often a legal requirement, as detailed in chapters 7 and 8. Many professional organizations now offer resources and services related to sustainable and green building techniques, as well as education on the value of sustainable practices to developers and investors. Groups such as the Rocky Mountain Institute provide comprehensive guides like, "How to Calculate and Present Deep Retrofit Value for Owner Occupants," which focuses on demonstrating the creation of value through sustainability.[2] The U.S. Green Building Council has created its LEED (Leadership in Energy and Environmental Design) rating system, which offers building owners and operators a framework for identifying and implementing practical, measurable solutions for green building design, construction, operations, and maintenance. It is heavily used by local jurisdictions for project approvals.[3] Going forward, sustainability and green building will be staples of the real estate development process.

A Much Longer Venture Capital Period

Chapters 10 and 11 cover the traditional financing cycle, which moves from land acquisition financing to land development financing to construction financing to permanent financing. This sequence still holds, but the time required to move from the early stages to the closing of the construction financing has lengthened. Why? Because building sites in infill locations are more complex and negotiations are more difficult as ever more participants enter the development process. Why does this matter? Because the cost of funds is considerably higher in the early stages of the development process. A lender putting up money for hard construction has relatively high-quality collateral. A lender or investor putting up the capital needed to carry out planning work and political negotiations over a period of many years before construction can start does not have good collateral. In fact, at this stage, financing is much like the financing that a venture capital company would extend to a new small business. If the business fails, not much is there to liquidate and sell. The longer time period before construction means a longer venture capital period and thus a longer need for expensive financing. This issue significantly affects how relationships among the development team are structured throughout the first five stages of the development process.

Feasibility from Another Perspective

It has always been important to understand the feasibility of a project as well as the feasibility of continued participation by all members of the development team. As the process grows more complex and the venture capital period lengthens, it becomes more important to focus on feasibility for the individual members of the team, sometimes called "level two" feasibility. As the timing of a project gets extended, everyone has to worry about how they personally are able to manage their finances and careers during what could be a long period with little or no cash inflow. As discussed throughout this book, it is the developer's responsibility to consider the viability of the venture for each member of the development team.

Wall Street (and Related Avenues)

During the 1990s, securitization became much more important in real estate investment. As will be explained in the chapters on finance, few large, publicly traded real estate companies existed before 1990. In fact, the market value of all REITs then was less than $10 billion. Today, with an equity market capitalization of more than $650 billion, REITs are included in numerous stock market indexes, such as the S&P 500.[4]

This change has had two obvious impacts on the development environment. First, it created a new level of reporting and thus made information more available. The Securities and Exchange Commission requires public companies to report their financial status, and Wall Street analysts provide considerable commentary on these public companies. Second, the investment banker mentality has hit real estate development because the major investment banks are now actively involved. In addition, large private equity firms such as KKR (of *Barbarians at the Gate* fame), Apollo, Blackstone, TPG, and the Carlyle Group now have extensive investments in real estate. Wall Street moves to a different beat than the commercial banks, insurance companies, and wealthy families that have traditionally financed development. To find the right investment partner, today's developer must contend with a faster-moving and often harsher world.

Increased Pressure on the Public Sector

A primary theme of this book is that the public sector is always a kind of partner in the development process. The evolution of community planning, environmental safeguards, hazardous waste cleanup, and other concerns has produced a more complex approvals environment. Government officials at all levels are under tremendous pressure to perform better (often with fewer resources) and to deal more rapidly with this more complex environment.

SUMMARY

As the book moves forward with the introductory framework in chapters 2 and 3, it is important to keep the following concepts in mind:

- Everyone is in some way connected to the development process. Consequently, the developer should see the public sector as a partner.
- The developer ultimately is responsible for creating buildings and spaces with appropriate associated services that meet society's needs over time.
- Because the decision-making environment of the development period is complex and interactive, a model is useful for evaluating the future ramifications of current decisions.
- Real estate development is an art that requires drive and creativity coupled with appropriate flexibility and risk management.
- Development of the built environment is a long-term activity that justifies considerable planning. Early consideration of future operational management needs should be a critical element of such planning.

Few people have the background needed to connect all the aspects of the development process. Readers of this book should skim the areas where they have the background to make the connections and focus their attention on the areas where they are less proficient.

TERMS

The following terms are introduced in this chapter:

- Asset management
- Built environment
- Capital markets
- Development team
- Entrepreneur
- Equity
- Feasibility studies
- Infrastructure
- Institutional investors
- Interdisciplinary
- Leverage
- Market research
- Operating costs
- Private sector
- Public sector
- Risk control
- Value

REVIEW QUESTIONS

1.1   What is real estate development?

1.2   Why does every real estate development project involve both the public and the private sectors?

1.3   What is the role of the developer in the development process?

1.4   What are the eight stages of development as delineated in this textbook?

1.5   What are the advantages of using such a model? What are the pitfalls?

1.6   Why is real estate development inherently an interdisciplinary process?

1.7   Why and how do developers use market research and feasibility studies?

1.8   Discuss the importance of good design in development.

1.9   Discuss the many roles a developer must play.

1.10   What role does time play in the real estate development process?

NOTES

1   www.gsa.gov
2   www.rmi.org/retrofit_depot_deepretrofitvalue
3   www.usbc.org/articles/about-leed
4   www.reit.com/REIT/REITbytheNumbers.aspx

Chapter 2

The Raw Material: Land and Demographics in the United States

The search for future opportunities benefits from ongoing examination of changes in basic demographic and economic indicators. The evolution of urban areas reflects changing social, technological, and political forces, and the developer should understand his place in this context. Reviewing the recent past and the present tells developers where the real estate markets have been, while carefully prepared projections can tell much about what future users of real estate will want. This chapter looks at five key indicators:

- Population growth;
- Employment growth and economic cycles;
- Land supply;
- The interaction of real estate values with gross domestic product, national wealth, and employment; and
- How the built environment will need to change to accommodate technological change and expected shifts in population.

It provides historical context on the basic issues that developers should consider as well as sources for current data and trends. It is not intended to be a resource for demographic trends but an introduction to some of the issues that developers should evaluate.

More context for these topics will be discussed as the book moves through the eight-stage model.

This chapter looks at broad, national data as background for the more exacting local analysis of these components that follows. It begins with *demographics* and market demand. It is important to understand that real estate is not like other products, in that it is location-specific. Unlike for other investments, such as stocks or bonds, the market potential of real estate is tied directly to its location and it cannot be moved to a more desirable location. Thus, it is important to understand local factors such as consumer wealth and education, and the density of the surrounding development.

POPULATION GROWTH

Population growth, new household formation, job creation, and increases in household income levels are key drivers of real estate demand. The best population data comes from the full census undertaken by the U.S. Census Bureau every ten years. Between the decennial censuses, the Bureau carries out regular updates that provide more current information at a less detailed level, as the survey sizes are smaller.

This chapter looks primarily at the ten-year reports to obtain an overview of longer-term national trends. Clearly, the developer will want local information and the latest estimates as well as these big-picture trends.

Figure 2-1	Population Growth in the United States: 1790 to 2020	
Census	Population	Increase over Previous Decade (Percent)
1790	3,929,214	–
1800	5,308,483	35.1
1810	7,239,881	36.4
1820	9,638,453	33.1
1830	12,866,020	33.5
1840	17,069,453	32.7
1850	23,191,876	35.9
1860	31,443,321	35.6
1870	39,818,449	26.6
1880	50,155,783	26.0
1890	62,947,714	25.5
1900	75,994,575	20.7
1910	91,972,266	21.0
1920	105,710,620	14.9
1930	122,775,046	16.1
1940	131,669,275	7.2
1950	151,325,798	14.9
1960	179,323,175	18.5
1970	203,302,031	13.4
1980	226,542,199	11.4
1990	248,718,302	9.8
2000	281,421,906	13.1
2010	308,745,538	9.7
2020[a]	333,896,000	8.2

a. Projected.

Sources: U.S. Census Bureau, Population Division, 2010 Census, Table 4, "Population: 1790 to 1990," and 2010 Census Briefs, "Population Distribution and Change: 2000 to 2010."

Populations grow in two ways: more people are born than die, and more people migrate in than leave. Figure 2-1 shows decade-by-decade changes in the number of Americans. In the earliest days of the country, immigration was the key source of population growth. This trend continued through the early part of the 20th century and then immigration dropped to a trickle during the 1940s and 1950s. In a dramatic reversal, both the number of newcomers and their share in population growth rose dramatically after 1980.

As shown in figure 2-2, legal immigration during the 1990s was at an all-time high. Yet the official immigration rate (the number of legal newcomers per 1,000 residents) was still less than half that seen at the start of the 20th century. Illegal immigrants, mainly from Mexico and Central America, add to these totals. Demographers estimate that in 2013, about 11.7 million undocumented immigrants lived in the United States, down from a peak of 12.2 million in 2007.[1]

In 2010, nearly 13 percent of U.S. residents were foreign born, compared with fewer than 5 percent as recently as 1970 (figure 2-3). And despite stricter scrutiny of potential entrants after September 11, 2001, immigrants continue to flock to the country's shores.

Although new Americans can strain local government resources, they are an important source of demand for housing, goods, and services. Homeownership rates for naturalized citizens are about the same as for native-born Americans. Sixty-five percent of naturalized immigrants live in owner-occupied housing units, in line with the 66 percent of U.S.-born citizens who are owner-occupants.[2]

National Demographic Trends

In the United States today, the rate of population growth (net natural increase plus immigration) is lower than that of most emerging nations, as seen in figure 2-4, but much higher than those of Western Europe and Japan. The population growth rate in the United States has been slowly decreasing since the 1960s. Nevertheless, the sheer number of new Americans is expected to be significant for years to

Figure 2-2   **Legal Immigration to the United States**

Decade	Legal Immigration by Decade	Population at Start of Decade	Average Annual Immigrants per 1,000 Population	Population Increase in the Decade	Legal Immigration Share of Population Increase (Percent)
1901–1910	8,795,386	75,994,575	11.6	15,977,691	55.0
1911–1920	5,735,811	91,972,266	6.2	13,738,354	41.8
1921–1930	4,107,209	105,710,620	3.9	17,064,426	24.1
1931–1940	528,431	122,775,046	0.4	8,894,229	5.9
1941–1950	1,035,039	131,669,275	0.8	19,161,229	5.4
1951–1960	2,515,479	151,325,798	1.7	27,997,377	9.0
1961–1970	3,321,677	179,323,175	1.9	23,978,856	13.9
1971–1980	4,493,314	203,302,031	2.2	23,240,168	19.3
1981–1990	7,338,062	226,542,199	3.2	22,176,103	33.1
1991–2000	9,095,417	248,718,302	3.7	32,712,033	27.8
2001–2010	11,342,055	281,422,246	4.0	27,300,198	41.5
2011–2020[a]	9,351,418	308,745,538	3.0	25,150,462	37.2

a. Projected.

Source: U.S. Immigration and Naturalization Service and Census Bureau, *2010 Current Population Survey (CPS) Data*, "2008 Immigration-Emigration Supplement."

Figure 2-3   **Foreign-Born Persons as a Percentage of U.S. Population**

Year	Number (Thousands)	Percent
1910	13,516	14.7
1920	13,921	13.2
1930	14,204	11.6
1940	11,595	8.8
1950	10,347	6.9
1960	9,738	5.4
1970	9,619	4.8
1980	14,080	6.2
1990	19,767	7.9
2000	31,107	11.1
2010	40,000	12.9
2020[a]	50,000	15.0

a. Projected.

Source: U.S. Census Bureau, *2011 Current Population Survey (CPS) Data*, "People and Households."

come. Census Bureau demographers project that the population of the United States will reach nearly 346 million by 2025.[3]

As the population expands, its composition is changing dramatically. In determining opportunities for future real estate development, these changes will be as important as total population size. Readily available demographic data show not only how many more people will reside in the United States over the coming decades but also their ages, household composition, and ethnicity. Looking beyond the totals helps predict and segment consumers' needs and desires.

Demographers used to refer to the *population "pyramid,"* showing large numbers of children on the bottom and relatively few old people at the top. In 1970, the nation's median age was 28. By 2000, it was greater than 35, and in 2010, it was greater than 37. In 2030, the age distribution will look more like a pillar than a pyramid (figure 2-5). Age cohorts younger than 75 will become more equal in size. The *baby boomers* (born between 1946 and 1963)

Figure 2-4	Projected Population Growth Rates: Developing Nations Versus Developed Nations	
	Projected Annual Rate (Percent)	
	2010	**2025**
Developing Nations		
China	0.5	0.1
Ecuador	1.5	1.1
Ethiopia	2.9	2.7
Honduras	2.0	1.3
India	1.4	0.1
Malaysia	1.6	1.2
Mexico	1.4	0.9
Pakistan	1.6	1.3
Philippines	1.9	1.5
Turkey	1.3	0.8
Developed Nations		
Canada	0.8	0.6
France	0.6	0.3
Germany	-0.2	-0.3
Japan	-0.1	-0.4
Norway	1.3	0.7
Russia	0.1	-0.3
United Kingdom	0.6	0.4
United States	0.8	0.7

Source: U.S. Census Bureau, International Database, "World Population Growth Rates: 1950–2050," 2010.

For retailers, it is crucial to understand the various market segments. Aging boomers mean better-educated and savvier consumers with higher disposable income, who spend more money on discretionary purchases than on necessities. Millennials lead more urban lifestyles, are likely to have less discretionary income, and do more purchasing online.

For housing, the relocation of some boomers from the suburbs to some urban cores has been a modest but noteworthy trend. A certain percentage of senior citizens will seek specialty housing catering to their lifestyle preferences, health needs, and ability to pay. However, the share of seniors who move during retirement is fairly small. As a result, absorption has been slow for some types of retirement communities. Demographics alone have been insufficient to gauge demand: increasingly, focus groups and other types of research are used to evaluate consumers' desires in terms of the features, functions, and benefits of the built product.

Speaking very broadly, millennials' preferences and lower incomes mean that large numbers will rent longer and live in smaller housing units. But as with boomers, gross generalizations do not fit all members of the cohort, and finely tuned market research is needed to gauge demand for specific product types and locations.

In the coming decades, the U.S. population will become more ethnically and racially diverse—partly because of differences in the age composition and birth rates of the minority population but also because of new immigrants and their offspring. Non-Hispanic whites constituted 76 percent of the population in 1990 but only 72.4 percent in 2010.[4] Hispanics (13 percent of the total in 2000) will continue to be the fastest-growing minority in absolute numbers, having reached 16.3 percent of the population in 2010. It is important to recognize that immigrants are not simply Asian or Hispanic or European. These broader categories contain numerous subgroups. Thais and Japanese, Puerto Ricans and Peruvians, Irish and Italians are very different subgroups of Asian, Hispanic, and European. Within each cultural group, many socioeconomic variations further segment the population. Real estate professionals need to be

constituted 35 percent of the population in 1970 but will account for only 20 percent in 2030.

As shown in figure 2-5, no single generation will be large enough to dominate public policy, and the cohorts will have more comparable numbers of real estate consumers (although their relative *purchasing power* will be quite different). Politicians and retailers will try to appeal to the various age groups in new ways. Overlaying the distribution of population by age with the distribution of variations in income and other household characteristics reveals the large number of discrete target markets. This variety creates opportunities for developers.

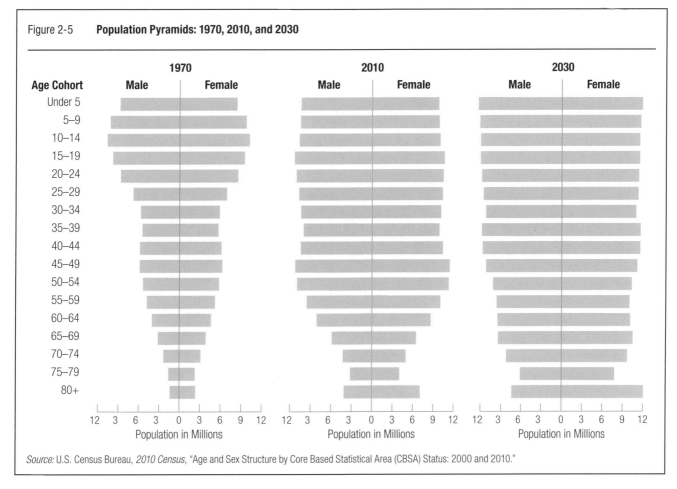

Figure 2-5   Population Pyramids: 1970, 2010, and 2030

Source: U.S. Census Bureau, *2010 Census,* "Age and Sex Structure by Core Based Statistical Area (CBSA) Status: 2000 and 2010."

sensitive to the different cultural and economic norms that are reflected in the shopping and housing choices of the various subgroups.

Similarly, households are not homogeneous, and neither are their housing preferences. Also, housing preferences change as each cohort ages and their needs change. For example, only 35 percent of millennials were homeowners in 2010, but 67 percent expected to be owners by 2015. Of those who expected to own, 82 percent expected to live in a single-family detached house.[5]

More than one-fourth of all households consist of a single person, and that proportion is rising rapidly. In the 2012 National Association of Homebuyers profile of homebuyers and sellers, 16 percent of all homebuyers were single women and 9 percent were single men compared with 20 percent in total for both categories in 1981. Growth in *single-person households* is fueled by adults who marry

later or never marry, by high divorce rates, and by an increase in the number of older widows and widowers.

The number of traditional married-couple-with-children families has declined sharply—from 40 percent of all households in 1970 to 20.2 percent in 2010 (figure 2-6).[6] Only 29.8 percent of all households include any children under 18. In a growing share of families with children, more than 32 percent have only one parent (or another adult relative) in the household, up from 11 percent in 1970.

To gauge demand, homebuilders focus on aggregate growth in the number of households in their market areas, within the context of national and regional trends. Average household size has been falling in the United States, from 3.14 persons in 1970 to 2.63 persons in 1990 to 2.59 persons in 2010.[7] But those statistics vary considerably between regions and population segments. Nationwide,

Figure 2-6 **Changing Composition of American Households**

Household Type	Percentage of All Households		
	1970	2010	2025
Family households	81.2	66.4	67.1
Married couple	70.5	48.4	51.3
With children under 18	40.3	20.2	20.4
Other family	10.6	18.1	15.8
With children under 18	5.0	9.6	7.6
Nonfamily households	18.8	33.6	32.9
Living alone	17.1	26.7	27.7
Not living alone	1.7	6.8	5.3

Source: U.S. Census Bureau, *2010 Census*, Households by Type 2000 & 2010, Table 2.

the number of households is still growing, but at a slower rate than in the past. Harvard University demographers project that the United States will gain between 11.8 million and 13.8 million new households between 2010 and 2020.[8] Consequently, aggregate demand for shelter will not grow at the same pace as in the past. Further tempering demand will be the long-term effects of the Great Recession, which is expected to reduce earning power for a generation.

Residential and retail developers closely monitor household income characteristics and are alert to how age, race, education, and household composition affect both spending power and preferences. As shown in figure 2-7, income can vary dramatically by age. Earning power is greatest in the 45 to 54 age bracket, followed by 35- to 44-year-olds, and then by people age 55 to 64. As the number of middle-aged households increases in coming years, the potential demand for discretionary goods and services and for move-up housing and second homes could increase. However, the astute analyst will evaluate all contributing factors.

Household income data vary dramatically by place of residence (metropolitan versus nonmetropolitan areas, central cities versus suburbs), by household type, and by race. For example, median

household income in the Northeast is about 14 percent higher than in the South. For non-Hispanic whites, it is about 70 percent higher than for African Americans.[9]

Census income data may underestimate household purchasing power because of the growing *informal economy*, which operates beyond the realm of traditional reporting practices. The magnitude of this economy varies among markets, and unreported activities take many forms (for example, second jobs, ad hoc tutoring, and various services paid in cash or barter). In addition, market analysts who focus only on current earnings miss part of the household wealth picture—those assets that can be used for home purchases and will be inherited by the next generation. In 2010, U.S. families had a median net worth of $77,300 and a mean worth of $498,800 held in investment vehicles such as equity in owner-occupied homes, interest-bearing accounts, stocks, bonds, and retirement plans. Net worth is highest for households of those aged 55 to 64: their 2010 median net worth was $179,400[10] and their mean worth was $880,500. Senior citizens, on average, have modest cash incomes but can tap into savings, investments, and home equity to pay for units in active retirement communities or assisted living facilities. Many young households, which may not be earning much now, will enjoy greater affluence upon inheriting family assets.

Figure 2-7 **2012 Median U.S. Household Income by Age of Householder**

Age	Annual Income
15–24	$30,604
25–34	$51,381
35–44	$63,629
45–54	$66,411
55–64	$58,626
65+	$33,848
All Households	**$51,017**

Source: U.S. Census Bureau, *Income, Poverty, and Health Insurance Coverage in the United States: 2012.*

Finding Demographic Data

Current and historical data about national demographic trends can be found in many different places. The U.S. Census Bureau's website (www.census.gov) provides a wealth of data that are constantly being updated and reinterpreted. The website provides easy access to population and housing data in the annual American Community Survey.

National income data can be found through the Bureau of Economic Analysis (BEA) on its website (www.bea.gov). Developers are likely to also require data for *metropolitan statistical areas (MSAs)* and even smaller areas, like zip codes, census tracts, or custom designated market areas. In addition, state, regional, and to a lesser extent, local governments often maintain websites that provide demographic data.

Usually these data are available from planning and research agencies. But most often a developer or analyst will purchase a complete set of data from a provider such as Esri (www.esri.com), Claritas (www.claritas.com), or Moody's (www.economy.com). These companies—and others—assemble raw data from a wide variety of sources and package it in formats to meet customers' needs, including manipulating the data to suit a customized geographic area. From these data, they also produce forecasts.

EMPLOYMENT GROWTH AND ECONOMIC CYCLES

Economics and job growth—both national and regional—have perhaps the greatest effect on real estate development. At the national level, economic cycles affect demand for space and the availability of capital for real estate development. At the regional level, developers analyze real estate markets at a fine grain. Regional economies are often described in terms of export (primary) and spin-off (secondary) employment. Primary employment is activity that results in the export of goods and services from a region, and spin-off employment is activity that supports primary employment. For example, Boeing and Microsoft are primary employers in the Seattle region; banks, barbershops, and architects there are secondary employers. Thus, when Boeing and Microsoft expand, so does the demand for all types of real estate. Without growth in primary employment, there is little demand for new space. Thus, when regional economies collapse, as did the Rust Belt of heavy manufacturing cities in the 1980s, demand dries up for all kinds of real estate.

Whereas demand for housing and retail space is primarily a function of population and of household growth and composition, demand for other commercial property development—office buildings, factories, research and development facilities, warehouses—is tied more closely to changes in the economy and employment. The office construction boom of the 1970s and 1980s was fueled, in part, by a dramatic shift in the focus of the U.S. economy from the production of goods to the delivery of services and the resulting growth of white-collar occupations. As a share of total employment, manufacturing jobs dropped but those in the *service sector*—a diverse mix heavily concentrated in business services and health care—grew dramatically. Women entered the labor force in ever-greater numbers, and new technology created opportunities for both professional and clerical services and knowledge workers. Typical anchor tenants of new office buildings were the expanding law, accounting, and investment firms, as well as corporations and private businesses.

At the turn of the 21st century, trends in employment suggested that the share of *office-prone employment* would continue to grow. The U.S. Bureau of Labor Statistics (BLS) predicted that the still rapidly growing service sector would create close to 14 million new jobs between 2012 and 2022 (figure 2-8). However, recent economic and social trends may temper those estimates.

In the near term, the demand for new office space will probably slow. Some of the growth in service sector jobs will be found at health care providers (home health care agencies, assisted living facilities, and nursing homes) that do not require office space. In most office-related sectors, a general focus on consolidation, greater efficiencies, productivity, and improved technology has resulted in job cutbacks and vacated office space. Employers are also cutting back on the amount of space per employee,

Figure 2-8   Employment by Major Industry: 2002, 2012, and 2022 Projections

	Number (Thousands)			Percentage of Total		
	2002	2012	2022	2002	2012	2022
Nonfarm wage and salary employment	131,028	134,427	149,751	100.0	100.0	100.0
Mining	512	801	922	0.4	0.6	0.6
Construction	6,716	5,641	7,263	4.7	3.9	4.5
Manufacturing	15,259	11,919	11,369	10.7	8.2	7.1
Utilities	596	554	498	0.4	0.4	0.3
Wholesale trade	5,652	5,673	6,143	4.0	3.9	3.8
Retail trade	15,025	14,875	15,966	10.6	10.2	9.9
Transportation and warehousing	4,223	4,415	4,742	3.0	3.0	2.9
Information	3,395	2,678	2,612	2.4	1.8	1.6
Financial activities	7,847	7,786	8,537	5.5	5.4	5.3
Professional and business services	15,976	17,930	21,413	11.2	12.3	13.3
Educational services	2,642	3,347	4,022	1.9	2.3	2.5
Health care and social assistance	13,556	16,972	21,966	9.5	11.7	13.6
Leisure and hospitality	11,986	13,746	15,035	8.4	9.5	9.3
Other services	6,129	6,175	6,823	4.3	4.2	4.2
Federal government	2,766	2,814	2,407	1.9	1.9	1.5
State and local government	18,747	19,103	20,032	13.2	13.1	12.4

Source: U.S. Bureau of Labor Statistics, "Employment by Major Industry Division, 2002, 2012, and 2022," Table 3, accessed December 19, 2013.

by moving from individual offices to cubicles or open-office plans and allowing more telecommuting. Many companies are encouraging employees to work from home or are using so-called hotel offices that are shared among employees, cutting back on the overhead allocated to office expense. Office-related growth is likely among high-tech industries, such as software developers and biomedical research, but they will be subject to the efficiencies just described. And the corner coffee shop is becoming the office for growing numbers of those who can work anywhere, anytime.

With the dramatic growth in online purchasing, the retail industry has also realized a significant change in the need for bricks-and-mortar space. Approximately 12 percent of all retail sales took place online in 2013, and that percentage is expected to reach approximately 17 percent by 2020. It is worth noting that these percentages were zero not long ago. The impact of this trend will be less demand for typical retail space in malls and shopping centers, but more demand for warehousing and distribution space for online retailers.

Regional and Metropolitan Shifts

Growth in population, households, and employment suggests opportunities for real estate development nationwide, but internal mobility data are what help identify specifically where development should occur. Movement across regions, between states, and within metropolitan areas creates demand for new homes, shopping centers, entertainment facilities, office buildings, and hotels. At the same time, a net loss of households or jobs leads to higher vacancies, lower rents, and softening home prices.

Mobility is the measure of population relocation. The U.S. population continues to shift from older metropolitan areas of the Northeast and Midwest

Figure 2-9   **Population of the United States by Region (Percent)**

	1970	1980	1990	2000	2010
Northeast	24.1	21.7	20.4	19.0	17.9
Midwest	27.8	26.0	24.0	22.9	21.7
South	30.9	33.3	34.4	35.6	37.1
West	17.1	19.1	21.2	22.5	23.3

Source: U.S. Census Bureau, *2010 Census Briefs*, "Population Distribution and Change: 2000 to 2010."

toward the Sun Belt, the mountain states, and the West (figure 2-9). More than half of all Americans lived in the Rust Belt in 1970. By 2010, that share had dwindled to 40 percent. Between 2000 and 2010, the population grew at a rate of 9.7 percent nationally, but at the state level growth varied dramatically (figure 2-10).

In the 2010s, energy and technology are driving the economies of the fastest-growing cities in the United States. According to *Forbes*, the five fastest-growing cities in the country in 2013 were Austin, Texas; Raleigh, North Carolina; Phoenix, Arizona; Dallas, Texas; and Salt Lake City, Utah,[11] all of which have economies based on energy or technology.

Population figures for MSAs, as shown in figure 2-11, underscore the Sun Belt/Frost Belt dichotomy. Lifestyle preferences encourage both young adults and retirees to seek milder climates, but location decisions are primarily economic. Many Sun Belt markets have lower real estate costs and lower taxes, factors that encourage both employers and workers to move to

Figure 2-10   **Percentage Change in State Populations, 2000–2010 (Total U.S. Growth = 9.7 Percent)**

Under 5 Percent	5–10 Percent	10–20 Percent	Over 20 Percent
Connecticut	Alabama	Alaska	Arizona
Illinois	Arkansas	California	Nevada
Iowa	District of Columbia	Colorado	Idaho
Louisiana	Indiana	Delaware	Texas
Maine	Kansas	Florida	Utah
Massachusetts	Kentucky	Georgia	
Michigan (-0.6)	Maryland	Hawaii	
Mississippi	Minnesota	New Mexico	
New Jersey	Missouri	North Carolina	
New York	Montana	Oregon	
North Dakota	Nebraska	South Carolina	
Ohio	New Hampshire	Tennessee	
Pennsylvania	Oklahoma	Virginia	
Rhode Island	South Dakota	Washington	
Vermont		Wyoming	
West Virginia			

Source: U.S. Census Bureau, *2010 Census and Census 2000*, "Population Change for the United States, Regions, States, and Puerto Rico: 2000 to 2010," Table 1.

Figure 2-11   **Population Change in the Ten Most Populous and Ten Fastest-Growing Metropolitan Statistical Areas, 2000–2010**

Metropolitan Statistical Area	Population		Change	
	2000	2010	Number	Percent
Most Populous				
New York–Northern New Jersey–Long Island, NY–NJ–PA	18,323,002	18,897,109	574,107	3.1
Los Angeles–Long Beach–Santa Ana, CA	12,365,627	12,828,837	463,210	3.7
Chicago–Joliet–Naperville, IL–IN–WI	9,098,316	9,461,105	362,789	4.0
Dallas–Fort Worth–Arlington, TX	5,161,544	6,371,773	1,210,229	23.4
Philadelphia–Camden–Wilmington, PA–NJ–DE–MD	5,687,147	5,965,343	278,196	4.9
Houston–Sugar Land–Baytown, TX	4,715,407	5,946,800	1,231,393	26.1
Washington–Arlington–Alexandria, DC–VA–MD–WV	4,796,183	5,582,170	785,987	16.4
Miami–Fort Lauderdale–Pompano Beach, FL	5,007,564	5,564,635	557,071	11.1
Atlanta–Sandy Spring–Marietta, GA	4,247,981	5,268,860	1,020,879	24.0
Boston–Cambridge–Quincy, MA–NH	4,391,344	4,552,402	161,058	3.7
Fastest Growing				
Palm Coast, FL	49,832	95,696	45,864	92.0
St. George, UT	90,354	138,115	47,761	52.9
Las Vegas–Paradise, NV	1,375,765	1,951,269	575,504	41.8
Raleigh–Cary, NC	797,071	1,130,490	333,419	41.8
Cape Coral–Fort Myers, FL	440,888	618,754	177,866	40.3
Provo–Orem, UT	376,774	526,810	150,036	39.8
Greeley, CO	180,926	252,825	71,899	39.7
Austin–Round Rock–San Marcos, TX	1,249,763	1,716,289	466,526	37.3
Myrtle Beach–North Myrtle Beach–Conway, SC	196,629	269,291	72,662	37.0
Bend, OR	115,367	157,773	42,366	36.7

Source: U.S. Census Bureau, *2010 Census Briefs*, "Population Distribution and Change: 2000 to 2010."

metropolitan growth magnets such as Dallas, Atlanta, and Miami. Note, however, that the New York, Los Angeles, and Chicago metropolitan areas—all high-tax, high-cost cities—grew in the 2000s.

Central cities were more successful in retaining their population base during the 2000s than in previous decades. Some cities that lost population in the 1970s and 1980s, such as Chicago, registered net gains. Redevelopment generated new office space, cultural facilities, hotels, and downtown housing. In the aggregate, however, the shift of households from

older cities to suburbs continues. Many Sun Belt cities can grow because they are able to annex adjacent unincorporated land—an opportunity not available to most cities in the Northeast or Midwest, which are ringed by incorporated suburbs.

For local public officials, growth is a source of civic pride and brings an expanding tax base, but it also triggers the need for public services and infrastructure. Rapid growth in the absence of adequate school, road, water, or sewer capacity often engenders no-growth attitudes among longer-term residents. Many states and metropolitan areas are implementing *smart growth* strategies designed to direct development into areas that have adequate utility capacity and transportation networks and to encourage walkable communities.

Like any other producer of goods and services, the real estate industry profits by satisfying buyers' needs and wants. The developers, builders, and marketers who pioneer new products and techniques spot trends early and attempt to profit from their innovation. Looking at broad demographic data is useful, not only to see the big national and regional trends, but also to stimulate obvious questions. Is the same trend affecting my local market? Will it continue in the future? What opportunities does it present?

Finding Employment Data

Employment statistics are compiled by the BLS (www.bls.gov). For more than 60 years, the BLS used the Standard Industry Classification (SIC) system to collect employment data by industry; however, the SIC system was not flexible enough to handle rapid changes in the U.S. economy such as developments in information services, new forms of health care provision, and high-tech manufacturing. The BLS now uses the North American Industry Classification System (NAICS), which was developed jointly with Canada and Mexico. The NAICS uses a six-digit coding system to classify employment into 20 industry sectors.

The BLS provides timely data for MSAs and the larger *consolidated metropolitan statistical areas (CMSAs)*. The Census Bureau defines CMSAs as two or more adjacent MSAs or smaller metropolitan regions that are combined, such as Washington, Baltimore, northern Virginia, and two counties in West Virginia, which make up the DC CMSA. The BLS uses MSA and CMSA data to produce forecasts of employment growth as well as population and income estimates. Two surveys provide current employment statistics: the 790 survey and the Quarterly Census of Employment and Wages (QCEW). The QCEW was originally called the ES 202 program, for the form it used. The primary

statistics derived from the 790 survey are estimates of employment, hours, and earnings. National, state, and county employment and wage data are provided by industry. Data from the 790 survey are timely because only a month elapses between data collection and release; however, as a survey, it is subject to sampling error and possibly bias in coverage. The QCEW is a census, published quarterly. Because of the complexity of the data it collects, there is a substantial lag before its release. Both series are subject to subsequent corrections.

Employment data can often be found at state departments of planning and research or employment. These data are usually current and broken down by NAICS categories. From these data, it is usually possible to track primary employment sectors to assess local economic trends.

LAND SUPPLY

The United States encompasses nearly 2.3 billion acres (about 3.6 million square miles of land),[12] which currently supports a population of approximately 319 million.[13] It is the fourth-largest country by area and the third largest by population.

Developed land takes up less than 6 percent or 113 million acres of the total land area (forest takes up 21 percent, pasture and range 27 percent, cropland 19 percent, federal land 21 percent, and other uses 6 percent).[14] The present land-to-people ratio in the United States is about 7.2 acres per person, or 89 persons per square mile, which may seem inconceivably low to someone living in New York City but may sound crowded to a Montana rancher.

Significant quantities of undeveloped land exist even in the urbanized metropolitan areas. These reserves result from leapfrog suburban development, abandoned or dying central-city neighborhoods, and relatively low-density development patterns in some urban areas. In recent years, however, the high cost of infrastructure—roads, water, and sewerage—and shrinking government funds for the extension of services has led community groups, planners, and real estate interests to seek ways to constrain suburban sprawl through farmland preservation programs, limits on utility extensions, impact fees, urban growth boundaries, habitat areas, and/or incentives for development in designated growth areas, resulting in higher-density commercial and residential land uses.

At the same time, metropolitan areas continue to expand outward geographically, so that the effect of population growth exceeds the impact of increased density. In 1960, metropolitan areas housed 63 percent of the U.S. population on 9 percent of the country's land area. In 2010, more than 80 percent of the nation's population lived in metropolitan areas. Urbanization of population is a worldwide trend. In 1960, only one-third of the global population lived in urban areas. In 2008, for the first time, more than half lived in urban areas; by 2050, the urban population is expected to include two-thirds of the world's people.[15]

A significant portion of developed land is occupied by residential development. Americans' love of space is exemplified by trends in homebuilding. Despite shrinking households, Americans continue to demand more interior living space. The median size of a new single-family house grew from 1,595 square feet in 1980, to 2,057 square feet in 2000, to 2,475 square feet in 2013.[16] Americans' tenacious demand for ever-larger single-family homes explains why small homes in desirable city neighborhoods and close-in suburbs are being torn down and replaced with larger—and more expensive—residences. Also, in high-cost areas, single-family detached homes are being built on smaller lots than in the past. In parts of California, it is common to find single-family houses built on lots of less than 3,000 square feet, at a density of nearly 14 units per acre. A significant corollary to this trend of less land and more house is the steadily growing share of new houses with two or more stories: 17 percent in 1970, 31 percent in 1980, and 55 percent in 2012.[17] Still, opposite trends are also occurring, such as a proliferation of micro-apartments in high-cost cities.

Who Owns the Land? How Is It Used?

With 402 million acres, or about 21 percent of the nation's 1.9 billion acres, the federal government is the largest single landowner in the United States; in fact, Uncle Sam owns 60 percent or more of four states: Nevada, Alaska, Utah, and Idaho.[18] As urbanization pushes the boundaries of metropolitan areas outward, farm acreage is declining. At its peak in 1954, more than 1.2 billion acres were under some form of cultivation. By 2010, only 387 million acres were considered active cropland—a 68 percent drop.[19] Moreover, individually owned farms are gradually being replaced by a smaller number of larger, corporate-owned agricultural holdings. The family farm certainly has not disappeared, but globalization of food production, processing, and marketing is changing farm ownership and operations.

Although government, forest product companies, utilities, and railroads control extremely large land holdings, real estate in the United States is widely owned by individual citizens and small partnerships. Throughout U.S. history, governments at all levels have actively promoted private ownership of land and homes, for social, political, and economic reasons. As explained in chapter 6, a variety of programs and policies have advanced homeownership: the Federal Housing Administration's mortgage insurance program and the Veterans Administration's mortgage guarantee program (which revolutionized home mortgage lending in the 1940s and 1950s); the federally facilitated secondary mortgage market for home loans (through the quasi-federal corporations known as Fannie Mae and Freddie Mac); tax legislation benefiting both homeowners and private investors in commercial and industrial real estate; and, most important, provision of the infrastructure needed to support private property ownership. In 2013, approximately 65 percent of all U.S. householders owned their homes. The value of owner-occupied housing (in terms of debt and equity) is far greater than that of commercial real estate.

Apartment ownership is diverse and widespread. According to the National Multi Housing Council (NMHC), the top 50 apartment owners in the United States in 2013 had an ownership interest in 2.90 million units, approximately 16 percent of the national apartment stock. Among these owners, ten are publicly traded REITs, accounting for 552,846 apartments or 19 percent of the units covered in the 2013 NMHC survey.

Foreign Ownership of Real Estate in the United States

The relative ease of acquiring property that U.S. citizens take for granted strongly attracts foreign investors to U.S. real estate. In many other developed nations, real estate markets are much smaller and laws dramatically restrict foreign investment. Property in the United States attracts offshore capital for several reasons: the perceived political and economic stability, the sheer size of the market, and the potential for appreciation. Data from the BEA indicate that foreign investment in U.S properties rose to $50.5 billion in 2012, up from $44.6 billion in 2010.[20] Forty-five percent of this investment comes from Europe; Asia and Latin America combined have invested another 40 percent. Looking at it another way, U.S. property owners closed more than $38.7 billion in foreign real estate investments in 2013 alone, a 40 percent increase over the preceding year.[21]

REAL ESTATE, GROSS DOMESTIC PRODUCT, WEALTH, AND EMPLOYMENT

Real estate is a significant component of gross private domestic investment in the United States. For individuals, real estate is an extremely important component of wealth, besides providing shelter and psychic benefits such as pride and security. Housing equity constitutes the largest portion of most households' net worth.[22] The importance of the real estate industry in the United States is also reflected in national employment figures. In 2013, the economy provided more than 137 million nonfarm jobs, of which 2.0 million were in real estate businesses and another 5.8 million in construction.[23] Overall, 5.7 percent of the nation's employment is attributable to real estate development, construction, management, and sales.

Figure 2-12	**Employment in Construction and Real Estate, 2004–2013 (Millions of Workers)**	
Year	**Construction**	**Real Estate**
2004	6.98	2.08
2005	7.33	2.13
2006	7.69	2.17
2007	7.63	2.17
2008	7.16	2.13
2009	6.01	1.99
2010	5.52	1.93
2011	5.53	1.92
2012	5.65	1.95
2013	5.83	2.00

Source: U.S. Bureau of Labor Statistics, Current Employment Statistics survey program, www.bls.gov/ces/home.htm.

SUMMARY

Understanding the present and past is the necessary first step in projecting future opportunities in real estate. Extrapolation is not simple, however. Economic conditions have a way of confounding forecasters who assume that past trends will simply continue. But technology, consumer preferences, government policy, demographics, sources of capital, and economic underpinnings all evolve—at times slowly and at other times rapidly in response to crisis. Many of these factors can dramatically affect what will happen in the real estate world. Moreover, not all real estate cycles operate in unison. Localities and regions vary, as do property types. It may be a weak market for the southeast, but a great one for the Pacific Coast; office demand may be weak while apartment demand is strong. The lesson for real estate practitioners is to stay well informed and to understand how events and trends affect real estate.

TERMS

- Baby boomers
- Consolidated metropolitan statistical area (CMSA)
- Demographics
- Metropolitan statistical area (MSA)
- Office-prone employment
- Population pyramid
- Purchasing power
- Service sector
- Single-person household
- Smart growth
- Informal economy

REVIEW QUESTIONS

2.1 Why is ownership of real estate more attractive in the United States than in many other countries?

2.2 Why have U.S. developers looked outside the country for development opportunities?

2.3 Why is real estate so important to the U.S. economy?

2.4 Describe the anticipated changes in the composition of the U.S. population.

2.5 How does immigration affect demand for real estate?

2.6 How does employment growth influence the demand for commercial space?

2.7 Why is it important for real estate players to stay well informed about trends?

2.8 How significant is the construction industry to the nation's overall economy?

2.9 How does the aging baby boom generation affect the population pyramid?

2.10 How might the housing market be affected by a population in which less than 30 percent of all households have children under the age of 18?

2.11 How will the significant growth in the "Professional and Business Services" and the "Health Care and Social Assistance" employment sectors affect the demand for real estate?

2.12 What portion of land in the United States is developed?

NOTES

1 Jeffrey Passel, "Population Decline of Unauthorized Immigration Stalls, May Have Reversed: New Estimate 11.7 million in 2012," Pew Hispanic Research Center, September 23, 2013.

2 Gregory Auclair and Jeanne Batalova, *Naturalization Trends in the United States*. Migration Policy Institute, October 24, 2013.

3 U.S. Census Bureau, *2012 National Population Projections: Summary Tables*.

4 U.S. Census Bureau, *Census 2010*, Summary Population and Housing Characteristics.

5 M. Leanne Lachman and Deborah L. Brett, *Generation Y: America's New Housing Wave* (Washington, D.C.: Urban Land Institute, 2011), pp. 5, 8, and 11.

6 U.S. Census Bureau, *Census 2010*, Households and Families 2010, Table 2.

7 www.statista.com/statistics/183648/average-size-of-households-in-the-us.

8 George S. Masnick, Daniel McCue, and Eric S. Belsky, "Updated 2010–2020 Household and New Home Demand Projections," Joint Center for Housing Studies, Harvard University, September 2010.

9 U.S. Census Bureau, Current Population Reports, *Income, Poverty, and Health Insurance Coverage in the United States: 2012*.

10 Jesse Bricker, Arthur B. Kennickell, Kevin B. Moore, and John Sabelhaus, "Changes in U.S. Family Finances from 2007 to 2010: Evidence from the Survey of Consumer Finances," *Federal Reserve Bulletin*, Vol. 98 (June 2012), p. 17.

11 Erin Carlyle, "America's Fastest Growing Cities," *Forbes*, February 14, 2014.

12 U.S. Census Bureau, *Statistical Abstract of the United States: 2012*, Table 1.

13 Census Bureau estimate as of October 2014.

14 U.S. Department of Agriculture, Natural Resources and Conversation Services, *Natural Resources Inventory Summary Report 2010*.

15 http://esa.un.org/unup/CD-ROM/Urban-Rural-Population.htm

16 http://eyeonhousing.org/2014/03/04/average-size-of-new-single-family-homes-at-the-end-of-2013.

17 U.S. Census Bureau, "Characteristics of New Housing, 2012."

18 NRCM, "Public Land Ownership by State," www.nrcm.org/documents/publiclandownership.pdf.

19 U.S. Department of Agriculture, Natural Resources and Conversation Services, *Natural Resources Inventory Summary Report 2010*.

20 Jeffrey H. Lowe, "Direct Investment Positions for 2009–2011: Detailed Historical-Cost Positions and Related Financial and Income Flows," *Survey of Current Business*, September 2012, p. 80; U.S. Bureau of Economic Analysis, "Foreign Direct Investment in the U.S.," Table 4.

21 REBusiness Online, "U.S. remains top destination for foreign commercial real estate investment," March 5, 2014.

22 Federal Reserve Bank, Flow of Funds Report, "Balance Sheet of Households and Non-Profit Organizations," Series Z.1, Table B.100, issued March 6, 2014.

23 U.S. Department of Labor, Bureau of Labor Statistics, *Current Employment Statistics 2013—National*.

Chapter 3

Developers and Their Partners

Developing a real estate project is like producing a movie in many ways: A developer (producer) assembles a team to create the project. A movie requires actors, scriptwriters, location scouts, accountants, attorneys, lighting technicians, and many other professionals. Similarly, a real estate project requires architects, accountants, attorneys, engineers, marketing specialists, and many others. Like a movie producer, a developer does not need the same team for each undertaking. Projects vary, so the developer composes a team having the skill set for the unique requirements of each project.

The developer's role is that of a generalist. He should have enough knowledge of a wide range of subject areas to effectively communicate his vision and manage the development team. Although deep technical skills are not always necessary, the developer's knowledge should be sufficient to evaluate the work and identify potential problems and conflicts.

To fully appreciate the role of developers in shaping the environment, it is necessary to understand the function and motivation of the major participants in the development process.

Development is a dynamic art that takes a considerable period of time—often several years. During that time, the many changes likely to be made to the original development plan may require new skills and different players.

THE MAJOR PLAYERS

- Private sector developers
- Public/private partnerships
- Architects
- Engineers
- Landscape architects
- Land planners
- Urban designers
- Building contractors
- Site development and grading contractors
- Environmental consultants
- Traffic and transportation consultants
- Biology consultants
- Geotechnical and soils consultants
- Hazardous substance consultants
- Air quality consultants
- Greenhouse gas consultants

- Noise consultants
- Market research analysts
- Lenders
- Construction lenders
- Permanent lenders
- Joint venture partners
- Appraisers
- Public finance consultants
- Attorneys
- Accountants
- Real estate leasing agents and/or sales brokers
- Marketing and public relations consultants
- Property managers
- Regulators
- End users

Private Sector Developers

Developers should have certain personal qualities. To be fully effective, they should possess clarity of vision. They must be persistent but also flexible and able to build consensus when they encounter opposition. Local authorities and community groups can have a powerful impact on a project, and developers may face an arduous approvals process that may require significant alterations to the project. Still, too much compromise can produce an unfocused project or financial failure.

Private developers range from straight fee to speculative developers. In the case of a fee developer, a client such as a retailer, health care provider, university, REIT, or public sector agency hires the developer to see a project through from concept to completion. Such developers usually receive a fee, possibly with a bonus for successful completion and timely delivery of the product. Speculative developers (and their investors) own the equity; they bear the downside as well as the upside risks of the relationship between final value and total cost.

Although many business models exist, developers generally receive financial compensation from one or more of the following sources:

- A *development fee*, which is payment for developing the project. It is often structured to cover the overhead of the developer that is directly attributed to the project.
- Profits on the sale of the project to end users (in the case of a for-sale project) or to an investor.
- A *promote* or ownership interest in excess of the developer's percentage contribution to the project's equity capitalization.
- Ownership of entities that sell services related to the development process, such as insurance agencies, mortgage banking firms, leasing and brokerage companies, management companies, or even general contracting firms.

Developers also receive many intangible returns, including the personal and professional satisfaction of advancing a new concept or improving the urban environment and an enhanced reputation, which creates future opportunities for development.

Like most businesspeople, developers seek to maximize return while minimizing risk. Financial risk for private developers arises in two ways. First, at the predevelopment stage, developers spend time and money before gaining assurance that a project will be built. Their expenditures may include due diligence, feasibility, and the community relations effort needed to formalize a development concept. Second, in addition to their own equity position (both contributed capital and debt for which developers are personally liable), developers may be required to guarantee investors and lenders protection against project cost overruns or initial vacancy losses. Developers' financial exposure depends on the amount of their direct financial commitment, plus the magnitude of any guarantees they make and the likelihood that the guarantees will be called on.

Developers come from a wide range of backgrounds, as indicated by the profiles featured throughout this book. Often contractors, architects, and other participants described in this chapter decide to move into development roles. The role is open to all who are up to the challenge.

INNOVATOR   **Gerald Hines** | Houston, Texas

Born in 1925 in Gary, Indiana, Gerald Hines learned at a young age that he did not want to follow in his father's footsteps as an employee of U.S. Steel. During the summers of World War II, while still in high school, Hines got the only taste he needed of manual labor. Determined to earn a university degree, Hines had to postpone his plans after his enlistment in the Army. After serving as a lieutenant in the combat engineers, Hines earned a degree in mechanical engineering from Purdue University in 1948. He then moved to Houston, where he began his career as one of the nation's most prominent developers.

Starting as a mechanical systems designer provided an easy transition into the development business. "I just got to know buildings very well," he said. "Then I thought I would like to build them." The Houston real estate market, then flush with oil money, provided an ideal environment. Hines erected his first building in 1952—a straightforward combination of office and warehouse space. After completing several similar buildings, he began his career in earnest in 1957 as a full-time developer.

As the sixties came to a close, Hines's firm—then called Hines Interests—had nearly 100 completed projects under its belt. Hines began office development along a stretch of I-610 known as the West Loop with the 22-story Post Oak Tower in 1970. In the same year, the first phase of the 420,000-square-foot Houston Galleria shopping center opened. This project proved to be a watershed for his career and the springboard for ambitious projects. Modeled after Milan's 19th-century Galleria Vittorio Emanuele, famous for its high-end shops and elegant design, the Houston Galleria attracted many upscale tenants and became a runaway success. The popularity of the design and its many retail and dining options led Hines to develop several more projects near the Galleria over the next 27 years.

Hines hit the mark again with the development of One Shell Plaza in 1971, his first high-rise venture in downtown Houston. For this project, he commissioned Skidmore, Owings & Merrill, the nation's preeminent corporate architecture firm, to design the building. It has several notable attributes: an Italian travertine marble exterior; wind-bracing columns at eight points, giving it an undulating façade; and its height—at 50 stories, then the tallest building west of the Mississippi River. Originally intended to serve as regional offices for Shell Oil Company, it was quickly requisitioned for the company's world headquarters. It became apparent that Hines intended to target the high end of the market while incorporating innovative structural and other cost-saving methods into the designs.

Riding on the success of One Shell Plaza, Hines was energized to undertake another bold project. For Pennzoil Place, he brought in acclaimed architect Philip Johnson of Johnson/Burgee Architects. The building, consisting of two trapezoidal towers only ten feet apart, has 45-degree angled roofs and an all-glass facade. It has been described as "one of the most architecturally influential buildings

constructed in the United States during the 1970s and 1980s." More than satisfying the company chair's request for "a building with character that would stand out from the undecorated glass boxes around town," Pennzoil Place, developed for $50 million, eventually was sold for more than $200 million. The handsome profits demonstrate the foresight and quality of Hines buildings compared with the commonplace structures offered by many of his competitors.

To Hines, designing an architecturally distinctive building makes perfect business sense. He strongly believes that "buildings of quality ... attract better tenants, command higher rents, and retain their value despite the ups and downs of the real estate market." Viewed as a patron of good design in architectural circles, Hines eschews simply budgetary considerations when developing a site. Obviously the object is to turn a profit, but Hines's calculus for doing so may include opting for a slightly more expensive material or systems if doing so will enhance overall quality and the eventual resale value. "A well-designed building," he says, "is the first to fill up—the main objective, after all—and the last to get vacated."

Despite the success of his signature corporate towers that grace the skylines of cities across the country, Hines prefers to erect building clusters that make a place. He takes special pride in the Diagonal Mar development in Barcelona, Spain. After acquiring the site in 1996 as an undesirable project, Hines turned the 84-acre development into a thriving $600 million mixed-use community. This prosperous makeover exemplifies his eye for opportune acquisitions, even in the tricky international arena.

Hines's mixed-use development, the 64-story Transco Tower (now the Williams Tower) and the 2.5 million-square-foot Galleria, created a completely new suburban-style business district outside Houston's downtown.

Continued on page 32

INNOVATOR **Gerald Hines** | Houston, Texas *Continued from page 31*

A man of detail, Hines considers every aspect of his projects and works to produce the highest result. According to Peter Rummell, a fellow developer, Hines knows how to put himself "in the consumer's position of how a project will be experienced." He seeks to improve energy efficiency in his buildings and drives innovation in that arena. Since 1992, his company has been a partner in the U.S. EPA's Energy Star program.

Emphasizing the theory that development is best performed by local firms, Hines has established a corporate structure that places decision making in the hands of local offices. As his company has grown, it has expanded to more than 110 cities and 18 foreign countries, employing about 3,000 people. Trusting bottom-up management has allowed Hines to decentralize his organization, tapping the wealth of knowledge in local places. He encourages a high level of communications throughout the development process to ensure a dynamic exchange of ideas and provide a system of checks and balances for executing decisions. Under this management structure, his is one of the largest real estate companies in the world, with control of an estimated $28 billion in assets.

Hines has proved that form can complement function in real estate development without fiscal abandon. His company has grown from a one-man operation to an international giant without losing sight of the mainstays of quality and innovative design. The company's numerous awards speak for the kind of product Hines strives for. In 2002, Hines was awarded the ULI J.C. Nichols Prize for Visionaries in Urban Development. He put the $100,000 from the award and a matched amount toward the funding of the ULI Hines Competition, which challenges students across the country to engage in quality urban design and planning. His is a legacy of high standards for the nation's future developers.

Public/Private Partnerships

A public/private partnership is one in which a private developer works with public authorities and public resources to develop a project that has both public and private components. The public/private developer is a private developer who works for profit but teams up with a public partner in exchange for access to public resources and assets. Public/private partnerships can be a way to address a pressing need for infrastructure and other public facilities (public/private partnerships are discussed further in chapter 8).

Architects

Architects offer a wide range of services to developers and, like other players, may work as outside professionals or as in-house members of the development team. Architects handle two major functions in the development process: they help develop the concept, and they create the detailed plans that enable a contractor to construct the project.

Architects are often involved at the early stages of the development process when they can help guide a developer in selecting a site for a specified use or develop alternative concepts for a site. They may be active participants in the regulatory process, helping a developer to secure approvals and working with community groups to understand their needs.

Architects are key to communicating a project concept to the community, including public officials, public sector staff, and the neighborhood at large. The architect can help explain and differentiate between design features. A good architect can be a great asset to a developer in the midst of a strenuous approval process.

Detailed illustrations or models of projects can be instrumental in winning public approval for the high-density and mixed-use projects that are becoming increasingly common. Moreover, architects may have a more favorable public image than developers and thus may be more effective in dealing with the public and public sector agencies.

During design development, more specialists are brought in to refine the design concept. *Structural engineers*, HVAC (heating, ventilation, and air conditioning) engineers, and others may be needed for the design of elevators, interior stairwells, plumbing, and other building components, especially in more complex buildings. After these refinements are incorporated into the architect's concept, the building assumes its final design. Each iteration requires key decisions by the developer and architect, working as a team.

During the working drawing stage, the architect creates the detailed plans that will enable cost estimates, public authority reviews and approvals, and creation of a bid package for contractors. Once construction begins, depending on the agreement with the developer, the architect is usually responsible for monitoring—but not supervising—the work site. The architect is expected to inspect the site periodically to determine whether contract documents are being followed faithfully. The developer and his financial sources rely on the architect, or an on-site construction manager in larger projects, to confirm that construction work phases have been completed satisfactorily. The architect's approval is usually required for each construction loan drawn from the construction lender. The architect attests to compliance with plans and specifications and bears legal *liability* for the plans and specifications for the number of years specified by the state government.

Architects are licensed under health and safety laws. They must pass an examination administered by the National Council of Architectural Registration Boards (NCARB), which has promulgated standards and criteria adopted by licensing boards as their standard for admission to licensing examinations. Registration takes eight to ten years—five to seven years of study at a university and three years of internship at an architectural or related practice.

Architects can be paid in several ways. Many developers hire architects initially on an hourly basis, until the project is fleshed out and the scope of services is clear. When the developer and architect establish that they will continue working together, they often negotiate a contract whereby the architect's fee is a percentage of the construction cost.

In addition to aesthetic considerations, the architect should have experience in the jurisdiction in which the project is to be built. She should have experience in the appropriate class of construction and in the use for which the building is intended. A walk-up wood-frame apartment project requires different skill sets than a high-rise mixed-use structure, for instance.

The selection process should be undertaken with care. The developer should evaluate finished buildings (not just unbuilt plans), and talk to clients

and other sources to help ensure that he selects an appropriate architect. Sometimes, the developer will build a team of architects, selecting a national firm for design and a local firm for detailed drawings. For example, developer OliverMcMillan paired Gensler, an international firm, with Architects Hawaii Ltd., a local firm, to design Symphony Honolulu, a LEED-certified 45-story luxury condominium tower.

Good design is important because a building stands for a long time. People experience it as part of their built environment, part of their everyday lives. It is part of the context of a city that creates a unique sense of place. It can be iconic, or it can blend into an existing urban context.

Engineers

Many types of engineers play important roles in the development process. In general, engineers are responsible for translating designers' work into more specific drawings and specifications that determine the technical aspects of the structure. They are critical to physical safety, comfort, and the efficient operation of a building. Their failure to deliver a safe product can have life-threatening consequences. Some engineers provide services related to the vertical structure; others are involved with site preparation and the impact of the project on the surrounding community. Several types of engineers with specific expertise—civil, structural, mechanical, and electrical—are required to ensure that the design can accommodate the required physical systems.

Civil engineers may be contracted for their expertise in land development, particularly for the design and construction of infrastructure, such as streets and systems for water, sewer, gas, electricity, telephone, cable, and storm drainage. They ensure that civil systems meet health, safety, and welfare requirements. Civil engineering firms often have a survey team that determines a property's physical and legal characteristics such as boundaries, easements, rights-of-way, and dedications, and then prepares a site map that plots these dimensions. This site map reveals how much of the site is buildable. Surveyors generally prepare two types of surveys: (1) a boundary survey, often called an ALTA (short for American Land Title Association) survey; and (2) a construction survey, which plots the location of relevant infrastructure to assist in planning connections to utility services.

Environmental engineers may be needed, particularly if a structure on the site—whether scheduled for renovation or for demolition—may contain hazardous substances.

Structural engineers work with the architect, particularly during the initial design phase, to ensure that plans are structurally sound. They can identify cost-saving measures that meet structural design and construction requirements. They are also responsible for producing drawings for the construction contractor that explain the structural system in detail, including connections and the size of the structural elements. Structural engineers assist the architect in ensuring a building's structural integrity. They work closely with soils engineers to determine the most appropriate foundation system and produce a set of drawings for the *general contractor* that explain that system in detail.

Mechanical engineers design HVAC, plumbing, life safety, and other mechanical systems and ensure that mechanical systems will serve the project adequately.

Electrical engineers design electrical power and distribution systems, including lighting, circuitry, and backup power supplies.

Engineers may be hired directly by the developer, or more typically, engaged by the architect. In either case, they maintain close relationships with the architectural staff as the project unfolds. Architects often hire engineers as the main design *subcontractor*. Typically, as head of the design team, the architect is responsible for the work of the engineers. Engineers' fees are often included in the architect's budget. However, developers have the option to negotiate contracts directly with different engineers. In more complex developments, engineers might also function as construction managers, supplementing the architect in supervising construction.

Engineers must be licensed by the state in which they operate, and plans cannot be approved unless they are signed by a licensed professional engineer. Like architects, engineers are licensed under health and safety laws and bear legal liability for their plans and specifications for some number of years. The duration of liability corresponds to the nature of the undertaking and the time allowed for recognizing defects.

In addition to being licensed, engineers are usually members of a professional engineering society such as the National Society of Professional Engineers (NSPE), the American Society of Mechanical Engineers (ASME), or the American Society of Heating, Refrigerating, and Air-conditioning Engineers (ASHRAE).

Landscape Architects

Landscape architecture encompasses the analysis, design, planning, management, and stewardship of the natural and built environment, which complement the primary structure. Developers often rely on the landscape design to help define the special nature or theme of the project, especially in residential master-planned communities and in mixed-use development projects, where the landscape design can help unite and define spaces. Landscape design creates a sense of place. It can create a sense of privacy within areas. Landscape forms can be used to soften the visual impact of development and transition between adjacent land uses. Architecture can create boundaries, and landscape design can humanize those boundaries, maintaining them but making them softer and more in scale with the people who use the site.

Landscape architects produce the master plans for all landscaping and hardscaping. They create the environment through the selection and siting of landscape forms and plant materials, and the strategic use of light and shade. They define the character of roadways and design walkways, outdoor lighting, outdoor seating, water features, railings, signs, grates, retaining walls, bus shelters, picnic shelters, outdoor waiting areas, outdoor play areas, and bicycle and walking trails.

Landscape architects help create memorable places. Examples are both large and small, classic

J. ALTDORFER PHOTOGRAPHY

Pittsburgh's Market Square provides flexible, pedestrian-only space for dining and events, surrounded by downtown businesses.

and recent: Frederick Law Olmsted's 1,100-acre "Emerald Necklace" series of parks, parkways, and waterways in and around Boston; Bradshaw Gill & Associates' plaza at CityPlace, in West Palm Beach, Florida; and the renovation of Market Square in downtown Pittsburgh, by Klavon Design Associates.

Landscape architects may also provide consulting services for wastewater management, wetlands mitigation, the preservation of wildlife habitats, *ecosystem management*, xeriscaping and irrigation, *sustainable site design*, and land reclamation. They are key contributors to the creation of sustainable environments, which limit the resources taken from the community and limit the impact of the project on the community. Sustainable site design can also contribute to more economic development by limiting the cost of infrastructure and ongoing maintenance.

The American Society of Landscape Architects (ASLA) is a national professional society representing the landscape architecture profession in the United States. Forty-seven states license landscape architects.

Land Planners

A land planner is often engaged for large, multistructure projects such as a master-planned community. A good site plan results in the most efficient use of property, taking into account topography, circulation, and land uses. It creates an environment that is aesthetically pleasing and that respects the characteristics of the land and its surrounding community.

Like the architect, the land planner bases his work on the project concept and the intended market. In so doing, he uses technical information about the land, including a topographic map, legal restrictions, environmentally sensitive areas, access, geologic conditions, and other factors. Often, the first step in the land planning process is an opportunities and constraints map that overlays the site conditions on a base map. Constraints are interpreted in light of the project concept and market goals for the project.

In a master-planned community, the land planner works with the developer and the marketing team to create themes for the overall site development. A theme is an expression of consistency in architecture, landscape design, signage, monumentation, and other elements to create an image and a sense of place. The master plan prepared by the land planner takes into consideration the natural amenities of the site (such as trees, water features, and rolling hills) and the constraints (floodplains, wetlands, and steep inclines). The planner is usually responsible for determining the traffic circulation pattern, the allocation of open space, the location of on-site amenities, and the mix of land uses.

Riverfront Park in downtown Denver is the result of a 25-year development process to create a

In Santiago, Chile, Territoria 3000 is a mixed-use building with premium offices, retail space, a hotel, and residences. The building leads the market in terms of rents and occupancy.

23-acre urban infill project. Thus far, the project includes nearly 2,000 units of housing, 49,000 square feet of retail and restaurant space, a museum, and three parks. East West Partners, the developer, hired Design Workshop as the master planner. The parks were designed by landscape architects Civitas, Inc., and the buildings by four architecture firms: 42/40 Architecture, Oz Architecture, Preston Partnership, and Humphries Poli Architects.

A large project often requires amendments to land use regulations, such as a jurisdiction's general plan. It may require supporting documents such as a specific plan, environmental impact documents, or zoning amendments, which are often discretionary approvals granted by an elected governing body. The land planner, working with other members of the development team, may be responsible for creating these documents.

Some of the land planner's expertise and contribution to the development can overlap with those of the urban designer and the landscape architect. Land planners may be independent practitioners or part of landscape architecture or architecture firms. The main professional society for land planners is the American Planning Association (APA), which has no licensing requirements but offers its members certification through the American Institute of Certified Planners (AICP).

Urban Designers

Developers of large projects often employ an urban designer to coordinate individual buildings with public spaces, open spaces, and the larger neighborhood. Urban designers create master plans, strategic plans, and detailed site plans, and help craft visions. Often, working closely with neighborhood groups and other interested parties, urban designers produce the plan and detailed drawings of key development elements that guide future growth in a neighborhood or a special district such as a waterfront or a master-planned community.

Urban designers and other professionals may engage in public outreach to identify and discuss the views of the stakeholders in a community. This outreach may consist of surveys, focus groups, or design charrettes. Charrettes are typically several-day workshops in which interested parties provide input or collaborate to arrive at an agreed-upon scheme for a city, site, or other specified area. Through this process, a shared vision arises, often facilitating the *entitlement process*. The results of such processes and subsequent efforts by the developer often contribute to a presentation of the development to government authorities and community groups to win their approval.

Urban designers may be trained as architects, landscape architects, or city planners who chose to concentrate in this specialty.

Building Contractors

Building contractors turn ideas into physical form. A large project typically involves a general contractor who is responsible for the overall project and who hires subcontractors to perform specialized work, such as excavation, HVAC installation, electrical wiring, plumbing, and dozens more construction line items. The responsibility of the general contractor is to schedule subcontractors' work and monitor its quality to ensure that it satisfies the general contractor's obligations to the developer.

The developer typically executes a contract with the general contractor to build the project, according to the plans and specifications developed by the architect and engineer, for an agreed-upon price (or price structure) and schedule. The general contractor, in turn, subcontracts with specialty tradespeople and pays them as their work is completed. In some cases, developers serve as their own general contractors and contract directly with subcontractors. However, many variations of these contractual arrangements are possible.

General contractors are often chosen through a selective bidding process in which the developer asks a number of contracting firms to submit proposals and general statements of qualifications that include descriptions of past projects, references from clients and lenders, résumés of key employees, and, possibly, verification that the company is bondable (that an insurance company will stand behind the contractor's contractual obligations). Often the construction lender has minimum requirements for general contractors' qualifications.

To start the bidding process, a developer sends out a notice requesting bids and statements of the required qualifications. The contractor (or subcontractor) that submits the lowest bid is not always the developer's best choice; the best player for the development team may have critical attributes, such as more experience or greater reliability, that outweigh their cost.

Contractors' fees are based on the size, difficulty, and risk involved in the project. The general contractor may charge a fee equivalent to 5 percent of hard costs plus project overhead and on-site supervision costs, but considerable variation can be seen in the marketplace. In a project funded by a construction lender, the terms of payment are governed by the terms of the loan documents as well as the construction contract. Those payment terms define the frequency of payment, the documents required before the release of each payment, and the amount of "holdback" that the lender retains until the work is satisfactorily completed. Associated Builders and Contractors (ABC) and Associated General Contractors (AGC) are just two of several trade associations for contractors.

Site Development and Grading Contractors

Before anything can be built, the site needs to be prepared. This work includes demolition of any old structures, excavation, grading, and utility work. Site development and grading contractors are most often hired and managed by the general contractor, though they can be hired and managed by the developer. The site development contractor works closely with the civil engineer and general contractor to ensure the site is prepared properly in accordance with the civil engineering plans and to resolve any issues that arise during site development.

Site development costs can vary significantly, depending on the complexity of the project, any subterranean obstacles, the location and quality of existing utilities, and the extent of any environmental remediation needed. Payment for the services of a site development contractor either follows the pattern described for subcontractors to general contractors or, when the developer hires the site development contractor directly, is based on a negotiated contract.

Environmental Consultants

Many developments require extensive technical work both as part of the entitlement process and as part of the construction of the project. Some of this work is required as part of the physical construction, but much is related to the regulatory process at the federal, state, and local levels of government.

Environmental consultants perform site reviews that may reveal important considerations in a developer's decision to go forward. Because environmental regulations are complex, developers may need expert help in navigating the maze to determine whether a project is feasible from a regulatory standpoint and if so, to produce the documentation necessary to receive approval from the appropriate agencies. Equally important are estimates of the cost of dealing with environmental issues.

Environmental consultants should be versed in the regulatory policies of all levels of government:

- The federal government regulates development through the Endangered Species Act and the Clean Water Act. Both pieces of legislation entail complex regulations that govern developmental impacts on plant and animal life and on wetlands. When a project may affect any area governed by these acts, those effects must be mitigated in accordance with those regulations, an effort that is time-consuming, costly, and complicated.
- Most state governments have adopted state-specific environmental legislation. Their regulations may go deeper and include subjects not addressed at the federal level.
- Local jurisdictions may have environmental regulations that go beyond state or federal regulations in level of detail and in scope.

The environmental consultant may hire more specialized consultants if warranted.

Traffic and Transportation Consultants

Few issues generate as much controversy during the approval process as traffic and transportation. Traffic and *transportation consultants* measure the impact of the project in terms of trips generated and the impacts of those trips on road segments and intersections. These measurements are based on *traffic models* that incorporate projections of future land uses. Improvements to mitigate the impact of projects on the surrounding community are identified as part of this process.

Transportation consultants may have experience in several specialties, including parking, traffic, signal technology, and other issues related to transportation. For example, if a jurisdiction has capped the number of parking spaces that can be built for a development, a transportation consultant can help the developer establish certain programs to accommodate office tenants—ride sharing, parking incentives for carpools, fare incentives for use of mass transit, and shuttle bus service between the project and transit facilities.

A parking consultant may be needed early in the design process to enable the architect to incorporate parking recommendations in the overall design. Parking is a significant and costly component, and parking consultants provide an array of solutions, from planning circulation for parking garages to designing access roads to developing shared parking plans for mixed-use projects. Shared parking is the use of parking spaces by two or more land uses, with peak use often concentrated at different times of the day. Parking consultants evaluate the relative cost-effectiveness of alternatives such as surface and structured parking. They assess the ingress and egress points, and the financial feasibility of alternatives.

A transportation consultant may be paid in one of several arrangements: a lump-sum fee, costs plus a fixed fee, salary, costs times a multiplier, time and materials, or a percentage of construction costs for the parking structure.

Biology Consultants

The federal Endangered Species Act (1973) and state environmental regulations identify classes of plant and animal species that are of interest, threatened, or endangered. Before construction, a site must be surveyed to identify the presence of any of these resources. For any that are identified, federal and state regulations have protocols that set forth the manner in which the species may be impacted and, if necessary, such impacts mitigated. Biology consultants undertake field surveys to determine the potential for or presence of biological resources. These reports become the basis for the negotiation of mitigation plans that range from payment of fees to on-site preservation, to the funding of habitat preservation.

Geotechnical and Soils Consultants

Geotechnical and soil engineers determine the ability of the ground to support the proposed development. Their surveys identify major structural features such as earthquake faults and landslides, as well as the *bearing capacity* of the soil. This information becomes part of the design requirements, in the specifications of the required depth and type of foundations, compaction, and setbacks. Geotechnical reports are also part of the information that excavation and grading contractors need for determining their scope of work.

Hazardous Substance Consultants

Generally, hazardous materials exist as the result of prior activity on a site. Such materials may be in a structure or in the soil. A hazardous materials study sets forth the procedures for safe removal of the substances from the site and disposal at an approved site.

The hazardous materials consultant will often begin with a "Phase I" report that identifies potential or existing environmental conditions at a site, on the basis of historic uses and known environmental issues at the property and in the vicinity. It may be followed by a "Phase II" report that entails a survey of the site and testing of suspicious materials. If hazardous materials are found, the consultant creates a mitigation plan that quantifies the amount of such materials, their potential danger, and the cost and proper means of disposal.

Air Quality Consultants

The federal Clean Air Act Amendment of 1990 instituted traffic control measures as a strategy for reducing air pollution emissions from cars, trucks, and buses. Enforcement of the act and provisions for reducing trips have increased the need for air quality consultants, who calculate the impacts of construction and operational traffic on the environment. Information about such impacts is usually included in environmental impact statements as part of the public approval process.

Professionals in this field are usually educated in environmental science or environmental engineering. They may hold certifications as a qualified environmental professional, certified hazardous materials manager, or certified industrial hygienist.

Greenhouse Gas Consultants

Global warming concerns have added another element to environmental reviews: the analysis of greenhouse gas contributions of a project. Like air quality consultants, greenhouse gas consultants work with models that calculate the contribution that a project makes to greenhouse gasses.

Noise Consultants

Any project will raise the ambient noise level during its construction and possibly during its operation. Noise consultants work with models that measure the impact of noise emanating from the project and the impact of noise from surrounding sources that may affect the project after occupancy. As with other environmental issues, the larger the proposed development, the more likely the developer will need technical consulting assistance.

Market Research Analysts

The key component of feasibility is market potential. The market study is based on the developer's vision for the property and will measure the supply and demand conditions for the project, determine potential pricing, and estimate the sales or leasing period.

The developer uses the market researchers' work to determine the revenue assumptions for the economic analysis of the proposed project. Market researchers may come from a number of disciplines, including urban planning, economics, and business. They are usually consultants and are paid a flat fee for their work. Chapter 13 covers feasibility in detail.

Lenders

Construction lenders, which are often commercial banks, are responsible for financing debt during project construction. Such lenders rely on a permanent lender or on sales proceeds for repayment of the loan. Thus, they face the risk that construction costs will exceed the amount of the loan that they provide. If the developer is unable or unwilling to cover overruns, construction lenders usually have the option to foreclose on the property or increase the amount of the construction loan beyond the amount specified in the original documents. Construction lenders thus must weigh the risk of these undesirable outcomes against the expected return in interest and loan origination fees.

Permanent lenders finance the completed project through a long-term mortgage. They essentially take over financing from the construction lender. Permanent financing may have a wide range of terms, involving fixed or variable interest rates, amortization periods, and repayment dates. The size of the permanent loan is determined by the value of the property and the cash flow that the property generates to service debt.

Permanent financing is available from a variety of sources, including commercial banks, savings and loans institutions, insurance companies, pension funds, REITs, private investors, and joint venture partners. These sources may include domestic as well as foreign investors. Lenders often specialize in property types, locations, and risk tolerances. Chapters 10 and 11 provide details on how the lending process works.

Joint Venture Partners

The term "joint venture" is not a precise legal term but in common usage refers to an individual or institution that provides the developer with equity funding during the developmental or operational period of a project in return for a share of profits from the development.

Appraisers

Appraisers produce an estimate of a property's value using three standard valuation methodologies: the *income approach*, the *market comparable approach*, and the *cost approach* (for a more detailed look at these approaches, see chapter 13). Appraisers may be involved before, during, and after project completion and often take part in the financing process. They can also provide a broad range of services, from investment analysis to litigation support.

The Appraisal Qualifications Board of the Appraisal Foundation has established recommended levels of education and experience for appraisers. The Appraisal Institute awards two designations: MAI (member of the Appraisal Institute), for those experienced in valuation and evaluation of all types of property, and SRA (senior residential appraiser), for those experienced only in residential valuations.

Public Finance Consultants

Some projects involve the creation of public debt instruments to finance improvements that benefit the general community. Such improvements include major roads, bridges, parks, schools, and other public facilities. These finance vehicles are commonly called assessment districts, benefit districts, or community facility districts, or other terms defined by state legislation. Proceeds from the sale of bonds are used to construct or acquire these facilities, and the bonds are often tax-exempt. The creation of these districts and the issuance of bonds require collaboration among local government agencies, attorneys, and investment bankers.

Attorneys

Attorneys are important players throughout the development process. Different legal specialists are required for different facets of the process. Land use, leases, and construction contracts require attorneys with different legal specialties or subspecialties.

Transaction attorneys are essential for producing purchase and sale agreements and leases. Land use attorneys are helpful in the rezoning and entitlement process, where understanding the local political environment is critical. Attorneys are also needed for setting up homeowners' associations (HOAs) and covenants, conditions, and restrictions (CC&Rs).

Attorneys are licensed by the state or states in which they practice. They are typically paid by the hour, although fixed prices for certain transactions are not uncommon.

Accountants

Accountants keep the numbers straight, from basic bookkeeping to reporting to the Securities and Exchange Commission. They review and validate project financial projections and ensure compliance with state and federal regulations on public and private investment offerings. Accounting firms perform audit, tax, and advisory services at all phases of development and project management.

Certified public accountants are accountants who have passed the Uniform Certified Public Accountant Examination and met the educational requirements to attain certification by the state in which they operate.

Leasing Agents and Sales Brokers

Real estate sales brokers and leasing agents are hired by the developer to implement the marketing plan. They sell or lease space to prospective buyers or tenants. They secure tenants and negotiate leases within the framework of the project's business plan and tenants' needs and creditworthiness. Lease negotiations cover multiple aspects, from tenant improvements to rent per square foot and assignment of responsibility for operating costs.

Developers usually decide early in the development process whether leasing or sales will be carried out by in-house staff or by outside professionals. They must find the right agent for the job and structure compensation to align the agent's motivations with the developer's objectives. Sales and leasing agents are most often paid a percentage of the value

of the sale or lease but in some instances may be salaried or paid on some other basis.

Marketing and Public Relations Consultants

Marketing and public relations consultants communicate the project vision to the users of space and the community at large. They translate the benefits of the project into imagery and material to create an image to appeal to the target audiences. Good public relations can generate positive attitudes toward a project before it is started and can even help diffuse opposition to the development during the permitting process. A marketing strategist may also work with the broker to find and sign tenants or to presell units.

The principals and employees of a marketing and public relations consultant may be members of the Public Relations Society of America or the American Marketing Association. For a short-term project, their payment can take the form of a fixed fee or an hourly rate. For large projects, many developers find it useful to establish a long-term relationship with a firm by keeping it on retainer throughout all phases of the project.

Property Managers

Property managers can provide valuable insight during the design stage, particularly in management-intensive facilities. They are typically employed full time when the development is close to opening and remain employed throughout the life of the project. They provide direct oversight of maintenance, repairs, security, and operation to preserve and enhance the property's value. They usually remain in constant contact with tenants, as they are the intermediaries between tenants and the owner.

Property managers may be independent firms or an in-house subsidiary of the developer. Compensation is typically a percentage of gross revenue—often 2 to 5 percent—but can also be a fixed amount. Commissions for leasing are usually separate from the management agreement. Property managers are often members of the Building Owners and Managers Association (BOMA) or the Institute of

---

INNOVATOR **James A. Graaskamp** | Former Chair and Professor, Department of Real Estate and Urban Land Economics, University of Wisconsin at Madison

The late Jim Graaskamp was a hero and mentor to his students and others who knew him. At the time of his death in 1988, the wheelchair-bound quadriplegic professor was the driving force behind the real estate program at the University of Wisconsin at Madison. Crippled by polio in his teens, Graaskamp, who turned lecture notes with a stick held in place with his teeth, viewed his handicap as a "materials-handling problem."

His disability did not prevent him from earning a PhD in 1964, teaching real estate, encouraging new theories of real estate, and consulting through his company, Landmark Research. Well-known for his articulate and spellbinding speeches, he was also often an outspoken critic—with many critics of his own—on national and local land use policies, often taking very unpopular positions.

Graaskamp understood that, in a world of change and uncertainty, determining a course of action is more important than merely pricing assets. He was a visionary with a strong system of ethics. He believed that the developer's profit should be the secondary motivation for a development project, for if a project fails, the negative consequences do not stop with the investor. In fact, Graaskamp wrote that a project should not be viewed as solvent if society has been shortchanged in its development. He conceptualized a real estate development process that would maximize the benefits not for just a few individuals, but for the greater society.

Feasibility analysis—the determination of what makes sense and why—was Graaskamp's major contribution to the field. He developed methods for solving problems based on the tenet that, because the key characteristic of real estate is its location, most problems are unique to the particular site. He developed the microanalytical approach to real estate problem solving, in which issues are defined in terms of the specific location, the individual developer, the micromarket, and other project characteristics.

According to Graaskamp, the real estate feasibility process should attempt to answer four questions:

1. *What is it that we are doing?* The three possibilities are a site in search of a user, a user in search of a site, or an investor seeking a development opportunity. If beginning with the site, the site's attributes should determine the project. Beginning with a user requires identifying a site that matches the user's requirements. When starting with an investor, the investor's objectives are the crucial element.

2. *For whom are we doing it?* Realizing that development occurs for many reasons beyond simply maximizing the investor's income, Graaskamp believed that it is important to understand the individual developer's goals.

3. *To whom are we doing it?* This question addresses understanding the market to adapt the product to its needs.

4. *Will it fly?* More than just the narrow concern of "will it sell?"; this question seeks to explore broader issues regarding the project's physical, legal, and financial viability.

Graaskamp expanded on the traditional concept of highest and best use with the more idealistic "most fitting use," in which the land use is measured by its optimization of consumer satisfaction, production cost, impact on third parties, and, finally, profit to the investor. He also defined the more pragmatic "most probable use," described as less than the most fitting use but constrained by political factors, short-term solvency, and the state of real estate technology.

Although better known for his speaking than his writings, Graaskamp nonetheless wrote *The Fundamentals of Real Estate Development*, published by ULI in 1981. In addition, his life and work were the inspiration for ULI's 1991 book, *Graaskamp on Real Estate*, and James R. DeLisle and J. Sa-Aadu's 1994 book, *Appraisal, Market Analysis, and Public Policy in Real Estate: Essays in Honor of James A. Graaskamp*. He remains an influential force in real estate thinking.

Sources: James A. Graaskamp, *Fundamentals of Real Estate Development* (Washington, D.C.: ULI–the Urban Land Institute, 1981); Stephen D. Jarchow, ed., *Graaskamp on Real Estate* (Washington, D.C.: ULI–the Urban Land Institute, 1991); and Mike Miles and Mark Eppli, "The Graaskamp Legacy," *Real Estate Finance*, Spring 1998, pp. 84–91.

Real Estate Management (IREM), which is part of the National Association of Realtors.

Regulators

The balance between the goals of the developer and the interests of other stakeholders is a primary theme of this text. Stakeholders include everyone affected by the impacts of the development. Their interests are formally represented by elected officials and appointed staff whose responsibility is to ensure that the development is consistent with the interests of the community. Those interests are codified in development regulations at the local, state, and federal levels of government, as explained in chapters 7 and 8.

End Users

The final participants in the development process are the future users of the space, such as businesses that lease office or warehouse space, retailers that lease stores, apartment residents who rent units, or households that purchase homes. When articulating the project concept, developers try to anticipate users' needs. Throughout the development process, they refine user needs by segment. The users ultimately determine the success of a project, as they choose how much to pay for the finished product when it is delivered to the marketplace.

PROPERTY TYPES

Developers tend to work in particular geographical regions and specialize in specific product types. Although all developers should possess a foundation of knowledge and skills, they are typically most conversant with the nuances of their own markets and product types.

There are various ways to categorize property types. The largest type is single-family residential, which makes up a very significant share of most households' wealth. The National Association of Real Estate Investment Trusts (NAREIT), which tracks only investment property, categorizes commercial property types as follows:

- Industrial/Office
  - □ Industrial
  - □ Office
  - □ Mixed use
- Retail
  - □ Shopping centers
  - □ Regional malls
  - □ Free-standing
- Residential
  - □ Apartments
  - □ Manufactured homes
- Diversified
- Lodging/resorts
- Self-storage
- Specialty

NCREIF, the National Council of Real Estate Investment Fiduciaries, has fewer categories: office, industrial, retail, apartment, and hotel. Like those of NAREIT, NCREIF categories do not include individually owned homes.

ULI categorizes real estate in various ways, depending on how it is being discussed. In real estate market analysis, the broad categories are residential, retail, office, industrial, hotel and resort, and mixed use.

Residential

Residential development encompasses a wide range of products from communities of single-family lots to multifamily apartments and condominiums. Apartment units are held by a single owner and rented to the end user, whereas condominium units are sold to an end user and the common property is owned and managed by a condominium association.

Typically, a residential land developer does not build single-family homes but develops finished lots that are sold to a homebuilder. Sometimes, however, the homebuilder is also the developer. If the project is a master-planned community, the developer is responsible for the overall character of the community, the infrastructure, the recreational facilities, any commercial facilities, and a unified marketing effort.

Retail

The United States has more retail space per capita than any other country. Retail development generally means shopping centers, and there is a hierarchy of types of shopping centers, based on size, tenant type, and market draw. Convenience, neighborhood, community, regional, and super regional are the typical geographical categories. Another way to categorize retail is by the types of products offered: those dealing in commodity goods and services, and those providing specialty goods and services—in other words, daily needs versus discretionary. In shopping for commodity goods, the customer seeks convenience and price, and the real estate reflects that. In specialty retail, the shopper's experience is a central motivation for choosing the venue, so the center should appeal to customers' emotions. More than just a place to buy things, specialty shopping centers provide entertainment, social opportunities, and an aesthetic experience.

Office

Office development includes multistory, pure of-fice buildings, as well as specialty buildings such as health care facilities, neighborhood-serving professional offices, and research and development (R&D) facilities. Traditional office development is classified in terms of quality. Class A buildings are well located and designed to appeal to first-rate tenants, who pay a premium for such desirable space. As a building ages, it may fall from class A to class B, or it may be renovated to maintain its status and desirability. Class B buildings may be less well located; they may be a bit older or have lower-grade finishes. Class C buildings are substantially older and not up to current standards in certain respects. Class C buildings are potential candidates for demolition, rehabilitation, or conversion to other uses.

Industrial

Industrial development falls into three primary categories: manufacturing, warehouse, and flex space, which overlaps with R&D office buildings. Self-storage buildings are a subset of warehouse development. A primary consideration for industrial development is transportation, so these facilities are often located near airports, rail lines, and freeways. Critical design factors are ceiling heights, loading dock configurations, and parking for the types of vehicles that must be accommodated. Industrial development is sometimes intentionally planned as an interim use for land that will eventually be developed at a higher use as the location evolves.

Hotel and Resort

Hotel and resort—or lodging—development targets two primary travel markets: business and pleasure. It encompasses an ever-expanding number of product types. For example, hotels run from full-service luxury to budget facilities. A separate category is extended-stay hotels, which offer more home-like units that usually include kitchen facilities; the property generally offers amenities to make the longer-stay traveler feel more like a resident.

Resorts may be developed around a hotel—or several hotels. Or they may be amenity-packed communities of second homes, or a combination of hotel and second-home development. Some resorts include conference facilities, to cater to business travelers who may be enticed to extend their trip for pleasure.

Mixed Use

The Urban Land Institute defines mixed use as three or more significant revenue-producing uses, such as retail/entertainment, office, residential, hotel, and civic/cultural/recreation, which in well-planned projects are mutually supporting. They are physically and functionally integrated and developed using a coherent plan. Mixed-use development can take many forms, including a single tower, a group of towers connected by a common concourse or shopping mall, or street-focused town centers with urban-style outdoor spaces.

The synergy between, say, an office component and a retail component is intended to expand the market for both. Many communities like mixed-use development because it enables shared parking, encourages pedestrian activity, brings more activity to areas that are revitalizing, and diversifies the tax base.

SUMMARY

Developers manage the creation of the built environment. They tend to be driven, innovative people who work with an extensive team of professionals through a complex and dynamic process. This process is described by the eight-stage model laid out in chapter 1. Chapter 2 discussed the land resource that makes real estate unique and underlies the built environment. This chapter completes the introduction by describing the players and their roles in the development process. Because each development is unique, developers must choose their consultants and coworkers with full knowledge of what skills are required for the specific project.

TERMS

- Appraiser
- Bearing capacity
- Civil engineer

- Development fee
- Ecosystem management
- Entitlement process
- Environmental consultant
- General contractor
- Landscape architect
- Liability
- Structural engineer
- Subcontractor
- Sustainable site design
- Traffic models
- Transportation consultant
- Valuation

REVIEW QUESTIONS

3.1 What are the most common forms of compensation for developers?

3.2 Describe the architect's role in the development process.

3.3 Why might development of a mixed-use project be more difficult than development of a single property type?

3.4 Why are contractors critical to the developer's work?

3.5 Describe the expanded role of the landscape architect.

3.6 Why do developers need environmental and transportation consultants more often now than 20 years ago?

3.7 Why are appraisers involved before, during, and at project completion?

3.8 Describe the various types of financial players and when they are involved in the development process.

3.9 How does the eight-stage model help the developer think about assembling the right team for a particular development?

PART 2

The History of Real Estate Development in the United States

One of the best ways to anticipate the future is to study the past. As Santayana said, "those who don't learn from the past are doomed to repeat it."

Part II reviews the evolution of real estate development in the United States from colonial days to the present. It covers the legal, economic, and physical history of development as illustrated through representative examples, and sets forth a full backdrop for the eight-stage model that follows. From a legal perspective, ownership of property is a cherished, fundamental right that evolved from centuries of English philosophy and common law. In the United States, it was adapted to a degree more widespread than in any other country. Real estate development has always played a key role in the financial life of the nation, and it has been the result and cause of major economic cycles. The physical expression of real estate development has been the response to the needs of the ultimate users of the built environment.

The role and degree of involvement of the public sector in real estate has changed over time, but it has always been an active partner in private development. Real estate development involves the interplay of the public and private sectors, the optimization of economic returns from the land, and the continual adaption of property to new purposes to meet the needs of society.

Chapter 4

The Colonial Period to the Late 1800s

Real estate has been a part of the American tradition since the country's beginnings. The era from the colonial period to the late 1800s covers most of the settlement period of the United States. This early period was defined by settlement patterns, first by the settlers and colonists who migrated here, and later by various actions of the federal government to open up the West. It was the period in which land was transferred from government (either the crown or the government of the United States) to private land owners. This chapter examines

- The transfer of land from the government to private owners which made real estate an American tradition;
- Land *subdivision* and residential development; and
- The role of railroads and railroad barons in real estate development.

By 1893, Frederick Turner concluded that the American frontier was closed. The nature of settlement and concepts of real estate would thereafter be much different.

REAL ESTATE AS AN AMERICAN TRADITION

Private ownership of real estate has been a part of the American tradition since well before the revolution. By then, the essentials for a real estate market had been in place for decades: contract law, measurement of land (to enable its conveyance), and related financial vehicles. Added to these prerequisites was the vast continent, on the threshold of settlement.

The patterns of settlement varied over the colonial period. Williamsburg, Virginia, was laid out "with formal axes adapted from the aristocratic mode in Europe."[1] Philadelphia was laid out in a grid pattern in 1682 by a surveyor commissioned by William Penn. Boston was oriented around the Commons. Cities in those parts of the continent claimed by Spain were laid out according to principles that can be traced back to Vitruvius, who established the template for Roman colonies. Each of these concepts established land patterns that dictate real estate development to the present day.

During the colonial period, most land was in the hands of governors, by authority of the English

This chapter was originally written by Marc A. Weiss, PhD, chair and CEO, Global Urban Development, Washington, D.C.

crown and other sovereign powers; beginning in the 17th century, it was purchased or appropriated from the Native American tribes that inhabited the continent when the European settlers arrived. In the early 1600s, British settlers were brought to this country to farm land owned by the Virginia Company; they were paid for their labors in both money and shares of stock. The early settlers quickly rebelled against this practice, however, and insisted on ownership of the land they were farming. (Laborers brought from Africa did not have such choices.) In 1616, the Virginia colonial governor acquiesced, granting free and clear title to a minimum of 100 acres for each farmer—an action that set an important precedent for patterns of settlement in the country.

Colonial governors had many methods of distributing the ownership of land. Outright grants were given for farming the land; settling the frontier; serving in the military, in a religious order, or as an educator; and demonstrating political connections. Large parcels of land were sold to investors, speculators, land developers, and settlement ventures. In the New England colonies, governors granted and sold land to groups for the purpose of establishing towns.

The largest transfer of land from the public to the private realm came as the result of the Land Ordinance of 1785 and the Northwest Ordinance of 1787. Together, they established the process by which the lands west of the Appalachians would be placed under the jurisdiction of the federal government, how the land would be divided according to the township and range system of legal description, and how that land would then be sold to settlers. Between 1800 and 1820, the United States sold over 13.6 million acres of public lands.[2]

After independence was achieved and the colonies became the United States, the federal and state governments together still owned the overwhelming share of all land. Much more land was added to the public domain during the next century through the Louisiana Purchase, the annexation of Texas, the war with Mexico, the purchase of Alaska, and several treaties with Spain and Great Britain.

Early Land Transactions

At first, public land was put into private ownership mainly through sales of large parcels to individual investors. The sales occurred as a result of negotiated deals, public auctions, and fixed prices per acre set by Congress. Many prospective frontier settlers could not afford to pay even the minimum government price to purchase federal land, let alone the often much higher prices asked by private speculators who bought public land wholesale and attempted to resell it retail. The huge numbers of land-hungry pioneers were also voters, however, and they rebelled in the mid-19th century as their forebears had done two centuries earlier in Virginia.

Fee Simple Real Estate Transactions

In 1862, Congress responded to this "Free Soil Movement" by passing the Homestead Act, enabling settlers who did not already own sufficient land to be granted title to 160 acres for each adult in the family simply by living on and improving the "homestead" for five years. No cash payments were required, thereby opening up ownership to a large segment of the population that had previously been excluded. Unfortunately, the system was subject to a great deal of fraud and abuse, allowing large landowners and wealthy investors to obtain substantial public acreage at bargain prices. Despite the abuses, the Homestead Act was extremely popular and was followed in the 1870s by additional federal laws granting free 20- and 40-acre parcels to settlers who engaged in mining and in forestry. In all, the government gave away nearly 300 million acres of public land to private owners through the various homesteading programs—almost as much land as it transferred through cash sales.

The creation of the *fee simple* system of complete property rights through private ownership—including the ability of one private party to convey those rights to another through sale, lease, or trade—generated a vibrant real estate market that attracted substantial amounts of investment capital. In the early years, the money moving into and out of real property was extremely volatile and subject to large fluctuations in amounts and prices. By the late 18th century, land speculation had already become a main preoccupation of Americans. Legendary fortunes were made and lost as the steady influx of immigrants entered the new nation. Rapidly rising prices frequently led to a mania for land gambling.

When new territory was opened for settlement and land was subdivided for sale, the speculative boom/bust cycles repeated themselves. "Land-jobbing" or "town-jobbing" by obtaining land and selling it through promotional schemes to specula-tors and settlers was one of the principal means of accumulating wealth in the early days of the United States, and all the major business and govern-ment leaders—from Benjamin Franklin to George Washington—engaged in it. Indeed, Washington was a professional land surveyor. An energetic entre-preneur in the real estate business, Washington was heavily involved in one of the country's first big de-velopment deals—the establishment of the District of Columbia as the nation's capital.

Developing the District of Columbia

The selection of the site for the District of Columbia and its development as the federal city was based on President Washington's plan for encouraging private land sales and trading.

TERMS of SALE of LOTS in the CITY of WASH-INGTON, the Eighth Day of *October*, 1792.

ALL Lands purchased at this Sale, are to be subject to the Terms and Conditions declared by the President, pursuant to the Deeds in Trust.

The purchaser is immediately to pay one fourth part of the purchase money; the residue is to be paid in three equal annual payments, with yearly interest of six per cent. on the whole principal unpaid: If any payment is not made at the day, the payments made are to be forfeited, or the whole principal and interest unpaid may be recovered on one suit and execution, in the option of the Commissioners.

The purchaser is to be entitled to a conveyance, on the whole purchase money and interest being paid, and not before. No bid under Three Dollars to be received.

Advertisement for the public auction of lots in Washington, D.C., in 1792, where the lowest acceptable bid was $3.00.

Much as China has done in recent years, the U.S. federal and state governments in the 18th century used land sales as a primary method of raising revenues to pay for public improvements. Washington, D.C., was to be developed on this basis, with President Washington and future presi-dents Thomas Jefferson and James Madison among the private bidders for the purchase of subdivided urban lots at the initial public auction in 1791. Only 35 lots were sold at that time, leading to additional promotional efforts that culminated in the wholesale purchase on credit of 7,235 lots by a *syndicate* headed by Robert Morris. Morris was a Philadelphia mer-chant, Revolutionary War financier, and real estate investor in Pennsylvania and New York. Morris and his partners, James Greenleaf and John Nicholson, promised to bring needed capital for *land develop-ment* and building construction into the federal city, starting with the "Morristown" project, 20 two-story brick houses near the capitol. George Washington also built several for-sale rowhouses in the same area.

In 1791, President Washington commissioned Major Pierre Charles L'Enfant to design a long-range plan for the entire city, including the layout of the street system and the public buildings. Though little of L'Enfant's grand scheme was adopted immediately, much of it was realized over the next two centuries. In the 1790s, the federal government tried to stimulate investment and economic and population growth by requiring all those who purchased lots to construct permanent, good-quality, two-story brick or stone buildings, with minimum and maximum prescribed heights to ensure uniformity in the appearance of the streetscape.

Unfortunately, Robert Morris's syndicate de-faulted on its payments for the Washington lots and failed to complete the construction of Morristown, and all three principals were sent to debtors' prison. Land prices fell precipitously, and the federal district remained for decades what Charles Dickens called "the City of Magnificent Intentions."[3] Nevertheless, the city named for George Washington eventu-ally proved him right: extensive public and private investment, good planning, quality development and construction, and a growing population would ultimately produce a healthy real estate market with rising long-term values.

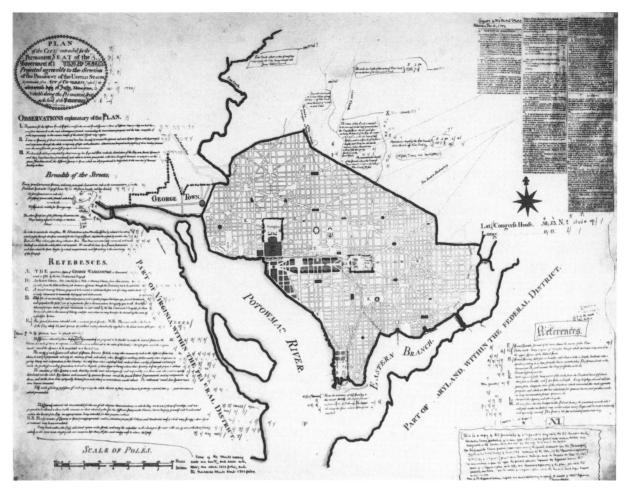

L'Enfant's 1792 plan for the federal city. Although implementation was slow, much of L'Enfant's original plan for a majestic city to rival any of the great European capitals is now complete.

Ground Leases

Ground leases formed the basis for the wealth of many early Americans. Under the provisions of long-term ground leases, landlords received rental payments for the use of land. Renters could occupy the land, lease it out for ground rent, sell their interest in the lease, or improve the property and then collect a building rent. Without surrendering the role of owner, landlords delegated control of the distribution, development, and use of land to the land tenants.[4]

The fact that this practice was common in 18th-century England was incentive enough for George Washington. By 1773, Washington owned 20,000 acres on the Ohio and Great Kanawha rivers. On July 15 that year, he advertised for settlers in *The Maryland Journal and Baltimore Advertiser*. He

indicated that he would divide the land "into any sized tenements that may be desired, and lease them upon moderate terms, allowing a reasonable number of years rent free, provided, within the space of two years from the next October, three acres for every 50 contained in each lot…shall be cleared, fenced and tilled."[5]

New York City's most noteworthy landlord was Trinity Church. Starting with a crown grant of 32 acres from Queen Anne in 1705, the vestrymen of the church had accumulated approximately 1,000 city lots by the end of the 18th century. Over the next several decades, the church leased lots under a single rate structure: £2 annual ground rent for the first seven years, £3 a year for the second seven years, and £4 annually for the remainder of the 21-year term. The vestrymen calculated graduated increases to cover the doubling of land values, which they expected after 21 years.

Trinity's common leases anticipated occupancy. the 21-year term was long enough to allow tenants to benefit from any buildings they constructed on the lot. In contrast, longer leases, especially those running from 63 to 99 years (with rent increases at intervals of 21 or 33 years), projected a property interest that extended beyond the tenant's lifetime. Under these longer leases, the tenant, who paid a fixed ground rent, retained any increase in the rent-generating value of the property.[6]

Even today, several of New York's important buildings sit on land leased from Trinity Church as well as from such families as Goelet, Rhinelander, and Astor, all of whom were active in the 18th-century real estate market.

The Holland Land Company

Although the tale of early American land and town sales is punctuated by get-rich-quick hype and a string of dreams and broken promises, it is also the story of the fundamentals of real estate development as the continent's rural and urban land was brought into productive economic use. One player was the Holland Land Company, a group of Dutch financiers and investors that bought 3.3 million acres of land in western New York from Robert Morris in 1792. Morris had purchased the vast property on credit, hoping that rising prices would yield huge profits through quick turnover.

The company acquired the immense territory with the intention of subdividing it into large parcels and rapidly disposing of the tracts wholesale to major investors. But a serious downturn in property markets brought on by the financial panic that ensued after the collapse of Robert Morris's syndicate in Washington, D.C., led the company to reassess its strategy. Out of necessity, the principals decided to engage in long-term, value-added investment and development. Land would be sold retail to new settlers who could be induced to migrate to the region on the promise of infrastructure and services that would make both farmland and town sites physically

accessible and economically viable locations for commerce, industry, and permanent residence.

In 1797, the Holland Land Company hired Joseph Ellicott, an experienced Pennsylvania land surveyor, to serve as chief land agent and to direct company operations in upstate New York. For the next two decades, Ellicott implemented a comprehensive long-term plan for the development of the territory and the retail sale of land. His work included laying out the city of Buffalo, at the western boundary of the company's holdings.

Ellicott's long-term development strategy included cutting hundreds of miles of roads through the wilderness and building towns at strategic points along the newly developed transportation routes. The company located offices in the towns, and Ellicott engaged in a wide variety of promotional activities to stimulate settlement in both the towns and the hinterlands. In addition to the roads, the Holland Land Company assisted in the construction of sawmills, gristmills, distilleries, and potash refineries to stimulate regional economic activity that would enhance demand for land sales and leases. Furthermore, when a town center was first platted and opened for development, the company often subsidized the pioneering private owners of general stores, inns, taverns, grain mills, ironworks, smithies, and other essential goods and services. The company also donated land for schools, churches, and public squares.

Ellicott sold a great deal of land. Within a decade, he had brought more than 200,000 new settlers to the company's vast territory, prompting the president of Yale College to write in 1810, "It is questionable whether mankind had ever seen so large a tract changed so suddenly from a wilderness into a well-inhabited and well-cultivated country."[7] Unfortunately, most of the settlers, who had bought land on credit with little or no downpayment, found themselves unable to meet the credit terms to complete their purchases and became essentially tenants of the Holland Land Company.

In 1820, the company attempted to bail out of the situation by reselling all its land to the state of

New York. The legislature refused to buy it, so the company was forced to squeeze more cash from the settlers or repossess their holdings. Neither approach proved economically or politically viable, and in 1830, the company helped organize the New York Life Insurance and Trust Company, which began to refinance Holland Land's creditors by converting the unpaid sales contracts into first mortgage loans. In 1836, a powerful local businessman and politician named William H. Seward arranged for Wall Street and European investors to purchase the loans, a popular act that helped elect Seward governor of New York in 1838. As Seward put it, "In less than 18 months, 4,000 persons whom I found occupying lands, chiefly under expired and legally enforceable contracts of sale, and excited and embarrassed alike by the oppression and uncertainty of ever obtaining titles, became freeholders."[8]

In 1835, the Holland Land Company sold its property to a New York investment syndicate for $1 million, leaving continuation of the massive enterprise for large-scale land development to a new group of real estate entrepreneurs. Fortunately for the Dutch owners of Holland Land, they managed to sell their holdings before the major economic depression of 1837. But the enduring heritage of Holland Land's nearly four decades in the land development business was not the record of financial deals; rather, it was Joseph Ellicott's establishment as a national role model of an early American "community builder."

John Jacob Astor

An alternative model to short-term speculators and long-term land developers of for-sale properties is the "Astor method," named for the real estate career of John Jacob Astor, one of the country's richest and best-known businessmen in the 19th century. Astor, who had started as a fur trader in the Pacific Northwest, owned a tremendous amount of real estate, including several land parcels and buildings in Manhattan, which he began accumulating in 1810. His approach was to purchase land at low prices and wait patiently for the market to change and for urban growth to drive values exponentially

higher. While waiting, he collected substantial rental income from his holdings.

Astor was always eager to buy properties when he could get a bargain, and he rarely sold except when he needed money to purchase more real estate or, occasionally, when values skyrocketed. He once sold a lot near Wall Street for $8,000 to a man who was convinced that he had outwitted Astor. The buyer said, "Why, Mr. Astor, in a few years this property will be worth $12,000." "No doubt," said Astor, "but with your $8,000 I will buy 80 lots north of Canal Street. By the time your lot is worth $12,000, my 80 lots will be worth $80,000." Needless to say, he was correct.

During the crash of 1837, Astor acquired several lots and buildings at "distress sale" prices and foreclosed on hundreds of properties on which he held or had obtained the mortgages. He seldom invested in any significant improvements, preferring to lease properties and earn profits primarily from rental income. Often, Astor settled for a 5 percent return on the current value of land and left the risk of construction and property management to others. By 1840, Astor was the country's wealthiest man, with an annual income of more than $1.25 million from ground rent alone and an estate worth more than $20 million, largely attributable to the tremendous growth in the value of his urban real estate assets. Shortly before his death in 1848, he declared, "Could I begin life again, knowing what I now know, and had money to invest, I would buy every foot of land on the island of Manhattan."[9]

Capital Improvement Projects

Financing has been an essential component in the success of real estate ventures, as the saga of the Holland Land Company demonstrates. Just as that company invested in infrastructure to enhance the value of its real estate assets, the federal, state, and local governments undertook wide-ranging development of roads, canals, ports, and other facilities to enable them to turn public lands into private holdings and, most important, to promote population and employment growth. Boosterism and public investment went hand in hand. Often *capital improvement projects* were financed either by issuing bonds to be repaid from user fees such as bridge, highway, and canal tolls or by combining rail and transit fares with revenues from the sale or lease of nearby land that had increased in value because of the new infrastructure.

For more than 200 years, private developers have used this same model when installing major improvements. Private utility, transit, railroad, and other companies have frequently relied on these methods, sometimes leveraging public powers of land acquisition or even outright grants of public land. At other times, taxpayers have voted to sell bonds for improvements, to be repaid through increased property taxes. Voters have anticipated that future population growth would increase the tax base and property values so that both the public treasury and private landowners who purchased real estate would benefit by boosting an area with expensive government-financed construction.

The government's role was crucial in facilitating development and widespread ownership of land. Forms of government intervention ranged from the ubiquitous rectangular survey that opened up the West to regulations such as building codes, the legal protection of property transactions, and land use controls that enhance the physical environment, public safety, and property values. In addition, the federal and state governments, through controls on currency, regulatory oversight of publicly chartered financial institutions, and macroeconomic policies, have played a major role in encouraging and monitoring the apparatus of money and credit that has enabled U.S. real estate development to thrive and grow.

LAND SUBDIVISION AND THE GROWTH OF CITIES

During the 19th century, the United States began to transform from an agrarian to a manufacturing economy. The creation of a manufacturing economy necessitated an urban form to meet its needs, and real estate markets responded in several ways. Existing cities began to grow outward from their cores. Growing populations led to increasing land values and higher densities. Subdivision of land by a grid came to be the most efficient way to achieve growth. In 1811, a commission prepared a plan for Manhattan that laid a gridiron street system over the entire island, largely because it would facilitate rapid growth.

The westward expansion in the 19th century precipitated the transformation of frontier towns into major cities. Many rural enterprises failed, leaving ghost towns in their wake, but some great metropolises did emerge from modest beginnings. Chicago, for example, grew in a brief seven decades from a tiny hamlet inhabited by a few hundred pioneers in the 1830s to the fifth largest city in the world by 1900, driven by its strategic location as a railroad hub. San Francisco grew from a remote trading outpost to "the great centre of a world-wide commerce"[10] by 1859, following the discovery of gold in the Sierra Nevada mountains in 1848. The single most common use of land in these metropolitan communities was housing for the steadily growing population. Land and, in some cases, buildings were continually carved up to provide dwelling units for new residents.

Because of the abundance of cheap land, inexpensive construction materials, and a constant stream of innovations in transportation technology that made residential dispersion possible, an enormous amount of urban housing in the United States consisted of single-family detached dwellings. In the older and more crowded cities of the early 19th century, attached row houses (typically constructed in block groups by speculative builders) and multifamily dwellings converted from spacious mansions accommodated a high-density population that walked to work and services. Later in the century, a number of other dwelling types made their debut, including luxury apartment buildings, squalid tenements, and two- to four-family structures whose modest-income owners often lived in one of the units and, in some cases, constructed the building themselves.

Unlike in most other countries, the U.S. urban real estate market allowed for mass participation. Vacant building lots were frequently sold on credit with only small downpayments required, making it possible for a wide range of purchasers to enter the market. Millions of people bought lots, including families who wanted to build their own houses, entrepreneurial builders who wanted to construct dwellings for sale or rent, and investors who wanted to turn over land for a fast profit or hold it for long-term gain. To reduce the costs of property ownership for people of limited means, subdivisions intended to house the working classes often included only the most rudimentary improvements such as unpaved streets and lacked basic amenities such as sanitary and storm sewers, fresh water supplies, or curbs and sidewalks. In higher-income communities, developers sometimes installed key improvements in advance of sales and added those costs to lot prices. More commonly, infrastructure and amenities were built after the initial sale of land, paid for by individual lot owners through special tax assessments. As with building and housing codes, society's minimum acceptable standards for neighborhood development today are much higher than they were a century ago.

Downtown Philadelphia, 1897, where streets were clogged with horse-drawn carriages, trolley cars, and pedestrians.

The Growth of Inner-City Slums

The Industrial Revolution changed the character of urban settlement patterns in the United States. While new housing was being built for the upper class, the middle class, and the more skilled working class, unskilled, low-income workers were still crowded into inner-city neighborhoods called *slums*. Close to the factories and warehouses that were the major sources of employment for people who walked to work, slums claimed the worst housing, the greatest overcrowding, and the highest rates of disease. In 1890, journalist and social reformer Jacob Riis attempted to arouse the nation's conscience with his photographically documented book *How the Other Half Lives*,[11] and, four years later, Carroll Wright, the U.S. Commissioner of Labor, systematically documented the deplorable conditions in his study of the slums of Baltimore, Philadelphia, New York City, and Chicago.[12]

Even though those living in the slums had low incomes, landlords often packed so many rent-paying customers into a building and spent so little money on maintenance that slum properties could be highly profitable. Not only were older structures regularly converted to house greater numbers of the cash-poor immigrants flocking to the central cities in search of economic opportunity, but new tenements and other forms of high-density residences were also built at a steady pace. Many of even the newest structures lacked such basic necessities as indoor plumbing and windows that brought light and air into all rooms. Lot coverage was extremely high, with little open space around buildings and no place for people to congregate and recreate other than in the streets and alleys, both of which were commonly covered with mud and littered with garbage.

During the late 19th and early 20th centuries in cities from New York to San Francisco, housing reform movements began to organize for stricter laws to regulate the minimum quality and standard features of new residential construction and existing housing. These movements frequently met stiff resistance from elements of the real estate industry. Where the movements did succeed, they often encountered the fundamental problem that many tenants could not afford to pay the higher rents necessary to finance the improvements needed.

One strategy to reduce rents was to encourage philanthropic capitalists to build housing for workers under limited-profit financial arrangements. These efforts were intended as both physical models of better construction and design, and economic and social models to stimulate more extensive investment. Most of the leaders in this movement came from business and professional fields not directly related to the real estate industry, although some real estate development firms, such as Alfred T. White's City and Suburban Homes Company of New York, became involved. However, these efforts did not produce enough housing to make even a dent in the immediate problem, though over the long run they had important symbolic value in helping to raise minimum standards and educate developers about better methods of planning and building low-cost housing.

Another approach, led by social workers, was to form settlement houses in slum neighborhoods that provided public health and education services to help residents improve their living conditions. Social workers in settlement houses also assisted community members in organizing labor unions and agitating for economic, political, and social reforms from business and government. Often the same people who contributed to the work of settlement houses were involved in attempts to regulate slum housing publicly and to promote the private, limited-dividend construction of new low-rent dwellings. The problem of housing the poor has a long history in the country, marked by many serious initiatives that have not yet achieved long-term success.

Company Towns, Utopian Communities, and Garden Cities

As living conditions in the industrialized cities deteriorated, development concepts arose that attempted to improve those conditions. In the early 1800s, mill towns such as Lowell, Massachusetts, provided housing for workers. Later in the century, entire model communities were built around large industries. Pullman, Illinois, for example, was built under a master plan to house workers for the factory

Living conditions were dismal in New York City's slums in 1888, when Jacob Riis took this photograph.

that built railcars. The plan included a town hall, parks, markets, and other elements necessary for a self-contained town. Other company towns were organized around extractive industries such as mining and logging. The primary reason for development of such towns was to make workers more efficient and more productive by providing a convenient place for them to live.

The conditions of the industrial cities in the 19th century gave rise to experimentation with utopian communities, each organized, populated, and governed by single religious or philosophical sects in the hopes of creating a society separate from and better than the urban one. In 1825, Robert Owen created "America's first secular utopian experiment," in the form of New Harmony, Indiana, a "community of equality" based on the idea that by changing the conditions of people's lives, it should be possible to change their characters.[13] Some utopian communities were influenced by the Communist Manifesto of 1848.

A farther-reaching real estate development concept that arose in the late 19th century in response to the urban conditions brought about by the Industrial Revolution was Ebenezer Howard's Garden City movement. Many discussions of 20th and 21st century land development patterns begin with this concept (see chapter 5).

Transportation Advances and the Rise of Suburban Development

A significant trend in the 19th century was the appearance of suburbs of large homes for upper-class commuters. At the time, most urban subdivisions lacked any significant controls on land use. Mixtures of lot sizes and shapes and of building densities, heights, forms, occupancies, and uses were typical. These characteristics could be limited only through actions by private owners. *Deed restrictions* in the form of private contracts were the sole regulatory device available, but they were difficult to establish and enforce and were used mostly in a small number of new, high-income residential neighborhoods.

Selling one's own—or someone else's—property as an agent was a completely unregulated activity

that occupied the time and energy of a substantial segment of the population, especially during boom times. Some vendors indulged in unethical practices that at times lent sales agents, developers, and landlords an unsavory image and later led to calls for reforms. By the 1920s, however, the extensive use of private deed restrictions and the introduction of public controls through zoning and subdivision regulations brought new stability and order to residential development. Not only was it possible for the first time for millions of people to own urban property, but many were also actively engaged in the real estate business.

In addition to property ownership, sales, and management, building construction was a widespread endeavor. Most contractors and subcontractors, particularly in the residential field, were small-scale operators, often shuttling between the roles of contractor and laborer. Nearly all houses were built under contract to the owners/users, many of whom constructed their dwellings with the help of family and friends. Stock architectural plans were readily available; only a small percentage of houses, mainly for the wealthy, were designed by professional architects. By the early 20th century, the Sears catalog was selling many models of ready-to-assemble houses that came in kits with instruction manuals. Contract work was the principal mode, but many large and small builders also constructed houses as speculative investments, though the norm was generally one or two and seldom more than five such houses per year. Merchant homebuilding, as this method came to be known, did not begin to dominate the housing industry until the 1950s. Instead, the standard approach for even sophisticated real estate developers was to sell finished building lots, not completed houses.

Llewellyn Park, New Jersey, and Riverside, Illinois

By the early 19th century, the spreading population of cities had begun to differentiate uses by location. The ability to plan and develop large-scale, primarily residential communities depended on transportation advances that enabled residents to reach their places of employment without being confined to the tight boundaries of the "walking city." Commuter ferry service by steamship across rivers and other bodies of water served as one means of circulation. Ground transportation started with the omnibus—a horse-drawn urban stagecoach—for short in-city trips and the steam railroad for longer, inter- and intracity travel. Later, horse-drawn passenger cars running on rail rights-of-way, cable cars, electric streetcars and trolley cars, elevated and subway rail transit, electric rail, and, finally, the gasoline-powered automobile all helped turn the landscape around cities into a vast, low-density suburban world of houses, highways, business parks, shopping malls, and parking lots.

The first generation of major residential land developers was spawned by the advent of long-distance railroads in the 1840s and 1850s. Their developments were essentially upper-middle-class suburbs in pastoral settings located on railroad lines connected to large central cities. Two of the earliest and best known of these suburbs are Llewellyn Park, New Jersey, and Riverside, Illinois.

Llewellyn Haskell, a successful New York merchant, purchased 400 acres of land near West Orange, New Jersey, in the 1850s with eight partners. The location was only 13 miles from Manhattan, on a railroad line into the city. Haskell was attracted by the natural beauty of the site, with its hills, streams, woods, and views of a mountain to the north and New York City to the east. His goal was to create a model community for "the wants of citizens doing business in New York, and yet wishing accessible, retired, and healthful homes in the country."[14] To further this goal, Haskell hired as his chief planner Alexander Jackson Davis, a well-known architect of luxurious and romantic country estates and author of *Rural Residences*, one of the bibles of stylish residential architecture at the time.

Haskell and Davis worked to make the most of the site's parklike environment. They discarded the familiar gridiron pattern of straight streets; instead, roads and lanes curved with the land's natural contours. Curvilinear streets later became a standard feature of suburban residential land development, but, in 1856, they were a bold innovation for a new

real estate venture. The developer and his architect-planner also created "the Ramble," a 50-acre park that followed a stream at the mountainside. The Ramble was left in its natural state except for the addition of some curving pedestrian paths. Haskell organized a property owners association to hold title to and maintain this common area, establishing another important precedent for new community projects—open space and recreation facilities dedicated by the developer and managed by a homeowners association.

Haskell also wrote into the deeds restrictions that prohibited industrial and commercial uses of the land, required large minimum lot sizes (three acres), and barred fences. These and other rules were all designed to preserve Llewellyn Park as a quiet, green paradise for its wealthy residents, who entered the exclusive private community through a security gatehouse. Haskell and Davis both moved there, the lots sold at high prices, and the partners earned an excellent return on their investment. The suburb's attractiveness as an elite enclave was so well conceived and executed that, more than 150 years later, the community remains as Haskell envisioned it.

Riverside is more familiar to many urbanists today because it was planned by the famous American landscape architects Frederick Law Olmsted and Calvert Vaux, the designers of New York City's Central Park. Emery Childs and a group of investors acquired 1,600 acres of undeveloped land on the Des Plaines River in Illinois and formed the Riverside Improvement Company in 1868 to build a new suburban community combining "the beauties and healthy properties of a park with the conveniences and improvements of the city."[15] The site lay nine miles west of downtown Chicago on the Burlington Railroad line. Olmsted and Vaux were impressed by its attractive natural features, calling it "the only available ground near Chicago [that] does not present disadvantages of an almost hopeless character."[16]

The pair planned a central 160-acre park along the river and several smaller parks and recreation areas, with the streets were laid out in a naturalistic curvilinear pattern. Several innovations in community planning were included. Deed restrictions provided an impressive array of controls, requiring everything from mandatory 30-foot setbacks, minimum home construction costs, and design review for houses to rules for maintaining private lawns. Olmsted and Vaux also proposed a limited-access parkway from Riverside to downtown Chicago, an unrealized idea for suburban development that in 1868 was a half-century ahead of its time.

The Riverside Improvement Company hired William LeBaron Jenney, Chicago's leading architect, to review the house plans of those who purchased lots and to design the Riverside Hotel (built in 1870) overlooking the river. Jenney built his own house in the new community and helped set the tone for the style that the developers and landscape planners desired.

Unfortunately, the luck of Childs and the Riverside Improvement Company was not as good as that of Haskell and his partners. The costly improvements installed to develop Riverside were not supported by vigorous land sales in the first few years. Many people considered Riverside too far away from the city. Market demand, access to capital, and lot prices all fell dramatically after the 1871 Chicago fire, and the company went bankrupt during the national depression of 1873. By the 1880s, however, sales of lots and construction of houses in Riverside had rebounded. Despite the early disappointments, Riverside—which today is a historic district—was eventually built as a middle-class suburb according to Childs's vision. It served as an important early model for many later suburban developments, from Roland Park in Baltimore to the Country Club District of Kansas City.

Although elite suburbs located along commuter railroad lines represent the earliest examples of large-scale residential subdivisions, further advances in transportation later in the 19th century enabled people of more modest means to move to suburban-style neighborhoods and to commute by electric transit. "Streetcar suburbs" began to appear on the outskirts of growing cities. Often these subdivisions, which today are urban neighborhoods, started as unincorporated areas that were later annexed to the nearby central city. In other cases (Brookline,

Massachusetts; Chevy Chase, Maryland; Shaker Heights, Ohio), they became incorporated towns themselves.

The development of subdivisions during this period was tied to the availability of mass transit. Sometimes the private transportation company was also the land subdivider, with the enormous profits on land sales helping to pay for an initially money-losing transit operation that used cheap promotional fares to encourage people to buy lots and build houses in a sparsely settled community. Real estate entrepreneurs of this type ranged from Boston's Henry M. Whitney, the leading subdivider of Brookline, Massachusetts, to F.M. "Borax" Smith, the largest land developer in Oakland, California. Developers who did not own transit companies usually had to pay subsidies to induce a transportation firm to extend its operations to the outlying locations. The subsidies were an essential business cost for the developer, because without transit service, there would have been no market for the subdivided land.

Samuel E. Gross

Most subdividers were small-scale dealers, though some, especially the transit and utility companies and other large landowners, sold a high volume of building lots. Rarely did any subdivision developer build more than a handful of houses, usually just enough to help define the character of the community and create an established image. One exception was Samuel E. Gross, a flamboyant residential subdivider who built thousands of houses in the Chicago metropolitan area in the 1880s and 1890s, mainly inexpensive ones for skilled blue-collar and white-collar workers earning modest incomes.

Gross had gone bankrupt in the Chicago real estate business during the 1873 panic but, after working as a lawyer and a playwright, he reentered the real estate market in 1880. By 1892, he had sold 40,000 lots and built and sold 7,000 houses. Many of his subdivisions were in the nearly 20 suburbs he developed. The best known is Brookfield, originally called Grossdale, located next to Riverside.

Gross engaged in extensive and dramatic advertising campaigns, emphasizing the simple requirements of his easy-payment financing plan: a 10 percent downpayment, low monthly installments, and generous refinancing for delinquent borrowers. Where he built houses, he charged a single price for the house and lot. He always made sure that a major transit line ran through his subdivisions, sometimes by working in partnership with Charles T. Yerkes, Chicago's "traction king." Gross also included major utilities and infrastructure in his developments and added special quality touches to the residential environment. His houses ranged from a modest four-room cottage that sold for $1,000 ($100 down and $10 a month) to a nine-room model that sold for $5,000. Most were built from orders with downpayments from customers, though Gross also maintained a small inventory for immediate sale. He built from stock plans but provided individualized touches and trumpeted this fact in his advertising.

Gross's somewhat bigger houses and more extensive amenities were reserved for middle-income subdivisions such as Grossdale. The marketing of his explicitly working-class subdivisions, however, stressed small houses and modest environments designed to keep down lot costs. Nonetheless, even in the least costly subdivisions, Gross always planted a considerable number of trees. His strategies for delivering low-cost housing were so well received that the Workingman's Party nominated him for mayor of Chicago in 1889. He declined the honor, but two years later the city's *Real Estate and Building Journal* crowned him "the Napoleon of homebuilders."[17]

Gross was aided in the production of inexpensive houses by the development of the balloon-frame method of construction a few decades earlier, during the 1830s and 1840s. This technique, which used light wooden two-by-fours hammered together with machine-made nails rather than heavy timbers held in place by elaborate joints, saved a tremendous amount of time, labor, and materials. By the time Gross entered the real estate business, the balloon-frame house had revolutionized homebuilding throughout the United States and, together with cheap land, made homeownership much more affordable in the United States than in Europe.

THE ROLE OF RAILROADS IN REAL ESTATE DEVELOPMENT

As noted earlier, one of the largest transfers of land from the public to the private sector came with the advance of the railroad in the mid-19th century. In the 18th and early 19th centuries, water-based transportation routes had made some land accessible, permitting many towns to develop mainly because of their location near navigable bodies of water. In the first half of the 19th century, canals had expanded the number of accessible sites available for land development, and steamships had provided for the movement of people and goods along the coast. However, railroads proved to be faster and more profitable than any water transport mode.

The speed and capacity of this new form of transportation profoundly affected life in the United States. Railroads quickly became the prime movers of people and goods around the nation, into and out of cities and towns. Municipalities came to depend on access to rail service for growth and even survival. In the early years, some organized their own short-haul rail corporations; later, many went deeply into debt from paying huge subsidies to private railroad firms for providing service to their communities. Once regular rail service was established, residents bought land and marketed it to newcomers. Because tracks could be laid almost anywhere, the volume of land potentially available for development expanded tremendously. At times, this expansion led to feverish speculation; no investor could predict with certainty which sites with access to rail transport would be in demand and at what price.

Following the Civil War, westward expansion was also facilitated by the development of the transcontinental railroad. Congress had chartered the Union and Central Pacific railroads in 1862. As an incentive, for each mile of track laid, each company was to receive ten square miles of land in alternate sections along the line. The railroads then sold this land, acquiring both cash and potential agricultural customers.

The giant railroad corporations, the country's first truly big businesses, were thus intimately involved in

The growth of railroad construction brought with it a frenzy of land speculation like that along this line connecting Houston and New Orleans, circa 1880.

real estate activity. The interstate long-distance rail carriers obtained their franchises and capitalization through the federal government's grant of not only rights-of-way but also millions of acres of additional land along their new proposed routes. Between 1850 and 1871, the federal government granted 130 million acres of public land to railroad companies. The companies received about half of the land within six to 40 miles of the rights-of-way, with the government retaining the other half. Continuing the pattern established for the transcontinental railroad, the land was divided into ten-square-mile sections, each made up of one-square-mile parcels, and the railroads were granted every other section. Public officials argued that once a railroad was built, the government could sell its remaining sections for at least twice as much as it could have otherwise, though it did not always work out that way in practice. After tracks were laid, the railroads and the government went into competition with each other in subdividing and selling their sections.

Railroads entered the real estate promotion business in an enormous way. Some of Southern Pacific's land was "perceived as potentially very valuable and was sold almost as soon as acquired by the railway, typically within a few weeks or months. Other more

arid or outlying land was of only modest value and sold gradually."[18] In addition to selling land, many railroad companies held onto vast expanses of their acreage, mortgaging it to bankers and bond buyers to obtain capital. Indeed, when some politicians and citizens tried to force the railroads to sell their publicly granted land, the companies responded that the assets were tied up as collateral and they could not sell the land without the permission of their lenders—an argument upheld by the U.S. Supreme Court.[19] Over the years, railroads have retained ownership of immense quantities of rural and urban land. They have sold it, leased it, and developed it. It has been used for agriculture, forestry, mining, and recreation, and for commercial, industrial, and residential developments as well as for railroad operations.

Railroads remained among the largest private landowners until the late 20th century, when they spun off much of their real estate holdings to development entities. Santa Fe–Southern Pacific's Mission Bay, a large mixed-use real estate development project near downtown San Francisco, is one such example. Another is the Hudson Yards Redevelopment Project on Manhattan's west side, the biggest private real estate development in U.S. history. In this case, the Metropolitan Transit Authority (which owns the Long Island Railroad) leased air rights over the rail yard for 99 years to a joint venture of the developers Related Companies and Oxford Properties Group. The project is the redevelopment of a vast railroad yard to commercial and residential high rises, a school, a hotel, and public open space. The Long Island Railroad will continue to operate beneath the development.

The Effect of Railroads on Industrial Development

The railroads completely reshaped the industrial landscape of cities. In the preindustrial era, everyone was packed together within walking distance of the city center, and artisan workshops were often located inside or next to people's homes. As cities expanded and manufacturing grew in importance, much manufacturing was located in separate multistory "loft" buildings with high ceilings and open floor space. The growing demand for industrial space made supplying such space an important branch of the real estate business. Small manufacturers still needed to be concentrated near city centers to take advantage of port facilities. With the advent of the railroads, however, manufacturing and warehousing could spread out along the rail lines, and rail spurs and feeder lines were built to connect local shippers to the main, long-haul trunk lines.

By the latter part of the 19th century, large factories and factory complexes with workers' housing were being built on new sites, owing to the railroads' cooperation in bringing in raw materials and shipping out finished products. Entire factory towns for large manufacturers began to sprout, such as the steel mill cities of Gary, Indiana, and Birmingham, Alabama. Decentralized industrial parks began to appear on the outskirts of large cities. Unlike the giant factories, industrial parks were primarily speculative real estate ventures. Some early ones were partially owned and financed by the railroad companies, to promote more intensive use of their land and transportation services.

By the early 20th century, Chicago real estate developers had established the Central Manufacturing

District and the Clearing Industrial District, both located on the city's southwest side, far from downtown. Many manufacturing and warehouse firms relocated to the new districts to take advantage of cheaper rents, larger one-story floor spaces, proximity to transit for workers, and, most important, excellent access to railroad sidings. These industrial parks were professionally managed and offered low-rise and low-density buildings, well-maintained grounds, clean sites, and attractive landscaping. Although this type of industrial development did not become prominent in the United States until the 1950s, the earliest models were established in the 1910s and 1920s.

Railroad Barons as Real Estate Developers

Two railroad barons each played a crucial role in shaping the patterns of real estate development and urbanization for an entire region: Henry M. Flagler on Florida's east coast and Henry E. Huntington in southern California.

Flagler and the Growth of Southern Florida
Flagler was one of John D. Rockefeller's original partners in the petroleum business; he became extremely wealthy through the growth of the Standard Oil Company. In the early 1880s, Florida was experiencing one of its periodic land booms. St. Augustine, where Flagler vacationed in 1885, was considered a favorable location because of its healthful climate. Flagler became captivated by the town and decided to develop it into a premier resort city for the upper classes, creating a southern version of Newport, Rhode Island. Flagler hired two young New York architects, John Carrère and Thomas Hastings, to design the massive and luxurious Spanish-style Hotel Ponce de León, named for the explorer who had searched in St. Augustine for the fountain of youth. The hotel opened in 1888 and proved so successful that, by the following year, Flagler had built the Alcazar, a large entertainment center that included mid-priced hotel rooms, ballrooms, theaters, swimming pools, and an array of other facilities. He also purchased a new, small luxury hotel called Casa Monica, which he renamed

The lobby of the luxurious Breakers Hotel, built by Henry M. Flagler in 1896 in West Palm Beach, Florida.

the Cordova. In addition, he built 14 expensive cottages for winter guests.

In the process of arranging for goods to be shipped to St. Augustine and marketing his hotels to the northeastern states, Flagler discovered that transportation to the site was a problem. To alleviate that problem, he began to acquire and reorganize local railroad lines. Eventually, he consolidated the lines and created the Florida East Coast Railway, laying tracks southward along the coast toward Daytona Beach and thereby acquiring thousands of acres of public land grants from the state for his railroad-building activities. When Flagler's rail lines reached the Lake Worth area, he created the new resort community of West Palm Beach, starting with the Royal Poinciana, which, with 1,500 rooms, was the world's largest hotel when it opened in 1894. Two years later, he built The Breakers, a 500-room hotel.

West Palm Beach soon eclipsed St. Augustine. From New York, Philadelphia, and Chicago, the elite traveled on Flagler's trains to this winter pleasure palace, and, by 1900, it had truly become the "Newport of the South."

During 1894 and 1895, Florida suffered a series of winter freezes, and Flagler decided to extend his rail lines farther south, where winters were even warmer. He settled on Dade County and negotiated thousands of acres in land grants from private landowners in exchange for promising to bring rail service to a little town called Fort Dallas on the Miami River and Biscayne Bay. When the railroad reached the site in 1896, the town was incorporated as Miami, and Flagler built the lavish Royal Palm hotel there, opening it in 1897 with 350 rooms for guests and another 100 for staff. He also built a rail terminal, an electric plant, a sewage system, waterworks, and—after dredging the Miami River—a harbor for ocean-going vessels. He laid out miles of streets; donated land for a civic center, public buildings, schools, parks, and churches; and started a newspaper called the *Miami Metropolis* at a time when the city had only a few hundred year-round residents. By 1910, rapidly growing Miami was already the state's fifth largest city, with a population of 11,000. Flagler took advantage of his extensive holdings to subdivide a tremendous amount of land for highly profitable sales and to develop additional hotels and other properties.

Besides the railroad land grants, Flagler had acquired several large landowning companies in Florida—including a former canal promoter—and consolidated them all into his Florida East Coast Canal and Transportation Company, which also became the holding company for his railroad lines. Flagler made enormous profits by the timely linking of his land sales and development activities to the provision of rail service. In 1897, he had added shipping to his transportation and development plans, founding the Florida East Coast Steamship Company to offer better access from Miami to Havana, Nassau, and Key West, again building hotels and other projects and selling land in Nassau and Key West. His final project was extending the railroad to Key West, a major engineering achievement. Flagler rode the inaugural train 225 miles over land and sea from his home in West Palm Beach to Key West for the grand opening in 1912. When he died a year later, the hotel, railroad, and land baron left an enduring legacy in the form and pattern of development and growth in the Sunshine State.

Huntington, the Southern Pacific, and Southern California's First Boom

The western segment of the first transcontinental railway was constructed by California's "Big Four": Collis Huntington, Leland Stanford, Mark Hopkins, and Charles Crocker. The Central Pacific joined the Union Pacific in 1869. Many other railways came under the control of the Big Four, including the Southern Pacific, in 1868, giving them control over most of the transportation routes in

California. Los Angeles was a small pueblo community of fewer than 6,000 inhabitants when it began negotiating in the early 1870s for the Southern Pacific to extend its lines to the town. The Angelenos offered free land, an ownership share in their local railroad, $600,000 in cash borrowed through municipal bonds, and other subsidies before Huntington finally agreed to the expansion during the 1880s.

The Atchison, Topeka, and Santa Fe Railroad was also building a new line to Los Angeles over the mountains, and, by 1887, the Santa Fe and the Southern Pacific were fighting a rate war to establish dominance in the market for coast-to-coast travel to southern California. At one point, they cut fares so low that passengers could ride from Kansas City to Los Angeles for one dollar. The rate war brought in vast numbers of tourists.

The new rail connections to the East and Midwest set off a subdivision boom that lasted for a single frenzied year before crashing. In Los Angeles County, 1,350 new subdivision maps were recorded in 1887, compared with ten in 1880 and 70 in 1890. In 1887, real estate transactions in the city of Los Angeles topped $100 million; only New York City and Chicago had more that year. Prices for acreage and for subdivision lots rose ten to 20 times within that year, only to drop back down again the next. In all, the 60 new cities and towns, covering 80,000 acres, that were laid out and marketed in 1887 and 1888 contained enough land to house several million people at low densities. Yet, by 1889, fewer than 3,500 people lived in those communities. Ultimately many of them became major cities and suburbs in the Los Angeles basin.

Though Los Angeles itself grew rapidly—to a population of 50,000 by 1890—other boom towns quickly became ghost towns. One was Border City in the Mojave Desert, platted by Simon Homberg on land bought from the federal government. With great fanfare, he sold lots that cost him about ten cents each to East Coast investors for $250 each; when the buyers found out the true nature of their nearly worthless purchase, the market dried up like desert air.

The land speculation boom and bust in 1887 and 1888 left the Los Angeles real estate market in a somewhat weakened condition during the 1890s, and the national depression of 1893 added to local difficulties. Nonetheless, the long-term prospects for Los Angeles's growth were promising. Even during the 1890s, the population doubled in size, and, by 1901, the city was poised for a major revival of real estate activity.

SUMMARY

Real estate contributed significantly to the country's overall growth from the colonial era through the early 1900s. Once the federal and state governments began privatizing public lands, real estate became the great American pastime. At the same time that large tracts of land were exchanging hands and undergoing subdivision and development, the public sector was becoming more involved in financing those activities. It was also looking to the real estate industry for new sources of public revenue. The railroads' twofold involvement in real estate—as transporters and as land developers and owners—strongly promoted new development.

TERMS

- Capital improvement project
- Deed restrictions
- Fee simple
- Ground lease
- Homestead
- Land development
- Slums
- Subdivision
- Syndicate

REVIEW QUESTIONS

4.1   How was public land put into private ownership?

4.2   Describe the fee simple system of private ownership.

4.3   What was the Holland Land Company noted for?

4.4   What effect did private deed restrictions and public controls have on real estate in the 19th century?

4.5   Who was Llewellyn Haskell?

4.6   What is the balloon-frame method of construction, and what effect did it have on residential development?

4.7   Describe the evolution of slums.

4.8   Discuss the role of the railroads in land development.

NOTES

1   Arthur Gallion and Simon Eisner, *The Urban Pattern* (Princeton: D Van Nostrand Company, 1963), p. 53.

2   Andro Linklater, *Owning the Earth* (New York: Bloomsbury, 2013), p. 220.

3   Larry Van Dyne, "The Making of Washington," *Washingtonian*, November 1987, p. 172.

4   Elizabeth Blackmar, *Manhattan For Rent*, 1785–1850 (Ithaca, N.Y.: Cornell University Press, 1989), p. 36.

5   Aaron M. Sakolski, *The Great American Land Bubble, The Amazing Story of Land-Grabbing, Speculations, and Booms from Colonial Days to the Present Time* (New York: Harper, 1932), p. 9.

6   Blackmar, pp. 31–32.

7   Sakolski, p. 82.

8   Ibid., pp. 84–85.

9   Eugene Rachlis and John E. Marqusee, *The Land Lords* (New York: Random House, 1963), p. 3.

10   Richard Henry Dana, Jr., *Two Years Before the Mast* (New York: Barnes and Noble, 1869), p. 378.

11   Jacob Riis, *How the Other Half Lives: Studies among the Tenements of New York* (New York: Scribner's, 1890).

12   Carroll D. Wright, *The Slums of Baltimore, Chicago, New York, and Philadelphia*. Seventh Special Report of the Commissioner of Labor (Washington, D.C.: U.S. Government Printing Office, 1894).

13   Ian Tod and Michael Wheeler, *Utopia* (New York: Harmony Books, 1978), pp. 83–84.

14   Kenneth T. Jackson, *Crabgrass Frontier: The Suburbanization of the United States* (New York: Oxford University Press, 1985), p. 77.

15   Ann Durkin Keating, *Building Chicago: Suburban Developers and the Creation of a Divided Metropolis* (Columbus: Ohio State University Press, 1988), p. 73.

16   Jackson, p. 80.

17   Keating, p. 76. See also Gwendolyn Wright, *Moralism and the Model Home: Domestic Architecture and Cultural Conflict in Chicago, 1873–1913* (Chicago: University of Chicago Press, 1980).

18   Richard J. Orsi, *Southern Pacific* (Berkeley: University of California Press, 2005), p. 69.

19   *Platt* v. *Union Pacific R.R. Co.*, 9 U.S. 48 (October 1878).

Chapter 5

The Late 1800s to World War II

The late 19th century marked the beginning of massive technological, demographic, and social changes that would transform land use in America. It was an era of contradictory forces: trends toward centralization and decentralization, unbridled growth and emerging land use regulation, growth of wealth and poverty, peace and war. Between 1890 and 1940, the population of the United States more than doubled, from 62 million to 132 million. Urban areas became magnets for an immense migration, from rural areas at home and abroad, of people looking for better economic prospects. Adna F. Weber's landmark 1899 study, *The Growth of Cities in the Nineteenth Century*, fully documents this rapid urbanization, which he called "the most remarkable social phenomenon."[1] As cities gained population, they spread across a great deal of additional territory, with improvements in transportation, utilities, infrastructure, and urban services encouraging the mass movement of industry and residences away from the crowded city center. All but the richest and the poorest moved to outlying neighborhoods in search of better housing and, in many cases, homeownership

on cheaper land. Factories and warehouses moved along with workers to industrial districts where land costs were lower, facilities were more modern, and it was now easier to ship goods.

This chapter looks at this transformation of cities and land use, beginning with a review of reforms that grew out of the Progressive Era and of changes in the urban landscape that resulted from the demographic, technological, economic, and political changes in the years leading up to World War II. The chapter ends with a discussion of how the financial and regulatory systems developed, and of the professionalization of real estate development.

CIVIC LEADERSHIP, REFORM, AND THE PUBLIC SECTOR

Except for the wealthy, cities of the late 19th century were not perfect places to live. Many people lived in overcrowded, substandard conditions. There were sweatshops and child labor abuses. Industrial activities polluted the air, water, and land. Municipal governments were sometimes run by corrupt political machines that used patronage to reward supporters.

This chapter was originally written by Marc A. Weiss, PhD, chair and CEO, Global Urban Development, Washington, D.C.

In time, pressure for change became institutionalized. Civic and business organizations commissioned master plans for future urban development. The Progressive Movement, supported by the middle class and some wealthy individuals, pushed for reforms at all levels of government. Adherents believed that scientific management techniques executed by professional managers would result in the delivery of more efficient municipal services.

A turning point in urban design was the 1893 Chicago Columbian Exposition. Promoted by local businessmen, the fair had an enormous impact on the public's perception of cities and city planning. Its success came from "three conditions: unity of plan, unity of architecture and magnitude."[2] It triggered the start of the *"City Beautiful" movement* to construct attractive and often monumental public buildings: city halls, libraries, museums, and schools, as well as public parks—both large "pleasure gardens" and smaller neighborhood parks and playgrounds. Plans were often based on classical architecture and land planning concepts, such as those of Daniel Burnham, or on pastoral and picturesque concepts such as those of the Olmsted brothers.

The largest example of the pastoral and picturesque approach was introduced in the 1850s with Fredrick Law Olmsted's design for New York City's Central Park. Olmsted spent the next four decades designing parks and parkways in cities across the country, including San Francisco's Golden Gate Park and park systems for Boston, Chicago, and Buffalo. Many cities in Europe were also enjoying a public park renaissance. Under the Crown Lands Act of 1851, London created eight large urban parks that, combined, encompass nearly 5,000 acres. Paris's Bois de Boulogne and Bois de Vincennes were created in the 1850s during Napoleon's reign. In 1862, the Stadtpark opened as the first public park in Vienna.

Along with parks came parkways—wide streets that coursed through parks or other natural settings—and boulevards—tree-lined thoroughfares bordered by buildings and other urban scenery. Although initially intended for leisurely drives, many of these roads later became principal transportation arteries overflowing with traffic.

The Progressive Movement also focused on the management of urban areas. In addition to structural reforms such as the city manager form of government, adherents also promoted the public ownership of major utilities such as water, electricity, and transportation systems. Structures such as docks, port facilities, bridges and tunnels, and railroad and transit lines all came to fall under the purview of the public sector toward the end of the 19th century. These new areas of activity added to the expanding demand for public infrastructure and utilities such as water and sewer systems and to the burgeoning growth of essential services, from police protection to street cleaning.

Two major kinds of real estate regulations that arose from the Progressive Movement were strong building codes and *zoning*. Social activism, provoked by the 1890 publication of *How the Other Half Lives*, by Jacob Riis, helped bring about legislation that set building standards in New York and other cities. Another impetus came from the fires that destroyed major portions of Boston, Baltimore, Chicago, and San Francisco in the late 19th and early 20th centuries. By the turn of the century, though, many cities had formalized building codes to govern new construction.

Land use zoning, which restricts the type of use and the configuration of buildings by geographic areas within a city, began to spread in the early 20th century. The rationale for such restrictions was that certain types of land uses are incompatible and threaten the health, safety, and general welfare of citizens. In 1905, Los Angeles adopted a code that separated residential and industrial land uses. In 1915, New York established a code that covered all land use categories and designated those uses on a map. It also created restrictions on setbacks and building heights. As discussed in chapter 7, these regulations were challenged in court but eventually upheld as a legitimate police power of the state.

Even before the introduction of zoning, real estate owners and developers had created restrictions that were written into property deeds as contractual obligations. Some communities relied on deed restrictions to control real estate transactions by race

Pittsburgh's downtown experienced remarkable growth in the late 1800s. Liberty Avenue, circa 1910, was one of the main streets leading to the convergence of the Allegheny and Monongahela rivers.

and religion—a condition that was not invalidated by the Supreme Court until 1948. Deed restrictions established the models used later in promulgating public sector development controls.

CENTRALIZATION

Cities exist because human interaction for commerce, government, religion, and protection required centrality. By the end of the 19th century, the need for dense urban cores was driven by the creation of industrial economies. The core of a city came to be called the "central business district" or "CBD," reflecting the amount of space devoted to commerce-based face-to-face interaction. Before the advent of electronic communication, for example, a manufacturing company needed to be physically near its financial institutions, attorneys, advertising

firms, brokers, transportation services, and all other services necessary to support its activity.

Central Business Districts and Commercial Development

The theory behind the CBD is simple: high-value activities compete for centrally located land. As the need for centrality decreases, so does the land value, in some proportion to the distance from the urban core. Thus, the CBD or "downtown" is a region's focal point for the largest banks, insurance companies, corporate headquarters, newspaper publishers, government functions, professional offices, retailing and wholesaling, hotels, cultural activities, and other functions supported by a large hinterland. Transportation corridors, initially railroad and streetcar lines and later freeways, radiate out from downtown, bringing in and taking home most of the metropolitan population every day to work, shop, obtain services, and be educated and entertained.

A living organism is often used as a metaphor for the city. It grows and in the process sheds some elements and adds others. Thus, as land values rose in the central core, many industrial and residential land uses were outbid, forced out, torn down, and replaced in an incredible commercial building boom. In downtown Pittsburgh, for example, more than 400 buildings were completed in just five years in the late 1880s and early 1890s, and nearly as many more were completed over the next decade.

The Growth of the Skyscraper

No symbol of the prosperous corporate-commercial city was more potent than the skyscraper. Most skyscrapers were office buildings and replaced church spires as the highest points of reference—though perhaps not reverence—for the urban community. The concept of the steel frame building, developed in Chicago in the 1880s, allowed buildings to attain greater heights and therefore offer more rentable floor space. With the advent of the elevator in 1852, *steel frame construction* rapidly evolved. The first skyscraper is typically acknowledged to be the 1884 Home Insurance Building in Chicago, designed by William Le Baron Jenney. Chicago architects such as Daniel Burnham and John Wellborn Root and Louis Sullivan quickly refined the concept. The Chicago "Loop" became the center of commerce for the entire midwest, largely enabled by the efficiency of steel frame construction. The architectural world began a long journey to understand and interpret the new technology, and the early Chicago buildings are recognized as significant steps in that process.

Life insurance companies erected many of the earliest and most prominent office buildings. The largest of these firms had substantial long-term capital to invest in real estate, needed their own headquarters, and desired to communicate their financial strength visually to current and prospective policyholders. In New York City in the late 19th century, Equitable, Prudential, Metropolitan, and others competed to build the tallest and most impressive structure. A similar battle took place among major

newspaper publishers, who desired the symbol of a distinctive office tower to boost circulation, advertising revenue, and prestige. In New York City, the Tribune and Evening Post buildings took the early lead but were soon eclipsed in 1892 by publisher Joseph Pulitzer's New York World Building, at 309 feet. Not to be outdone, the *New York Times* fought back a decade later with the 362-foot Times Tower.

Two years later, the Singer Sewing Machine Company, whose consumer products were distributed globally, stunned both the insurance and the newspaper businesses by announcing plans to construct a new headquarters building more than 600 feet tall. When completed in 1908, the Singer Building, designed by the distinguished architect Ernest Flagg, was twice as high as nearly all of New York's and the world's other skyscrapers—and 40 feet taller than the Washington Monument in the nation's capital.[3] The Singer Building, however, was overshadowed in 1909 by the Metropolitan Life Tower, which was nearly 100 feet taller.

Some city residents became so alarmed by the perceived negative impact of the new towers on urban density, sunlight, and safety that they lobbied municipal authorities to impose limitations on building height. By the 1890s, Boston and Chicago had already passed such restrictions, to be followed by Washington, D.C., Los Angeles, and several other cities. In most cases, the maximum permitted building height ranged between 100 and 200 feet. But by the 1920s, many of these regulations had been lifted or modified to allow continued vertical expansion.

Corporations put their names on skyscrapers for advertising value and usually owned their headquarters buildings, but they typically did not occupy all the office space. A great deal of it was leased to a variety of business and professional tenants. Not surprisingly, the new downtowns spawned a specialized real estate industry in architecture, construction, brokerage, and property management. The demand for office space was sufficiently strong that developers and investors also put up purely speculative buildings to compete with the large company headquarters structures. In New York City, the Trinity Building and the United States Realty Building were both built speculatively without an anchor or "name" tenant. A more famous example is the iconic triangle-shaped Flatiron Building on Fifth Avenue and Broadway, designed by the well-known Chicago architect Daniel Burnham and completed in 1903. The Flatiron Building was occupied primarily by wholesalers and other small firms.

The most important early developers of commercial office buildings were the Brooks brothers from Boston. Peter and Shepherd Brooks were investors who in 1873 acquired the seven-story Portland Block, Chicago's first office building equipped with a passenger elevator. From this initial investment, the Brooks family developed many buildings pioneered by the world-famous Chicago school of architecture, which was noted for the design and construction of large commercial buildings during the late 19th century.

In 1881, Peter and Shepherd Brooks had decided that the downtown Chicago real estate market was robust enough to support construction of the city's first ten-story building, the Montauk Block. Peter Brooks wrote to his attorney and partner Owen Aldis that "an office building erected to suit modern notions, thoroughly equipped with modern appliances, would fill up with modern tenants, leaving the old and un-remodeled houses to the conservative fogy."[4] He wanted a building whose modern construction techniques, attractive and simple design, and quality materials, methods, and maintenance would project a businesslike image of efficiency and strength: "The building throughout is to be for use and not for ornament. Its beauty will be in its all-adaptation to its use."[5] The architectural partners Burnham and Root designed the Montauk Block plus two other Brooks-Aldis office buildings, the Rookery and the Monadnock Block. The Brooks brothers and Aldis also teamed up to develop the Pontiac Building and the Marquette Building, both designed by another famous architectural firm, Holabird and Roche.

Brooks's and Aldis's guidelines for the design of their numerous buildings included "height sufficient to warrant the use of elevators, as much light as possible, easy maintenance, high percentage of rentable space, and ornament sufficient to avoid absolute plainness."[6] Aldis also wrote eight rules for building management when the Marquette was completed in 1894, with the basic thrust being that building first-class space and providing first-class services are the best investments. It certainly turned out that way for Peter and Shepherd Brooks, who earned a substantial return on their investments. Aldis also did extremely well financially from his investments and fee income.

Interestingly, Aldis's leasing strategy was to "arrange [a] typical layout for intensive use." He noted:

> A large number of small tenants is more desirable than large space for large tenants because: a) a higher rate per square foot can be added for small tenants; b) they do not move in a body and leave the building with a large vacant space when hard times hit; c) they do not swamp your elevators by coming and going by the clock.[7]

Once New York City's most famous skyscraper, the Flatiron Building (originally known as the Fuller Building) stands at the intersection of Fifth Avenue and Broadway.

The buildings developed by Brooks and Aldis were fully rented when they opened in the 1880s and 1890s. Though the Montauk was demolished in 1902, the others maintained high occupancy rates through the mid-1960s.

Downtown Hotels and Department Stores

High-rise office buildings were the most distinctive new features of the rapidly growing urban downtowns in the early 20th century, and they were soon joined by other prominent structures and land uses. Large hotel towers became a vital feature of downtowns, attracting business customers and the rapidly expanding tourist trade to meetings, social functions, entertainment, and, most important, the thousands of new guest rooms. Henry Flagler's thriving Florida hotel operations, though winter resorts, also anchored the downtowns of several growing cities, particularly Miami. In New York City, the heirs and descendants of John Jacob Astor built the luxurious Waldorf-Astoria Hotel in the 1890s on the site of their parents' mansions. Potter Palmer in Chicago, Henry Huntington in southern California, and other developers elsewhere built similar "grand hotels."

The other major urban innovation was the massive, multistory department store. These structures, often designed as "pleasure palaces" with ornate exteriors and lavish interiors, catered especially to women shoppers. The stores employed service-oriented sales personnel and offered special events and promotions. The earliest department stores go back to the 1700s in Great Britain. The large-scale modern prototype appeared in the mid-1800s, and some of these vast emporiums still thrive. Kendals in Manchester, England, was among the first and is still operating, albeit with a new name (House of Fraser). In London, Harrods and Bainbridge's (now John Lewis) also date back to the mid-1800s. In the United States, the first department store was Alexander T. Stewart's elaborate dry goods center, the Marble Palace, which opened in 1846 on Broadway and Chambers Street in New York City. Later in the century, larger and more spectacular department stores covering entire city blocks and serving as major downtown institutions flourished in

The Waldorf-Astoria Hotel, built in the late 1890s by the descendants of John Jacob Astor in the Second Empire style.

many cities. Examples include Selfridges in London, Le Bon Marché in Paris, Filene's in Boston, and Marshall Field's in Chicago. In every case, these stores acted as magnets for the real estate market. When Marshall Field's changed locations in Chicago from Lake Street to State Street in 1867, its new site became the prime "*100 percent corner*" almost immediately.

One of the greatest American department store ventures was Wanamaker's in Philadelphia. John Wanamaker and his partner, Nathan Brown, opened Oak Hall, a men's and boys' clothing store, on the ground floor of a six-story building in downtown

Philadelphia in 1861. Their business philosophy, which Wanamaker elaborated throughout his long retailing career, called for selling high-quality merchandise at one "everyday low price" and guaranteeing money-back returns on all goods. Wanamaker emphasized a democratic, egalitarian ethic with his slogan, "no favoritism."[8] Every customer was to be treated with equal respect, to be charged the same low prices, and to be served properly. In the early years, Wanamaker's made only cash sales, refunded only cash, and paid its workers daily in cash.

By the 1870s, Oak Hall proved so successful that John Wanamaker purchased an abandoned rail depot from the Pennsylvania Railroad and built the world's largest department store, a huge two-acre dry goods emporium at Thirteenth and Market streets dubbed "the Grand Depot." It opened in 1876 in the midst of the centennial celebration of the Declaration of Independence, which brought 10 million visitors to Philadelphia. And one of the big

Built in 1900, the 15-story Continental Building in downtown Baltimore was a classic early skyscraper in the Chicago style.

The grand atrium of Wanamaker's downtown Philadelphia store in 1911. The neoclassical, 13-story building was a block long.

tourist attractions was Wanamaker's Grand Depot. A year later, Wanamaker was already building an addition on Chestnut Street that connected through a stylish arcade to the main store. The Chestnut Street store, with its separate and ornate entrance, was designed to specialize in ladies' goods, which eventually became an even bigger business for Wanamaker's than its already brisk trade in men's and children's clothing. Linens, appliances, housewares, furniture, pianos, and everything else imaginable were eventually added to various departments in the acres of retail space.

For many years, the Grand Depot, with its distinctive clock tower, was known around the world as one of Philadelphia's central landmarks. In 1908, the Chestnut Street store was demolished and replaced by a much larger, block-long structure, complete with its own subway station. By the time its founder died in 1922, Wanamaker's, like other major department stores, was beginning to build suburban stores at prime locations near commuter train stations.

Despite the subsequent urban decentralization, the role of Wanamaker and other central-city department store owners in creating the modern commercial downtown produced an enduring legacy.

Office Building in the Roaring Twenties

After a relatively dry spell immediately before, during, and after World War I, the construction of downtown office space burgeoned in the 1920s, in structures of all shapes, sizes, and heights. Near the end of the decade, the Thompson-Starrett Company of New York, one of the world's largest private construction firms that specialized in skyscrapers, surveyed the country's 173 largest cities and found nearly 5,000 buildings ten stories or higher, many of them built during the 1920s. This list included hotels, department stores, manufacturing lofts, civic centers, and other private and public structures, but private office buildings predominated.[9]

Although New York City accounted for more than half of all skyscrapers in the entire country, many other cities had significant and growing numbers. Chicago, Los Angeles, Philadelphia, Detroit, and Boston all had more than 100 buildings taller than ten stories. The growth in height and bulk was made possible by new building technology but fueled by the increasing urban wealth and productivity of the 1920s and the consequent tremendous

---

The Story of the Empire State Building

The site of the Empire State Building was attractive to its investors because a very large parcel of land, 197 feet by 425 feet, was available. The old Waldorf-Astoria Hotel, which sat on that parcel, was slated to be demolished when the new hotel on Park Avenue was completed. After developer Floyd Brown, who had bought the site in 1928, defaulted on his mortgage payments, the property was sold to the Empire State Company, and the hotel was demolished just a few weeks before the stock market crashed in October 1929. Despite the crash, the Empire State Company, partially owned by the du Pont family and headed by former New York Governor Al Smith, decided to move forward with the project in the face of what it incorrectly perceived to be a brief economic downturn. The company invested a total of $45 million to acquire the site, demolish the hotel, and design and construct the world's tallest building, all in less than 18 months. The construction, managed by the general contracting firm of Starrett Brothers and Eken, took less than a year. At the peak of activity, 3,500 construction workers were adding one story a day. By the official opening on May 1, 1931, the building stood 1,250 feet tall, with 85 floors of offices and the equivalent of another 17 floors devoted to the magnificent mooring mast and observation decks.

When completed, the Empire State Building's skeleton consumed 57,000 tons of steel. The finished building contained 51 miles of pipe, 17 million feet of telephone cable, and seven miles of elevator shaft.

One reason for the speed of construction was that in those days commercial leases in New York expired on April 30, and if the Empire State Building were not ready for occupancy on May 1, the company would have to wait an entire year to attract tenants—a costly delay. The rationale for building it so tall was that the syndicate had paid record high prices for a location at 34th Street and Fifth Avenue that was less than ideal for a quality office skyscraper: the principal office districts were at 23rd Street near Madison Square, 42nd Street near Grand Central Station, and downtown around Wall Street. The Empire State Building stood alone in the middle of a low-rise section of hotels, department stores, shops, and loft buildings, relatively far from the Grand Central and Pennsylvania Railroad stations and several blocks from the nearest subway lines. The extreme height and distinctiveness of the building were designed to serve as an advertising beacon to attract office tenants.

Similarly, key architectural features were intended to maximize the net revenue that could be generated by the rentable space. For example, the building is less bulky than was permitted under the zoning laws. By designing almost the entire building as a setback tower over a wide, five-story base, the developers increased the rents per square foot by offering offices that were quieter and had more natural light. By building shallow floors with window access for every office, the developers also eliminated the disadvantage of their location relative to other tall buildings, offering prospective tenants panoramic and unobstructed views. In this design, constructing less space per floor made each square foot more valuable. Similarly, rather than building a simple flat rectangular structure that would have produced four corner offices on each floor, the Empire State Building was recessed in the north and south towers so that the extra angles of the structure would yield eight to 12 corner offices per floor, adding significantly to the potential rent.

The physical achievement of the Empire State Building obscures the fact that, like today's projects, it too had to meet legal

Continued next page

expansion of cities both outward and upward. By the late 1920s, financing was flowing freely from institutional lenders, equity syndicators, and *mortgage* bond houses, further encouraging the construction of speculative office space. New organizations and methods of equity financing through the sale of stock (under the aegis of such firms as the Fred F. French Investing Company or Harry Black's United States Realty) and debt financing (through the likes of the S.W. Straus mortgage bond company) fed the rapid private development of high-rise commercial and residential buildings.

By the late 1920s, office buildings were going up so fast and American business tenants, investors, and real estate developers were all in such a confident mood that several new structures, including the 77-story, 1,030-foot-high, art deco Chrysler Building, far surpassed earlier buildings in height and prominence. The building that was to become the world's tallest for more than four decades, the Empire State Building, was not a corporate headquarters like some of the other giant skyscrapers but rather a purely speculative office building built quickly in what many considered a poor location.

The Story of the Empire State Building   *Continued*

and financial requirements for feasibility. John Jacob Raskob, one of five partners in the development, asked his architect, William Lamb, "Bill, how high can you make it so it won't fall down?" The real question was, how high and still profitable? The answer depended on a stipulation in New York City's 1916 zoning ordinance that above the 30th floor, a building could occupy no more per floor than one-fourth of the total area on its lot. With two acres of ground, the Empire State tower could cover half an acre. Lamb determined that 36 million cubic feet would be a profitable size; he then began playing with alternatives. The 16th iteration (Plan K) was it: an 86-story tower. His client Raskob declared, "It needs a hat" and in a creative burst suggested a mooring mast for a dirigible. The 200-foot mast, intended to be an international arrival point for lighter-than-air craft, extended the building's total height to 1,250 feet. Because of high winds, the mast never worked as intended, but it was eventually used for observation. During the Great Depression, income from the observation platform offset large office vacancies and kept the Empire State Building in business.

Unfortunately, all the developer's sophisticated planning and marketing strategies designed to cope with the basic circumstances of no preleased tenants, a poor location, and a terrible office market during the Great Depression were in the short run to little avail. The building stood mostly vacant throughout the 1930s and was widely nicknamed "The Empty State Building." With the return of full employment and prosperity in the 1940s, however, the building filled up and has proved successful. Rather than being a symbol of a corporate, government, educational, medical, or cultural institution, the Empire State Building stands as a symbol of commercial real estate development.

The completed Empire State Building in 1931—the symbol of New York for nearly a century. The facade is made of limestone, granite, aluminum, and nickel, with art deco ornamentation.

Rockefeller Center: Mixed-Use Innovation

During the 1930s, most big projects were funded or subsidized with public money. One of the few that were privately funded was Rockefeller Center in New York City a major development that replaced several blocks of tenement housing and stands as the forerunner of today's large-scale urban mixed-use developments. It remains one of the best known and most successful of such projects.

The original parcel of land for the development lay between Fifth and Sixth avenues and 48th and 51st streets. It belonged to Columbia University, which leased it for 46 years to John D. Rockefeller, Jr., in October 1928 at an annual rent of nearly $4 million—ten times the existing rental yield. The Rockefeller family, which lived on 53rd Street near Fifth Avenue, already owned a great deal of property in the neighborhood. That fall, New York City was in the midst of the real estate boom that preceded the stock market crash, and Rockefeller was extremely optimistic about his prospects for redeveloping the area.

Once the Depression hit, it became highly uncertain how such a large site could be redeveloped and space occupied in the market-wide context of falling rents and rising vacancies. Teams of architects worked for several years on many schemes, both with and without an opera house as a focal point. The buildings were planned using a unified architectural theme and materials, enhancing the new and unusual image of a mixed-use center in a single development project. Innovative design features included the addition of private streets to cut up the long east-west blocks and the creation of the first privately developed public plaza in the city, which today houses the world-famous outdoor ice-skating rink.

Rockefeller originally planned to build a new Metropolitan Opera House on the site, knowing that the directors of the opera company wanted to relocate from 40th Street and Broadway to escape encroachment by the garment industry. When the directors eventually turned down the opportunity, Rockefeller turned to mass culture as his best prospect for attracting commercial tenants to this untested location. By the mid-1930s, he had filled the 70-story RCA Building (now called the GE Building)—his main high-rise office tower—with radio, motion picture, and vaudeville businesses, including RCA, RKO, and NBC, which were thriving even during the Great Depression.

He also developed on Sixth Avenue an entertainment facility for the general public, Radio City Music Hall, as well as the Center Theatre for opera and large-scale musical shows. The Sixth Avenue side of the site had been considered a blighted area because elevated railroad tracks ran along the avenue. By 1939, though, a new subway had been constructed and the elevated tracks removed, opening up new opportunities for private redevelopment.

Publishers also gravitated to new office buildings in Rockefeller Center. By the early 1940s, the development had clearly succeeded in becoming a desirable location for corporate office space, and since the 1950s, it has expanded to the west across Sixth Avenue with high-rise office buildings whose major tenants range from Bank of America to NBC's headquarters and studios. On the Fifth Avenue side, Rockefeller constructed low-rise structures for international retail and office tenants, taking advantage of proximity to prestigious retailers across the street. These smaller tenants, a network of below-ground shops and restaurants, and a tightly controlled and well-maintained environment all helped turn a risky, speculative, expensive, money-losing venture into the premier private real estate development of the Great Depression decade.

Urban Apartment Buildings

Another innovation of the late 19th century was the apartment house. As land values rose in cities, it became increasingly uneconomical to build or maintain single-family houses, other than as mansions for the wealthiest people. Spacious apartments complete with the latest amenities and services provided an attractive alternative for many upper- and middle-class urbanites desiring to live close to the action.

By 1900, apartment buildings accounted for a growing and important use of land in New York City, Chicago, Boston, San Francisco, Washington,

D.C., and a few other cities. Luxury apartments and working-class tenements were located in separate neighborhoods close to downtown, and middle-class multifamily dwellings were built farther out along avenues and boulevards traversed by streetcar lines.

One of the most notable trends of the 1920s was the tremendous acceleration in the construction of apartment buildings. Outside of a handful of major cities, earlier waves of urbanization in the United States had been based on a relatively low-density pattern of single-family houses, attached rowhouses, or duplexes. Some cities, including Boston, had triple-decker houses, and in many cities, large older houses had been subdivided into multiple apartments. This pattern began to change dramatically during the 1920s. Real estate investors, developers, lenders, and contractors all became active participants in the production of new apartment buildings, primarily built as rental units, though in a few cities, some were sold to occupants for cooperative ownership.

The new structures ranged from fashionable luxury residences with doormen and other services to more modest housing and from individual six-unit buildings to high rises and large complexes equipped with schools, parks, and community centers. Some buildings offered hotel-like amenities and were called apartment hotels. This vertical lifestyle had already become popular in Paris by the mid-19th century, and, when the idea was first transplanted to the United States, the apartments were often referred to as "French flats."

Perhaps the largest private rental housing development of the decade was the 2,125-unit, moderate-income Sunnyside apartment complex in New York City, with rents subsidized through a ten-year property tax abatement provided by the municipal government. The Metropolitan Life Insurance Company developed the apartments in 1922 to help ease the city's severe housing shortage. As an experiment in direct ownership and management of rental housing, Sunnyside proved economically successful and induced the insurance firm to build many larger apartment projects across the country during the 1930s and 1940s.

Apartment living suddenly became more fashionable for many middle- and upper-income people. Rents were relatively high because of the lack of supply resulting from the lack of construction during and immediately after World War I. With the growth in postwar housing demand, apartments became a good investment. The volume of apartments increased steadily throughout the decade, with new construction peaking in 1928. Starts of single-family housing, by contrast, peaked in 1925 and dropped sharply thereafter. That peak was not surpassed until 1950. Nearly 40 percent of all the dwelling units built during the 1920s were multifamily units. Furthermore, the share of total residential construction devoted to multifamily dwellings rose from approximately 25 percent in 1921 to more than 50 percent of all residential building permits issued in 1928. In every region of the United States and in all urban areas, the absolute number and relative percentage of apartments expanded significantly.

Nonfarm homeownership escalated by more than five percentage points from 1920 to 1930. Urban decentralization and suburbanization spread in all directions across the metropolitan landscape, the number of private automobiles increased by the millions, disposable income and savings among the middle class rose substantially, and land subdividers carved up an astonishing amount of acreage at the periphery of cities into building lots for sale. Massive land speculation and wild price escalation ensued in many rapidly growing areas of the country, helping to induce an unfortunate degree of mismanagement and fraud. In Florida alone, enough lots were subdivided, many of them in swampland or literally under water, to house the entire population of the United States.

DECENTRALIZATION

At the same time that economic forces were creating powerful central cities, forces for decentralization were at work. Outward expansion has been a characteristic of urban settlement throughout history, especially during periods of an expanding middle class. With the rise of the industrial city, the concept of entire planned communities emerged as an alternative to urban living for the middle and upper classes. Riverside, Illinois, was developed in 1869 according to a master plan created by Frederick Law Olmsted, as noted in chapter 4. In other cities, outward expansion followed the extension of streetcar lines.

The Streetcar Suburbs

Throughout the 19th century, the expansion of cities had been facilitated by the extension of streetcars, initially horse-drawn and later electric powered. In the late 1890s, when Henry Flagler was building the Hotel Ponce de León on the Atlantic Coast, southern California was in the midst of a wildly speculative land boom brought on by the arrival of transcontinental railroad service (see chapter 4). Following the bust, in 1901, Henry E. Huntington, nephew of Southern Pacific president Collis Huntington, formed the Pacific Electric Railway company to provide streetcar service to serve suburban communities, many of which were his own land ventures.

Huntington laid out a transportation network that stretched from the San Fernando and San Gabriel valleys of Los Angeles County all the way south to Newport Beach in coastal Orange County. By 1910, his railway companies covered more than 1,300 miles, making him the owner of the largest private interurban transit system in the world. Many southern California communities owed their rapid growth in the first two decades of the 20th century to Huntington's rail service. By 1920, the population of Los Angeles City reached 576,000, and Los Angeles County was home to nearly 1 million. The landscape of the metropolitan region was strongly shaped by Huntington's rail network: many of today's freeways follow the old Pacific Electric rights-of-way.

Before Huntington's undertaking, the normal practice for streetcar extensions called for landowners to pay the transit company for its capital costs in anticipation of the appreciation in their property values once service began. Huntington did not bother to pursue such an incremental strategy. He had his own capital and easy access to lenders and investors. The Huntington Land and Improvement Company and several of his other entities bought, subdivided, and sold real estate wherever the Pacific Electric's "big red cars" rolled along their tracks. Huntington brought rail service to areas he considered ripe for land development, even when the existing ridership was minimal. In many cases, those areas did grow rapidly once they became accessible through electric rail. For different target markets, Huntington developed a wide variety of residential subdivisions, with different lot sizes and prices and different deed restrictions, landscaping, street plans, and utilities.

Eventually the areas between the outlying suburbs filled in, creating additional grade crossings and lengthening the travel time. For a time, the automobile offered a more efficient travel alternative, and by the 1950s use of the big red cars was discontinued.

Sears, Roebuck and Co. had a booming do-it-yourself homebuilding business in the early part of the 20th century. On the cover of this catalog of houses from 1929, Sears advertises itself as the world's largest building material dealer, a different Sears from the one of today.

Huntington's ambitious development strategy included moving into the utilities business as a way of providing services necessary to enhance the value of the land he was selling. Given that the Los Angeles Railway and the Pacific Electric transit system were major users of electricity, Huntington established the Pacific Light and Power Company to provide hydroelectric and steam power both to his transit operations and to the areas that he was developing. By 1913, Pacific Light and Power was supplying 20 percent of the region's electricity and natural gas as well as all the power for Huntington's streetcars. Having acquired so much rural land to obtain a source of water to generate power, Huntington also organized the San Gabriel Valley Water Company to supply fresh water to San Marino, Alhambra, and the greater Pasadena area.

The interrelationship of transportation, infrastructure, utilities, and real estate development that Henry Huntington's development efforts exemplified on such a grand scale is aptly illustrated by a local joke from 1914: A mother was taking her daughter on a trolley ride to the beach. The daughter asked, "Whose streetcar are we riding in?" Her mother replied, "Mr. Huntington's." Passing a park, the girl asked, "What place is that?" "Huntington Park," responded her mother. "Where are we going, mother?" "To Huntington Beach" was the answer. Finally arriving at the sea, the child ventured one more query: "Mother, does Mr. Huntington own the ocean or does it still belong to God?"[10]

In addition to good transportation networks, water was the other factor behind California's growth. In 1908, the city of San Francisco obtained the right to dam the Tuolumne River inside Yosemite National Park for municipal water service. In 1902, the city of Los Angeles began work on one of the largest engineering projects in history, to bring water from the Owens Valley to the Los Angeles basin. (That project was backed by civic leaders, some of whom were investors in large land holdings in the San Fernando Valley that would benefit from the project.)

The Emergence of the Garden City

The intellectual concept of a suburban community planned as an alternative for the industrial city was articulated in 1898, with the publication in England of *Garden Cities of Tomorrow* by Sir Ebenezer Howard. The *garden city* concept was based on a master plan containing a mix of residential, business, industrial, and agricultural land uses surrounded by a buffer of open space, or a *greenbelt*. As a response to overcrowded, grimy industrial cities, the concept was to incorporate the best elements of "town" and "country" that would improve the living conditions of residents. The basic elements of the garden city—a master plan of mixed land uses conceived and implemented by a single developer—were the elements of the master-planned communities of the late 20th century. The first garden city, Letchworth, was developed in England in 1904.

Examples of Early Planned Communities

By the first decade of the 20th century, the forces behind decentralization were well in place: a

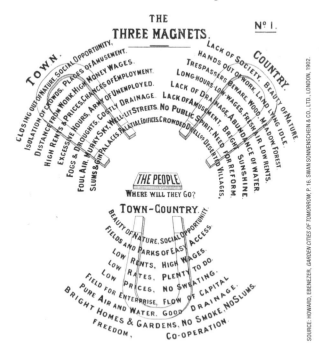

SOURCE: HOWARD, EBENEZER, *GARDEN CITIES OF TOMORROW*, P. 16. SWAN SONNENSCHEIN & CO., LTD., LONDON, 1902.

Ebenezer Howard's Three Magnets describe the political, economic, and social factors that underlay his vision for the utopian "town-country" community.

response to blight, slums, congestion, and unhealthy conditions in the central city; rail transportation corridors bringing new subdivisions within commuting distance; and an intellectual examination of the role of cities and suburbs sparked by the garden city movement. The automobile then displaced rail transportation, creating freedom of personal mobility. Land use patterns quickly changed in response. New community planning concepts arose, and those concepts influenced future suburban development.

Radburn

The most ambitious attempt to give full expression to Ebenezer Howard's ideas in the United States was the community of Radburn, New Jersey, which was developed by the City Housing Corporation (CHC) of New York, headed by Alexander Bing. Bing, who along with his brother Leo had been a successful developer of luxury apartment buildings in Manhattan before World War I, had become more public-spirited during his service as a housing consultant to the federal government in the war years. After the armistice, he was determined to embark on a path of social reform.

Linking up with a group of visionaries called the Regional Planning Association of America—headed by critic Lewis Mumford and architects and planners such as Clarence Stein, Henry Wright, and Catherine Bauer—Bing attracted sufficient investment capital to establish the CHC, with the intention of building a garden city in the United States. After developing a successful preliminary project called Sunnyside Gardens in New York City, the CHC bought a large parcel of land in Fair Lawn, New Jersey, within commuting range of Manhattan, and, in 1928, began developing Radburn, "a town for the motor age." Planned and designed primarily by Clarence Stein and Henry Wright, Radburn incorporated many innovative features that responded to the realities of the automobile and remained principles of master-planned communities until the late 20th century. The plan segregated vehicular and pedestrian traffic through the use of bridges, underpasses, and footpaths. It incorporated "superblocks" with interior parks and culs-de-sac to create common open spaces,

keep automobile through-traffic away from houses, and economize significantly on the typical costs of land and infrastructure development. Homes were to be oriented toward rear yards and open spaces. Radburn also modeled new ways of establishing an unincorporated self-governing community through strict, comprehensive deed restrictions and an active, well-funded homeowners association. Although Radburn received global publicity and many of its planning ideas were widely imitated, it ran into the economic crisis of the 1930s, and only a small portion of the original design was built. The CHC encountered serious cash flow problems and was eventually forced into bankruptcy. Yet the development of Radburn remains one of this country's best-known and most-admired experiments in for-profit, speculative community building by a private real estate developer.

Shaker Heights

Shaker Heights is a model suburban community near Cleveland, Ohio, where the Van Sweringen brothers developed the financial skills that enabled them to take over a major railroad and an important section of downtown Cleveland, using almost none of their own money. Oris P. and Mantis J. Van Sweringen were minor land developers in the Cleveland area in 1900 when they first approached the Buffalo syndicate that owned property formerly occupied by a Shaker religious community. For more than ten years, the syndicate had been attempting to sell the property, which was valued at $240,000. The Vans, as they became known to Clevelanders, eventually convinced the syndicate to give them a free 30-day option on a small section of the property. The agreement contained an option for an additional section twice the size of the first for a period twice as long as the first. If they exercised that option, the Vans would receive additional options. The Van Sweringens were consummate salesmen and convinced a number of Cleveland's leading citizens to join their development syndicate. After exercising a few of the options, they bought the entire property of 1,400 acres, which they later expanded to 4,000 acres. The brothers had learned during an earlier venture that transportation was critical to successful suburban development, but the president of the Cleveland Railway Company rejected as impractical their proposal that the company contribute an extension to the existing railway line to serve the new Shaker Heights community. Consequently, they decided to build their own railroad.

First, they identified a ravine in which the railroad tracks could run without hindering any grade crossings and then began to buy the needed land. Eventually, to complete the right-of-way, it became necessary to purchase an entire railroad (called the Nickel Plate) for $8.5 million. In addition, they acquired four acres of land in downtown Cleveland's

Public Square to construct a terminal for their new commuter railroad. By June 1929, they had spent more than $2 million on their development of Public Square, including a new railroad station, a 36-story office tower, a department store, and a hotel. By then, more than 15,000 people lived in Shaker Heights, on land valued at more than $80 million.[11]

THE EVOLUTION OF REAL ESTATE FINANCE

Before the advent of the *Federal Housing Administration (FHA)* mortgage insurance and Veterans Administration (VA) home loan guarantee programs, "builders' mortgages" were an essential

---

J.C. Nichols and the Country Club District

The garden city model comprised four elements: environmental reform, social reform, town planning, and regional planning. Many development efforts, including J.C. Nichols's Country Club District in Kansas City, Missouri, were motivated primarily by interests in environmental reform and town planning, with far less stress placed on the other two elements.

Upon graduating from Harvard University in 1903, Jesse Clyde Nichols returned home to Kansas and entered the real estate business. He started as a small, speculative homebuilder, building and selling single-family houses on vacant lots in a partially improved subdivision. Two years later, he acquired a ten-acre subdivision just south of the city limits of Kansas City, Missouri, and began planning his vision: the long-term development of a large, high-quality urban community. Part of what inspired J.C. Nichols to build his ideal of a stable, family-oriented, and beautifully landscaped community was his exposure to the garden city movement during his college years. By 1908, with capital from a group of wealthy investors, he had gained control of more than 1,000 acres on Kansas City's south side, calling it the Country Club District to emphasize its proximity to the Kansas City Country Club. Eventually, those 1,000 acres would contain 6,000 houses, 160 apartment buildings, and 35,000 residents.

By the 1920s, Nichols had already established the Country Club District as one of the most attractive and expensive communities in the region. For the initial planning and landscaping, he employed the well-known landscape architect George Kessler, who had previously designed a "City Beautiful" plan for Kansas City. Later, S. Herbert Hare became the chief landscape designer. Nichols worked with the city to extend and build two of the new parkways, the Ward and the Mill Creek, through the Country Club District, giving the community excellent transportation connections

to downtown and a vital community amenity. Ward Parkway became among the most fashionable addresses in Kansas City.

Nichols relied on long-term deed restrictions to control the design, cost, and use of all private property in the district—as well as to prohibit racial, ethnic, and religious minorities from owning property in the community. For years, he advertised the Country Club District as "the one thousand acres restricted." Nichols invested heavily in a wide range of community facilities from landscaped parks to public art and in an ambitious program of community activities. In addition, he was one of the first developers to establish a mandatory homeowners association that collected fees to help legally enforce, revise, and renew deed restrictions; finance and maintain community facilities and activities; and establish an active, participatory community identity.

Nichols engaged in practices that were unusual for real estate developers in his day. He installed first-rate infrastructure in advance of development, adding its costs to the prices of the lots for sale. He also engaged architects to design model homes and built many houses both on a speculative basis and under contract with lot purchasers. In addition, Nichols saw the potential in developing and owning retail centers as a profitable enterprise and as a strategy for building community. Over the years he developed and owned many neighborhood shopping centers. His flagship regional retail and office complex in the heart of the district, called Country Club Plaza, is generally recognized as America's first suburban shopping center. Designed with a Moorish-Spanish architectural theme and controlled by centralized management, the plaza provided both on- and off-street parking, was well located for public transit, and drew a walk-in trade from residents of apartment buildings and workers in office buildings that Nichols developed nearby.

Continued next page

J.C. Nichols and the Country Club District *Continued*

J.C. Nichols's Country Club District promised "spacious grounds for permanently protected homes, surrounded with ample space for air and sunshine."

Even today, the district and the plaza are the desirable places to live and shop in Kansas City.

The restrictive covenants discriminating against minorities were a standard practice before the U.S. Supreme Court ruled such provisions legally unenforceable in 1948. The district in general catered primarily to upper-income residents, though beginning in the 1930s, Nichols shifted focus in some of the newer subdivisions to smaller houses and lots for a middle-income clientele. Yet through creative and successful real estate entrepreneurship over half a century, Nichols's achievements stand out. He provided leadership to the real estate community as an officer of the National Association of Realtors, to the urban planning community as a founding member of the American Planning Association, and to large-scale developers as the founder of the Urban Land Institute.

component in the sale of one- to four-unit housing. Developers acquiring acreage from farmers and other rural landowners often negotiated complex transfers of ownership and repayment schemes in an attempt to bridge the gaps of time and cash flow. Brokers also entered the field; many real estate sales firms maintained mortgage and loan departments as a service to their clients and helped generate a greater volume of sales (and thus sales commissions) and additional profits from the loan business itself. By the early 20th century, they called themselves mortgage bankers and in 1914 formed the Farm Mortgage Bankers Association.[12]

Other traditional suppliers of funds for real estate have been networks of local investors, including direct financing from friends, relatives, and wealthy individuals; lending through a trust company or mortgage company; and providing equity capital by forming or joining syndicates and limited partnerships. Richard Hurd, most famous today for writing the classic *Principles of City Land Values* in 1903, for many years headed the Lawyers Mortgage Company in New York City. There he gathered money from prosperous investors and then made first mortgage loans on commercial and residential real estate that was strictly limited to high-quality rental buildings or "income properties" in the best locations.[13] Hurd's instincts for good value and his low-risk strategy led to a successful track record in loan safety and relatively high yields.

In contrast to Hurd, mortgage bond houses such as S.W. Straus flourished during the 1920s by selling securities backed by frequently overinflated values of new office and apartment buildings. Before the 1929 stock market crash, funds flowed into mortgage bond sales, and securities dealers arranged for highly speculative new construction simply as a minor detail associated with issuing and selling more bonds. After the crash, even the most optimistic appraiser had to admit that the buildings were grossly overvalued; not only did the borrowers default for lack of sufficient tenants to generate cash flow but the bond houses themselves went bankrupt and left vast numbers of investors with little or nothing but the promise of a guaranteed high yield and timely return of principal and interest.

Commercial banks are the oldest of the institutions that have been involved in making both construction loans and mortgage loans. These banks have participated heavily in real estate lending, often to the point of insolvency during periods of economic and financial crisis. Financial "panics" and banking problems were so common in the 19th century that when the federal government introduced national bank charters in the 1860s, the charters expressly prohibited mortgage lending for urban real estate. State-chartered commercial banks were under no such constraints, however, and continued to be major real estate lenders. National banks were permitted to get back into urban mortgage lending beginning in 1916, and they expanded their real estate lending significantly during the 1920s.

Because commercial banks relied primarily on short-term deposits to obtain funds for lending, they generally preferred and were often required to lend for short terms, either through construction loans or through mortgages for as short a term as one year. Until well into the 1930s, most bankers considered a three- to five-year mortgage loan to be both long term and risky. Normally, though, short-term mortgages were renewable; in fact, borrowers simply assumed that they could keep rolling the loans over for years to come. When the market turned down and the banks got into trouble, however, lenders called the loans or refused to refinance them, often forcing borrowers into default and foreclosure. Historically, the system of real estate credit has been far more unstable than it is in today's volatile world.

Life insurance companies have always been important players in real estate, both as owners and as lenders. Since the mid-19th century, real estate assets have made up a significant portion of their investment portfolios. Life insurance companies have traditionally been involved in financing and purchasing large-scale projects such as office buildings, shopping centers, and apartment complexes. Beginning in the 1920s, some also entered into residential mortgage lending.

A century earlier, mutual savings banks, primarily in the northeastern United States, had been significant institutions in some cities. Nationally, however, their role and influence in residential lending was eclipsed by the advent of savings and loan associations (S&Ls) in the 1830s. Also called building and loan associations, homestead associations, cooperative banks, and thrift institutions, S&Ls evolved specifically to promote homebuilding and homeownership for people of modest incomes. Savings were pooled through monthly savings plans, and money was loaned for the construction or purchase of homes. Though S&Ls charged higher interest rates than other mortgage lenders, in order to pay a higher return to their depositors, their loan terms were more favorable in two ways: through higher leverage—they lent up to 75 percent of a property's appraised value while most other lenders advanced only 40 or 50 percent on first mortgages; and through longer terms—S&Ls used amortized monthly loan repayment plans for up to 12 years while most other lenders used nonamortized balloon mortgages with semiannual interest payments and made the entire principal due in one to five years.

By the 1920s, S&Ls had become the major residential lender, particularly for single-family homes. Life insurance companies and commercial banks dominated commercial and industrial real estate lending. Although syndications, mortgage companies, and a variety of other noninstitutional lenders remained important, the major trend in real estate lending was the increasing role of financial institutions, especially in the field of housing. More and more, "sweat equity" was being supplanted in real estate by a debt-driven system that encompassed entrepreneurial producers and institutional financiers.

THE GREAT DEPRESSION AND WORLD WAR II

The long boom of the 1920s came to an abrupt end when the stock market crashed in October 1929. Though most people believed that the economic downturn was only a temporary setback—that prosperity was just around the corner—in fact the Great Depression would be the longest and most severe economic depression in U.S. history. Starting in 1929, output and employment fell steadily for four straight years, finally hitting bottom in 1933. At the low point, one of every four people was out of work, desperately seeking but unable to find any kind of job.

The bubble had burst on the real estate boom even before the stock market crash. Real estate markets reached their peak in 1926, the same year that the Florida land boom collapsed. Since then, investment in real estate, construction, property sales, and values had been slowly spiraling downward. Real estate activity, though declining in most markets, still continued at a high level relative to the early 1920s or the previous decade, and in certain categories, such as construction of new urban office and apartment buildings, the markets still appeared to be flourishing.

By the late 1920s, however, the speculative craze for subdivision lots was abating, and many of those who had bought on credit in anticipation of rapid and profitable re-sales were defaulting on their loans and property tax assessments. A major disaster loomed. Soon most of the mortgage bond issues were in default and foreclosure, with many bondholders losing their capital, leading to widely publicized investigations of fraud and corruption during the 1930s, similar to the S&L collapse in the 1980s. As banks faced a worsening crisis of liquidity after 1929, they refused to make new real estate loans or to refinance existing ones, often calling in loans to be repaid immediately. That approach was self-defeating because it brought about the further collapse of markets and the failure of thousands of banks. Millions of depositors lost much or all of their savings.

Through 1931, new investment, development, sales, and leasing continued in many markets, and real estate entrepreneurs kept hopes alive; in the following year, however, everything began grinding to a halt, and bankruptcy became the normal state of affairs. Financing was unavailable, and real estate

plummeted in value. Much of the market was frozen, flooded with for-sale and rental properties that no one wanted—even at heavily discounted prices and rents. By 1933, nearly half of all home mortgages were in default and 1,000 properties were being foreclosed each day. Annual construction starts of new housing had dropped by more than 90 percent from the record-breaking peak of 937,000 units in 1925 to the dismal trough of 93,000 units in 1933.

Soup lines formed in major cities across the country to feed the many unemployed workers during the Great Depression.

Into this escalating crisis stepped the federal government, at first gingerly under President Herbert C. Hoover—with considerable prodding in 1931 and 1932 from the Democratic Congress. Under the New Deal of President Franklin D. Roosevelt, failing banks and securities markets were reorganized and stabilized as federal deposit insurance, and a new regulatory apparatus helped restore the public and investor confidence. Public works programs were initiated on a massive scale that dwarfed any previous peacetime federal spending, with billions of dollars spent to employ millions of jobless workers in building and rebuilding the nation's infrastructure—roads, bridges, tunnels, highways, dams, power plants, airports, waterways and ports, railroad and transit lines and terminals, parks, playgrounds,

INNOVATOR   Robert Moses

Robert Moses directed the construction of parks and parkways for the state of New York beginning in the 1920s. In 1933, Mayor Fiorello LaGuardia appointed him parks commissioner for New York City. During the New Deal era, LaGuardia lobbied in Washington for billions of dollars in federal public works funds, and Moses built many of the projects, including the complex and expensive Triborough Bridge, which opened in 1936. As chair of the Triborough Bridge Authority, Moses discovered that semi-independent public authorities could amass considerable long-term power so long as the authority's management continued to control an activity that generated sufficient revenue to repay debt and accumulate a surplus. These authorities could successfully finance their operations through the sale of bonds and then retire those bonds through a dedicated revenue source, such as bridge tolls. (In the early days of the Triborough, the federal Reconstruction Finance Corporation was the only willing bond buyer, though later private investors bought the bonds.)

Moses's extensive multibillion-dollar development activities as head of several authorities for more than three decades helped establish public authorities as critical organizations in real estate. During the early 1970s, for example, under the leadership of Austin Tobin, one of Robert Moses's most powerful competitors among public authority chief executives, the Port Authority of New York and New Jersey built the massive twin office towers of the World Trade Center in lower Manhattan, at that time the world's tallest buildings.

schools, health clinics, community centers, civic administration buildings, public housing, and a host of other facilities.

These mainly federal public works initiatives helped encourage two forms of entrepreneurship that flourished during the New Deal: the powerful public works manager, best symbolized by New York's Robert Moses, and the large-scale private contractor, exemplified by California's Henry J. Kaiser (see profiles).

Bailing Out the Financial Institutions

Public works was only one of the strategies New Dealers used to revive both the general economy and one of its most important sectors: the construction and development industry. By 1933, the private housing sector had suffered an almost complete collapse, and the entire system of residential financing that had grown so rapidly during the 1920s—with its crazy quilt of land contracts, second and third mortgages, high interest rates and loan fees, short-term maturities, balloon payments, and various other high-risk and speculative practices—had come crashing down. In the wake of this panic of defaults and foreclosures, the federal government intervened to transform the rules of the financial game and move the sale and construction of private housing out of the doldrums.

The first federal actions in housing finance focused on bailing out the S&L associations. S&Ls had mortgaged 4.35 million properties during the 1920s, lending out more than $15 billion to homebuilders and purchasers. By the early 1930s, thousands of these institutions were insolvent as a result of bad loans, overvalued properties, and the inability to raise sufficient new capital. President Hoover and the Congress responded to the crisis in 1932 by establishing the Federal Home Loan Bank System, which merged and reorganized bankrupt S&Ls, encouraged the creation of federally chartered S&Ls that would be better capitalized and more strictly regulated, and, most important, provided vitally needed liquidity for federal- and state-chartered thrifts, helping to free them from their traditional dependence on short-term commercial bank credit. Two years later came the Federal Savings and Loan Insurance Corporation, which greatly strengthened the attractiveness of S&Ls to savers by insuring deposits and helping to standardize the management of thrift institutions. S&Ls also were granted a series of income tax and regulatory benefits in exchange for the requirement that they continue to lend money primarily for residential mortgages (a requirement that remained in force until the Reagan Administration's monetary reforms of 1982).

Other dramatic structural changes occurred in the 1930s. The federal government created the Home Owners' Loan Corporation (HOLC) in 1933 and the FHA in 1934. The HOLC refinanced more than $3 billion of shaky or defaulted mortgages and introduced long-term (15-year) self-amortizing loans to many borrowers who were not familiar with the idea, before it stopped making loans in 1936.

The Federal Housing Administration

Stabilizing the real estate finance markets of the 1930s required two things: the correct identification of the problem and the correct solution to the problem. The problem was the prevalence of short-term loans securing long-term assets. The solutions were standardized terms, standardized underwriting criteria, and a secondary market.

The FHA revolutionized housing finance. Its mutual mortgage insurance system reduced the investment risk for lenders and brought the twin S&L principles of long-term amortization of mortgage loans and high loan-to-value (LTV) ratios into the world of commercial banks, life insurance companies, mutual savings banks, and mortgage companies—institutions that had not previously used such underwriting practices. The FHA's initiatives encouraged lenders to increase the first mortgage LTV ratio to an unprecedented 80 to 90 percent, to extend the length of the loan repayment period to 20 and 25 years, to eliminate second mortgages, and to lower interest rates and total loan origination fees significantly.

Among its many reforms, the FHA rationalized, standardized, and improved methods and practices of appraisal, universalized the use of title insurance, required the lender's monthly collection of property taxes and property insurance as part of the loan payments, and helped popularize other methods for stabilizing real estate transactions and financing procedures. The FHA's insured mortgages became a standardized product and a safe investment that helped establish a nationwide mortgage market in place of previously idiosyncratic and localized sub-markets. The entire home mortgage lending system began to shift from lending based primarily on the security of the property in the event of foreclosure to lending based primarily on the borrower's projected income and ability to repay without default—a major conceptual change.

The FHA also promoted the cost-efficient production of small houses and affordable

---

INNOVATOR   Henry J. Kaiser

Henry J. Kaiser was a general contractor who built public works. Initially a road builder for governments in the western United States and Canada, in 1930 he put together a consortium of six large construction firms and successfully obtained the federal contract to build the massive Hoover Dam on the Colorado River in southern Nevada.

Beginning in 1933, Kaiser established a close working relationship with U.S. Secretary of the Interior Harold L. Ickes. Ickes was one of a handful of key New Deal officials controlling the federal purse strings for public works and dispensing billions of dollars in government contracts. During the 1930s, Kaiser-led teams won federal contracts to build both the Bonneville and the Grand Coulee dams, in addition to doing part of the work on the San Francisco–Oakland Bay Bridge and constructing Oakland's Broadway Tunnel and several other large projects. Headquartered in Oakland, Kaiser achieved national recognition as a shipbuilder during World War II and as a manufacturer of cement, gypsum, aluminum, chemicals, steel, automobiles, jeeps, and cargo planes.

During the war, Kaiser built a substantial amount of emergency housing for the workers flocking to Richmond, California; Portland, Oregon; and Vancouver, Washington, to construct Kaiser's "liberty ships" for the U.S. Navy. After the war, Kaiser became interested in mass-producing houses; in 1945, he formed a partnership with Fritz Burns, a major southern California developer. Their new company, Kaiser Community Homes, built thousands of small, inexpensive, two- and three-bedroom single-family detached houses on the West Coast until it ceased production in 1950. During the mid-1950s, Kaiser retired as chief executive of Kaiser Industries and moved to Hawaii, where he became a major developer of resort hotels, recreational subdivisions, houses, shopping malls, golf courses, and convention centers until his death in 1967 at the age of 85.

---

homeownership for middle-income families. The agency's conditional commitment enabled subdivision developers and merchant homebuilders to obtain debt financing for the large-scale construction of new residential communities, with homes ready for immediate occupancy by people who were able to buy with modest savings because they qualified for FHA-insured mortgages. The FHA model of real estate development represented a dramatic advance over the subdividing and selling of unimproved lots that had been fairly common in the 1920s.

The FHA's standards for property and neighborhoods raised the minimum level of quality in the design, engineering, materials, equipment, and methods of land development and housing construction. The agency's Land Planning Division encouraged private planning by developers and builders, and public planning by state and local governments to ensure the coordination of accessible transportation, recreational facilities, utilities, services, and land uses through comprehensive plans, official maps, zoning laws, requirements for setbacks, and regulations for subdivisions. The Land Planning Division also played a key national role in reshaping the design of suburban housing tracts, upgrading the use of deed restrictions for private planning and development, and reorganizing and extending the role of local and metropolitan public planning.

In addition, the FHA introduced new techniques for analyzing market demand and using stricter underwriting criteria to limit overbuilding and excessive subdividing. This element of market control was explicitly aimed at eliminating "curbstone" subdividers and "jerry-builders" and replacing them with community builders. More sophisticated market analysis and greater market control became necessary as a result of the FHA's emphasis on long-term financing of large numbers of homes in newly developed neighborhoods. FHA underwriters needed to know before development began that the market commanded a sufficient number of potential buyers for the planned houses, and that purchasers' incomes, market demand, and property values would either remain stable or rise over the 25 years during which the mortgages would be insured. The FHA's risk-rating system weighed several factors affecting the supply of and demand for housing, including patterns of urban employment, distribution of income, population growth, changes in the housing stock, formation of households, locational dynamics of residential neighborhoods, and future land uses and property values.[14]

Within two years of the FHA's creation, new federal and state laws to stabilize and restructure the commercial banking system—along with the creation of the Federal Deposit Insurance Corporation

in 1933—enabled commercial banks to participate in the FHA's program. Life insurance companies and mutual savings banks also took advantage of FHA insurance. They acted as primary lenders and also purchased and sold standardized and relatively low-risk FHA-insured loans. FHA-insured mortgages made possible the 1938 creation of the *Federal National Mortgage Association (Fannie Mae)*. Fannie Mae, capitalized by the federal government's Reconstruction Finance Corporation, initiated a strong secondary market for FHA-insured mortgages, purchasing loans from primary lenders to provide them with both the liquidity to make new loans and additional income gained through the retention of servicing fees. This national secondary mortgage market helped smooth out fluctuations in real estate business cycles as well as compensate for geographic differences in the availability of mortgage funds. Fannie Mae was particularly vital to the growth of modern mortgage banking companies, many of which started their high-volume businesses in the 1930s and 1940s based mainly on making FHA-insured loans for resale to Fannie Mae or to a life insurance company, a savings bank, or another group of lenders and investors.

The FHA's underwriting guidelines strongly favored new housing over existing homes, suburban locations over central-city sites, entire subdivisions over scattered building lots, single-family houses over apartments, and Caucasians over African Americans. For older cities and racial minorities, these policies were inequitable, discriminatory, and disastrous. But for the growth of white, middle-class suburbs, they were crucial. Though the FHA did insure mortgages on suburban garden apartments, its overall policy helped reverse the late 1920s trend toward increased construction of apartment buildings and instead boosted large-scale suburban homebuilding and homeownership.

By the late 1930s, the U.S. economy and housing markets were reviving, and the FHA was insuring more than one-third of all new homes; 98 percent of FHA-insured mortgages were on single-family detached houses in new suburban subdivisions. The highest volume was in California, where the

Housing in a Washington, D.C., alley, circa 1937.

country's suburban future was already under construction in the late 1930s. Fred Marlow, who headed the FHA's southern California office from 1934 to 1938, and Fritz Burns formed a private development company and, beginning in 1942, built more than 4,000 FHA-insured houses in a new southwest Los Angeles subdivision called Westchester. The purchasers of the houses were primarily workers in the nearby and rapidly growing aircraft industry. Westchester became a model for postwar suburban tract housing, and Fred Marlow and Fritz Burns both served as presidents of the National Association of Home Builders.

HOUSING AFTER THE GREAT DEPRESSION

While construction of new homes finally began rising after the long slump, conditions in much of the older housing stock were badly deteriorated and getting worse as a result of overcrowding, lack of maintenance, and other direct effects of the Great Depression. In 1937, President Roosevelt declared in his second inaugural address that "one-third of a nation [was] ill-housed, ill-clad, and ill-nourished."

In 1919, Edith Elmer Wood, a talented housing reformer, wrote *The Housing of the Unskilled Wage Earner*, an eloquent book documenting the problems of low-income shelter and arguing for government aid as part of a positive solution. In 1935, the federal *Public Works Administration (PWA)* under Harold Ickes published Wood's *Slums and Blighted Areas in the United States*. Wood demonstrated in considerable detail that more than 36 percent of the American people were living in very substandard housing. In her 1919 book and in her 1931 publication *Recent Trends in American Housing*, Wood described private, philanthropic, and public sector efforts to build decent and affordable housing in many areas of the country.[15] Except in New York City and a handful of other cities, however, substantial government involvement did not begin to emerge until the early 1930s. The collapse of the private housing industry opened the way for public support and programs to stimulate employment and economic activity in urban real estate development.

In 1934, the federal government established the PWA Housing Division, which was followed by the U.S. Housing Authority (USHA) in 1937, to support the removal of the worst slum dwellings and their replacement with publicly owned rental housing. Under the USHA formula, local governments owned the housing, which was built by private contractors. Local authorities borrowed the funds by selling 40-year tax-exempt bonds to private investors, and the federal government repaid the principal and interest on the bonds through annual contributions. The operating costs of the housing were to be paid by the local government through rents collected from the tenants. By the time that World War II interrupted and changed the nature of the public housing program to one of providing temporary shelter for war workers, the USHA and its predecessors had already produced more than 100,000 units of decent, safe, and sanitary dwellings in low-rise buildings. These well-constructed and attractively landscaped buildings provided a welcome new environment for many low- and moderate-income families.

Nathan Straus, chief administrator of the USHA from 1937 to 1941, had been an early pioneer of private, limited-dividend housing development in New York City. During 1934 and 1935, he developed Hillside Homes in the Bronx, which was the largest private housing development built with a federal loan from the PWA. Clarence Stein served as the architect for Hillside Homes, and Starrett Brothers and Eken were the general contractors. The 26-acre project consisted of low-rise and garden apartments

Zlin, Czechoslovakia: A Workforce Housing Model

The Bata Shoe Company was one of the most influential manufacturers in Europe in the early 20th century. An innovative employer that sought to improve the lives of its employees, Bata built company towns to provide housing, schools, and other amenities for its workers.

When he was just 18, Tomas Bata started a cobbling business in Zlin, Czechoslovakia, with his brother Antonin. Bata's adoption of mechanized production, which he learned from trips to America, made Bata Shoe Company one of the most modern and successful companies of its time. After his brother died in 1908, Tomas was the sole owner. Throughout the 1920s and 1930s, wherever Bata established a factory, he also created a master-planned community for his workers. Plans for Bata's towns were largely influenced by the architectural modernism of Le Corbusier as well as the Garden City movement. Bata believed that a clean urban environment with plenty of green space would keep workers comfortable and happy, thereby making them productive.

By 1938, the company managed approximately 65,000 employees worldwide. Zlin, which was home to fewer than 5,000 inhabitants in 1921, had grown to more than 40,000. In addition to a shoe factory and thousands of homes for workers, Bata established department stores, a hotel, a cinema, a network of schools, film studios, scientific facilities, and a large hospital. A testament to Bata's unique approach, Zlin became the only city in Czechoslovakia to be centered on a factory rather than a cathedral, marketplace, or castle. The city's buildings were designed in a functionalist architectural style with unadorned building materials such as brick, concrete, and steel, and surrounded by greenery. The city owed so much of its economic growth and identity to Bata that it elected him mayor in 1928.

Camille Galdes

Workforce housing in Zlin, Czechoslovakia, the headquarters of the Bata Shoe Company.

for 1,400 families and included landscaped interior garden courts, a public school, a large central playground, clubrooms, a nursery school, a community center, and other recreational facilities. Though initially a private developer, Straus wrote a spirited defense of America's public housing programs in 1941, in *The Seven Myths of Housing*.[16]

THE PROFESSIONALIZATION OF REAL ESTATE DEVELOPMENT

The vigorous spirit of reform and modernization that characterized the early 20th century paralleled the tremendous growth and institutional development of the real estate industry through the movement for "professionalization." Many elements of the flourishing real estate business organized *trade associations* to upgrade standards of practice; to isolate, ostracize, and, where possible, eliminate unsavory activities; and to cooperate with the public sector and other segments of the business world and the general public to protect the interests of real estate and enhance its political stature and economic viability.

The National Association of Realtors (NAR), for example, was established in 1908 to seek government licensing of the brokerage business. Operating through local boards of Realtors, the NAR lobbied for public regulation of all participants in the larger industry combined with self-policing of smaller and more select groups of members. The NAR promoted real estate education and research, and played a role in many public policy issues, from urban planning to property taxation. Its Home Builders and Subdividers Division was a national leader in the formulation of federal housing policy in the 1920s and 1930s.

Two other groups organized during this period were the Building Owners and Managers Association (BOMA International) and the Mortgage Bankers Association of America (MBA). BOMA represented the owners and property managers of the rapidly growing number of skyscrapers and other large commercial buildings in central cities and later also in the suburbs. Its focus was on

professional training for management combined with a unified voice for relevant public policy issues. The MBA was originally called the Farm Mortgage Bankers Association, but it adopted an urban focus and assumed a new name during the early 1920s. At that time, mortgage bond houses and mortgage lending companies—allied with real estate brokers, developers, and life insurance companies—were rapidly evolving and expanding the variety of capital financing instruments available to use in acquiring and developing property. The MBA later increased its national prominence with the advent of the federal government's new housing finance system in the 1930s and 1940s.

Two new private organizations, both spin-offs of the NAR, emerged from the crucible of economic crisis and political reform that characterized the 1930s. The Urban Land Institute (ULI) started as a small, elite organization of primarily large commercial and residential developers. ULI was charged with focusing on education and research, public policy issues, and improving standards and practices of private development. Initially, ULI organized into two key subgroups. The Central Business District Council sponsored a series of studies on urban decentralization and urged federal, state, and local government officials to establish and provide funds for urban renewal, urban highways, and other programs to redevelop physically and revitalize economically the commercial core of older central cities. The Community Builders Council, which sponsored ULI's *Community Builders Handbook*, published in 1947, concerned itself with promoting high-quality, large-scale residential and commercial development in suburban areas.[17]

The National Association of Home Builders (NAHB) was formed in 1943 to lobby the federal government during wartime to allow the continued private development of for-sale and rental housing with the aid of FHA mortgage insurance. Some government policy makers favored limiting new housing to public construction and ownership during the wartime emergency, arguing that such an approach would be more cost-efficient and easier to manage in the context of allocating scarce resources for the war effort. The Home Builders Emergency Committee, led by Hugh Potter, a former lawyer and judge who developed River Oaks in Houston, fought for publicly subsidized housing for war workers to be built and owned by the private sector. In the end, a compromise permitted the development of housing under both public and private ownership. In the process, the Home Builders and Subdividers Division of NAR split from the parent organization and merged with a completely separate group called the National Home Builders Association. Together, the two groups became the NAHB. Fritz Burns of Los Angeles was the founding president of the new organization, which grew from an initial 1,300 members to more than 25,000 in less than a decade.

During World War II, the real estate industry in certain locations received an enormous economic boost from the surge in demand for new construction, land, and space in existing buildings. Yet many ventures not directly related to the war economy were put on hold for the duration. Some people were apprehensive about the war's end, fearing a replay of the Great Depression after the war effort wound down. Others were more optimistic, seeing a wave of growth precipitated by the rising disposable incomes and pent-up consumer demand that were accumulating during the war. By 1948, the optimists' predictions were proved correct, and the development of the postwar suburbs—dependent on the automobile, homeownership, and a consumer boom—was in full swing.

SUMMARY

Expansion of the real estate industry characterized most of the period from the end of the 19th century through the first half of the 20th century. Aggressive commercial development in downtowns and residential movement to the suburbs changed the face of the nation's cities and metropolitan regions.

The growing involvement of the public sector reinforced the private development process. Changes in lending policies brought about by the creation of

the FHA made residential development easier and dramatically increased the number of homeowners in the United States.

TERMS

- 100 percent corner
- Central business district (CBD)
- City Beautiful movement
- Community builders
- Federal Housing Administration (FHA)
- Federal National Mortgage Association (Fannie Mae)
- Garden city
- Greenbelt
- Mortgage
- Public Works Administration (PWA)
- Skyscraper
- Steel frame construction
- Trade associations
- Zoning

REVIEW QUESTIONS

5.1   What happened to downtowns as transportation networks allowed people to move farther and farther out of the city?

5.2   Discuss the history of the skyscraper—its construction, its symbolism, and how it shaped cities.

5.3   Discuss the role of the downtown department store at the turn of the century.

5.4   What was the City Beautiful movement?

5.5   What was a garden city and how did the movement evolve?

5.6   How did real estate trade associations come about?

5.7   How did the advent of creative financing change real estate markets in the United States?

5.8   What strategies were used in the New Deal to revive the Great Depression economy?

5.9   What was the role of the Federal Housing
        Administration in financing housing and
        homeownership?

5.10   Why was Rockefeller Center such an impor-
        tant project?

NOTES

1   Adna Ferrin Weber, *The Growth of Cities in the Nineteenth Century:
A Study in Statistics* (New York: Macmillan, 1899), p. 1.

2   Christopher Tunnard and Henry Reed, *American Skyline* (New
York: Mentor, 1956), p. 143.

3   Paul Goldberger, *The Skyscraper* (New York: Alfred A. Knopf,
1981), p. 7.

4   Kenneth Turney Gibbs, *Business Architectural Imagery in America,
1870–1930* (Ann Arbor, Mich.: UMI Research Press, 1984), p. 45.

5   Ibid.

6   Ibid., p. 54.

7   Earle Shultz and Walter Simmons, *Offices in the Sky* (Indianapolis:
Bobbs-Merrill, 1959), pp. 33–34.

8   *Golden Book of Wanamaker Stores* (Philadelphia: John Wanamaker,
1911), p. 47.

9   Thompson-Starrett Company, "A Census of Skyscrapers," *The
American City*, September 1929, p. 130. See also Marc A. Weiss, *The
Rise of the Community Builders: The American Real Estate Industry and
Urban Land Planning* (New York: Columbia University Press, 1987);
and Marc A. Weiss, "Skyscraper Zoning: New York's Pioneering
Role," *Journal of the American Planning Association*, Spring 1992, pp.
201–212.

10   William B. Friedricks, "A Metropolitan Entrepreneur Par Excellence: Henry E. Huntington and the Growth of Southern California,
1889–1927," *Business History Review*, Summer 1889, p. 354.

11   Eugene Rachlis and John E. Marqusee, *The Land Lords* (New York:
Random House, 1963), pp. 60–86.

12   Ibid, p. 1.

13   Richard M. Hurd, *Principles of City Land Values* (New York: Real
Estate Record and Guide, 1903).

14   Marc A. Weiss, "Richard T. Ely and the Contribution of Economic
Research to National Housing Policy, 1920–1940," *Urban Studies*,
February 1989, pp. 115–126; Marc A. Weiss, "Marketing and
Financing Homeownership: Mortgage Lending and Public Policy in
the United States, 1918–1989," *Business and Economic History*, 1989,
pp. 109–118; and Weiss, *The Rise of the Community Builders*.

15   Edith Elmer Wood, *The Housing of the Unskilled Wage Earner* (New
York: Macmillan, 1919); *Recent Trends in American Housing* (New
York: Macmillan, 1931); and *Slums and Blighted Areas in the United
States*, Public Works Administration, Housing Division Bulletin No. 1
(Washington, D.C.: U.S. Government Printing Office, 1935).

16   Nathan Straus, *The Seven Myths of Housing* (New York: Alfred A.
Knopf, 1941).

17   Community Builders Council, *The Community Builders Handbook*
(Washington, D.C.: ULI–the Urban Land Institute, 1947).

Chapter 6

The Modern Era: World War II to the Present

From the end of the Second World War to the present, the United States has experienced a dramatic transformation of its built environment, driven by a population increase from 132 million in 1940 to 318 million in 2014, by gains in technology, by prosperity, and by the transformation of the global economy. In a 1964 speech, Lyndon Johnson said "in the next 40 years we must rebuild the entire urban United States,"[1] and to a remarkable extent, that happened. Over this period, the economic and employment bases of cities shifted from manufacturing toward service, while electronic communication eroded many of the bonds that held businesses to central locations. The forces behind centralization and decentralization became increasingly complex, giving rise to intense debates on the management of growth.

Against this backdrop of postwar economic growth, this chapter explores the evolution of the real estate industry since World War II, examining

- Suburbanization and the postwar boom;
- The mid-20th century office building boom;
- Urban renewal, decline, and regeneration;
- The expansion of interstate highways and the growth of the suburbs;
- The urban crisis in race, housing, and neighborhoods;
- New development patterns from the 1980s through today; and
- The cyclical nature of real estate.

For the duration of World War II, most new private construction was put on hold except for that directly related to the war effort. On the heels of the decade-long economic depression, most U.S. real estate markets were thus badly underbuilt by 1945. The demand for housing was particularly pressing with 11 million servicemen and servicewomen returning home. By 1947, more than 5 million families had either doubled up with other families in overcrowded dwellings or were occupying temporary shelters. Housing construction quadrupled to a half million new homes in 1946, but production remained far below demand, and newly deregulated housing prices were skyrocketing.

After a bumpy start, the homebuilding industry eventually rose to the challenge. With government

This chapter was originally written by Marc A. Weiss, PhD, chair and CEO, Global Urban Development, Washington, D.C.

assistance in the form of mortgage financing, new highways and infrastructure, and more permissive zoning and planning, by 1950 housing starts reached an all-time high of more than 1.5 million new units, mostly single-family homes.

SUBURBANIZATION AND THE POSTWAR BOOM

In 1944, Congress prepared for postwar growth by passing the Servicemen's Readjustment Act—better known as the *"GI Bill"*—which established both the *Veterans Administration* (now the *Department of Veterans Affairs*) and the *VA home loan guarantee program*. Under the VA program, an eligible veteran could obtain a low-interest, highly leveraged mortgage to buy a home, in some cases with no downpayment. In the original legislation, homeownership loan guarantees were available to veterans only for the first two years following their return to civilian life, but by 1946 the housing shortage became so severe that Congress soon extended the program for ten years. Billions of dollars were authorized for the FHA, VA, and Fannie Mae during those postwar years, most notably in the landmark Housing Act of 1949, which declared as a national goal "a decent home and a suitable living environment for every American family."

The production of housing reached an unprecedented volume. Fifteen million houses and apartment units were built in the 1950s, more than

Inexpensive two-bedroom Levittown homes made it possible to purchase a home with little money down and low monthly payments—a real boon to World War II veterans who were starting families in the late 1940s and early 1950s.

double the number for the 1940s and more than five times the number for the 1930s. Two-thirds of new housing was constructed in the rapidly expanding suburbs. Concurrently, many central cities began losing population after 1950.

Production

To accommodate growth, agricultural land was subdivided into suburban tracts on a grand scale. The new form of building occurred in, for example, New York (Levittown), Chicago (Park Forest), and Los Angeles (Lakewood and Panorama City).

By 1949, 10 percent of builders were constructing 70 percent of new homes, a radical change from the prewar years. The consolidation trend would continue, with the large homebuilders expanding further in size and in volume. Part of the postwar change in the real estate industry can be attributed to the experience gained during the war, when the federal government encouraged and subsidized residential developers to mass-produce private housing for war workers, and part can be traced to experiments with mass production in earlier decades.

One challenge was the inefficient building industry, which was hampered by outdated construction methods, financing, and building codes. In the early postwar years there was also a debate about the role of the federal government versus the private sector in the production of housing, with many of the New Deal era interests arguing that the federal government should assume more responsibility for providing shelter.[2] Countering that argument was the newly formed National Association of Home Builders, led by William Levitt.

The biggest homebuilder immediately after the war was Levitt & Sons, developers of Levittown, New York, the country's largest private housing project. The first homes were completed in fall 1947. By the early 1950s, Levitt & Sons had built 17,500 homes on 4,000 acres of potato fields in Hempstead, about 30 miles east of New York City. *Time* magazine devoted a cover story to Levittown in July 1950, calling the firm's president, William Levitt, "the most potent single modernizing influence in a largely antiquated industry."[3] Levitt & Sons priced most of its homes at $7,990—about $1,500 less than any of the competitors—and still managed to earn a $1,000 profit per home.

Abraham Levitt and his two sons, William and Alfred, started in the housing business on Long Island in the late 1920s. During the war, the firm entered into government contracts to construct 2,350 homes for war workers in and around Norfolk, Virginia; what the Levitts learned there about high-volume methods of production became the basis for their postwar planning and development. At Levittown, William Levitt turned the entire development into a mobile assembly line, with teams of workers moving from house to house to perform 26 specific, repetitive tasks. Everything was carefully programmed and tightly controlled. The Levitts bought materials in bulk, to their own specifications. Subcontractors were required to work exclusively for them. The Levitts specially trained and managed construction crews. Materials were preassembled in central facilities and delivered to each construction site just in time for that day's assignments. The emphasis was on speed, and, at peak production, homes in Levittown were completed at the astounding rate of 35 per day.

Levitt & Sons built two other Levittowns, both in the Philadelphia suburbs: in Bucks County, Pennsylvania, in the early 1950s, and in Willingboro, New Jersey, in the late 1950s. They built their last large housing project, Belair, in Bowie, Maryland, during the early 1960s. The production housing format was repeated in Chicago by Philip Klutznick, and in Los Angeles by Fritz Burns, Louis Boyar, Ben Weingart, and Mark Taper. Klutznick purchased land south of Chicago to create a new town for returning veterans. The project, Park Forest, was designed in the tradition of what are now called master-planned communities. Burns had developed large residential communities in Los Angeles between the wars. Following the end of the Second World War, he teamed with Henry Kaiser to build mass-produced housing, including Panorama City, a 430-acre project in California's San Fernando Valley. Boyar, Weingart and Taper developed 17,500 homes

for a community called Lakewood, near Long Beach. Although many other big developments flourished during the postwar years, the original Levittown in Hempstead, Long Island, still stands as an American cultural symbol of postwar housing construction.

Transportation: The Expansion of Interstate Highways and the Growth of the Suburbs

A major influence on postwar land use was the 1956 interstate highway program. It had many purposes, including support of the national defense through easy movement of troops and materiel, as well as safety and promotion of interstate commerce. A clear urban goal of the system was to help revitalize central cities. Downtown corporate interests lobbied heavily for the federal government to fund the interstate highway program. These new superhighways were considered the last, best hope for downtowns. New expressways radiating in all directions were expected to bring workers, shoppers, tourists, and middle-class residents to urban downtowns while reducing traffic congestion on city streets and improving speed and accessibility. However, the sheer size of limited-access highway infrastructure facilities had adverse impacts on the fabric of downtown areas and on neighborhoods. In the process of building this grand and expensive automobile-based transportation system, displacement hit inner-city communities and created new land use patterns. Some of these effects were already being felt. "One Mile," Robert Caro's dramatic chapter on New York City's Cross-Bronx Expressway in *The Power Broker*, paints a vivid portrait of the human drama behind a limited-access facility that Robert Moses built in 1952.[4]

Ironically, the downtown expressways turned out to be two-way streets that allowed city businesses and residents to leave as well as to enter the center city, thereby exacerbating urban flight. Together with the suburban highways that surrounded and bypassed the urban core, the highways radiating from the cities' centers enabled the hallmarks of downtowns—office buildings, department stores, and hotels—to move or expand to the interchanges of major suburban transportation arteries.

INNOVATOR Alan M. Voorhees

Alan M. Voorhees was an engineer, planner, entrepreneur, and decorated veteran of World War II. His pioneering forecasting technique assisted in the development of highway and transit systems in metropolitan areas. He went on to become an entrepreneur in real estate and other businesses.

Following his distinguished service in World War II, Voorhees returned to Rensselaer Polytechnic Institute, earning his civil engineering degree in 1947. He earned a masters degree in city planning at MIT in 1949 and completed the Yale University traffic program in 1952. While at Yale, he pioneered the use of the "gravity model" for forecasting urban travel patterns based on future land development patterns. His groundbreaking work, "A General Theory of Traffic Movement," was published in 1955 in the *Proceedings of the Institute of Traffic Engineers.*

In 1949, Voorhees became the first city planning engineer for Colorado Springs, Colorado, where he developed a master plan for land use and transportation. He was part of a committee that put together a proposal that led to the location of the Air Force Academy in Colorado Springs. In 1952, he became a planning engineer for the Automotive Safety Foundation, a nonprofit corporation in Washington, D.C., where he further developed and applied his methodology for urban travel forecasting and assisted the federal government in developing computer programs for use by American cities that needed metropolitan transportation plans to complete urban portions of the growing interstate highway network. His gravity model work and its later derivatives became the basis of standard practice throughout the world for planning and designing highways, mass transit, and other systems.

In 1961, Voorhees founded Alan M. Voorhees and Associates (AMV), a transportation planning and engineering firm that grew to become one of the largest such firms in the United States. During the next two decades, AMV prepared transportation plans

for new national capitals, including Canberra in Australia and Abuja in Nigeria. The firm designed transportation networks in the area surrounding the New York World Trade Center, then being planned. It assisted in the development of new rail transit systems in Washington, D.C.; Caracas, Venezuela; São Paulo, Brazil; Hong Kong; and Atlanta. It prepared transportation plans for a number of new towns including Reston, Virginia, and Columbia, Maryland. It prepared comprehensive transportation plans for Boston, Detroit, Miami, Minneapolis, St. Louis, Pittsburgh, and Seattle, as well as Adelaide, Australia, and San Jose, Costa Rica. It also prepared financial and operating plans for the conversion of private bus companies to public operation in numerous cities, including Washington and Boston. In 1967, AMV was bought by Planning Research Corporation, thereafter operating as an independent subsidiary.

In 1977, Voorhees became dean of the College of Art, Architecture, and Urban Sciences at the University of Illinois at Chicago. The following year, he established an endowment named for his wife and founded the Nathalie P. Voorhees Center for Neighborhood and Community Improvement in the university's College of Urban Planning and Public Affairs.

In 1979, Voorhees left academia to return to Washington, D.C., and the practice of real estate development. He also engaged in extended entrepreneurship with firms in technology, air transport, and space exploration. His real estate development career included building mixed-use projects in the historic districts of Washington, D.C., and Richmond, Virginia. His consulting firm conducted the first "Parking Requirements for Shopping Centers" study for ULI in 1965. Voorhees, a member of ULI, was one of a small group of transportation leaders to recognize the importance of the connection between transportation and land use.

Robert T. Dunphy

Financing

Promotion by the FHA and VA of large-scale home-building was a major factor in allowing residential developers to grow rapidly in size as the entire housing industry dramatically increased total production. Levitt simplified the sales transaction to two half-hour steps that made purchasing easy for people who had never before owned a home. Many of the purchasers were veterans who could move in with no downpayment other than $10 in closing costs and then pay $56 a month for principal, interest, taxes, and insurance—considerably less than the monthly

rent for a comparable apartment. The two-bedroom homes came equipped with modern appliances, and the quarter-acre lots offered plenty of room for expansion.

Regrettably, the Levitts restricted their American Dream to whites only. Before the civil rights movement of the 1960s, restrictive practices were common in most new housing developments. Even the FHA and VA—federal government agencies—actively supported discriminatory policies against racial minorities.

Employment: The Growth of Suburban Office and Industrial Parks

The decentralization and suburban growth fostered by the new highway system led to residential and retail relocation. Industry and commerce began moving to suburbia to locate near major transportation arteries. Manufacturing plants that had previously depended mainly on railroad lines now relied more heavily on trucking. They found highway-accessible suburban locations, whose land costs and rents were cheaper than urban sites, to be increasingly attractive. In the 1950s, *industrial parks*, office parks, research and development parks—with full utilities, plenty of parking, access roads, attractive landscaping, and nearby services—sprouted across suburbia, particularly near the interstate highways. Cabot, Cabot & Forbes (CC&F) of Boston earned a national reputation for successfully developing many of these projects.

CC&F was an old-line real estate investment management company founded in 1897. In 1947, 26-year-old Gerald Blakely convinced senior partner Murray Forbes to hire him to develop suburban industrial parks. The role of the Massachusetts Institute of Technology and Harvard University in pioneering new science and technology for the war effort suggested that the Boston area could become a significant center of research and manufacturing for electronics and related industries. Blakely also assumed that engineers and scientists then moving to suburban neighborhoods would appreciate shorter commuting times to nearby industrial and office parks. He focused his development strategy on Route 128, a circumferential state highway then under construction about 12 miles outside of Boston.

Blakely acquired land in Needham and Waltham, two suburban towns along Route 128. It took several years to raise the private financing, win zoning approvals, and convince the state government to build the necessary highway interchanges and access roads. In the mid-1950s, CC&F finally opened three large facilities: the New England Industrial Park in Needham, the Waltham Industrial Center, and the Waltham Research and Development Park. All three centers were soon fully occupied, and CC&F was

quickly searching for more sites to capture a major share of the rapid economic growth then taking place along Route 128.

By the mid-1960s, CC&F alone had built 13 of the 19 industrial parks along Route 128. It also developed the 800-acre I-95 Industrial Center near Boston's I-495, Technology Square in Cambridge, industrial parks in Pennsylvania and California, and several office buildings and shopping centers. In 1967, the National Association of Industrial and Office Properties (now called NAIOP) was formed to represent developers, owners, and managers of such parks.

With manufacturing comes distribution and wholesale trade; for developers, that means warehouses and showrooms. Trammell Crow, the country's largest developer of the postwar period, started out specializing in developing warehousing and wholesaling facilities. Crow built millions of square feet of warehouses and trade marts in his hometown of Dallas and across the country. As the U.S economy grew, especially in the Sunbelt, so did Crow's ambitious development, construction, and leasing activities (see profile).

The Growth of Suburban Shopping Centers

Even before the federal interstate highway program was launched, state and local highways in the suburbs offered promising locations for a new type of large-scale development, the shopping center. By 1954, total retail sales in suburban centers already exceeded that in major central cities. Though antecedents to the modern shopping center existed before the war—J.C. Nichols's Country Club Plaza in Kansas City, Hugh Prather's Highland Park Shopping Village in Dallas, and Hugh Potter's River Oaks Center in Houston—these centers were built primarily to serve existing communities. It was only after World War II that construction of the first freestanding regional shopping centers—not tied to any specific residential development—drew patrons from a wide geographic area.

By the early 1950s, shopping centers were springing up on the periphery of cities everywhere. One of the most widely heralded of the

---

INNOVATOR **Trammell Crow**

Initially a leasing agent for warehouse space, Trammell Crow began building new warehouses in 1948 in Dallas's Trinity Industrial District, along the Trinity River. A federally funded flood control construction program in 1946 had rendered this area newly ripe for development when Crow first approached owners John and Storey Stemmons to negotiate a deal to obtain land. The Stemmons brothers decided to go into partnership with Crow. With financing from life insurance companies and several local banks, Crow and the Stemmons brothers developed more than 50 warehouses over the next two decades. Working with different partners, Crow built another 40 warehouses in the Trinity Industrial District, then branched out to Denver, Atlanta, and many other cities. Crow has been a partner in constructing tens of millions of square feet of warehouse space—more than any other single developer—ranging from speculative multi-tenant facilities to custom-built single-tenant projects.

Seeking tenants for his inventory of warehouse space, Crow traveled to Chicago and became fascinated by the city's massive 24-story, 4 million-square-foot Merchandise Mart, built by Marshall Field in 1934 as the world's largest wholesale showroom facility. By the mid-1950s, Crow launched a new plan to build trade marts in the Trinity Industrial District. Over the next three decades, the Dallas Market Center became Crow's largest and best-known development. The project became feasible in 1955 when the Stemmons brothers donated 102 acres of land to the state of Texas for a planned interstate highway with service roads for the Trinity District, making the site for Crow's trade center just two blocks from an on/off ramp and a short commute to downtown Dallas and the airport. The highway (I-35), known in Dallas as the Stemmons Freeway, opened in 1959.

Rather than build one enormous multipurpose structure like the Merchandise Mart, Trammell Crow's strategy was to build an entire complex of attractive, modern buildings—one structure at a time—that would specialize in specific product lines. In partnership with the Stemmons brothers, Crow constructed the Dallas Decorative Center in 1955 for decorators and the design trade, and then developed the Home Furnishings Mart in 1957 for the furniture and fixtures business, the Trade Mart in 1960, the Apparel Mart in 1964, the World Trade Center in 1972, and the Infomart in 1984 for the high-tech information industry. He also built Market Hall in 1963, which was the largest privately owned exhibition center in the United States, and the 1,600-room Loew's (now Hilton) Anatole Hotel, which opened in two stages in 1979 and 1981. This hotel has so many amenities and facilities that it helped turn the Dallas Market Center into a focal point for nighttime activity and added to the center's attractiveness as a location for conducting business and holding conventions and trade shows.

Trammell Crow entered the hotel business through his association with architect-developer John Portman of Atlanta. This team built the Atlanta Decorative Arts Center in 1960 and over the next two decades developed two huge urban renewal projects, the Peachtree Center in Atlanta and, with David Rockefeller, the Embarcadero Center in San Francisco. Both projects involved the construction of multiple high-rise office buildings and a large Hyatt Regency Hotel.

Beginning in 1960 with the opening of the Trade Mart in Dallas, Crow included large indoor atrium lobbies in his buildings. The atrium lobby has since become a standard feature of Crow's wholesale market centers, office buildings, hotels, apartment buildings, and even industrial parks. As chief architect, Portman achieved public recognition for the large atrium lobbies in the Atlanta and San Francisco Hyatt Regency Hotels, and the ensuing publicity accorded this innovative hotel design helped set off a wave of similar developments during the series of booms in downtown and suburban hotel construction that ebbed and flowed during the 1970s and 1980s.

---

new suburban malls was the Northgate Shopping Center, about 20 miles from downtown Seattle. Developed by Allied Stores and opened in 1950, Northgate featured a Bon Marché department store as the anchor tenant. Smaller stores flanked its major design innovation: a central outdoor ground-level pedestrian mall with an underground truck tunnel that hid deliveries and trash removal. Surrounding the mall was the necessary sea of parking spaces, and it was considered a bold step to turn the storefronts away from the automobile traffic and parking lots. In 1954, Northland Center outside Detroit, developed and anchored by J.L. Hudson's department store, opened as the largest regional shopping center at that date and the first to offer attractive amenities and open space. *Architectural Forum* even compared Northland, which was designed by Victor Gruen, to Rockefeller Center.[5]

Two years later, another department store company, Dayton's of Minneapolis, built Southdale Center, the first fully enclosed, heated, and air-conditioned suburban shopping mall. Located in Edina, Minnesota, Southdale was also designed by Gruen, who had won critical acclaim for Northland

Before 1956, Southdale, Minnesota, was farmland. But that year, Dayton's opened Southdale Center, often considered the first enclosed suburban shopping mall.

and went on to design nearly 100 other malls. To block the construction of a nearby competing mall and thus protect its investment, Dayton's broke with previous practice by inducing another department store, Donaldson's, to come to Southdale as a second anchor. Southdale set new standards for the design, construction, leasing, and management of shopping malls.

The year after Southdale opened, James Rouse, an independent developer, built the fully enclosed Harundale Mall in the Baltimore suburbs. In 1961, Rouse and Victor Gruen teamed up to design and develop Cherry Hill, a 78-acre shopping center in Delaware Township, New Jersey, outside Philadelphia. The shopping center became such a symbol of the township's economic and cultural life that residents later voted to change the community's name to Cherry Hill.

Many of the early shopping centers proved to be highly profitable, and, into the mid-1990s, those with available land to expand increased the number of stores and the number, size, and type of anchors. Anchors no longer had to be department stores, but could also be big-box stores as well as movie theaters, eateries, or other entertainment venues. The number of shopping centers in the United States grew exponentially, from a relative handful at the end of World War II to 7,000 at the beginning of the 1960s to more than 100,000 by 2014, including 1,500 enclosed malls.

The enclosed shopping mall model in the United States reached its peak in the mid-1990s, and by 2000, the concept began to tarnish as big-box stores and open-air town centers gained market share. In 2007, for the first time in 50 years, not a single enclosed mall was built in the United States. Besides competing new formats, other factors are to blame, including changing demographics and weakened sales due to online shopping.

While shopping mall development in the United States has stalled, such development has continued in much of the rest of the world. Asia's rapid growth and increasing prosperity has spawned significant new shopping center development.

Europe—especially Russia—continues to develop new shopping centers as well. Nearly 100 new shopping centers were built in Russia between 2012 and 2014, including Avia Park, outside Moscow, Europe's largest shopping mall. Avia Park comprises 2.5 million square feet of retailers and entertainment facilities on four levels.

The Growth of the Lodging Sector

The postwar growth of the interstate highway system and suburbanization dramatically affected the lodging business. Before the late 1940s, most hotels were located in city centers. The exception was resort hotels located near vacation destinations. When most travel was by railroad, hotels served travelers through their proximity to train stations.

A typical motel outside Washington, D.C., in the early 1950s.

Beginning in the 1920s, "roadside inns" opened along major thoroughfares to accommodate automobile drivers, but this type of lodging was usually small and nearly always a local mom-and-pop business. Further, roadside inns quickly acquired a seedy image.[6]

In 1952, Kemmons Wilson and Wallace Johnson opened the nation's first Holiday Inn "hotel court" in Memphis, with free parking, modest prices, and a respectable family image bolstered by the widely advertised offer of free accommodations for children under 12 when accompanied by their parents. The Holiday Inn hotel chain expanded rapidly during the 1950s and 1960s, initially taking advantage of key locations on the new interstates. Holiday Inn later moved into urban areas and resort communities and, by the 1980s, became the world's largest hotel chain.

Early hotel chains such as Hilton and Sheraton evolved from large downtown hotels that, in general, were independently owned and managed. But, with the 1950s explosion of motels at freeway interchanges and near airports, chains such as Ramada, Howard Johnson's, and TraveLodge proliferated, as did cooperative referral organizations such as Best Western and Friendship Inns, which represent large groups of independently owned hotels and motels. By 1954, the number of motel rooms in the United States exceeded the number of hotel rooms, and, by 1972, the nation had twice as many motel rooms as hotel rooms.

Not only did the focus of new development shift from the center of town to the outskirts; much more of the growth occurred in the Sun Belt states and the intermountain West than in the Northeast and Midwest. In addition, the size of hotels and motels grew steadily larger. In 1950, a typical motel consisted of fewer than 20 rooms and hotels averaged about 40 rooms. In 2013, there were a total of 52,500 hotel and motel facilities, with 4.9 million guest rooms—an average size of 93 rooms.

The line between hotels and motels has blurred, with a broad range of offerings that include conference centers, budget motels, residence suites, and a multitude of other categories in every kind of location. A major change in the lodging industry was the entry of investors into the business and the reemergence of many large chains, such as Hilton, Hyatt, Marriott, and Sheraton, as contract management firms. The many new and complicated methods by which hotels and motels are owned and operated have created an opening in development of hotels, both freestanding and as components of mixed-use developments. Some developers own and operate hotels, conference centers, and resorts as long-term investments, although many more are involved on a shorter-term basis in the construction and sale of such properties. Today, lodging is considered a key sector of the real estate development industry.

THE URBAN CRISIS: RACE, HOUSING, AND NEIGHBORHOODS

Suburbanization hit the country like a tidal wave in the 1950s, but the movement of population and employment away from the central cities was already evident three decades earlier. While downtown development flourished in most cities during the 1920s, the neighborhoods surrounding the central business district, sometimes called "the zone of transition," had already started to deteriorate. Once the Great Depression took root, development in most central cities ground to a halt and remained stagnant through World War II and immediately after. By the mid-1950s, many U.S. cities had not seen new office building construction in nearly 30 years. Most were also losing large numbers of manufacturing jobs after the war-induced growth spurt. Rail yards, factories, and warehouses were abandoned, with little demand for new occupancy. Many old houses and apartments in the zone of transition deteriorated and lost occupants. Offices, stores, hotels, and restaurants all suffered from declining markets, and civic leaders feared that the hearts of cities would die a slow economic, political, and cultural death.

The American Dream—a typical FHA-financed residential subdivision in San Diego circa 1964.

Urban Renewal

The remedy proposed by many business, real estate, and civic groups was first called district replanning, then urban redevelopment, and, finally, *urban renewal*. The idea was to rebuild centrally located blighted areas—clear away underused commercial and industrial structures, move out poor (and often minority) residents, and tear down their housing—and replace it with new office towers, convention centers, hotels, shopping malls, and housing. Local governments would use their *powers of eminent domain* to condemn and acquire the land, demolish the structures, redevelop the infrastructure and public amenities, and sell the land to private developers, who would construct new privately owned developments.

Initially, state and local governments operated urban renewal programs. One of the most ambitious efforts was the Pittsburgh "Renaissance," which was spearheaded by a coalition of corporate executives headed by Richard King Mellon, scion of the family that owned Gulf Oil, Alcoa, and Mellon Bank, and by Mayor David Lawrence, an energetic New Deal Democrat. Working through the Allegheny Conference on Community Development, state and city officials and private sector leaders devised a master plan that guided the rebuilding of downtown's "Golden Triangle" as well as part of the nearby Lower Hill District, which was populated largely by African Americans. Several new high-rise office buildings, luxury apartments, a state park, two highways, a convention center/sports arena, and other public and private developments replaced the older buildings that had occupied these two key downtown Pittsburgh sites.

The main obstacle to extensive urban renewal was its high public cost. Local taxpayers balked at the magnitude of the funding needed for full-scale renewal, although occasionally subsidies provided sufficient economic incentive in the form of real estate tax abatements for large investors and developers to bear the direct expenses. Such was the case with the Metropolitan Life Insurance Company's

Stuyvesant Town and Peter Cooper Village, two massive private residential redevelopment projects built on Manhattan's East Side during the 1940s.

Drawing on the precedent of the 1930s, when the federal government had, for the first time, granted billions of dollars to state and local governments to rebuild the infrastructure and amenities of central cities, several lobbying groups demanded that Washington pay for urban renewal through a federal grant program. *Title I* of the Housing Act of 1949 created such a program, which was strengthened and modified by the Housing Act of 1954 and by many subsequent legislative enactments. Under Title I, the federal government paid two-thirds or more of the "write-down," the total direct public subsidy minus the revenue from the sale of land to private redevelopers.

By the 1960s, the impact of Title I was apparent, with new private and public buildings in central cities throughout the nation. Most of these developments brought needed investment into the urban economy. They helped create jobs, increase the tax base, improve the physical and cultural environment, and add attractive structures as well as public open spaces.

Some land clearance efforts, however, merely produced holes in the urban fabric but no new development; projects such as St. Louis's notoriously nicknamed "Hiroshima Flats" cleared sites that failed to attract bids from private developers. These sites became a more blighting influence on the community than the buildings that had been demolished. Urban renewal projects also meant dramatic displacement of small businesses and of low- and moderate-income residents. Unless they owned property, those who were displaced received no compensation and, in most cases, little or no relocation assistance—in the form of money or new facilities or dwellings. Even when relocation housing was available, it was seldom in the same neighborhood. Between 1949 and 1967, some 400,000 residential units were demolished under Title I, but only 10,000 new public housing units were built on urban renewal sites. By the middle 1960s, such statistics led to outcries against "Negro removal" and

considerable controversy. As a result, the program underwent substantial improvement from 1968 to 1970, but in 1974 it was abolished.[7]

With suburbia's powerful attraction and the long period of downtown stagnation uppermost in their minds, lenders and investors in downtown space were very cautious during the 1950s and early 1960s. Despite all the financial incentives, most local governments found it difficult to persuade private developers to participate in downtown renewal efforts. One successful high-risk developer who bucked the conservative mood and plunged headfirst into urban renewal programs across the country was William Zeckendorf (see profile).

In the early days of urban renewal, the largest investors, lenders, and joint venture partners were the major life insurance companies. They had emerged

---

INNOVATOR   William Zeckendorf

As head of Webb & Knapp in the 1950s and 1960s, William Zeckendorf was America's best-known national developer, buying and selling land and buildings in and near many large cities and constructing major projects from the Mile High Center in Denver to Plâce Ville-Marie in Montreal to Century City in Los Angeles. He assembled the land for the site of the United Nations in New York and achieved distinction in urban design through the work of his chief architect, I.M. Pei.

Zeckendorf's most aggressive efforts were federally subsidized urban renewal projects. Beginning in the 1950s, Webb & Knapp built L'Enfant Plaza, a mixed-use office complex; the Town Center apartments; and the Waterside Mall shopping center in Washington, D.C. In Philadelphia, Zeckendorf developed the Society Hill Towers and townhouses near the waterfront of the historic city and restored many of Society Hill's colonial rowhouses. Webb & Knapp, using the talents of architects I.M. Pei and Henry Cobb, won the contract to redevelop Society Hill through a design competition. Webb & Knapp also won design competitions to build the University Gardens apartment complex in the Hyde Park neighborhood of Chicago and an even larger project in Pittsburgh's Lower Hill District. In New York, where Webb & Knapp had its headquarters, Zeckendorf and Pei teamed up to develop three major Title I urban renewal residential developments in Manhattan: Park West Village, Kips Bay Plaza, and Lincoln Towers. Zeckendorf was also involved with downtown redevelopment planning in Cincinnati, St. Louis, San Francisco, Cleveland, and Hartford.

from the war with tremendous amounts of cash to invest, and real estate assets appeared to offer a good economic return. Companies such as Equitable, which developed the Gateway Center office complex in downtown Pittsburgh; New York Life, the developer of Chicago's racially integrated middle-income apartment complex, Lake Meadows; Prudential, which built and occupied the main office tower in Boston's Prudential Center; and Metropolitan Life and John Hancock were all players in the urban renewal game.

In 1957, the editors of *Fortune* magazine published *The Exploding Metropolis*. The title referred primarily to the burgeoning postwar suburbs, but the book included articles on central cities and rising racial conflict. A chapter on "the enduring slum" concluded with an ominous statement: "One way or another, we will continue to pay plenty for our slums."[8] Written at the time of the first stirrings of the civil rights movement, the words proved a perfect introduction to the 1960s; the book's title was a harbinger of the events that would unfold in American cities during the decade. Along with the migration of white middle-class homeowners to the suburbs, another great migration was taking place: African Americans were moving from the rural south to central cities in record numbers, particularly to the older industrial cities of the North, where they overflowed the boundaries of established and highly segregated ghetto areas. Three million African Americans migrated from the South to the North and West in the 1940s and 1950s; by 1960, two-thirds of that population was concentrated in the 12 largest cities. The percentage of African Americans in Chicago, for example, jumped from 8 percent in 1940 to nearly 25 percent in 1960, and to 37 percent in 2000 (then declined, to 33 percent in 2010).

The unfortunate legacy of racism cast a cloud over this dynamic process of urban growth and change. Newly arrived African Americans were often forced to live in overcrowded, overpriced, poor-quality housing because they were restricted from buying or renting in white neighborhoods. When they did attempt to break through the "color line,"

African Americans frequently met with intimidation and violence. In response, some metropolitan areas launched interracial antidiscrimination movements for "open housing." At the same time, however, most cities were beginning to lose industrial jobs, either to the suburbs or from the entire metropolitan region. As a result, the rural-to-urban migrants during the 1950s and thereafter had fewer economic opportunities than their predecessors. The competition with existing residents for jobs contributed to racial tensions. Many city government agencies, bureaucracies, and politicians proved unreceptive to these African American newcomers, who were often denied access to adequate municipal services and political representation. In particular, schooling became a volatile issue, with numerous battles fought over racial desegregation.

Other groups of "new minorities" also gained a foothold in some cities during this period, most notably Puerto Ricans in New York City, Cubans in Miami, and Mexicans in many parts of Texas, Arizona, Colorado, and California. By the 1970s and 1980s, large numbers of Hispanics from Central and South America and a dramatic influx of Asians from China, Japan, Korea, and Vietnam had become major forces in U.S. urban life. What came to be called the "urban crisis" of the 1960s, however, largely revolved around the economic and social injustice suffered by African Americans.

The struggle against these injustices grew increasingly heated throughout the 1950s and 1960s, with violence exploding during the 1960s. Local police and white residents directed much early violence against their African American neighbors and coworkers. Later, African Americans fought back, battling in the streets with law enforcement officials, including the National Guard, looting stores, and burning or vandalizing buildings, usually in their own neighborhoods. Long hot summers of riots broke out in U.S cities, from New York's Harlem in 1964 and Los Angeles's Watts in 1965 to Detroit and Newark in 1967 and dozens of other cities in 1968 in the wake of the assassination of Dr. Martin Luther King, Jr. In all, nearly 200 people were killed and 20,000 people arrested nationwide, with property damage estimated in the hundreds of millions of dollars.

Eventually, many concerned citizens mobilized to address the interconnected set of problems that had spawned dissatisfaction and disorder. The most obvious inequity was the legally and officially sanctioned segregation and discrimination that had long pervaded U.S. life. Beginning in the 1940s, the powerful political coalition and moral force of the civil rights movement began to sweep away many discriminatory barriers through a series of federal, state, and local laws and court decisions. In 1962, President John F. Kennedy issued an executive order banning racial discrimination in federal housing programs, and, after his assassination the following year, President Lyndon B. Johnson carried through on a host of successful legislative efforts, including the landmark *Civil Rights Act of 1964* and the *Voting Rights Act of 1965*.

To solve the underlying problems, legal rights had to be supplemented by economic and social action. In 1960, the Ford Foundation launched its Gray Areas Program to foster the revitalization and redevelopment of urban neighborhoods with minority populations, simultaneously trying to improve housing, social services, employment opportunities, crime prevention, and public education. These pilot projects paved the way for a vast array of public efforts, from the many programs and organizations grouped under the *War on Poverty* starting in 1964 to the comprehensive neighborhood-based *Model Cities Program of 1966*. One of the most innovative public/private partnerships was the creation of *community development corporations (CDCs)*, entrepreneurial institutions that attempted to combine the best features of business investment and management with government services and citizen participation.

In 1967, the Ford Foundation worked with New York's two U.S. Senators, Robert F. Kennedy and Jacob K. Javits, to establish the Bedford-Stuyvesant Restoration Corporation in a predominantly African American neighborhood of Brooklyn. Since the 1960s, a combination of public and private funding has helped many other CDCs grow. Today, CDCs continue to build and manage affordable housing, health clinics, and commercial development; and provide preschool education, child care, job training and placement, and a host of other services. Much of today's minority and urban political, business, and philanthropic leadership emerged from these organizations and movements.

The Federal Government's Response to the Urban Crisis

One major response to the 1960s urban crisis was the 1965 creation of the U.S. Department of Housing and Urban Development (HUD). Robert

Washington, D.C., after the 1968 riots. The destruction of the inner city was extensive, and evidence of it remained nearly 50 years later.

C. Weaver, a lifelong activist for better-quality affordable housing and a strong opponent of racial discrimination, was appointed first secretary of HUD, becoming the first African American member of a U.S. president's cabinet. Under Weaver's direction, federal involvement in subsidized housing changed dramatically. Since the 1930s, the federal focus had been largely limited to mortgage insurance and guarantees and the secondary mortgage market, mostly for the benefit of middle-income homeowners and to foster the development of middle-income suburban rental apartments. In encouraging private development, these activities received active support from the real estate development industry. The other emphasis at that time concentrated on public housing for low-income households. Public housing was a small program nationwide, directed primarily to large cities, and was extremely unpopular within the real estate community.

By the late 1950s, the postwar demand for new suburban single-family houses had largely been satisfied, and builders and developers sought new products and markets. One potential market yet to be tapped was those whose incomes were too modest to afford homes in the private market. Such households could, however, be served by the private sector if public subsidies were available. Proponents of low-income housing began to view the subsidized public/private approach as a solution. The NAHB, recognizing the economic potential for its members, reconsidered its position and became a key supporter of federal subsidies to produce privately owned housing for moderate-income families.

With the NAHB's backing, the federal government launched new affordable housing programs in the 1960s. These programs generally served people with somewhat higher incomes than public housing residents. By the 1970s, these assisted housing programs were producing a large volume of new rental apartments. In addition, passage of the landmark *National Housing Act of 1968* had set forth the ambitious goal of producing 600,000 subsidized homes in each of the next ten years. The 1968 act included both a program to assist in the production of rental housing (Section 236) and a mortgage subsidy

program to encourage homeownership for low- and moderate-income families (Section 235). Both programs expanded rapidly in the early 1970s but ran into problems, ranging from poor management and outright fraud to the economic recession 1973. In 1974, the Section 236 program was replaced by the Section 8 New Construction and Substantial Rehabilitation programs.

During the 1960s and 1970s, these programs helped produce hundreds of thousands of new homes, many of good quality. The federal government drastically cut back most of these programs during the 1980s, entirely eliminating some and reducing others by as much as three-fourths of their annual budget compared with the late 1970s.

State and local governments as well as nonprofit organizations and for-profit companies have contributed resources to the nation's complex system of housing production. Some for-profit builders have made development of housing for low- and moderate-income households a major component of their business. For example, Corcoran Jennison Companies in Boston has been building affordable housing since its founding in 1971. The company has produced more than 34,000 units of housing, most in mixed-income developments. Jonathan Rose Companies produces innovative affordable and mixed-income housing with an emphasis on environmental sustainability. The company often works in partnership with local government agencies, nonprofits, and other institutions.

Development Movements in Inner-City Neighborhoods

As the clearance and displacement associated with urban renewal grew increasingly controversial and expensive in the 1960s and early 1970s, many community activists and urban policy makers searched for alternative methods to save and improve the existing housing stock and revitalize neighborhoods. Over time, the idea of neighborhood conservation and housing renovation led to new government programs, such as Section 312 home rehabilitation loans, federally assisted code enforcement, and community development block grants (CDBGs), to assist the revitalization process.

One of the biggest stumbling blocks was *redlining*—real estate lenders' refusal to lend money, often with the implicit or explicit backing of the federal government, for properties in neighborhoods inhabited largely by those with weak credit—and insurance companies' denial of homeowners' insurance in those neighborhoods. For many years, the federal government redlined properties through the FHA and VA, but, by the late 1960s, various legislative and policy directives led to reform of this practice. After these reforms, most private lenders and insurers continued redlining, and the FHA and VA became the primary sources of home loans in many inner-city neighborhoods.

INNOVATOR   Abraham Kazan

Perhaps the biggest of all of America's private builders of affordable housing was Abraham E. Kazan. Kazan was a Russian Jewish immigrant who joined the Amalgamated Clothing Workers, one of the newly emerging labor unions of the early 20th century. Kazan helped organize a credit union and a union-sponsored bank to make financing more available for affordable rental housing and homeownership. In the 1920s, his union was instrumental in passing the New York State housing law that provided subsidies for moderate-income rental apartments. Kazan formed the Amalgamated Housing Corporation in 1927 and, with property tax abatements under the new state law, built the first two affordable developments: Amalgamated Houses in the Bronx and Amalgamated Dwellings on the Lower East Side of Manhattan. These historic landmark residential complexes were financed primarily by the Metropolitan Life Insurance Company and the Amalgamated Bank. Both developments were structured as limited-dividend cooperatives to make the attractively designed new housing permanently affordable for moderate-income working families.

In 1951, Kazan formed the United Housing Foundation, a nonprofit organization that built numerous large-scale cooperative housing developments in New York City during the 1950s, 1960s, and 1970s. His final project was Co-op City, which, with more than 15,000 apartments, is still the largest private housing development in the United States. All told, Kazan constructed more than 33,000 cooperatively owned affordable apartments in over half a century of real estate development. Today, the United Housing Foundation and other institutions like the National Cooperative Bank help to carry on his legacy.

In the 1960s, a movement emerged to reverse this development. Gale Cincotta, a housewife and leader of the Parent-Teacher Association in the west-side Chicago neighborhood of Austin, crusaded for community stabilization and improvement. She began her efforts with the discovery that banks and thrift institutions were taking millions of dollars in deposits from local residents but refusing to lend even thousands of dollars to those very same customers. Cincotta's neighborhood battle against redlining and in support of *"greenlining"* united people across racial and geographic boundaries. Starting with the Organization for a Better Austin, Cincotta later helped establish the Chicago Reinvestment Alliance and the National People's Action, which led to city, state, and federal intervention and eventually to a variety of fair lending and insurance agreements with banks, thrifts, and insurance companies. These agreements helped bring needed loan and grant money and homeowners' insurance back into long-ignored communities, where property owners were eager to reinvest and upgrade their homes and where developers were ready and willing to invest.

From Cincotta's movement came two national laws: the Home Mortgage Disclosure Act (HMDA) of 1975 and the *Community Reinvestment Act (CRA)* of 1977. Both laws discourage redlining and encourage affirmative lending. A related initiative is the federally supported *Neighborhood Reinvestment Corporation*, which promotes conservation of communities through the successful Neighborhood Housing Services plan pioneered in the mid-1970s on Pittsburgh's North Side. Congress and the federal financial regulatory agencies strengthened the Community Reinvestment Act in 1989. President William J. Clinton and Comptroller of the Currency Eugene Ludwig further strengthened the CRA in 1994. Congressional amendments to the Fair Housing Act in 1992 plus subsequent civil court rulings have helped reduce property insurance redlining. The Community Reinvestment Act played an essential role in expanding available capital for neighborhood development in the 1990s.[9] (Chapters 7 and 8 look at current best practices and prospects for the government's continuing role.)

DOWNTOWN REVIVALS

While residents of inner-city neighborhoods were struggling to pump life back into their communities, corporate and civic leaders were engaged in an identical process focused on their cities' central business districts. Many downtowns that experienced real estate booms during the 1920s languished for the next two or three decades without any significant new development. The postwar urban renewal and interstate highway programs were designed to jump-start downtown redevelopment through the combination of land assembly, public improvements, and subsidies. By the 1960s, these government programs were beginning to yield results. The growth of the service economy and the white-collar workforce stimulated the construction of new office buildings, and the rising incomes and changing lifestyles of both young and old led to new investment in retail development and, in some cities, the construction and renovation of downtown housing.

In 1985, the Urban Land Institute published a survey conducted by the Real Estate Research Corporation that documented the long hiatus in office building development in 24 of the nation's biggest cities from the 1920s to the 1950s, and the massive growth that followed, from the late 1960s to the mid-1980s.[10] The survey documented the completion of new, privately owned, large high-rise office buildings (100,000 square feet or larger) located in central business districts. In some cities, no office towers had ever been built before the postwar years; most other major cities lived through several decades without any development of these symbols of progress and prosperity. Cities like Atlanta, Houston, and Miami had no office development between World War II and the 1960s, while St. Louis, St. Paul, and Washington, D.C. saw no office development until the 1970s.

Beginning in the 1970s, cities began to make up for the long drought in office tower development.

Community Development Financial Institutions

Since the late 1800s, lower-income communities across the nation have sought alternative credit solutions because traditional financial institutions have not addressed their needs. Community development financial institutions (CDFIs) have provided one solution. CDFIs are non-governmental financial institutions that provide credit and financial services to underserved markets, such as low-income neighborhoods. CDFIs can be non-regulated institutions (e.g., venture capital funds) as well as banks and other regulated institutions. There are six basic types of CDFIs, all of them locally controlled, private-sector entities:

- Community development banks,
- Community development loan funds,
- Community development credit unions,
- Microenterprise funds,
- Community development corporation-based lenders and investors, and
- Community development venture funds.

CDFIs operate in every state and serve both rural and urban communities. Today nearly 1,000 CDFIs are certified by the CDFI Fund, within the U.S. Department of the Treasury. The Treasury provides funds to certified CDFIs through programs such as direct investment, training loan providers, technical assistance, and a tax credit program.

Some notable CDFIs include the following:

- OneUnited Bank, the largest African American–owned CDFI in the United States. Based in Boston, the bank concentrates on serving urban communities in Boston, Miami, and Los Angeles.
- The Center for Community Self-Help, headquartered in Durham, North Carolina, has provided more than $5 billion in financing to underserved urban and rural borrowers. In addition to providing mortgages and business loans, the center also develops commercial and residential real estate.
- ShoreBank, founded in Chicago in 1973 as the South Shore National Bank, initially served low-income African American communities, providing loans, deposit-banking services, venture capital for small business and real estate development, job training, and social services. It was formerly the oldest and most expansive CDFI in existence, with over $2 billion in assets. In 2010, ShoreBank was declared insolvent and taken over by the Urban Partnership Bank, which continues to provide similar services.

Among the most active downtown office markets in the latter part of the 20th century were New York City, Chicago, San Francisco, Houston, Washington, D.C., Denver, Boston, Los Angeles, Dallas, Philadelphia, Atlanta, and Seattle.

Office development has been cyclical, with the economic climate determining the demand for space and developers responding accordingly. During the mid-1980s boom, 200 million square feet of office space was built annually.[11] That pace dropped significantly during the recession of the early 1990s, then rebounded in the early 2000s, but fell precipitously following the Great Recession of 2007 to 2009; from 2011 through 2013, less than 20 million square feet of office space was built annually.[12]

Although many cities built downtowns full of gleaming high rises, and suburban office nodes competed successfully with downtowns, New York City remained the premier office market in the United States. The city boasted the most prominent developers, the most prestigious tenants and owners, and the highest rents. Signature buildings added to New York's skyline included the 59-story Pan Am Building, built in 1963 (now the MetLife Building); the 1984 AT&T building (now the Sony Tower), designed by Philip Johnson with its controversial Chippendale-style roofline; the Time Warner Center, a mixed-use complex topped with two 55-story office towers, which opened in 2004; and the first LEED (Leadership in Energy and Environmental Design) Platinum office high rise, the 55-story Bank of America Tower, built in 2009 by the Durst Organization.

But no office building was taller, larger, or more iconic than the twin skyscrapers of the World Trade Center. In 1968, construction started on a complex of seven buildings, including the landmark "twin towers." Completed in 1973, the towers were the world's tallest buildings, at 1,727 feet and 110 stories. On a typical weekday, 50,000 people worked in them.[13]

The attacks of September 11, 2001, which caused the buildings to collapse, killing more than 2,600 people, raised concern that the loss and sense of vulnerability would mean the end of skyscrapers, the end of urban living, and the start of a bunker mentality. ULI's president at the time, Richard Rosan, called for a continuing commitment to urban development. Gradually, the city and the nation began to heal, and Rosan's statement held true: "What draws people to cities is stronger than any attempt to scare them away."[14] Recovery from this tragic event was difficult, but within five years, development resumed and life returned to the Lower Manhattan neighborhood.

Along with the 1970s resurgence of downtown office development came a gradual revival in the fortunes of urban retail space, with large department stores partially eclipsed by new specialty multistore shopping malls—often part of mixed-use developments. The success of Chicago's Water Tower Place, an enclosed vertical mall with two department store anchors and 130 retail stores on seven levels, completed in 1975, had led to similar developments in other cities. Boston's Copley Place, for example, was developed by the Urban Investment and Development Company, the same firm that built Water Tower Place. Another innovative development is the TrizecHahn Company's Horton Plaza in downtown San Diego, an architecturally distinctive vertical downtown shopping mall that is not fully enclosed, to take advantage of the city's year-round dry and temperate climate. The long-term success of these urban retail centers has been mixed. Many were hurt by the consolidation of department stores that occurred from the 1980s through 2005, decimating the pool of potential anchors. A number of malls have gone through bankruptcies, buyouts, and repositionings—some emerging strong, but others failing.

Vertical urban shopping malls have proliferated in Asia, where nearly all the world's largest ones now exist. They too have had mixed results. The Dubai Mall opened in 2008. At nearly 6 million square feet, it was the world's largest mall at the time and was so successful that it began a 1 million-square-foot expansion in 2013. The New South China Mall, built in 2005 in Dongguan, China, remained 98 percent vacant for several years after completion.

Other large urban shopping malls have been built in cities in China, Indonesia, Malaysia, and Thailand.

Another urban retailing trend that began in the 1970s was tourism-, entertainment-, and food-oriented "festival marketplaces" that relied on specialty shops rather than on department store anchors. Unquestionably, the leading developer in this field was the Rouse Company, headed in the 1970s by its charismatic founder James Rouse. The first two such marketplaces, both early successes, were Boston's Faneuil Hall, opened in 1976, and Baltimore's Harborplace, opened in 1980. *Time* magazine was so enthusiastic about the impact of these two developments on the revitalization of urban downtowns that it featured James Rouse on its cover in 1981 under the heading, "Cities Are Fun!"[15] By 1990, the Rouse Company was operating 14 such centers in cities around the country, the largest being Pioneer Place in Portland, Oregon. Many downtown retail projects, including Harborplace and Horton Plaza, were urban renewal projects whose initial costs were heavily subsidized by their city governments.

The notion that the urban shopping experience is fun accelerated in the 1980s and 1990s with a new concept: urban entertainment centers. These complexes combine stores with entertainment facilities such as cinemas, skating rinks, and even roller coasters. In many cases, the stores themselves are designed for play, ranging from Niketown to the Apple Store to grocery stores that offer wine tastings and a party atmosphere. Many of these urban entertainment centers highlight the joys of strolling along to enjoy the crowds and action, and some have made that aspect the most prominent feature of their names, such as Third Street Promenade in Santa Monica, Coco Walk in Coconut Grove near Miami, and Universal CityWalk near Universal Studios in Hollywood. Some of these centers have an ethnic appeal, like Harlem USA in New York City or Jump Street USA in Philadelphia. The re-creation of city street life as a key aspect of shopping and entertainment is a trend not just in urban retail development but even in suburban malls, where the look and feel of "Main Street" has become popular.

Corvin Promenade in Budapest has revitalized one of the city's most dilapidated areas with a vibrant mix of uses, including street retail.

Along with the effort to bring back street life in urban areas came a reexamination of the urban freeways that were built in the 1950s and 1960s. A number of cities decided that it was time to remove these elevated freeways—so disruptive to urban life—and replace them with more urban-style boulevards, bike lanes, and linear parks. In 1978, Portland, Oregon was the first to dismantle a major urban freeway, which ran along the Willamette River, and replace it with a boulevard and park.

After a 1989 earthquake damaged San Francisco's Embarcadero Freeway beyond repair, the traffic that the road carried was absorbed by other roads, and the city made the decision to demolish it. In 2000, a new surface boulevard replaced the highway with positive results. Not only was the new boulevard less expensive to build than a new elevated freeway would have been, but once the freeway was removed, real estate values in the area went up by 300 percent. The site was redeveloped with a public plaza, waterfront promenade, and private-sector commercial and residential development. Also in 2002, an elevated highway in Milwaukee was dismantled and replaced with an urban boulevard. Freeways are "a rural form visited upon the city, that destroys property values, commerce, and vitality," said the former mayor of Milwaukee, John Norquist.[16]

Not all cities have benefited from revitalization efforts. The "Rust Belt," the region that stretches from central New York through Pennsylvania, Ohio, Indiana, Michigan, Illinois, and Wisconsin includes many cities that once thrived on heavy industry. Beginning in the mid-20th century, as the auto and steel industries of that region declined, the cities that were so dependent on them deteriorated. Some cities have been so devastated that it will take decades before they turn around—if they ever do.

Detroit is a case study in urban decline and an experiment in downsizing a city. It suffered from the same factors that led to decay in many American cities, but on a massive scale. Detroit was once the richest city in America, with a population of 1.9 million and a thriving economy built on the colossal U.S. auto industry. But beginning in the 1950s, the city fell victim to white flight, then to the decline of the auto industry, leading ultimately to the city filing the largest municipal bankruptcy in American history in 2013. By then the population was 701,000,[17] and block after city block held rotting or burned-out buildings. Entire blocks were scraped clean and had begun to reforest. City services were virtually nonexistent because there was no tax base left to support them.

Even as Detroit suffered, there were glimmers of hope. Urban pioneers moved in, renovated decaying houses, and opened restaurants and galleries. A few business leaders made major commitments to the city, moving into downtown office buildings and encouraging employees to live in the city. Symbolically, the city turned the streetlights back on in 2013. While most observers believe that the new Detroit will be a much smaller city than it was in 1950, the downtown has seen reinvestment, much of it powered by a public/private partnership backed by local business leaders, foundations, and community organizations pumping billions of dollars into the urban core.

Whereas Detroit's decline occurred over more than half a century, New Orleans was taken down in an instant. On August 29, 2005, Hurricane Katrina caused the failure of the levee system that protected the city from Lake Pontchartrain and the Mississippi River, leaving about 80 percent of the city severely flooded. It was one of the most deadly and destructive storms in U.S. history, causing more than 1,000 deaths, and displacing thousands. Nearly a decade later, the city still suffers from its damage. The population declined by about a quarter, from 485,000 to 369,000.[18] Like Detroit, New Orleans is expected to become a smaller city. Over time, both will offer lessons for downsizing a city.

THE EVOLUTION OF PLANNED COMMUNITIES

Another key trend of the 1960s and 1970s was the creation of large-scale, mixed-use, master-planned communities. Called "new towns," they were an alternative to both big crowded cities and suburban sprawl. Master-planned communities are usually a product of long-term multiphase development programs that combine a complementary mix of land uses.[19] They are generally large scale and controlled by a master developer who provides physical and sometimes social infrastructure. Master-planned communities can range from a few hundred acres to ten thousand acres or more.

James Rouse, known for reinventing urban retail, was also identified with this trend. Beginning in the early 1960s, a Rouse Company subsidiary called Community Research and Development began planning the new town of Columbia, Maryland. Rouse convinced his main lender, the Connecticut General Life Insurance Company (CIGNA), to provide financial backing for the massive project, beginning with several hundred secret transactions to purchase more than 16,000 acres of mostly contiguous farmland in Howard County, halfway between Baltimore and Washington, D.C.

Rouse assembled a team of distinguished city planners and social scientists to advise on how to produce a better design for modern living. They devised such innovations as a prepaid community health insurance plan; a minibus system; shared multipurpose community facilities for worship, recreation, and other uses; and a focus on quality education and active community participation. Columbia survived the collapse of its homebuilding program during the national economic recession from 1973 to 1975, to become a thriving community of almost 100,000 residents and 60,000 workers.

Built around ten self-contained villages and manmade lakes, Columbia has a "downtown" that features a regional shopping mall (owned and operated by the Rouse Company until 2004, when the company was purchased by General Growth Properties), business centers, entertainment and cultural facilities, and branches of several colleges. In 2010, a new master plan created by architects Cooper, Robertson & Partners and landscape architects Sasaki Associates was approved, to redevelop Columbia's commercial core as a more urban-style downtown.[20]

Housing in the community is targeted to a wide range of income groups and includes everything from single-family homes valued at more than $1 million to subsidized, moderate-income rental apartments. Racial integration, one of Rouse's explicit goals, has been achieved through a policy of nondiscrimination: nearly one-fourth of Columbia's population is African American. The Rouse Company also helped launch a successful homebuilding firm, Ryland Homes, which now operates nationwide but is still headquartered in Columbia.

Columbia was among a wave of privately developed new towns during the 1960s and 1970s. Most were concentrated in the rapidly growing Sun Belt states of California, Texas, and Florida, though many other states were also represented. Some of the developments were associated with resource-based corporations such as oil or logging companies that already owned large amounts of land. For example, Gulf Oil was a major investor in Reston, Virginia, another early new town, founded in 1964 by Robert E. Simon (his initials form the first part of the name). Other new communities such as Las Colinas, Texas, evolved from large agricultural and cattle ranches.

Several developments in California were the legacy of Spanish land grants whose massive, contiguous, undeveloped acreage survived into modern times under single ownership. California's early master-planned communities include Thousand Oaks, Valencia, Laguna Niguel, Mission Viejo, Rancho Santa Margarita, and, the biggest of them all, the Irvine Ranch, now known as the city of Irvine. Owned by the Irvine Company, the ranch consisted of more than 100,000 acres, nearly one-fifth of all the land in Orange County. By the early 1960s, metropolitan growth had reached the northern boundaries of the Irvine Ranch. The Irvine Company hired architect William Pereira to design a master plan for the new city of Irvine to be built around a new campus of the University of California. In 1971, Irvine had a population of 10,000 residents. Growth has continued at a rapid pace and today the city is home to more than 230,000 residents and 190,000 jobs.[21]

Niche types of master-planned communities include retiree- or adult-only communities such as Leisure World and Del Webb's Sun City brand, and recreation-oriented second-home communities in resort areas of the country. Perhaps the most far-reaching movement in master planning has been new urbanism, a concept of land planning based on the most attractive and livable communities of the pre–World War II era.

New urbanism began in 1981, with the founding of Seaside, an 80-acre beach town developed by Robert Davis on a quiet stretch of Florida's panhandle. Davis hired the design team of Andrés Duany and Elizabeth Plater-Zyberk, who established the basic principles for new urbanism: an emphasis on community space over private space and the importance of valuing the pedestrian experience over expediting vehicular traffic. Although the principles of new urbanism have been expanded over time, the concept rests on several key elements:

- The neighborhood has a center and an edge. The center includes a public space, shops, and places of work. It is the focal point of the community.
- It is compact. Ideally, most residents live within a five-minute walk of the center.
- It includes a mix of uses; for example, shops, workplaces, parks, a school, and a variety of housing types.
- It consists of an interconnected network of streets and blocks, usually laid out in a modified grid pattern.
- It gives priority to public space. Open space (squares, parks, and plazas) is provided. Civic buildings are offered prominent locations. Streets are designed to be part of the public realm.[22]

The initial costs of land acquisition, planning, infrastructure, and development are high and require many years to pay back through sales and leasing of land and buildings. So, an important lesson learned from large, master-planned communities is that patient investors are essential. These communities require strong, long-term financial investment to succeed. In the 1970s, the HUD-managed *New Communities* Program sponsored developers who, for the most part, were too thinly capitalized and received inadequate operating support from the

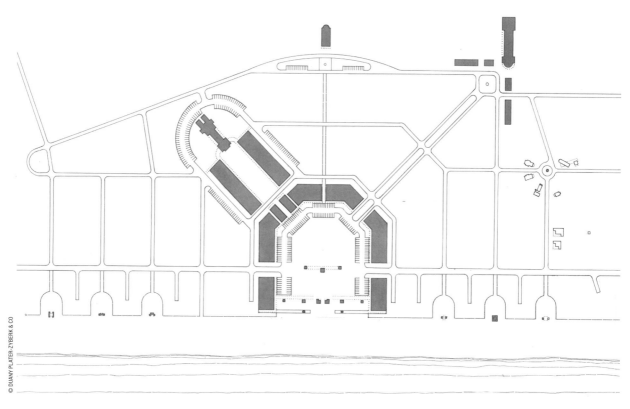

© DUANY PLATER-ZYBERK & CO

Plan for Seaside, Florida.

agency. Consequently, most of the HUD-supported new community projects went bankrupt. One exception is the Woodlands, near Houston, which has been owned for nearly three decades by the Mitchell Energy and Development Corporation. The Woodlands was able to draw from both the corporate resources of its parent firm and the substantial personal commitment of the company's owner and chief executive, George Mitchell, to build the town of his dreams.

One of the most catalytic events in master-planned development was the entry of the Disney Corporation into central Florida. In 1965, Disney purchased 27,000 acres of swampland near Orlando and began to develop Walt Disney World, including the Magic Kingdom and EPCOT Center. Two years later, Florida's legislature created Disney's own private government, the Reedy Creek Improvement District, which enjoys full powers of taxation, borrowing, servicing, and regulation. Disney's intention was to control the pace and type of development surrounding its main facilities, something the company had been unable to do with its 250-acre Disneyland in Anaheim, California.

Disney continued to expand, building a motion picture and television theme park and studios (together with MGM), a wild animal park, many distinctive resort hotels designed by well-known architects such as Michael Graves and Robert A.M. Stern, a themed shopping district called Downtown Disney, office buildings, recreation facilities, and the whole new communities of Lake Buena Vista and Celebration. For a time, Disney was heavily involved in residential development throughout Florida, acquiring the Arvida Company, a major land development and homebuilding firm now owned by the St. Joe Company. The result of Walt Disney's choice of a sleepy spot in central Florida is that Orlando today draws about 55 million visitors annually—the most of any U.S. city.

EDGE CITIES

The heavy investment in large-scale development at the periphery of established central cities led to

The Waterway Square entertainment and commercial district in the Woodlands, completed nearly 40 years after the HUD-supported planned new community was launched.

TED WASHINGTON VISUAL COMMUNICATIONS

a new phenomenon in the 1970s and 1980s—the growth of suburban nodes of development sometimes called "edge cities," a term coined by journalist Joel Garreau and explained in his book *Edge City: Life on the New Frontier*.[23] These concentrations of regional shopping malls, office and industrial parks with enormous quantities of space, major highway interchanges, and low- to medium-density housing create a prime activity area away from the traditional central-city downtowns—sometimes even eclipsing them in terms of growth and employment. Some of these suburban mixed-use edge cities have grown around a large suburban shopping center, such as Tysons Corner Mall in northern Virginia or Woodfield Mall in Schaumburg, Illinois. In other cases, a highway such as Route 1 in the vicinity of Princeton, New Jersey, or I-285 north of Atlanta has been the focal point. The world's center of innovation, Silicon Valley, is an edge city that began as a suburban office park with ties to Stanford University.[24] Nearly every major metropolitan region now has multiple edge cities that compete with their downtowns for corporate headquarters, industrial development, and other commercial activity.

Today, edge cities can be found in most developed countries around the world. Some examples are Rivas-Vaciamadrid, about 12 miles southeast of Madrid, Spain; Bundang-Gu, about 20 miles north of Seoul, Korea; and the Bole District around Bole International Airport in Addis Ababa, Ethiopia.

THE CYCLICAL NATURE OF REAL ESTATE

Real estate development has always been a cyclical industry, with fluctuations precipitated by a wide variety of factors. A boom in the late 1960s and early 1970s fueled by strong economic growth, military spending, and modest inflation heralded a bust from 1973 to 1975 that was induced by quadrupled oil prices, double-digit inflation, and a severe economic recession. A boom in the late 1970s stimulated by the entry of the baby boom generation into housing and job markets gave way to a crash in the early 1980s caused by extremely high interest rates and a contraction in financing, combined with high

unemployment. In the mid-1980s, money flowed freely again, job growth was strong, and real estate development took off on a speculative binge that by 1990 was squeezed by extraordinarily high vacancies; large unsold inventories; falling prices, rents, and yields; and defaults, foreclosures, and bankruptcies. Yet, by 1993, relatively low mortgage interest rates and rising job growth led to a new boom in residential construction and sales. In 1994, single-family construction starts reached 1.2 million homes, the highest total in nearly two decades, and the national homeownership rate reached a new all-time high of 65.7 percent. It continued to rise each year thereafter, reaching 68.6 percent in early 2005.[25] And then, in 2007, the worst global recession since the Great Depression hit, wiping out the previous round of gains.

Boom and Bust

Beginning in the mid-1970s, the Southwest boomed while the Northeast stagnated, both affected by the dramatic rise in energy prices. In the 1980s, energy prices fell and the fortunes of the Southwest sank while those of the Northeast rose again. The relative fortunes of real estate also differed cyclically by product type. During the late 1980s, when office buildings and hotels were overbuilt in most markets, many developers turned to apartment buildings and warehouses. By 2004, downtown office buildings and luxury hotels had once again become "hot" properties, only to decline again during the Great Recession.

Residential development was affected by a number of factors, including the transition of the massive postwar baby boom to adulthood, the shift in population from the Rust Belt to the Sun Belt, the increase in single-person households, and the rise in the numbers and wealth of senior citizens. Beginning in the 1970s, condominiums as a form of individual apartment ownership became a significant portion of new and converted multifamily housing.

On the East and West coasts, housing sales and prices rose and fell in successive waves of speculative frenzy followed by recessionary panic. The easy availability of low-cost, fixed-interest mortgages at a time of rapidly rising interest rates in the late 1970s, for example, helped finance and encourage the boom in homeownership. It also led to the near insolvency of S&L institutions. Under deregulation, thrifts began to compete for funds from 1980 to 1982 by paying interest on deposits that was often higher than the interest they received on their mortgage loan portfolios. The S&Ls were borrowing short term and lending long term—a very risky proposition. This disaster of deregulation was followed by another in 1982, when S&Ls were permitted to move away from home mortgage lending and into commercial real estate markets, to engage in equity deals, to purchase "*junk bonds*," and to get involved in many high-risk ventures while bearing no risk of failure to depositors, because deposit accounts were federally insured.

A combination of factors, especially the real estate recession of the late 1980s, led to widespread bankruptcy among S&Ls. Consequently, in 1989, the government began taking over much of the thrift industry. The federal Resolution Trust Corporation, created to handle the S&L crisis, became the owner of real property worth billions of dollars. Indeed, it became a major force in the future fortunes of the real estate industry as it sold off property amassed from failed S&L holdings, often for pennies on the dollar.

The collapse of many thrifts, the difficulties experienced by a large number of commercial banks, and tighter federal regulations on real estate lending meant that, in the early 1990s, developers faced considerable challenges in financing new projects. The mood of lenders had reversed to one of cautious, selective practices, especially for commercial development—only to reverse again a few years later.

Although the decline of the thrifts left a temporary vacuum for financing new commercial development, it had little impact on financing home purchases because of the growth in securitization and mortgage banking and the expansion of the secondary mortgage market. Through the large government-backed agencies such as Fannie Mae, Freddie Mac, and Ginnie Mae, and a host of private

securities firms, mortgage companies have been able to draw capital from a wide range of institutional investors.

Since the 1970s, pension funds, life insurance companies, private investment funds, and other institutional investors also began playing a much greater role as lenders, purchasers, and joint venture partners for development and financing. Real estate investment funds have grown into an industry in which financial advisers play a prominent role in property development and management.

Another change since the 1970s was the increasing involvement of large corporations in real estate. Previously, industrial and commercial firms had ignored the profit potential of the land and buildings they owned and used. Beginning in the 1960s, however, many resource-based companies that

Via Verde, an innovative mixed-income community, was developed by the Jonathan Rose Companies in partnership with Phipps Houses, a nonprofit developer of affordable housing. (See http://uli.org/case-study/uli-case-studies-via-verde.)

DAVID SUNDBERG

owned surplus land, such as the railroad, forestry, oil, mining, and agricultural giants, entered the real estate business to develop everything from rural recreational subdivisions to urban mixed-use complexes. The federal government also encouraged corporate entry into the high-volume production of housing through HUD's Operation Breakthrough.

The growing presence of large institutions in real estate was matched by the growing size of many development firms. As early as the 1960s, large national developers emerged in the homebuilding field, including Kaufman & Broad (now called KB Home), Centex, and Ryan Homes. Similarly, shopping center developers such as Edward DeBartolo, Melvin Simon, Alfred Taubman, and James Rouse went national. In the 1970s and 1980s, they were joined by nationwide office developers such as Trammell Crow, Gerald Hines, and Tishman Speyer, along with major life insurance companies such as Prudential, Equitable and several large Canadian development firms, including Olympia & York, Cadillac Fairview, and TrizecHahn. The entry of the Canadians into the U.S. development market signaled a trend toward international development, as many North American developers looked to Europe for new projects and prospects beginning in the 1990s—and even more aggressively in the first decade of the 21st century. During the Great Recession, when U.S. markets were depressed, Asia also became a draw for American investors in search of stronger markets.

The Great Recession

Real estate plays a significant role in the U.S. economy. It can help create prosperity, but it can also trigger economic collapse. The Great Recession officially lasted for about 18 months, but it continued to affect worldwide economies—and, of course, real estate—for years. On October 9, 2007, the stock market reached an all-time high, with the Dow Jones at 14,164. Unemployment was at 4.7 percent. But by December, the U.S. economy was in recession and over the next months, things got far worse—ultimately spurring worldwide recession. The stock market finally hit bottom on March 9,

2009, having lost more than half of its peak value, with the Dow reaching a 12-year low of 6,547. By October of 2009, unemployment had climbed to 10 percent. Overall real estate values had declined by an estimated 40 percent from the 2007 peak.[26] Florida and Nevada, the two boom states of the preceding era, were the hardest hit, but nearly every state suffered. The recession affected countries around the world.

There is general agreement that the Great Recession was caused by a housing bubble collapse, along with decades of financial deregulation that allowed unsustainable lending practices. In January 2011, the federal government issued a report by the Financial Crisis Inquiry Commission (FCIC), which was tasked to learn what caused the crisis. The report states[27]:

> While the vulnerabilities that created the potential for crisis were years in the making, it was the collapse of the housing bubble—fueled by low interest rates, easy and available credit, scant regulation, and toxic mortgages—that was the spark that ignited a string of events, which led to a full-blown crisis in the fall of 2008.

By June 2009, 18 months after it began, the Great Recession was officially over, but the damage would be felt for years. In 2011, it was estimated that about 4 million households had lost homes to foreclosure, with another 4.6 million at risk. Nearly $11 trillion in household wealth—in the form of housing equity, retirement accounts, and life savings—had vanished. The FCIC report notes, "The collateral damage of this crisis has been real people and real communities. The impacts of this crisis are likely to be felt for a generation."[28]

The FCIC concluded that the crisis was preventable and held both private and public sector players responsible. On the private side, residential overbuilding was supported by a proliferation of risky subprime mortgages, predatory lending practices, and outright fraud. Borrowers were sold mortgages they could not afford, with little documentation or equity required. When housing prices fell, sometimes tied to ballooning mortgage payments, borrowers—who in many cases had no equity—defaulted in large numbers, and the system unraveled.

On the public side, a history of deregulation and reliance on the financial industry policing itself had eliminated meaningful safeguards that may have helped to avoid the crisis. In some cases, regulators failed to use the tools they did have.

Fannie Mae and Freddie Mac, the two government-sponsored enterprises, played a role in the financial crisis, and there has been some debate about the degree of their responsibility. They had been allowed to operate with minimal oversight and took risks that ultimately led to huge immediate losses and federal conservatorship; they had become too big to be allowed to fail. Eventually, they recouped their losses and rebounded to profitability, repaying their debt to the federal government.

Another factor was inaccurate credit ratings. As lenders issued more than $3 trillion in mortgages to unqualified homebuyers, rating agencies—such as Moody's—continued to rate these lenders as AAA. Rating agencies were paid by the very investment banks that benefited from the ratings, a conflict of interest that made objectivity unlikely.

Critics of the Community Reinvestment Act believe that federal affordable housing policies were a key factor in the subprime mortgage failure, but others, including the FCIC, argue that many of the delinquent lenders were not subject to CRA regulations and that CRA-regulated loans were half as likely to default as similar loans made by independent mortgage lenders not subject to the law.

PLANNING MOVEMENTS

Up to the mid-20th century, planning was a technical process. The land use plan was a product of "urban activity systems and a carefully studied estimate of future land requirements for expansion and renewal…recognizing local objectives and generally accepted principles of health, safety, convenience, economy, and the general amenities of urban living."[29] By the 1960s, the decision-making process was coming under attack, partly as a result of the displacement effects of urban renewal and

the interstate highway programs, but also because of the rising environmental movement and changing attitudes toward sprawl. The reaction was a shift in focus from the physical product of planning to the process itself. "Advocacy planning" was the result. Described in 1962 by Paul Davidoff and Thomas Reiner,[30] advocacy planning sought to give a voice in public decision making to those—especially minorities—who had no voice in the planning process.

The conflicts between planning by technical specialists and planning by advocacy groups were difficult to reconcile. Among the issues:

- Who is allowed to participate in the decision-making process, and to what degree?
- Who holds the ultimate responsibility for determining policy?
- What are the roles of the professional planner and the elected decision makers?

Different models of public participation emerged, each with varying degrees of interaction between advocates and professional planners. By the 1980s, though, public participation had become an essential element of the planning process.

Public Interests

One growing interest has been a concern for the effects of real estate development on the natural and human environment. The 1969 National Environmental Policy Act and its state equivalents led to public regulators' and legislators' use of environmental impact reviews to decide whether proposed development projects should be approved. The 1966 National Historic Preservation Act helped focus attention on conserving structures rather than permitting their demolition to make way for new developments. These and other new laws and practices—growth controls, sewer moratoriums, impact fees, linkage payments—all slowed the approval process and added to the costs of development.

In the 1950s and 1960s, California was considered a developer's paradise for obtaining public infrastructure and services along with fast and favorable regulations. But beginning in the 1970s, it became an embattled and difficult state in which to build new projects, with active protests by citizens, strict time-consuming regulatory processes, and costly taxes and fees. This change in the political scene helped reduce overbuilding, but it also contributed greatly to the rapid escalation of housing prices. Much of the California experience was repeated in the Northeast during the housing boom of the mid-1980s. In some cases, developers joined the ranks of civil rights and affordable housing activists to attack exclusionary zoning and other related practices. The New Jersey State Supreme Court's *Mount Laurel* decisions (1975 and 1983) mandated regional "fair share" housing; Massachusetts's statewide "antisnob" zoning law attempted to deal with the exclusionary practices of many suburban towns. Public and private organizations, including the NAHB, HUD, and ULI have searched for solutions to housing affordability through regulatory reform.

Smart Growth

Since the 1970s, government at all levels has attempted to trim its expenditures for infrastructure and services. The long-running tax revolt that began in the 1970s led to reduced maintenance and the replacement or expansion of key facilities. In the context of overburdened infrastructure, new development often appeared to exacerbate traffic congestion, air and water pollution, school crowding, and other undesirable outcomes without generating sufficient tax revenues to finance needed improvements. Developers found themselves increasingly involved in public relations campaigns and public policy initiatives to build support for proposed projects. The need to resolve the conflicts between development and environment led to the "smart growth" movement.

Smart growth is a set of principles that aims to balance the need for new development with protection of the environment. Community-centered processes are essential elements of smart growth. Smart growth recognized that growth is inevitable but should be directed in ways that curb sprawl by reinvesting in already-developed areas, increasing urban densities, and preserving agricultural land, recreational land, and open space. Many states and localities have embraced smart growth concepts.

Smart Growth America, a coalition of public, private, and nonprofit groups, was founded in 2003 to advocate for more sustainable growth practices. Sustainable development, the next iteration of smart growth, is defined as development that meets "the needs of the present without compromising the ability of future generations to meet their own needs."[31] The emphasis is on the following:

- Minimizing the consumption of land through compact development,
- Reducing consumption of energy and nonrenewables,
- Using existing resources, such as infrastructure and historic structures,
- Enhancing the sense of place, and
- Increasing access to jobs, affordable housing, and transportation choices.

Related to smart growth and sustainable development is the green building movement, which grew out of similar environmental concerns beginning in the 1970s. Green building uses resource-efficient materials and building techniques. Some of the greenest buildings require no heating, ventilating, and air-conditioning (HVAC) systems. In 2001, the U.S. Green Building Council created a rating system called LEED (Leadership in Energy & Environmental Design). Increasingly, office tenants demand green buildings to mitigate rising utility costs and for the public relations value of occupying environmentally correct space. Office building owners find that LEED certification is becoming critical if their buildings are to be competitive.[32]

The Green Building Finance Consortium is a research and education initiative that focuses on sustainability from a financial perspective. Founded in 2006 by Scott Muldavin, an internationally known leader in sustainable property finance, investment, and valuation, the organization provides resources to advance sound decision making in this area. (see www.greenbuildingfc.com).

Successful green projects come in all sizes and shapes—from single-family houses to office skyscrapers. One of the earliest green buildings, the Johnson Diversey global headquarters in Sturtevant, Wisconsin, was built in the late 1990s before many current technologies and products became available. With a tight building envelope, a heat-recovery system, efficient mechanical systems, and energy management systems, it is estimated to use 60 percent less energy than the average for a comparable office building.

SUMMARY

In the period since World War II, real estate development has become a much more sophisticated and professional endeavor. Developers have increasingly specialized in different product types but have also created mixed-use developments that take advantage of synergies created among the various uses. Development companies have consolidated and grown larger, but small niche companies remain an important part of the industry. Some larger developers have established an international presence, with offices in cities across the globe.

Concern for the entire community as well as the environment has spawned multiple advances in both planning concepts and land use regulation.

TERMS

- Civil Rights Act of 1964
- Community development corporation (CDC)
- Community Reinvestment Act (CRA)
- Department of Veterans Affairs
- GI Bill
- Greenlining
- Industrial parks
- Junk bonds
- Model Cities Program of 1966
- National Housing Act of 1968
- Neighborhood Reinvestment Corporation
- New Communities
- New urbanism
- Powers of eminent domain
- Redlining
- Title I
- Urban renewal
- VA home loan guarantee program
- Veterans Administration
- Voting Rights Act of 1965
- War on Poverty

REVIEW QUESTIONS

6.1 How and why did homebuilding production methods change after World War II?

6.2 Describe the urban renewal efforts of the 1950s and 1960s.

6.3 How and why did retailing change in the 1950s and 1960s?

6.4 What spurred the urban crisis of the 1960s, and what housing-related programs were initiated because of it?

6.5 What is a CDC, and what is its role in community building?

6.6 What is a new community?

6.7 Real estate is always said to be a cyclical business. What are some of the financial cycles that have occurred since 1970?

NOTES

1 Lyndon Johnson, Commencement address speech at the University of Michigan, Ann Arbor, May 22, 1964, www.lbjlib.utexas.edu/johnson/lbjforkids/gsociety_read.shtm.

2 Rosalyn Baxandall and Elizabeth Ewen. *Picture Windows: How the Suburbs Happened*. (New York: Basic Books, 2000), p. 91.

3 "Housing: Up from the Potato Fields," *Time*, July 3, 1950, p. 67. See also Marc A. Weiss, *The Rise of the Community Builders: The American Real Estate Industry and Urban Land Planning* (New York: Columbia University Press, 1987).

4 Robert A. Caro, *The Power Broker: Robert Moses and the Fall of New York* (New York: Random House, 1974), pp. 850–894.

5 "Northland: A New Yardstick for Shopping Center Planning," *Architectural Forum*, June 1954, pp. 102–119. See also Howard Gillette, Jr., "The Evolution of the Planned Shopping Center in Suburb and City," *Journal of the American Planning Association*, Autumn 1985, pp. 449–460.

6 Kenneth T. Jackson, *Crabgrass Frontier: The Suburbanization of the United States* (New York: Oxford University Press, 1985), p. 254.

7 Marc A. Weiss, "The Origins and Legacy of Urban Renewal," in *Federal Housing Policy and Programs: Past and Present*, ed. J. Paul Mitchell (New Brunswick, N.J.: Rutgers University Center for Urban Policy Research, 1985), pp. 253–276; and Ann R. Markusen, Annalee Saxenian, and Marc A. Weiss, "Who Benefits from Intergovernmental Transfers?" *Publius: The Journal of Federalism*, Winter 1981, pp. 5–35.

8 Daniel Seligman, "The Enduring Slums," in *The Exploding Metropolis* (Garden City, N.Y.: Doubleday, 1957), p. 132.

9 Marc A. Weiss, "Community Development," *Private Finance and Economic Development: City and Regional Investment* (Paris: Organization for Economic Cooperation and Development, 2003), pp. 55–73.

10 Real Estate Research Corporation, *Tall Office Buildings in the United States* (Washington, D.C.: ULI–the Urban Land Institute, 1985).

11 Joel Kotkin, "American Cities May Have Hit 'Peak Office,'" Forbes.com, www.forbes.com/sites/joelkotkin/2013/11/05/american-cities-may-have-hit-peak-office/.

12 Jones Lang LaSalle Research, *Construction Outlook, United States, Fall 2013*, 2013, p. 16.

13 Eric Darton, *Divided We Stand: A Biography of the World Trade Center* (New York: Basic Books, 2011), p. 204.

14 Richard M. Rosan, "Celebrating America's Cities," *Urban Land*, October 2001, p. 99.

15 "He Digs Downtown: For Master Planner James Rouse, Urban Life Is a Festival," *Time*, August 24, 1981, pp. 42–53.

16 Amy Crawford, "The Future of Urban Freeways is Playing Out Right Now in Syracuse," *CityLab*, February 18, 2014, www.theatlanticcities.com/commute/2014/02/future-urban-freeways-playing-out-right-now-syracuse/8419/.

17 U.S. Census, State and County QuickFacts, Detroit, Michigan. http://quickfacts.census.gov/qfd/states/26/2622000.html.

18 Allison Plyer, "Facts for Features; Katrina Recovery," *The Data Center*, August 28, 2014, www.gnocdc.org/Factsforfeatures/HurricaneKatrinaRecovery/index.html.

19 Adrienne Schmitz and Lloyd W. Bookout, *Trends and Innovations in Master-Planned Communities* (Washington, D.C.: ULI–the Urban Land Institute, 1998). p. vi.

20 www.columbiamd.com.

21 www.cityofirvine.org/about/demographics.asp.

22 Robert Steuteville, "The Elements of a (Neo) Traditional Neighborhood," *New Urban News*, July/August 1996, p. 2.

23 Joel Garreau. *Edge City: Life on the New Frontier* (New York: Doubleday, 1991).

24 www.paloaltohistory.com/stanford-research-park.php.

25 U.S. Census Bureau, "Residential Vacancies and Homeownership in the Fourth Quarter," news release, January 31, 2014. www.census.gov/housing/hvs/files/qtr413/q413press.pdf.

26 The Urban Land Institute and PricewaterhouseCoopers LLP, *Emerging Trends in Real Estate® 2010* (Washington, D.C.), p.1.

27 Financial Crisis Inquiry Commission, *The Financial Crisis Inquiry Report*, Washington, D.C., February 25, 2011, p. xiv, www.gpo.gov/fdsys/pkg/GPO-FCIC/pdf/GPO-FCIC.pdf.

28 Ibid., p. xvi.

29 Stuart Chapin, *Land Use Planning* (Urbana: University of Illinois Press, 1965) p. 355.

30 Paul Davidoff and Thomas Reiner, "A Choice Theory of Planning," *JAPA*, volume 28, issue 2, 1962.

31 www.iisd.org/sd/.

32 The Urban Land Institute and PricewaterhouseCoopers LLP, *Emerging Trends in Real Estate® 2009* (Washington, D.C.) p. 10.

PART 3

The Public Interest

Chapters 4 through 6 gave the reader background on how the practice of real estate has evolved since colonial days. Part III begins to lay the groundwork for today's practice of real estate development, beginning with the public's role in the development process. Few, if any, real estate projects can be developed without the involvement of the public sector. The right to use and develop property is created and governed by laws. Those laws establish the land uses allowed to an owner and they regulate the impact those uses may have on the community.

Real estate development involves the public sector in two ways. Most development plans require approval from a public decision-making body. Development also requires conformance with local, state, and federal land use regulations. Because the developer initiates the development process, it is up to him to align private and public interests in a relationship that will lead to a successful project. Without this alignment, approvals are not likely to be granted and there will be no project.

Real estate development is sometimes mistakenly perceived as a purely private sector enterprise. In this view, the developer exercises private property rights, obtains capital from a private financial system, and executes a project according to a set of private contracts. Yet public interests touch nearly every aspect of the development process and shape every project from feasibility through execution. Successful real estate development thus lies at the intersection of private and public interests.

The public sector plays multiple roles: It may be a collaborator that brings resources to the project. It may be a regulator that ensures the project conforms with complex regulations. It may be a facilitator that balances the interests of the developer and the community. And it sometimes may be an adversary that tests the limits of property rights through the judicial system. Those involved in protecting the public interest include government regulators who grant approvals according to their interpretation of laws, elected government officials who have the power to grant discretionary approvals for a project, and a broad range of nongovernment stakeholders who may have direct or indirect interests in how the development process is executed.

The responsibility for addressing the public sector rests with the developer, who starts the process by proposing the project. If he fails to reach out to stakeholders and tries to impose a project on the community behind the shield of property rights, the risk of failure is substantially heightened.

The relationships among stakeholders are not static. The positions of the developer, the public, and the landowner are continually refined and redefined, sometimes within the development period. This refinement and redefinition occurs in two arenas: the regulatory and the political.

Chapter 7 explores the regulatory environment through which the public sector controls and mitigates the external effects of a development project. Chapter 8 addresses the more fluid aspects of understanding the needs of other stakeholders and obtaining their necessary support to achieve project approvals. It discusses all of the components of the process. For a given project, only a select subset may apply. Still, an overview of the spectrum of land use rules provides good background for all developers, as the spirit of certain legislation may apply even when the specific rules are not articulated in a given locality.

Chapter 7

The Role of the Regulatory Sector

"This land is your land, this land is my land."
—*Woody Guthrie*

The scenario is well established. In the public hearing, a developer stands behind the podium to address staff comments on his project. A group of homeowners sits in the first row, holding small potted plants and ready to testify that the proposed building will cast shadows over their backyard gardens. The third-generation landowner sits in the rear, awaiting an outcome that will determine if his property is worth $5 million or $500,000.

These participants represent three often conflicting positions in the development process: private enterprise, public interests, and property rights. Each participant fervently believes in the legitimacy of his position, often to the exclusion of the other two. The participants, including the developer, are *stakeholders*. The private sector is represented by the developer and landowner who seek to exercise their property rights. The public sector is represented by government agencies, citizen groups, and other non-government stakeholders who seek to express their interests through representative democracy.[1]

THE ALLOCATION OF POWER

The public and private sectors each have limited rights in the real estate development arena. The rights of a real estate developer are controlled by a system of land use regulations and discretionary approvals necessary to build a project. The rights of the public sector are constrained by a system of private property rights. The allocation of power between the two sectors changes continually as new regulations are enacted, challenged by property rights interests, and tested in the judicial system.

Land use regulations, which are enacted at all levels of government, establish the legal framework within which changes to the built environment may occur. The regulations are administered by professional staff employed by government to execute the decisions made by elected officials.

All projects require public sector approvals at some point in the development process. Approvals may be "by right" or "discretionary" or some combination:

- By right approvals are for developments that are consistent with the rules and regulations. These can be approved without further action.

■ Discretionary approvals are granted when developments that comply with rules and regulations still may require approval by elected officials. Before a discretionary approval is granted, public sector staff evaluate the project within the context of the regulatory framework to enable elected officials to make an informed decision.

■ Some development proposals may not be consistent with rules and regulations and thus require discretionary approvals from elected officials to change, amend, or grant a variance from rules and regulations. Such projects often have a higher profile and, by their nature, involve more stakeholders. For such projects, it can take extended periods of time to obtain approvals.

PROPERTY RIGHTS AND ENTITLEMENTS

A landowner on the coast incurred significant expenses to advance her development vision: a marina with a breakwater constructed from boulders blasted from the mountains behind the shoreline; the level land created would be used for custom home sites and a destination resort. The vision conflicted with many layers of land use regulation, beginning with the local general plan, the state's coastal legislation, and the federal Clean Water Act. To promote the project, the landowner had to seek extensive exemptions from the rules. To her, the plan seemed reasonable: it was her land.

The coastal landowner misunderstood property rights as absolute freedom of a landowner to benefit from the unencumbered economic use of her property. The freedom is not absolute, however; every property has an impact on the surrounding community. Those impacts may be externalities that affect the community at large, such as additional traffic. They may be environmental consequences to the property, such as damage to wetlands or animal habitats.

Property ownership is a collection of rights to the economic use of land, and those rights are limited. Ownership is sometimes expressed as "a bundle of rights" which set the parameters within which a developer may operate." These rights may be enhanced

or diminished through the development approval process. The developer must understand these rights because they determine what can be built, how intensively the site may be used, and how much the effort will cost.

The rights to use and to develop property are commonly referred to as *entitlements*. They include approvals, granted by all levels of government, necessary for the development of the project. Entitlements are the subject of land use law, a set of rules that enable all participants to understand their rights in the development process and the consequences of a proposed project. The ability of a developer to calculate such consequences is critical. Without a thorough understanding of the project's legal framework, the developer cannot make informed decisions about the amount of resources to spend on promoting a project or about the amount of risk exposure to take on.

At the local and regional levels, entitlements address land use, environmental concerns, and design issues through general plans, specific plans, zoning, conditions of approval, and other regulations. At the state and federal levels, entitlements address environmental issues though the Clean Water Act; the Endangered Species Act; the Clean Air Act; the Comprehensive Environmental Response, Compensation, and Liability Act (CERCLA); and corresponding state laws. Many jurisdictions impose additional layers of regulations, depending on the location and nature of the property.

Entitlements originated as part of the *police power* of state governments to protect public health and safety, and the general welfare of citizens. Most states enacted enabling legislation in the 1920s and 1930s to give local governments the power to regulate real estate for these purposes. One of the first forms of land use regulations was the *zoning ordinance*. Courts have upheld the rights of local governments to create zoning regulations. Two early Supreme Court challenges, *Welch v. Swasey* (1909) and *Hadacheck v. Sebastian* (1915), established the right of local governments to regulate development. The former established the right of a city to regulate building heights, and the latter upheld the right of a city to prohibit a manufacturing use.

One of the best-known cases supporting zoning and police power was *Euclid v. Ambler Realty* (1926). A property owner, Ambler Realty, contested the right of the city of Euclid, Ohio, to establish land use and height and setback requirements for its land, asserting that such zoning restrictions reduced the economic value of the property. The Supreme Court held that "the constantly increasing density of our urban populations make it necessary for the state to limit individual activities to a greater extent than formerly."[2] The Court's reasoning was based on the impact of the proposed land use on the greater community. *Ambler* addressed two themes of contemporary land use regulation: the "increasing density of …urban populations" and the impacts of a proposed land use on the community, both necessitating greater regulation of land use.

Zoning alone did not address all of the issues arising from rapid urban growth. It controlled the use of a specific parcel, but it did not solve the long-term land use and *infrastructure* needs of a large urban area. A broader concept, the *comprehensive plan*, was required to address these concerns. In 1928, the federal Standard City Planning Enabling Act was passed; eventually it was adopted by virtually every state. It set forth the "principal duty of the city planning commission as the preparation, adoption, and maintenance of a long-range, comprehensive, general plan for the physical development of a city."[3] The model statute "encouraged states to empower cities, towns, and counties to prepare comprehensive plans."[4] It was to be a "proposal for the future use of land and the structures built on the land,"[5] and the official statement of policies concerning future development. It was intended that the document "include a single, unified general physical design for the community and … attempt to clarify the relationships between physical development policies and social and economic goals."[6]

By the 1960s, the impacts of urban growth extended beyond municipal borders. Air and water pollution spread across political boundaries, and the effects were felt far beyond the points of origin.

Atlantic Wharf, located on Boston's waterfront, is a 2.18-acre redevelopment that includes nearly 800,000 square feet of office space, 25,000 square feet of retail space, and 86 residential units. Completed in 2011, the project went through a complex entitlement process that included numerous federal, state, and local reviews. The state Department of Environmental Protection required the developer to maintain public access to the waterfront as well as provide public spaces and associated programming.

Unplanned growth, or "sprawl," affected critical natural resources and habitat. Public awareness of the negative side of growth and development was heightened by influential books such as Rachael Carson's *Silent Spring* (1962), Jane Jacobs's *The Death and Life of Great American Cities* (1961), and Peter Blake's *God's Own Junkyard* (1964).

The response was the enactment of the environmental laws of the 1970s, which moved many land use decisions away from local governments into the federal arena. Local general plans and zoning laws were overlaid with regulations controlling endangered species and water and air quality. Some states and local jurisdictions enacted additional environmental regulations, called growth management plans, and created regional land use authorities to better regulate multijurisdictional areas. The promulgation of land use regulation increasingly restricted the rights of a landowner to benefit from unrestrained economic use of his property. The range and intensity of allowable uses became increasingly narrow under a matrix of federal, state, regional, and local laws. By the 1990s, such limits to the regulation of property rights began to be tested. Those limits were asserted through interpretation of the Fifth Amendment, which affirms the power of government to take private property over the owner's objection but only on the payment of "just compensation." Several Supreme Court cases began to define the line between regulations and takings, among them *Nollan v. California Coastal Commission* (1987), *First English Evangelical Lutheran Church of Glendale v. the County of Los Angeles* (1987), and *Dolan v. City of Tigard* (1994).

A 2005 Supreme Court case, *Kelo v. City of New London*, set a new standard for the use of eminent domain and transfer of land from one private owner to another for the purpose of economic development. The city of New London, Connecticut, condemned privately owned property for use in a project that was part of a comprehensive economic redevelopment plan. The benefits that a community enjoys from economic development qualified as a permissible public use under the Fifth Amendment. Property rights activists and others have criticized the decision as a violation of individual rights in favor of broader community economic development goals. Adverse public reaction to this court decision has resulted, in a number of states, in the adoption of restrictions on the use of eminent domain with the express purpose of sharply limiting the legal authority that the Supreme Court decision otherwise confirmed.

LOCAL AND STATE-MANDATED REGULATION

A landowner and developer open discussions. The market would support the development. The financial feasibility seems to work. However, in walking the site, the developer sees an area that looks suspiciously like a wetland that could be habitat for endangered or threatened species. Gaining approval to develop that part of the site could take up to two years and add several hundred thousand dollars to the entitlement costs. The current general plan designates the site commercial, and a general plan amendment would be required for the developer's mixed-use concept. The city has limited experience with mixed-use projects, and the concept might trigger staff requests for additional technical studies over the course of the approval process. A quick assessment leads to the conclusion that this opportunity may require the investment of a significant amount of time and money in due diligence just to assess the regulatory environment. However, all other potential sites in the developer's market have issues: the easy sites are gone, and there is going to be competition for this property. How does the developer make a decision to proceed or drop the opportunity?

From a regulatory perspective, real estate development is a local business. A framework of local, state, and federal regulations establishes general restraints on the use of any development site, but the impact of those regulations must be analyzed specifically for each site. Although the federal Clean Water Act establishes general rules for impacts to U.S. waters, the specific application and impact of those rules depend on the length, width, hydrology, and biology of wetlands on each site. Furthermore, state regulations often supplement the federal rules. At the local level, each jurisdiction has its own process for land use approvals.

The success of a project concept depends on the developer's detailed knowledge of the regulatory environment as it applies to his site. In some states, regulations may be minimal and the establishment of entitlements simply administrative. In others, such as California, the extremely complex entitlement processes can take years to navigate.

Most state and local jurisdictions govern land use through a hierarchy of regulations, ranging from long-term regional plans to specific project-level plans. At the highest level are broad, long-term plans that describe intended land uses but do not establish final development rights. At the lowest level are final development rights that are granted only after a greater level of specificity is set forth in extensive documentation.

General (Comprehensive) Plans

The general or comprehensive plan is a statement of the goals and policies of cities and counties that govern land use for a specified, extended period of time. The planning period can be up to 20 years. It sets the framework for all other local land use regulations. Each section of the general plan expresses a statement of goals and policies supported by statistical tables, maps, and graphics.

The general plan is a political document in that it is prepared and approved by members of an elected body who represent the desires of the community. The plan is usually created by the local government's planning staff, drawing on a body of technical material. It is a public process that entails commentary from other government entities and public testimony from the general public. It often can take years to prepare and adopt.

The general plan usually contains sections that summarize its underlying technical studies, including the following:

- Land use, which addresses the location and relationship of types of land use in the jurisdiction, including residential, retail, office, industrial, open space and recreation, and public facilities. It is based on projections of population, employment, available land, and circulation systems.
- Circulation, which identifies future transportation needs that will support the projected land uses. It may include improvement of

---

Figure 7-1   **Typical Procedures for Development Approval**

The following is the typical process used by many communities for subdivision plan review, rezoning, or comprehensive plan amendments.

Concept Phase			**Application Phase**	
Developer	➤	Identifies site, defines preliminary development concept	Developer ➤ Prepares reports, drawings, plans for application	
	➤	Evaluates feasibility of concept with consultants	Public Staff ➤ Routes application to other agencies	
	➤	May test ideas with citizen groups	➤ Meets with developer to resolve questions, problems	
Preapplication Phase			➤ Initiates official notice of upcoming public hearing(s) to public, adjacent owners	
Developer	➤	Prepares basic descriptions of proposed project, including location, types of uses, general densities, public facilities	Developer ➤ Prepares final plans	
			Public Staff ➤ Prepares final report and recommendations to public officials	
	➤	Meets with public staff to discuss concept, define initial issues, determine appropriate approval procedure	**Public Decision Phase**	
			Public Officials ➤ Conduct one or more public hearings at which developer presents plans (perhaps before multiple agencies)	
Public Staff	➤	Checks conformance of proposal with official plans and regulations	Public Officials, Staff, and Developer ➤ Propose modifications or conditions necessary for approval	
	➤	May test preliminary concept with other agency staff	Public Officials ➤ Approve, approve with conditions, or deny application	

existing facilities as well as construction of new ones. It is supported by traffic engineering models that forecast the origin and destination of trips throughout the planning area. It may also project an assumed distribution of trips between private and public transit.

INNOVATORS   Managing Urban Transformation for Livability and Growth

Just as developers adjust practices to meet the changing growth demands and public attitudes, so must public sector partners. These two public officials are noteworthy for their creativity, tenacity, and skill in moving cities forward.

Harriet Tregoning is an intrepid public service leader who has applied her interests in smart growth policies to comprehensive operational plans at the local, state, and national levels. Appointed as the director of the U.S. Department of Housing and Urban Development's Office of Economic Resilience in 2014, she works with the departments of Agriculture, Energy, and Transportation to bring about the kinds of advances in cities that she accomplished when she was director of the District of Columbia's Office of Planning, from 2007 to 2014. In her tenure there, Tregoning worked to make the District a walkable, bikeable, livable, globally competitive, and sustainable city–rewriting the city's zoning code for the first time in 50 years, planning the revitalization of the poorest part of the city as part of the plan for consolidation of the Department of Homeland Security's headquarters, and collaborating with her transportation colleagues to bring ever more transportation choices to the District, including the nation's largest bike-sharing program, with more than 1,670 bicycles operating from more than 190 stations.

Tregoning cultivated her pragmatic knowledge of development and city planning in previous roles in policy advocacy and implementation. As the director of Development, Community, and Environment at the EPA, she headed projects related to waste policy, which sparked an interest in doing more than just cleaning up spoiled lands. In 1994, she participated in President Clinton's Council on Sustainable Development, through which she became an expert on smart growth and eventually its most ardent advocate.

In 2005, Tregoning directed the Governors' Institute on Community Design. With former Maryland Governor Parris Glendening, she cofounded the Smart Growth Leadership Institute and served as its executive director. Before establishing the Governors' Institute, she served as Maryland's Secretary of Planning and then as the nation's first state-level Cabinet Secretary for Smart Growth.

Tregoning's academic training is in engineering and public policy. She was a Loeb Fellow at the Harvard University Graduate School of Design for 2003–2004.

Amanda M. Burden, as commissioner for the New York City Department of City Planning from 2002 to 2013, made a remarkable contribution to the physical development of the city. She spearheaded the largest planning effort in the city since 1961, initiating comprehensive rezoning plans for 124 neighborhoods—almost 40 percent of the city—and catalyzing the development of significant new housing opportunities in diverse communities throughout the city's five boroughs.

A champion of design excellence, Burden emphasized community consensus-building in helping to improve the city's streetscapes, reclaim the waterfront, and create dynamic public spaces that include the East River Esplanade and the High Line (see chapter 18). Before her city appointment, Burden assisted in the launch and administration of the Midtown Community Court in Times Square, acclaimed as a model of community-based justice in New York City.

"New York is a global city, but most importantly, it's a city of neighborhoods. The essence of good planning is to really understand the constraints and opportunities in each neighborhood, and to build from the characteristic strengths found in each one," Burden explains. "Underlying all our efforts is a focus on the human scale of the city. An overriding goal is to create great places that will keep people in the city—keep them loving what brought them here in the first place. There's an overarching sense of creating a sustainable city—a city that has great diversity, accessibility, and affordability for all its people."

From 1983 to 1990, Burden served as vice president for planning and design at the Battery Park City Authority, developing building design guidelines and supervising the design of the Esplanade and the 30 acres of parkland incorporated in the project. Burden is a 2009 laureate of the ULI J.C. Nichols Prize for Visionaries in Urban Development.

Shortly after the end of her tenure with the city, she joined Bloomberg Associates as principal for urban planning. This philanthropic venture seeks to help city governments improve residents' quality of life. Burden supports the consultancy's work to improve urban environments by collaborating with cities to develop best practices, build consensus, and foster key relationships.

Alison Johnson

- Housing, which projects overall housing needs for the planning area, often with a focus on demand for and supply of workforce housing.
- Resources, which focuses on agricultural, mineral, biological, and other natural elements that may require special measures for protection.
- Recreation and open space, which identifies areas targeted for environmental preservation and parkland.
- Safety, which identifies issues associated with earthquakes, floods, wildfires, and other natural hazards.

These elements are examined in greater detail when specific projects are proposed. Every new project is examined for consistency with each element of the general plan.

Because forecasts are imperfect, amendments to the general plan may be required in order to respond to changes in growth rates, community needs, or the plan's underlying assumptions. Amendments may also be initiated by a developer seeking a land use change that will make possible a proposed project. The process for amendments to the general plan often follows the same technical examination and public hearing process as the creation of the document itself.

Specific Plans and Planned Unit Developments

Many jurisdictions recognize that some situations benefit from greater flexibility than allowed under their current general plan and zoning regulations. The kind of flexibility usually considered includes land use mixes and densities, clustering of land uses to preserve open space, and latitude in the negotiation of land use mitigation measures. The vehicles through which these more flexible entitlements are delivered vary by jurisdiction. They are called specific plans, *planned unit developments*, area plans, precise plans, and other terms that define their place in the hierarchy between specific planning areas and general plans. They may involve one or more property owners, and they may be initiated by a developer

or a government entity. They may designate future specific plan areas within the general plan, or they may be proposed as an amendment to the general plan in response to a project proposal.

Specific plans consist of text, maps, statistical tables, and other graphics that describe the project, the location and setting, the legal authority for the plan, the project's consistency with the general plan, and the mix and location of land uses. It may provide detail on design standards, conditions of approval, phasing, public financing, and steps for implementation and enforcement. The adoption of a specific plan may be supplemented by ordinances that create the corresponding zoning for each of the land use areas.

The specific plan may include several elements:

- A project description, which describes the local setting, the site, proposed land uses, existing regulations, and project goals. The project description is often critical because it is the legal standard by which the specific plan's other development regulations are measured.
- A detailed site-specific discussion of the elements that appear in the general plan. It addresses land use, open space, circulation, infrastructure, and public services.
- Design guidelines, which address architecture and landscape standards.
- Implementation, which discusses phasing, financing, maintenance, and public sector monitoring and oversight of the plan.
- Consistency with the general plan and other regulations.

Conditions of Approval

Beginning with the specific plan and continuing through subsequent steps, jurisdictions may add conditions that developers must satisfy before a project can move forward. These conditions are detailed requirements necessary to ensure that the project is built to the standards of the community and in accordance with the parent document. They may include a diverse range of requirements related to construction standards, bonding, mitigation of project impacts, approval by other agencies, environmental mitigation, completion of infrastructure improvements, or other measures. They may be standard conditions that are attached to every project, such as design specifications for infrastructure improvements. They may also be unique to the specific project and location, setting forth the design standards unique to that development. They may be tied to specific project milestones, such as grading, issuance of building permits, completion of off-site improvements, or other approvals.

Zoning

The zoning ordinance is a local law that addresses the specific conditions under which land may be developed. It consists of a map that establishes land use classifications for each area and text that describes how the land in that area may be used. Typical descriptions for each land use area may include building types, floor areas, floor/area ratios, permitted uses, parcel sizes, height limits, lot coverage allowances, setbacks, densities, and other standards. A jurisdiction's zoning ordinance is usually updated to conform to its general plan. It may be amended to be consistent with the approval of a specific plan or a project that does not require a specific plan. Some projects may be granted variances from certain elements of the zoning code to accommodate uses, heights, setbacks, or other elements deemed appropriate for the development.

Subdivision Maps

A *subdivision* is the partitioning of any unit of land for the purpose of sale, leasing, or financing. Regulations governing subdivisions are intended to ensure that the partitioning is done in accordance with the state's map act and with local ordinances. Subdivisions may be created by *tentative maps* and *final maps*, depending on the jurisdiction. Variations of subdivision maps include condominium maps, common interest developments, financing maps, and parcel maps. The map act also addresses other subdivision actions such as lot line adjustments and lot mergers.

Subdivision maps are usually processed in two steps. The first is a tentative map, which is a discretionary approval reviewed by a planning department and submitted to a public hearing. A tentative map illustrates the proposed legal parcels, including the dimensions and locations of lots, the layout and sizes of streets, the location of utilities, land uses, topography, and other information sufficient to enable the public body to approve or deny the application. A tentative map typically must meet certain requirements: it should be consistent with applicable general and specific plans and zoning; the site should be physically suitable for the proposed development; and the project should be consistent with public health and safety interests. Conditions of approval attached to a tentative map can include dedications for streets, parklands, school sites, and other public facilities; payment of impact fees; execution of reimbursement agreements; final engineering requirements; indemnifications; responsibility for off-site improvements; and environmental mitigation requirements. The second step is the final map, which creates the recorded legal parcels in the subdivision. Approval of the final map usually requires final engineering drawings for grading and infrastructure, together with financial assurance that those improvements will be completed.

Infrastructure

Infrastructure consists of roads, water, sewer drainage, gas, electric, communications, and other systems necessary to support the built environment. Developers are usually responsible for the provision of infrastructure within the project site ("on-site" improvements). Governments have traditionally been responsible for the provision of infrastructure outside the site, infrastructure that may serve a broader area ("off-site" improvements). Off-site infrastructure may involve critical major facilities that must be built before any construction can occur in an area, such as a sewage treatment plant. Off-site improvements also may be comparatively minor, such as the extension of existing sewage lines to a project site.

The BW is an urban infill project located in the Brentwood neighborhood of Los Angeles consisting of 78 apartments and 2,000 square feet of retail space. The project underwent a ten-year entitlement process, beginning with a proposal for a high-rise office building but ultimately scaling back to an eight-story, 80,000-square-foot residential building.

The responsibility for regional off-site infrastructure may lie with city or county governments or special taxing districts. These agencies forecast long-range infrastructure needs that are expressed in their own long-term improvement plans. They provide or arrange for the design, scheduling, financing, and construction of the facilities. They are intended to meet the future needs of many residents and may be funded internally, by bond issues, or by grants from other levels of government.

Many jurisdictions have adopted the position that "growth is expected to pay its own way." Existing residents do not want to generate the financial burden of added population by underwriting the facilities that enable growth. Thus, off-site infrastructure facilities that are required for specific projects are often the developer's responsibility. These facilities can include roads, sanitary and sewer facilities, storm drain facilities, water facilities, parks, and other public facilities deemed necessary to support the project. Where multiple landowners may benefit from these off-site improvements, the developer may reach an agreement wherein she is responsible only for her fair share of the cost. The balance of the cost may be funded by the payment of fees, by reimbursement agreements with other owners, or by various forms of public financing.

In certain situations, the developer may work with local government to create public finance vehicles to provide infrastructure. The forms of these vehicles vary widely. They may be called assessment districts, benefit districts, community facility districts, road and bridge districts, or other names given under the state enabling legislation. In general, these financing vehicles provide for the issuance of bonds to finance the needed facilities. The debt service on the bonds is paid by the future owners of property that will benefit from the infrastructure improvements. The debt service is often added to the real estate tax bill for those property owners.

Exactions

Exactions are financial or other conditions imposed on the developer as a condition of project approval. Most often, they take one of two forms:

- Scheduled fees imposed by city and/or county agencies, school districts, transportation districts, and water districts as a condition of service. The scheduled fees collected by these agencies may go toward funding a variety of purposes. Some monies may be applied to the agency's improvement programs to provide area-wide community facilities. Some also may be applied to reimburse the agency for staff time for processing and inspection. Fees are imposed by the board of the governing agency and applied uniformly to all projects or according to formulae that reflect size, improvement costs, or other indices.

- Mitigation exactions are monetary amounts or in-kind contributions that are applied toward offsetting a project's direct impacts. For example, a project may generate additional traffic, resulting in a requirement for an additional traffic signal. That signal may be constructed by the developer or by the appropriate public agency, depending upon the specific circumstances of the project. Other types of mitigation can include the provision of on-site or off-site environmental resources to replace those that would be affected by the project.

CASE STUDY   The Irvine Tech Center Regulatory Process

The regulatory environment in California is probably the most complex in the country, and the entitlement phase there is one of the highest-risk segments of the real estate development cycle. The layers of local, state, and federal rules change frequently and are subject to different interpretations. Instead of creating certainty, the process and regulations add uncertainty. The risks are compounded when the rules change midstream, as they did for the Irvine Tech Center (ITC).

Greenlaw Partners initiated the entitlement process for the ITC project and had retained consultants to prepare its draft Environmental Impact Report (DEIR). Midway through the process, the city of Irvine became concerned about the level of proposed development activity in the Irvine Business Complex (IBC). The applications were arriving one by one , and changes in land use were being proposed without the context of a master plan. The city wanted new development standards and the opportunity to create an organized, master-planned, mixed-use urban district within the IBC. Thus, the city initiated its IBC Vision Plan, and the ITC was folded into the city's IBC Specific Plan and DEIR. Fortunately for the ITC, the project concept was consistent with the goals of the Vision Plan and the project was relieved of several steps in what would have otherwise been a lengthy process. Originally, the ITC plans had anticipated a general plan amendment, a zone change, a conditional use permit, a park plan, a tentative tract map, and a development agreement, as well as the DEIR. Following adoption of the Vision Plan, the ITC required only a master plan, park plan, and tentative tract map. The important lesson is that Greenlaw conformed its project to the goals of the city.

Even so, the entitlement risks were substantial. The IBC had a system of transferrable development rights (development intensity values, or DIVs), that the project had to obtain before the city would accept the entitlement application. When Greenlaw CEO Wilbur Smith acquired the ITC parcel, he immediately began to acquire DIVs in the market.

Another phase of the entitlement process was a required amendment to the 1965 Declaration of Restrictions (CC&Rs) which prohibited residential uses inside the IBC. This part of the planning process required that the private parties in the surrounding properties had to sign off on the rezoning to residential. This was a private party restriction set in the context of a public process. The CC&Rs required that 65 percent of the property owners in the IBC approve the rezoning of the ITC property. In 2006, Greenlaw hired Munro and Associates to tackle the project of acquiring signatures. Although there was a lull in activity during the recession, by late 2011, well before the sale of the project in 2013, Munro had acquired nearly two-thirds of the signatures. The CC&Rs were set to expire in 2015, thus making way for the approval process to continue without getting the sign-off from the remaining one-third of the property owners. Ultimately the buyer would not require a pursuit of the remaining CC&R sign-off.

Continued on page 141

Although many exactions and fees are specified in development regulations, many jurisdictions negotiate with developers to obtain additional contributions. Public officials and other stakeholders often find that exactions and fees offer an opportunity to request additional fees beyond those for which developers are legally obligated. Debate over the extent to which local governments can demand contributions from developers, and for what purposes, has generated a considerable amount of litigation in state and federal courts. Three constitutional concepts—just compensation, equal protection, and due process—establish limits on the size and scope of exactions. Exactions must be related to a public purpose, they must be applied equally in similar situations, and they must not be imposed arbitrarily or capriciously. Under the police power that allows local governments to regulate land development, exactions must be necessary for protecting health, safety, and public welfare.

A general test is that exactions should bear a *rational nexus* to a development's impacts on local public facilities. A local government may, for example, require a developer to improve a certain road intersection if the developer's project will generate enough traffic to warrant the improvement. The local government cannot, however, legitimately require developers to pay for improvements to distant intersections that will seldom serve traffic generated by the developer's project.

State Environmental Regulation

The specific plan and map required for the various government levels of approval describe a proposed project in terms of its basic components. In many jurisdictions, this description is inadequate for public approval because it does not measure and assess the impact of the proposed project on the community. To address this need, some states have adopted measures that assess the environmental impact of proposed projects, adding a layer of entitlement approvals to the public hearing and approval process. These environmental approvals are similar to but separate from the National Environmental Protection Act (NEPA), which focuses primarily on

federally initiated projects. State-level environmental legislation often extends to private projects.

The intent of the environmental review process is to offer the opportunity for all government agencies and all stakeholders to participate in the decision-making process. The scope of the environmental review includes the identification of all impacts that may affect the community and the measures that can mitigate those impacts.

The topics addressed in an environmental assessment often parallel those covered in the general plan, specific plan, and map documents themselves, but with a greater reliance upon technical studies. These studies typically include the following:

- Land use analysis, which determines the proposed project's consistency with surrounding land uses and the general plan.
- Traffic, analyzing the impact that the project will have on existing streets. It is supported by a technical study, usually a traffic model, which assigns the projected trips to existing street segments and intersections on the basis of agreed-upon trip generation standards for each land use. These project-specific models are based on broader traffic models that forecast the origins and destinations of trips throughout the planning area. The traffic study may also project an assumed distribution of trips between private and public transit. The model then determines the level of service (the efficiency of the segment or intersection) under existing conditions and the level of service if the project were to be built. If the addition of trips attributable to the proposed project causes the segment or intersection to worsen, the project may be required to provide improvements to remedy the situation.
- Impacts from noise, air quality, and greenhouse gases, which are usually derived from the traffic study: the sources of all three are most often a function of vehicular trips, unless the proposed land use itself—such as certain manufacturing uses—is a point source.
- Biology, based on background studies to determine the types of plants and animals that are likely to occur on the site and entails field

surveys to determine their actual presence. The species are usually identified according to one of several classifications of sensitivity, depending on standards set by state and federal environmental agencies. Those classifications include candidates for listing, threatened species, and endangered species. The biology study may also include an analysis of wetlands that fall under state and federal jurisdiction and may require separate permitting.

- Visual impact, or aesthetics, which analyzes current and proposed views of the project from off-site locations.
- Hazards, including the remediation of hazardous materials and the risk of wildfires, flooding, and other natural threats.
- Hydrology and water quality, which studies the additional runoff created by the project and its potential impacts on downstream facilities and resources.
- Public services, including the availability of schools, fire, police, ambulance, and other support necessary to accommodate the project.
- Recreation, including the availability of open space, recreation facilities, and parks to serve the project.
- Resources, which focuses on the agricultural, mineral, and other natural elements that may require special measures for protection.
- Utilities, including the availability of water, sewer, and power services.
- Geology, which identifies natural features such as slopes, soils, faults, landslides, and other site characteristics that may affect the feasibility and safety of the project.
- Cultural resources, based on secondary research and field surveys, which determine the presence of archeological resources on the site.

The impacts identified in the environmental document can be mitigated in a variety of ways:

- Avoidance, which means designing the project in such a way as to avoid any impact on sensitive areas;
- On-site mitigation, which establishes offsets to the impact within the project site, usually at a stipulated ratio (for example, two acres of mitigation for one acre of impact);
- Off-site mitigation, which establishes offsets to impacts to be implemented at a separate site, usually through the acquisition of land or the payment of fees to an existing mitigation bank (an area designated for the preservation of one or more species); and
- Fees, which provide for monies paid to an agency that are designated for the direct or indirect mitigation of project impact.

Other State and Local Agencies

A variety of other state and/or local agencies may be involved in the approval process.

Councils of Governments

Councils of governments are associations of local governments and agencies that address regional issues. Membership is made up of representatives of government bodies within a given area. These councils address issues such as regional and municipal planning, economic development, and transportation planning. They may provide technical assistance to their members and in some cases be responsible for the administration of state and federal programs. Although entitlements are granted by local governments, the plans of councils of government may contain information critical to a project's feasibility. For example, these councils often prepare regional traffic models, for which the assumptions must be consistent with the cities and counties that are represented on the councils.

Special Taxing Districts

Many areas have special taxing districts and entitlement mechanisms to manage the entitlement process. These districts, which may span multiple city or county boundaries, have the power to establish their own regulations and fees. The mission of some is to address infrastructure needs: water, sanitary and sewer, storm drainage, transportation, and school districts are usually limited to the provision of functional services. Other districts address environmental issues. Water quality and air quality districts are concerned with regional impacts that cross municipal boundaries and cannot be regulated locally. Both often have the power to set and negotiate their own fees and mitigation agreements with the developer.

Coastal and Special Focused Commissions

Some states and local governments have established regional special-purpose agencies, such as coastal zones, historic districts, and airport land use commissions to govern land use in sensitive areas. Each type of agency manages an overlay of special restrictions that affect how land in its jurisdiction may be used. Coastal agencies establish allowable land uses within specified distances from bodies of water. Historic districts are concerned with the preservation of existing buildings and the design, scale, and aesthetic character of areas under their jurisdictions. Airport land use commissions establish density restrictions to mitigate noise and limit population within approach areas surrounding their facilities. Special commissions create rules that can affect the feasibility of a project and usually require a separate level of approval.

Other Site-Specific Development Control Mechanisms

The land use controls implemented through the general plan, specific plan, and zoning; environmental approvals; and special district regulation are often inadequate to address all of the issues and impacts in the development process. Accordingly, many jurisdictions have other entitlement mechanisms.

Development Agreements

A developer's right to proceed with development of the project without the risk of changes in the rules is known as a *vested right*. Until a developer has obtained a vested right, the possibility exists that the development regulations could change and preclude the developer from proceeding as planned. The point at which a developer achieves a vested right to develop varies from state to state. In some, a building permit vests the developer's right to proceed with the development for a period of time equal to at least the life of the building permit. However, the issuance of a building permit does not occur until after the investment of considerable time and money. An earlier point of vesting is usually desirable from the developer's perspective.

A development agreement is a contract between a local government entity and a landowner that defines the entitlement obligations of each party with respect to the development of the property. In a typical agreement, the developer receives assurance that the development standards and fees will be fixed as of the date of the agreement for the life of the agreement. In return, the jurisdiction may receive the implementation of mitigation measures, exactions, off-site improvements, and other conditions over and above those required in the ordinary entitlement process.

The development contract confirms the understanding between the developer and jurisdiction regarding two aspects:

- The project's entitlements, fees, exactions, and dedications, for which the project will be responsible; and
- The right of the developer to develop the project in accordance with the jurisdiction's rules, regulations, and official policies as those rules existed on the date of the contract.

Transferable Development Rights

Transferable development rights (TDRs) are a device to move densities or other entitlements from one planning area to another. The planning areas may be located within a larger master plan or may be separated by geography and ownership. In the former situation, the developer is afforded a mechanism to adapt to changing market conditions or to plan a complex site more creatively. In the latter, a developer may purchase the development rights of certain properties within a designated district and transfer the rights to his own district to increase its density. The mechanism may be used to promote certain planning objectives—such as environmental, agricultural, or historic preservation—without resorting to zoning or other mechanisms that may otherwise diminish the values of properties in those areas.

Form-Based Zoning

Form-based zoning is a fine-grained planning mechanism that defines the aesthetic appearance of an area. Its purpose is to create an attractive urban form by stipulating key elements such as the visual relationship of form, mass, color, scale, proportions, and design details. The zoning codes are established through text, diagrams, and maps that define the physical appearance of an area beyond what can be articulated through traditional zoning codes, which establish only heights and setbacks. Unlike traditional zoning, form-based zoning also attempts to facilitate mixed-use as opposed to single-use development (see box).

Transect Zoning

Transect zoning, an outgrowth of the new urbanism discussed in chapter 8, is a system that establishes six areas of increasing density as one moves toward the urban core: rural preserve, rural reserve, edge, general, center, and core. The rural areas are undeveloped, the edge and general areas lower density but with some mixed-use elements, and the center and core areas more urban.

Growth Boundaries

Urban growth boundaries are lines around an urban area that separate areas intended for development from those intended to be preserved in their current use. Their purpose is to curtail sprawl by encouraging higher densities within the boundaries. Areas outside the boundaries are restricted to low densities through the general plan and zoning.

Ballot Box Planning

In some jurisdictions, decisions about urban planning have shifted from being made through representative democracy, by elected officials, to being made through direct democracy, by local voters. Some of the reasons for the shift are discussed in

Form-Based Codes

A product of the new urbanism, form-based zoning is a regulatory system used to control development through the shape of buildings instead of through land use. Form-based codes support a building policy aligned with an area's design principles, rather than a simple "one size fits all" policy. Proponents of this method of zoning see land use as secondary to a development's context. Form-based codes often address building frontage, form, scale, and massing. These regulations cover the relationship between public areas, such as streets and sidewalks, and buildings. Factors that may be incorporated in a form-based system include build-to lines, numbers of floors permitted, size of street blocks, and building orientation. Form-based codes put much less emphasis on division of buildings by type, generally allowing for a mix of uses.

This method of zoning can be employed to encourage the preservation of a historic downtown district or to dictate a desired aesthetic direction of a new community. Form-based codes can be used to encourage architectural continuity by promoting better transition from outer areas to an urban center. A smooth transition can be accomplished with a "transect," which is part of the code that ensures gradual shifts between high- and low-density areas.

Traditional zoning (often called Euclidian Zoning for the town where it began) is based primarily on more abstract building parameters and separation of uses. Considerations such as floor/area ratio, building density, residences per acre, building setbacks, and building height are used to create guidelines, often without a building design component. This primary focus on regulating development on the basis of building density can lead to a wide range of results. Two developments that differ significantly in height or arrangement could still maintain the mandated density. The ambiguous nature of conventional zoning makes it a less predictable way to create a community vision than form-based zoning. Instead, it is more conducive to supporting individual development proposals. Because of its focus on separation of uses, traditional zoning often prohibits the mixed-use environment that is conducive to pedestrian-friendly development, with multiple uses within a short distance.

Form-based codes emphasize aspects of development, such as visual appeal and character of community, that are often difficult to encourage with traditional zoning. It can be used to help integrate new development into the surrounding neighborhoods and support a community vision.

the next chapter, but the genesis is public distrust of elected officials to effectively manage or curtail growth. In these situations, the developer's entitlement risk is significantly increased: instead of working through an established set of regulations with professional staff and an elected body, the approval of a project is subject to the outcome of an election, usually financed by the applicant. Just to reach the stage of an election requires a significant investment of money for feasibility analysis, environmental analysis, and public outreach.

FEDERAL REGULATION

Federal land use regulation is focused on the environmental impacts of development. The landmark federal legislation consists of the Clean Air Act (1970), the Clean Water Act (1972), the Endangered Species Act (1973), and CERCLA (1980). The enforcement of these laws is the responsibility of the Environmental Protection Agency (EPA), the Fish and Wildlife Service, the National Oceanic and Atmospheric Administration (NOAA), and the U.S. Army Corps of Engineers. These agencies are also responsible for promulgating regulations that interpret and update the laws—an ongoing process that balances expansion of regulatory requirements against occasional court tests of taking. In this respect, an important aspect of the environmental laws has been their focus on the acquisition of land necessary to meet the goals of the program.

Knowledge of the scope of federal environmental legislation is critical for the developer's decisions. For example, a developer could spend millions of dollars in the local entitlement process only to find that mitigation for a federally protected species would affect half of the project site. If the developer had a working familiarity with trends in the regulatory community, he would have known that the particular species has a foraging radius of ten miles from its nest, that 95 percent of the nests are on private land, and that regulations governing mitigation requirements were becoming increasingly stringent. These conditions may be sufficient to persuade the developer not to pursue an acquisition opportunity.

Detailed biological knowledge is not required for a developer to recognize an environmental issue; the presence of a certain type of habitat is sufficient to raise concerns. Some habitats require professional analysis, but an informed observer can often recognize their signature features. Vernal pools, for example, are not only habitat for the protected fairy shrimp but also for the California tiger salamander which has a migration range of one mile, which makes many sites undevelopable. This example also illustrates the dynamic nature of federal regulation. The California tiger salamander was listed as endangered when it was designated a separate species from the ordinary tiger salamander. As a result, certain properties in California became almost undevelopable.

The Clean Water Act

A developer is conducting due diligence on a piece of land. Its historic and current use is a meadow used for seasonal grazing. It is periodically irrigated from a manmade channel along one edge. Grading imperfections from decades earlier created minor depressions that hold water for short periods before percolating into the ground. There is no connectivity between these depressions and any larger stream or body of water. The question is whether improvement of the site would be subject to the Clean Water Act. The answer is not self-evident. The developer's technical consultants say the site is not jurisdictional (that is, not subject to the act); the Corps of Engineers says otherwise.

Wetlands, which include bogs, swamps, and marshes, are one of the earth's most productive natural ecosystems. They shelter fish and wildlife, cleanse polluted and silt-laden water, and protect against floods. More than half of North American ducks nest in wetlands in the north central United States and southern Canada, and about two-thirds of U.S. shellfish and commercial sport fisheries rely on coastal marshes for spawning and nursery grounds. In the past, the federal government encouraged the draining, plowing, and planting of wetlands. They were considered nuisances. Developers and farmers alike converted these "worthless" areas into economically productive uses. Since the passage of the Clean Water Act of 1972, however, the situation has changed and wetlands are now valued for their enormous environmental and economic importance. The U.S. Army Corps of Engineers, in consultation with the EPA, is responsible for the enforcement of the Clean Water Act. The scope of that act covers "any work, including construction and dredging, in the nation's navigable waters."

The determination of impacts to the "waters of the United States" is a complex process that includes scientific, legal, and regulatory considerations. The first level of analysis is the definition of "waters," which includes waters used in interstate or foreign commerce; interstate waters including interstate wetlands; waters such as intrastate lakes, rivers, streams (including intermittent streams), mudflats, wetlands, sloughs, wet meadows, playa lakes, or natural ponds; tributaries of waters; and wetlands adjacent to waters. For application in the field, the regulations further define each of these features. For example, "wetlands" includes "areas that are inundated or saturated by surface or ground water at a frequency and duration sufficient to support, and that under normal circumstances do support, a prevalence of vegetation typically adapted for life in saturated soil conditions."[7]

Yet these definitions are not sufficiently refined to enable determination of the extent to which the wetland features may be jurisdictional. The specific site must be analyzed in its scientific context and a more meticulous regulatory context. Three characteristics define wetlands: vegetation, soil, and hydrology. Wetlands may be characterized by thousands of plant and soil types, and hydrology standards measure the presence of water at or above the soil surface for defined time periods. Interpretations of these characteristics in the field may differ.

If a technical analysis determines that potential impacts to a site may fall within the scope of the Clean Water Act, a permit must be obtained prior to the initiation of any form of construction activity. Such permits are issued pursuant to Section 404 of the Clean Water Act; there are two types:

- Nationwide permits are issued for activities that have minimal impacts as defined by then-current regulatory thresholds. The impacts eligible for nationwide permits are outlined in the Corps regulations.

- Individual permits are issued for impacts that exceed the standards for nationwide permits. Their issuance is more complex, involving a process of public notice and, under certain circumstances, public hearings. The evaluation process includes an analysis of less environmentally damaging alternatives and identification of mitigation measures, if it is determined that the impacts will be significant. Under certain circumstances, the Corps may be required to consult with state and federal wildlife agencies regarding any impacts of a proposed project.

The issuance of a permit will be conditioned upon "mitigation," which is intended to offset the impact of the proposed development.

The permitting process is complex for several reasons:

- First is the definition of wetlands. Using the federal definition, land that appears dry may constitute wetlands. For example, federal jurisdiction extends over dry washes in the Southwest, where a two-foot-wide wash that carries water only after a rare rainfall is considered jurisdictional.

- Second is the difficulty of confirming the presence of wetlands. There is no way to obtain judicial review of a determination by the Corps that wetlands or other waters are present, other than by either seeking a permit or defending against an enforcement action that seeks to punish a landowner for developing wetlands without a permit.

- Third is the considerable disagreement about the type of activity that is subject to regulation under Section 404. For instance, building in wetlands clearly qualifies as "fill" under the act. Under current court decisions in some areas, however, certain dredging, agriculture, and irrigation projects may not require a Section 404 permit.

- Fourth, the Corps has drastically limited the type and size of projects eligible for pre-approved permits under the Nationwide

Permit Program. Developers of projects that are not eligible for preapproved permits must obtain an individual permit through a complicated process subject to environmental review under the National Environmental Policy Act. The Corps permitting program is time-consuming and often involves review by several other federal agencies, including the EPA and the Fish and Wildlife Service, and by state agencies, including water quality and coastal zone management boards. Given the growing complexity, cost, and duration of permitting, most developers seek to minimize the time required by designing their projects with reduced impacts so as to qualify for the preapproved permits.

■ Fifth, the Corps usually issues permits on the condition that developers mitigate any adverse impacts on wetlands stemming from their developments. Both the Corps and state regulators generally require developers to compensate for any wetlands lost during development by restoring or creating wetlands nearby. This process is referred to as *wetlands mitigation*.

Mitigation may take several forms: a fee may be paid to compensate for the loss of the wetland feature; purchase of an amount of similar environmentally sensitive acreage in another location may be required ("off-site mitigation"); or an amount of acreage may be required to be preserved within the site ("on-site mitigation"). The amount of mitigation required is usually expressed as a ratio between the feature affected and the preserved acreage (that is, if two acres are affected, "2:1 mitigation" would require the purchase or preservation of four acres).

Mitigation, particularly the creation of wetlands, has been controversial. Wetlands are complex, dynamic ecosystems, and early attempts to create them yielded mixed results. Environmentalists have argued that artificially created wetlands can scarcely be considered adequate substitutes for natural wetlands; however, a number of successes have occurred as biologists have continued to improve wetland creation and maintenance techniques. The Corps has

also gained substantial experience in how to write and enforce permit conditions that ensure successful mitigation and that provide fallback systems and other provisions to protect the environment if the mitigation is not as successful as expected. Even with these improvements, however, federal permitting for projects involving wetlands or other waters of the United States remains very problematic. And many states have adopted wetlands protection laws that are more stringent than the federal laws.

In addition, a project that may discharge dredged or fill material or pollutants into U.S. waters may require a permit from a local Regional Water Quality Control Board or water quality certification under Section 401 of the Clean Water Act. Such a discharge may be the result of activities granted under a Section 404 permit and may extend to other sources of pollutants, such as stormwater runoff.

The Endangered Species Act

The Endangered Species Act protects endangered and threatened plants and animals and their habitats. It is administered by the U.S. Fish and Wildlife Service. Under the act, species may be listed as either endangered, threatened, or a candidate for listing. Endangered means a species is in danger of extinction throughout all or a significant portion of its range. Threatened means a species is likely to become endangered within the foreseeable future. A candidate for listing is a species that is under consideration for endangered or threatened status. All species, subspecies, varieties, and population segments are included under the act.

The protection of habitat has the greatest impact on many real estate development projects. The definition of habitat includes, among other things, the needs of a species for open space, food, water, breeding sites, and lack of disturbance.

A project that has an impact on the habitat of a listed species requires a permit. A developer has two alternatives. The first is avoidance of the sensitive area, which is determined by scientific criteria for each species. If an impact (taking) is unavoidable, a permit may be required under several provisions of the Act. Some of these provisions may involve on-site or off-site mitigation, including the acquisition of suitable sites for preservation or contributions to an approved mitigation bank.

The Clean Air Act

The Clean Air Act regulates air emissions from stationary and mobile sources. It authorizes the EPA to establish national air quality standards to regulate emissions of hazardous air pollutants. A project is subject to the requirements of the act during the construction and operational phases.

The Superfund Act

"Brownfields" are sites that contain a hazardous substance—either in existing structures or in the soil or groundwater. Typically, the source of the substances is prior industrial uses on or near the site. The approach to these sites varies with the type and extent of the hazardous material. Some sites lend themselves to private cleanup and redevelopment; others may be so contaminated that their cleanup is feasible only with government assistance.

Due diligence on any property suspected of containing hazardous materials begins with a Phase I Environmental Site Assessment. The Phase I includes a number of elements:

- An on-site visit to view present conditions and evaluate likely environmental hazards;
- Evaluation of risks from neighboring properties upon the subject property;
- Review of records of land uses surrounding the site;
- Interviews of persons knowledgeable about the property history;
- Searches of public agencies' files;
- Examination of historic aerial photography; and
- Examination of drainage patterns and topography.

Depending on the outcome of Phase I, a Phase II study may be undertaken for on-site soil and water testing. If contamination is present, a remediation program is designed to remove or otherwise neutralize the hazardous material prior to development of the site.

To address sites with significant contamination, Congress enacted CERCLA in 1980. Also known as the "Superfund" law, CERCLA was adopted to provide funding for the cleanup of toxic waste sites and to establish powerful legal tools to enable regulatory agencies to force the responsible party to undertake a cleanup program. Under CERCLA, present owners and certain past owners of land contaminated with hazardous substances can be liable for the entire cost of cleanup, even if the disposal of the material was legal at the time, the owner had nothing to do with the disposal, and the disposal occurred years before passage of CERCLA.

In the early days of the law, its all-inclusive liability scheme caught many developers and lenders off guard. In 1985, for instance, Shore Realty Corporation and its principal stockholder were each held responsible for cleaning up hazardous waste on land only recently purchased, even though the corporation had neither owned the property at the time the wastes were dumped nor caused the release of toxins. The court did not need to rely on the traditional (and often difficult) process of "piercing the corporate veil" to find the stockholder that was liable. Instead, it relied on a principle included in the Superfund legislation to determine that the stockholder had enough of a role in managing the hazardous materials after the corporate acquisition to qualify as an "operator." According to the background summary included in the court's opinion, the cleanup was estimated to cost more than Shore Realty had paid for the property.

In response to such excessive provisions of the Superfund law, the Superfund Amendments and Reauthorization Act of 1986 (SARA) created a defense for so-called "innocent landowners," who did not know and had no reason to know that the property they purchased was contaminated. This defense was expanded in 2002 with the Brownfields Amendments, which were designed to facilitate the acquisition and development of properties believed to be contaminated. These amendments expanded the defense to include three classes of protected land buyers: (1) the innocent purchaser who buys the property without knowledge of the on-site contamination, (2) the contiguous landowner who buys the neighboring property without knowledge that the property has been contaminated by a nearby property, and (3) the bona fide purchaser who buys the land knowing that it is contaminated. Even if a landowner qualifies for one of the defenses under the Brownfields Amendments, the problems of dealing with contaminated property may have only just begun. Contaminated property probably cannot be sold, except at a discount reflecting the cost of cleanup. If a public health threat is associated with

---

CASE STUDY The Irvine Business Complex and Transferable Development Rights

The original Irvine Ranch comprised 98,000 acres in Orange County, California, between Los Angeles and San Diego. In the 1960s, recognizing the magnitude of southern California growth, the Irvine Company retained architect and planner William Pereira to develop a master plan to guide the development of the land. Pereira's plan included a series of master-planned villages, a new campus for the University of California, and 2,800 acres for industrial and office use. The last area, the Irvine Industrial Complex West (later renamed the Irvine Business Complex, or IBC) was completed by 1970. It was adjacent to the Orange County airport on the southwest and to the Tustin Marine Corps Air Station on the north. It was bisected by Interstate 405 and bordered by the Interstate 5 and State Route 55 freeways.

The IBC was originally intended for industrial and office uses. Large parcels of land were sold to major users such as Douglas Aircraft, and smaller parcels were sold to developers who built multitenant tilt-up buildings. By the early 1980s, economic growth exceeded that anticipated in the original master plan. The site's strategic location supported much more intensive uses and land values. Parcels planned for industrial uses were being developed as mid-rise office complexes: even Douglas Aircraft established a real estate development group to take advantage of the opportunity. Feasible development projects went from tilt-up industrial to low-rise office to mid-rise office with structured parking in less than 20 years, with development pressures also coming from addressing business accommodation needs (hotels, services, and higher-density residential use for employees).

By the late 1980s, concerns were rising about the impact that the more intensive uses would have on traffic. In response to predicted traffic gridlock and a lack of funds for roadway improvements, the city of Irvine conceived a plan to cap the number of vehicular trips in the IBC as a *growth management tool*. The cap was to be based on then-existing zoning, thus creating a market in which excess trips could be exchanged among property owners. An owner of a site zoned for less intensive use could sell its excess trips to the owner of a site who wished to develop a more intensive use. The concept was further developed by a business and property owners' advisory group working with the city, then implemented as a program adopted by the city council.

By the late 1990s, the IBC was entering another land use phase. Multifamily housing projects began to appear along one of the major IBC corridors. In 2004, the city initiated a vision plan for the IBC that outlined goals and design criteria for residential and mixed-use projects and increased the allowed number of residential units from 9,015 to 15,000, which—with density bonuses—could be increased to 17,038. In addition, the vision plan established design criteria and proposed urban amenities and infrastructure improvements to better create a more urban environment.

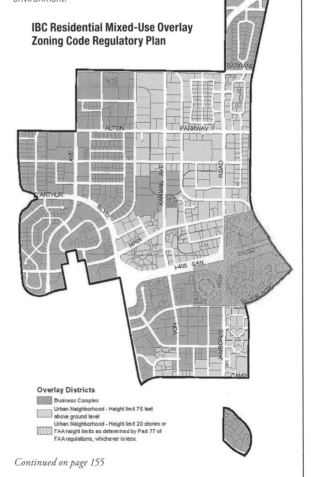

IBC Residential Mixed-Use Overlay Zoning Code Regulatory Plan

Overlay Districts

- Business Complex
- Urban Neighborhood - Height limit 75 feet above ground level
- Urban Neighborhood - Height limit 20 stories or FAA height limits as determined by Part 77 of FAA regulations, whichever is less.

Continued on page 155

the contamination (such as the release of poisonous vapors into structures above and below ground), the exculpation against cleanup costs provided by the defenses to CERCLA liability may prove ineffective as a shield from tort liability, if the facts indicate a breach of duty to the public by the owner of the property where the problem originated.

Asbestos

Asbestos was used extensively for decades to insulate, fireproof, and soundproof all kinds of buildings, particularly commercial and industrial buildings. In the mid-1970s, however, following mounting evidence that asbestos posed significant health risks, the EPA adopted regulations that ended the use of asbestos materials in newly constructed buildings and set guidelines for removal of certain forms of asbestos from existing buildings.

Asbestos is a natural, fibrous, mined material. Its mere presence does not necessarily pose a hazard; only when it exists in a "friable" condition—that is, when it can be crumbled by hand pressure, thereby causing its fibers to become airborne—does it pose a danger. When the fibers are inhaled, they may lodge in the lungs, which, research indicates, can lead to lung disease such as asbestosis and cancer. Fear of asbestos-induced illness and the potential resulting claims has made bankers and investors cautious of loans for projects that include buildings containing asbestos. Lenders and investors will consider such buildings only if the price is low enough to make remediation economically feasible or if the asbestos is in a condition that does not pose a threat to human health.

In the mid-1980s, Congress enacted the Asbestos Hazard Emergency Response Act (AHERA) to address concerns related to risks created by the use of asbestos in the construction of public schools. The program required all schools to be inspected by certified inspectors trained under EPA guidelines. It further mandated preparation of a management plan if asbestos were identified. Commercial building owners have not yet been brought within a regulatory net similar to AHERA, but under the Clean Air Act, asbestos must be handled in a manner that protects public health before a building is demolished. Building owners and managers may face common law liability as a result of claims by people exposed to asbestos. A few states have adopted regulations governing buildings containing asbestos. In California, for instance, owners and lessees of such buildings must inform their employees and certain other people of the location and condition of asbestos, the results of any studies to monitor the air, and any potential health risk stemming from exposure to the asbestos.

Americans with Disabilities Act

The Americans with Disabilities Act (ADA) was signed by President George H. W. Bush in 1990. Its objective is to provide people with disabilities access equal to or similar to that available to the general public. The ADA is considered civil rights legislation; it is not a building code. Title III of the law affects places of public accommodation, including commercial real estate. The law also affects alterations to existing properties. Residential real estate is largely excluded from the ADA as it is already covered by the Fair Housing Act of 1988. However, in cases in which a residential building or community makes spaces available to the public, these spaces must comply with the ADA. Such spaces may include rental offices, pools, gyms, or other amenities that are not limited exclusively to owners, residents, and their guests.

The law is administered and enforced by the U.S. Department of Justice. Congress incorporated a provision into the ADA stating that "good-faith efforts" and "attempts to comply" should be considered in enforcing the law. The Department of Justice has identified a compliance plan as a good-faith effort when accompanied by constructive actions. Priorities in a compliance plan include entryways, routes from entryways to public places, and public facilities such as restrooms and drinking fountains.

The cost of complying varies significantly from property to property, depending on specific building conditions and original project design. For additional insights into ADA compliance, see "Guide to the 2010 ADA Standards," published by the Building

Owners and Managers Association International, or www.ada.gov.

PACKAGING THE ENTITLEMENTS

A typical project will involve a package of entitlements, and usually construction does not begin until all of the entitlements are complete. The entitlement package may involve a vertical stack of internally consistent approvals from a single jurisdiction or it may be horizontal, spanning multiple agencies. An example of a single jurisdictional vertical stack is a project requiring from a city a general plan amendment at the top, a specific plan, and tentative and final maps, together with their conditions of approval. The same project may require a horizontal package that includes the city approvals, plus coastal commission approval, a Corps of Engineers 404 permit, and a Fish and Wildlife Service habitat mitigation plan. The approval agency with the most stringent conditions usually governs.

The Process

The entitlement process begins with the developer submitting an application for a proposed project. The material required for the application is determined by each jurisdiction, the type of project, and the scope of the entitlements required. In some jurisdictions, the application may consist of the completion of a standard form; in others, a complete draft set of the entitlement documents themselves may be required.

The receiving staff reviews the application to determine whether it is complete. Being "deemed complete" is critical to the ability to proceed to subsequent steps. If a project is found to lack critical requirements, such as the developer's right to represent the owner of the property, the application can be rejected.

Once an application is accepted, the staff arranges with the applicant for a kickoff meeting to review the project, identify critical issues, and discuss timing.

City Creek Center, a 23-acre redevelopment of two enclosed shopping malls, created 536 residential units, 1.7 million square feet of office space, and 760,000 square feet of retail space in a pedestrian-oriented plan that helped revitalize downtown Salt Lake City.

THE TAUBMAN COMPANY

A staff planner is assigned to the project to review subsequent documentation and coordinate those documents with other staff departments and outside agencies. The kickoff meeting may include representatives from all of the agencies that will be involved.

Once an application has been deemed complete, the developer begins to prepare the documentation required for the entitlement process. The documentation may entail the work of a wide range of environmental, legal, processing, engineering, and design consultants. The work may take months to complete, and the initiation of some studies may depend on the completion of others. On larger projects, the costs may run into millions of at-risk dollars before the initial submission of the documentation.

When the lead government agency receives the documentation, it circulates the entitlement documents to all other affected agencies and departments. A process of review and comment begins, with comments returned to the developer and his team, appropriate changes negotiated, and revised drafts circulated.

When the documents are completed, the government agency prepares a report for the decision-making body or board that will approve or deny the entitlements. The report summarizes the project and its regulatory issues, and recommends action by the body or board.

Projects involving discretionary approvals are usually opened to a public hearing, during which testimony may be received from any stakeholders who wish to comment on or influence the outcome of the process.

The Risk Profile

A developer is planning a residential project. Three years into the process, the regional water quality agency adopts new standards regarding stormwater runoff, resulting in the loss of six home sites and requiring that all of the specific plan, environmental documents, and accompanying exhibits be redrafted. Shortly thereafter, an environmental manager for the city looks anew at a site condition where oak trees lie within a riparian corridor. The planner re-interprets the conclusion of his predecessor and determines that the 50-foot setback required from a riparian corridor and the 50-foot setback from oak trees are additive and not inclusive. The specific plan, environmental documents, and accompanying exhibits must again be redrafted. Each redraft costs about $50,000 and takes one month to complete.

Assembling an entitlement package entails two challenges. First, the process is sequential, creating a significant risk that the project concept will not be certain until the final approval is granted. Second, the applicability of regulations to a specific site often requires interpretation, creating a risk of unanticipated changes and costly replanning.

The regulatory environment may be ambiguous. When complex or expansive development regulations are enacted, the intent of the legislation may be articulated, but the details may be vague. The scope of the regulations may be so broad that it becomes impossible to foresee every situation that may arise on a specific site. The interpretation of the regulations then falls to public staff, sometimes at a departmental level and sometimes at the level of the individual project manager.

Entitlement regulations are not static. The span of impacts in the environmental arena expands as federal agencies make new interpretations and ebbs with judicial curbs on those interpretations. Air quality standards, the definition of wetlands, and the number of listed species, for example, are constantly evolving. At the local level, general plan updates, mitigation exactions, and growth control measures affect the regulatory environment of a project.

Dependence on Others and Management of the Entitlement Process

By design, the entitlement process is in the hands of staff and elected officials who are beyond the developer's control. The effectiveness of the developer in managing the process depends on his knowledge of the process and his ability to assemble a knowledgeable entitlement team to position the project within the regulatory framework and to work with staff to process the application.

The developer's land use attorney is the key consultant in the regulatory process. His span of expertise includes the following:

- Local land use approvals, such as general plans, specific plans, and zoning, together with representation through the legislative and administrative process;
- State and federal environmental law, including the Clean Water Act, Clean Air Act, Endangered Species Act, and CERCLA, and the corresponding state legislation;
- Development agreements and exactions; and
- Approvals from other state and local commissions and compliance with specialized local development regulations.

The land use attorney will advise on the impact that the regulatory framework will have on the proposed project, suggest changes to the project concept that will accommodate those impacts, and assist in the negotiation of exactions and mitigation requirements. Complex projects may require land use attorneys who specialize in a particular arena, such as the Clean Water Act, and who have a working relationship with the regulatory staff of the appropriate organizations.

The developer's entitlement team consists of technical and processing consultants who analyze the project in terms of their area of expertise. On larger projects, this team will include traffic engineers, biologists, archaeologists, geologists, and other engineering and scientific specialists.

Selection of the right entitlement team members is critical. They should have the technical expertise to analyze the project as well as familiarity and credibility with the agencies involved in the entitlement review process. They also must be sensitive to the objectives of the project: it is very difficult to optimize the technical position of every discipline involved in the entitlement process. The entitlement team's ability to suggest compromise and find solutions is an asset.

THE IMPORTANCE OF NEGOTIATION

Many areas of the entitlement process have the look of technical analysis but in fact may be highly subjective. In many areas, flawed analytical tools lead to illogical or inconsistent results. Even sophisticated computer models fail to capture all of the variables in a project or its environs. Inevitably, the technical analyses can sometimes lead to irreconcilable conclusions. The complexity and detail of the entitlement process is such that perfect mitigation of every project impact is often impossible. Finally, the appropriate level of mitigation is often unique to each project: guidelines cannot anticipate site conditions for every property in every circumstance.

All these issues are resolved through negotiation. Illogical or inconsistent results can be resolved, and tradeoffs between project impacts can be negotiated: for example, an extra traffic lane may be added at the expense of affecting a wetland. Mitigation of impacts may be addressed through a variety of measures.

The developer's assessment of the negotiating environment is important. In an anti-growth jurisdiction, the complexity of the entitlement matrix may be used to stop a project or make it financially infeasible. Other jurisdictions may have a mix of growth philosophies across staff groups and elected decision makers. Knowledgeable developers are aware of the regulatory environment before they commit significant funds to pursue a project.

SUMMARY

The relationship between private and public interests cannot be underestimated. From stage one forward, a project's feasibility depends on the developer's ability to create a process in which he and the public sector ultimately stand as partners with common interests. The entitlement process may add great value or result in great loss in the development process. The uncertainty involved makes entitlements the most risky phase of the development process, with the consequence that it is the hardest and most costly to finance.

TERMS

- Clean Water Act
- Comprehensive plan

- Entitlements
- Exactions
- Form-based zoning
- Growth management tools
- Impact fees
- Infrastructure
- Planned unit development (PUD)
- Police power
- Rational nexus
- Stakeholders
- Subdivision
- Takings
- Transferable development rights (TDRs)
- Vested right
- Zoning ordinances

REVIEW QUESTIONS

7.1 What is police power and how is it enforced? Who has a stronger obligation in the exercise of police power—the federal government or the states? Why?

7.2 What are the mainstays of local governments' regulatory programs and how do they affect development?

7.3 What are the roles of state and regional agencies in regulating development?

7.4 Discuss how developer fees and exactions work.

7.5 Explain the bundle of rights of property ownership.

7.6 What are special taxing districts?

NOTES

1 In this regard, "political" does not have a negative connotation. It pertains to the organization of those interests that influence the actions of government.

2 J. Sutherland, Opinion of the Court, Supreme Court of the United States, 272 U.S. 365, *Village of Euclid v. Ambler Realty Co.*, Appeal from the United States District Court for the Northern District of Ohio.

3 T.J. Kent, Jr., *The Urban General Plan* (San Francisco: Chandler Publishing, 1964), p. 33.

4 Henry L. Diamond and Patrick Noonan, *Land Use in America*, (Washington, D.C.: Island Press, 1966), p. 25.

5 F. Stuart Chapin, *Urban Land Use Planning*, 2nd ed. (Urbana: University of Illinois Press, 1965), p. 356.

6 Kent, p. 18.

7 U.S. Army Corps of Engineers, "Recognizing Wetlands, An Informational Pamphlet," www.usace.army.mil/Portals/2/docs/civil-works/regulatory/rw_bro.pdf.

Chapter 8

Decision Makers and Stakeholders

A developer has control of a site in a declining commercial area, and he believes his proposal for a mixed-use, infill project would rejuvenate the neighborhood. Before committing significant resources to the project, he arranges a meeting with the city councilman representing the district in which the site is located to learn of any concerns he may have. The councilman is enthusiastic about the project and indicates that he and two other councilmen would also be in favor.

The developer decides to proceed and arranges financing to carry him through the entitlement period. The planning staff, sensing emerging community opposition to what is perceived as a high-density project, requires additional traffic, visual, and economic impact studies. Securing entitlements takes twice as long as the developer had estimated and extends beyond the city council elections. The elections are influenced by an antigrowth group, and the two councilmen who were favorably disposed to the project are defeated.

The developer tries to meet with the newly elected councilmen but his requests for the meeting are denied, on the grounds that they want to reserve judgment until the staff recommendation has been submitted.

The developer now believes he is facing a possible 3-2 negative vote by the council, and opposition has been mobilized. His choices are to press forward or abandon the project. The opportunity to redesign the project to meet community concerns has passed. There is no one to negotiate with.

This scenario is an example of "entitlement risk." In this case, it arose after completion of the *regulatory process* and the investment of considerable time and resources. Adherence to the regulatory framework by itself was not sufficient to ensure success. The developer could have taken additional actions to prevent failure if he had developed a better understanding of the public sector and reached out to the public. The public sector includes community stakeholders and their representatives, who express community values through the political process. Members of the community are elected to public office, and those elected officials are charged with making decisions for their constituents.

Elected officials rely on staff reports and land use regulations to help them make decisions. They also balance their views with the desires of their constituents, who often are competing stakeholders. As is often the case in the political process, no one is fully satisfied.

MANAGING CHANGE

Change is often opposed by communities because it threatens to disrupt daily life: a new project will alter the visual landscape, it will bring new people into the community, it will increase traffic, and daily habits will be affected. When change occurs rapidly, a gap may emerge between the interests of local stakeholders and the decisions of elected officials. If the gap is significant, the power to make land use decisions can be reallocated. Concerned residents may form groups to oppose growth, sometimes leading to the election of representatives who will better represent their interests. This reallocation of decision making has deeper roots than dissatisfaction with elected officials. In the 1960s, a planning theory called *advocacy planning* emerged as a reaction to the sometimes autocratic planning process of that time. Advocacy planning greatly expanded the public's role in land use decisions. It was based on the premise that "any group which has interests at stake in the planning process should have those interests articulated."[1] Processes once the domain of professionals were opened to the public.

The Nature of Change

A driving force behind change is growth. Growth creates demand for places to live, places to shop, and places to work. However, reactions to growth are not always positive: debate more often arises over how to stop it, direct it to other places, or make it happen more slowly. The motives are varied: people want control over their environment, do not want their neighborhoods to shoulder their share of regional growth, and want to determine their own destiny.

Discretionary Approvals

As described in chapter 7, every jurisdiction has a regulatory framework that establishes what may be built. The purpose of the regulations is to create a reasonable environment of certainty on behalf of all stakeholders on how a community may develop. This expectation of reasonable certainty creates a problem: There is a reasonable expectation that a long-range plan, once adopted, should govern growth. Yet the long-range plan cannot anticipate everything that may happen during the planning period. The impetus for changes to a plan arises for a number of reasons:

- The general plan may have recognized the need for future land use changes but deferred the implementation of those changes to a later date when better information would be available. The economic structure of a region changes, and those changes are reflected in its rate of growth and patterns of land use. Market conditions evolve, affecting the design and type of real estate products. Environmental regulations change, resulting in decreases in the inventory of land available to accommodate growth. Thus, recognizing that long-range plans cannot accurately predict all growth patterns, the general plan usually contains mechanisms for amendments to the plan.

- Elected officials may recognize the right of a landowner to realize the highest economic use of his property, subject to the goals of the community, and be willing to consider new opportunities for the exercise of those property rights.

- The political constituency that gave rise to existing plans may be supplanted by new stakeholders with different perspectives on growth.

- Complex projects may raise issues that go beyond those addressed by existing regulations.

When a jurisdiction recognizes the need for flexibility in addressing land use issues and has a process to accommodate unique situations or to better manage growth, public participation in the process is reopened, creating an opportunity for stakeholders to participate in land use decisions.

Accommodating Stakeholders

The public's acceptance of growth is cyclical. Growth may initially be welcomed because it offers economic opportunity and new community facilities. As the negative effects of growth become apparent, progrowth jurisdictions become antigrowth. Residents "want more roads built, but fewer houses. They want to freeze the peaceful hominess of the town that was growing when they moved there five minutes before."[2] Old elected boards are voted out of office and replaced by new ones that promise to stop or slow the rate of change. Elections are won or lost over issues of neighborhood character, traffic, loss of open space, and visual impact. A perception of the influence of special interests emerges. Some jurisdictions return to a middle ground; others do not.

Sometimes stakeholder groups persist beyond the resolution of the growth event that sparked their creation. They became institutionalized, and the stakeholder environment becomes populated with vocal and focused antigrowth groups, against a backdrop of a general population base that may or may not share the same values. *Discretionary approvals* become suspect merely because they are discretionary, a departure from the plan. Decisions are placed in the hands of a small group of elected officials. The entitlement and regulatory process that leads up to the discretionary approval is complex and little understood by the general public. There is a vague suspicion that a discretionary approval creates financial value for the developer and landowner and is therefore an "unearned increment" rather than a means of meeting the community's needs.

THE PARTICIPANTS

The variety of participants include the developer's team, public sector staff and officials, and others.

The Developer's Team

A developer acquires a transitional property in a working-class neighborhood. She arranges an outreach meeting to present her project to the community. The residents are already concerned about the amount of traffic the project will generate. The developer arrives in a Mercedes, wearing an expensive suit, and spends most of her presentation promoting her architecture. She loses the audience, and her opportunity for gaining community support evaporates.

The key position on the developer's team is the individual who represents the project in the community. It may be the developer, her project manager, or one of her consultants. The individual in this role personalizes the project. His is the face that creates trust or distrust, accommodation or defiance. Fulfilling this role requires community involvement, listening skills, the ability to deal with all kinds of personalities, and the skill to negotiate compromises.

The developer is often perceived as an outsider. New projects are viewed as changes initiated by powerful groups from outside the community: it is "they" who are planning the apartment project or shopping center down the street. Some development companies have refined the job description of the project representative to fit the culture of the community. The person in this role is expected to join local civic organizations, give financial assistance to efforts that are valued by the community, and identify ways to satisfy critical community needs, as well as speak about the project's benefits and allay fears about its impacts. Perceptions change when a development project is proposed by the person who has worked on the public safety task force of the Chamber of Commerce with community members for the past year and who has supported the fundraising effort for the high school athletic program.

The primary responsibility of the project representative is to listen. The developer needs to understand the possible impact that her proposal will have on the community and with this knowledge take specific action: change the project, mitigate its impacts, or provide appropriate offsetting benefits. Above all, the developer must communicate with honesty and respect. Neighbors are quick to sense whether someone is listening to their concerns or trying to buy her way into the community.

Public Outreach and Public Affairs Professionals

Community outreach is the process of engaging local stakeholders, learning and responding to concerns, and building support. There are both individuals and firms that specialize in this process. Their role begins at due diligence and continues throughout the development cycle. During due diligence, the development team member charged with outreach may undertake surveys to determine the community's attitude toward growth in general and the proposed project in particular, and their key concerns about both. This information may be used to anticipate critical issues and shape the project concept. In the period leading up to public hearings, the development team needs to develop collateral material that explains the project, organize public informational meetings, and identify individuals—especially those from the local community—who may support the project in public hearings.

Lobbying, the process of gaining access to or influencing decisions made by elected officials, is usually considered an activity that occurs at the state or federal level of government. The same factors that give rise to lobbying at higher levels of government are also present at the local level: elected officials have many constituencies, receive conflicting information and have limited time. In many communities, there are individuals or firms whose role is to facilitate communications with key decision makers. These individuals usually have had local political experience as elected officials or government staff members. This work may be done by a developer directly or by a public affairs consultant who understands matters of concern to office holders and the community and can advise the developer on issues that may contribute to a project's success or failure. The person in this role can act as a channel of communication between the developer and the elected officials and their staff.

A public affairs consultant can advise the developer of particular barriers to approval that can be anticipated in the entitlement process. For example, the consultant could advise the developer that the elected official may be focused on traffic issues and

may want the project to demonstrate mitigation measures beyond those called for by technical studies. The political arena is characterized by compromise and tradeoffs, so an elected official's support for a project may wax and wane over the entitlement period. The public affairs consultant's role is to keep the developer advised of the political trends and issues that may impact the project.

The Land Use Attorney

As described in chapter 3, developers rely on several types of attorneys throughout the development process. The land use attorney engages in due diligence and plays a significant role in the regulatory process. His participation remains critical as the project moves forward through discretionary approvals. He will advise on negotiations with stakeholders and translate agreements into entitlement documentation, ensure that documentation is consistent across

Masonvale is an employer-assisted housing development for faculty at George Mason University, in Fairfax, Virginia. The public university partnered with a private development team to create a nonprofit development entity.

agencies, and review documentation for its integrity in the event of legal challenges.

The Public Sector's Team

Localities differ somewhat in the makeup of their decision-making team. Described below is a typical organizational structure.

The Board

The final authority for local land use issues resides with the senior elected body for the jurisdiction, generically called the "board." The board may be the city council, a board of supervisors, or a similar panel, elected at large or by district.

In large jurisdictions, elected officials typically have professional staffs who are responsible for office management and constituent interaction. The staffs include a chief of staff and sometimes a land use representative who deals directly with developers and the community on proposed projects. Such representatives summarize key issues from project proponents and opponents, coordinate with the jurisdiction's planning staff, synthesize the information for the decision maker, and evaluate broader political implications of the project decision.

The Planning Commission and Other Commissions

The planning commission is an elected or appointed panel that serves several purposes: it may make final land use decisions, make land use decisions subject to appeal, make land use decisions for subsequent approval by the board, originate studies and regulations, or initiate updates to plans and regulations. The span of its activities may include decisions on land use proposals, including subdivisions, master plans, development agreements, and annexations.

The board may also create and appoint members to advisory commissions on specialized subjects such as environmental issues, parks and recreation, education, public facilities, affordable housing, transportation, and subdivisions. These groups meet to review issues related to development in general or to specific project proposals and forward their recommendations to the board.

The Planning Staff

A developer submits an application for an infill project. The application conforms to all of the current zoning regulations except for a minor variance for building height for one of the buildings in the center of the site, which would be mitigated by lower building heights along the street. This variance was reviewed by the developer's land use attorney who felt it should not be a problem, and the planning staff agreed. The developer proceeds to invest hundreds of thousands of dollars over the next six months on architectural and engineering drawings. The variance is denied by the city council under opposition led by one member who believes that building heights in the zoning ordinance are absolute.

As discussed in chapter 7, most local jurisdictions have a professional planning staff that reviews and advises decision-making bodies. The staff's influence varies. In some jurisdictions, the professional city management staff, including the planning director, may provide strong leadership. In other jurisdictions, the elected and appointed decision-making bodies provide strong leadership, and the professional staff does not take action without specific direction from the board. The developer should know where leadership and power resides, especially with controversial development proposals. Misinterpretation of community leadership is a fatal flaw in a developer.

Stakeholders

A stakeholder is a person or group who may be affected by or have an interest in a proposed development project. The impacts of any change in the built environment are far-reaching. The developer should fully understand how the project will change the community and how people will be affected by those changes.

Individual Stakeholders

Every project has an impact on its neighbors. A view is altered, traffic is increased, and local everyday experiences are changed. Not all negative impacts can be resolved, but some concerns can be eliminated and others mitigated. Some can be addressed in the project design stage, and others can be resolved as they arise.

Many of the concerns of those directly affected by the project can be identified in advance. The developer's team reaches out to direct stakeholders early in the process and listens to their objections. Information may be gathered through direct contact, as the project representative meets with each neighbor. At the other extreme, the developer may retain a public outreach firm to conduct blind surveys to cover a broader population and obtain more objective data.

Ad Hoc Groups

As news of a proposed project spreads through a community, ad hoc groups may form to organize opposition. The concerns of these groups may be the same as those of direct stakeholders, and they may be formed despite the developer's initial outreach to individuals directly affected by the project. The community may organize if the impacts of the project are too far-reaching or if the initial outreach information is inadequate. In the absence of being provided with facts, stakeholders often assume the worst outcomes.

The members of informal opposition groups may come from the immediate neighborhood or they may be drawn from outside the sphere of direct impacts of the project. These groups may obtain financial support—from their own members as well as from sympathetic external organizations—to retain legal counsel and to mount opposition campaigns. Leaders may emerge from these groups, and they may use the opportunity as a platform for election to local political office in an effort to overturn what may be perceived as an overly favorable climate for development.

A developer's early engagement with a community can sometimes defuse the organization of these groups: facts can be disseminated to correct misinformation; changes to the project concept can be discussed; people can be engaged in the process of shaping their community; and the stakeholders can feel that their concerns have been heard.

Formal and Semiformal Groups

A community experiencing growth or change often contains formal groups whose purpose is to oppose new projects as they emerge. Sometimes these began as informal groups formed to oppose a single project but lived on as standing antigrowth organizations. They are often support groups for elected candidates who represent their interests. These groups may or may not reflect the values of the community as a whole. The developer usually identifies these groups and determines their influence as part of his due diligence, in the community assessment study.

Issue-Based Groups

Issue-based interest groups are standing organizations whose purpose is to protect or advance a set of values. They may be focused on specific matters such as biological species, wetlands, historic structures, views, or equestrian facilities, or they may be more generally antigrowth. They may be local organizations or national organizations with local chapters. They are often well funded and have technical resources that can be directed toward the critique of a proposed project. Litigation by such groups can slow a project or drain it of financial resources.

Supporters

With few exceptions, active stakeholders represent a small portion of the population in a community. Active stakeholders have something to gain or lose in the board's vote on a project. The balance of the population may not. In many cases, the community may include supporters who welcome the change brought about by a new project. They may support specific aspects, such as aesthetic or economic benefits. They may be ideologically responsive to the concept of private property rights. Or they may be uncommitted but willing to listen to reasonable arguments in favor of the project. As the developer moves forward with the project, she will reach out to and attempt to engage those who may be willing to support the development when they are fully informed.

INNOVATOR **Richard M. Daley** | Mayor, Chicago, Illinois

Daley is the longest-serving mayor in Chicago's history, holding office from served 1989 to 2011. During his tenure, Chicago was transformed into a prominent player in the global economy. Today, Standard & Poor's ranks the city among the world's top 10 economic centers, and in 2010 *Foreign Policy* magazine ranked Chicago sixth among global cities worldwide. Daley earned a reputation—both in Chicago and around the world—for improving Chicago's quality of life, acting to improve its public schools, strengthening its economy, and helping it become one of the most environmentally friendly cities in the world.

Under Mayor Daley, Chicago became a leader in the environmental movement. The beautification of Chicago stems from Daley's unrelenting focus on sustainability—a goal he pursued even as other cities scaled back sustainability initiatives during the Great Recession. Every new building in Chicago is required to strive for LEED certification for energy efficiency and conservation. As of late 2009, 88 Chicago buildings had achieved LEED certification, a record high among U.S. cities.

Daley led by example. In 2001, to lower energy costs and help mitigate the urban heat-island effect, he had a 20,300-square-foot green roof installed on City Hall. Today, more than 600 rooftop gardens and green roofs cover more than seven million square feet on public and private buildings around Chicago. "If you invest in an environmental manner, it saves money in the long run. It saves your health, the air, everything around you," Daley says.

Since 1998, the city has added 1,300 acres of new open space, and planted hundreds of thousands of trees along miles of major roadways. One green space—Millennium Park—has most likely changed the city's image more than any other amenity. The 24.5-acre park, which opened in 2004, is the city's top tourist destination and a model for public/private partnership, drawing more than $200 million in private donations. It is an economic development engine for downtown Chicago and has enriched the city's portfolio of significant public art, including Anish Kapoor's iconic Cloud Gate sculpture.

A former state senator and county prosecutor, Daley was first elected mayor to complete the term of the late Harold Washington, then re-elected five times. He has received many awards, among them the ULI J.C. Nichols Prize for Visionaries in Urban Development in 2010. In more than 40 years of public service, Daley left his mark on his city for years to come.

Since his retirement from public service, Daley has continued to help cities grow responsibly. Soon after leaving office, he founded Tur Partners LLC, an investment firm that partners with leaders and innovators to drive growth in global urban environments. The University of Chicago appointed Daley a distinguished senior fellow in the Harris School of Public Policy, where he is responsible for coordinating a guest lecture series on critical urban policy challenges with influential policy makers from around the world. Daley was named senior advisor to JPMorgan Chase, where he chairs the new Global Cities Initiative, a joint project of JPMorgan and the Brookings Institution to help cities compete more effectively in the global economy. He was also appointed the cochair of President Barack Obama's 100,000 Strong Initiative, which aims to increase the number and diversity of American students studying in China in order to foster a stronger people-to-people tie between China and the United States. Through his continuing endeavors, Daley continuously finds new and creative ways to influence the built environment.

PUBLIC OUTREACH

The attainment of entitlements is the highest-risk phase of the development process. But the risk can be mitigated by putting in place an effective public outreach strategy. Communication is a two-way street involving gathering information about community concerns and disseminating information about the project. It is an opportunity for the developer to determine whether the project is politically feasible and to shape the project to respond to community objections before committing significant resources.

Information Gathering

There are many ways to gather information about the political climate and community attitudes toward a proposed project, including surveys, informational meetings, and *charrettes*.

During the due diligence phase, community attitude surveys may be commissioned. Surveys can take a variety of forms. A common process uses a mailed or telephone survey targeted to directly affected and other selected stakeholders to determine their views on growth and specific issues that may shape their opinions on the proposed project. A well-structured survey enables the analysis of this data by geographic area and other metrics to uncover underlying themes. Armed with the knowledge about community concerns gleaned from the survey, the developer may arrange small-group meetings to gain a greater understanding of issues identified in the surveys. These meetings are often informal and focused. As the process unfolds, developer outreach may begin to identify stakeholders by their potential to support the project as well as those who will be opposed regardless of the developer's efforts.

The initial survey can also identify highly regarded thought leaders who may be able to influence the attitudes of other stakeholders. Thought leaders may include elected officials, heads of civic organizations, or neighbors. The outreach process may include personal meetings with these people to determine their attitudes toward the proposed project and their assessment of community needs.

Charrettes

Charrettes are meetings of stakeholders to influence the character of a proposed project. They are intended to be collaborative. By promoting the idea of joint ownership of solutions to project impacts, charrettes are intended to defuse later adversarial confrontations. The meetings are often extended workshops that involve a variety of tools to elicit meaningful input. The tools may include multiple support professionals and even multiple design architects so that a range of solutions can be visualized.

Participants are often organized into teams under the direction of a skilled facilitator. The facilitator is critical to the process, to keep it on target and to avoid raising false expectations about participants' input. Because charrettes convey the aura of empowerment, they run the risk of raising such expectations or creating infeasible solutions. The results of the charrette are usually recorded and later may be disseminated in published form.

Disseminating Information

It is important that the proposed project is accurately portrayed to the community. As noted by urban policy researchers Robert Burchell and David Listokin, "Direct communication prevents the public from learning of the development from secondhand sources that often spawn rumors and misinformation."[3]

The developer's outreach team organizes a program that accurately describes the proposed project's benefits and addresses the ways in which it will mitigate its negative impacts. Many developers use visual simulations that provide still or animated characterizations of how the project will appear when finished. Tours of similar projects completed by the developer help lessen concerns about the impact of the project on the values of surrounding properties. The developer may choose to meet with thought leaders one on one to get a better understanding of the specifics of their concerns and perhaps negotiate mutually acceptable project changes. Sometimes the developer meets with directly affected stakeholders, such as groups of neighbors, to explain the project and perhaps offer ways to mitigate the project's construction or operational impacts.

Larger community meetings offer the opportunity to have members of the developer's team explain specific aspects of the proposed project. Technical consultants can review in greater detail aspects such as traffic, design, and environmental mitigation. As appropriate, some of these meetings may take place on the project site. Some projects use a website to give the public the opportunity to study the project in greater detail and provide feedback.

Building Support

The goal of the outreach program is to build support for the project. It is important to remember that the developer is asking for a privilege and not exercising an absolute right. The purpose of the outreach program is to identify supporters and neutralize potential opposition. The message should allay fears about the impact of the project on the community and communicate its potential benefits.

Some parties may be neutral. Although they may not necessarily support the development, their concerns can be mitigated so that they will not actively oppose it. Other groups may eventually withdraw their active opposition in exchange for some type of mitigation. Some groups, particularly those that have broad antigrowth agendas, will never support any project. Attempting to influence them is often a waste of resources.

The outreach program is a high-stakes effort. The developer should have control over the process at all times to ensure that accurate information is being disseminated, that all of the efforts are coordinated with other parts of the development process, and that the effort reflects the developer's ethical values. Some common pitfalls to avoid are

- A drift to the mechanical. The tools of community outreach are well known. Some outreach consultants fall back to using the same tools for every job, regardless of context. The community usually knows the methods of the developer's outreach program, to the extent that they can recognize messages that are off point, inaccurate, or blatantly promotional. The development team must understand these tools to know which are appropriate for the project and to resist pressure to use those not likely to work for the given community.
- A drift to the passive. A project can involve issues that do not fit the regulatory structure. To that extent, the developer and jurisdiction are in a negotiating environment. Failure to recognize that some issues are negotiable can lead to suboptimization of the project and problems later in the development cycle.
- Identifying the wrong leaders and issues. The community environment is complex. Often, the most vocal individual or most repeated issues dominate the debate but they may not accurately represent the views of the community at large.
- Negotiating too soon. Entitlements are generally granted at the public hearing. Early settlement carries the risk that the agreement will be forgotten by the time of the public hearing or that splinter groups will emerge after an agreement has been reached with the lead opposition organization. Furthermore, additional issues may arise, making the initial negotiated solution impractical.

The Public Hearing

The public hearing is often an opportunity for political theater. The major participants are the developer (and other members of the development team), the staff, the decision-making panel (the board), and the stakeholders.

A developer should enter into a public hearing reasonably assured of the outcome. A negative decision, especially if it cannot be appealed, can close off subsequent efforts to gain approvals. A successful outreach effort will have identified the likelihood of a positive vote from each board member, with sufficient positive votes to gain approval. Other members may favor the project but, knowing that it will be approved, vote against it to maintain appearances. To avoid alignment with any political factions, other members of the panel may abstain.

Stakeholders at a public hearing show their strength through demonstrations of solidarity. They sit as a group, stand in unison to show their numbers, and often carry badges to identify themselves.

CASE STUDY **Irvine Tech Center: Greenlaw's Political Process**

Discretionary entitlements are subject to a vote of an elected body according to the merits of the proposal. A project can proceed on paper through the regulatory process, but unless there is an understanding of its political support, it will collapse in the hearing or be dragged out through staff processing. This creates a sequential problem for the developer: an elected official cannot vote on a project until all of the facts are presented in accordance with the rules of the entitlement process. But an investment in the entitlement process cannot be justified without some likelihood of approval. How does a developer gauge the outcome of the political process?

At the outset of the entitlements process, Greenlaw added two key consultants to its team. One, a former senior city staff member, coordinated efforts as the project proceeded through the regulatory process. The second was a political consultant.

Coordination with staff was critical. Once the project was folded into the IBC Vision Plan, Greenlaw had to ensure that its desired entitlement package would be preserved. Factors such as unit count, building height, land use mix, setbacks, coverage, and other factors had be expressed in technical terms

Continued next page

in the city's documents to preserve the project concept. There are many risks in this process: the project could be modified to accommodate the broader plan; the environmental impacts of that plan could be greater than the impacts of a project; the number and distribution of stakeholders could be expanded; and conflicts between planning theory and market realities could be heightened. Greenlaw's processing consultant worked with city staff to ensure that the project remained commercially feasible.

Alignment with the values of the locality is also necessary to the granting of discretionary entitlements. An elected official usually has no reason to vote for a project unless it advances the interests of the jurisdiction. The first requirement of a political consultant is to communicate with those elected officials to determine the needs of the jurisdiction and express how the proposed project meets those needs. A discretionary entitlement for a major project carries additional negotiable issues. The city may impose exactions beyond those called for in the regulatory framework. In the case of ITC, those exactions took the form of development impact fees paid to the locality to be used to mitigate the additional traffic generated or for parkland, affordable housing, or other needs of the community.

At the end of the process, the city of Irvine had a new vision plan that articulated new development standards, laid the groundwork for a total of 15,000 residential units in the IBC, and completed a new environmental impact report (EIR) that would dictate the trip requirements, park and open land requirements, and other aspects that would affect development in the IBC. The goal of an organized approach to the IBC's residential rezoning had been realized.

The new EIR and new development standards ended up working in Greenlaw's favor by helping to reduce entitlement costs and streamline the process. Furthermore, during this time, Greenlaw was able to sit on the sidelines, learn from the mistakes of other developers, and stake out a new game plan for ITC that would maximize the return for its stakeholders.

Incorporating that knowledge and some feedback from the city, the new plan comprised 1,800 apartment units and 17,000 square feet of retail and restaurant space. Office space was eliminated because of the high vacancy rates in the area. The project was to be executed in three phases and would include a mix of uses.

The retail component is often the Achilles heel of a mixed-use project. Place-making theory usually locates retail at the center of

IBC Residential Development Fee Estimate, October 2011

Type of Fee	$/Unit
IBC transportation fee	1,862
Transportation corridor fee	2,102
School fee	2,673[a]
Community park fee	5,980[b]
Water and sewer connection fees	5,300
Systems development charge	1,200
Subtotal	$19,117
IBC neighborhood infrastructure fee	7,410[c]
Subtotal	$26,527
Affordable housing in-lieu fee	16,693[d]
Neighborhood park in-lieu fee	6,000[e]
Total	$49,220

a. Fee based on Santa Ana fees of $2.97/SF for new construction and average unit size of 900 SF.

b. Fee based on new land appraisal of $2.3 million/acre as approved by the Community Services Commission in February 2011. Assumes no on-site affordable units.

c. Fee varies from $5,700 to $14,820 with product type and affordable housing implementation; $7,410 is the fee for rental units that do not provide on-site affordable housing.

d. Fee based on recent land appraisal of $3.3 million/acre as approved by the City Council in January 2011.

e. Fee may be charged, depending on amount of on-site neighborhood park amenities. The IBC Vision Plan changed the requirement for on-site public neighborhood park space. ITC may be exempt.

the development, within walking distance of the most units possible, to serve as a focus of community activity. Often, this theory leads to a greater amount of retail than can be supported internally by the project itself. From a commercial viewpoint, retail needs exposure to traffic and must be supported by a trade area that extends beyond the project. Using other properties as an example, Smith was able to negotiate less retail than the city proposed. His argument was supported by proof that retail space in other projects was subsidized by the owner and could end up vacant.

Continued next page

CASE STUDY   Irvine Tech Center: Greenlaw's Political Process   *Continued*

In 2007, another political factor arose. The neighboring cities of Newport Beach and Tustin became concerned about the impact that the development surge in Irvine would have on their streets. They decided to challenge all new approvals of residential projects in the IBC and sued the city of Irvine. The Allergan and Deft corporations, both of which were operating industrial/manufacturing/testing plants within the IBC, also had concerns about residential development in the surrounding areas. Allergan decided to join in the fight against the proposed rezoning and sued to maintain a buffer zone around its manufacturing plant.

Allergan asserted that it was necessary to protect future residents from any ill effects from their manufacturing/testing operations. (The Deft Corporation did not end up suing but brought a unified presence to the city council meetings, sending dozens of employees in matching shirts, to illustrate their commitment against residential uses in the IBC.) The lawsuits were filed in 2007, just as the market began to decline. The cases were heard by the Orange County Superior Court in late 2008 and through early 2009.

The court found in favor of the cities of Newport Beach and Tustin. Each was awarded funds for the improvement and widening of their streets and infrastructure, to help alleviate traffic conditions. The judge also found in favor of Allergan, awarding the company a buffer zone that restricted residential development around its facility. The judge, in the statement of his findings, noted that the 1992 EIR that was used to analyze all new applications was stale and needed to be revised. He also took issue with the process of "piecemealing"—that is, the way that the city of Irvine was approving projects individually when it should have analyzed the entire area as a whole, as prescribed under the CEQA (California Environmental Quality Act). The judge therefore recommended that the city analyze all pending 6,000 units as a whole. This led to the development of a new traffic study and the cap of 15,000 residential units in the IBC. As of this writing, the city has processed 10,461 units.

Allergan Buffer Map

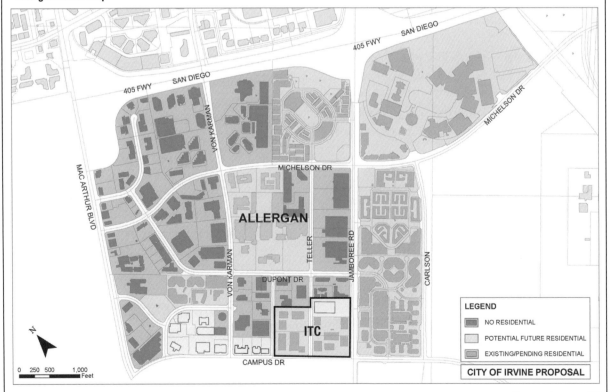

Continued on page 179

There may sometimes be public demonstrations outside the hearing room. Because public input is usually limited to minutes, stakeholders organize their scripts to be certain that all of their points are addressed. The talking points are the project impact issues that were identified by the developer's public opinion research. There should be no surprises, as the critical issues should have been addressed by the developer in the project concept.

THE INTERSECTION OF PLANNING THEORY AND ENTITLEMENTS

Planning theory, an evolving body of thought on the built environment expressed through academics and practitioners, articulates the principles of a regulated land use system. Entitlements deal with the real-world land use regulation system as expressed through regulations created by elected officials and administered by public and private sector professionals. Since the mid-20th century, planning theory has led or influenced the entitlement process in three areas:

- Participation—the inclusion and representation of all stakeholders in the entitlement process;
- Process—the means by which stakeholders are empowered to influence the character of the development; and
- Physical design—the final form of the proposed development to meet the needs of the stakeholders.

The connection between theory and practice is not always direct. The regulatory system is complex and often presents barriers to the absorption of planning thought:

- Regulatory lag: Planning theory evolves, and entitlement regulations are slow to adapt to change.
- Conflicting agency objectives: Land use regulations are promulgated by many single-purpose agencies whose goals may conflict with trends in planning theory. For example, the street width standards of neo-traditional planning theory and those of fire authorities

usually conflict. There is no mechanism to balance priorities.

- Market resistance: There is often a perception that some dictates of planning theory will not be acceptable to the market.
- Entitlement barriers: The cost and time required to navigate the regulatory environment may preclude a developer from taking on the additional risk of requesting a variance for an innovative project.

Planning theory and regulatory practice form the boundaries within which the developer operates. An understanding of both the spirit and the letter is essential in stages one and two of the development process, when the project concept is formed. The alternative is to be held captive to a costly, reactionary process as the project is confronted with continuous regulatory challenges.

Advocacy Planning

Advocacy planning has greatly complicated the approvals process, expanding the amount of time and money that must be allocated to this phase. As described in chapter 6, advocacy planning arose in the mid-20th century, out of dissatisfaction with the decision-making process and the public's lack of a voice in the process, and a desire to better respond to long-term community goals. A number of planning movements have advanced to the point that they now are mainstream and have considerable influence over community planning as a way to address environmental and quality of life issues. The major movements include smart growth, new urbanism, and environmental sustainability, all of which are described in chapter 6.

PUBLIC/PRIVATE PARTNERSHIPS

A *public/private partnership* is a development venture operated through the collaboration of one or more government entities and private sector developers. Each party brings resources to the venture in the form of approvals, financing, management skills, or land. There is increasing interest in such so-called P3 projects, especially at the federal and state levels.

Development in the United States has traditionally occurred through a process in which the public and private sectors perform independent, arm's-length functions, as described in part II. The public sector was expected to perform the functions of land use regulation and planning and to provide the needed services—schools, roads, water, sanitation, fire and police protection—to support new development. The public sector did not assume any of the entrepreneurial risks or absorb any project-specific costs typically borne by the private sector.

This development model changed dramatically in the late 1970s with a proliferation of real estate projects defined by their special public/private status. Variously referred to as partnerships, joint developments, co-developments, or just public/private deals, these projects reshaped the conventional development process by expanding the public sector's traditional sphere of activity. In a number of roles—as developers, lenders, equity investors, land lessors, and, in selected cases, operators—public agencies have become more active in the development arena. In so doing, they have assumed new risks. With each succeeding decade, the number of public/private projects has continued to grow and the concept has been applied to a more diverse array of projects.

Several forces contributed to the public sector's heightened engagement in the development process. Cutbacks of federal urban aid in the 1980s pushed local governments to innovate and improvise to meet their city planning and economic development objectives.[4] A rash of tax-cutting referenda (beginning in 1978 with California's Proposition 13) made raising taxes or going to the voters for approval of new bond issues a political risk and compelled local governments to search for new sources of funds. In the environment of fiscal restraint and rising land values, local governments came to view development as a strategic resource that could be harnessed to revitalize downtowns, capture hidden land values, finance needed infrastructure, stimulate economic growth, and generate jobs.

Public/private partnerships dramatically redefine the traditional roles of the public and private sectors in the development process. Each partner shares risks and benefits in such ventures. Even though joint efforts involve many steps similar to conventional development, they differ in several ways:

- Business agreements between private firms and government detail the terms and conditions of development and involve the private sector in the public planning process much earlier than is traditionally the case.
- Relatively limited public financial resources are used to attract larger amounts of private investment for community and economic development.
- Public approvals as well as commitments of financial resources engender concerns about public accountability and create expectations for financial returns in exchange for the risks taken.
- The active involvement of the public, private, and community sectors creates more complex sets of public/private interactions.
- Public objectives (including community goals, design criteria, affirmative action, and hiring of residents) must be considered in addition to private objectives.

Public/private projects are diverse in scope. For any city, individual characteristics and history determine the types of projects and forms of assistance that best meet local public goals. Generally speaking, public entrepreneurship is most beneficial in the case of complex projects proposed for weaker markets, where a city's active involvement can make a real estate project attractive for both public and private participants. In contrast, in strong markets, the public sector may be presented with select opportunities to capture benefits from the rising values of publicly owned land.

Even during times when property markets have experienced severe distress, public/private development has still been appealing as an economic development strategy. Throughout these cycles, the public/private approach has been particularly evident in development of brownfield sites, waterfronts, affordable housing, and transit-oriented developments.

Private versus Public Sector Resources

The private sector is often presumed to be more likely to be able to construct a large capital project in a shorter period of time than a public agency counterpart and do so at or under budget. There is a further presumption that the private sector is likely more able to operate and maintain an infrastructure project less expensively than the public sector, even factoring in an allowance for profit. This is not always the case.

After the cutbacks in federal aid in the late 1970s, cities received fewer categorical aid dollars from Washington with which to fund their projects, yet they continued to support projects through the issuance of tax-exempt bonds—at least until the 1986 Tax Reform Act curtailed the use of such bonds for private-purpose projects. Continually pushed to rely more and more on local resources, cities established a broad inventory of incentive tools and financing techniques from which to fashion their assistance packages: tax increment financing (TIF), special assessment districts, tax abatements, dedication of sales or special-purpose taxes, urban development action grant paybacks, eminent domain, land write-downs, land swaps, *ground leases,* lease/purchase arrangements, loan guarantees and credit enhancements, loan subsidies, capital improvements, leases for office space, and value-creating tradeoffs based on zoning bonuses.

Specific circumstances determine whether the private sector is more efficient. For very large and capital-intensive projects, it is difficult to overcome the significant advantage that tax-exempt debt financing provides to the public sector as long as the public agency has the demonstrated ability to bring projects in on time and within budget. Increasingly, as public agencies shift from design-bid-build construction management programs to design-build ones, projects undertaken by the public sector are being effectively managed and the performance differential in favor of the private sector is closing.

Examples of Public/Private Partnerships

Intervention in the market has successfully stimulated revitalization in center-city commercial cores and suburban downtowns, inner-city neighborhoods, and waterfront districts through the development of mixed-use projects, retail centers, commercial buildings, stadiums and convention centers, and residential clusters. Many cities have earned acclaim for their joint public/private efforts. Each city develops its own method of leveraging private investment to improve that city's economy and quality of life. Some more entrepreneurial local governments have, through their initiative and their willingness to take risks, become joint venture partners with private developers on projects. Following are five examples of how public/private partnerships have been implemented by cities.

AUSTIN, TEXAS: MUELLER

Mueller, a joint project of the city of Austin and Catellus Development, is a 700-acre master-planned community on the site of a former municipal airport, along the first phase of a planned urban rail line. Mueller was planned to be a model of sustainability and community health promotion. The first phase opened in 2007 with about 800 homes and 240,000 square feet of retail space.

Continued next page

JOSEPH FREED AND ASSOCIATES/GILBERTSON PHOTOGRAPHY

Sullivan Center is a restoration of the Carson Pirie Scott building to its former glory.

Debate about the long-term operating cost performance is ongoing.

Organizations and the Public/Private Process

As public/private ventures have evolved, the involvement of state and local organizations has expanded in innovative ways. Various types of government structures, including an array of *quasi-public* government bodies, development corporations, and city departments with expanded functions, have been organized to handle public/private development. Other actors have joined as well—nongovernmental institutions such as health care providers and educational institutions, nonprofit organizations, and intermediary groups such as business improvement districts.

Via Verde, a mixed-income residential development in the Bronx, New York, began as a design competition to determine a viable plan to build affordable housing on a city-owned site. The result was an innovative health-focused community developed by two private developers with support from various city agencies and multiple layers of financing from 19 public, private, and nonprofit funding sources.

Public/private development is frequently organized under a quasi-public institutional structure that permits an organization to operate with greater flexibility and fewer restrictions than a city agency involved in development. Though partially publicly funded, a quasi-public development organization can conduct negotiations in private—a particularly useful feature as developers are reluctant to negotiate when the details of their financial dealings are made public.

Civic San Diego is a city-owned nonprofit development partner that focuses on developing in urban neighborhoods. Goals include providing affordable housing and public improvements, and stimulating job creation through partnerships with private developers.

Examples of Public/Private Partnerships   *Continued*

The city owns and holds the land until it is taken down for development or infrastructure. Catellus funds the infrastructure costs and is reimbursed for public infrastructure through tax increment financing or land sales revenue.

At buildout, projected for 2020, the community will include nearly 6,000 homes and 4 million square feet of commercial and office space.

CHICAGO, ILLINOIS: SULLIVAN CENTER

The Sullivan Center project involved renovation and repositioning of a historic downtown department store complex made up of nine buildings on a 2.35-acre site in the heart of Chicago's Loop. The upper floors of the building have been converted to modern office space, and the lower levels are now occupied by several retail and restaurant tenants, including a new three-level CityTarget store. The project unfolded over more than ten years and involved historic tax credits and tax increment financing. The project's financing and long-term success rely on partnerships and collaborations with the Office of the Mayor, the alderman's office, the Chicago Department of Housing and Economic Development, the Chicago Loop Alliance, the Chicago Central Area Committee, Friends of Downtown, the Illinois Historic Preservation Alliance, and the National Park Service.

PORTO, PORTUGAL: MERCADO DO BOM SUCESSO

Mercado Do Bom Sucesso is a redevelopment of a 60-year-old city-owned fresh goods market in central Porto, a city with a 1,200-year history. The redevelopment of the original building adds civic office space, a hotel, and retail kiosks and retains the historic market, which became the main entrance for the entire project. The 85-room Hotel da Música takes its theme from the Casa da Música, a major concert hall venue located off the same traffic circle.

The Porto Municipality owns the property and saw a need for reinvestment at this important location, so in 2008, it launched a design competition for the property. Two things were clear: (1) there was little market potential for new office or retail development, and (2) local citizens would want to preserve the historic market. The solution addresses these concerns by preserving the original building and adding a careful mix of uses that do not depend on expanded market potential. The building continues to be owned by the city, which signed a 50-year lease with the Urban

Continued next page

Examples of Public/Private Partnerships *Continued*

Market Company to manage the market and retail areas. The hotel is managed by Hoti Hotéis, a Portuguese hotel chain.

VANCOUVER, BRITISH COLUMBIA: WOODWARD'S

Woodward's is a mixed-use, urban redevelopment project in the Gastown neighborhood, close to downtown Vancouver. Located on the site of the former Woodward's department store, the redevelopment involved the demolition of several buildings, the restoration of one historic structure for office space, and the construction of two new residential towers, new educational and cultural space for Simon Fraser University, an atrium, a daycare center, and ground-level retail space—all within the confines of a 2.32-acre site in an area with a variety of social and poverty issues. The project includes 1.08 million square feet of space.

Public partners included the city of Vancouver, the province of British Columbia, and Simon Fraser University. The city contributed the land in exchange for the developer performing demolition and remediation of the site, and providing municipal office space and public open space. British Columbia provided C$62 million for the university building and C$44 million for a social housing component. The federal government committed to leasing 30,000 square feet

of office space and also provided the C$205 million construction loan for the project through the Canadian Mortgage and Housing Corporation. The project's owners include Westbank, Peterson Investment Group, the university, the city, and the province of British Columbia.

WASHINGTON, D.C.: CITY VISTA

City Vista is a $200 million public/private project spearheaded by the D.C. National Capital Revitalization Corporation (NCRC) on the 3.2-acre site of the former Wax Museum in Washington, D.C. Selected as developer by the NCRC through a request for proposals, Lowe Enterprises created a mixed-income community of affordable and market-rate residences: 244 rental apartments and 441 condominiums. The project also includes a 55,000-square-foot supermarket and 60,000 square feet of additional commercial space designed in the style of European food markets. The city's goal was to create a mix of commercial space, affordable and market-rate housing, and underground parking. The city's contribution to the developer included below-market sale of part of the land, and two ground leases. The city also agreed to participate in the project's financing.

The many responsibilities carried out by the public partner—brokering regulatory approvals, negotiating with other public agencies, shepherding the development proposal through the environmental impact and community review processes, and providing financial assistance—can expedite progress through the inevitable hurdles encountered by these projects. More so than with other types of development, the risks of public/private development are political. Gauging both the level of political commitment to carry through with a project and the government's ability (in terms of financial resources and personnel) to deliver on agreements is central to a developer's qualitative assessment of project feasibility.

Principles of Public/Private Partnerships

Although the terms and conditions of public aid are tailored to the needs of individual projects, local government assistance falls within the framework of three widely held (if informal) general policy principles:

- Public aid should be delivered through cost-sharing mechanisms.
- Investment of public dollars requires a return for risk taking apart from increased collections of property taxes, based on some form of loan recapture or profit participation in future project revenues.
- The timing and conditions of public commitments should be linked to specific private obligations and responsibilities that must be performed.

In each instance, the public sector seeks to create binding ties in the form of mutually dependent commitments and business interests that establish incentives for the completion of an economically viable project. Generous upfront subsidies can carry risky projects through the first uncertain years, but experience has shown that they cannot turn weak projects into successful ventures. Beyond the task of making development feasible, the hard part of crafting public/private deals is finding ways to ensure the efficacy of public investment in joint development ventures. When deciding on the measures to apply in helping developers close *financing gaps*, public entities must define and measure the public risk of and reward for their actions.

The terms of assistance and conditions of development contained in public/private agreements are complex. This complexity reflects the many tradeoffs made during the course of negotiations in which the public's set of objectives is reconciled with both its limited resources and the demands of private investment. Similarly, the roles adopted by the public sector—broker, facilitator, lessor, builder, lender, investor—reflect both the range of multi-faceted issues (bureaucratic, financial, and political) to be addressed and the conditions in local real estate markets at the time those roles are defined.

The Objectives of Public/Private Development

Increasingly, public/private partnerships are structured as creative alliances that are intended to produce net benefits for all parties. Public sector entities can leverage and maximize public assets, strengthen their control over the development process, and create a more vibrant built environment. Private sector entities may have greater access to developable sites and typically have the experience to develop and manage a real estate project.

Whether for urban revitalization, economic development, or to capture value, the growth of public/private development initiatives has been fostered by a shift in public values favoring entrepreneurial behavior. Further, the broad definition typically accorded "public purpose" provides a rationale that allows every type of public agency to become involved in real estate development: local governments, redevelopment authorities, transit agencies, port authorities, school districts, quasi-public development corporations—even the U.S. General Services Administration, the U.S. Navy, and the U.S. Postal Service.

The public/private approach has proved critical to large-scale projects with complex site conditions, infrastructure demands, or environmental contamination. The open-ended and unpredictable nature of

environmental cleanup, for example, requires high rates of return to attract private capital. The major impediment to redevelopment of brownfield sites is often risk, not cost, and a public entity can bear the risk better than a private company.

Each decade since the 1940s has seen the promulgation of federal, state, and local public policies aimed at stimulating the development of projects that otherwise would not occur. The ways in which government has sought to influence private investment decisions span a broad spectrum of policy approaches. At one end of the continuum are "carrot-oriented" regulatory actions (incentive zoning and transfer of development rights) and programmatic assistance (tax abatements) through which local government provides subsidies to attract desired types of private investment. With these policy approaches, the benefits of public assistance are available to all who meet the qualifying conditions of entitlement. At the other end are more active "stick-oriented" public intervention strategies that rely on bargaining and custom-tailored negotiations with private firms over the terms and conditions of individual projects. In such instances, selective processes of competition rather than prescribed incentives determine private firms' access to development opportunities.

Many kinds of development benefit from a public/private partnership strategy. One example is transit-oriented development—uses that attempt to create synergies and enhance the value and usage of a transit node. Such projects may be developed as part of station construction or after a station is built, or even before, if plans are in place. Joint development of transit-related sites often seeks close coordination of residential and commercial development at transit stations.[5] From the perspective of transit, joint development aims to meet many goals—generation of additional sources of revenue, increased rail ridership, enhanced convenience for riders, creation of a public amenity, and achievement of architectural distinction through direct physical connections between private building entrances and rail stations.

Formation of Public/Private Partnerships

Two levels of government—city and state—worked together with multiple developers over a 30-year period to execute the cleanup and redevelopment of New York's Times Square/42nd Street district, long known as a center for crime, pornography, and sleaze. In 1980, Mayor Edward Koch announced the plan to redevelop the area using eminent domain to take over derelict properties so private developers could build four office towers and a merchandise mart. The city would also rejuvenate the Times Square subway stations. But the original plan faced much resistance—including 47 lawsuits. A recession and declining market conditions caused the city to reexamine the plan. It was the Walt Disney Company that led the way to a new concept. Disney wanted to develop its own Broadway theater, and it was crucial that the surrounding neighborhood be compatible with Disney's image. With state financing, Disney took over the New Amsterdam Theater and worked with officials to facilitate redevelopment of nearby properties. Over time, with the city and state governments taking an active role, more properties followed and the area became a booming commerce and entertainment and district.[6]

Public/private partnerships offer many advantages but a nearly equal number of challenges. Developers anticipate a more cooperative regulatory environment when a government agency is their partner.[7] Developers perceive government entities as more apt to approve and often to accelerate the approval process for those projects in which public agencies have an investment. For the public sector, public/private partnerships afford more control over projects throughout the development process and enable cities to achieve a variety of social objectives; for example, affirmative action, use of minority contractors, and the creation of jobs for low-income residents.

Public/private projects typically involve greater public review and comment, specific contracting requirements, and attention to political concerns. In most cases, the receipt of public monies and the participation of a public partner also mean greater disclosure than in a private project. At the same time, politically active pressure groups are more likely to be a problem for private developers as a result of the publicity that usually accompanies public/private ventures.

Strategic Decisions in the Implementation of Public/Private Projects

In implementing a public/private project, the public sector faces three fundamental tasks:

- Selecting a developer;
- Determining appropriate terms for the deal; and
- Negotiating the deal.

Selecting a Developer

From a strategic perspective, some of the decisions a city must make in the early stages of planning a public/private venture ultimately come to shape both the agenda for negotiations and the tools available for managing the initiative. These choices often must be made when city decision makers are least informed about a project's development potential or are still evaluating possibilities. One such decision concerns the process of selecting a developer. The choice is typically between a bid competition or a development-prospectus competition, through which a parcel is offered for disposition and a developer selected on the basis of comprehensive responses to a *request for qualifications* (*RFQ*) or a *request for proposals* (*RFP*). For nearly all public/private ventures, the RFQ/RFP has been the preferred option; the bid approach generally offers the government less flexibility in controlling the development process and less control over the composition of the benefits package.

In attracting private developers' interest and specifying the ground rules for participation in the project, the RFP sets the stage for future implementation of the project. The RFP can be short and open ended or long and detailed with respect to a project's land uses, design guidelines, and business terms. Regardless of its length, however, it requires the public entity to assess its specific objectives for the project with an eye to

- Broadly defining the character of the private development,
- Identifying public roles and available types of assistance,
- Structuring a set of project-specific planning conditions and business points to which developers must respond, and
- Providing for an orderly and clearly understood procedure for evaluating proposals.

These tasks are roughly analogous in timing to the activities in stages one through three of the conventional development model. The level of specificity for each element is often a matter of market conditions. For example, when the market is weak and the site untested, attracting the attention of qualified developers may require a detailed prospectus and thorough feasibility study. Conversely, when the market is strong, less documentation may be needed, but correspondingly more attention must be devoted to other matters, particularly the detailed terms and conditions for the contemplated business deal. Differences in market dynamics, site characteristics, a given project's public objectives, and the legal alternatives available for designating developers are all important considerations when selecting a developer—and thus make generalizations about the "best" approach inappropriate.

Terms of the Deal

In determining whether significant levels of public assistance for development and financing may be required, public officials typically proceed through the following steps:

- Determining total development costs by project component; and
- Determining the level of private financing available (discussed in part IV) by
  - □ Identifying the gap between project costs and available private resources; and
  - □ Structuring assistance to close financing gaps and to gain reasonable project returns.

When land for public/private development is publicly owned, a second strategic decision is whether to sell or lease the parcel to the developer. A sale can generate substantial upfront revenues for use in other

public projects, eliminate the risk of future nonpayment, and under certain conditions, promise higher dollars for the public treasury than lease arrangements. In terms of controlling land use, restrictive covenants can be attached to property deeds as a condition of sale, as was the case with urban renewal dispositions. As a means for managing the development of large-scale public/private projects, many big

---

The Ground Lease as a Public/Private Partnership Tool

The ground lease form of land disposition creates an ongoing business relationship. It is usually long-term—often 99 years. At the end of the lease, the land and all improvements revert to the owner of the land. For the developer, leasing minimizes the upfront capital investments; for the government agency, retaining ownership of the land allows the public to benefit from rising land values through lease escalations and/or percentage rents.

Structuring a ground lease that is acceptable to a long-term lender is the developer's major concern. In strong markets, government often does not subordinate the land lease to the development financing. To control its exposure to the political as well as the business risks of assuming a proprietary interest in a private investment, the public sector seeks tight lease conditions and, through participation formulas, protection against charges that the developer is earning a "windfall." Both positions present problems to institutional lenders seeking protection from the potential loss of control through foreclosure by the government fee owner.

In the case of percentage rent, lenders hesitate because they fear a reduction in the amount of income to be capitalized when a large percentage of the income stream is committed to a ground lessor. In the event of foreclosure, the valuation impact would be substantial unless the lessor had agreed to subordinate the percentage provision in the lease.

Portland State University in Oregon negotiated a ground lease with American Campus Communities as part of its public/private partnership to develop campus housing. The developer bears all development costs and pays ground rent to the university for the duration of the lease, which is 65 years with two ten-year options. Upon termination of the lease, the university will own the buildings.

In Washington, D.C., a site that was once a gravel parking lot is now 77H, a mixed-use development that includes an urban-format, 75,000-square-foot Walmart; 10,000 square feet of other retail; and 303 rental apartments. The city owns the land and has established a 99-year ground lease with developers JBG Companies and the Bennett Group.

cities have found that leasing affords more strategic advantages.[8]

It should be generally presumed that the public agency will prefer to retain ownership of property rather than to sell it outright, especially if it is deemed well located and difficult to replace. The exception would be in those instances where the agency has made a formal determination that it has land or facilities that are truly surplus to its needs.

Public investment in projects has taken the form of subsidies for land redevelopment and such capital improvements as infrastructure, parking garages, transit systems and stations, stadiums, and public amenities (for example, outdoor plazas and other open space). Such improvements ready a site for private development, provide needed amenities, and/or create an improved programmatic environment in which a project is more likely to succeed. Indirect forms of assistance designed to improve project feasibility can be passed on to developers in several ways: through density bonuses, commitments or guarantees to lease space in a new development, transfers of development rights, land and/or building exchanges, air rights transfers, regulatory relief from zoning and building codes, reduced processing time for approvals, coordinated design of projects in an area, arbitration of any disputes that might arise, and work with or organization of neighborhood and business groups. These public actions typically do not require an outlay of public money but provide the developer with savings in time and money, reduced risk, and/or increased opportunities for development.

For example, Levi's Stadium, in Santa Clara, California, was built for the San Francisco 49ers on land acquired from the city under a 40-year ground lease (see box on page 165). The deal was approved by ballot, with 58 percent of voters approving. The city expects to gain $40 million in revenue over the 40-year lease. The city also benefits from the stadium-naming rights, for which Levi Strauss will pay $220 million over 20 years, with 70 percent going to the quasi-public agency, the Santa Clara Stadium Authority.

Negotiating the Deal

Public agency lease negotiations can be much more complicated and time consuming than comparable private sector discussions. Part of the difficulty is associated with the levels of approvals that are required. It is not uncommon for deal terms to be debated anew once the governing body is involved so the developer should not presume a deal is final prior to that round of review and approval. Furthermore, property leases and ground leases always pose some challenges for lenders who prefer "clean collateral" on which they can place first liens. Government agencies usually argue that they will not subordinate their ownership position or allow ultimate ownership of the land or property to be jeopardized by a default of the developer or subsequent property owners. This illustrates just one of a number of deal points that take time to resolve to the parties' mutual satisfaction.

The practical problems of implementing public/private development require that the public sector partner take an active role in decision making. Reconciling initial differences, finding efficient cost-sharing arrangements, coordinating public and private construction schedules, recasting the deal when crisis threatens the project, and managing the process in light of public review all call for flexibility in responding to the economic and political events that often challenge public/private projects. For private developers, participation in a public/private development means changing normal business practices to accommodate the demands of a politically accountable partner. As discussed in later chapters, time pressure increases dramatically in stage six of the development process, causing stress for both the private developer and the public sector participants. Consequently, the terms of agreement between the parties negotiated in stage four and signed in stage five must be even tighter and more goal-aligning in public/private ventures.

In return for the risk involved, the public sector partner can take a direct financial stake in projects to secure a specified percentage of a project's cash flow (a pseudo-equity interest) through such mechanisms as participatory leases and profit-sharing agreements. An example of profit sharing is the 2014 deal between Louisville, Kentucky, and developers Omni Hotels and the Cordish Company to redevelop a city-owned site as a $261 million mixed-use development. Under the agreement, the city and state contribute about $138 million in exchange for a share of the long-term profits, with a guarantee of at least $10.3 million per year. The city's contribution includes the site, which is valued at about $17 million.[9]

Profit-sharing agreements have not always produced substantial revenues for cities. The economic logic of the subsidy tends to work against a big return. To kick off a project, the city invests funds early in the development process. Then, so as not to burden the project before it reaches an economically viable operating position, profit-sharing revenues typically are structured as triple-net revenues, with the city last in line to receive any cash flow. In other words, the cost-revenue ratio is likely to be negative for many years.

Sharing profits does afford cities nonfinancial benefits. Although large public subsidies can be controversial, profit-sharing arrangements in effect provide a political solution to the buy-high/sell-low problem of writing down the cost of redevelopment. They offer political protection to city officials vulnerable to charges of giving away too much. Even if the anticipated revenues are small or expected far in the future, a financial agreement to share returns is perceived as a sign that the city is acting responsibly and effectively.

PRACTICAL PROBLEMS AND POLICY ISSUES

The public interests at stake in joint venture projects draw governments into management and decision making associated with stages four through seven of the development process. These are decisions typically left to the private sector. As cities share more of a project's financial risk, they often ask for more control.

As the public sector has become more involved in making deals, concerns have surfaced about its objectivity in regulating development and about whether public/private development leads to a conflict of interest for the public sector. The dual role of the public sector creates a dilemma: the potential conflict of interest inherent in the public sector's roles as land seller and as land regulator. At its simplest, the conflict arises because a city's goals in selling versus regulating land are potentially at odds, with the city's role as seller perhaps improperly influencing its regulatory role.

The following questions should be considered in examining whether such a conflict exists:

- Is the city overlooking longer-range public interest goals?
- Can the city make good deals, especially when bargaining with sophisticated private parties?
- Are regulatory concessions given away too cheaply?
- As deal makers, are planners focusing on short-term real estate activity rather than on long-range comprehensive planning?
- Can traditional notions of due process be fulfilled when deals are hammered out behind closed doors?

Ideally, a full accounting of costs and benefits should accompany the evaluation of a deal; with multiple agencies involved, however, it is often hard to track all the direct costs and indirect subsidies. Certain aspects of a deal are simply too difficult to value. Although amenities, subway improvements, and below-market loans can be valued by referencing market equivalents, other benefits such as employment preferences and environmental mitigation commitments have no obvious market comparables. These differences make it hard to standardize evaluation techniques and to define the value of tradeoffs in a public/private deal. As a result, public officials must devote substantial time and resources to effectively communicating the objectives of public/private development and to disclosing public commitments, risks, and expected returns.

INNOVATOR | **Joseph P. Riley** | Mayor, City of Charleston, South Carolina

With no formal education in architecture or urban design, Mayor Joseph P. Riley has demonstrated an uncanny knack for creating a powerful sense of place for citizens and tourists alike while revitalizing the centuries-old city of Charleston, South Carolina. With a developer's vision and an architect's attention to detail, his best education was gained not in the classroom but in walking the streets, examining urban design blemishes and triumphs, and being receptive to the city's voice.

Riley's tenure as mayor of Charleston began following a six-year term in the South Carolina House of Representatives. In his early years as a representative, his reformist position on civil rights and social equality was controversial. Indeed, once elected mayor of Charleston in 1975, Riley increased the number of African Americans on the city council by 50 percent and appointed the city's first black police chief. In 2000, his "Get in Step" campaign to march four days to the state capital to remove the Confederate flag from atop the South Carolina State House was met with national media coverage and credited with the flag's ultimate removal. Racial harmony and equitable consideration of the needs of all citizens, regardless of social class, are pillars of Riley's mayoral canon. In fact, to confront the port town's slavery-dominated past, he has proposed the construction of a $75 million international African American history museum.

His resolve to cure social issues is matched by his unrelenting attention to the public domain. Riley often works with private developers to bring to fruition buildings and spaces that will prove most beneficial to the community. While touring Europe on a Marshall Fellowship, Riley noticed the costly materials that were used in public areas. He learned from his travels that it is a city's duty to provide beauty for communal enjoyment and that it should view such costs as investments. In the long run, Riley posits, thoughtful improvements pay dividends by making the city more attractive to vacationers, businesses, and investors. He likens cities to family heirlooms in that "we are to pass them on to future generations in just as beautiful condition—if not more beautiful—as the way we found them."

Charleston's Waterfront Park has become iconic of Riley's determination and the city's celebrated revival. Riley began plans for the park in 1975 and after years of planning, fundraising, environmental hurdles, and hurricane damage, it finally opened in 1990. Riley described the 13-acre park as "a gift to the future," saying it would add tax revenues to local coffers and raise the value of surrounding real estate. Riley's foresight paid off: nearby land prices rose significantly and a meaningful public space was created that could be enjoyed by all. In another instance of Riley's commitment to the public and innovative land use, after a 2007 fire that destroyed a local store and killed nine firefighters, Riley announced that the city would purchase the property and create a public park and memorial on the site in remembrance of the tragedy.

Riley is adamant about the preservation of Charleston's historic features. The developments he inspired coupled with stringent regulatory guidelines have rejuvenated Charleston since he first took office. Guidelines he initiated include concealing parking facilities behind shops and restaurants whenever possible, and setting

Continued next page

SPORTS FACILITIES

Sports facilities deserve special mention. Believing that they are an important component of economic vitality, cities and states have typically been eager to compete with other cities and states to keep sports franchises from leaving, spending whatever is necessary to accomplish this goal. But cities—and taxpayers—are becoming more wary about claims of benefits from projects like stadiums and arenas, and are critically scrutinizing the cost/benefit ratio attached to such projects, especially when voters are being asked—sometimes through the ballot box— to pay the price. If voters want stadiums, they often do not want to shoulder the costs or to subsidize a team's owner.

Some economists have argued against public funding of sports facilities, showing that they are often a bad deal for the city. Geoffrey Propheter of George Washington University has found little evidence to support the notion that basketball arenas are catalysts of economic development.[10] Urban theorist Richard Florida argues that although arenas may sometimes add to regional income, the tax subsidies they enjoy often erase those gains.[11]

Sports franchises have used their power to pressure governments for new or substantially refurbished stadiums; the present stadium may be too old or too small or lack the amenities or luxury suites that raise the revenue to develop a top team. Alternatively, city officials may actively seek a franchise when the city has no sports team or may

---

INNOVATOR   **Joseph P. Riley** | Mayor, City of Charleston, South Carolina *Continued*

noise ordinances in residential neighborhoods to preserve quality of life. Immediately following Hurricane Hugo, which stripped many structures' rooftops in 1989, Riley allowed property owners to repair damages as quickly as possible, but he set the conditions of the repairs to abide by the city's high design standards; if the original material were not available at the time to fix a roof, it would later be replaced with a more historically appropriate material.

In 1986 Riley helped found the Mayor's Institute on City Design. Convening twice a year nationally and four times a year regionally, the institute invites six to eight mayors from cities around the United States to introduce a critical urban design problem from their city. An interdisciplinary team offers suggestions and potential solutions the problem. Since its inception, more than 900 mayors have participated in the institute. Reflecting Riley's stance on diversity and identifying similarities among the challenges in both small and large cities, much of the success of the program has been in its inclusion of mayors from all sizes of cities and every major region of the United States.

Mayor Riley is one of the longest-serving American mayors, having served ten consecutive terms since he was first elected in 1975. For his tireless efforts as a statesman at the local, regional, and national levels, he has won much praise. In 1985, he was presented a Presidential Award for Design Excellence by Ronald Reagan for public housing in Charleston, and in 2000, he became the first recipient of the ULI J.C. Nichols Prize for Visionaries in Urban Development. In 2009, he received the National Medal of the Arts, presented by President Barack Obama for his work in

urban design and revitalization of the city's historic resources and character. Riley believes that the true job of a leader is to understand the "best aspirations of citizens." His attitude toward his position as a civil servant is best summarized by his insistence that public administrators have a "moral imperative" to create beautiful, meaningful places.

BILL MURTON, CITY OF CHARLESTON

Located on the shore where the Cooper River flows into Charleston Harbor, the 13-acre Waterfront Park is one of Riley's successes.

view an additional franchise as an element of its economic development strategy for downtown or an enhancement to the community's quality of life.

In either case, cities have to figure out how much and in what form they should contribute to the building of a new stadium for a privately owned team or risk losing that team to another city that seems (at least during the heat of negotiations) only too willing to promise team owners a new stadium. Some highly successful stadiums and arenas have been built entirely with private funding. MetLife Stadium, the New Jersey home to the Giants and Jets, was completed in 2010 with no public funding. In Grand Rapids, a stadium for the West Michigan Whitecaps, a minor league baseball team, opened in 2014, built entirely with private funds. Older

examples include AT&T Park, home of the San Francisco Giants, and the Verizon Center in downtown Washington, D.C., which is home to the city's basketball and hockey teams.

The political stakes of such debates are high, with pros and cons targeting both economic and strategic issues (see box). Economists continue to cast doubt on the monetary benefits that cities reap from subsidizing new stadiums. Heavy public financial assistance is highly controversial, so the way that the public assistance package is put together is key to the political acceptance of a city's decisions. To partially finance stadium construction, cities and developers may rely on specialized types of so-called export taxes such as hotel and motel taxes, car rental taxes, or a tax on visiting athletes; cities also have

The Pros and Cons of Publicly Subsidized Financing for Sports Stadiums and Arenas

PROS FOR NEW STADIUMS

- Foster local economic growth.
- Generate new jobs and new tax revenue.
- Stimulate spending in neighborhood restaurants, bars, and hotels.
- Create spillover opportunities for real estate development.
- Meet local citizens' desires for entertainment and pride of place for local sports teams.

CONS FOR NEW STADIUMS

Stadiums are poor sources for economic development, as most empirical studies have shown, because

- The projected economic impacts rarely materialize.
- Stadium-related jobs are often seasonal and pay low wages.
- Rather than generating new revenue, stadiums merely change where people's entertainment dollars are spent.
- The value of publicly subsidized financing is often distorted in economic studies.
- Costs typically exceed benefits.
- Cities have more pressing needs—schools, transit, infrastructure—competing for scarce public funds.

Economic studies need to answer four questions:

- How do the costs of a proposed stadium compare with its benefits?
- Who benefits and who pays?
- What is the impact of a new stadium on local per capita income?
- What is the likely impact of a new stadium on the rate of growth of the local economy?

COMMON CRITICISMS OF ECONOMIC STUDIES

- Impact or cost/benefit studies are rarely commissioned by independent players, and the results typically are consistent with the positions (pro or con) of their sponsors.
- Estimates of benefits (direct revenues and spillovers) are imprecise because data are limited and assumptions suspect or optimistic.
- Multipliers—one of the key variables of any economic impact analysis—used by most studies are based on decades-old data.
- Econometric studies of economic impacts are also suspect, because economists disagree on methodological approaches and conceptual models for measuring impacts are weak.

Source: David C. Petersen, *Developing Sports, Convention, and Performing Arts Centers*, 3rd ed. (Washington, D.C.: Urban Land Institute, 2001).

---

created sports lotteries and put in place an ostensibly temporary sales tax or surcharge on an existing sales tax, in addition to many other forms of assistance. The private side of the equation offers a number of special sources of funds: corporate sponsorships, stadium-naming rights, luxury boxes and charter seats, concession rights, advertising revenues, and parking fees.[12]

SUMMARY

This chapter began with a description of a public hearing where the economic interests of the land owner and developer were to be decided by an elected body. The developer was attempting to create a project that met the demands of a future market and the concerns of an existing community. Opponents to the project saw the developer reaping a windfall through the granting of rights that did not theretofore exist.

Differing stakeholders' perceptions are often difficult to understand and reconcile.

Growth management regulations usually attempt to channel and guide the inevitable impacts of growth on the existing environment. However, land use regulations are often difficult to navigate. Entitlements can be very costly to obtain, and the capital to finance entitlements requires very high returns to compensate for the risk. Lengthy entitlement processes also may lead to supply constraints. Accordingly, much of the value in the development process is created through entitlements. Some critics of the growth management system note, "the inevitable result of restricting the supply of land…is a rise in prices."[13]

The success of public/private development has made it an important strategy for stimulating local economic development and financing selected items of capital infrastructure. It is also a means of implementing complex redevelopment projects. The tangible results of this type of development approach contrast sharply with the legacy of controversy, acres of cleared but eerily vacant land, and years of frustration that resulted from failed urban renewal projects developed under a strategy of command and control on the part of the public sector in the 1960s and 1970s. Consequently, city governments, public authorities, and other special-purpose agencies have strong incentives to build a foundation for public/private partnerships by establishing planning and consensus-building processes, resource mobilization efforts, and institutional mechanisms the set the groundwork for successful joint ventures.

The scope and focus of urban public/private development activity continues to evolve. Building on experience, much of it concentrated in large-scale building of downtowns, cities today tend to focus more on smaller-scale projects targeted at rebuilding neighborhoods, creating transit hubs, revitalizing waterfronts, and creating town centers with a mix of uses. And there is little reason to expect that the drive for off-budget financing of public infrastructure and civic amenities among suburban governments will abate. Land-owning public authorities are also likely to continue to pursue efforts to capture value through joint development.

TERMS

- Advocacy planning
- Charrettes
- Discretionary approvals
- Financing gap
- Ground leases
- Public/private partnership
- Quasi-public (organizations)
- Request for proposals (RFP)
- Request for qualifications (RFQ)
- Tax increment financing (TIF)

REVIEW QUESTIONS

8.1 Who are the various stakeholders involved in the approvals process?

8.2 Describe how the approvals process has changed over time.

8.3 What are some ways the development team can build public support for a project?

8.4 Describe the key decisions the public sector faces in implementing a public/private partnership.

8.5 What advantages does a city gain by working within a public/private partnership? What advantages does a developer gain? What are some of the practical problems or points of tension in such a business relationship?

NOTES

1 Lisa R. Peattie, "Reflections on Advocacy Planning," *Journal of the American Institute of Planners*, vol. XXXIV, no. 2, March 1968, p. 81.

2 David Brooks, "Patio Man and the Sprawl People, America's Newest Suburbs," *The Weekly Standard*, vol. 007, issue 46, August 12, 2002, p. 14.

3 Robert W. Burchell, David Listokin et al., *Development Impact Handbook* (Washington, D.C.: ULI–the Urban Land Institute, 1994), p. 19.

4 See Lynne B. Sagalyn, "Explaining the Improbable: Local Redevelopment in the Wake of Federal Cutbacks," *Journal of the American Planning Association*, 1990, pp. 429–441.

5 See Robert T. Dunphy et al., *Developing around Transit: Strategies and Solutions That Work* (Washington, D.C.: ULI–the Urban Land Institute, 2004).

6 For a detailed history of the redevelopment of Times Square, see Lynne B. Sagalyn, *Times Square Roulette: Remaking the City Icon* (Cambridge, Mass.: MIT Press, 2001).

7 Richard F. Babcock, "The City as Entrepreneur: Fiscal Wisdom or Regulatory Folly?" in *City Deal Making*, ed. Terry Jill Lassar (Washington, D.C.: ULI—the Urban Land Institute, 1990), p. 14.

8 See Lynne B. Sagalyn, "Leasing: The Strategic Option for Public Development," Working Paper, Lincoln Institute of Land Policy, Cambridge, Mass., 1993; Robert Wetmore and Chris Klinger, "Land Leases: More Than Rent Schedules," *Urban Land*, June 1990, pp. 6–9; and Lynne B. Sagalyn, "Negotiating Public Benefits: The Bargaining Calculus of Public/Private Development," *Urban Studies*, December 1997, pp. 1955–1970.

9 Braden Lammers, "Omni Hotel Headlines $261 Million Downtown Development Project," *Louisville Business First*, March 6, 2014.

10 Propheter, Geoffrey, "Are Basketball Arenas Catalysts of Economic Development?" *Journal of Urban Affairs*, vol. 34, issue 4, pp. 441–459, October 2012.

11 www.theatlanticcities.com/jobs-and-economy/2012/08/do-basketball-arenas-spur-economic-development/2804/

12 David C. Petersen, *Developing Sports, Convention, and Performing Arts Facilities*, 3d ed. (Washington, D.C.: ULI–the Urban Land Institute, 2001).

13 Robert Bruegmann, *Sprawl* (Chicago: University of Chicago Press, 2005), p. 209.

PART 4

Ideas

Some of the best development ideas seem so simple that people assume they appear like the proverbial lightbulb over cartoon characters' heads. Unfortunately, that "ah, ha!" experience is rare. Instead, most ideas arise from a combination of intuition, creativity, and rigorous market research. Sometimes opportunities result from a developer's deliberate efforts. At other times, an almost unconscious processing of information leads to ideas for the next development.

Chapter 9 sets the stage for the development process by laying out various ways ideas are generated. The idea for a project may begin with a piece of land that becomes available and a developer considering what might work on that site. Or a developer might have an idea that meets some new need in the community. Only with considerable thought and investigation does the idea move forward. Chapters 10 and 11 provide the basic financing background and tools that developers use throughout the development process. Chapter 12 picks up on refining the idea, which is typically based on a significant amount of data collection and analysis supported by discussions with team members, lenders, investors, public officials, and others involved in the project.

Chapter 9

Stage One of the Development Process: Idea Inception

Knowing the roles of the participants in the development process and the historical evolution of the relationship between the public and private sectors, it is time to move forward with stage one of the development process—idea inception. Of all the activities that constitute real estate development, this is the least mechanical and most creative. The excitement of identifying an unfilled need and creating a product to fill it is the stimulus that drives development. Success is predicated on finding the right idea. It is difficult, if not impossible, to manage one's way out of a bad development idea.

Where do developers get their ideas? How do they know which ideas deserve further analysis and which do not? No magic formula exists for generating good development ideas because everyone receives different data and processes that data into information differently. The spark comes from the way pieces of information are put together to solve a problem—as well as from the quality and uniqueness of multiple insights. One thing is certain: developers need background information to turn insights into good ideas. Such information, along with experience, produces a feel for the market. This feel does not earn the developer any money, but

without it, a developer is likely to lose money and do a disservice to the community.

Human experience and observation go a long way when a developer tries to understand real estate markets. The developer, members of the development team, investors, regulators, and policy makers can be more effective and successful if they look at all the data (history, current conditions, and forecasts). In a sense, the development players unconsciously perform market research during almost all their waking moments when they read, drive, eat, play, meditate, or interact with other people. They perform more structured market research when they rigorously analyze the regional economy, local population growth, employment figures, zoning provisions, traffic counts, occupancy rates, and consumer surveys. Curiosity, interest, and observation enhance the formal approaches to generating ideas.

This chapter explains a developer's need to fully understand how to market the product: finding out what customers want, ensuring that the product responds to those demands, and persuading customers to purchase or rent the product at a price that produces an adequate return. Such a comprehensive approach to marketing provides a decision framework in which the development team's creative juices can flow productively into an idea that can become a profitable physical reality.

Although marketing and market research underlie every stage of the development process, the basics of marketing and market research are highlighted at four points in the development process: idea inception, idea refinement, feasibility analysis, and project marketing.

As a starting point to the eight stages of the development process, this chapter covers the following topics:

- The motivations behind ideas,
- The *back-of-the-envelope pro forma*,
- Techniques for generating ideas, and
- Risk control during stage one.

MOTIVATIONS BEHIND IDEAS

For a developer, every new insight serves as a catalyst, which, when melded with the developer's background and experience, generates still more ideas. In this way, the developer moves repeatedly through stage one many times a day.

Developers are constantly involved in informal brainstorming, always searching their knowledge and experience for an idea that offers potential. In the development process, ideas may emerge in many

---

CASE STUDY   **Envisioning Shortbread Lofts**

Shortbread Lofts is an 85-unit, 271-bedroom student housing development, the first new construction, for-rent multihousing community in downtown Chapel Hill since 1999. The neighborhood around the Rosemary Street site is the epicenter of the picturesque college town, with restaurants, storefront retail, and the entrance to the University of North Carolina (UNC) campus.

UNC has nearly 30,000 students. Freshmen are required to live on campus, but that leaves more than 25,000 students in need of housing, of whom almost 60 percent are women. University dorms for freshmen located two blocks from the Rosemary Street site charged room and board fees ranging from $4,500 to $9,000 per semester for a one-bedroom suite. Other than such accommodations for freshmen, there were no other equally well-located student rentals except the Warehouse, Short's largest development at that point. It was targeted to upscale female students (85 percent of the occupants) but had become a bit dated in terms of its fixtures and amenities.

Short was selling the Warehouse, as the partners were no longer compatible. Some wanted to refinance to secure lower rates and pull out cash. Others preferred to avoid the significant prepayment penalty associated with in-place financing. The project had done well and had considerable equity.

To envision Shortbread Lofts, Larry Short drew on this background and his awareness of changes in market needs. The idea for Shortbread Lofts was to go after the same market as the Warehouse but with significantly better features, functions, and benefits. As the Rosemary Street site was very close to campus, the target market segment was clear. With only 271 bedrooms planned for the project, overestimating the size of the segment was not expected to be an issue.

What were the ideas that ultimately became Shortbread Lofts? First, upscale student housing—particularly for women—had already proven to be a viable market. Second, from Short's experience with the Warehouse, he knew that the target consumers desired certain features, functions, and benefits that were not currently available in the market. Third, he knew that an appropriate site might be assembled from two contiguous parcels on West Rosemary Street. These three insights collectively generated an idea worth pursuing—that is, it passed the back-of-the-envelope pro forma.

Early Rough Estimate of Total Costs

Land	$4 million
Hard construction	$21 million ($70,000/unit)
Soft costs and fees	$4 million
Total	**$29 million**

Early Rough Estimate of Value

Average rental rate	$850
Annual income per unit	$10,000
Estimated units	300
Total annual revenue	$3,000,000
Operating expenses (30%)	$900,000
Expected annual income	$2,100,000
Cap rate	6%
Expected value at completion	$35,000,000

Back-of-the-envelope feasibility: value of $35 million exceeds total cost of $29 million.

Continued next page

ways. For example, developers sometimes discover a site looking for a use. For one reason or another, the owners of a particular parcel, whether public or private, want the site to be developed, thereby creating possibilities for a developer. Sometimes the site is already developed and the existing structure needs to be redeveloped. Perhaps a building stands on the site and must remain, but the owner is seeking a new use for it. Or perhaps the existing building will be expanded or additional buildings built on the site. Alternatively, developers sometimes encounter a use looking for a site, which is frequently the case when corporations want to expand, introduce a new product, or restructure their operations. These

goals create a need for constructed space (a fast-food restaurant, for example, looking for a high-traffic corner in a specific trade area, or a residential developer seeking lots in a target neighborhood that will fit an existing house plan series). Finally, powerful forces of the capital market might be at work, setting owners of capital to looking for a development opportunity. This is the raison d'être of development companies. They are in the business of employing capital to provide economic returns from the asset class of real estate.

In all these cases, the developer must have the tools—the relevant experience in development and the familiarity with the latest changes in the

---

CASE STUDY   **Envisioning Shortbread Lofts**   *Continued*

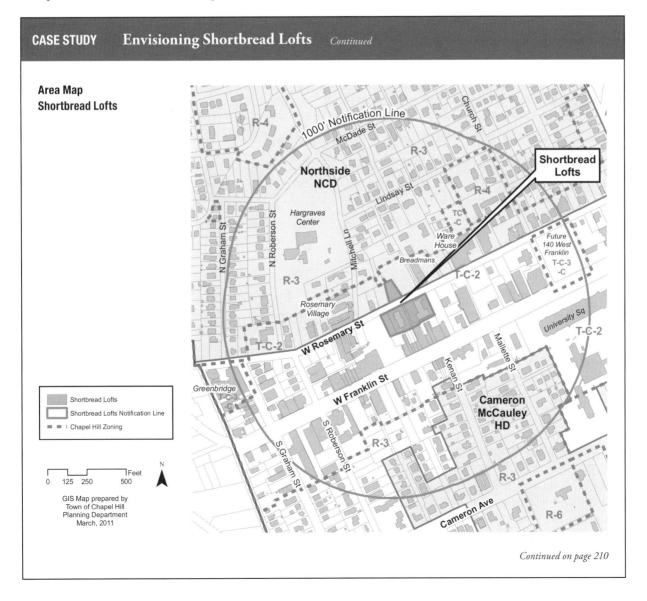

**Area Map
Shortbread Lofts**

GIS Map prepared by
Town of Chapel Hill
Planning Department
March, 2011

Continued on page 210

industry—to be able to respond to the stimulus. Successful developers also have extensive contacts who function as a sounding board for new ideas and who can suggest potential members of the development team.

Although an initial idea may be rough, the key concerns at this early stage are all the ways that a project affects its surrounding environment as well as all the effects of that environment on the project. Known as a property's *situs*, from Graaskamp's Situs Theory,[1] these locational factors inform the decision-making process by which a location is deemed suitable for a development. In addition to fitting the location, the site must, in turn, fit the tenant and fit the financing. Ultimately, this fit usually reshapes the original idea, as demonstrated in the next several chapters. When fit and reshaping are being considered, it is important not to lose sight of ethical obligations. As the pressures of the development process intensify, the developer must remain alert to any moral hazards lurking in the substructure.

THE BACK-OF-THE-ENVELOPE PRO FORMA

Stage one of the development process ends when the developer tests the new idea with a "back-of-the-envelope" pro forma—a simple comparison of value and cost. At this stage, ideas are not sufficiently refined to be subjected to the type of detailed analysis that incorporates the computerized discounted cash flow models described in chapter 11. And because most ideas generated at this stage are never carried out, the developer cannot justify the expenditure of a great deal of money or time to fully analyze every aspect of each idea.

To prepare a quick pro forma for an income property, the developer typically uses his concept of the target tenant to estimate how much rent a tenant might be willing to pay for a particular type of space with appropriate services in a particular location. The projection consists of a rough estimate of income per square foot and operating expenses per square foot without detailed attention to the configuration, length of lease, number of elevators, and the many

---

INNOVATOR Wilbur H. Smith III | Principal, Greenlaw Partners

Wil Smith, a California native, has a pedigree in the development business. His uncle is a leading and highly respected California developer, and his father was a successful commercial developer. Smith learned the business from the ground up: He worked in construction, leased and managed properties, made acquisitions, and conducted other facets of the business. He has always had a huge drive to succeed as well as a nose for a deal, with an understanding of markets and deals with high potential across all product types.

Smith earned his bachelor's degree in agriculture from California Polytechnic State University, San Luis Obispo, and a master's degree in real estate development from the University of Southern California. Before founding his own firm, he was the director of asset management and vice president of entitlements for Makar Properties LLC, a privately held real estate company.

In 2003, Smith and John Tumminello formed Greenlaw Partners and Greenlaw Management Inc. According to John Brady of Guggenheim Real Estate (GRE), "John was the perfect counterpoint to Wil. John was a transplanted New Yorker with a strong financial and management background. He was several years older but possessed the same hunger for the business. They played off each

other very well. They also had extensive contacts in what I called the 'next generation' of broker stars. These guys drove SUVs and 300 series BMWs on the way to Porsches and 700 series BMWs. Their network provided access to quality under-the-radar deals."

Today, Greenlaw is a full service real estate investment management and operating company that has completed more than $2 billion in acquisitions and dispositions of commercial real estate properties. The company manages a portfolio in California of four million square feet of office, industrial, retail, resort, and commercial assets. Smith oversees all aspects of the company's acquisition, operations, and investment development/redevelopment programs.

Innovation abounds in Orange County, allowing Smith to borrow ideas from multiple sources. For example, during the idea inception stage of the ITC project, Smith's connection to Reed Brady at Guggenheim and thus to Brady's industry contacts was a key factor. Smith saw the potential of the site but knew he needed investors with deep pockets for "patient cash," as the project was difficult to define. Smith knew that his dream for the development would go through many iterations before the final approvals, detailed design, and eventual reconstruction.

other factors that will be determined during the later stages of development decision making. The next step is to multiply the project's leasable square feet by the estimated revenue per square foot. The developer then subtracts the projected operating expenses to obtain an estimate of operating income, which can then be translated into an estimate of value. If cost exceeds value, it is back to the drawing board.

This back-of-the-envelope pro forma follows the same format as the more complete one described in

---

CASE STUDY   Envisioning Irvine Tech Center

Wil Smith had purchased and sold a site in the city of Anaheim in advance of the city's initiative to develop a "24/7" district. Known as the Platinum Triangle, the district was to have a mixed-use residential/retail/office framework. The template for the project at that site was carried over to the ITC site, where the real estate dynamics were similar: an area of rapid economic transformation and rising land values. The idea for the site began with the application of the principles of the Anaheim experience to an area with a unique regulatory environment. Although the basics were the same, it required insight born of experience to understand the latent opportunities in the area. Some cues were evident in earlier developments along Jamboree Road, which fronts the property. There, a few multifamily projects that had been started before the S&L crisis had finally stabilized. Another high-density master plan, Central Park West, had been caught in the 2008 financial downturn after construction had started, but it established the development

concept that was beginning to take root on the Jamboree corridor. Smith's success with ITC thus depended on five key elements:

- Experience with the concept, based on Smith's Anaheim experience;
- Knowledge of the market dynamics of the airport submarket;
- Market analogues in the IBC and the lifestyle changes that would support more growth of that market segment;
- Knowledge of political changes that would open the door to high-density residential uses; and
- Appreciation of the location and land values.

All of these elements provided the confidence that the market was solidifying and that Smith would not bear the risk of being "the first man in."

Continued on page 200

Irvine Tech Center Site Plan

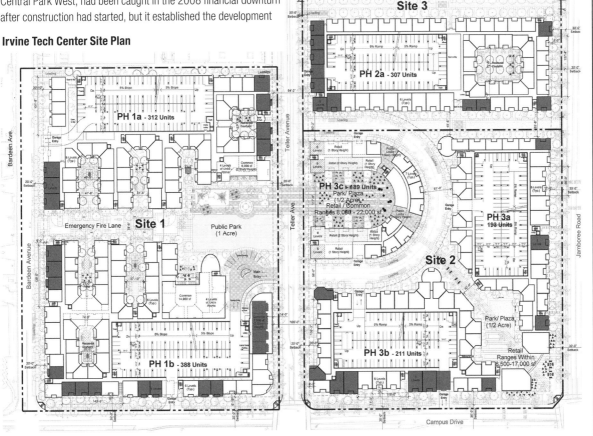

---

chapter 11. It differs only in the level of detail. The rough estimate of value thus inelegantly generated is then compared with a rough estimate of cost, which at this point typically is projected from estimates of what the land might sell for plus site development costs and the construction costs per square foot of the proposed structure. If cost exceeds value, the developer goes back to the drawing board. If, however, value exceeds cost, the idea remains viable and may proceed to the next stage.

In stage one, it is critical to get the "big picture" right. In subsequent stages, much more detailed rigor is needed. For example, with his idea for Shortbread Lofts, Larry Short thought he could get about 300

Willowsford: Downzoning as an Opportunity

When Rockpoint Group LLC learned that a 4,100-acre property in Loudoun County, Virginia, was becoming available owing to the owner's failure to obtain a rezoning, the company saw a unique development opportunity. It was clear that the county would not approve a large number of lots on the site, so instead a plan evolved to use the farmland on the site as the theme for a new residential community based on a sustainable "farm-to-table" lifestyle. This theme differentiated the community, provided a marketing strategy, and created a more desirable product that yielded higher sales prices and drew buyers from a broader market area than a more generic community would have. Rockpoint's back-of-the-envelope estimates showed potential and ultimately a successful project was developed.

Developers of Willowsford, in Loudoun County, Virginia, turned zoning limitations into an opportunity by using farmland as a theme. An on-site farm produces fruits, vegetables, eggs, honey, and other goods that are sold to residents.

rental units on the site and could assemble and secure the site for about $4 million. With a construction cost of about $30 million (rough estimate of major cost items below), the all-in cost would be about $34 million.

With the newest features, functions, and benefits, Short expected a rental rate average of $850 per month or about $10,000 per year per unit, for total annual revenue of $3 million. Using an equally rough estimate of expected operating expenses at 30 percent, the expected annual income was $2.1 million. The market capitalization rate in the Chapel Hill apartment market at the time was about 6 percent. (The capitalization rate is explained in chapter 10. It is essentially income divided by value, for an average of comparable properties in the particular market.) The expected value of the completed development was $35 million ($2.1 million divided by 0.6), which is greater than the expected total cost of $29 million. Although the finances never turn out to be as easy as the back-of-the-envelope pro forma, Short decided that the idea had enough potential to justify the expenditures he would have to make in stage two—idea refinement.

Like most research-driven activities, the vast majority of development ideas are not financially viable. Thus, most of the time, stage one ends with recognition that the smart decision is to stop. The prospect of a "no-go" decision is a fact of life for developers and a natural part of the development process. But the compensation for nine (or 999) ideas that die on the back of the envelope is one good idea worth refining in stage two.

It is important to note, too, that when developers calculate a back-of-the-envelope pro forma and the idea looks like a go, it is no guarantee that the idea will live beyond the next stage. Developers are part dreamers, and everything to this point is a rough estimate. Once other players become more involved—which occurs upon getting a positive value from the back-of-the-envelope pro forma—they may temper the dream with realities and improved information that make it impossible to go ahead with the project.

IDEA INCEPTION IN THE CORPORATE CONTEXT

The rise of large development companies, corporate real estate departments, and a large body of professionals with extensive university training has accelerated the application of more formal strategic planning to the creative side of real property development. This trend is noteworthy because the public often views developers as freewheelers unfettered by bureaucracy.

The choice of a project affects the organization of the development company. Before deciding on a project, a developer should think about how large an organization he wants to control, the extent of desired vertical or horizontal integration (that is, the amount of structure he is willing to accept), and the talent, ambition, and money available. Any idea selected for implementation becomes part of an organizational strategy; in fact, a developer can identify specific projects and locations, and consider those choices to be part of the organizational strategy he wants to pursue. Ideally, a developer should consider how a particular project fits into the strategy for his company.

To use marketing research effectively for a project, a developer should have a clear idea of why he wants to undertake the project and how much of his money, personnel, and reputation he is willing and able to commit to it. (Note how Graaskamp's definition of feasibility fits easily into a strategic planning framework: "A real estate project is 'feasible' when the real estate analyst determines that there is a reasonable likelihood of satisfying explicit objectives when a selected course of action is tested for fit to a context of specific constraints and limited resources."[2]

Organizational strategies differ in detail and formality with the size and focus of the development company. Small developers may have a strategy that

Altmarkt-Galerie | Dresden, Germany

The Altmarkt-Galerie is a key retail center that has helped to redefine the urban core of the war-torn city of Dresden in the former East Germany. In 1990, the city and ECE Projektmanagement, a private developer based in Hamburg, realized that they had shared goals. ECE thought there was commercial development opportunity in Dresden, and the city sought economic revitalization, especially in its urban core. During World War II, the city had endured the destruction of 1,600 acres of its downtown, and commercial activity had subsequently been largely located on the periphery of the city. ECE and Dresden's city council decided to partner to work on revitalizing the downtown. The goal was to create a retail shopping center that would drive foot traffic to the city's urban core and spur further development downtown.

The city and ECE created a steering committee that included representatives from both parties and met regularly until the project was completed. A municipal coordinator promoted the project and ensured that all the stakeholders stayed invested in its success. One of the steering committee's first decisions was to finance a competition among architectural firms to generate design ideas for the retail center. The most important aspect of the project would be its ability to define an urban core for Dresden. Because the city contained several locations that could be considered its center, the architectural competition was critical in deciding to place the Altmarkt-Galerie between the historic district and Prager Strasse. The historic district offers tourist sites, such as the Zwinger Palace and the Semperoper Opera House, while Prager Strasse offers well-established shopping destinations. Other components of the design, such as architectural style and strategies for creating a human scale, were also aided by the competition.

The partnership between the developer and city, as well as the architectural competition, were instrumental in making the Altmarkt-Galerie a success. The cooperative nature of the development process generated ideas for how to transform downtown Dresden and also carried the project through to completion. The development opened in 2002 to such success that in 2008 a major expansion got underway to add 93 shops, offices, and a hotel. That expansion opened in 2011. The Altmarkt-Galerie has attracted a variety of retailers and driven foot traffic of over a million people a month to Dresden's new urban core.

The Altmarkt-Galerie combines historic buildings with new construction and links a historic district with a commercial one.

exists only in their heads. In contrast, the development arm of a large corporation must usually prepare an organizational strategy for its real estate business that fits into the larger corporate strategy. In such an environment, fairly rigid procedures exist for making a go/no-go decision should be followed.

TECHNIQUES FOR GENERATING IDEAS

Ideas often appear to arise intuitively; however, certain formal techniques can be used to stimulate creativity. *Brainstorming*, the *nominal group process*, the *Delphi method*, *environmental scanning*, *focus groups*, and surveys (or a combination of these types) are the techniques used most frequently to generate and test development ideas. These techniques are sufficiently systematic and precise to help generate ideas without making exorbitant demands on limited time and money.

Brainstorming is a group (or individual) exercise devoted to producing the largest possible number of creative ideas during a given period of time. To encourage an atmosphere of creativity, the group or individual initially accepts every idea, no matter how unusual. Whether pursued in a group or individually, brainstorming should follow several rules:

- Write down every idea, and defer judgment on their value.
- List as many ideas as possible.
- Try not to let participants get too far afield while still pursuing radical thoughts.
- Most important, look for combinations of listed ideas.

After completing a brainstorming session, a development team can study the lists of ideas more closely and select the most promising combination of ideas for potential projects.

The nominal group process is a technique for establishing priority among ideas identified by a group. It can be used to analyze in more detail ideas generated through brainstorming. It is particularly useful when a development team is responsible for achieving consensus on goals and courses of action to achieve those goals. Participants are first asked to write ideas in silence after a facilitator has explained

the problem or issue. The facilitator lists the ideas that participants have developed, helps clarify them, and screens opinions based on the group's preferences. Members then submit a written, confidential vote on the various alternatives, and preferred projects emerge. The usefulness of the nominal group process depends on the developer's willingness to work with a group—usually the development organization or a larger development team that includes outside consultants—to establish priorities among project ideas. The process is often used in public sector development, where consensus is critical.

The Delphi method, first used to analyze military strategies and the impacts and implications of new technologies, brings expert opinion to bear on a research question. A developer can use the technique to gather the informed opinions of market experts about a complex question without having to bring them together at one time. One obvious application in real estate development is in forecasting the supply of and demand for kinds of space. Aiming for a consistent set of answers, the developer prepares a set of questions for a diverse group of experts, perhaps a politician, a market researcher, and a broker. After examining the experts' independent responses, the developer can prepare more structured and closed-ended questions and then ask the experts to compare their views with others and to consider revising their opinions. The process may require several rounds of review. If the process is successful, the developer can elicit a single, coherent picture of the environment under study. Developers find the Delphi method attractive when the questions are complex, the experts are dispersed and few in number, or antipathy exists in the proposed development team.

Environmental scanning is a systematic way for developers or a development team to monitor the local, regional, national, and global environments and to predict the possible implications of environmental events. For example, a developer engaged in a large-scale project with a lengthy completion period might consider the implications of a recession on the project's feasibility. Scanning can be simplified by identifying a few readily available, easily interpreted indicators for monitoring environmental events.

Examples include the prime interest rate or quarterly changes in the GDP. The developer or team specifies the events and the actions that those events would trigger, and often writes scenarios to use in playing out the implications and results of alternative courses of action. Although environmental scanning is widely used and highly recommended for strategic organizational planning, it is a time-consuming way to generate project ideas. It is more commonly used in stage three, in conjunction with computerized sensitivity analysis.

Focus groups are most often used in modifying a proposed project to meet the desires of a potential consumer group, although they sometimes are used to generate ideas for future developments. Focus groups have one primary advantage over other processes: they allow a free flow of thoughts that can sometimes generate a wide range of interesting ideas. The groups typically consist of eight to 12 people who meet for about two hours. A moderator leads a discussion from a set of carefully prepared questions or objectives, but is flexible enough and sufficiently knowledgeable about the topic to know when to delve deeper. The moderator should be trained to avoid steering the group to affirm preconceived notions. Critics of focus groups say that the technique is not rigorous and that its results can be misleading if the wrong participants are chosen. However, when

---

INNOVATORS   Fresh Approaches to Community Building

Public communications and stakeholder engagement can be difficult efforts—especially if a proposal does not reflect a community's vision or master plan. The two practitioners profiled here have managed major community planning projects that have championed diversity and inclusion, propelling growth in their respective communities.

Kishore Varanasi is principal and the director of urban design at CBT Architects in Boston, where he leads a studio that focuses on innovative city-building practice both locally and internationally. As a master planner for the 113-acre Boston University Campus, Varanasi redefined the objectives from traditional campus planning to a city-building exercise. By engaging the investors, public agencies, and surrounding towns through hundreds of meetings and coordinating their visions, he found implementation and financing efficiencies and also produced specific projects that provided larger benefits. This strategy allows the university to densify rather than expand into surrounding communities. Most recently, Varanasi served as a member of the mayor's Complete Streets Advisory Committee, which has made radical changes to streets as public spaces through deployment of electric car stations, parklets, bicycle-friendly infrastructure, and improved pedestrian safety.

Varanasi has been in the business for only 15 years but has already shaped some of Greater Boston's highest-profile projects, encompassing more than 400 acres and 30 million square feet of development. His training in architecture, urbanism, and real estate, coupled with his energetic personality, inspires great collaborations and successful community building.

Brian Allan Jackson is a partner with EYA LLC, an urban infill development company in the Washington, D.C., area. Jackson serves as senior vice president of land acquisition and development, and leads EYA's Investment Committee. He directs strategy and planning for the firm and serves on EYA's Executive Committee.

At EYA, Jackson has played a leading role in $1 billion worth of public/private development partnerships, creating mixed-income communities that are integrative, walkable, and sustainable. He has led development projects that exemplify equitable place making and transit-oriented best practices, such as these:

- *Old Town Commons.* A partnership with the Alexandria, Virginia Redevelopment and Housing Authority to redevelop an underperforming public housing site into a pedestrian-friendly, mixed-income community with 365 units of affordable rental and market-rate for-sale housing.
- *Capitol Quarter.* A 323-unit mixed-income community that is part of the Arthur Capper/Carrollsburg HOPE VI redevelopment in Washington, D.C.—one of the largest urban redevelopment areas in the country.
- *McMillan Reservoir.* A 25-acre mixed-use/mixed-income redevelopment partnership with the District of Columbia government, Trammell Crow Company, and Jair Lynch Development Partners.
- *Shady Grove Station.* A 90-acre mixed-use/mixed-income/ transit-oriented redevelopment partnership with Montgomery County, Maryland.
- *National Park Seminary.* One of the largest adaptive reuse developments in the state of Maryland.

Before joining EYA, Jackson served as chief of staff at the U.S. General Services Administration (GSA), the single largest owner and operator of real estate assets in the United States. While at the GSA, he played a key role in several high-profile development projects as well as in the GSA's response to the 9/11 terrorist attacks.

Alison Johnson

focus groups are used to search for ideas that will be tested further, these weaknesses are not critical.

Surveys are another tool that developers use to generate ideas for new products and projects and to modify projects that are underway. Many times surveys are given to residents or tenants in a developer's existing projects to assess customer satisfaction. Or they are given to prospective customers who visit or call the sales office for information. Developers can put together a profile of probable customers, including the kind of product they want and their willingness to pay for it. The advantage of this method is that the profile is generated by sales center traffic—people who have already shown a certain amount of interest by making the effort to gather information about the development.

All these generic techniques can be modified to fit the particular situation.

Although these formal methods can be quite useful, entrepreneurs should not rule out some less formal techniques used by creative people, such as daydreaming, carrying a notepad, and writing down anything that is remotely related to the problem, or changing routines to open oneself to fresh experiences. So long as the developer enters these activities—formal and informal—with an open mind and does not merely look for confirmation of an initial idea, new ideas and reshaped ideas will emerge.

Even at this early stage, it is useful for the developer to consider whether the idea meets the public sector's interests and goals. Developers should have some instinct for local politics and an understanding of the development climate and public needs. An idea that does not meet the requirements of those granting entitlements or gets tangled in long legal battles may not be a good one.

Developers kick a lot of tires, show colleagues a lot of sketches and photographs, and visit other cities and countries to get ideas. Sometimes a developer builds a project in small phases, allowing market response to shape the later phases. But because the products are so expensive, good market research is particularly important. A successful developer is adept at identifying a need and responding to it.

Sometimes the idea is a startling new combination of elements such as Chelsea Piers Sports and Entertainment, a 30-acre sports and film center on four giant finger piers on the Hudson River in New York City. The sports center was started because the developer, Roland Betts, had a daughter who was a figure skater and was himself a hockey player; he knew too well that the few ice rinks available in the city were inadequate. His frustration led him to develop the piers, which now house a sports center, ice-skating rinks, bowling, a fitness center, a rock-climbing wall, and golf facilities. About 30 sports are accommodated, as are a park, restaurants, and other amenities. After Chelsea Piers was well established as a destination recreational center, the owners added a large event space with water views—something almost unheard of in Manhattan.

Successful developers have coped with too little relevant information, too much data, inaccurate data, and rapidly changing conditions, while managing to synthesize successful new ideas from insights gained from imperfect sources. Sometimes the idea is a small change in familiar elements—perhaps developing a fairly standard 300-unit apartment complex, but with slightly larger master baths, in a new city. Or it might be a new concept, such as a more urban version of a product that has been successful in suburban markets. The multilevel big-box stores that have been built in dense, urban locations are an example. Behind almost all these ideas lies some form of market research.

RISK CONTROL DURING STAGE ONE OF THE REAL ESTATE DEVELOPMENT PROCESS

Knowing when to hedge bets plays a big part in a developer's longevity. A pragmatic developer can follow several principles to reduce risk in stage one of the development process:

- *Know yourself.* A developer who honestly evaluates his own capabilities (financial, intellectual, and emotional) is better situated to deal with the pressures of development. It is helpful to have well-positioned contacts in financial institutions, in groups of prospective tenants, and in construction companies. A high—and liquid—net worth is also usually helpful. Yet a developer with a net worth in the six figures and no construction experience beyond garden apartments would be stretching to attempt a $50 million high-rise residential tower without strong development partners to fill the gaps.

Ideas that can be executed successfully by one developer may be less viable for another. Some participants enter the development process "not knowing what they don't know," especially for projects that lack an immediate market analogue. In some cases, ignorance of risk can lead to an innovative project; in others it can lead to disaster. Knowing oneself means being aware of aspects of a project that are not or may not be revealed until later in the development process.

- *Know your image.* Often the public perception of a developer is that of a black-hatted gunslinger. Successful developers often see themselves as risk averse and functioning more like movie producers. By drawing on several individuals' talents, they package ideas and create a product intended to satisfy society's needs for space. Aspiring developers should understand both what a developer does and how the public views the development profession. Keeping the public perception firmly in mind makes it more likely that a developer will document ideas appropriately to win the support of others.

- *Know your team.* Self-perception and public perception are useful background for self-preservation. A developer needs to determine the quality of all participants in the development process at an early juncture. During stage one, as a developer decides on a general type of project, a general location, and a general type of tenant, she also thinks about players she might recruit for the development team to make the development possible. People who demonstrate both excellent track records and financial strength, and who are

easy to work with reduce the long-term risk. Naturally, such people often cost more. The developer must decide which costs are justified for reducing risk.

- *Coordinate.* From the beginning, a developer needs to coordinate the activities and functions of the individuals involved in the development process. This task becomes even more critical in later stages, when the developer adopts a more managerial role. Even at the beginning, however, the developer must talk to—not just read about—contractors, subcontractors, potential tenants, city managers, and community groups. The team coordinated by the developer should function more smoothly than a collection of talented free agents.

- *Keep current.* A developer who stays current in her reading and networking is more likely not to move beyond stage one when available information suggests that an idea is not feasible, economically or otherwise. Trends in the national economy, supply conditions, the political climate, and tax laws can shift quickly and interact in unexpected ways. Reading newsletters and attending local and national meetings cannot guarantee profits, but keeping abreast of major events can help minimize financial losses.

- *Behave ethically.* Personal relationships and ethics are critically important in the development process because it is often difficult to rely on the courts for a speedy resolution when problems arise. In development, time is money—a lot of money—and developers lack the luxury of time to stop and sue. The stronger the personal relationships and business ethics of all those involved, the safer the development for all concerned, including the general public.

- *Pay attention to global financial cycles.* It is not just the cost of financing that cycles, but also its availability. A developer who locks into high-cost, long-term financing with limited prepayment options takes on a very real financial risk. If, for example, at a more attractive time in the financial cycle, a competitor down the street obtains cheaper financing, he may quickly price the first developer's space out of the market. Yet, a developer who fails to have long-term financing commitments in place can soon find the bank owning the property when credit conditions tighten. As this text moves through the eight-stage model, it reviews appropriate risk control techniques for each stage. One takeaway point for stage one is that a developer may need to defer some otherwise promising ideas until the financial markets are more accommodating.

RORY DANIEL

Miro is a 31-story residential high rise In Singapore. All 85 loft-style units feature balconies for private outdoor space. Community space includes sky terrace gardens on eight levels that bring nature into the dense urban environment.

SUMMARY

Stage one is clearly the most important stage of the development process. Several techniques are available for generating ideas, but no matter the source, any idea must be tested with a quick, back-of-the-envelope pro forma. Ideally, idea generation is integrated into a development company's strategic planning, with market research adding rigor to the process. Regardless of the level of rigor or the techniques employed, though, several potential pitfalls can derail even the most promising proposed project. Accordingly, formal consideration of risk control is necessary even during the first stage of the development process. The best risk control technique is "don't." Advice to "stay within the boundaries of the market" is good; however, the boundaries should not be those of the current market but those of where the market will be upon completion of the project.

TERMS

- Back-of-the-envelope pro forma
- Delphi method
- Charrette
- Environmental scanning
- Focus groups
- Nominal group process
- Situs
- Strategic planning

REVIEW QUESTIONS

9.1 What are the three most common motivations from which ideas for new developments emerge?

9.2 Describe a back-of-the-envelope pro forma and what it is used for.

9.3 What are some of the formal techniques that developers can use to generate ideas?

9.4 Describe the techniques of risk control that developers can use at this stage. How do they help developers hedge their bets?

NOTES

1 James R. DeLisle, "Graaskamp: A Holistic Perspective," reprint, Runstad Center for Real Estate Studies, College of Architecture and Urban Planning, University of Washington, August 2004, p. 5.

2 James A. Graaskamp, *A Guide to Feasibility Analysis* (Chicago: Society of Real Estate Appraisers, 1970).

PART 5

Financing the Project

Part 4 discussed the many ways that ideas are generated for projects. Regardless of the source of the idea for a real estate project, it is important to find the appropriate financial resources to move it forward early in the development process. Without financing (debt, equity, or some combination), no real estate development is possible. Consequently, it is critical for developers to keep up with trends in real estate finance and the various sources of capital. Part 5 provides that foundation, covering both the basic theory and the analytics of real estate finance.

On big-picture finance issues, developers need only an "order of magnitude" appreciation. As they move into decision making during the development period, the needs become much more specific and detailed. Chapter 10 reviews basic finance theory to provide the context for the decision maker to understand the tools laid out in chapter 11. It begins with a review of the relationship between the space and the capital markets followed by a macro view of financial markets. With that foundation, it then reviews the traditional real estate financing process, elaborating on the usual sequence of development financing. The chapter then looks at the motivations of the major institutions involved, since developers are likely to make better decisions if they better understand the sources of capital.

Chapter 11 covers analytical techniques used to implement the basic finance theory in development period decision making. The analytical techniques are applied to the continuing case study on Shortbread Lofts. The chapter concludes with an expansion of the chapter 10 discussion of the forms of equity ownership and structures for real estate ventures. Building on this foundation, the rest of the book then delves into complexities of the development environment and the investment logic used for making decisions at each stage of the development process.

Real Estate Finance: Background

The real estate market is driven by two funda-mental elements: users of space and providers of capital. The strength of the space market determines a property's rent (or sales price in the case of for-sale development). Stated another way, the property's rent is determined by the local space market and by the relative quality and location of the subject prop-erty in that market—that is, the specific property's features, functions, and benefits to a tenant. The strength of the tenant market is apparent in the lease contracts—the lease term, rental rate, and tenant's creditworthiness.

The availability and cost of capital, both debt and equity, determine if and how demand for space can be met. Historically, real estate markets in the United States—both space and capital markets—have been largely local. When new space was need-ed, local developers would gather several wealthy investors and form a limited partnership to provide the equity (ownership capital). A local bank would fund the construction loan (short-term construction debt underwritten by the credibility of the developer and the strength of the project in its market), and a life insurance company would fund a permanent loan (long-term debt underwritten by the property's prospective income). That old model is now only one of several models available to developers.

THE BIG PICTURE

The global, macro view of real estate financial markets starts with numbers of people and dollars. In the United States in 2013, GDP was about $17 trillion, spread (unevenly) across about 316 million people. That equates to a GDP per capita of roughly $53,000. In comparison, GDP in Mexico was about $17,000, in China $12,000, and in India $5,000.[1]

Moving from global GDP and population to more real estate–specific national statistics, it is useful to review some aggregate measures of wealth and the size of investment cohorts. Total national wealth is about $80 trillion. Depending on what is counted and who is counting, the value of U.S. housing is $22 trillion to 28 trillion, and the value of commercial real estate is $6 trillion to 10 trillion. (See the Federal Reserve and Bureau of Economic Analysis websites for current detail.) Clearly, real estate is an important part of the economy and thus considerable regulation is not unexpected.

Abu Dhabi's new central business district is anchored by Sowwah Square, a five-building waterfront complex that houses the Abu Dhabi Securities Exchange headquarters and several international financial firms. The project, built and owned by Mubadala Real Estate & Infrastructure, involved an international development team.

The capitalization (total market value) of publicly traded U.S. real estate is nearly $1 trillion. A significant component of privately held commercial real estate appears in in the NCREIF Property Index of the National Council of Real Estate Investment Fiduciaries. Developers should periodically review the National Association of Real Estate Investment Trusts publications and website for information about innovations in everything from property type segmentation to daily pricing. They should periodically review the NCREIF website for new research findings and performance statistics.

THE RELATIONSHIP BETWEEN THE SPACE MARKET AND THE CAPITAL MARKETS

The most common form of property valuation in the United States is *capitalization* of a property's income stream. In this approach, the property's net operating income (NOI, or the property revenue stream after operating expenses) is divided by a *capitalization rate*, or cap rate (a measure of the property's growth prospects and perceived risk relative to other investment opportunities) to derive value:

$$Value = \frac{Net\ Operating\ Income}{Capitalization\ Rate}$$

If the perceived risk per unit of return—the risk-adjusted expected return—from investing in real estate is lower than from investing in other financial and nonfinancial assets (stocks, bonds, private equity, etc.), then investors will acquire more real estate, driving down property capitalization rates as property prices are bid up. Property prices will continue to increase to the point where the risk-adjusted return matches that of other investments. Conversely, if the perceived risk-adjusted return for real estate investment is lower than other investment alternatives, capital flows away from the sector, reducing the price of real estate until risk-adjusted rates of return increase to the point where returns are appropriate for the perceived risks. In short, capital market participants are relatively efficient at chasing risk-adjusted returns across investment alternatives worldwide.

At the same time, a particular property's income stream depends primarily on trends in the local space market. The ability of a property to generate an income stream depends on the demand for space, competing properties, and locational factors that include everything from the quality of the local labor force to the price of electricity. The NOI reflects a location's relative quality.[2] As a result, the conceptual relationship between the space and capital markets can be thought of as

$$Value = \frac{Space\ Market}{Capital\ Market}$$

The intersection of the space market and the capital market is where real estate value emerges. As the tenant market begins to strengthen, landlords secure leases with higher rents and property income streams increase. The strengthening of the space market may also reduce a property's perceived investment risk. Prospective investors are willing to pay a higher price for a less volatile income stream, thus accepting a lower capitalization rate. Alternatively, as *space markets* weaken and rents and the viability of tenants in a building become less secure, the risk premium embedded in the capitalization rate increases and property values decline. All else being equal, the risk premiums of income-producing real estate move in the same direction as the perceived risks of the space markets. Property values move in the opposite direction of property risk premiums and capitalization rates.

Appraisers apply these concepts when they use recent sales of similar (comparable) properties in a particular market to calculate a capitalization rate for any particular (subject) property. By dividing a comparable property's annual income by its sales price, the appraiser gets a measure of what that same relationship might be if the particular subject property were sold. Because no two properties are exactly alike, appraisers often use a grid approach to adjust each comparable sold property's cap rate for their differences from the subject property—such as better location, weaker tenants, and so on.

Capitalization rates are calculated from trailing annual income (for the prior 12 months), in-place income, and/or prospective annual income. As shown in the case studies later in the chapter, it is not a simple task to obtain accurate and consistent data to use in estimating capitalization rates. Although a developer often creates his own capitalization metrics, several national sources provide information for local markets by property type. Depending on the need, it may be useful to draw data from Altus, REIS, CoStar, RCA, IDP, NCREIF, and other information providers.

EXPECTED RATE OF RETURN: A FUNDAMENTAL UNDERPINNING OF CAPITAL MARKETS

Most investors eventually move beyond valuation based on a single year's income to consideration of the rate of return over the expected holding period. Like the capitalization rate, the expected rate of return on real estate investments is determined in a market where stocks, bonds, real estate, and other investments compete for investor capital. Within the real estate sector, different sources of investment capital—individual investors, *REITs*, pension funds, and *private equity firms*, for example—compete for investment opportunities. Thus, the expected rates of return on real estate (and all other investments) are determined in a competitive marketplace. Generally speaking, the greater the number of people who follow the investment market, the more "price efficient" it is thought to be. When a market is more price efficient, investment opportunities are said to be fairly priced. The less price efficient a market, the more likely one is either to find a bargain or to overpay.

When evaluating prospective rates of return among investment alternatives, most investors start with the rate of return on U.S. Treasury obligations as the baseline. Investors add a risk premium to this "risk-free" rate. In real estate, the risk premium is project-specific and based on the risks associated with the particular project.

Over the last half century, the average ten-year U.S. Treasury rate of return has been about 7 percent. After the Great Recession, the Federal Reserve's bond purchasing program held yields on the ten-year Treasury notes artificially low, with the rate hitting 1.39 percent in July 2012. Because the U.S. ten-year yield (promised interest rate divided by current price) is so important in global asset pricing, it is useful to reflect on how yields have varied over time (figure 10-1).

Inflation and Time

Yields on the ten-year bonds move with changes in the expectation of future inflation. The more inflation investors expect, the higher the *required return* on this risk-free (in terms of default) instrument. Consequently, it is helpful to think of the ten-year yield as composed of a real return (net of inflation) and an *inflation premium*. With the advent of a ten-year inflation-protected Treasury security, investors have a way to determine the inflation expectation being priced in the market. The inflation-protected instrument pays a stated rate plus actual inflation

Figure 10-1	Ten-Year Treasury Bond Yields, 1970–2013		
Year	Ten-Year Treasury Bond Rate (%)	Year	Ten-Year Treasury Bond Rate (%)
1970	6.39	1992	6.77
1971	5.93	1993	5.77
1972	6.36	1994	7.81
1973	6.74	1995	5.71
1974	7.43	1996	6.30
1975	8.00	1997	5.81
1976	6.87	1998	4.65
1977	7.69	1999	6.44
1978	9.01	2000	5.11
1979	10.39	2001	5.05
1980	12.84	2002	3.82
1981	13.72	2003	4.25
1982	10.54	2004	4.22
1983	11.83	2005	4.39
1984	11.50	2006	4.70
1985	9.26	2007	4.02
1986	7.11	2008	2.21
1987	8.99	2009	3.84
1988	9.11	2010	3.29
1989	7.84	2011	1.88
1990	8.08	2012	1.76
1991	7.09	2013	2.35

Source: Compiled from U.S. Federal Reserve data.

so that the investor gets the stated return, as well as compensation for inflation. The difference between the regular ten-year Treasury yield and the inflation-protected yield is the market's expectation of inflation over the next ten years.

Rates are normally lower for shorter-term loans than longer-term loans. In finance speak, the relationship between rates and maturity is called the "yield curve." It normally slopes upward, because more can go wrong over a longer period and thus the lender is more exposed to market risks. In certain periods, however, capital may be very scarce and investors in short-term debt may be able to get a higher rate than long-term lenders. This occurs when borrowers want to avoid committing to pay the higher

rates over the longer period, expecting that rates will come down.

RISK PREMIUM

Investments other than those in U.S. Treasury securities and similar "risk-free" instruments are priced to include a risk premium. The risk premium or risk spread (the difference in rate between any particular investment and the risk-free security with a similar maturity) compensates investors for their willingness to make an investment that may default, be difficult to sell, or experience extreme price volatility. Even supposedly risk-free securities will experience price variation over time as market interest rates change. The buyer of a ten-year Treasury note in 2015 is safe from default in 2025 because final payment is guaranteed by the federal government. However, if interest rates rise in 2016, the Treasury security bought in 2015, which pays the lower 2015 rate, will be less attractive and its price will fall. Risk premiums are intended to compensate the investor for risks beyond this fundamental risk of changing market rates.

As with all investments, risk premiums in real estate vary based on the perceived risk of the investment. A 50 percent loan on a high-quality building with credit tenants on long leases carries a lower-risk premium than investment in the equity of a new development in a pioneering location with a new design type by a first-time developer. Throughout the eight-stage model of the development process, investors see many types of investments with varying risk premiums. As the risk exposure changes over the development process, so do the risks associated with any particular investor position (mortgage lender, *joint venture partner*, or equity investor). The critical skills for a developer are first to minimize risks, then not to overpay investors for taking any particular risk position.

Because the construction phase is generally more risky to a lender/investor than financing the completed project, the rate for construction loans may be higher, despite their shorter maturity. Still, the risk of the specific loan is most important.

CAPITAL MARKET SEGMENTS

Capital sources have varied over time, with banks being the largest source and government agencies and *commercial mortgage–backed securities* (CMBS) the most volatile in terms of percentage of total lending. The real estate capital markets have been described as having *four quadrants*: *private debt*, *public debt*, private equity, and *public equity*. This can be a helpful starting point in understanding real estate capital markets; but, given that there are several types of intermediaries, it is only a starting point. The differences between the quadrants lie in how capital is accessed and how the entity providing that capital is traded. Although banks and life insurance companies may be publicly traded (that is, shares of their stock trade on a public stock exchange such as the New York Stock Exchange), if the mortgage debt they issue is not publicly traded, the debt is considered private debt.

Commercial banks are intermediaries that make loans directly to developers but are capitalized by the sale of equity in public markets. A developer is said to access the market directly when dealing with a bank that retains ownership of the loan. The developer is using the public markets when the bank loan is then securitized in a pool of CMBS. Since the early to mid-1990s, a growing share of capital for real estate has come from such public sources.

The flow of capital into commercial real estate from the quadrants has varied dramatically over the years. The original REITs, dating from the early 1970s, provided considerable debt but had to be bailed out by the Federal Reserve in the downturn of the mid-1970s. Lending heated up again in the 1980s, with newly deregulated S&Ls leading the way. In the subsequent meltdown, once again, the federal government had to step in. All the while, insurance companies have been major lenders, and in the 1980s they became major equity holders as well. With the turn of the century, public debt in the form of CMBS took a larger market share. In the Great Recession, defaults in this sector played a big part in the ensuing financial crisis.

In all financing decisions, it is helpful if the developer is able to stand in the lender's or investor's shoes. This perspective enables the developer to approach the right sources of capital with the right requests. The developer should also keep pace with changes in the ever more complex lending market[3]—in particular, the regulation of real estate lending, which has evolved in response to economic cycles and the associated lending problems. Today, for example, the industry is trying to understand all the implications of the most recent legislation, the massive Dodd-Frank Act.

Private Sources of Real Estate Debt

Historically, commercial banks provided *construction financing* while insurance companies provided long-term financing. The banks have shorter-term capital (checking and saving accounts), while the insurance companies have longer-term capital and liabilities associated with the various forms of life, health, and property insurance. Consequently, it was natural for banks to offer shorter-term lending and insurance companies to offer longer-term loans.

Although this is still the case, the complexity of financing alternatives has increased almost exponentially. Large financial institutions now do a little of everything. They can make long-term loans, then securitize them and take the long-run exposure off their books. Insurance companies have moved forcefully into equity real estate as well as debt and then backed off from equity investment with the advent of risk-based capital regulations, only to return to equity investment as the risk-based capital rules were modified.

Public Sources of Real Estate Debt

For decades, the quasi-government entities Fannie Mae and Freddie Mac provided guarantees that enabled single-family loans to be efficiently packaged and sold to end investors. In this way, an investor with a modest amount to invest could help fund a pool of loans, along with other small investors. This meant greater availability of financing for homebuyers at lower cost. With a bit of help and motivation from the financial crisis of the late 1980s, Wall Street found a way to apply the same securitization concepts to commercial lending through CMBSs.

These fixed-income investments are similar to corporate bonds and are collateralized by pools of

commercial mortgages rated and sold in the fixed-income (bond) markets.

A number of large commercial banks have established their own conduit for CMBS operations in which some of the loans they underwrite, originate, and service are pooled and sold in the form of mortgage-backed bonds on Wall Street. The pools are usually diverse in terms of property type and geographic location but fairly homogeneous in their loan terms. These pools are then rated by third-party debt rating agencies that determine the size of the credit tranches and assign credit ratings: AAA, AA, A, BBB, BB, B, or nonrated.

Beyond commercial CMBS, additional publicly traded capital flows from federally guaranteed pools of multifamily debt (Fannie Mae and Freddie Mac). Today, equity in both entities is traded publicly on the New York Stock Exchange, but both were initially chartered by the federal government. As such, the debt issued by these two organizations has the implicit guarantee of the U.S. government. Therefore, Fannie Mae and Freddie Mac often can quote loan originators a lower risk spread than most CMBS pools. Because the two entities are chartered for housing debt only, Fannie Mae and Freddie Mac can pool mortgages only against commercial properties that are primarily residential. At this writing, the federal government is trying to decide how to restructure these organizations; there is considerable pressure to keep them functioning, but many in Washington want to eliminate both and rely on the private sector alone. Clearly, the smart multifamily developer keeps abreast of impending changes.

Indications are that publicly traded instruments will continue to make up a sizeable share of the total market for permanent loan financing. According to the Commercial Real Estate Finance Council, CMBSs valued at $48 billion were issued in 2001. By 2007 the figure had jumped to $230 billion before free-falling to less than $3 billion in 2009, at the height of the Great Recession. In 2013, about $90 billion in CMBS loans were originated.[4]

CMBSs have brought greater liquidity and greater competition for commercial real estate mortgages. Now the institutions and brokers supplying real

---

INNOVATOR Crowdfunding for Real Estate Investment

Financing drives the real estate development process, and investment trends evolve quickly to keep up with demand, new regulations, and other changes. Traditional investment-capital vehicles are still the foundation of real estate development, but new models are constantly emerging to fund projects. Among the many players involved, one is notable for being at the forefront of investment evolution, keeping up with market innovations, and adapting the methodology for real estate investors.

Jilliene Helman is CEO and cofounder of Realty Mogul, an online peer-to-peer marketplace for real estate investing, based in Los Angeles. This method of internet-based investment sourcing has become a feasible way to finance a real estate project, and Realty Mogul is the leading crowdfunding real estate company in the country. Helman established Realty Mogul in 2013 with the simple objective of making it easy for investors to invest. In the company's first 12 months, it financed over $100 million in property value, all facilitated with investors over the internet. The firm has more than 14,000 active accredited and institutional investors who are invested in a wide range of projects, including residential, retail, office, hospitality, self-storage, and industrial properties. Unlike with REITs, participants can choose to invest in individual projects.

For those looking to raise equity or secure a loan, the firm provides access to funds that are usually far more difficult and time-consuming to secure through traditional means. Like more traditional funders, Realty Mogul performs due diligence, typically accepting developers that have experience of at least five years and with $100 million in real estate projects.

By financing development and acquisitions over the internet, real estate investment is opened up to a broader group of investors, many of whom never had access before. They include software engineers at Google, product managers at Facebook and Yahoo, and finance folks at Amazon. These investors now have a way to invest in real estate that they are comfortable with—the internet. Realty Mogul has also been good for developers, expanding the sources of capital to get real estate transactions done.

Crowdfunding is one way the real estate financing industry is changing. It is an unfolding act, with many of its opportunities and difficulties yet to be discovered. Helman has not gone unnoticed by the business world. In 2013, she was named Crowdfunding CEO of the Year and one of the "100 Most Influential Real Estate Leaders" by Inman News. In 2014, she was named one of *Forbes* magazine's "30 Under 30."

Alison Johnson

estate debt have the option to hold the debt or to securitize it, which enhances the institution's liquidity and thus facilitates the flow of funds to real estate.

Private Sources of Equity

Equity, both private and public, is higher-risk financing than debt financing. Consequently, providers of equity capital have the most to say about how a project will be developed. More equity in a project usually means that debt will cost less and be more available. However, equity is a more expensive source of capital, so the developer faces a tradeoff. Using more equity makes debt financing easier but means that the project may need to earn more—that is, the weighted average cost of capital may be higher.

The last paragraph captures several fundamental financing concepts, so it bears repeating. The development must generate sufficient income to satisfy the various sources of capital, which are most simply characterized as debt and equity. Although an almost infinite variety of both debt and equity structures is available in today's capital markets, the distinction is fundamental. The higher the percentage of low-risk debt capital, the better—so long as using more debt does not cause too much of an increase in the cost of the equity. Classic finance literature suggests that in a perfectly efficient capital market, the higher cost of equity exactly negates the benefit from using more debt. In practice, this theoretical concept seldom holds exactly, so a developer looks to find the best combination for the particular situation.

Unfortunately, from the developer's perspective, using more debt means that the equity provider will usually want a higher return and/or more control. The objective is to get the right balance for the particular project, keeping in mind that beyond the weighted average cost of capital, the developer needs to make sure there are no legal restrictions or stipulations in the documentation connected with the sources of capital that will cause difficulties as the development progresses. As the book moves on through the eight-stage model, more details are provided about such legal provisions.

The ten-year Treasury yields shown earlier explain a good part of the changing returns on private real estate equity. Individual investors are still very important in the equity sector, particularly for smaller properties. However, large institutions (along with the public markets) have now become critical actors. To get a feel for what equity returns on larger, lower-risk properties have been, figure 10-2 shows what large institutional investors have received from their commercial real estate investments over the last few decades. (The NCREIF returns are for unleveraged,[5] privately held real estate equity.) Note that NCREIF returns are based on appraisals and have nowhere near the volatility seen in publicly traded real estate (as shown on the NAREIT website).

The term "quadrants" is common in the real estate literature, but it can lead to some terminology confusion. Private equity is distinguished in this characterization as different from public equity, private debt, and public debt. That is a useful distinction, but the term "private equity" is now commonly used in the press to apply to investment funds set up for wealthy individuals, foundations, endowments, and pension funds to make aggressive investment plays across the universe of investment opportunities (not just real estate). Such private equity funds have become active participants in the equity real estate markets. Because private equity has been growing rapidly both in aggregate and in its share of the capital markets, it is important for the developer to maintain an ongoing connection to how this source of capital is viewed.[6]

A considerable portion of private equity investment has come from foreign sources, particularly sovereign wealth funds. In addition to participating in private equity funds, international sources also make considerable direct equity investment. The countries of origin have varied over the years, with the Japanese dominating in the 1990s (as in the 1990 sale of Pebble Beach for $841 million) and the large Middle Eastern sovereign wealth funds such as the Abu Dhabi Investment Authority more recently.

Figure 10-2	NCREIF Historical Quarterly Returns			
	Returns (%)			
Year	Q1	Q2	Q3	Q4
1978	2.90	3.07	3.39	5.89
1979	3.81	4.32	4.75	6.19
1980	5.54	2.36	3.79	5.32
1981	2.96	4.23	3.21	5.29
1982	2.49	2.07	1.52	3.04
1983	1.75	2.54	2.96	5.31
1984	3.35	3.16	2.46	4.21
1985	2.08	2.60	2.39	3.73
1986	2.03	1.96	1.50	2.57
1987	1.83	1.19	2.09	2.67
1988	1.84	2.00	2.39	3.07
1989	1.75	2.00	2.05	1.75
1990	1.38	1.52	0.84	−1.43
1991	0.05	0.01	−0.33	−5.33
1992	0.03	−1.03	−0.44	−2.81
1993	0.77	−0.24	1.10	−0.25
1994	1.31	1.54	1.51	1.88
1995	2.11	2.08	2.06	1.09
1996	2.40	2.29	2.63	2.61
1997	2.34	2.82	3.38	4.71
1998	4.14	4.19	3.46	3.55
1999	2.59	2.62	2.81	2.89
2000	2.40	3.05	2.94	3.33
2001	2.36	2.47	1.60	0.67
2002	1.51	1.61	1.79	1.67
2003	1.88	2.09	1.97	2.76
2004	2.56	3.13	3.42	4.66
2005	3.51	5.34	4.44	5.43
2006	3.62	4.01	3.51	4.51
2007	3.62	4.59	3.56	3.21
2008	1.60	0.56	−0.17	−8.29
2009	−7.33	−5.20	−3.32	−2.11
2010	0.76	3.31	3.86	4.62
2011	3.36	3.94	3.30	2.96
2012	2.59	2.68	2.34	2.54
2013	2.57	2.87	2.59	2.53
2014	2.74	2.91	2.63	3.04

Source: www.ncreif.org/property-index-returns.aspx.

Public Sources of Equity

The flow of public equity capital into commercial real estate comes from three major sources: master limited partnerships, C corporations, and—particularly—REITs. Master limited partnerships are partnerships (for legal and tax purposes) that have been listed on stock exchanges so that investors may buy partnership interests, just as they buy common stock. Shares of operating companies that are publicly traded (such as IBM common stock) are referred to as C Corporations; and several such entities operate in various sectors of the real estate market. REITs can be publicly or privately traded. Either way, they enjoy tax-free status as long as they adhere to certain investment and income distribution rules.

REITs have been a congressionally approved means of publicly holding real estate since the early 1960s. However, they were underused as an investment vehicle until 1993, when the umbrella-partnership REIT (UPREIT) structure was created. The UPREIT structure allows private real estate partnerships to transfer ownership interests to an operating partnership controlled by the UPREIT. This arrangement was very appealing to U.S. private investors in limited partnerships, because the transfer could be completed without triggering a federal income tax obligation. During the early to mid-1990s, UPREITs were one of the few sources of equity capital in a market experiencing extremely thin trading volumes. As UPREITs acquired partnership interests, they bought out some limited partners and paid off some debt obligations through money raised on Wall Street in new REIT offerings.

For more insight, it is useful to review the NCREIF and NAREIT websites. The NCREIF return series is based on appraisals of unlevered property. The NAREIT return series is based on continuous trading prices of leveraged public companies. Clearly both have varied over time, with the public markets showing much more volatility. A huge volume of academic literature has dealt with the differences between the two return series. The main take-away points from these voluminous databases and the extensive literature are five:

1. Returns have varied considerably over time.
2. The data contain a great deal of useful detail and segmentation by both property type and geography.
3. Because both series represent U.S. commercial real estate during the same underlying national economic cycles, there is a strong correlation between the two.
4. With continuous trading, the public markets tend to lead the private markets.
5. Public markets are far more volatile due to both the daily trading effect and the leverage effect.

Both total return histories are useful background as a real estate decision maker seeks to find the right financing for a particular development possibility.

Non-traded REITs (entities with a REIT structure that are not publicly traded) have waxed and waned in popularity over the years. They have recently come under scrutiny from regulators questioning the products' fees, their valuation methods, and how their value appears on client account statements.

REAL ESTATE CYCLES

Two kinds of cycles are of interest: local market rental cycles and national market financial cycles. At the national level, few investments made in 2006 looked good in 2009. In contrast, investments made at the bottom of the market in 2009 have done relatively well over the last few years. At the same time, each local market and even each property type in each local market has its own "space market" cycle independent of what the national financial markets create. It is no secret, for example, that Detroit rents have been on a long downward trend—a trend that it is hoped will be one phase of a cycle. Conversely, San Francisco has recently been on a huge up-cycle driven by the tech sector.

From a strictly financial standpoint, maintaining liquidity through a downturn is a major concern for a developer because the cash flows dictated by the cycle in the local space market need to carry him through financial market cycles, and vice versa.

Developers of the global headquarters for Biogen Idec, in Cambridge, Massachusetts, used a highly collaborative project delivery method, shortening the development schedule by four months and saving $2 million in construction costs. The project was completed in 2013.

Several commercially available data sources have shown that local metropolitan markets are in different phases of the classic cycle (recovery, expansion, hypersupply, recession) at different points in time.[7]

THE REAL ESTATE FINANCE PROCESS

Real estate development typically involves a series of financing arrangements: predevelopment financing, short-term construction financing, possibly *interim financing*, and finally *permanent financing*. As a project progresses, its investment risk varies and consequently so do the interest rates and rates of return required by lenders and equity investors. Predevelopment debt and equity usually carry the most risk and the highest expected returns. Financing the purchase of well-designed and well-located buildings with creditworthy tenants carries lower risk and correspondingly has lower expected returns.

Lenders are primarily concerned about two risks: nonpayment of debt service (principal and interest payments) and loss of loan principal. Equity investors, by contrast, focus more on after-debt-service cash flows, value appreciation, and tax benefits. Debt investors generally are more risk averse than equity investors. They are inclined to offer stricter terms for risky stages of development such as land acquisition, land development, and preconstruction activities. Although all these general principles are valid, real estate finance is as much an art as a science. Creativity is important; numerous combinations and alternative sequences of the process described in the following sections are possible.

Financing Predevelopment Activities

Generally speaking, real estate projects in the predevelopment stage are the riskiest: any positive cash flow from rents lies in the future, and the more distant the time until income is received, the riskier the investment. The probability that a project in the predevelopment planning stage will be completed and occupied is smaller than the probability that a project in more advanced stages will be completed and occupied. Yet, developers need front-end capital for a number of predevelopment tasks: obtaining entitlements, completing conceptual designs, conducting technical studies, and possibly securing tenant commitments. Developers can cover predevelopment costs with their own equity capital or with capital from a joint venture partner.

A joint venture agreement can take many forms. It is often a limited liability corporation or a limited partnership composed of a financial partner and the developer as the managing or general partner. Other joint venture forms include partnerships with a landowner or a future owner/user. The joint venture agreement allows participants in the development process to define their relationship in a legally defensible manner. The agreement should cover responsibilities for performance, financing shortfalls, and other potential risks.

Land Acquisition Financing

The land acquisition process involves an agreement between buyer and seller. That agreement can take many forms, ranging from an all-cash purchase to various types of option arrangements wherein the closing occurs after the passage of time or the completion of certain events. In most cases, the agreement contains a "due diligence" period" during which the buyer conducts an investigation of the site to ensure that the property is suitable for development. The buyer and seller negotiate the payment of deposits, which may be refundable or nonrefundable, and applicable or nonapplicable to the purchase price.

Landowner Financing

Landowners sometimes provide financing for the land, perhaps in the form of a seller-financed loan ("purchase money mortgage"). In a purchase money mortgage, the deed to the land is transferred to the developer, and the developer makes loan payments that are negotiated as part of the transaction. The same effect can be achieved by an option to purchase, with a closing date at some future point.

Seller financing can be an attractive alternative for the developer, who needs to raise only the difference between the purchase price of the land and the amount of the loan. The seller/lender may agree to a subordination clause that allows a construction loan to be recorded on the property and have priority over the land loan, giving the construction lender a first lien position. By doing so, the seller makes it easier for the developer to obtain construction financing since in the event of default, the construction lender will receive the first distribution of any foreclosure proceeds. Only after the first lien holder is paid in full will the second lien holder, the seller in this illustration, receive any proceeds from the foreclosure. Because of this risk, sellers usually require additional compensation in the form of a higher price for the land or a higher interest rate when subordinating the land financing.

An alternative form of seller financing is a land purchase option. In this arrangement, the seller retains title to the land and the buyer/developer agrees to pay the landowner to take the land off the market during the option period. The payment can take a variety of forms. It may be a lump sum paid when the agreement is signed, or it may be paid in installments. The payments may be refundable, nonrefundable, applicable, or nonapplicable. In an option arrangement, the land price is usually higher than it would be in an all-cash purchase, in part because the seller defers receipt of the price and takes on the risk that the transaction may never close. However, the agreed-upon purchase price can reflect the value of the site after the completion of entitlements, such as zoning, that convert the land use to one that is more valuable for development. Thus, the seller participates in the increase in the property value and is, in essence, a partner with the buyer until the property closes.

For the developer, a land purchase option is a relatively low-risk method of controlling the site before committing significant resources to the project. While the site is under option, the developer can work on other steps in the development process—further land assembly, environmental assessment, rezoning and other government approvals, leasing, design, and financing.

Ground Lease

Ground leases are another form of land finance. Instead of purchasing the land, the developer enters into a long-term lease. Such an arrangement allows the land owner to re-acquire control of the property at the end of the lease and take advantage of any higher values at that time. At the same time, it enables the developer to begin the project with less capital.

A ground lease is usually structured as a triple net lease, meaning that the lessee is responsible for all expenses associated with the property. Ground rents may escalate according to a predetermined schedule or an agreed index such as the consumer price index (CPI) or changes in the property's rental income.

A ground lease offers advantages and disadvantages for developers. The advantages are that no front-end land payment is needed and the developer's leverage is increased. Among the disadvantages are that negotiations can be difficult and time-consuming, escalations in ground rent can grow faster than the building's cash flow, and the developer does not participate in future land appreciation since, when the lease term ends, improvements revert to the landowner.

For the landowner, a ground lease also offers advantages and disadvantages. The advantages include the opportunity to capture increases in value over time, to have an income stream with few management responsibilities, and to own improvements at the end of the lease. Among the disadvantages are the risk of default by the lessee, less control over the land, and forgone development opportunities during the ground lease period.

Construction Financing

Most projects involve a construction loan. The timing of construction financing varies with myriad development period concerns, from the method of land acquisition to the qualifications of the general contractor to the decision on whether to secure a permanent loan commitment before starting construction. Depending on the point in the real estate cycle and the type of property, construction lenders seek terms that reduce the risk that the loan will not be paid off at the end of the term. In some cases, a permanent financing commitment may be required. In other cases, some preconstruction leasing may be required. In these situations, the amount of preleasing required will vary depending on market conditions, the developer's experience, and the complexity of the project. As further assurance, the construction lender may require personal guarantees beyond simply recourse to the property.

The interest rates and terms of construction loans vary with economic, financial, and underwriting factors. Lenders rely heavily on the developer's creditworthiness and the level of equity investment by both the developer and any development-period equity partner. Many construction loans carry adjustable rates and have terms that extend 6 to 18 months beyond the completion of construction, which allows the income stream to stabilize so that permanent financing may be obtained at a lower cost.

Commercial banks, whether local or global, have traditionally been the primary source of construction financing. Banks traditionally have concentrated on assets that require the kind of loan management that they can provide. The construction lender wants to know the qualifications of the builder and be able to monitor the construction process, which usually requires a local presence. Developers of large or multiphase projects that require longer-term construction loans may obtain financing from a consortium of lenders formed to share the risk of a large loan or a loan with a long time horizon.

The interest rate on short-term bank loans is often tied to a short-term money market rate. Reflecting the higher risk of construction loans, the risk premium is usually higher than for permanent loans. That said, given the usual upward-sloping yield curve, the overall interest rate may be higher for the long-term permanent loan. Interest spreads usually are based on a major index like LIBOR. Upfront loan fees also vary with the market and the perceived risk of the project or the developer.

Most construction loan agreements allow interest to accrue (be periodically added back to the principal) through the construction period rather than requiring periodic interest payments. When construction is complete, the developer obtains a permanent loan or sells the project and pays off the balance of the construction loan, including accrued interest.

Permanent Financing

Long-term loans based on the continuing income stream are referred to as "permanent loans." Historically, the primary sources of long-term debt financing for real estate developments have been life insurance companies, with commercial banks playing a more limited role. As noted earlier, many large

---

CASE STUDY   Irvine Tech Center: Greenlaw Partners and Guggenheim Real Estate

The introduction of Greenlaw Partners to Guggenheim Real Estate (GRE) came about through a longstanding relationship with a respected member of the mortgage banking community. His exact words were, "You have got to meet these guys. They may be working out of the trunk of their car right now, but they will be stars."

The first meeting between Greenlaw and GRE took place in what would become Greenlaw's first office space. The team set up their materials for the meeting (which included aerial photos of Orange County and other southern California markets) and for the next hour, they delivered one of the most impressive market presentations GRE had seen. They presented each submarket with positive and negative recommendations on each product type and identified areas where there was potential value creation. At the end, the team outlined an office opportunity on which they had the inside track.

So, why was GRE a good match for Greenlaw? First, GRE liked the concept of the partnership structure they outlined. And there were not many institutional partners willing to make a $45 million investment on the say-so of two guys just starting out on their own and working from the trunk of their car.

Why was Greenlaw a good match for GRE? Greenlaw filled a remaining vacant space in GRE's partner model. Goal alignment was easy, there was mutual respect, and both teams' objectives matched.

Through Greenlaw's local contacts, the partners learned that an 18-acre parcel fronting on Jamboree and the major cross-street, Campus Drive, might be coming to market. As described in preceding chapters, this was a true "Main and Main" location and one of the largest potential redevelopment parcels in the submarket. The rectangular property is divided almost in half by a city street. This configuration would allow for future redevelopment of the site to occur from back to front, leaving development of the premium land fronting on Jamboree until the end, when it would return the most value.

GRE was founded in 2001, inspired by a vision to bring to real estate investment the same level of sophistication enjoyed by other asset classes. An unusual part of GRE's program is the application of the NCREIF Property Index. This index is a time-series composite measure of the performance of a large pool of commercial real estate properties. GRE uses it as the measure for calculating the operating partner's incentive compensation on each deal. Traditionally, the financial partner and the operating company play a kind of "Pac Man": any downturn in the market results in the evaporation of any upside position in a deal. With the GRE model, the index trails the market up or down, and in theory the operating partner's position is protected, if they perform.

GRE sought to identify and bring on board the best operating partners by region and product type. On the West Coast, the company had in place a strong network of contacts in disciplines serving the real estate industry (legal, accounting, appraisal, mortgage banking, brokerage, etc.) to identify and vet prospective partners. GRE was looking not just for talent but for developers with integrity and a philosophy that fit with the GRE program. Many were interviewed, but only a select few made the list.

GRE's objective was to put together partnerships to ensure that it received the best market intelligence and saw all of the deals in the market across all product types. This sometimes means that two partners in the same geographic area may have "positive

Continued next page

CASE STUDY   Irvine Tech Center: Greenlaw Partners and Guggenheim Real Estate   *Continued*

Irvine Tech Center Location Map

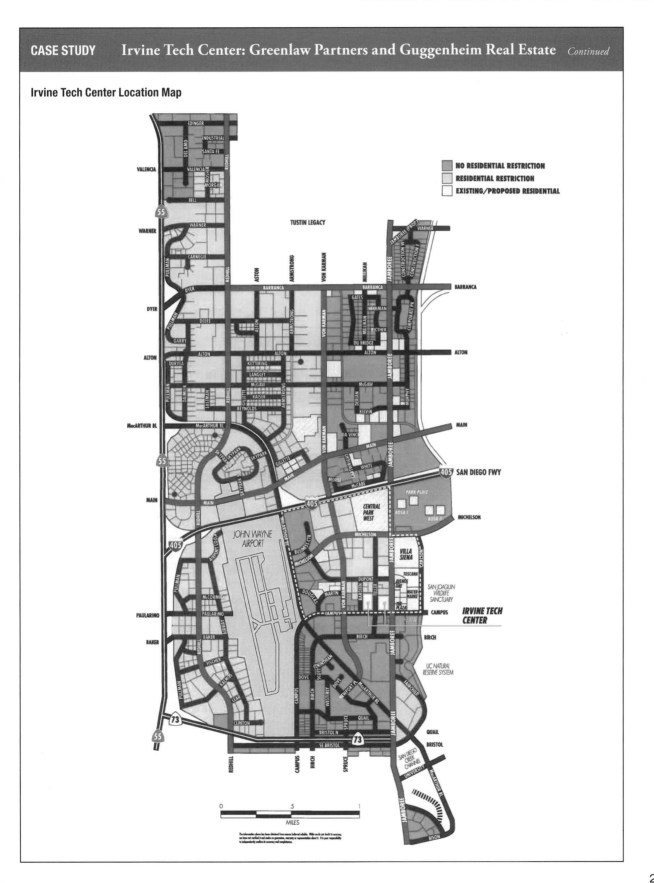

competition," meaning local partners have to find better-than-market opportunities to invest in by looking for opportunities that are not yet on the market. GRE's first relationships were formed with established companies that provided access to the "old lions" of the brokerage community and specific market segments.

Late on a Friday afternoon, Greenlaw learned that a senior member and key decision maker of the subject property's ownership was in town for the weekend. Wil Smith had a positive relationship with this owner. A meeting was arranged, and the GRE principal from the San Francisco office planned to fly to Orange County early the next morning for it. The key issues for the seller were not only a good price but also certainty that the deal would close. GRE had earned a reputation for closing deals that went to contract, and the seller knew the GRE principal. Greenlaw had

done such an excellent job in the preliminary underwriting that over the weekend the outline of a deal was negotiated and sealed with a handshake. The deal was closed with underwriting of the project based on its current use, with the expectation of negotiating with the city of Irvine a redevelopment agreement that would provide for the maximum density in office, hotel, residential, and retail use.

The ITC development is a good example of a positive relationship between a local developer and national investors. It is a relationship combining the talents of GRE as an institutional partner able to respond quickly to a unique opportunity generated by Greenlaw, and the ability of Greenlaw to identify and underwrite good projects ahead of the market. But most important, this relationship has been successful because it is based on trust, honest communication, mutual respect, and alignment of interest.

Continued on page 230

JOHN BRADY (RETIRED), GUGGENHEIM REAL ESTATE, SAN FRANCISCO

institutions now originate loans for securitization so that CMBSs are an important source of funds in permanent financing.

Life insurance companies can invest a large amount of capital in long-term mortgages because

their liabilities are long term and predictable. They receive a regular flow of funds from premium payments, and from actuarial tables they can predict with reasonable accuracy their future outlays. Therefore, they often lend to developers of better properties, underwriting the investment conservatively. When a life insurance company issues a permanent loan and holds it in its general account, the company monitors the success of the project and will consider reworking the terms of the loan over its life if such a restructuring of amount or rate is in its interest. From the developer's perspective, this allows more long-term flexibility than is the case with CMBSs. CMBS pools require considerable standardization of loan terms on origination and are less flexible in terms of loan modification over the life of the property.

Interim and Mezzanine Financing

At times, interim financing is needed to bridge the gap between construction loans, permanent loans, and equity. Sometimes, there is a temporary mismatch between what the developer wants to do in the longer term and what is feasible in the short term. In such situations, it may make sense to bring in someone or some institution to bridge the difference. From the developer's perspective, an interim loan may be necessary to buy time for the project to succeed. It may be required if things did not go as expected during construction and lease-up (construction delays, difficulty obtaining municipal approvals, problems leasing, etc.). To compensate for this risk, the interim lender's terms will reflect the added uncertainty in the form of larger origination fees or higher interest rates or both.

REGULATORY CHANGES RESULTING FROM THE GREAT RECESSION

Like the rest of the U.S. economy, the real estate industry is still digesting lessons from the Great Recession. Experience in previous financial meltdowns suggests two events will occur: more regulatory changes and a period of learning how those changes play out in day-to-day financial transactions. The aggressive lending practices before the Great Recession and the subsequent defaults on mortgages and mortgage-backed securities have resulted in significant new regulations that alter some of the rules of development finance.

The Dodd-Frank Act increases the stringency of appraisal practices, the oversight of the securitization of mortgages, and the requirements for loan underwriting. The act affects both the commercial and the residential real estate industries. Among other changes, it created an agency responsible for implementing and enforcing compliance with consumer financial laws. How it will change what financial institutions can and want to finance is an unfolding story.[8]

SUMMARY

Real estate development is a capital-intensive enterprise. Most developers do not have the wealth or desire to fund an entire project on their own, so they seek debt and equity investment capital from other sources. Because real estate finance is global, projects compete with stocks, bonds, and other investment opportunities worldwide. However, the supply of and demand for tenant space is local. The financing challenge for the developer is to balance the two appropriately. The space market must be strong enough to produce the returns required by the capital markets. At the same time, if the developer overpays for financing, he will need higher rents from the local market, which may cause leasing problems.

The process of financing real estate involves a series of arrangements based on the types of risk present at each stage of development. During the predevelopment stage, the project carries the greatest risk. As a property is constructed and occupied, many risks are dramatically reduced. Consequently, different sources of capital are appropriate at different stages.

This chapter presents a broad summary of real estate finance. It is important to remember that the basic concepts laid out in finance textbooks apply to real estate—from Irving Fisher on interest rates to Merton Miller on capital structure, to Bill Sharpe on investments, to Fisher Black and Myron Scholes on options pricing. The following chapter builds on the conceptual foundation established here to apply those basic concepts to real estate development.

TERMS

- Capital markets (and four quadrants)
- Capitalization rate
- Commercial mortgage–backed securities (CMBS)
- Construction financing
- Ground leases
- Inflation premium
- Interim financing
- Joint venture partner
- Permanent financing
- Private debt
- Private equity firms
- Public debt
- Public equity
- REITs
- Required return

REVIEW QUESTIONS

10.1 Discuss the market for commercial real estate in terms of its space market and capital market components.

10.2 Explain how the quality and stability of a property's income stream are determined by its space market.

10.3 Describe the four quadrants of the capital markets.

10.4 How can one determine the market expectation of inflation?

10.5 How is the required rate of return different from the cap rate?

10.6 What are CMBSs?

10.7 What is the normal sequence of financing for real estate development?

10.8 What are the largest sources of equity capital for commercial real estate? Which has grown fastest over the past decade?

10.9 In the early stages of the commercial real estate development process, what are the primary sources of capital? Why?

10.10 What are the primary differences in risk between a construction loan and a permanent loan from the lender's perspective?

NOTES

1   Estimates based on World Bank statistics.

2   The supply of and demand for space in geographic markets are analyzed by national, regional, and local firms. At the national level, Reis Reports, Torto Wheaton Research, Dodge, CoStar, and PPR (Property and Portfolio Research) are well known. Most commercial real estate brokers and appraisers maintain space market data for their locales. See chapter 16 for more information on specific providers.

3   The gold standard for the performance of real estate mortgagees is the Giliberto-Levy Index, which reports quarterly.

4   CRE Financial Council, Compendium of Statistics, https://www.crefc.org/compendium/.

5   NCREIF reports property returns before any debt service.

6   For an analysis of how private equity returns compare with other market returns, follow the academic literature evolving from "Private Equity Returns: What Do We Know," *Journal of Finance*, October 2014, by Robert S. Harris, Tim Jenkinson, and Steven N. Kaplan. For a view on the major players, see http://alphaipartners.com/pdf/PR-2013-05-05.pdf.

7   For diagrams of market cycles, see *IRR Viewpoint* annual reports, www.irr.com/Publication-PublicationList/Index.htm.

8   To learn more about Dodd-Frank, see http://dodd-frank.com, www.acc.com/legalresources/quickcounsel/dfrrrlp.cfm, and http://realtormag.realtor.org/commercial/conversations/article/2011/07/what-dodd-frank-means-for-commercial-real-estate.

Chapter 11

Real Estate Finance: The Basic Tools

To evaluate the feasibility of a real estate investment, investors and lenders use the same measurement tools, but their objectives differ materially. An investor's primary objective is to maximize the value of the investment, while a lender's primary objective is to avoid losing money by ensuring that the underlying collateral value remains intact and property cash flows are sufficient to cover debt service payments. For both, the estimation of value starts with an estimation of property cash flows. Property cash flows come in two forms: the periodic payment of rents (net of *operating expenses and other cash outflows*) and the eventual sale of the property.

Recall from chapter 10 that individual real estate investments differ fundamentally from stock market investments, in which every share of stock for a given company is identical. Because every real estate asset is associated with a unique location, every building is unique. Furthermore, information about real estate assets is more dispersed, and there is no entity like the Securities and Exchange Commission that requires regular, standardized financial reports. Markets are said to be efficient when numerous analysts regularly follow the securities and everyone has roughly the same information. When this is not

true, it is more likely that a few investors may have a comparative advantage in a particular market. When it is possible for some participants to have better information, the premium on more and better legwork goes up. From an investment standpoint, comparative advantages are more likely to exist when markets are less price-efficient, which is often the case in real estate investing.

To provide proper context for valuation in price-inefficient markets, investors and lenders seek to understand how the physical asset complements its unique location and how it fits society's needs over the long term, relative to the competition. A real estate asset's long expected life in a fixed location suggests a longer investment holding period. Furthermore, real estate usually has higher transaction costs than do stock and bond investments. Individual common stocks, for example, can be sold almost instantaneously for a very small commission. In contrast, a commercial property sale may take many months from the start of marketing to final close. The total sales cost, including costs for brokers, lawyers, and inspections, may amount to several percentage points of the final price. Such fundamental differences make more extensive advance legwork a smart move.

Later chapters deal with the more nuanced aspects of getting the numbers to accurately reflect what is likely to happen. In this chapter, the basic tools for assembling that information are covered. Specifically, this chapter discusses three things:

- Calculation of *net operating income (NOI)* and property cash flow,
- Direct *capitalization* and discounted cash flow (DCF) valuation methods, and
- Capital structure—debt and equity financing and related tax considerations.

The tools are put in context using the Shortbread Lofts case study. To facilitate illustration of the basic financial tools, the cash flow estimates used here are at the level of rigor found in stage four. Subsequent chapters examine the legwork needed to produce the estimated cash flows.

THE COMPONENTS OF NET OPERATING INCOME

One of the most frequently used terms in real estate financial analysis is *net operating income* (NOI), a concept introduced in chapter 10. NOI measures a property's productivity and is the source of the returns to lenders and equity investors. As the term suggests, NOI is the income from the operation of a property. It is not easily controlled by the owner or manager, as rents, vacancies, and operating expenses depend to a large degree on the local space market. Information that is included in a property's NOI pro forma should be verifiable through a comparison with rents, market vacancy rates, and operating expenses of comparable properties as well as with industry norms. The following sections discuss the components of NOI.

Potential Gross Income

In its simplest form, potential gross income is the rent a property could generate if it were fully occupied, with no discounts. Potential gross income includes contract rent, rent escalations, and expense reimbursements by tenants. Contract rent is the

stated rent per square foot times the number of square feet occupied. In apartments and hotels, rent is usually stated in per-unit terms rather than per square foot.

Many multiyear lease agreements for office, retail, and industrial properties include a rent escalation clause. Rent escalations are rent increases used to keep rents in line with market rents. Rents are typically escalated on the anniversary date of the lease. Escalations can be stated as a dollar increase per year (or dollar increase per square foot per year), a percent increase in rent per year, an increase based on an inflation index such as the Consumer Price Index, or, in the case of retail, a function of retail sales.

With the exception of indexed and overage rents, the calculation of rent escalations is largely self-explanatory. Indexed rents use published inflation indices as the basis for increasing rent on a period-to-period basis. Indexed rents protect landlords from unexpected increases in inflation during multiyear lease terms; they can also protect tenants, as a fixed-rent escalation may outpace the rate of inflation. Overage rents, also referred to as "percentage rents," are used primarily in retail leases. They are based on tenant sales: If tenant sales exceed a threshold, the landlord receives rent escalations that are based on a percentage of the sales over the threshold.

Many office, industrial, and retail leases require tenants to reimburse landlords for certain property expenses or increases in property expenses. These reimbursements are usually recorded as a part of the income to the property owner. Clearly such reimbursements can be quite significant and therefore are negotiated strenuously.

There are three general types of expense reimbursement clauses (note that each real estate market may use slightly different names):

- Gross—The landlord pays for property operating expenses and expense increases. Apartment lease agreements are gross leases in terms of property taxes and maintenance, but the tenant usually pays for utilities.
- Modified Gross or Full Service—The landlord pays all expenses up to a lease-defined

CityCentre is a 47-acre mixed-use development in Houston, Texas. The equity for the land acquisition came from a number of high-net-worth investors with whom the developer had worked on other projects.

expense stop, and all expenses over the expense stop are passed through to (or paid for by) tenants. An expense stop usually excludes per-square-foot expenses incurred in the first year of the lease term, allowing only increases in expenses in lease year two and beyond to be passed through to the tenant. Modified gross expense pass-through clauses are most commonly found in office leases.

■ Net—A net lease is essentially a modified gross lease with an expense stop of zero. The tenant is responsible for all property expenses and expense increases (with the possible exception of management fees). Industrial and retail leases often include net lease pass-through clauses. There are typically three forms of net leases: single net, net net, and triple net. Each "net" refers to property taxes, building insurance, and property maintenance, in that order. In a single net lease, the tenant is responsible for property taxes, and the landlord or lessor is responsible for building insurance and property maintenance. In a net, net lease, the tenant is responsible for property taxes and building insurance, while the landlord is responsible for property maintenance. In a triple net lease, the tenant is responsible for property taxes, building insurance, and all building maintenance (with some exceptions for structural repair); the landlord takes on very minimal responsibility. Clearly, a very careful reading of the specific leases is the only way to establish accurate operating income estimates.

Vacancy, Collection Loss, and Rent Concessions

Similar to income statements for large corporations, income statements for real estate contain negative income items, or items that decrease the amount of income received. After accounting for all contractual sources of revenue, these negative income items are netted against the gross rental revenue to arrive at net rental income. In corporate income statements such items might include loss on merchandise returns and missing or stolen merchandise. On real estate income statements, negative income items typically include rental vacancies, collection losses, and rent concessions.

When underwriting an investment, investors and lenders usually include a rental vacancy rate on a property, to account for periods when space is not rented. Even if the property is "stabilized," a 5 to 10 percent vacancy rate is typically applied to the gross potential rental revenues for valuation purposes. One possible exception would be single-purpose buildings with creditworthy tenants on long-term leases.

Investors also consider collection loss, which is the loss of income from tenants that occupy space but do not pay the contractually agreed-upon rent. Although no tenant or landlord expects this situation when a lease is signed, a savvy investor includes a modest credit loss in certain projects.

Landlords may give rent concessions to tenants in the form of free rent when the market for tenant space is overbuilt; these concessions should be included in the pro forma. Even when the market is not overbuilt, landlords often offer new tenants free rent while the space is being fitted out with tenant *improvements.*

Miscellaneous Income

Miscellaneous income, additional income obtained from real estate that is ancillary to contract rents, can be a significant addition to gross potential income. Miscellaneous income includes income from other sources that are not the primary use of the property, such as parking, vending machines, and rental of rooftop space. Many tall buildings lease their rooftops to cellular phone companies and police and fire departments for transponder towers. Buildings near freeways may rent their rooftops to advertising companies.

Miscellaneous income can be verified through parking receipts, rent payments, and contracts with vendors. During the due diligence process, the purchaser of a real estate investment attempts to verify all property income streams. In most cases, sellers recognize the need to provide the information necessary to do so. For projects under development, the developer is responsible for providing credible estimates of all these items. For Shortbread Lofts, Short treated a broader than typical range of items as "miscellaneous" and expected extensive miscellaneous income from double occupancy in units, parking, and balcony premiums, as well as retail activities on the first floor.

Operating Expenses

To determine NOI, operating expenses are subtracted from total revenue. Operating expenses are the periodic expenditures necessary to maintain a property—real estate taxes, common-area maintenance, utilities, insurance, management fee, and so on. Periodic debt service payments, property depreciation, and capital expenditures are not considered operating expenses. Most operating expenses should be verifiable with invoices and payment receipts and through a review of audit reports.

The largest operating expense is often real estate taxes. These taxes are paid to the local municipality to fund municipal services such as public schools, police and fire protection, and road repairs. Because of the impact that real estate taxes have on pro forma income, it is strongly recommended that investors evaluate the municipality's financial condition so as to estimate the likelihood and scale of future property tax increases. The second-largest expense typically is common-area maintenance; that is, the cost necessary to maintain the property in good working order. Such expenses include cleaning of lobbies, hallways, and restrooms; maintenance of landscaping and parking areas; servicing of the HVAC (heating, ventilating and air conditioning) and elevator systems; and similar day-to-day operations. Other significant expenses include utility costs, such as the gas, electricity, and water necessary to operate a building, and liability insurance to insure a building physically and protect it from tenant actions. As a former accountant, Short liked greater detail (more individual line items) in operating expenses than is typical (see figure A in case study).

Management fees are often stated as a percentage of revenue and are paid to the parties that manage the day-to-day needs of buildings and tenants. Depending on the building, they usually run from 2 to 5 percent of revenue. A single-tenant warehouse building may have a management fee lower than 2 percent, but a busy shopping mall with high turnover, many inline retailers, a constant flow of customers, and large common areas may require a management fee greater than 5 percent.

Periodic longer-term costs are treated as capital expenditures. Most property owners put capital expenditures "below the line" (that is, below the NOI line). Although capital expenditures are material cash outflows for the landlord, they are not considered operating expenses. Getting the distinction between operating expense and capital items right is very important, as cap rates are usually estimated before capital items occur whereas discounted cash flow analysis puts those expenditures in the future year of expected occurrence. In apartment buildings, the convention is to put capital items associated with each move-out (such as carpet cleaning) above the line as "reserves."

Calculating Net Operating Income

NOI is total revenue less operating expenses. NOI does not include mortgage debt service, capital expenditures associated with significant building improvements and re-leasing of tenant space, or property depreciation (a tax, not a cash flow expense). These items are not included in NOI because they are not periodic expenses directly associated with the productivity of the property. Instead, the timing of these expenditures is controlled by the property's ownership and management preferences. NOI, therefore, serves as the most standard performance measure across properties because it minimizes the "noise" that can be created by below-the-line expense items. NOI measures the amount of regular income expected to be available to debt and equity investors. How that income is divided between them depends on financing decisions, which are typically viewed separately from decisions about the property's operations.

PROPERTY CASH FLOW

Although NOI is the industry standard for assessing property performance, it does not account for all of the costs to operate the property. Capital expenditures significantly impact property cash flow. They typically include tenant improvements (furnishing necessary to make the space habitable for a new tenant such as carpets, moving walls, and drop ceilings), leasing commissions (paid to a leasing agent to secure a tenant), and capital improvements (items intended to extend the building's economic life, such as a new roof). Capital expenditures are not regular periodic expenses like operating expenses; instead, they are triggered by an event such as a new lease or management decision to significantly improve the property. The distinction between these below-the-line items and above-the-line items enables investors to evaluate properties on a relative basis because NOI remains fairly steady year over year, whereas capital expenditures can drastically affect cash flow in any given year. An investor comparing cash flows between properties in a single year could be misled

CASE STUDY   Shortbread Lofts NOI

Because Short had developed a similar property in the same neighborhood, his building costs and operating income estimates had considerable credibility with the lender. For operating income, Short was estimating $2 million in the first year, with modest growth over the next five years. Figure A shows the pro forma NOI for Shortbread Lofts as presented to the construction lender.

Figure A   **Net Operating Income**

	Year 1	Year 2	Year 3	Year 4	Year 5
Current market rents	$2,799,360	$2,799,360	$2,911,334	$2,998,674	$3,088,635
Rent increase (market)	–	111,974	87,340	89,960	92,960
Scheduled market rents	2,799,360	2,911,334	2,998,674	3,088,635	3,181,294
Loss to lease	–	43,670	44,980	46,330	47,719
Gross potential rent	2,799,360	2,867,664	2,953,694	3,042,305	3,133,547
Vacancy loss	–83,981	–86,030	–88,611	–91,269	–94,007
Non-revenue units	–21,840	–22,495	–23,170	–23,865	–24,581
Net rental income	**2,693,539**	**2,759,139**	**2,841,913**	**2,927,171**	**3,014,986**
Double occupancy	48,025	49,466	50,950	52,478	54,053
Parking income	140,400	144,612	148,950	153,419	158,021
Balcony premium	9,860	10,156	10,460	10,774	11,098
Miscellaneous services and fees	94,860	97,706	100,637	103,656	106,766
Total revenues	**$2,986,684**	**$3,061,079**	**$3,152,910**	**$3,247,498**	**$3,344,924**
Operating Expenses					
Payroll	$162,600	$166,665	$170,832	$175,102	$179,480
Gas and electricity	75,880	77,777	79,721	81,714	83,757
Water and sewerage	60,675	62,499	64,062	65,663	67,305
Trash and pest control	9,485	9,722	9,965	10,214	10,470
Repairs and maintenance	37,940	38,889	39,861	40,857	41,879
Turnover-related loss	32,520	33,333	34,166	35,020	35,896
Cable and internet	51,000	52,275	53,582	54,921	56,294
Marketing and advertising	33,875	34,722	35,590	36,480	37,392
Administrative	40,650	41,666	42,708	43,776	44,870
Security	24,390	25,000	25,625	26,265	26,922
Controllable expenses	529,315	542,548	556,112	570,014	584,284
Management fee	89,601	91,832	94,587	97,425	100,348
Taxes	271,000	277,775	284,719	291,837	299,133
Insurance	19,125	19,603	20,093	20,596	21,110
Total operating expenses	**$909,041**	**$931,758**	**$955,511**	**$979,872**	**$1,004,856**
Replacement reserves	40,375	41,384	42,419	43,479	44,566
Total expenses	**$949,416**	**$973,142**	**$997,930**	**$1,023,351**	**$1,049,422**
Net operating income	**$2,037,268**	**$2,087,937**	**$2,154,980**	**$2,224,147**	**$2,295,502**

Continued on page 213

by the fluctuations that take place in years when management decides to reinvest in the property or signs a large lease that requires expending capital up front for tenant improvements. Subtracting capital expenditures from NOI yields expected cash flow from operations. Subtracting financing costs (annual principal and interest payments) from the cash flow from operations yields cash flow after financing:

NOI
– Tenant improvements
– Leasing commissions
– Capital improvements

Cash flow from operations
– Financing costs

Cash flow after financing

Because Shortbread Lofts is an apartment building, there are no outside leasing commissions or tenant improvements as would be the case with an office building. Furthermore, all rollover expenses were included above the line in reserves. Because it is new construction, no major capital items were expected in the first five years of operation. Consequently, in this situation, the net operating income was the same as the annual cash flow before debt service.

ESTIMATING VALUE USING CAP RATES

Using estimates of NOI and cash flow, an investor or lender can estimate the value of the underlying asset. Two approaches typically are used: direct capitalization and discounted cash flow. In the *capitalization rate approach*, a single-year income estimate is capitalized to estimate value. In contrast, the discounted cash flow analysis uses a multi-period estimated stream of cash flows to value a property.

Direct Capitalization

The Appraisal Institute defines the direct capitalization approach to value as "a method used to convert an estimate of a single year's income expectancy into an indication of value in one direct step, either by dividing the income estimate by an appropriate rate or by multiplying the income estimate by an appropriate factor." In other words, a cap rate is

the relationship between the NOI that an investor expects to receive and the price the investor is willing to pay for the asset. For example, if an investor is willing to pay $1 million for an asset that generates $80,000 of NOI, the investor is paying an 8 percent capitalization rate.

Clearly, cap rates vary significantly across property types, locations, and quality. Ideally, cap rates are derived from recently sold properties. It is important to obtain verified property income streams and confirmed sale prices when calculating cap rates because even small errors in cap rate estimation can lead to serious misevaluation. The closer the match of the comparable properties with the subject property in terms of location, quality of construction, tenant mix, and other characteristics, the more accurate the valuation derived from capitalizing the property's income stream. Cap rates may be "trailing" (last year), "in place" (current), or "expected" (next year). Local Realtor associations and independent organizations (REIS, CoStar, Altus, CBRE, Axiometrics, Real Capital Analytics, and others) provide cap rates for markets throughout the United States. One limitation of the capitalization rate approach is that cap rates explicitly value the NOI of only one year of operations, which is why a prudent investor also incorporates a multi-period discounted cash flow valuation in the investment analysis.

Discounted Cash Flow and Internal Rate of Return

Discounted cash flow (DCF) analysis is an alternative to the direct capitalization method of valuation. It calculates the present value of expected future project cash flows to estimate the current value of the project. Instead of dividing NOI for year 1 by a capitalization rate, this method discounts future cash flows at the investor's required rate of return to take into account the time value of money across the expected project time horizon. In DCF analysis, near-term cash flows are valued more highly than more distant cash flows. This difference increases with the required rate of return.

How does the investor determine the required rate of return for any given investment?

Understanding Cap Rates

The formula for the direct cap rate approach to estimating the value of a property is relatively simple: cap rate (R) is a function of the property NOI divided by the property value (V). That is:

$$R = NOI \div V,$$

where

V = the value of the property,
NOI = the property NOI, and
R = the capitalization rate.

Alternatively, to determine the value of a property using a cap rate,

$$V = NOI \div R.$$

In the context of the broader financial markets, the cap rate (or initial yield) can be seen as the total required return less the expected net growth in income. Thus,

Cap Rate = Required Return − Net Income Growth

The investor's required return can be divided into two components: the risk-free rate plus a market risk premium. The risk-free rate can be derived from government bonds that align with the investor's expected hold period. The market risk premium that an investor requires derives from factors that influence the future value of the underlying asset, including uncertainty about expected future cash flows and illiquidity. Net income growth is a function of the rate of rental growth expected for new buildings in the market and the rate of depreciation suffered by a property as it ages.

To make a comparison with the stock market, a capitalization rate is the reciprocal of a price/earnings ratio, with real estate market value serving as price and NOI substituted for earnings.

Source: Andrew E. Baum and David Hartzell, *Global Property Investment: Strategies, Structures, Decisions* (Hoboken, N.J.: Wiley-Blackwell, 2012), p. 128.

Conceptually, it is the market "risk-free" rate of return (the rate on a Treasury security with the same maturity) plus an estimated risk premium. In practice, many investors also look at the rate of return expected from similar investments as well as the return they need to satisfy internal needs; for example, when private equity funds have told their investors that they would receive a certain level of returns.

This method not only values ongoing cash flows from operations but also the terminal cash flow when the property is sold. To calculate the terminal value, an investor uses the direct capitalization method with the projected NOI from the final year. For example, if the time horizon of the investment is ten years, the investor typically capitalizes the projected NOI for year 10 with an appropriate cap rate for expected market and project conditions at that date. Because this terminal value is in gross terms, expected selling costs (usually expressed as a percentage of sale price) are subtracted.

After calculating the annual cash flows and expected proceeds from sale, the investor determines what discount rate to use to calculate the present value of the cash flows. Discounting each cash flow back to year 0 and subtracting the initial investment (the total development costs), the project will have either a positive or a negative net present value (NPV). If the NPV is positive, the analysis suggests that the investor should move forward with the project because expected returns exceed the discount rate (which is the return appropriate for this level of risk). A negative NPV does not imply that the project will lose money, only that it is not expected to achieve the investor's desired rate of return.

In addition to valuing the property before leverage, it is useful to look at the value of the equity after the proposed financing. This is done by subtracting both the annual debt service and the loan balance from the pre-debt service cash flows. The cash flows to equity consist of cash flows after financing for the expected holding period as well as the expected cash flow from disposition after paying off the final loan balance. Clearly, the required return will be higher for this equity valuation, as leverage increases the risk.

Along with the NPV calculation, investors may incorporate a calculation of the *internal rate of return (IRR)*. An IRR calculates the annual return that a stream of cash flows generates over the life of a project, relative to the initial investment. Therefore, the first cash flow is an outflow and shown in the IRR calculation as negative (the investment); future cash flows are inflows and shown as positive (income and proceeds from sales). Investors contextualize an IRR by comparing it with their required rate of return, or hurdle rate. If the IRR that is expected from a project exceeds their hurdle rate for that project, given their cost of capital and the level of perceived risk of the project, then investors likely move forward with the project.

The basic formula for the NPV and IRR calculation is as follows:

$$PV = \sum_{n=1}^{N} \frac{ECF_n}{(1 + r)^n}$$

where

PV = present value,
N = number of periods,
n = the particular period,
ECF = expected cash flow, and
r = required return.

If the price today (PV) is known and the expected cash flows are estimated, then solving for r yields the project IRR. In the old days, this calculation was done by hand. Today, few people remember this basic formula, as both the NPV and IRR calculations are typically performed using spreadsheet software. Regardless of the software used, the decision maker must decide on the appropriate discount rate. The components of the discount rate are easy to understand: a risk-free rate, as measured by a Treasury bond with a similar maturity, and a risk premium. For example, on a ten-year investment, the calculation starts with the current yield on a ten-year Treasury bond and then adds a risk premium appropriate for the particular investment.

Assume the investor has determined that a 9 percent rate of return is appropriate for a particular investment that is expected to produce $200,000 at the end of two years. How much should the investor pay for that investment today? The present value of $200,000 to be received in two years is $200,000 ÷ $(1 + .09)^2$, or $200,000 ÷ 1.1881, or $168,336. Alternatively stated, if the investor invested $168,336 today and earned 9 percent on it, he would have $183,486 after one year ($168,336 + $168,336 × .09). At the end of the second year, he would have $200,000 ($183,486 + $183,486 × .09). If the $200,000 was expected at the end of three years, then the factor 1.09 would have been cubed—$200,000 ÷ $(1 + .09)^3$—and the present value would be lower. If the required rate of return

---

CASE STUDY   **Shortbread Lofts Cap Rate**

Short's mortgage banker, CBRE, looked at estimates of stabilized capitalization rates from NCREIF and other sources to determine that at the end of the expected five-year holding period, Shortbread Lofts should command a 5 percent "trailing" capitalization rate. Because the project was nothing more than an idea and not an operating property, the banker determined that a 6.5 percent forward-looking capitalization rate was appropriate prior to construction. Therefore, the estimated "end of year 5" value was

$2,295,501 (year 5 expected NOI) ÷ 0.05 (the cap rate) = $45,910,020.

Similarly, the valuation based on first-year cash flow is

$2,037,268 (year 1 expected NOI) ÷ by 0.065 = $31,342,584.

Clearly such estimates are not precise, so the estimates were conservatively rounded to $45 million for the year 5 valuation (net $44 million after sales costs) and $31 million for the value at the start of the project.

Continued next page

---

was 11 percent, then the factor 1.09 would instead be 1.11, and again the value of the investment today (the present value) would be lower.

These mechanics are deceptively simple. In practice, it is quite difficult to forecast cash flows into the future. It is even harder to choose a discount rate that properly reflects all the risks identified in the cash flow forecasting exercise. Often it is helpful to create the first model in a spreadsheet program such as Excel so that all the unique aspects of the proposed development can be clearly identified and tracked. Subsequently, for ease of communication with others in the capital markets, it may be helpful to move to a well-established program for discounted cash flow analysis such as Argus.

The next exercise that the savvy investor undertakes is sensitivity analysis. Even if a project yields a positive NPV or a favorable IRR, the investor wants to determine how sensitive these metrics are to changes in the underlying assumptions. For example,

if the project's exit cap rate changes by 50 basis points (0.5 percent), what effect will that have on the IRR of the project? If rents escalate at only 3 percent instead of 5 percent, how will that impact the NPV of the project? Although these exercises are predictions, they provide investors with valuable quantitative data by establishing ranges or cushions around the set of assumptions used in underwriting a project.

CASE STUDY   Shortbread Lofts Calculations

With no expected below-the-line cash flows, Shortbread Lofts had a projected set of cash flows that were identical to the NOI

estimates. Short worked with CBRE to decide that investors would want a 12 percent unlevered return.

Figure B   **Total Present Value**

	FY1	FY2	FY3	FY4	FY5
NOI	$2,037,268	$2,087,936	$2,154,980	$2,224,147	$2,295,501
Capital items	0	0	0	0	0
Cash flow	2,037,268	2,087,936	2,154,980	2,224,147	2,295,501
Residual value					44,000,000
Total cash flow	2,037,268	2,087,936	2,154,980	2,224,247	46,295,501
PV factor $1/(1 + r)^n$ ($r = 0.12$)	0.893	0.797	0.712	0.636	0.567
PV	1,819,280	1,664,085	1,534,346	1,414,557	26,249,549
Total PV	32,681,818				
Cost estimate	29,000,000				
NPV (unlevered)	$3,681,818				

Short thought that the land he was assembling had a value of about $8 million (including associated soft costs) and that the total construction costs would run in the range of $21 million for an early total cost estimate of $29 million. Therefore, the NPV is $3,681,818. Because the NPV is positive, the project is financially feasible. Now, how does the equity position look after debt service? At the time, shorter-term interest rates were very low, and Short felt that he could justify a low-risk premium to the lender if the lender ratios (discussed later in this chapter) indicated a relatively safe loan. Initial preliminary discussions with lenders suggested an interest-only loan of $21 million at 4.8 percent interest was possible. Working with CBRE, Short determined that the return required by an equity investor would be 15 percent, with the attractive tax situation described near the end of this chapter.

The discussion on risk premium in chapter 10 explains that the investor's "required" or "desired" rate of return is composed

of a risk-free rate (usually taken from the same maturity treasury security) and a risk premium appropriate for the particular investment. As shown in figure 10-2, the total annual rate of return on existing institutional real estate has been about 9 percent over the last 35 years. Looking forward, the risk-free component is comparatively low, with the ten-year U.S. Treasury bond yielding only 2 percent at the time. In contrast, investing in development is far riskier than investing in operating properties. CBRE looked at their database of recent sales and came to the conclusion that the property unlevered would need to generate a 12 percent return to interest investors. If Short chose to put debt on the development before selling, the risk to equity would be higher. Again, from its database of recent sales, CBRE determined that investors would want a 15 percent return, given the increased risk with the debt having a prior claim on property cash flows.

Continued next page

Shortbread Lofts Calculations *Continued*

Figure C **Value with Proposed $21 Million Financing**

	FY1	FY2	FY3	FY4	FY5
Total cash flow	**$2,037,268**	**$2,087,936**	**$2,154,980**	**$2,224,247**	**$46,295,501**
Debt service	1,008,000	1,008,000	1,008,000	1,008,000	1,008,000
Loan payoff					21,000,000
Equity cash flow	1,029,268	1,079,936	1,146,980	1,216,247	24,287,501
PV factor	0.870	0.756	0.658	0.572	0.497
PV	895,463	816,432	754,713	695,636	12,070,888
Equity PV	$15,233,132				

Value with proposed financing = $36,310,233

With these assumptions, obtaining financing clearly increased the value of the equity and improved Short's position. Because the loan would cover the construction cost (all rough estimates at stage one), Short saw an opportunity to charge a higher development fee and/or retain a disproportionate share of project equity. This opportunity is discussed in more detail as the text moves though the eight-stage model.

Continued on page 219

CAPITAL STRUCTURE

As explained in chapter 10, a real estate project is typically financed by at least two capital sources: debt and equity. In some cases, there is a complicated financing structure, or "capital stack," with multiple sources of debt and equity each controlling partial interests in the property cash flows. Why does the capital structure occasionally become quite complex? The short answer is that each interested party desires a different risk profile, which dictates how their claims on the cash flows should be structured. The first major distinction is that debt financing is more contractual, while equity financing is more residual. Debt capital providers (lenders) have the first claim on cash flows from the property on the basis of contractual agreements that specify the property (and sometimes personal assets) as collateral for the loan. By contrast, equity investors receive cash flows from the property after the debt holders have been paid. This distinction causes debt providers to require a lower return on capital than equity holders, who assume a higher level of risk and therefore require a higher return on capital.

Senior debt usually constitutes the largest portion of the capital stack but carries the most conservative risk profile because of its contractual interest in property cash flows and ability to foreclose on the asset if the contractual terms are not met. Senior debt is usually sourced through banks and other institutional lenders. Mezzanine debt is subordinate to senior debt; in the capital stack, it fills the gap between senior debt and project equity. Typical providers of mezzanine debt include hedge funds, mortgage REITs, and private sources. Equity capital takes the form of either preferred equity or common equity. Preferred equity, as the name suggests, takes a senior position over common equity in the capital structure. Although it maintains a residual interest in the property cash flows, it functions more like debt, with a set return that is paid, or accrued, on a regular basis. Preferred equity providers expect a higher return on investment than both senior and mezzanine debt providers, but a lower return than common equity providers require, as shown in figure 11-1. Preferred equity is sourced through private investors such as individuals, private equity funds, and real estate investment firms. The capital source that maintains the highest risk profile and highest expected return is common equity.

Numerous potential ownership structures provide flexibility for all levels of investors to take part in a real estate project. A common format is the partnership that involves both a general partner and limited partners. Usually, the general partner is responsible for sourcing and managing the project; the limited partners provide the capital necessary to fund the equity portion of the project but do not typically get involved in management. General partners typically invest a modest percentage of the overall equity, perhaps 5 percent, to demonstrate their commitment to the project; the limited partners contribute the remainder. To establish the distribution of project cash flows, multiple legal structures are available. They are usually negotiated at the beginning of the project and depend on the track record and sophistication of the sponsor as well as the deal itself.

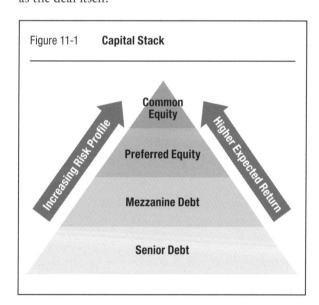

Figure 11-1 **Capital Stack**

Increasing Risk Profile · *Higher Expected Return*

- Common Equity
- Preferred Equity
- Mezzanine Debt
- Senior Debt

Loan Underwriting Process

As explained in chapter 10, a sequence of lenders is typically involved in financing a property: a construction lender and a permanent lender. The permanent lender commits to a loan on the basis of the proposed development's long-term economic viability. The construction lender relies on the permanent lender's commitment as a "takeout." This relationship between lenders inherently leads to different objectives and incentives for each lender.

Construction loans typically begin with a zero balance. During construction, the construction lender funds "draws" to cover portions of the cost of the building completed to date. Most construction lenders are not paid interest during the construction of a building because there is no property income to cover the mortgage payments; instead, interest is accrued and added to the principal of the loan. Therefore, the construction lender often receives no debt service payments until late in the loan, if at all, making the construction lender's exit strategy very important. The principal and most, if not all, interest on construction loans are received when the loan matures.

Once construction is complete and the property income stabilizes, the construction loan is usually taken out by a permanent lender. Since the payoff is critical, it is common for the developer to arrange for permanent financing before obtaining the construction loan, even though the construction loan will be funded first. The amount of the permanent loan depends on the amount of income the property is expected to generate, as shown in the ratios that the permanent lender applies to that income stream. Therefore, the amount of the takeout loan, which pays off the construction loan, usually determines the size of the construction loan. Because the construction lender receives most, if not all, of the principal and interest on the construction loan at maturity from a permanent lender, the construction lender pays close attention to the permanent lender's specific criteria, outlined in the loan commitment.

The loan underwriting process for a development proposal can be illustrated in six steps, although the number, terminology, and sequence of steps varies from lender to lender. When a developer submits a loan application to a lender, the proposal usually includes information on the space market, the property's location, proposed improvements, the borrower's creditworthiness, the construction team, and financial analyses. In the process of underwriting the development, the lender verifies the developer's assumptions, adjusts them as needed, and then independently assesses the project's viability. Each step includes a series of questions that both the developer and the lender need to address.

The six steps begin with a broad or macro view of the market and the property's location in the market, and then narrow to a micro view of the improvements and borrower. The final step combines all the collected quantitative and qualitative data into an analysis of the development's financial viability. With relatively minor variations, for most lenders a loan proposal includes these elements:

1. Market and submarket analysis,
2. Location analysis of the subject site,
3. Assessment of the appropriateness of the proposed improvements for the site,
4. Determination of the creditworthiness of the borrower,
5. Evaluation of the developer's construction team and property management plan, and
6. Evaluation of the financial viability of the proposed improvements.

Much of the loan underwriting process flows from the lender's analysis of the property's market and submarket in the first step. In this work, the lender asks many questions: What is the market's demand for this kind of space over time? How much competition does the development face from existing and future competitive properties? Timing of the loan is also an important consideration that depends on a number of issues. How long will it take for the new space to be absorbed? Are unanticipated construction delays possible or likely? How would the developer pay for any increased costs associated with delays? Are market conditions likely to change adversely before the project's completion and lease-up?

The second step—a location analysis—involves evaluating the site's accessibility and suitability for its target tenants within the submarket. Is the development convenient to the kinds of amenities, services, and resources that the target tenants need or prefer? Can the site physically accommodate the intended development? Is the proper zoning in place? Do the community and the project's neighbors generally support the development? Are utilities available? Is the site in a growth corridor?

Step three is to determine the appropriateness of the proposed improvements for the site. Does the site have physical constraints to development? Does it contain species habitat that needs to be protected? Will the site require environmental remediation? Do the subsoils support the planned development? Does the proposed building suit its location? For instance, a highly finished flex building might be deemed out of place in a heavy-industrial park and, for that reason, considered less economically viable.

As mentioned, a developer typically gets a permanent loan commitment first, then a construction loan. The permanent lender is very concerned with these first three steps, as they drive long-term value. The construction lender is more concerned with the fourth and fifth steps, as they determine the likelihood of completing the project on time and on budget and hence being able to count on the permanent loan takeout.

Step four is the evaluation of the borrower's creditworthiness. Many development and construction loans are recourse loans; that is, in the event of default, the lender has recourse to the borrower's other assets, in addition to the property pledged as collateral. Thus, the lender's analysis of the collateral may include an investigation of the borrower's other assets and associated liabilities. In addition, the lender must investigate the borrower's other activities and repayment obligations on existing liabilities, which might deplete the assets available to satisfy the contemplated loan if the lender must resort to assets other than the subject property for repayment.

Step five qualifies the developer's construction team and property management plan, both of which are major considerations for the construction lender. Lenders prefer construction teams with a proven record of completing projects on time, on budget, and in accordance with architectural and engineering specifications. Missing development and construction deadlines can cause costs to escalate, and missing completion dates can give preleased tenants the right to renegotiate or cancel their leases. If a project is not developed to project specifications, the structural and mechanical integrity of the project may be compromised, which can lower the collateral value of the property.

The permanent lender is also concerned about what happens after construction is complete. Does the borrower have the necessary property management skills or the appropriate property management team to market and lease the asset and maintain the property's collateral value? The operating management team is responsible for ensuring that tenants' creditworthiness is adequate. The signed leases—and the tenants' willingness and ability to pay the rent—are key considerations in assessing the value of the collateral. Preconstruction lease commitments of strong (creditworthy) tenants ensure that their portion of the rental income will be generated when the building is complete, thereby reducing the risk that the property's cash flow will not be adequate to cover debt service for the permanent lender. Although good management cannot save a poorly conceived and executed project, poor management

can severely damage a good project. Hence, the proposed management plan is an important factor in the decision to lend money to the borrower.

In the sixth step, the lender assesses the financial viability of the proposed improvements and the project's economic feasibility. This analysis uses the data, findings, and conclusions from the preceding analyses. Step six essentially covers everything from the project's concept to its cash flow and its ultimate sale to the next investor or, if the developer plans to hold the property, the management plan. The lender's primary analytical tools are the *pro forma cash flow statement* and a multi-period DCF analysis. The lender's goal is to determine whether the development will be a safe investment from the lender's perspective. The following section discusses the ratios that a lender uses to determine whether the project is feasible and a good risk.

Lender's Calculations

When underwriting a loan, commercial lenders use two major metrics to analyze the financial viability of the development being financed: the *debt service coverage ratio (DSCR)*, and the *loan-to-value (LTV) ratio*. The DSCR measures the property's ability to cover debt service payments, while the LTV ratio assesses the property's collateral value.

In the past, real estate textbooks commonly included amortization tables showing interest rates and maturities. Today, most analysts use the functions in a spreadsheet program. A user enters the loan amount, the interest rate, and the amortization period, and the program calculates the monthly (or annual) payments.

A higher interest rate or a shorter loan amortization period causes the annual debt service for a given loan to rise. The higher the mortgage constant (annual debt service divided by the loan amount), the lower the justified loan amount. Developers pursue a strategy of bargaining for the lowest interest rate and the longest amortization term that the lender will accept, knowing that such a strategy will result in the lowest mortgage constant, the smallest debt service payment, and ultimately the largest loan amount.

FOREST CITY RATNER

Located in lower Manhattan, 8 Spruce Street is a 76-story residential apartment building developed by Forest City Ratner. The developer and NEBF, a large pension fund, provided the equity.

Debt Service Coverage Ratio

The DSCR is probably the single most important measure for determining the acceptability of a loan application. It is calculated by dividing the project's NOI by the project's annual debt service as follows:

$$DSCR = NOI \div Annual\ Debt\ Service.$$

A property with a 1.80 DSCR produces $1.80 of NOI for every $1.00 of debt service. The DSCR determines the adequacy of the development's projected cash flow to service the debt and is an indication of the lender's risk. The lower the DSCR, the smaller the cushion of available NOI per dollar borrowed and therefore the higher the lender's financial risk. If, as in the case of Shortbread Lofts, the developer asks the construction lender to proceed without a permanent loan takeout commitment in place, the construction lender will want a high expected DSCR.

For real estate projects, lenders generally require a DSCR between 1.20 and 1.60. Note that the DSCR in the Shortbread Lofts case is a strong 1.80 in the first year. Given the lack of a permanent loan takeout and the non-amortizing construction loan, this high ratio was appropriate.

Loan-to-Value Ratio

The LTV ratio expresses the relationship between the amount of a mortgage loan and the value of the property securing it:

$$LTV = Loan\ Amount \div Property\ Value.$$

The higher the LTV ratio, the larger the loan relative to the value of the property and thus the lower the equity invested in the property. When less equity is invested in a project, the risk to the lender is greater. If the property values erode, the equity cushion may not be sufficient. For projects in the conceptual stage, most lenders use a loan-to-cost (LTC) ratio in place of the LTV ratio. The LTC ratio divides the loan amount by the total construction budget, as follows:

$$LTC = Loan\ Amount \div Total\ Construction\ Budget.$$

CASE STUDY **Shortbread Lofts Project Loan Metrics**

Short contemplated going without a permanent loan commitment. Consequently, he needed very strong ratios to attract a construction lender. The construction lender needed both a high DSCR (in case no permanent loan was forthcoming at the end of the five years) and a low LTV ratio (in case of default prior to loan maturity).

Debt service:	4.8% × $21,000,000 = $1,008,000
NOI in year 5:	$2,295,501
DSCR at maturity:	2.02

As derived by direct capitalization, the Shortbread Lofts value is $31 million, so the LTV ratio is 61.8 percent ($21 million ÷ $31 million). Both ratios are strong, suggesting that Short could probably get a construction lender to commit without first arranging a permanent loan commitment.

Continued on page 237

To ensure that the developer provides an adequate equity cushion, lenders often apply both the LTC and the LTV ratios, to assess the amount of equity needed.

As a matter of policy, banks and insurance companies often mandate maximum LTV ratios for their investments in different types of real estate. Furthermore, federal and state regulators often specify maximum LTV ratios for the real estate investments of regulated institutions.

When a lender is considering a loan proposal using the LTV ratio and the DSCR, he underwrites the property to the lower of the two justified ratios. For instance, if the maximum indicated loan amount using the DSCR is $12 million and the maximum indicated loan amount using the LTV ratio is $12.5 million, the maximum loan the lender would make is $12 million. As noted, the ratios quantify different risks. The DSCR measures the adequacy of the property's cash flow to meet debt service; the LTV ratio measures principal preservation—that is, how far property value can fall before the collateral value of the property is less than the mortgage amount.

Benefits and Costs of Using Debt Financing

A basic benefit of debt is that it can be used to leverage up the equity return. Such "positive" leverage occurs when the cost of debt financing is lower than the overall return generated by the property. In such situations, the percentage return to the equity investor is greater using debt than it is with no debt. A simple example illustrates the point. Consider a project that returns 6 percent with no debt. If the investor finances 80 percent of the project with debt that costs 4 percent, then the return on the investor's equity goes from 6 percent to 14 percent. For example, if a $1 million property produces an NOI of 6 percent—or $60,000—and leverage is 80 percent ($800,000) at 4 percent interest, then the equity cash flow is calculated as follows: $60,000 in NOI less interest of $32,000, producing equity of $28,000 (14 percent on $200,000 in equity).

Moreover, by combining various debt and equity structures, a developer can create risk/return opportunities to fit specific investors' needs. The flexibility to tailor the investment to suit the investor client is an additional benefit of debt financing. If a property maintains positive leverage, it appears to be a free lunch for the borrower—that is, positive leverage creates a return multiplier and a better tax position, as discussed in the next section. Still, the basic relationship between risk and return remains. When equity investors borrow money to magnify equity returns, they assume the cost of greater variability in equity cash flows, and therefore higher risk. And, if the project's income drops below the level of debt service, investors may face the choice of paying the monthly debt service from other income sources or defaulting on the loan. Clearly, the risk to the equity investor goes up when a prior claim is added. This is why CBRE and Short used a much higher required return (15 percent) when estimating the value after debt service, despite the tax benefit (see case study on page 219).

Adding Income Tax Considerations

Tax benefits to the investor in real estate parallel those to investors in corporate finance, as interest payments are tax deductible. However, in real estate the story gets better because of the interplay between debt and depreciation. Simply put, the depreciation deduction improves with the use of debt. Consider the following very simple example. A building is valued at $1 million with an NOI of $70,000. The investor is considering borrowing $700,000 at 5 percent interest. Thus the interest payments would be $35,000. If the weighted average life of the structure is 25 years and the land is 20 percent of the investment value (land is not depreciated), then annual depreciation is $32,000 ($800,000 ÷ 25).

Financing with Your Money versus Other People's Money

When looking to secure financing for a project, developers often debate whether to use their own money (if they have enough capital) or someone else's. There are advantages to both approaches. Following are a few guidelines:

- *Try not to sign anything but the carve-outs.* In standard nonrecourse financing, lenders often have "bad boy" provisions. These specify that the borrower becomes liable if he does certain things, such as file for bankruptcy. Borrowers want to keep risks as low as possible, so they only want to be on the hook for specific acts that they know they are not going to commit, rather than all the "standard provisions" in the particular lender's documents. Therefore, borrowers want to carve out from the rest of the provisions the lender desires those recourse provisions they can live with.

- *Make the other guy cross-collateralize.* Cross-collateralization entails guaranteeing the loan with properties other than the subject development. If a developer's investment partner cross-collateralizes the development loan with other properties, the lender is happier and the developer is less likely to run into financial trouble. However, if the developer cross-collateralizes with his other properties, then his risk of loss extends beyond the subject property. This is not good.

- *Clawbacks are good, if you get the claw.* Clawbacks are previously distributed funds that may be taken back under certain specified circumstances. For example, if early-period cash flows on a multistage development have been distributed to a developer's financial partner, the developer would like to be able to recall them in the event of a future cash squeeze. However, he does not want the financial partner to be able to claw back the development fee.

In this very simplistic example, an investor using no debt has taxable income of $38,000 ($70,000 less $32,000 depreciation). With the use of the debt, the investor's taxable income is nearly zero: $70,000 less interest of $35,000 and depreciation of $32,000. With debt, the required equity is lower, but depreciation is unchanged. Note that depreciation is tax deductible, but it is not a cash expense. This advantageous tax situation occurs in addition to the leverage impact on returns noted earlier.

INDUSTRY TOOLS FOR PROJECT UNDERWRITING

Any modern hand calculator can easily solve for the DCF done by hand in the Shortbread Lofts example. In fact, even that simplification is now a bit obsolete. There are two widely used calculation tools—Microsoft Excel and Argus Enterprise—and many firms develop custom adaptations of one or both. Microsoft Excel remains the most widely used spreadsheet program among real estate practitioners because of its flexibility and its horsepower for complex calculations. It is recommended for early development-period forecasts where many items are still in flux. At some point, it may be to the developer's advantage to switch to Argus to facilitate ongoing negotiations, as many institutional lenders and investors use this software.

Developers use Excel because it is straightforward to use for building out development budgets, construction timelines, and detailed line items. In Excel, users can create and link nearly unlimited tabs and data tables, enabling developers to model the on-the-ground situation and the particular financial structure of each project. Once the situation has been modeled, sensitivity analysis can be done expeditiously. For example, the analyst can easily evaluate rent realization scenarios, expense escalation scenarios, and so on.

Investors who focus on income-producing properties also use Argus software. Argus offers streamlined property-type templates, enabling users to input assumptions in a standard format and arrive quickly at property cash flow projections and related valuations. The standardization of the Argus software is valuable in the real estate industry because it enables investors, bankers, and developers to communicate through a familiar model, facilitating negotiation.

SUMMARY

Real estate development is both an art and a science, requiring both technical skills and intuition. Numerous players are involved, and many complications challenge decision makers. All that said, it is smart to bring together all that can be known about an idea in a consistent format early in the process. The finance tools discussed in this chapter enable the developer and other parties (such as lenders) to achieve that objective.

The development process starts with an examination of the proposed project in its market, to estimate what the income and expenses are likely to be. From the projection of NOI, the analysis moves to a calculation of expected cash flows. The cap rate is used to estimate value from a single-year forecast of stabilized NOI. The present value technique is used to estimate value from the projected cash flows over time. All the capital market participants use these basic tools to evaluate their position in the proposed development.

An understanding of the finance needs of all participants requires more scholarship than is presented here. Continued study is recommended, using more detailed real estate finance texts. Several are included in the bibliography (for example, Bruggemann, Fisher, Geltner, Giliberto, and Lynn).

As this book moves through the eight stages, the financial estimates produced in stage one become ever more exacting as more insight is added. As construction progresses, developers use the financial models to evaluate new tradeoffs without losing sight of how all the players come together to create the final product.

TERMS

- Capitalization
- Capitalization rate (cap rate)

- Debt service coverage ratio (DSCR)
- Discounted cash flow (DCF) analysis
- Improvements
- Internal rate of return (IRR)
- Loan-to-value (LTV) ratio
- Mortgage constant
- Net operating income (NOI)
- Operating expenses
- Positive leverage
- Pro forma cash flow statement

REVIEW QUESTIONS

11.1 Discuss the three ways that property owners escalate tenant rents in multiyear leases.

11.2 What is an expense stop, and how is it used in gross, modified gross, and net leases?

11.3 What is a capitalization rate, and how is it used to value commercial real estate?

11.4 What is the most difficult part of DCF analysis?

11.5 What are the primary ratios that commercial property lenders use? What risks does each ratio assess?

11.6 What are the six steps in underwriting a commercial loan? Why is each important?

11.7 What are capital expenditures, and why are they usually not included as an expense in the calculation of NOI?

11.8 Who decides the capital structure of a development?

11.9 How does financial modeling facilitate loan negotiation?

PART 6

Proving the Concept

Real estate development usually begins with a very rough idea that the developer refines by further examining and exploring the idea's feasibility. The original vision needs to take physical form in sketches. It must be buildable on a particular site. It needs to pass regulatory scrutiny and draw interest from investors. It needs to appeal to a large enough market.

Chapter 12, Idea Refinement, describes stage two, the beginning of formal market research, preliminary design sketches, and exploration of public sector considerations, all tied to a development concept at a particular location and site. During stage two, the stage one back-of-the-envelope pro forma evolves into a much more rigorous set of financial forecasts. If the idea continues to pass muster, the developer is then willing to move to stage three—formal feasibility.

Chapter 13 describes the feasibility study, which informs the developer's decision-making process. It is also the sales tool that the developer uses to assemble the development team, including investors, tenants, and appropriate public officials. The feasibility study becomes the primary risk control device to be used in all subsequent stages of the development process.

Chapter 12

Stage Two: Idea Refinement

The ideas formulated in stage one come in different packages. They may be a new type of development or a refinement of an existing product. Retail developers adapt their product to shifting consumer demands, and homebuilders update their models to reflect current tastes. In such situations, an idea is looking for a site. In other situations, a developer may encounter a site with unique location or economic characteristics, perhaps a site that has been vastly underutilized. Montage Laguna Beach, for example, is a high-end resort on a spectacular oceanfront site in Laguna Beach, California, that had been a trailer park. This was a site looking for an idea.

Most ideas do not survive even stage one. For qualitative or quantitative reasons, they cannot rise to fulfill the original vision, or they die in red ink on the back-of-the-envelope pro forma. Occasionally, the developer's back-of-the-envelope figures show promise. When that happens, the process moves to stage two: idea refinement.

One of the biggest challenges at this point is effective communication of the project concept. Once built, real estate is tangible, and most people can relate to an example of an existing building. In the concept stage, the project exists only in the mind of the developer and is expressed in spreadsheets, drawings, and studies. These media are often inadequate for communication to all but experienced professionals, and the communication hurdles are even greater for projects that lack a direct market analogue. At this point, the developer is usually not willing to spend a great deal on sophisticated computer simulations or graphic communication devices, so the advancement of the concept falls to his ability to convey the project's merits to potential team members. This is a key skill; in the ears of the listener, there is a fine line between effective communication and shallow promotion.

In stage two, a developer can solicit input to refine the idea. The object at this point is to identify the critical assumptions, modify them as appropriate, and prepare them for validation through the due diligence process. Idea refinement is complex because many activities are carried out simultaneously and interactively. Essentially, all of the disciplines and considerations that go into the determination of feasibility move forward at a similar pace. (Figure 12-1 attempts to capture this complexity.) The

Montage Laguna Beach in California is a luxury resort built on a site overlooking the Pacific Ocean.

answer to the overarching question—is this idea feasible on this site?—is conditioned on the answers to multiple questions posed at about the same time but not always answerable quickly, completely, or at all.

OBJECTIVES OF STAGE TWO

Considering the complexity of stage two, the phrase "refining the idea" is deceptively simple: the developer's idea either evolves into a feasible concept for a specific piece of land or is abandoned before making large, unrecoverable expenditures. The developer moves from, for example, the idea of an office building for tech firms in a particular geographic submarket to the preliminary design for a 100,000-square-foot, four-story office building with specific characteristics.

Finding and controlling the right site while making an initial determination of a project's feasibility are primary tasks of stage two. Associated with these primary physical tasks are marketing, financial, and construction management disciplines, which combine with the site selection to allow the developer to feel reasonably confident at the end of stage two about the project's feasibility. This comfort level permits a significant increase in resource commitment by the developer during the next stage. In stage two, it is the developer who must be convinced of the project's feasibility because it is largely his own funds that will be put at risk during stage three to convince the other participants of the project's viability.

Creating a Plan

For ideas that were not associated with a specific site in stage one, creating a plan for land acquisition is the first task of stage two. In the process of finding a site and specifying a proposed project, developers undertake many, if not all, of the following tasks simultaneously:

- Analyzing the areas or neighborhoods in the market that might offer an appropriate site;
- Analyzing the competition—both competing development companies and competing projects—and refining the idea to maximize the project's competitive position;
- Discussing the project with elected and appointed officials and city planners to ascertain their interests and any possible constraints on the project;
- Determining initial design requirements for the site;
- Analyzing potential sites to identify one that best satisfies the criteria;
- Negotiating for the selected site and structuring a contract to secure the site; and
- Continuing to refine financial feasibility—periodically retesting the back-of-the-envelope numbers.

Completion of these tasks culminates in a decision to move the idea to stage three (formal feasibility), rework the concept, or abandon the idea.

Developers must tolerate some disorder and uncertainty as they bring an idea to reality. Each development requires a slightly different approach, and the work does not provide the certainty of a manufacturing process. Sometimes developers press hard and commit substantial resources early in stage two. At other times, they let certain political pressures "work themselves out" before proceeding. Still, at some point, the developer must acquire control of the land, make contact with other potential members of the development team, and undertake initial project design. There are often good reasons to deviate from the sequence outlined in the eight-stage model. For example, one site might be far superior to all others and the owner might want to sell only for cash. At the right price, the developer may be smart to close on the land without having done all the work described in stages two and three. Still, it is important to remember that developers frequently incur penalties—through increased risk or decreased reward—when tasks are completed too far out of the logical sequence of the development process.

Controlling the Site

In the acquisition process, risk and return considerations are critical. It is sometimes appropriate to acquire a site for cash at a lower cost; however, this potential savings conflicts with the desire to control the level of financial risk early in the development process. The dilemma: the developer should tie up a site before fully demonstrating its feasibility to capture the maximum profit on the land. But, if the project proves infeasible, the developer may have to resell the land at a lower price and with significant transaction costs. Consequently, developers typically use some type of an "option to buy" to tie up a site during stage two. (See "Negotiating for the Site" in this chapter.)

For each property type, there are general rules of thumb for how much land should cost as a percentage of total cost or as a per-unit cost. Still, there is no universal rule: the readiness of the land for development in terms of entitlements, infrastructure, and remediation are all factors that give rise to wide variances. Location is the most obvious consideration, but one that varies according to land use. One approach that developers may employ in stage two is a land residual analysis. This calculation arrives at land value by determining the value of the improvements to be constructed on the land and deducting the direct and indirect costs of constructing those improvements.

The public sector influences the developer's site selection decision. As discussed in chapters 7 and 8, entitlements determine the potential uses of the land. Regulations usually set forth a process by which land uses can be changed, but the costs (and likelihood of success) vary considerably from one jurisdiction to another.

A MORE DETAILED SCAN OF THE ENVIRONMENT: GOVERNMENTS AND COMPETITORS

Developers need to understand the ways in which evolving local politics and regulations are likely to affect the viability of their projects. They need to

Figure 12-1   **Activities Involved in Refinement of the Idea**

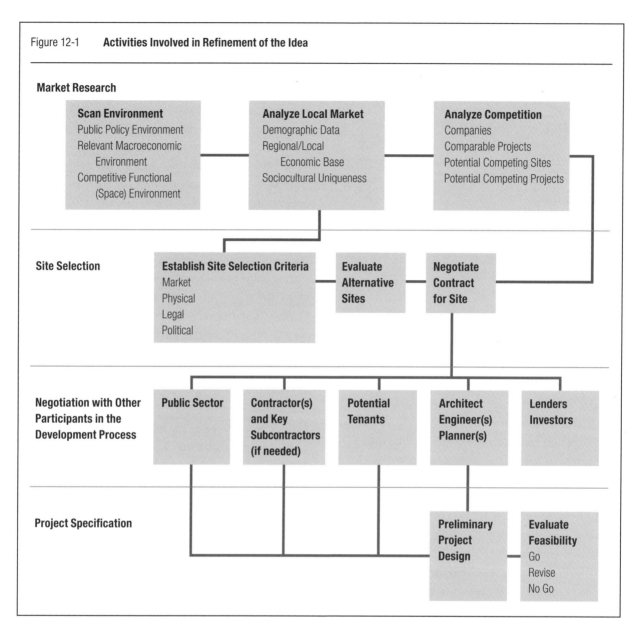

Market Research

Scan Environment
Public Policy Environment
Relevant Macroeconomic
   Environment
Competitive Functional
   (Space) Environment

Analyze Local Market
Demographic Data
Regional/Local
   Economic Base
Sociocultural Uniqueness

Analyze Competition
Companies
Comparable Projects
Potential Competing Sites
Potential Competing Projects

Site Selection

Establish Site Selection Criteria
Market
Physical
Legal
Political

Evaluate Alternative Sites

Negotiate Contract for Site

Negotiation with Other Participants in the Development Process

Public Sector

Contractor(s) and Key Subcontractors (if needed)

Potential Tenants

Architect Engineer(s) Planner(s)

Lenders Investors

Project Specification

Preliminary Project Design

Evaluate Feasibility
Go
Revise
No Go

forge and maintain relationships with city officials, politicians, and the general public. Understanding the human and organizational sides of the public sector is as important as understanding the physical infrastructure, interactive land uses, and urban growth patterns.

Competition, regulation, and politics are all subject to continuous change. A developer might find an apparent opportunity for development only to confront rigid opposition from the public sector. For example, a market for apartments might exist simply because area residents successfully opposed previous project proposals. Or, the local council or planning board might decide to limit apartment construction as part of a strategy for avoiding perceived adverse impacts on a neighborhood. In other instances, constraints imposed through building codes could represent more subtle impediments to development. Lengthy project reviews might prevent a developer from retaining site control at an affordable price. Infrastructure might appear to be adequate, but other projects scheduled for completion before the developer's proposed project could consume available service capacity and lead to moratoriums on new development. New impact fees and exactions may reduce a project's profitability below the level needed, given its perceived riskiness.

It is essential that developers know the projects, financial depth, and political clout of their competitors in the local market. A developer might perceive an opportunity to build apartments in a submarket, only to find that an established apartment developer with solid political connections and a favorable public image is already planning such a project. Unless the new entrant can clearly distinguish its project from those of established developers, the newcomer might be well advised to find another submarket, as he could be at a regulatory competitive disadvantage relative to the locally established developer.

URBAN GROWTH MODELS

Models of urban growth provide developers with a useful framework for understanding a market's current patterns of land use and potential directions of change. These theoretical urban models focus on where growth takes place and how land uses interrelate. People and businesses cluster in concentrations, rather than spreading uniformly over the land. Historically, such concentrations have been for reasons of defense, religion, government, and trade. Modern economic theories of location discuss the "friction of distance." Because resources are needed to move people, goods, and information, agglomerations can reduce costs and thereby foster economies of scale. Most large cities evolved around nodes where transportation lines met, often at break or transfer points between modes of transportation such as water and rail.

As technical and social forces evolve, so does the role of cities. The dominance of social, cultural, or economic forces continually changes the nature of optimal land uses in urban areas and therefore how a developer should respond to those changes to meet the needs of the market and the community.

Urban geography theories attempt to explain growth patterns that evolve with changes in employment patterns and technology. Land acquisition is the practical application of urban growth theory,

and developers should use this broad theoretical context to facilitate site analysis. The following are four early examples of urban growth models. Each attempted to explain and predict land use patterns based on distance, transportation, and growth nodes.

The *concentric zone theory* held that, assuming no variations in topography or transport corridors or limits on land use, cities would grow in concentric rings, with the most intensive uses located at the center. Accordingly, land values would decline with distance from the central, most intensive uses. Over time, more competitive land uses replace less competitive uses.

The *axial theory* modified the concentric zone theory and took into account more intensive land use patterns along transportation corridors, which typically radiate outward from the city center.

The *sector theory* holds that because of geographic features and differential access, waves of development tend to move outward from the center, forming wedge-shaped sectors that follow the path of least resistance to natural and built features and provide the lowest transportation costs. Careful analysis of development over many years often reveals a sectoral pattern of growth, possibly overlain by the network of circumferential highways that have created new suburban nodes. In fact, during the late 19th and early 20th centuries, Homer Hoyt (the originator of the sector theory) based his general model of urban sectors on such an evolution of U.S. cities.[1]

The *multiple nuclei theory* recognized that even though a city may have initially grown around a central business district, smaller commercial cores develop on the outskirts, allowing shorter commutes. This theory anticipated the later common notion of "edge cities."

Urban land use patterns are today more complex and dynamic, but these theories still provide a useful frame of reference. Transportation, communication, and information technology change the fundamentals of business and therefore business location decisions. An example is Atlanta, a city with no major geographic restrictions preventing concentric

CASE STUDY	Irvine Tech Center at Stage Two

Real estate submarkets can be active or dormant. If dormant, an initial project concept can remain largely intact through all stages of the development cycle. If active, that same project is exposed to changes in market conditions, political perceptions, and the regulatory environment. The developer should have an intuitive understanding of all aspects of his project to understand how these changes will affect the feasibility of the venture. In midstream, changes may come so quickly that there is no time to prepare detailed analysis and submit it to investment committees for consideration. Immediate decisions often are needed to exploit opportunities and respond to challenges, and the subjective aspects of these changes often defy quantification.

Greenlaw encountered both market and political changes. The Great Recession required the ability to evaluate longer-term prospects when many investors took immediate losses and walked away from what would have become profitable projects. The Greenlaw team recognized the value of the real estate fundamentals in their deal and believed that the value of the ITC site would be greater on the other side of the recession.

At the same time, the city was re-examining its regulatory approach to the IBC through its Vision Plan. Greenlaw was able to adapt its project to the new political goals for the area. The downturn gave Greenlaw an opportunity to reassess the market and recast the project concept to align more with the firm's expectation about the post-downturn environment. It also provided the opportunity to acquire additional land as well as what would prove to be extremely valuable trip allocations, both at the bottom of the market.

Smith had the insight to recognize that his market and political environment were dramatically changing. Not only had the economy collapsed, but the feasibility of what could be built on the site was now open to the risk of unknowns in the political process. The single thread running through these changes was the knowledge that the real estate fundamentals of the property, vested largely in its location, would yield great value if the moving parts—the market and the politics—could be properly interpreted to reshape the original idea.

Continued on page 253

spread. A railroad line and its terminus established the original city center, which still serves as the central business district. As strong north–south corridors developed in response to the influence of road networks, upper-income neighborhoods expanded to the north on physically attractive land. The major industrial zone moved outward south of downtown and today extends to Hartsfield-Jackson Atlanta International Airport. As the perimeter highway around Atlanta developed, new nodes of office and retail development sprang up, pushing Atlanta's urban fringe farther out, and created a multicentered pattern and many more new low-density edge cities.[2]

In addition to edge cities, sprawling "edgeless cities" have developed that never reach the scale, density, or cohesiveness of edge cities.[3] The evolution of these areas can be particularly difficult to explain. Depending on the era and their location, some have proven to be excellent opportunities for redevelopment into desirable areas for living and work places. Others, lacking critical elements, have become sociologically and economically obsolete.

In addition to economic activity and transportation, other forces are rapidly affecting settlement patterns and land uses. Among them:

- Technology as a force for decentralization. Electronic communication has enabled telecommuting and electronic retailing, which has weakened the need for face-to-face contact that was a primary force for central cities.
- Growth management policies as a force for centralization. The perceived negative aspects of decentralization, particularly higher costs, have generated land use regulation to encourage growth into higher-density urban cores.
- The changing role of central cities. High-density urban areas have evolved into cultural and entertainment centers, attracting residents to a dynamic lifestyle.

CHOOSING THE SITE

The land acquisition process involves a wide range of participants, entails agreements that range from quite simple to extremely complex, and takes place in a market that is sometimes opaque and often price inefficient. Opportunities to acquire land vary with the real estate cycle. When the market is down, there may be opportunities to acquire distressed properties. However, sources of capital are generally reluctant to invest at this point in the cycle, and many potential sellers withdraw from the market to wait for better times. At the top of the market, land appears more attractive, leading to higher prices. This phase of the cycle is characterized by intense competition, possibly resulting in either overpaying or overpromising the seller.

Types of Buyers

The land acquisition process varies according to the type of developer. At one end of the spectrum is a build-to-suit developer providing a product for a single user, such as a retailer or distributer, whose location requirements are extremely specific and depend on the character of a trade area or transportation system. Typically, these buyers enter the process through the brokerage community or through negotiations with a land developer who has created a marketable site ready for development.

Next are developers who specialize in the vertical construction stage of the development cycle. They acquire land that may or may not be subdivided or improved. These buyers typically build structures that are then sold or leased to final users. The acquisition process usually involves working through the brokerage community or through master developers who have removed much of the entitlement and timing risk from the land.

The most complex form of land acquisition is the purchase of raw land: property that has limited or no entitlements or improvements. This is a highly opportunistic market and typically involves sellers who are not in the real estate industry. The acquisition process is lengthy and the success rate is lower.

Types of Sellers

Sellers may include
- Families who have held property for generations and are not in the real estate business;
- Speculators who have acquired land for passive investment in the hope of an increase in value arising from growth pressures;
- Corporations and government agencies which have surplus property not required for their core operations;
- Financial institutions that may have taken land back through foreclosure; and
- Land developers who have created land parcels intended to be built upon by others.

The sellers of unentitled land are rarely real estate professionals. They usually face one of the largest transactions of their lives and are conflicted between obtaining the highest price possible and apprehension about making an error in judgment somewhere in the process. The acquisition process can extend for many months and depends on the creation of trust on both sides of the table, which may be the dining room or living room of the seller's farmhouse.

The Deal

As noted above, a developer has several objectives in the acquisition process: a favorable price, terms that allow sufficient time to analyze risks and undertake due diligence, and the option to arrange financing with the minimum cash exposure. The seller's goals are the opposite: a high price and the minimum time for the property to be taken off the market before the transaction is closed.

The negotiating process may differ, but the objective is the same: an agreement on terms followed by a contract. In many cases, the process is initiated by preliminary discussions that lead to a nonbinding letter of intent that outlines the terms under which the parties would be willing to enter into a contract. Among other terms, the letter of intent includes
- The price to be paid at closing;
- Deposits paid to the seller as an inducement to take the property off the market;
- A determination of whether the deposits will be refundable or nonrefundable to the buyer, and if they will be applicable or inapplicable to the purchase price;
- Conditions of closing;

- Responsibility for brokerage commissions;
- Responsibilities of the buyer and seller;
- Due diligence rights, including entry, testing, interviews, and other acts; and
- Right of assignment.

If there is agreement on terms, the letter of intent is converted into a formal purchase and sale agreement. At one end of the spectrum, that may provide for a cash closing for the full purchase price. At the other extreme, the agreement may take the form of a joint venture in which the seller participates in the uplift in value created by the development process. An *option agreement* is midway between the two. It allows the property to be taken off the market for a sufficient period of time for the developer to significantly reduce the project's risks, including entitlements and financing. Depending on the landowner's

objectives and the current attractiveness of the site, negotiations lead to a tradeoff between the developer's desire to pay as little as possible for the option with as long a lead time as possible and the owner's desire to receive a large payment for a short option period. The strike price for the option would in theory be the value of the land with the uncertainties removed.

The option should specify all requirements necessary for the transfer of title from the seller to the buyer, including any details about financing by the seller (such as release clauses and subordination agreements) that facilitate subsequent financing (see the finance chapters for a discussion of option types and structures). The option grants the buyer the opportunity to examine the land's title, conduct due diligence, arrange financing, and complete

---

Preliminary Due Diligence Checklist

Due diligence investigates the major aspects of the anticipated development. The activities can be broadly grouped as follows:

Existing Site Conditions

- Opportunities and Constraints Analysis
  Determination of the unusable portion of the site; identification of impacts on neighboring properties and other restrictions; identification of access, views, and other site assets
- Biological Surveys
  Identification of endangered, threatened, or "of interest" species and the feasibility of mitigation for impacts to their habitat
- Wetlands
  Identification of potential wetlands, as defined under the Clean Water Act and state and local regulations, and the feasibility of mitigation of impacts to these resources
- Geology Surveys
  Determination of fault lines, potential landslides, and other features that may impact the buildable portion of the site or the cost of site improvements
- Soils Analysis
  Determination of the ability of the soils to support the expected load of planned structures
- Environmental Hazards Review
  Survey for toxic materials or other conditions that may require removal or that would preclude development
- Flood Zone Mapping
  Determination that any portion of the site may be subject to flooding or exposure to similar risks

- Cultural Resources
  Determination of the likelihood that archaeological assets may be present on-site
- Infrastructure
  Determination of the capacity of streets, water, sanitary sewer, stormwater, gas, electricity, and telecommunication facilities to serve the site, together with the cost of upgrading these facilities, if necessary

Property Issues

- Review of Title Report
  Identification of any legal constraints on the site, including financial issues, such as liens; quality of title, such as contested ownership claims; and physical issues, such as easements, that may give third parties rights that could interfere with the productive use of the land
- ALTA or Boundary Surveys
  Property surveys that show the physical location of boundaries, encroachments, and other physical impairments that could affect the buildable portion of the site (boundary surveys show property lines; ALTA surveys show boundary lines and the location of improvements and easements that may affect ownership and use)
- Property Taxes
  Development of an understanding of the property tax structure, how reassessments through the development period are determined, and the amount of any levies for special service or improvement districts

Continued

entitlements. The agreement includes escape clauses based on the results of environmental or engineering tests.

At times, it can be useful to include landowners in the development process. Sometimes landowners want to take a long-term equity position in a developed structure. At other times, when the seller owns surrounding parcels, that can be the incentive needed to encourage the landowner to participate as a financer of the development.

A release clause and/or a subordination clause in the option or purchase agreement are useful techniques for controlling risk. A release clause enables a borrower or developer to obtain fee title on a portion of the land by paying a portion of the seller's note. For example, if a developer purchases 100 acres for $10,000 an acre, a release clause might provide

that any one of ten ten-acre parcels included in the overall tract could be released from the *lien* if the developer makes a $150,000 payment. Subordination clauses accomplish a similar objective while providing developers with something extra. An agreement to subordinate by the seller is a promise to move from a first lien to a second lien position under specified circumstances. For example, a seller who owns thousands of acres in a particular area and wants to encourage a particular developer to develop one site within that area might agree to subordinate its claim on that one site to the bank's construction financing. Subordination is superior from the developer's perspective because it enhances her ability to borrow from others. From the construction lender's perspective, the landowner's subordinated interest looks almost like equity in that it is an investment that is

---

Preliminary Due Diligence Checklist   *Continued*

Entitlement and Public Opinion Research

- **General Plan, Specific Plan, Zoning Determinations, Other Ordinances**
  Review of these regulations to determine whether the proposed project fits within them, whether an amendment is required, and if so, the feasibility of obtaining such a change.
- **Development Agreements**
  Determination of whether a site that has progressed through the entitlement process is subject to a previously negotiated development agreement that spells out further obligations of the developer and the government entity
- **Environmental Impact Requirements**
  Identification of the various levels of environmental reviews—often part of the discretionary approvals granted a project—that examine the impacts of a proposed project and how the project may mitigate those impacts
- **Biology Studies**
  Determination of the presence of any species that are of interest, threatened, or endangered under federal, state, or local regulations
- **Growth Controls**
  Identification of any measures implemented by state, regional, county, or local jurisdictions to govern growth patterns and rates, and whether any such measures may be modified only in an election ("ballot-box planning"), which would make any change very costly or impossible

- **Inclusionary Housing**
  Determination of whether a jurisdiction requires a certain number of affordable units on or off-site, or a mitigation fee in lieu of meeting any requirements
- **Tentative Map/Final Map Status**
  If an acquisition candidate has progressed through entitlements to the step of a tentative or final map, careful review of the map status and conditions of approval to establish their utility and implementation costs
- **Special Districts/Zones**
  Identification of any special districts or zones for coastal protection, historical preservation, agricultural protection, or other concerns that carry additional entitlement and regulatory oversight requirements
- **Public Opinion Surveys**
  In areas of particular public sensitivity or where discretionary approvals are required, identification of groups with particular concerns and the ability to address those concerns in the project concept, possibly entailing formal public surveys or local meetings to better articulate the project and solicit public input
- **Processing Feasibility**
  In jurisdictions with complex regulatory structures, retention of processing feasibility consultants to determine project feasibility through analysis of the regulatory environment and assessment of the feasibility of obtaining approvals

paid after the bank's loan. In effect, if the landowner subordinates its claim, the land serves as collateral for the development, even though the developer has not yet paid for it.

Information Sources

Many computerized tools exist to assist in the acquisition process. An app called Zonda brings local demographic and market data to a smartphone to enable access to key information while in the field. Google Earth enables a quick desktop view of property that can reduce the time devoted to site visits.

Many cities and government agencies have developed data-rich *geographic information systems* (GISs) that combine spatial data such as road maps, parcels, and satellite imagery with real estate databases. Much data can be found quickly and easily, and much of it is available free online. Many local and regional government agencies use GISs to support economic development. They can be used to identify locations for transit-oriented, mixed-use, and high-density residential developments and for low-density projects where physical constraints such as geologic features and floodplains are included in the computerized maps. Local governments use software packages like ESRI (www.esri.com) to determine which areas should be subject to increased densities, financial incentives, and infrastructure enhancements. Such packages are also used to help locate sites for fire stations, schools, and other public facilities. ESRI offers information that can assist businesses that are looking to relocate or expand. The application enables users to create, view, and print maps and to customize demographic and business data.

Two main types of GIS models are used to forecast where development will occur and what the impacts will be. Spatial interaction models (also known as gravity models) offer the capability to forecast traffic flows, store patronage, and shopping center revenue for use in assessing the desirability of a retail site. Spatial diffusion models can help predict population movements, growth or decay of neighborhoods, and development of new neighborhoods. Such models enable developers to visualize complex spatial information and anticipate future opportunities. Government agencies use these models to develop policies and programs to support future growth.

Despite the evolution of such advanced computer models, technology has not replaced old-fashioned tire kicking. To anticipate emerging trends, developers continue to rely on personal contact—with people and with sites. Furthermore, developers recognize the advantages of imperfect information and will not readily give up any comparative advantage by transferring personal insights or proprietary information to publicly available databases.

Developers love land, are fascinated by it, and think about it most of the time. As they gain experience in their asset class and markets, they acquire knowledge of their area and reach a point where they have a database in their heads: they instinctually identify good sites and bad sites, remember the transaction history of the major parcels, and know the potential value of those sites at any point in the market cycle. For added perspective, they go to professional meetings to get new ideas and more background. They regularly take time wherever they are visiting a city to get out and talk to people.

The Site's Physical Characteristics

One way to begin the analysis of the physical characteristics of a site is to create an opportunities and constraints map. This map identifies all of the site features that may affect the suitability of the site for its intended purpose. Such constraints include geologic, soils, wetlands, biologic, and cultural resources, as well as topography, easements, development regulations, and other factors that limit the amount of the site that can be used. A more complete list appears in the due diligence checklist (see box); however, reliance on checklists can produce a mechanical process in which critical elements may be underdeveloped. For example, a fatal flaw in a property may not appear on a checklist.

Usable Area

The entire area of a site is called the gross area; the amount of a site that can be utilized for development is the net area. Although simple in concept, the definitions of gross and net may vary by region or discipline. A local government may use one formula to define net area, and an engineer may use another. The definition may change as the development concept advances. For example, the area dedicated to circulation is usually figured into the calculation of net area and may be treated differently if the project is a master-planned community or an industrial site. Urban sites often use the concept of a *floor/area ratio* (FAR) to determine the amount of square footage that can be constructed on a parcel. The precise definition of land area under local entitlement regulations is an important factor in assessing feasibility.

Sometimes a developer may acquire some surrounding land, to capture some of the increased value that accrues from the development of the primary parcel. Doing so increases land costs, but the potential return may justify the cost. It is important to consider the concept of *situs*—the interactions of a project with surrounding sites and the impacts of those surrounding uses on the subject property. This principle is basic to real estate. No site operates in isolation. A graphic example of the impact of situs is the difference between the development of Disneyland in Anaheim, California, and Disney World in Orlando, Florida. At Anaheim, all the peripheral value creation was captured by others. Recognizing this loss of profitable opportunities, Disney acquired a huge site in Florida for the Magic Kingdom, enabling the company to reap much of the benefit of subsequent surrounding development such as resort hotels and shopping districts that feed the theme park's facilities.

Geology

Soils determine a site's potential for development as adequate load-bearing capacity is required for the structures that the developer plans to construct. Developers should not take soil conditions for granted; unless geologic reports are provided by the seller or available from the local government, preliminary studies may be appropriate. The problems are not always evident from a visual survey. Even where soils appear suitable for construction,

unique conditions such as abandoned landfills may create problems that even long-time residents have forgotten. A developer who is unfamiliar with local conditions should solicit preliminary geologic and soils studies from a knowledgeable geologist or soils engineer. Some problems that may arise include poor bearing qualities, expansiveness, rock, subterranean drainage patterns, landslides, alluvial material, and faults. These can add extra costs in the excavation and foundation work.

Hazardous Materials

It is customary for a buyer to obtain a preliminary hazardous materials study to determine whether a site is likely to be contaminated. Contamination is a legal as well as a physical issue. The liability associated with being in the chain of title for a property with hazardous material on it can give rise to significant costs. In negotiations, neither the buyer nor the seller wants to assume this liability, so the hazardous materials clause in a purchase agreement can be the subject of lengthy negotiation. Some situations warrant elaborate and costly hazardous waste studies conducted by environmental professionals. In stage two, however, a developer wants to hold down major cash outlays and make careful tradeoffs between expenditures and the assumption of risk. Ideally, the developer structures contracts that allow him to back out of a land purchase if significant environmental contamination is discovered. Even with such contracts, however, the developer is still out of pocket for the cost of the environmental study.

Cultural Resources

Some government agencies require an archaeological survey. In some states, a mere application for entitlements triggers a notification to Native American groups for their review of the proposed project and their identification of any cultural resources that may be present on the site. If a survey turns up artifacts, archaeologists may have to excavate the area by hand, possibly delaying development for months. In New York City, when an African American cemetery was discovered on a site in lower Manhattan, construction of a federal courthouse was delayed until a decision could be reached about the proper means

---

INNOVATORS   Moving the Needle of Sustainability

Sustainable development has evolved from an ancillary project element to a component of good business practice. Two consultants who specialize in sustainability stand out for their integrative efforts to address sustainability by pioneering concepts to influence market behavior:

Lauren Yarmuth, cofounder and principal of YR&G, a sustainability consulting firm based in New York City, helps businesses find innovative, meaningful, and beneficial ways to succeed in their work. After starting her career at the Rocky Mountain Institute in Colorado, at age 30 Yarmuth was elected to the National Board of the U.S. Green Building Council (USGBC), where she supported its strategic planning and refinements to LEED (Leadership in Energy and Environmental Design), the group's certification program for rating building sustainability. That same year she cofounded YR&G, which has become one of the most influential consulting firms enabling better, more sustainable development and business practices worldwide. She has worked with the LEED rating system since its inception, including helping hundreds of projects to earn LEED certification.

Yarmuth consistently pushes the boundaries of what sustainability means and how to get there. She has been on the forefront of major trends such as urban agriculture, active and regenerative design, health and wellness in buildings, and community resilience. She is a presenter, educator, and facilitator, and a LEED faculty member for USGBC. She teaches at several universities, including as adjunct faculty at Columbia University. Yarmuth is supporting the launch of the International Well Building Institute's (IWBI) WEI L Building Standard®, an evidence-based system for measuring, certifying, and monitoring the performance of building features that affect health and wellbeing. She is developing an educational initiative aimed at a "Renaissance man" approach to knowledge to inform complex decision making.

Ioannis Orfanos, another innovator in sustainable business practices, founded Green Value Associates in 2010 and serves as its director and investment advisor. Splitting his time between the London and Athens offices, Orfanos focuses on identifying, originating, and managing sustainable real estate investments. He also advises investors, corporate occupants, and public sector entities on sustainable property portfolio strategies.

The implementing concept of Green Value Associates (GVA) is to bring together a collaborative professional network of independent subject experts and freelance professionals, of different seniority and expertise, who team up on a project basis to increase the impact of sustainability in real estate. GVA also advises clean tech service providers and mentors start-ups on market penetration strategies, fundraising exercises, strategic partnerships, and merger and acquisition initiatives.

As part of a senior GVA team, Orfanos counseled companies making a strategic capital investment funded by the European Union (€30 million) that aimed to save up to €20 million in annual operating costs through better energy efficiency. The team assessed the companies' portfolios using defined strategic criteria, analyzed their energy performance and management operations, and proposed strategic solutions for improvement.

Orfanos, who has a civil engineering background, has overseen real estate development investments across Europe for Europa Capital Partners in London. He has also worked on two projects for METKA SA as part of the Athens 2004 Olympic Games infrastructure program.

Alison Johnson

---

of dealing with the remains. In other cases, artifacts may require further analysis to determine their significance. At times, development must be designed to leave them in place. The threshold is low. In some cases, even midden mounds—essentially historic trash heaps—require preservation.

Infrastructure

A site cannot be developed without infrastructure: roads, water, sanitary sewer, and storm drainage. Developers need to ascertain whether the local municipality can and will provide sufficient capacity for these facilities. Where municipalities have reached capacity, new development may be prohibited until

additional public facilities can be planned, financed, and constructed. These may include major facilities that are beyond the capacity of any but the largest projects to financially support, such as water and sewage treatment plants, and freeway interchanges. In some cases, for the purposes of growth control, a jurisdiction may deny access. Such denials can turn an otherwise attractive site into an infeasible one—despite high demand, ideal topography, and good parcel configuration. Where additional infrastructure is needed, the developer may have to absorb some or all of the costs or participate in a local assessment district with other landowners to provide the funding for these facilities. Once such facilities are completed, the developer usually dedicates the infrastructure to the local government entity, which, in turn, is expected to provide ongoing maintenance.

The Site's Development Rights

As discussed in chapters 7 and 8, a critical consideration in evaluating a site is the entitlement package that defines the permitted uses and the intensity of uses for the parcel. A site may be zoned for multi-family housing, for example, but at such a low number of dwelling units per acre that the development costs make the idea infeasible.

Developers look at current entitlements for the tract under consideration as well as at the feasibility of obtaining changes to those entitlements. The avenue of least resistance is to work within the existing rules. Next most difficult is to apply for a variance as provided in the existing code. Whether to attempt to go further and actually change the rules through the legal and political process is an important consideration. Finding a way to obtain the needed entitlements, given the particular political climate, is a major way developers add value to a site—even before any physical development occurs.

The process for obtaining such changes may include many tiers of regulation ranging from general plan amendments to environmental impact analyses, to specific plans, to zoning. Other regulations

---

CASE STUDY   Shortbread Lofts at Stage Two

The town of Chapel Hill views the development of student housing downtown as beneficial because it reduces the pressure to convert single-family housing in traditional neighborhoods to student rentals . Consequently, Larry Short was not overly concerned about getting support for his overall idea. In contrast, he was very concerned about the town allowing the right parking mix.

Short already owned some of the land that supports the project. He had previously worked on upgrading the small rental property known as Rosemary Street Apartments. This project was adjacent to the original location of a very well-known restaurant that had expanded to a location across the street. Joining his land with the now available former location of the restaurant created sufficient total size (1.2 acres) to support the proposed development. Short formed a partnership with the two brothers who owned and operated the restaurant. The 60-40 basis (Short controlling

with 60 percent) allowed Short to assemble land without any new debt or new cash investment. (Short did have debt on Rosemary Street Apartments, but he moved it to another project to facilitate the Shortbread Lofts development.)

The rest of the idea refinement process was straightforward, as Short already knew the precise market segment he was seeking to address—upscale female students. In fact, from his experience with the development and marketing of the Warehouse, he knew what had been missing in the market and thus what new features, functions, and benefits were cost-justified for Shortbread Lofts. The new project would offer many more amenities, including a high-end bathroom for each bedroom in every suite, a state-of-the-art fitness center, a tech-friendly lobby outfitted with computers and printers, and more security features.

Continued on page 249

Among the amenities is a state-of-the-art fitness center.

ALEXANDER ELKINS PHOTOGRAPHY

Woodward's: A Site Looking for a Use

Woodward's is a mixed-use urban redevelopment project in the Gastown area of Vancouver's east side, near downtown, located on the site of the former Woodward's department store. The redevelopment involved the demolition of several buildings, the restoration and adaptive use of a historic structure, and the construction of two residential towers, educational and cultural space for Simon Fraser University, an atrium, a daycare center, and ground-level retail space—all within the confines of a 2.32-acre site in an area with a variety of social and poverty issues. The project includes more than 1 million square feet of space.

After Woodward's department store closed in 1993, it stood vacant for 11 years, causing further deterioration to the neighborhood. Previous attempts to redevelop the property had failed, and eventually, in 2001, the British Columbia provincial government acquired the site for C$22 million. Meanwhile, city officials were exploring ways to respond to the problems of the poor in the area. In 2003, the city negotiated a deal to acquire the property for only C$5 million. After acquiring it, the city undertook an RFP process. One proposal came from a team that included the developer

Westbank, the Peterson Investment Group, and Henriquez Partners Architects. In 2003, the team was selected to restore the 1903 building, add a tall tower, and develop social housing, office, retail, and university space. A deal was struck with the city that involved no land cost in exchange for the developer providing city office space, an atrium, and public open space, as well as demolition and remediation of the site.

Market-rate housing was essential to the financial viability of the project, but integrating a substantial amount of low-income housing was a major objective of the city. Preserving the site's historic elements was also important. Many drivers and entities came together to make the project work. The city and provincial governments, the university, the private development team, the anchor tenants, and numerous community groups were all committed to making it a success. The redevelopment, completed in 2010, changed the perception of the neighborhood, provided much needed housing, and increased property values and the tax base, generating new revenue for the city. For the complete ULI case study, see http://uli.org/case-study/woodwards.

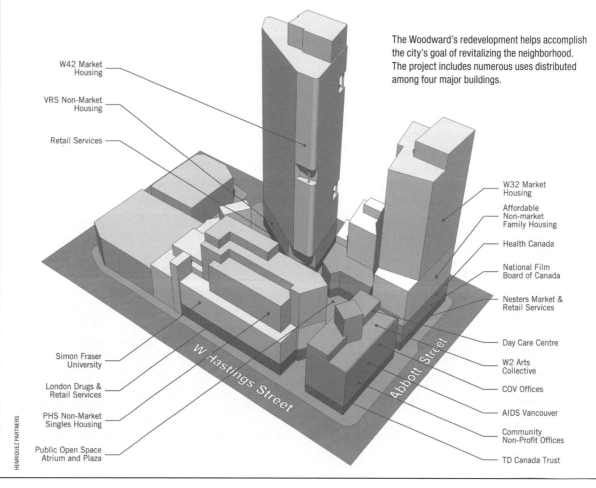

The Woodward's redevelopment helps accomplish the city's goal of revitalizing the neighborhood. The project includes numerous uses distributed among four major buildings.

W42 Market Housing

VRS Non-Market Housing

Retail Services

Simon Fraser University

London Drugs & Retail Services

PHS Non-Market Singles Housing

Public Open Space Atrium and Plaza

W32 Market Housing

Affordable Non-market Family Housing

Health Canada

National Film Board of Canada

Nesters Market & Retail Services

Day Care Centre

W2 Arts Collective

COV Offices

AIDS Vancouver

Community Non-Profit Offices

TD Canada Trust

HENRIQUEZ PARTNERS

created to address the health and safety of the community, such as subdivision regulations and building codes, are less negotiable. Subdivision regulations, for example, typically specify the required quality of necessary infrastructure.

INITIAL FEASIBILITY

In stage two, developers test concepts in the context of specific sites. This requires moving forward to validate assumptions on every aspect of the project, including the physical character of the site, the entitlement environment, and the competitive market for the particular space, all culminating in the financial feasibility. At this stage, a developer engages the project team to assist in refining the concept to a point that will justify the expenditure of additional due diligence funds.

It is a misconception that this step is led by design: the site constraints and allowable uses under existing or proposed entitlements establish the framework within which the designer must work. It may be helpful to prepare concept drawings, but the real design work begins only after thorough analysis of the site and its constraints. The investigation begins with the ground. The due diligence checklist suggests the range of areas that should be considered, but because every site has its unique characteristics and issues, some may not appear on the checklist. Each area to investigate may involve the engagement of a specialist. Potential subsurface problems may justify the opinion of a geologist or soils engineer. Groundwater and stormwater runoff might require a hydrologist. The on-site wetlands and vegetation may necessitate the analysis of a biologist knowledgeable in local, state, and federal habitat regulations. A land use attorney may be needed to assess entitlement risks. Although all of these specialists working in concert may be able to advise the developer on better ways to address the site, it is unlikely that an all-disciplinary team can or should be assembled at this point. The decision about whom to engage and when is the developer's responsibility; it is made based on her expertise in land acquisition. The development process is taking

place in the developer's head at this point, and she is the only person capable of making the tradeoff in time and money against the need for additional data and insights.

With an understanding of the site constraints and opportunities, the developer can provide direction to designers such as land planners and architects. Starting from the developer's initial idea of building configuration, the architect or land planner lays out an initial building footprint on the site and, given intended access points, determines whether the building and its associated parking can be placed on the site. The layout should honor environmental features as well as setbacks and guidelines specified in local subdivision regulations without compromising the image the developer hopes to create. Most important, it should do it all with an eye toward how end users will perceive the final product. Sensitivity to the natural environment and situs at this stage can pay off with easier permitting later.

NEGOTIATING FOR THE SITE

At this point, the developer faces another dilemma. Work during stage two has shown that the site is probably feasible physically, legally, and politically. Still, it has yet to be subjected to a complete feasibility study. To minimize the amount of money at risk during this period, the developer does not want to purchase the land. Yet, the more publicly known the idea for development becomes, the higher the price that the landowner is likely to ask. Thus, assuming the refined idea and subsequent feasibility study will prove positive, the developer's objective is to obtain the right to buy the land at the current price without committing a great deal of money.

The most obvious solution is an option. Ideally, the developer would like to pay a minimal fee for the right to buy the land at today's stated price at any time over the next five years. Not surprisingly, owners are not enthusiastic about tying up their land for a long time without significant remuneration. Thus, depending on the landowner's objectives and the current attractiveness of the site, negotiations lead to a tradeoff between the developer's desire to pay as little as possible for the option with as long a lead time as possible and the owner's desire to receive a large payment for a short option period.

An option agreement is a more complex document than first meets the eye. Even in the most straightforward transaction, the option, if exercised, becomes a contract of sale and legally drives the entire process of land purchase. Accordingly, the option should specify all necessary requirements for the transfer of title from the seller to the buyer, including any details about financing by the seller such as release clauses and subordination agreements that facilitate subsequent financing The option almost always grants the buyer the opportunity to examine the quality of the seller's title as well as time to arrange financing, permits, and possibly even a zoning change. The agreement should not only specify the price and any warranties in the deed (and any possible deed restrictions) but also include escape clauses based on the results of environmental or engineering tests.

The option is a forward-looking agreement that should be as complete as possible and anticipate future actions as well as reactions to those actions. If the developer, for example, needs to rezone the site, the option agreement might contain a clause specifying that the developer has 120 days to propose the change to the local jurisdiction and that the option runs until 90 days after the jurisdiction's decision or for one year, whichever comes first.

As with all real estate contracts, the economic content of the option agreement is in theory very flexible and limited only by developer's imagination. In fact, the agreement might not, strictly speaking, be an option. For example, in a low-downpayment, nonrecourse purchase, the developer buys the property but the seller provides 95 percent (or more) of the financing, with the seller's only recourse being to retake title to the property. In economic terms, this particular arrangement differs little from paying 5 percent of the asking price for an option.

STAGE TWO PARTICIPANTS

At this stage, the developer begins to consider who will be joining the development team, as either a

consultant or a staff member. The developer also begins to consider in more detail the needs of the potential end users.

Contractors

During the project's early stages, developers have to determine who has the expertise needed to construct the project. Some general contractors take on all types of projects; others specialize in a specific type of project. In a dynamic market, developers should also determine which general contractors have the time to take on the construction of an additional project.

Interestingly, the business cycle affects the quality of available building tradespeople. Construction workers tend to move up the line during a boom period when ample work is available. In other words, the rough carpenter becomes a finish carpenter, the finish carpenter becomes a superintendent, and the superintendent becomes an independent general contractor. As the business cycle peaks, construction costs may escalate and quality may suffer, as less-experienced people become the only ones available to do the labor.

Typically, contractors estimate the cost of construction. Their input is one of the critical elements in both the informal feasibility in stage two and the formal feasibility in stage three. As input to marketing efforts, contractors can also outline for developers the typical functions and features as well as the quality of materials and finishes in comparable buildings in the market area.

End Users

During stage two, developers begin discussions with a range of possible tenants to determine users' specific requirements and to refine the general idea of market demand established during stage one. As the idea becomes better defined and tied to a particular site, developers often begin serious discussions with likely tenants. Despite appropriate use of market research techniques, they may find that the initially targeted users do not want precisely what has been proposed. Redesigning a project to have the features, functions, and benefits likely users want is much more cost-effective than retrofitting a completed structure.

Property Managers

Early in the process, the developer usually begins working with a property manager knowledgeable in the particular product niche. That person's input is particularly important when a proposed project will involve extensive, ongoing services. Keeping tenants satisfied requires good management, and good management requires a building realistically designed to accommodate the targeted tenants and their day-to-day needs. Property managers can be very valuable in helping developers avoid costly design mistakes and in planning design features that will make the building easier to manage and/or reduce operating costs. Knowledgeable managers can advise developers about everything from appropriate floor plans to the right tradeoff between elevator cost and speed.

Lenders

Developers usually contact potential lenders and investors early in the process. A typical sequence of events begins with discussions with permanent lenders—institutions that might finance the project for the long term and be willing to take the long-term market risk or at least some portion of it (see chapters 10 and 11 for more detail). The developer then contacts construction lenders, who finance the project during construction and initial operations.

Lenders have preferences; some finance only certain types of projects, and others finance projects only in certain ways. To obtain the most advantageous and compatible sources of financing, developers may rely on their knowledge of financial markets or they may obtain assistance from a mortgage broker. Hiring a mortgage broker represents an additional expense and does not relieve the developer of the responsibility to make financial decisions. After getting professional advice, developers themselves choose the appropriate sources of financing and the appropriate structure for the particular transaction.

At this early stage, developers seek an understanding of lenders' interests in the geographic area and the project type. They need to learn any specific guidelines that lenders have, such as parking requirements that exceed city minimums or sprinkler systems that surpass code requirements. By determining lenders' interests in stage two, developers

HafenCity is a redevelopment of a seaport brownfield site in Hamburg, Germany. The public and private sectors collaborated in a multiyear development process that resulted in a lively urban space with offices, residences, retail space, and culture, leisure, tourism, and educational facilities.

THOMAS HAMPEL/ELBE & FLUT, HAFENCITY HAMBURG GMBH

can often refine a project to increase the number of potential lenders, heighten lenders' interest, and possibly lower financing costs.

Investors

Depending on the developer's financial position, the nature of the project, and lenders' demands, the developer decides by the end of stage three when to involve outside equity investors. By anticipating some of their needs at this earlier stage, the developer can refine his ideas more effectively. Early equity investors typically want a greater portion of the project's cash flow because they assume more of the development risk. Yet, early involvement of equity investors reduces the risk to permanent and construction lenders, thereby lowering the cost of debt financing.

Just as developers can use a mortgage broker to help them determine the best source of debt financing, they can also seek outside counsel on equity investments. For larger projects, the counselor might be a national or international investment banker, for medium-size projects a mortgage brokerage firm, and for smaller or tax-oriented projects a local syndicator. Although specialized assistance may increase the developer's awareness of options, it does not remove the developer's responsibility to make the final decisions.

Because the development process in certain locations takes a long time and requires a substantial amount of early financing, many projects endure a period that requires something resembling *venture capital*, in that none of the money will be returned to investors if the project does not proceed. Consequently, money for preconstruction expenses is the most difficult and costly kind of money to raise. It often comes from wealthy individuals. Other sources of very high-risk financing are the "opportunity funds" managed by Wall Street firms and independent investment boutiques.

The Public

At this stage, developers should again talk to the general public, as represented by government, neighborhood associations, and other advocacy groups.

Because the public sector is always the developer's partner in a long-lived investment that requires substantial infrastructure, it is important that the developer "sell" the project and its benefits to elected and appointed public officials and to relevant citizen groups. The hope is that, by the end of stage three, the public will have a favorable impression of the project.

Just as lenders and investors exhibit preferences and concerns, so do government officials and agencies. Public officials can offer suggestions that enhance the value of the finished project and reduce the time required for approvals. Developers should investigate regulators' desires and how the project might satisfy public needs in various jurisdictions. Sources of information on local policy and politics include news media, the municipality's master plan, conversations with elected and appointed officials and other developers working in the local market, and political consultants who specialize in the local market, as well as public meetings and local blogs where multiple groups express their opinions.

Completed in 2011, ECO Modern Flats, in Fayetteville, Arkansas, redeveloped a 1960s-era complex into a 96-unit Platinum LEED–certified rental apartment community. Green features include a ductless, energy-efficient heating and cooling system, solar hot water, and reflective roofs.

SEGMENTING THE MARKET AND DIFFERENTIATING THE PRODUCT

While talking with other players, developers continually think about who will use the proposed space and how the general public will react to the project.

They need to move from the broader idea of building apartments in Madison, Wisconsin, for example, to the narrower plan of building 225 one- and two-bedroom units in a mid-rise apartment complex located on a specific site and targeted to young professionals earning more than $60,000 per year.

How do developers accomplish this task? They consider the features, functions, and benefits offered by the competition. In searching for the winning strategy, one that will capture sufficient market share, developers move back and forth between considerations of cost and market appeal. They segment demand and differentiate their product from the competitors' products. In terms of market research,

idea refinement can be viewed as the interactive process of segmenting the market and differentiating the product.

FINANCIAL FEASIBILITY

Developers rarely build projects for money alone, yet financial feasibility is a primary concern. During stage two, the analysis of financial feasibility goes a critical step beyond stage one as developers begin estimating cash flows during the development period. Can the developer finance the project through startup? It hardly matters that the project's completed value exceeds cost if the developer cannot survive

---

ULI Credo

As responsible citizens, we shall leave this land enhanced … thereby enriching the lives of all who live on it.

ULI CODE OF ETHICS

1. Respect for the Land
I know that each parcel of land is a precious, distinct, and irreplaceable portion of this distinct and irreplaceable planet. I will treat it with the respect that it deserves, recognizing that I will be judged by the integrity and permanence of my developments, which will survive my lifetime.

2. Respect for the Profession
ULI–the Urban Land Institute has pioneered many of the practices and techniques that have become the standards in the land use and development profession. I will support the profession's continuing efforts to create a wider understanding of sound land use and development principles and practices and to disseminate knowledge thereof through its research and educational programs. I will observe the highest standards of professional conduct and will seek continually to maintain and improve my professional skills and competence.

3. Respect for the Consumer
Recognizing that a good reputation is a possession beyond price and that the quality of my product will determine the quality of my reputation, I will strive at all times to ensure the professional quality of my enterprise.

4. Respect for the Public
I will endeavor at all times to enhance public understanding of the development process, to preserve the public's confidence and trust in my profession, and to protect the public welfare.

5. Respect for Equality of Opportunity
I will support the private enterprise system that can provide the widest latitude of equality for opportunity, creativity, and innovation.

6. Respect for Others in the Land Use and Development Profession
I will treat others in my profession fairly and honestly. I will share with them my knowledge and experience, recognizing that both the people and the land will benefit from the dissemination of that knowledge.

7. Respect for the Larger Environment
In attempting to provide adequate staging for decent environments in which people will live, work, and play, I will be ever vigilant toward preserving the quality of the larger environment—the air, the water, and the land.

8. Respect for the Future
Recognizing that change is inevitable, I will pursue excellence with an open mind, challenged by the need to provide housing and facilities for employment, distribution, relaxation, and enjoyment.

9. Respect for Future Generations
Recognizing that younger generations will be more affected by what we do than by what we say, I will do my utmost to set a good example and will participate wholeheartedly in the development community's efforts to inform and encourage future generations of land use and development professionals.

10. Respect for Personal Integrity
I will employ the highest ethical principles and will observe the highest standards of integrity, proficiency, and honesty in my professional and personal dealings. I will remain free of compromising influences or loyalties and will exercise due diligence in ensuring that my performance is at all times creatively, competently, and responsibly managed.

to completion. A key part of the analysis at this stage is figuring out how much startup capital is needed and where it will come from.

Site Evaluation Factors

Market Area and Competition
- Population and job growth trends and projections
- Economic characteristics
- Existing competitive inventory
- Similar products that may compete
- Development pipeline

Location and Neighborhood
- Proximity to key metropolitan-area locations
- Quality of surrounding environment
- Existing housing stock, other buildings
- Schools, other public facilities, houses of worship
- Parks and other recreational facilities
- Other amenities
- Shopping and entertainment
- Public improvements (existing and planned)

Utilities
- Water and sewer or septic
- Electricity and gas (availability and quality)
- Telecommunications (broadband, cable TV)

Physical Conditions
- Visibility and accessibility
- Slopes and grading requirements
- Soils and hydrology
- Vegetation, forestry, and agriculture
- Existing structures on-site
- Toxic wastes and nuisances
- Wildlife and ecological features

Legal Constraints
- Zoning, likelihood of obtaining variances
- Utility and private easements
- Covenants and deed restrictions

Regulatory Environment
- General climate for development
- Exactions and impact fees
- Future infrastructure work or takings
- Approval process and timeline
- Methods of citizen participation
- Administrative vs. board approvals
- Upcoming elections and rule changes

Developers continually revise the initial back-of-the-envelope analysis as they refine an idea. Refinement means better estimates of costs and better projections of revenues. The pro forma need not be complex, but the more rigorous and insightful it is, the better. To assess feasibility, a developer puts all of the financial information in a risk/return framework.

It is important to remember the concept of level two feasibility: The project must be feasible for the developer and the lenders/investors and should be feasible for all the other development team members—the general contractor, architects, engineers, and so on. As quarterback of the process, the developer is concerned not only with whether the overall project is viable but also with whether participation in the process is a financial winner for each prospective member of the development team.

RISK CONTROL DURING STAGE TWO

The method of land acquisition is one means of controlling risk during stage two. Because a developer seeks to limit financial exposure before formally committing to a project, controlling the site through an option or a low-downpayment, nonrecourse, seller-financed purchase are ways to minimize risk exposure.

In most real estate transactions, constructive notice to the general public takes place by recording the instruments as they are executed. The first is typically the option agreement to acquire the land. So long as it is in the proper form and, in most states, notarized, it can be recorded. Recording places the agreement in the chain of title and thus gives notice to all others of the developer's right to the land. At times, this step can be particularly helpful in reducing the possibility that a landowner will execute subsequent contracts that use the land for purposes other than the one the developer intends.

In addition to eliminating uncertainties associated with a site's availability, developers can control risk by helping to ensure that a project is acceptable to the community. If they can show from the beginning that the development plan fits or coordinates well with the city's master plan, fewer time-consuming delays are likely. Informally presenting the project to city officials and building inspectors to elicit their responses can eliminate potential opposition later in the process. Because elected officials may leave office during the approval process, it behooves developers to seek approvals and opinions in writing. Documentation does not always secure a developer's position against changes in rules, but it does help.

More and better market research is a primary technique for controlling risk, but, as noted earlier, it is not always cost-effective at this stage. The best risk control technique in stage two is to control the invested time and money so that the option to stop remains viable.

SUMMARY

Stage two in the development process involves what many people see as the heart of real estate development: refining the big-picture idea generated during stage one. Toward the end of stage two, the rough idea is linked to a specific site that is legally, politically, and physically capable of supporting the idea. Moreover, the developer, through a series of conversations, believes that one or more general contractors will be available to construct the project, that end users will be interested, that lenders will want to lend money, and that appropriate equity interests can be attracted to the project.

By this time, the developer has probably decided whether the development idea is feasible. Nonetheless, a formal feasibility study is often necessary to convince other participants such as investors, lenders, tenants, and the public sector. Although the vast majority of ideas generated in stage one fail the back-of-the-envelope pro forma test, the pass rate is a little higher in stage two. If the refined idea still seems feasible, the developer takes it to stage three, at which point financial and emotional commitments become much greater.

The ULI Code of Ethics (see box) is an eloquent statement of principles that can guide the developer through what is becoming an increasingly complex process.

TERMS

- Axial theory
- Concentric zone theory
- Geographic information system (GIS)
- Lien
- Option agreement
- Sector theory
- Subordination clause
- Venture capital

REVIEW QUESTIONS

12.1 Describe some of the key concepts involved in site selection and how developers go about assessing potential sites.

12.2 What issues do developers face when they find a site that meets their initial criteria but that has not yet been subjected to a thorough feasibility analysis?

12.3 What services can architects provide to developers at this stage of the development process?

12.4 What are market segmentation and product differentiation? Why are they important in the real estate development planning process?

12.5 How can developers control risk during stage two?

NOTES

1 For discussion of these and other urban economic concepts, see John F. McDonald and Daniel P. McMillen, *Urban Economics and Real Estate: Theory and Policy* (Oxford, U.K.: Blackwell, 2006); Alan Rabinowitz, *Urban Economics and Land Use in America: The Transformation of Cities in the Twentieth Century* (Oxford, U.K.: Blackwell, 2004); Arthur O'Sullivan, *Urban Economics*, 5th ed. (New York: McGraw-Hill, 2002).

2 For more about edge cities, see Joel Garreau, *Edge City: Life on the New Frontier* (New York: Anchor, 1992).

3 Robert Lang, *Edgeless Cities: Exploring the Elusive Metropolis* (Washington, D.C.: Brookings Institution Press, 2003).

Chapter 13

Stage Three: The Feasibility Study

Developers usually have a strong intuitive feel for a project's viability on the basis of their work in stages one and two. Nonetheless, in most cases, they must formally demonstrate the project's viability to other participants. The formal demonstration of viability—the feasibility study—constitutes stage three of the development process. At the end of this stage, developers may still decide not to undertake a project but that decision will come at a significantly higher cost than at the end of stage two. The cost goes beyond dollars—it includes relationships, time, reputation, and credibility.

The feasibility study is an important management tool that provides multiple forms of risk control over several subsequent stages of the development process. Even the most creative, intuitive developers who bring new concepts to the marketplace benefit from running all the numbers and systematically addressing all the issues. Among its other uses, the feasibility study is an excellent organizational tool. It brings together every aspect of the development in a consistent format, usually using a computer program. As the project moves through the eight stages of development, the feasibility study is continually refined and modified, with estimates becoming increasingly concrete.

A complete feasibility study is an extensive undertaking. To ensure its full benefit, the study should not end with a mere finding of "sufficiency"— that is, a determination that the project's value exceeds the cost, making the development feasible. Rather, the feasibility study should be considered an *optimization tool*. By using *sensitivity analysis*, the developer can examine every major decision and every significant feature, function, and benefit of the proposed project to determine whether it is the best plan, not simply an acceptable plan.

The developer should produce one feasibility study, with relevant sections for each participant in the development process. He probably does not want to share the details of the equity financing with the contractor or the lead tenant, but would want to be certain that all the assumptions in the equity section are internally consistent with the assumptions in the construction cost and leasing sections. The developer should not prepare an independent feasibility study for each participant, even though each must be induced to make an individual commitment. A single feasibility study for the entire project enables the developer to see how the individual participants will achieve the development goal collectively.

The feasibility study might not always be fully delineated during the third stage. It might start during the second stage (idea refinement), and the final design might spill over into the fourth stage, contract negotiation. Like the entire development process, the feasibility study should be seen as inherently interdisciplinary. This chapter begins with a comprehensive definition of feasibility and then discusses the elements of the feasibility study.

THE DEFINITION OF FEASIBILITY

The best definition of feasibility remains the one that renowned real estate educator James A. Graaskamp (see profile in chapter 3) advanced in his classic 1972 article, "A Rational Approach to Feasibility Analysis": "A real estate project is 'feasible' when the real estate analyst determines that there is a reasonable likelihood of satisfying explicit objectives when a selected course of action is tested for fit to a context of specific constraints and limited resources."[1]

Each phrase of Graaskamp's definition is important. First, feasibility never demonstrates certainty. A project is feasible when it is reasonably likely to meet its goals; favorable results from a feasibility study do not guarantee a project's success.

Second, feasibility is determined by satisfying explicit objectives that should be defined before initiating the feasibility study. It is not just a matter of satisfying the developer's objectives, though such objectives may be the initial driving force. The other players have objectives to be met, the most important of which are the objectives of the financial partners, the public sector, and the end users.

Third, the definition points to selecting a course of action and testing it for fit. In other words, execution—particularly timing—matters. It is not simply a question of whether an idea might work; rather, it is a question of whether a particular plan for turning an idea into bricks and mortar is likely to work within a specific time frame.

Fourth, the selected course of action is tested for fit in a context of specific constraints, which include all the legal and physical limitations enumerated in stage two. In addition to the obvious constraints associated with both the public sector's involvement and the land itself, there are limits to capital and other resources. For a project to be feasible, it must be feasible with the amount of capital and the number of people to be dedicated to the project, according to the selected course of action at a particular time.

This broad definition of feasibility goes far beyond the simple idea of value exceeding cost. When the word "constraints" is pushed into the ethical dimension (as suggested by Graaskamp), then both personal and social ethics as well as formal legal and physical constraints must also be satisfied.

INITIATING THE FEASIBILITY STUDY

A typical feasibility study includes an executive summary, a market study, revenue projections, preliminary drawings, maps, cost estimates, information about the terms and sources of financing, government considerations, and an estimate of value.

Depending on the size and complexity of the development, the feasibility study can vary significantly in length, scope, and cost. At one extreme, if the project is a set of duplexes in an area already developed with similar properties and is to use architectural drawings from a previously built project and the same contractor and lender, then the *feasibility analysis* is a simple activity that involves applying updated market information to a proven course of action. In other words, new market data are used to project rent and absorption, with most other factors refined modestly from preceding developments. In such a simple case, developers would probably choose to perform the feasibility study with in-house staff at limited cost.

This simple case contrasts sharply with a 5,000-acre master-planned community of multiple housing types with office and retail components. Such a community requires extensive infrastructure as well as aboveground construction and is likely to take many years to complete. Because of its long time frame, the recognition of long-term trends is important—even for designing the first stage of the project. An idea for a complex, expensive, long-term project often results in a complex, expensive feasibility study that involves outside professionals such as architects, land planners, soils engineers, hazardous waste experts, and public relations consultants.

With a large project, the involvement of various government bodies will probably be substantial from the outset. In some jurisdictions, developers use political consultants who function like pollsters to test the local political waters and then help prepare and

deliver the developer's message. Likewise, market analysis and tenant relations in a large project are more complex because of the possibility that people will move to the location not simply from within the locality, but also from around the country and possibly from around the world. The developer coordinates all the professionals and ensures that they understand all the details of the project so that they can collectively determine its feasibility.

CASE STUDY   **Shortbread Lofts at Stage Three**

Larry Short confirmed his rental rate assumptions in two ways. First, he hired CBRE, a real estate broker, to estimate potential rents. Second, he canvassed five property manager prospects (some local, some national) to see what rents they would recommend. Drawing on his accounting background, Short pushed hard to obtain multiple sources for the rent estimates.

CBRE's work also became the background information for the development's presale package. Short explored the possibility of preselling the project but ultimately chose to hold the equity himself because he felt that the postdevelopment value would be much higher than the offers he received for the idea at stage one. Still, being a conservative accountant by training, he remained flexible

Continued next page

Floor Plan Level One

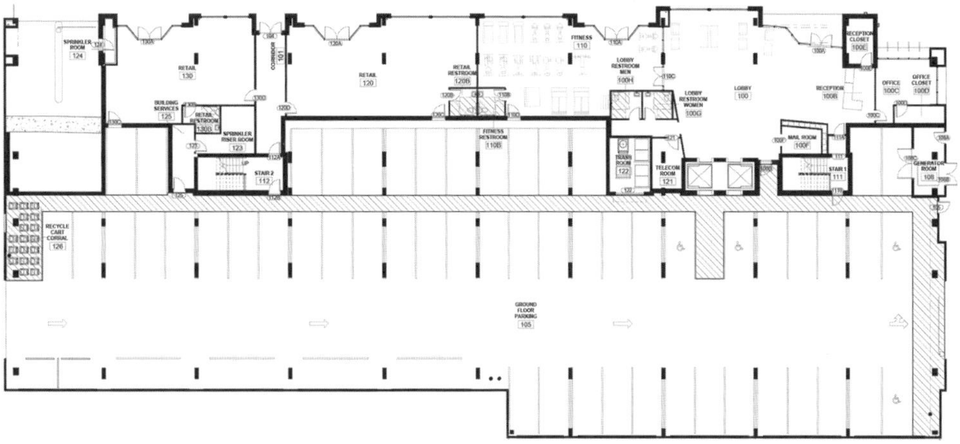

Floor Plan Level Two

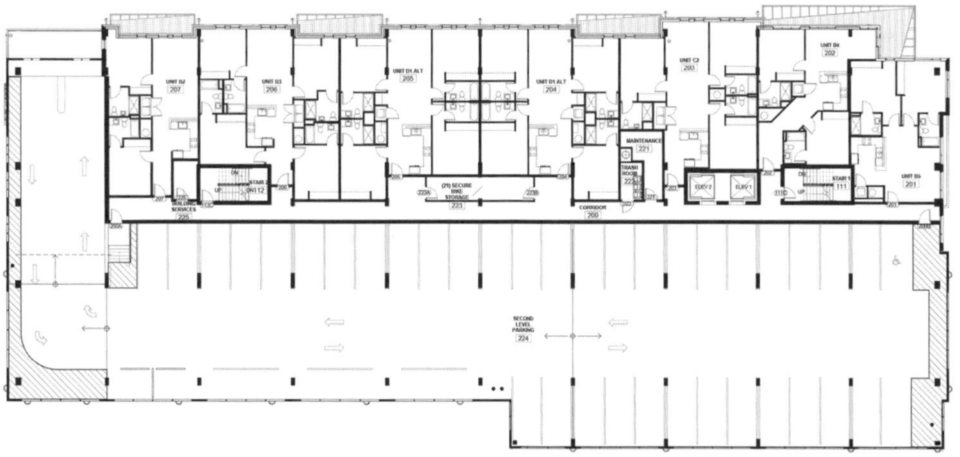

CASE STUDY *Shortbread Lofts at Stage Three* *Continued*

by negotiating a loan with no prepayment penalty. He chose a bank loan package that was designed to accommodate either alternative—hold or sell during the development process.

At this point, the prospective development cash flows were as follows:

Item	($ millions)
Construction cost (from budget)	20.5
Land (at estimated market value)	8.0
Cost, predevelopment fee	28.5
Development fee	1.8
Total cost	30.3
Loan	21.0
Cash flow	0.5

From this point, the only cash cost to the developer is construction, estimated at $20.5 million. Because cash into the project includes the loan of $21 million, there is a negligible positive cash flow of $0.5 million, an excellent situation for the developer.

Short included a very large development fee in the CBRE package, but the plan was to not take a development fee if the original group continued to be the sole equity holders. The large developer fee was intended as compensation should the majority of the development profit go to the buyer on a presale. If the decision was to hold through development, the plan was to have enough financing so that the soft costs could be covered by the loan with neither partner having to put in cash.

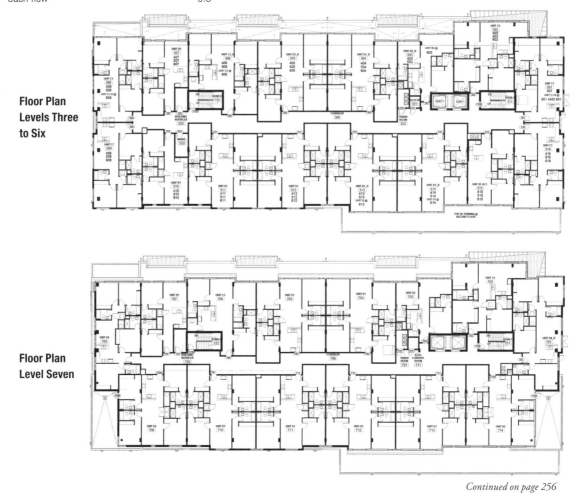

Floor Plan Levels Three to Six

Floor Plan Level Seven

Continued on page 256

Many specialized companies are available to perform feasibility studies or their various components. Real estate advisory firms, appraisal companies, business consultants, and the real estate divisions of some large accounting firms can be commissioned to perform feasibility studies.

Because various regulatory agencies oversee the lenders who bear a portion of the risk in developments, financial institutions are usually required to include feasibility work among the items they examine in underwriting loans. An outside feasibility study prepared by a well-respected firm meets this requirement. The Federal Home Loan Bank Board's Rule R-41c ("Appraisal Policies and Practices of Insured Institutions and Service Corporations") requires lenders to mandate that appraisals of development projects constitute more than mere data illustrating current conditions based on a few comparables. Instead, lenders are required to formally estimate a project's "highest and best use" based on a schedule of space absorption over time. Furthermore, as a measure of risk control, appraisers estimate the "as is" value of partially completed projects as well as their projected values upon completion. (See chapters 10 and 11 for more detail.)

In establishing this rule, the government hoped to end the unsubstantiated assertions of financial feasibility and property values that led to many financial disasters during the 1980s. Given the real estate implosion during the Great Recession, it is clear that more regulation was needed and more recent regulations have placed greater responsibility on lenders. When loans are to be packaged and sold in some form of mortgage-backed security, the rules become considerably more complex.

Regulators do not spell out every item that lenders should require of appraisers and market analysts; instead, lenders require whatever analyses are necessary and appropriate in the particular situation. Lenders can find this difficult. If they do not require substantial analysis by an independent party and a loan subsequently goes into default, then the regulators will fault them for not performing sufficiently detailed due diligence. They do not want to put too much cost burden on their customers (developers/borrowers), but they want to leave a paper trail in case problems develop later. Most important, lenders want to make money, so they aim to avoid loans for losing developments.

COMPONENTS OF THE FEASIBILITY STUDY

Among the possible components of a feasibility study, the essentials include the following:

- Executive summary;
- Maps of the site and surrounding area;
- Photographs of the site;
- Renderings of the proposed project;
- Market study, including analysis of market demand and competitive supply;
- Revenue and operating cost projections;
- Electronic valuation model derived from an appropriate market study;
- Documented cost projections;
- Development schedule; and
- Background on key players, including project consultants.

Critical analytic elements for the developer include

- A sensitivity analysis with an evaluation of each component and variation of the plan, to move from feasible to optimal;
- A review of risks in the optimal configuration, with appropriate risk management techniques; and
- Confirmation that the project is feasible for each participant.

The Market Study

The market study is the basis of the feasibility analysis. It analyzes the long-term global, national, regional, and local trends that were identified during stage two as relevant to the particular development. These trends are now formally examined in light of the local situation, helping the analyst to develop an absorption schedule for the project.

The first step in a market study is an examination of national economic conditions (including international influences) and projected trends, in light of the characteristics of the region, locality, neighborhood, and site. Segmentation of the population forecast and the job growth forecast is usually an extremely important part of the analysis. It has been well documented, for example, that there is a growing mismatch between the types of jobs available and types of job seekers in many areas. The

Using Design to Revitalize Cities

Architecture and design can help revitalize an entire city. Bilbao, Spain, for example, has centered its economic development plans on striking architecture, beginning with the Bilbao Guggenheim Museum, which opened in 1997. The museum, designed by Frank Gehry in his signature style, was expected to bring perhaps 500,000 visitors to Bilbao the first year. Instead, it brought 1.36 million visitors and $160 million in revenue to the former shipbuilding town that few tourists had ever visited before. The city has used the museum as a catalyst for further investment—both public and private—with an emphasis on design. Today Bilbao features a subway with stations designed by Norman Foster, two bridges and an airport designed by Santiago Calatrava, and a cultural center designed by Philippe Starck. The city's once dismal riverfront has been enhanced with a linear park, widely used by both tourists and residents. Private investment includes a wealth of trendy hotels, restaurants, galleries, and shops. The city has continued to draw more than a half million visitors annually.

Many cities have followed Bilbao's lead and commissioned a high-profile architect to design a public building—including quite a few by Frank Gehry. For example, Miami Beach commissioned Gehry for the New World Center concert hall, which opened in 2011. Other notable examples include Zaha Hadid's Guangzhou Opera House, in Guangdong Province, China, which opened in 2010; the shimmering museum building by Rudy Ricciotti for the MuCEM on Marseille's waterfront, built in 2013; the Copenhagen Concert Hall, by Jean Nouvel, which opened in 2009; and Rem Koolhaas's design for Casa da Música, a multivenue concert hall opened in 2005 in Porto, Portugal.

Since the opening of the Guggenheim Museum, Bilbao has reinvented itself from a declining industrial town to a center of arts and culture.

labor market in the United States has continued to move away from lower-skill manufacturing jobs and toward jobs that require specialized skills and education. Market analysts should not lose sight of such important national trends as they project demand for a specific site. They should also remember that for planning, construction, and sales or leasing, even modestly sized projects have two- to five-year time horizons, which increases the importance of sound forecasting.[2]

As the second step in a market study, analysts investigate comparable properties to determine the features, functions, and benefits of those properties that are important to the market. The analysis focuses on projects that are most directly competitive with the proposed development, hence most

useful for providing insights into market preferences. Understanding and quantifying the value of particular features can help developers refine the key features of the proposed development. If the best leasing in the area has been achieved by an office building that has no fitness center but more parking than the competition, then extra parking is more important than a fitness center and the subject property should be designed accordingly. Still, it is important to understand the market's preferences and not to just assume that a particular feature is desirable because a given project with that feature leased well.

The market study concludes with projected absorption schedules for the market segments that are appropriate for the specific property. How many units at what price over what time period will the target market be likely to absorb?

Preliminary Drawings

If an idea's viability is established (at least in the developer's mind) during stage two, money must usually be committed to more detailed drawings in stage three. Preliminary drawings show exterior elevations and specify floor layouts with rentable square feet or salable units, parking, type of HVAC systems, and the like. Part of this work was done in stage two, but the *formal feasibility* study requires drawings that are much closer to final design plans so that cost estimates can be more exact.

Although different architects and engineers can be used for the initial architectural layout and the final construction drawings, it is usually more efficient to use the same architect and engineer throughout the entire process. Keeping the same teams throughout helps to maintain consistency in the underlying assumptions and methodologies, minimizes the learning curve involved in bringing in new players, and promotes commitment to and understanding of the developer's objectives. Developers should decide on the level of expertise needed of the architect and the engineer as well as the amount of their time to use at each stage, all of which affect costs. The more complex and innovative the job, the more technical skills the team members will need and the earlier they should be brought into the process. In addition, communication among the members of the development team is essential from the beginning. An architect cannot design a project unless he understands other players' activities and objectives.

High-quality design is much more than aesthetics; it can make buildings more functional and cost-effective to operate and can go a long way toward ensuring the successful leasing and management of the finished project. A successful project is marketable, manageable, and cost-effective. A beautiful building that costs too much to construct and is difficult to manage will not be successful; a low-budget project can be both visually unappealing and difficult to manage and therefore even less successful.

The development team's clear communication of marketing information to the architect stimulates the design of manageable space that is attractive to prospective tenants.

Preliminary drawings must reflect consideration of three basic items: marketing appeal (the project's eye appeal to prospective tenants), cost, and ease of ongoing management. A balance among the three cannot be achieved without fitting the project to a specific site, as exemplified by the designs of the legendary Frank Lloyd Wright. The primary distinguishing characteristic of real estate is its specific,

---

CASE STUDY **Irvine Tech Center: Feasibility**

Feasibility analysis in the course of changing circumstances requires a tolerance for a reasonable level of ambiguity. It also requires an understanding that the uses of feasibility analysis change as a project moves forward. The initial feasibility analysis for the ITC project was a reflection of conditions at the first two stages, idea inception and idea refinement. It was relatively straightforward. However, as the project moved forward, the developer needed to focus more incrementally on feasibility. First, the impact of changes being imposed on the project from external sources had to be analyzed. Second, the opportunities for additional acquisitions of land and trip allocations had to be understood. The tradeoffs were complex. Smith needed approvals and could benefit from additional capacity. However, each possible move affected other options. If he paid for adjoining land to obtain the trips associated with that parcel, he then had to redo plans already submitted to the town for approvals.

Ambiguity arose from the timing of the project in the market cycle. The California real estate market is characterized by extremely sharp turns often described as "throwing a light switch." In such an environment, current analogous data points provide little comfort. How long would the current high demand for residential in this location continue, and would the features currently satisfying residential tenants change before Smith could deliver the constructed space?

In this environment, Smith's feasibility analysis not only communicated data to his investor but also aided his own decision making. This is the kind of feasibility analysis that only an entrepreneurial developer can undertake. The information that goes into the decision-making process is shaped by the developer's broad understanding of the market and its opportunities but is often not entirely quantifiable. It goes to the core of the developer's personality as the locus of creativity. *Continued on page 278*

unchangeable location. A project that fits one site well is often far less successful when replicated on a second site. Fitting the project to the site requires creativity and is frequently time-consuming. Early refinements in the design can prevent the development of structures that are hard to build, manage, or lease. Good planning can also reduce or eliminate opposition from the public sector.

Besides being concerned about how a building fits its site and serves its intended tenants, developers also need to think about how a building blends into the urban setting. An individual building may appear attractive in isolation and may function well for its occupants, but once built, it should also interact aesthetically with its surroundings.

Context is thus an important element of design. Size and scale, massing and setbacks, landscaping, circulation, lighting, stylistic details, relationships, image, range of difference—not to mention form and materials—are all important in what is usually referred to as "the context of the building." Likewise, foreshadowing and the entry, contrast and consistency, form and space relationships, volume, ordering systems, edges in transition, activity areas, levels, circulation in movement, building footprint, human scale, surfaces and materials, varied elements, ornamentation and color, and landscaping are important design considerations.

For a non-architect, this list may sound like an expensive set of intangible combinations. A good way for developers to learn about architecture is to visit great buildings and study how they fit with the city and how the space functions for those who inhabit it. This is one of the most enjoyable parts of kicking tires in the real estate business.

Space that appeals to people can generate a new market beyond the demand indicated in the market study. Heightened interest in the functionality and aesthetics of constructed space has led to research into the value created by outstanding architecture. This work specifically addresses the question of whether or not buildings that are design landmarks (or are particularly attractive) bring a higher return to the developer and the investor.[3] Whether or not such research eventually proves that higher returns

Chicago's skyline is filled with unique, well-designed buildings that fit within their neighborhood context. These high rises help define the edge of Millennium Park.

accrue to great architecture, developers often find that some lenders and investors want to be associated with big-name architects.

Construction and Total Cost Estimates

Although it is easy to list cost categories, it is difficult to estimate actual costs. The cost of the land is probably known after stage two, though with some variability for more complex options, lease fees, subordination agreements, and the like. In most cases, the most difficult cost to estimate accurately is the cost of the site preparation. Without extensive soil borings, it is difficult to know where rock is located and hence how expensive it will be to remove it or route underground infrastructure around it. Even with the advice of the best soils engineer, the handling of surface and subsurface water may be more expensive than expected. To obtain an estimate of the total cost of infrastructure, any off-site infrastructure costs for water, sewers, streets, and the like (whether assumed voluntarily or imposed by regulation) must be added to on-site costs. In some cases, a developer acquires additional land after the primary land purchase, further complicating initial cost estimates.

For estimating construction costs of aboveground elements, readily accessible guides are available. Examples include the annual *RSMeans Building Construction Cost Data* series and Sage Estimating software.[4] The guides break down cost elements and include monthly updates for cost inflation as well as adjustments for geographic location, based on cubic, square, or linear feet.

Developers typically use standard industry cost guides to compile in-house cost projections to compare with local general contractors' estimates. In-house cost projections should yield an estimate that is close to the general contractors' cost estimates. When a significant difference occurs, developers need to recheck the figures and discuss them in more detail with the general contractors. If discrepancies remain, they should at least be explainable. At times, the estimating process requires a developer to meet with individual subcontractors. For example, if the project will use an unusual amount and type of glass, the developer might find it advisable to discuss with the glass subcontractor the specifics underlying the cost estimates used in the feasibility study. Information gleaned from talking to contractors and subcontractors helps the developer refine and improve parts of the project so that the proposal becomes more attractive to tenants, less expensive to construct, more cost-effective to operate, or some combination of these three.

In addition to the costs of land with improvements and aboveground construction, an estimate of total costs includes the soft costs of marketing, financing, insurance, consultants, and other administrative work. Depending on the type of project, marketing could start well before construction is complete. Market research starts even earlier. Advertising, commissions, consultants, and special concessions to tenants during the initial leasing period represent the major portion of the costs of marketing the development. Postconstruction costs for operations during initial periods of moderate occupancy are also a part of the total cost estimate.

Fees for outside professional services vary depending on circumstances. For example, at the bottom of the market, consultants may offer guidance to favored clients at lower costs so as to gain an opportunity for later work. Although astute developers minimize costs and capitalize on past relationships appropriately, successful developers also know when to spend additional dollars. Part of

the developer's role is to decide which items require additional investment as a means of controlling risk and enhancing future returns.

Lenders' fees go into the estimate of total costs. Long-term lenders charge a commitment fee for the promise to take out or replace the construction lender. Construction lenders typically charge origination fees (points) on top of interest.

Carrying costs, which are time-related, must also be counted. Local governments collect property taxes throughout the development process, and the total cost of those taxes will increase with delays in construction and absorption. Insurance should include fire and extended coverage in addition to various forms of liability coverage. Accounting costs and a variety of overhead costs should also be included in the overall cost estimate. The inclusion of both expected overhead and a development fee over and above overhead costs indicates that the developer is planning to draw some profit during the construction period.

Most estimates of marketing, financing, property taxes, insurance, and administrative costs can be based on experience and a projection of trends. It is possible, for example, to know what market brokerage fees are and to estimate both the amount of print collateral needed for advertising and the cost of those materials. Based on trends in the marketplace, one can project the lease-up period, an essential part of accurately estimating the cost of initial periods of low occupancy. Likewise, estimates of financing costs can be based on a combination of projected construction time and projected interest rates.

Finally, funds for contingencies should be included. In an uncertain world, where feasibility is only "reasonably likely" and not guaranteed, it is important to have financing for unexpected costs and cost overruns. Because the total cost estimate is based on several other estimates, it is important to provide contingency funds commensurate with the level of certainty in the rest of the estimates. The contingency allowance typically ranges from 5 to 10 percent, depending on the perceived accuracy of the other estimates. The contingency allowance can be reduced in budget updates as risks are eliminated.

Although the cost estimate for each development has features specific to that development, a typical estimate includes the following elements:

- Land cost,
- Site and infrastructure costs (on-site and off-site),
- Design fees (architecture and engineering),
- Hard costs by category (labor and materials),
- Entitlement costs (consultants, public agency fees),
- Financing costs (permanent loan commitment fees, construction interest, construction loan fees),
- Marketing costs (promotion, advertising, leasing commissions, broker fees),
- Preopening operating costs,
- Legal fees,
- Accounting and audit costs,
- Field supervision (inspection) costs,
- Overhead,
- Property taxes,
- Contingencies, and
- Development fees.

Ideally, each estimate is confirmed by market data. Some items, such as land costs, may be based on contracts. The largest item, hard costs, should be confirmed by comparison with (1) the cost of similar recently constructed projects, (2) input from cost estimation services, and (3) input from the prospective general contractor.

The Value Statement and Formal Estimate of Feasibility

The result of the market study is an estimated schedule of leasing or sales that forecasts rent or sales revenue, occupancy, and related expenses. During the feasibility study, developers should ensure that perceptions cohere—that the marketing staff is planning to sell the same product that the builders are planning to construct, which is the same project that the public sector is expecting to review and that lenders or investors are planning to finance.

The features and amenities included in the project should be determined, to a large degree, by analyzing the success of comparable developments

---

CASE STUDY   **Shortbread Lofts**

Figure A   **Budget Items**

Soft costs	
Architecture	$364,895
Design fees	100,000
Civil engineering	279,500
Mechanical, electrical, plumbing engineer	158,089
Structural engineer	81,403
Environmental engineer	20,000
Energy Star certification	31,375
Architectural and engineering reimbursable	11,000
Owner fees and permits	445,151
Owner's liability insurance	5,000
Appraisal	8,000
Development overhead	200,000
Advertising	75,000
Real estate taxes	140,000
Legal	169,930
Accounting	4,244
Contingency	175,000
Total soft costs	**$2,268,587**
Hard costs	
Construction	$15,530,839
General conditions	910,251
Fee	514,773
Standard liability 1.1%	185,123
Bond for JMA (contractor)	144,623
Total hard costs	**$17,285,609**
Finance costs	
Capitalized interest	490,000
Loan fees	105,000
Total finance costs	**$595,000**
Development contingency	402,984
Development costs	**$20,552,180**

Continued on page 274

investigated in the market study. It is critical that projected rents or sales are based on truly comparable projects. A well-prepared feasibility analysis includes a comparison grid in the market analysis section. The grid identifies competitive projects and shows the specific adjustments for differences between those projects and the proposed development. The comparison should be sufficiently rigorous to give readers confidence in the estimate of the project's NOI. That calculation is straightforward: potential revenues minus vacant space equals effective gross revenue. Effective gross revenue minus operating expenses equals NOI. The difficulty comes in making reasonable assumptions for each element. (See chapters 10 and 11 for information on the mechanics of these statements.) The larger the adjustments that the analyst makes to the comparables, the more likely that some misestimate will be made and, thus, the greater the need for a larger budget for contingencies and/or a higher risk premium in the discount rate. Unique ideas for which no comparable projects exist are more risky, and the developer of such projects thus should have greater reserves.

The value side of the feasibility analysis is based on discounted cash flow, with the discount rate taken from the market. That said, feasibility is a forward-looking concept. In preparing the feasibility study, the analyst reviews historical investment return numbers and adjusts them for the expected inflation rate as well as for any other projected changes in financial conditions that may affect the relative risk of the project. Once a discount rate has been determined in this manner, the analyst should confirm it by questioning investors who are actively seeking this type of investment.

Using the estimated discount rate, the analyst reduces projected cash flows to a current value that incorporates everything that can be known about the project. In other words, all the information about the market, the quality of the space relative to the competition, future trends, and the risks associated with all the projections are brought back to one value at one point in time. The analyst then compares this value with the projected total cost.

A project satisfies Graaskamp's definition of feasibility if

1. The value (adjusted for risk) exceeds the total cost, where the total cost includes all physical items as well as all planning and other soft costs;
2. Legal and ethical rules have been satisfied; and
3. The developer commands the financial and human resources necessary to bring the project to fruition.

Thus, the developer uses both appropriately defined value and completely specified costs to determine formal feasibility. It is critically important to remember that the value shown in the feasibility study is based on the cash flows that the project is expected to generate over its lifetime. How the project is expected to perform in its market is captured by the revenue and expense streams laid out in the cash flow statements. As shown in chapters 10 and 11, standard industry practice is to lay out in some detail the expected cash flows for each of the next ten years. The final year includes the expected cash flow from the sale of the property, with the sale price usually based on a capitalization of the final year's income. That capitalized value is itself a proxy for the remaining expected cash flows after the first ten years. Expected cash flows drive value, as they are the bottom-line composite of all the preceding analytical work.

There is nothing magical about ten years. Using the next five years or the next 20 years could work as well, depending on the particular investment. As noted, discounted cash flow analysis typically includes capitalizing the final year's income to get an expected sales price and hence the cash flow from the final disposition. The primary concern in deciding on the length of the analysis period is to capture the effect of any unusual cash flows anticipated at the time of the analysis. If a major cash flow is expected shortly after the end of the analysis period, then capitalizing the last year's income is not the best way to estimate the disposition cash flow.

For example, if the subject property is a warehouse leased to a single tenant, the discounted cash flow period should include what is expected when the existing tenant lease expires. If seven years are left on the lease, the investment analysis period should be longer than seven years. Similarly, if the investment is a shopping center and a competing center is planned for a nearby site, the analysis period should be at least long enough for the subject property to feel the impact of the proposed new development.

For the Shortbread Lofts development (see its NOI statement in chapter 11), a five-year cash flow was used. Because Short is approaching the age when he plans to scale back his work, the plan was to finish and sell everything while he is still working full-time. Consequently the partners agreed to a five-year time horizon on all activities. The partners do not currently anticipate any unusual cash flows beyond five years, so they used a five-year model for the discounted cash flow analysis.

After estimating the value, the analyst should construct an after-financing and after-tax scenario to show how all the participants fit into the project. Ideally, the sum of the parts should be greater than the whole. If tax benefits result, they accrue to the appropriate investor.

Once the cost and value statements have been determined, the developer runs a sensitivity analysis to see whether some aspect of the project can be improved. For example, a slight increase in operating costs may be justified if it substantially lowers the project's construction cost. If the cost and income statements are set up on a simple computer spreadsheet, it is easy to check the tradeoff between operating costs and visual appeal, between construction costs and management costs, and so on. By using sensitivity analyses, a feasibility study transitions from a static financial analysis to a dynamic planning tool.

An important caveat is in order. Electronic spreadsheet models can easily be used to force feasibility: it is easy to change a number here or there to produce a value that exceeds costs by an appropriate amount. But forcing the numbers will surely come back to haunt a developer during the highly stressful stage six or the very long duration of stage eight.

The Enterprise Concept

Treating real estate as an ongoing business is an important consideration during stage three. Operations management has an important role in all phases of real estate and is critical as a developer considers the complex combination of real estate development with the ongoing needs of a tenant's business and its customers. The enterprise concept, as originally espoused by Graaskamp, portrays real estate as an enterprise and sets the stage for business-like, aggressive management. Graaskamp campaigned for years for a change from the concept of real estate as bricks and mortar to the concept of a building as an operating entity—that is, a living, breathing business with a cash-flow cycle similar to that of other operating businesses. He urged developers to recognize that, like businesses, buildings continually need to redefine their market positions and seek new niches in the marketplace. Treating real estate as a business means that the entity must be managed aggressively to remain viable. Although real estate assets have a long life in a fixed location, it is important to remember that the demands of building users are constantly evolving. In this dynamic environment, design flexibility is required for long-term operating success.

The more a building entails significant management operations—such as a hotel, to which food, beverage, and other services are critical to realizing income—the more complex the feasibility study. Two sets of questions arise: (1) How crucial are management operations to the project's long-term success? And how good is the management (on a relative basis) selected for this development? (2) Is the developer or the tenant responsible? Or has the developer passed this risk on through an unconditional presale to a long-term investor?

Bringing It All Together

Three additional items complete the feasibility study:

1. The overall construction schedule, a composite of the various components, which is usually compiled by the project manager, who

GLP Misato III, in Misato City, Japan, is a state-of-the-art logistics facility that includes everything needed to continue doing business in the face of a natural disaster, such as backup generators, emergency sewage systems, showers, a cafeteria, and a convenience store for workers. The solar-powered facility earned LEED Platinum certification.

is charged with coordinating the participants to facilitate timely completion;

2. Applicable portions of the resumes of the key participants, to give investors and lenders confidence that the development team has the capacity to complete the project successfully; and

3. Maps, drawings, and other visuals, which show the location and site of the development to orient reviewers. Architectural renderings and photographs of the subject property as well as complementary and competitive projects help complete the visual summary.

INVESTORS AND LENDERS

The preliminary discussions with investors and lenders that began in stage two now progress to a more formal level. Based on initial reactions to his

overtures, the developer is now close to finding the most appropriate long-term investor, permanent lender, construction lender, and, possibly, development-period joint venture partner. In stage three, the developer presents prospective lenders and investors with more specific information about the target market, the design and costs of the project, and the financial structure of the proposed transaction.

Investors

For a large-scale mixed-use project, two to six years might elapse between stage two and stage six, the beginning of construction. During that time, the formal feasibility study is undertaken, much of the design work is done, extensive government relations are worked out, and long-term tenant relations are negotiated. All these activities require out-of-pocket cash from the developer. Consequently, the source of operating money is an extremely important consideration. Because the amount of money may be large and because developers usually take great pains to minimize the amount of their own money involved before committing to a project, substantial front-end funds from other sources may be needed.

In such a situation, it is probably appropriate to judge this interim period between the end of stage two and the beginning of stage six as more of a venture capital period than a traditional real estate financing period. The amount invested may be substantial. Furthermore, a great deal of risk is associated with the investment because of uncertainties as to whether the project, whose exact size and value are still unknown, will ever be undertaken. Consequently, investors during this period look for extraordinarily high returns, not unlike venture capitalists. (This is not to suggest that such financing comes from venture capitalists, but that this financing comes from higher-risk investors—like venture capitalists—and is usually expensive.)

An extended venture capital period changes the investor's, the lender's, and even the developer's traditional role. All the traditional players are still important, but the need for financing during this venture capital period introduces an additional level of complexity. If the project does not proceed to stage six, the investors do not receive a low return. Instead, they lose all their money because plans for an infeasible development have little or no resale value.

The astute developer uses as much of the less expensive financing (such as commercial banks) as possible and as little of the expensive financing (such as early-stage joint venture partners) as possible. The development company is a business, and its collection of development projects should be structured so that the development company remains viable. To keep the development company solvent, the developer may at times need to trade longer-term profits (the percentage of the difference between value and cost) for a smaller developer contribution to preconstruction financing.

Lenders

At this stage, the developer uses the project's estimated value in his search for debt financing.

Permanent lenders look at their prospective return and the associated risk. This exercise usually involves calculating a projected debt service coverage ratio, a loan-to-value ratio, and an estimation of the project's ability to maintain value through long-term appeal in a particular market. Construction lenders usually prefer a simple project designed and built by highly skilled individuals with whom they have worked before. However, if developers always followed lenders' guidelines, their profits would likely be slim. Lenders want both low risk (often interpreted as "it's been done successfully before") and high interest rates or loan fees. Lenders have been known to deviate from their general preferences, but only for logical reasons and usually only if those reasons are supported by a high-quality feasibility study. Beyond minimizing the costs of financing, developers try to maximize their flexibility by minimizing the number of rules and other constraints imposed by lenders in the loan documents.

To find the appropriate financiers for a proposed development, developers should know lenders' and investors' particular interests, their histories, their self-images, and the current preferred mix for their portfolios. Why does a particular investment fit one lender better than another? On the surface, the answer is fairly straightforward. Larger life insurance companies typically finance larger projects developed by national firms. Regional life insurance companies and some commercial banks are more likely to finance smaller, more local projects. Many commercial banks, because of their predominantly short-term sources of funding, are more often found acting as construction lenders on safer projects.

Recalling the typical sequence presented in chapters 10 and 11, usually the developer first lines up the largest, lowest-cost permanent loan possible. This permanent loan is the *takeout loan* for the construction lender. The difference between the total project cost and the available financing is the required equity. If the developer does not have sufficient capital (or does not want to risk that capital), he needs an equity investor for the development period.

The critical concept is matching the right lenders and investors with the particular development. With consolidation in the financial markets, the mega-institutions typically engage in a variety of real estate lending through subsidiaries and affiliates, if not directly. As with the selection of an architect and an engineer, the more complex and crucial the financing arrangement, the more skilled a developer and his agent needs to be in dealing with the financial community. A developer does not have to personally arrange financing; instead, he could hire a mortgage banker or an investment banker. Still, even with a top national banker on the team, it remains the developer's job to make the project happen, and financing is critical to that outcome.[5]

ENTITLEMENTS AND OTHER GOVERNMENT CONSIDERATIONS

Government agencies are responsible for issuing the necessary entitlements for the project. In some areas, obtaining entitlements is a highly political process. Developers who misjudge the local political environment or suggest a project that does not fit the community's long-term interests can have difficulty even if they technically meet the letter of the law (see chapters 7 and 8 for more detail).

Clearly, some representatives of local government need to be involved in the determination of feasibility. If the regulators understand all the pressures on the development and how the development meets both public and private objectives, they are more likely to support the project and less likely to delay the development approval process. Many municipal staff are technically well trained and will support a development concept so long as it fits with the city's master plan. If the public sector is recruited early in the development process and is fully committed to the concept, it is less likely to throw up time-consuming roadblocks as the process unfolds.

Turnover in public offices can pose other problems for developers when projects conflict with the platforms of newly elected officials. When administrations change, earlier approval of a project does not necessarily guarantee that the newly elected officials will be good partners.

FEASIBILITY: THE PROJECT AND THE PARTICIPANTS

Although a project may eventually be profitable, the developer and his team need to eat every day, well before the project reaches completion; therefore, it is instructive to think of feasibility not just in terms of the project, but in terms of each player's ability to maintain financial stability for the duration of the development process. As mentioned in chapter 12, this is referred to as "level two feasibility."

Just as a project must appear feasible—that is, its value must exceed its costs—so all participants in the process should see a greater value in participating in the process than in their cost of participation. If, at any point, any of the participants find that participation ceases to be profitable for them, the whole project may be endangered. Despite legal obligations to perform, most people become less enthusiastic about even the most exciting project when their participation ceases to generate the expected profit. As an ongoing risk control technique, the developer uses the feasibility study not just to monitor the project's viability, but also to think about each participant's perspective.

RISK CONTROL TECHNIQUES DURING STAGE THREE

Several techniques are available to control risk during stage three. The most common ones are described in this section.

Using the best available information and doing rigorous data analysis in the feasibility study is clearly a major risk control technique, one that will be used throughout the remainder of the development process. The better the information and the effort that go into estimating all revenues and costs, the more likely it is that the development decisions will be sound. In almost all cases, the better the forecast, the less risk involved in the development. Yet, the feasibility study for a large project is expensive and time-consuming. Overdoing the feasibility analysis is a waste of time and money that can seriously extend the length of the development process—much to the detriment of the developer. How much is enough but not too much? That is where the developer's judgment comes into play.

The *financing* arranged during stage three critically affects the sharing of project risks. Different lenders and equity investors have different preferences. The construction lender wants early equity contributions, a floating-rate loan with strict procedures for dispensing funds, and both the developer's and any equity investors' guarantees and personal liability. The developer prefers an interest rate cap, easy draw procedures for requesting payments, no personal liability, and the right to contribute his own cash after the bank puts up its cash. How these desires are traded off depends on the quality of the project, the relative strength of the lender and the developer, and current conditions in the capital markets. In a lender's market, the developer may have to take on greater risk. When financing is readily available from many sources, lenders are more likely to accommodate developers' desires and take a greater share of the risk.

Permanent lenders likewise focus on the tradeoff between risk and return. The higher the DSCR and the lower the LTV ratio, the more likely it is that the lender will be paid on schedule and, in the event of default, collect the total loan balance.

Investors bring their own perspectives to the financing arrangement. They want to make their cash contributions late and receive assurance that, in the event of the need for additional cash, the shortfall would be made up by the developer or the lenders. Investors do not want to be personally liable; they do want to maximize their after-tax returns.

A formal review of the architect's design plan by operating, marketing, and construction professionals as well as by public officials is critical in controlling risk. More review by all players in stage three will make the negotiations in stage four much easier.

The developer should check to ensure that *utilities and other infrastructure* are available. Even though a project is legally feasible and publicly desirable, a city may ultimately be unable to provide sewer, water, or other infrastructure services in the expected manner. The developer should begin discussions early, document the meetings, and—whenever possible—obtain formal commitments for public facilities and services.

In a competitive world, it can be useful to share costs. When considering all the costs of infrastructure for a project, a developer may ask a city for concessions in return for providing the public with something of value. Alternatively, a *joint venture* with other private sector users or a public/private partnership might be a possible and appropriate way to share the costs and risks.

Checking details helps control risk. The developer should check to make sure that a building permit has been issued to the chosen contractor; in addition, in some cities, it is important to make sure that subcontractors have obtained the appropriate permits. In their haste to get a job, contractors sometimes overlook certain rules or promise something that the company cannot deliver. Furthermore, it is wise to ensure that both contractors and subcontractors are properly licensed to do the work.

It is often useful to provide *structural warranties* in the architect's contract. (When the architectural firm is a small one, some developers consider insuring the contract.) After the windows fell out of the John Hancock building in Boston, it became obvious to many developers that they were not adequately prepared to undertake a final review of all the technical aspects of construction. Warranties from the architect, suppliers, and builders along with assurance that all participants have sufficient financial worth to support a lawsuit mean that the developer has a remedy in the event of disaster. Although it is seldom a good idea to stop development for a lawsuit, the potential for a successful suit often encourages players to perform up to their commitments. The more concrete the legal documentation of responsibilities, the easier it is to convince individual players that serious problems will result if they fail to perform. Thus, structural warranties and, even more important, clearly drawn contracts can be tools that facilitate negotiating from strength. These possibilities should be anticipated during the economic discussions in stage three; if they are not, the legal negotiations in stage four will be far more difficult.

SUMMARY

The definition of feasibility presented in this chapter is noticeably broad. It begins with a formal definition of the development's objectives, which may involve money, ego, civic enhancement, and other related items. The defined objectives are then tested for fit in the context of specific market, legal, physical, and ethical constraints as well as limited financial and human resources. A project is feasible when it is reasonably likely (almost never certain) that objectives can be achieved in a particular situation.

A primary task in the feasibility analysis is producing a sound market analysis that culminates in a projection of net operating income for the subject property over the relevant time frame. The expected rate of return should be commensurate with the project's risk and should compare favorably with other investment options. Based on these projections, the developer estimates a value for the project using discounted cash flow analysis. A project is said to be feasible when that value exceeds all the projected costs of development.

The feasibility analysis should be more than a technique for controlling risk during stage three of the development process. Once completed, the formal feasibility study is the sales tool used to bring together all the players needed to accomplish the development. During stages four through seven, the feasibility study is constantly refined, and it remains probably the single most important management tool in the development process.

TERMS

- Enterprise concept
- Feasibility study

- Formal feasibility
- Market study
- Optimization tool
- Preliminary drawings
- Sensitivity analysis
- Takeout loan
- Venture capital period

REVIEW QUESTIONS

13.1 Define feasibility.

13.2 What is a feasibility study, and why is it necessary for a development?

13.3 What are the essential elements of a feasibility study?

13.4 What is the role of the architect at this stage of the development process?

13.5 How do developers know whether general contractors' estimates of construction costs are appropriate?

13.6 How and why do construction contingencies change?

13.7 Describe some of the techniques that can be used to control risk during stage three.

13.8 Discuss the enterprise concept and the impact it can have on the type of space that is developed.

NOTES

1 James A. Graaskamp, "A Rational Approach to Feasibility Analysis," *Appraisal Journal*, October 1972, p. 515.

2 A good source for broad trends is Emerging Trends in Real Estate®, produced annually by the Urban Land Institute and PricewaterhouseCoopers. It examines the outlook for real estate capital markets and contains a comprehensive annual forecast for all categories of commercial real estate. Reports are published for the United States, Europe, and Asia Pacific.

3 See, for example, "The Design Dividend," a research project on the investment return accruing to owners of well-designed projects by the Property Council of Australia, published in 2006, www.propertyoz.com.au.

4 Other sources include Marshall & Swift (www.marshallswift.com) and McGraw-Hill Construction (a network including *Architectural Record*, *Design-Build*, *Engineering News-Record*, Dodge, and Sweet's Group) at www.construction.com.

5 Morgan Stanley, Goldman Sachs, Citigroup, and others describe the risk profile and property cash flows that attract certain larger lenders to particular transactions in publications and on their websites.

PART 7

Making It Happen

The diverse, creative work that goes into starting a development comes together in stages four, five, six, and seven. During stages four and five, the nitty-gritty negotiations and detailed agreements are completed, allowing construction to begin. Many decisions are made that affect how well and how quickly the development will be completed. This stage is when the developer changes his primary role from creator/promoter to negotiator. He must ensure that all contracts are aligned and that each of the various participants involved in the project will interact consistently. By the time a developer initiates stage six—construction—his commitment to a project is nearly irreversible, because from that point on the decision to back out would result in a tremendous financial and professional loss. Stage seven—completion and formal opening— is the initial test of how well everything was done.

Chapter 14

Stages Four and Five: Contract Negotiation and Formal Commitment

Stage three of the development process—the formal feasibility study—brings together all the previously completed research and projections into summary statements of value and costs. If the project is feasible, its estimated value is expected to be sufficient to provide returns that will attract capital to the project. With data, analysis, knowledge, and experience indicating that the project is feasible, a developer has the information necessary to complete the assembly of the development team. The feasibility analysis serves as a sales and negotiating tool and as a coordinating device in stage four, contract negotiation. During stage four, contracts are arranged to implement the decision to proceed with the project; during stage five, these contracts are executed.

Contracts are the usual method of allocating and controlling both responsibility and risk. They set forth the rules for the physical, financial, marketing, and operating activities that occur during construction, formal opening, and operation (stages six, seven, and eight, respectively). The stage four effort progresses based on the conviction that all of the contracts will be consummated. That conviction is the driving force that enables the development to move forward. If all contracts are drawn properly and are consistent with each other, then the collective risk of all members of the development team is reduced. With proper structuring of the contracts, a developer can appropriately allocate the risks and rewards among the participants.

A detailed agreement should be negotiated with and documented for each member of the development team. The developer should ensure that the collection of individual contracts covers all aspects of the project and clearly defines the relationships among all participants in the project. The agreements should make the costs and responsibilities explicit and as free of ambiguities as possible.

A major transition occurs as a development moves from stage three to stage six. During the earlier stages, the developer is primarily the idea generator and promoter. As the process moves toward construction, the developer's role becomes that of the primary negotiator, who brings together all the members of the team. In stage six, the developer's role shifts to manager of the development team.

The authors are indebted to the law firm of Cox, Castle & Nicholson LLP, Los Angeles, for its contributions to this chapter.

Because so many elements must be clarified and potential conflicts resolved during these middle stages, this chapter covers a variety of issues. It begins with negotiating financing and then moves to the handling of environmental concerns; consideration of contracts with architects, engineers, and building contractors; and leases with tenants. Because of their many complex interactions, the topics are covered in a somewhat arbitrary order. Nowhere is this complexity more evident than in the financing. For example, the players do not negotiate financing without first considering the impact of the timing of financing on construction. And lenders like to know that environmental concerns have been addressed, acceptable contractors have been located, the prescribed preleasing has been accomplished, and equity investors are committed. All these topics are covered in this chapter.

STAGE FOUR: CONTRACT NEGOTIATION

A developer conducting due diligence calls one of his longstanding consultants and asks for a "quick cost estimate." The consultant delegates the task to a staff member. The estimate arrives late and contains far more detail than necessary to make a decision at this point in the process. The developer receives an invoice for the estimate that is three times what he expected.

Relationships in real estate development rely on written contracts. The work is too complex and the needs too explicit to be captured accurately in solely oral communication. Because transactions and contracts can be quite complex, accurate expression of the parties' understanding and intent is critical. In even the simple example above, reliance on oral instruction and previous relationships failed because team members, locations, and the scope of work were not made clear. Delineation of the timing, scope, and cost of tasks requires some thought and resources, but that work can ultimately save significant time and money. Decades of experience have defined the basic terms that should be considered in each situation; the context may change but the actions to be accomplished remain the same.

In stage four, the developer formalizes the business arrangements necessary to implement the project. This is a process of proposals and eventually commitments. Up to this point, the developer has made representations about what the project will be when completed, in a series of statements on all aspects of the project made to gain stakeholders' approvals. Those statements addressed the project's income stream, physical appearance, schedules, and community impacts. At this point, the pool of stakeholders has expanded to include the financial community and possibly the landowner. To move beyond stage four, the developer's representations need to be formalized as commitments. The commitments take the form of contracts, legal documents that formalize the intentions of the parties involved.

Agreement on contract terms is usually reached through negotiations that span a wide range of subjects as the project advances. The developer must adapt to a wide range of changing circumstances. More than in other fields, in real estate development, "the ideal negotiator should have a high tolerance for ambiguity and uncertainty," as negotiation trainer Chester Karrass notes.[1]

DECISIONS ABOUT FINANCING

The feasibility study completed in stage three is the primary tool used to arrange financing in stage four. The market study and the investment analysis contained in the feasibility study are part of the raw material for the loan application.

As described in chapters 10 and 11, developers often begin arranging financing by seeking a permanent lender and obtaining a permanent loan commitment, and then finding a construction lender and negotiating a construction loan. However, at times developers find it advantageous to arrange the construction financing in stage four and wait to arrange permanent financing until a later stage.

Potential tradeoffs can be complex. The developer trades off exposure across the development-period investors (equity, long-term lender, and construction lender), seeking to find the terms that best balance

INNOVATOR   Pamela Bundy Foster

In the male-dominated real estate development industry, it is no surprise that an African American woman who achieves flying success would garner attention. Such has been the case for Pamela Bundy.

Bundy was born and raised in rural Virginia; neither of her parents earned a high school diploma. Her first job was in the family business, farming. During the summers, she and the rest of her family traveled to her uncle's fields to pick tomatoes for 20 to 25 cents per basket. From these modest beginnings, she developed skills that would prove beneficial in her real estate career—a hard work ethic, for one, and her financial savvy, acquired through her weekly trips to the bank to review the family's finances. "I knew from an early age that to control my own destiny, I had to control my money," Bundy remembers.

Farm life was not for Bundy, so after graduating from high school, she set out for Lincoln University in Pennsylvania. After earning a degree in psychology, she considered graduate school but ultimately headed to the West Coast to enter the corporate world.

As a middle manager at Southland Corporation's 7-Eleven, Bundy returned to the East Coast, where she eventually settled in Washington, D.C. Being laid off ignited an entrepreneurial fire that led Bundy into real estate. She became a certified appraiser. To cut costs, she moved into her grandmother's house and worked from there.

Her first investment was the renovation of a 5,000-square-foot, four-story house in a low-income neighborhood. After turning over the house for a profit, she sought out similar residential projects she could flip. After a decade, she had accumulated enough capital to make the leap into the realm of upscale residential and commercial development.

Persistence led to one of Bundy's first major commercial deals. She pored over the market in search of the ideal location for a high-end residential development. Settling on a parcel at Logan Square, she found herself in line to speak to the owner behind several larger, established developers. Undaunted, she stopped by each morning on her way to the gym to try to meet with the owner.

This diligence paid off and she was granted the right to develop the property, much to the chagrin of the other developers.

Under Bundy's leadership, her company is developing more than 1.3 million square feet of renovation and new construction, which includes more than 1,430 housing units and approximately 510,000 square feet of retail and commercial space. Her persistence and confidence have helped her land spots in the development of downtown Washington's two largest mixed-use projects. Her company is the co-developer and an equity partner in City Vista, a $300 million development that includes more than 685 condominium units and approximately 100,000 square feet of retail space. She is also a development partner in City Center DC, a $1 billion, ten-acre, mixed-use development at the old convention center site.

Larger projects thrill Bundy because she works with a different team for each one. She has no in-house employees save for an accountant/assistant and commits only to projects that she selects. She stresses that no cookie-cutter formula can be applied to new developments: "Each deal is like a piece of artwork with its own different needs."

Civic engagement is a priority for Bundy, and she generously gives her time to local causes. In 2011, she was selected for the Capital One Advisory Board. For her pioneering accomplishments in real estate, she has received several awards, including the Commercial Real Estate Woman (CREW) Network Impact Award in 2008, *Washington Business Journal*'s Minority Business Leader Award in 2008, and the "Women Who Mean Business" Award in 2004. She also was acknowledged as the 2004 Entrepreneur of the Year by the Parren J. Mitchell Foundation.

To stay competitive in Washington's evolving market, Bundy obtained a master's degree in 2008 from Harvard Business School. Bundy attributes her success to being a good student. She has found role models in the industry who became mentors and followed their counsel. Her advice to aspiring developers: "Be willing to walk away from a deal. If you are bringing substantial equity for a project, and they are not offering you a fair share of the profits, walk away."

cost against risk. Often, the developer's profit potential and her exposure to risk changes materially with different sources of debt and equity financing. Using the feasibility study's spreadsheet as an optimization tool, the developer performs sensitivity analyses on revised cash flows, using alternative forecasts of events to determine the impact of each scenario on the cash flows of the various investment participants. The developer relies on experience and

intuition when specifying alternative scenarios and estimating their likelihood.

The ideal project is one whose value is so far above cost that the developer can obtain a loan that is sufficiently large to cover all costs, including a development fee, major reserves to cover any operating deficits before lease-up, and a large reserve for contingencies. However, even in the best situations, lenders usually rely on conservative underwriting criteria, so the financing nearly always requires some equity investment by the developer or some other equity investor. Furthermore, lenders usually prefer that developers have "skin in the game." Only a truly great idea attracts 100 percent debt financing and even then, some guarantee of the debt by the developer is often required.

When a developer cannot finance an entire project through senior debt, he must find additional sources of capital. Four basic alternatives are possible: he can provide the necessary equity from his own funds or his firm's funds; he can bring in an outside equity investor for the development period; he can obtain a second loan, subordinate to the first, in which the lender may get part of the equity in return; or he can use some combination of these three alternatives. These approaches have numerous variations, all of them compensating investors according to the risk associated with their contributions to equity.

Amazon's 1.8 million-square-foot headquarters complex in Seattle was a catalyst for revitalizing an urban neighborhood. With two preserved historic structures and nine new LEED Gold–certified buildings, the project houses 10,000 workers in a transit-accessible, urban location and has brought economic benefit to the city and local businesses.

Chapters 10 and 11 explained the concepts and tools relating to the basic development period. This chapter summarizes them again to shine a sharp light on how the various financing options must integrate multiple stakeholders' concerns during stage four.

In structuring the financing, the developer can demonstrate great creativity as the number of possible deal structures is almost limitless. Whatever the deal, however, the components need to be arranged in stage four and formally executed in stage five.

Finding a Permanent Lender and Securing a Loan Commitment

Using the material developed during the feasibility study, the developer tries to attract the most suitable long-term lender. Beyond the project characteristics, the developer (or his mortgage broker) should understand the specific needs and expertise of potential long-term lenders. Which lender wants to expand in a particular property type or geography? Which lender has specific expertise in a particular property type that may increase his willingness to do a project? The analysis includes not just the institution, but also the individuals in the institution who will handle the loan. Are they satisfied with the participants that the developer plans to bring to the team? What may seem to be the right institution can in fact be a bad choice if the individuals who will manage the loan are not right for the situation.

Beyond the dollar amount, the terms of the permanent loan takeout are major concerns and will be extremely important in obtaining the construction loan. When negotiating both the construction loan and the equity financing, the developer's position is strengthened or weakened by any permanent loan commitment. Therefore, paying a slightly higher rate may be a smart move if it means getting the right kind of permanent loan commitment from the right permanent lender—one that maximizes the usefulness of the takeout commitment in assembling the team. For example, as part of the takeout commitment, construction lenders sometimes require a permanent lender to preapprove certain closing conditions in the permanent loan commitment.

Onerous permanent lender conditions in the takeout agreement make construction lenders less willing to lend.

Once a lender decides to make a loan on a project, it either issues a *commitment letter* or accepts the developer's application for financing. Both the letter and the application typically include the loan amount, interest rate, term of the loan, and a period of time within which the loan must be closed, i.e., funded by the lender. In the context of the takeout loan, both documents provide that the lender will make the described loan within a certain period, say, 24 to 36 months, upon the satisfaction of certain terms and conditions. Such conditions usually include completion of the project in accordance with approved plans and specifications, satisfaction of any leasing requirements, acceptable title insurance, and an ALTA (American Land Title Association) survey.

Finding a Construction Lender and Securing a Loan Commitment

As noted previously, construction lenders traditionally made development loans conditioned on the developer obtaining a commitment from a permanent lender. The permanent lender then provides assurance to the construction lender that, if the project is built on time, on budget, and consistent with approved construction drawings, the construction lender's loan will be paid off ("taken out") at a certain time. With a permanent loan commitment in hand, the construction lender does not have to assume market or other long-term risk.

Depending on the state of the market, some construction lenders may not require permanent commitments as a condition of loan approval. Even without the express requirement, however, construction lenders typically expect that they will be paid off in a short time. Without a permanent loan commitment, a developer can expect to be required to provide more equity, more personal guarantees, and more documentation of ongoing marketing efforts during construction.

As described in chapters 10 and 11, short-term loans tend to come from institutions that hold

shorter-term liabilities in their portfolios. Balancing the maturities of assets and liabilities reduces the institution's risk. For that reason, commercial banks are the leading construction lenders. With thousands of such banks located across the country, the institutions (or their branch operations) are likely to be located near a given project; accordingly, they can monitor construction and better control risk through their draw procedures. Construction lenders that are not located near a project often engage local construction disbursement agents to supervise the project for them.

Construction lenders take on execution risk, whereas long-term lenders are more exposed to market risk. Consequently, construction lenders examine the experience and reputation of the developer, the architect, and the general contractor, as well as the complexity of the project and any site risks specific to the project. The more complex the project, the more experience the construction lender will require on the development team.

A single lender may not want to assume the risk inherent in a large project. For such projects, it is not unusual for a number of lenders to collectively provide construction financing. The structures for such an arrangement range from a traditional loan participation arrangement in which a lead lender commits to making the loan and seeks out loan participants who have no direct relationship with the developer, to an agency lending arrangement in which each lender executes its own commitment with the developer and one of the lenders acts as an agent on behalf of all the lenders in dealing with the developer. The latter option is riskier for the developer, as no lender agrees to fund any shortfall that may arise as a result of another lender's failure to fund its share of the loan.

The interest rate on a construction loan typically varies and is most often tied to an index, generally the lender's *prime rate* or LIBOR (London Interbank Offered Rate). The lender typically charges a spread over the index, so that the rate the developer pays moves up and down with "market" short-term rates. Because the budgeted interest in the construction loan may not be large enough to accommodate unanticipated increases in market interest rates, developers may arrange for an interest rate hedge. Typically the hedge is purchased from a financial institution and stipulates that the institution will pay interest over a specified rate so that the developer's maximum rate exposure is limited. The hedge thus reduces risk, but it also increases costs.

During periods of low interest rates, lenders often require a minimum (or "floor") interest rate, ranging from 4 percent to 6 percent. Borrowers, mindful of the potential for rapid escalation of the rate, often bargain for a maximum (or "ceiling") rate as well.

The conditions under which the developer may draw down the construction loan can be the subject of a great deal of negotiation. Typically, the developer and construction lender agree on a line-item budget for the project (usually based on the feasibility study), with draws advanced against that budget. Many lenders do not permit draws against a particular line item if, in the opinion of the lender, the draws will leave insufficient funds in the line item to complete that portion of the project. Some lenders permit the developer to use a portion of the contingency line item in the budget to cover a shortfall or to move savings on other line items into a line item that is over budget. If neither of these devices is available, the loan may become "out of balance," meaning sufficient funds will not be available to complete the project. In this circumstance, the lender may then require the developer to deposit sufficient funds with the lender to bring the loan into balance; the lender then disburses the developer's funds first. Developers can generally persuade a lender to agree, however, that demonstrable cost savings on a particular line item can be added to the "contingency" line item.

As the "quarterback" of the development process, the developer needs to negotiate terms from the construction lender in stage four that will enable the team to react to unexpected conditions during stage six. Unfortunately, this flexibility usually comes at an upfront cost.

The developer of 1450 Brickell, in Miami, Florida, pursued a strategy of targeting small and medium-sized tenants. As a result, the 576,000 square feet of office space is leased to 67 tenants. The structure features impact-resistant glass throughout, making it able to withstand hurricane winds of 300 miles per hour.

Using Mezzanine Financing to Complete the Financing Package

In the past, developers have used a variety of equity structures (partnerships, syndications, private placements, and others) to raise the money to cover any shortfall in the financing needed to complete the development. In recent years, such financing has been referred to as *mezzanine financing*.

Originally, mezzanine financing typically was used for speculative developments for which the goal was to sell the project in three to five years. Now, it is used in circumstances in which a developer wants to get his equity investment out earlier or to obtain financing in lieu of equity.

Basically, the mezzanine lender makes a loan to the developer or the equity holders in an amount ranging from 50 percent to as much as 100 percent of the shortfall between the construction lender's (or permanent lender's) loan and the equity investment. For example, assume that the total costs for a particular development are $10 million and that the developer can obtain $7.5 million in construction financing. As an alternative to raising the $2.5 million shortfall in equity investment or investing the $2.5 million himself, a developer might consider obtaining mezzanine financing for a substantial portion of the shortfall, say $1.5 million. The developer thereby limits the needed equity investment to $1 million and, through the leverage, improves the residual equity's tax position. For this financing to work, the project should generate sufficient cash flow to cover the higher debt service of the permanent and mezzanine debt and/or produce a value that allows a large enough permanent loan to "take out" both the construction loan and the mezzanine loan.

Mezzanine lending is inherently riskier than conventional lending. The mezzanine lender usually requires the loan to be secured by a subordinated deed of trust. More often than not, however, the "senior lender" (the construction lender or the permanent lender) does not permit a junior encumbrance, and the mezzanine lender is forced to secure the loan with a pledge of the equity in the development. In either situation, the mezzanine lender's security is less secure than the first-priority lien granted to the conventional lender.

The inherent risk underlying mezzanine financing translates into higher borrowing costs, which come in the form of greater loan fees and higher interest rates than conventional development loans. In addition, mezzanine lenders may require a share of the profits. So-called "participation interests" usually amount to both a share of the project's cash flow after other financing until the project is sold or the mezzanine loan is repaid, and a percentage of the profits from the sale.[2]

If the loan becomes out of balance, who steps in with the needed cash (equity)? The developer, or the mezzanine lender? This is the kind of detail that is negotiated in stage four.

Entitlements and Financing

Entitlements are often complex, especially if the project is vulnerable to political controversy or if the site has environmental features that will require permits from federal, state, regional, or local agencies. Financing sources are keenly aware of the related risks and look to the developer to provide assurances that the risks are manageable. In the case of discretionary entitlements, developers must continue discussions with governmental entities throughout the early stages of development. In stage four, a developer needs to conclude as much as possible on the entitlement front so as to be able to wrap up financing and other contracts that depend on the entitlements.

A developer's right to proceed with development without concern about the rules changing is known as a *vested right*. Until a developer has obtained a vested right, the possibility exists that the local rules could change and preclude the developer from proceeding as planned. The point at which a developer achieves a vested right to develop varies from state to state. In some states, merely pulling a building permit vests a developer's right to proceed with the development for a period equal to at least the life of the permit.

In Massachusetts, for example, a developer's interests are vested if a building permit has been issued and construction starts within six months. Also in Massachusetts, if a plat map for a new subdivision is filed before a rezoning hearing is held, zoning in that area is frozen for a period of years. Down zoning is therefore not an immediate risk once a plat map is filed. In other states—California, for example—no right is vested to complete construction until a building permit has been obtained and until substantial work has been undertaken and liabilities incurred in good-faith reliance on that building permit. A grading permit therefore would not satisfy the California standard for vested rights.

As noted in chapters 7 and 8, some states allow cities and counties to enter into formal development agreements that confirm these vested rights. They address the fees, exactions, and dedications for which the project will be responsible. Under such an agreement, a developer is assured of the right to proceed with the development of the project during the term of the development agreement. She is assured that the project may be developed in accordance with the rules, regulations, and official policies of the municipality that were in effect on the date on which the development agreement was entered into. Where development agreements are available, some financing sources may require such agreements as a condition of closing.

The Common Thread in All Forms of Financing

The developer's role in stage four is to negotiate financing terms that fit with both the planned

logistics of the construction process (stage six) and the longer-term operations strategy (stage eight). The developer should ensure that financing options are explored, whether by a member of the development team or by a third party retained to obtain the financing.

Whoever is seeking the financing should try to stand in the lender's shoes. Only when a developer anticipates all the ways the lender may be compensated (interest rates, points, participation, and so on) and appreciates any nonmonetary objectives the lender may have (civic duty and compliance with new regulations, among others) can he obtain the lowest overall cost of financing with the fewest restrictions. For example, most lending institutions picture themselves as experts in certain areas or pursue leadership in certain fields. When a project fits a lender's self-image, the lender tends to stretch a little to get the business. Likewise, individual loan officers have self-images, and the smart borrower fits

---

CASE STUDY   Shortbread Lofts

Larry Short stressed the need to have a lawyer with general contracting experience in order to successfully complete the contract negotiations. At stage four, he chose to bond the general contractor for the Shortbread Lofts project, realizing that he had unusual exposure because of the nature of the target market: Students must move in at a certain time in the fall (a classic seasonal rental issue). Still, the penalty in the construction contract for time delays was not sufficient to protect the developer fully. Consequently, Short focused on anything that could delay construction.

Following the decision not to presell the project, the bank loan negotiation became the critical item. Short used the CBRE package but agreed not to draw any development fee. He made the choice to take interest rate risk, negotiating an extended construction loan (maturing in December 2015). The rate on the construction loan was very attractive. Nonetheless, waiting to secure long-term financing increases the developer's risk. Given the low LTV ratio and extensive preleasing (the project was fully leased in November 2013 for occupancy in August 2014), the lender was not significantly exposed. Both the restaurant-owner brothers and Short personally guaranteed the loan. At this stage, Short was still listening to long-term loan proposals from BB&T, his construction lender.

The site had no natural staging area for construction. However, Short knew that the owner of the adjacent property had a problem with his now-vacant land: it had a sewer down the middle and was not developable in that condition. Short arranged with the adjacent owner to reroute the sewer to an unused side of the Shortbread Lofts property in return for allowing Short to use the adjacent property as a staging area during development.

Chapel Hill thinks of itself as a very progressive town; it is also a town where relationships are important. Short's strategy exemplified the importance of relationship building throughout the development process. He ingratiated himself with town officials, agreeing to host a local job fair for low-income workers. Although the fair began well, few of the aspirants who attended were employable. Another community endeavor proved much more successful. Short worked with a local muralist and fifth-grade class from a low-income neighborhood school to design the art contribution that is required as part of development projects by town ordinances. The resulting mural is installed in a local school. Short is very pleased with the outcome, as is the town. Well-known problems at other major developments in Chapel Hill (140 West and Greenbridge) have affected the approval process by offering fuel for NIMBYism in town, but they had no direct spillover to Shortbread Lofts in part because of Short's efforts to build relationships.

Continued on page 301

the financing to the individual loan officer as well as to the institution.

WORKING ENVIRONMENTAL REVIEWS INTO CONTRACT NEGOTIATIONS

Awareness of the environment increased dramatically in the 1970s as Congress took an active role in protecting the nation's natural resources through the *Clean Water Act*, the Endangered Species Act, the *Clean Air Act*, and other legislation. The administration of these laws has become more complex in recent years. Developers today realize that they must do more than simply ensure that their property does not violate any environmental protection laws.

Several federal and state laws profoundly affect real estate development. Issues relating to two federal laws—*CERCLA*, or the *Superfund* law, and the Clean Water Act—are representative of the types of issues that may arise in the financing process.

Lenders, developers, buyers, and sellers have all been touched by these far-reaching laws.

In stage four, the developer confirms decisions made in preparing the feasibility study. At this point, the contracts negotiated need to conform with environmental regulations; the following sections briefly review some of the key issues.

Hazardous Wastes: Everyone's Concern

Congress enacted CERCLA in 1980 not only to provide funding for at least a portion of the cleanup of the nation's worst toxic waste sites but also to establish powerful legal tools to enable regulatory agencies and, in some cases, private parties adversely affected by contamination to force the responsible party to undertake a cleanup program or to recover costs if the claimant undertakes the cleanup. Under the Superfund law and its amendments, present owners and certain past owners of

LUCA SANTIAGO MORA

A new 54,000-square-foot building for the privately owned Danish Maritime Museum is located in an abandoned dry dock. The site came with many challenges: to preserve views of the adjacent Kronborg Castle, the building was not allowed to protrude above ground level; the museum's space requirements were far larger than the dock's footprint; and laws require all workspaces to have both daylight and views. The solution was to build the museum below ground level, around the dry dock rather than inside it. A series of two-level bridges span the dry dock, serving as public walkways and providing access to the sections of the museum.

land contaminated with hazardous substances can be liable for the entire cost of cleanup, even if the disposal of the material was legal at the time, even if the owner had nothing to do with the disposal, and even if the disposal occurred years before the passage of the Superfund law. "Potentially responsible parties" that can find themselves liable for the cost of remediating contamination include (1) current owners and operators of a property, (2) former owners and operators of a property, (3) people who arranged for the disposal or treatment of hazardous materials at a property, and (4) people who accepted hazardous materials from a property for transport to disposal or treatment facilities. Liability under CERCLA can be joint and several, meaning that an owner of property found to be contaminated can be held responsible for the entire cost of the remediation. Such an owner is thus left on his own to try to recover costs from the culpable parties. CERCLA is discussed in detail in chapter 7.

Most real estate lenders have developed their own environmental standards, which generally require purchasers to conduct environmental site assessments based in part on the standards of the American Society for Testing and Materials (commonly known as the ASTM). Many states have enacted laws intended to require investigation and cleanup of *hazardous waste* sites within their borders. Some states impose penalties if the landowner does not address the requirement for cleanup. Many state laws provide for the imposition of a lien to allow the jurisdiction that conducted the remediation to recapture the public monies spent for the cleanup, thereby avoiding a windfall to the owner (that is, the restoration of market value to a previously contaminated site). A handful of those states have adopted so-called "superlien" laws that give the state claim priority over all other liens. Obviously, lenders do not want their collateral to be subject to such risks. Consequently, properties with such problems are very difficult to finance. Nonetheless, certain companies specialize in buying and cleaning such sites.

The design tradeoffs to maximize market appeal while conforming to regulatory safeguards enumerated in stage three are finalized in stage four.

Financing sources are typically unwilling to move forward without assurance that this has happened. The *EPA* website provides assistance by topic or sector. Planning guides for construction and development of a property can be found at www.epa.gov/laws-regulations. Information about state regulations can be found at the website of the Construction Industry Compliance Assistance Center, http://cica-center.org.

Asbestos

For projects that require partial or complete demolition of existing structures as well as those that require renovations, the presence of asbestos can add considerable time and cost. Depending on the condition of the asbestos in those buildings, owners may be sitting on a time bomb of future remediation. Although asbestos remediation is a manageable issue in most cases, often it poses a considerable challenge during construction. It can cause scheduling issues, particularly if the hazardous waste removal contractor is separate from the general contactor. Schedules need to be coordinated as part of the contracting process in stage four.

Wetlands

As understanding of wetlands expands, so do the number and scope of federal and state laws that protect them. Under Section 404 of the Clean Water Act, as described in chapter 7, developers must secure a permit from the U.S. Army Corps of Engineers before building in certain wetlands and other waters of the United States. Development without a permit can lead to substantial fines and, in some cases, jail time. The permitting process is complex for a number of reasons:

- First is the definition of wetlands. Using the federal definition, land that appears dry may constitute wetlands. For example, federal jurisdiction extends over dry washes in the Southwest, where a two-foot-wide wash that carries water only after a rare rainfall is considered jurisdictional.
- Second is the difficulty of confirming the presence of wetlands. There is no way to

obtain judicial review of a determination by the Corps that wetlands or other waters are present, other than by either seeking a permit or defending against an enforcement action that seeks to punish a landowner for developing wetlands without a permit.

■ Third is the considerable disagreement about the type of activity that is subject to regulation under Section 404. For instance, building in wetlands clearly qualifies as "fill" under the act. Under current court decisions in some areas, however, certain dredging, agriculture, and irrigation projects may not require a Section 404 permit.

■ Fourth, the Corps has drastically limited the type and size of projects eligible for preapproved permits under the Nationwide Permit Program. Developers of projects that are not eligible for preapproved permits must obtain an individual permit through a complicated process subject to environmental review under the National Environmental Policy Act. The Corps permitting program is time-consuming and often involves review by several other federal agencies, including the EPA and the Fish and Wildlife Service, and by state

agencies, including water quality and coastal zone management boards. Given the growing complexity, cost, and duration of permitting, most developers seek to minimize the time required by designing their projects with reduced impacts so as to qualify for the pre-approved permits.

■ Fifth, the Corps usually issues permits on the condition that developers mitigate any adverse impacts on wetlands stemming from their developments. Both the Corps and state regulators generally require developers to compensate for any wetlands lost during development by restoring or creating wetlands nearby. This process is generally referred to as *wetlands mitigation*.

Mitigation, particularly the creation of wetlands, has been controversial. Wetlands are complex, dynamic *ecosystems*, and early attempts to create them yielded mixed results. Environmentalists have argued that artificially created wetlands can scarcely be considered adequate substitutes for natural wetlands; however, a number of successes have occurred as biologists have continued to improve wetland creation and maintenance techniques. The Corps has also gained substantial experience in how to write

UC Davis West Village, a 130-acre mixed-use neighborhood, is the nation's first zero-net-energy planned community. The result of a public/private partnership, the development mixes student apartments and single-family homes with office, retail, parking, and recreational space. The buildings consume 50 percent less energy than the state's maximum requirements and meet all their energy needs with a photovoltaic solar system.

277

and enforce permit conditions that ensure successful mitigation and that provide fallback systems and other provisions to protect the environment if the mitigation is not as successful as expected. Even with these improvements, however, federal permitting for projects involving wetlands or other waters of the United States remains very problematic. And many states have adopted wetlands protection laws that are more stringent than the federal laws.

Like asbestos, wetlands on or near projects create risks for lenders and investors. The feasibility study will have addressed such issues, as their mitigation is essential to obtaining financing. In stage four, attorneys for all parties should be careful to cover their clients for such risks. As always, the developer is the one responsible for ensuring that the language in the different contracts is compatible.

Sustainable Development

Developers understand that environmentally sustainable practices help establish a strong image for a project and, in some cases, save money. In stage four, the developer needs to ensure that what the marketing group is counting on in terms of community and client appeal from green or sustainable features is what the construction team is contracted to build.

Developers should be aware of the many tools and the information available for green and sustainable development. One of the most valuable tools is the voluntary Leadership in Energy and Environmental Design (LEED) rating system developed by the U.S. Green Building Council, which provides guidelines and a recognition system to promote green building and development practices. The LEED Neighborhood Development (LEED ND) program measures developments in terms of their location efficiency, resource efficiency, environmental preservation, and establishment of compact, complete, and connected neighborhoods. Ratings are based on such factors as density, transit access, balance between housing and jobs, share of mixed-income housing, and energy-saving features.

DECISIONS ABOUT DESIGN AND CONTRACTORS

By the time a developer enters stage four, he usually has at least preliminary drawings of the project.

CASE STUDY **Irvine Tech Center at Stage Four**

Wil Smith's contract negotiations were many:

- The development rights acquisition required an ongoing program to obtain as many rights in the market as possible. The justification was straightforward: Smith knew that his land value would increase if it were entitled for residential use and that those entitlements would require more development intensity values (DIVs), the measureable unit of density transfers created for the IBC. The biggest opportunity came through the bankruptcy of a neighboring builder/developer, which enabled Smith to acquire the DIVs that would be needed to obtain city approval of the original development concept.
- The holding period—between the point of acquisition and the start of construction—required the cash flow stream from existing improvements to be managed in such a manner as to optimize income and yet retain the flexibility to initiate development at the appropriate time.
- Flexibility in the development process enabled Smith to acquire the final phase of the project, ITC 3, in 2012.

The ongoing entitlement process with the city of Irvine was based in part on following the vision plan and in part on negotiations that would lead to fitting ITC within that plan. Originally, Smith had anticipated that gaining entitlements for the project would entail a general plan amendment, a zone change, a conditional use permit, a park plan, a tentative tract map, and a development agreement as well as the DEIR. Each of these elements would have required extensive negotiations. Following the city's adoption of the vision plan, ITC required only a master plan, a park plan, and a tentative tract map. The smaller number of requirements reduced many of the negotiations to the interpretation of conditions of approval governing the details of project implementation.

For ITC, the formal commitments were spread over several years: the acquisition of ITC I and II in 2005, the acquisition of ITC III in 2012, and the ongoing acquisition of DIVs. Along the way, the entitlement process began to shape the project and narrow the options for development.

Continued on page 317

In order to obtain bids from contractors, he will need final plans and specifications from the architect. Without such final plans, construction cost estimates will be inexact, increasing the risk for all parties. At some point before the architect draws final plans, a contract should be drafted to establish the formal relationship between the developer and the architect.

It is often useful and necessary to designate the architect as the responsible party for all design matters, as the developer has difficulty closing the permanent loan unless someone has been made professionally responsible for the quality of all work. Thus, the contract with the architect drives related contracts with other design professionals.

Architects' Contract

Most architects prefer to use the most current version of the American Institute of Architects (AIA) standard contract, known as AIA Document B-101™. Like all contracts in stage four, it should be negotiated and executed so that all parties agree to produce an appropriate product, and all risks and responsibilities are clearly defined. Because the standard contract was drafted by AIA, it protects the architect in various ways; therefore, the developer may need to negotiate changes to it. In fact, lenders may require several changes to the contract.

What is omitted from the standard AIA contract is as important as what is included. For example:

- Only some preliminary budgeting (estimating costs) is included in the basic services portion; any other budgeting is charged for in addition to the basic price of the architectural design.
- Two important elements—public hearings and interior layouts—are excluded from the basic contract price. If a developer wants any of these services, he needs to clarify whether he will pay extra for them.
- The architect is given the right to notify the developer of his need for certain additional services. If the developer does not respond promptly, the architect has the right to do the work and bill the developer for those services.

- Insurance of any kind (such as professional errors and omissions insurance, commercial general liability insurance, and worker's compensation insurance) is not included. Developers should specify the proper amount of insurance and the appropriate carrier.
- The architect has the right to make decisions binding on the developer and the contractor regarding disputes between the parties, unless the developer or the general contractor takes specific actions to challenge the architect's decision.

At a minimum, then, the contract should be modified to add such items as responsibility for professional errors and omissions insurance, indemnification, and any expanded scope of services.

Other elements that developers should consider modifying relate to certification of the work done, ownership of the plans, and assignment of the contract. The standard contract does not specify the exact form of certification that the architect must execute regarding the quality of the work—certification that the developer needs when the permanent loan is closed. Thus, the developer should specify the form so that problems do not arise at the loan closing.

The standard contract states that the plans drawn belong to the architect, not to the developer, even though the developer has paid for them. This provision should be changed to give the developer ownership rights, provided that the developer makes payment to the architect in accordance with the contract.

Another provision prohibits the assignment of the contract to any other developer without the architect's consent. This provision should be deleted because it could seriously affect project financing. If the original developer cannot perform, the lender might want another developer to step in and finish the project, to salvage the lender's position. That said, the AIA has spent a great deal of effort developing the standard contract. In stage four, the developer should go to the AIA's website (www.aia.org/contractdocs/forarchitects) and carefully review all

Working with an Architect

WHAT TO EXPECT FROM AN ARCHITECT

- High-quality design that satisfies the owner's program.
- Timely answers to the owner's requests and suggestions.
- Alternative suggestions and schemes during the early phases of the project; an architectural problem never has only one solution. An open mind to requests for modifications of the project when necessary.
- Sensitivity to and understanding of zoning and building codes, environmental issues, and other government restrictions.
- An understanding of construction costs relating to particular types and uses of buildings.
- Ability to interact constructively with government agencies and to understand the positions of groups opposing the project.
- Ability to be a team player, joining and frequently meeting with owners, consultants, and others who contribute to the project.
- Suitable graphic presentations that portray the project in its best light to government agencies and local interest groups.
- Good (not perfect) construction documents that are well coordinated with documentation from other consultants.
- Architectural supervision throughout the construction of the project, with field reports on each site visit; it is easier to respond to a contractor's questions on the job than to make serious corrections later.
- Timely and accurate processing of all paperwork—change orders, bulletins, pay requests, and final certifications as required by lenders (with the wording not in conflict with what an architect is allowed to sign under professional liability insurance).

WHAT NOT TO EXPECT

- Cut-rate fees, free services, or work on "spec"; high quality service with the proper amount of time spent by experienced professional personnel requires proper remuneration; if a large, upfront payment is a problem for the developer, deferred payments should be an option.

- The ability to design anything; special consultants with proper training and experience should be used for traffic, parking, interiors, graphics, landscaping, and so on.
- A guarantee of the contractor's work; architects cannot guarantee work over which they have no control or have not put in place.
- Work on a fixed fee before the program and final scope of the project are determined.
- Changes by the owner without affecting the architect's fee, construction costs, and schedule.
- Detailed, highly accurate cost estimates unless a professional cost estimator is on staff or has been retained to perform such work.

HOW TO SELECT AN ARCHITECT

- An architect should not be hired on the basis of aesthetic competence alone. The most attractive project can be totally unsuccessful in terms of financial performance, profitability, and quality of construction.
- An architect or the key person on staff who will manage the project should be highly experienced in the specific project type.
- An architect should not be hired based on an extensive portfolio of renderings of unbuilt projects.
- You should talk to the owners and/or users of other projects the architect has designed to determine the project's success and the architect's responsiveness throughout the project.
- It is essential that the owner can relate to and respect the individual assigned to the project.
- The owner should make sure the architect's current workload allows for the required attention to the project and its on-schedule completion.

Source: Adapted from Charles Kober, the Kober Group, Santa Ana, California.

---

the enumerated provisions. Although the contract's bias is toward the architect (as would be expected), the coverage is extensive. Hence it is a great review tool in stage four.

Construction Contract

Drafting the design contract typically transitions into drafting the construction contract. Some developers—especially those with a general contracting background—may designate in-house staff as the primary builder of the project. Most developers,

however, rely on outside construction contractors for much of the work. As in all aspects of the development process, many variations are possible, depending on the developer's in-house capabilities. Regardless of these variations, there are several critical items to consider as the construction contract is negotiated.

First, it is important to determine at this stage whether disputes are to be handled by mediation, arbitration, or litigation. Architects often prefer arbitration, although some developers may fare better

Figure 14-1   **Checklist for Construction Contracts**

	OWNER	ARCHITECT	CONTRACTOR
Program Development			
Project requirements, including design objectives, constraints and criteria, space requirements and relationships, flexibility and expandability, special equipment, and systems and site requirements			
Legal description and a certified survey; complete, as required			
Soils engineering; complete, as required			
Materials testing, inspections, and reports; complete, as required			
Legal, accounting (including auditing), and insurance counseling, as required			
Program review			
Financial feasibility			
Planning surveys, site evaluations, environmental studies, or comparative studies of prospective sites			
Verification of existing conditions or facilities			
Construction Cost			
Budget and funds			
Estimate of probable costs			
Detailed estimates of construction cost			
Control of design to meet fixed limit of construction cost			
Design			
Schematic			
Design development			
Consultants: structural, mechanical, electrical, special			
Construction Documents			
Final drawings and specifications			
Bidding information, bid forms, conditions of contract, and form of agreement between owner and contractor			
Filing for government approvals			
On-site maintenance of drawings, specifications, addenda, change orders, shop drawings, product data, and samples			
Bidding			
Obtaining bids or negotiated proposals			
Awarding and preparing contracts			
Documents for alternate, separate, or sequential bids; extra services in connection with bidding, negotiation, or construction before completion of construction documents			
Administration of Construction Contract			
General			
Owner's representative			
Periodic visits to the site			

Figure 14-1 **Checklist for Construction Contracts**

	OWNER	ARCHITECT	CONTRACTOR
Administration of Construction Contract *(continued)*			
General			
Construction methods, techniques, sequences, procedures, safety precautions, and programs			
Contractor's applications for payments			
Certificates for payment			
Document interpretation/artistic effect			
Rejection of work; special inspections or testing			
Shop drawings, product data, and samples			
Submittals			
Review and action			
Change orders			
Preparation			
Approval			
Closeout			
Date of substantial completion			
Date of final completion			
Written warranties			
Certificate for final payment			
Coordination of work of separate contractors or by owner's forces			
Services of construction manager			
As-built drawings			
Schedule			
Design schedule			
Development			
Maintenance			
Construction schedule			
Development			
Maintenance			
Payment			
Basic design services			
Accounting records			
Construction (the work)			
Progress payments			
Final payment			
Evidence of ability to pay			
Secure and pay for necessary approvals, easements, assessments, and changes for construction, use, or occupancy			

Figure 14-1   **Checklist for Construction Contracts**

	OWNER	ARCHITECT	CONTRACTOR
Construction			
General			
Labor, materials, and equipment			
Correlation of local conditions with requirements of the contract documents			
Division of work among subcontractors			
Right to stop work			
Owner's right to carry out work			
Review of contract documents for errors, inconsistencies, or omissions			
Supervision and direction of the work			
Responsibility to owner for errors and omissions in the work			
Obligation to perform the work in accordance with contract documents			
Provide and pay for all labor, materials, equipment, tools, machinery, utilities, transportation, and other facilities and services for the proper execution and completion of the work			
Enforce discipline and good order among those employed on the job			
Warranty for all materials and equipment			
Sales, consumer, and use taxes			
Secure and pay for all permits, fees, licenses, and inspections			
Compliance with all laws, ordinances, regulations, and lawful orders			
Employment of superintendent			
Cutting and patching			
Cleaning up			
Communications			
Payments of all royalties and license fees; defense against suits and claims			
Indemnification; hold harmless agreements			
Award of subcontracts			
Owner's right to perform work and award separate contracts			
Award			
Mutual responsibility			
Cleanup dispute			
Miscellaneous			
Performance bond, labor, and material payment bond			
Tests			
Protection of persons and property			
Insurance			
Contractor's liability insurance			

Figure 14-1   **Checklist for Construction Contracts**

	OWNER	ARCHITECT	CONTRACTOR
Insurance *(continued)*			
Owner's liability insurance			
Property insurance			
Changes in the Work			
Uncovering and Correction of Work			

Source: G. Niles Bolton, architect, Atlanta, Georgia.

using at least the threat of litigation as a negotiating point. It is often beneficial to the developer to use the same dispute resolution procedures in all the contracts.

Second, a provision in the construction contract, which is coordinated with the loan agreement, can make it possible for the developer to withhold a portion of the money due to the contractor for work completed. Known as "retainage," these funds are held until completion to ensure that the work is done properly and the job completed. The developer draws down the amount of money owed on the construction contract from the lender net of the retainage, protecting both the developer and the lender.

Although all terms should be tailored to fit the specific development, developers are generally well advised to guard against the designation of allowances, as opposed to fixed prices, for certain budgeted items in the construction contract. Allowances—such as $20,000 for carpeting rather than a fixed price, for example—can lead to serious problems in stage six. Allowances make it possible to draw a set amount from the construction lender. If costs exceed this amount, serious financial pressures can result, as the developer is responsible for costs in excess of the allowance.

Bidding versus Negotiations: Fixed Price versus Cost Plus

The developer and general contractor can reach agreement on a construction contract in several ways. The two ends of the spectrum are the bid contract and the negotiated contract. In a *bid contract*, the developer puts out plans and specifications to

general contractors who are considered technically and financially qualified and asks them to offer a set price or a base price plus a fixed rate for certain items whose exact specifications will be known only as the leasing is completed, such as the number of electrical outlets. In a *negotiated contract*, the developer negotiates with one general contractor, agreeing that the general contractor will perform the work and bill the developer for a fixed price or cost plus a certain profit margin.

Developers prefer a fixed-price contract, while contractors prefer a cost-plus agreement without a guaranteed maximum price. Consequently, many projects fall somewhere between the two extremes. It is common for a developer to negotiate with only one contractor and to obtain a "not-to-exceed price" that is based on the contractor's estimate of cost plus a reasonable profit margin. If the cost of the work plus the reasonable profit margin comes in below the not-to-exceed price, then the developer and contractor may share any savings.

Most developments involve many unknowns, even after completion of the formal feasibility study and construction drawings. Often, marketing feedback received during construction requires the introduction of change orders. Thus, the developer is to some extent always exposed to renegotiation, no matter how tightly the original construction contract is drawn.

On jobs that tend to require few change orders and where public scrutiny is more intense, bidding is more common. Projects involving the federal, state, or local government, where the plans are set firmly in advance and no formal marketing occurs, are usually bid. The bid process satisfies the public's need to know that the price is fair. Formulating a bid requires the general contractor to spend considerable time motivating subcontractors to submit their bids, consolidating the bids, and submitting the complete bid package to the developer.

When contractors have some clout, such as when they have plenty of other work, they may even refuse to bid on smaller jobs. At other times, they may bid high on the theory that they do not need the work but will obviously benefit if they are awarded the contract at the high price. In such situations, developers who have established long-term relationships with quality contractors might find it preferable to negotiate directly with one contractor.

Typically, the developer and the general contractor sign one contract, and the general contractor and the subcontractors sign another set of contracts. The developer negotiating a contract with the general contractor may have concerns about the quality of the subcontractors. Depending on the job's complexity, certain subcontractors may play critical roles in construction. In such situations, the developer may specify in the bid package or during negotiations for a cost-plus contract that particular subcontractors be used and/or specific trade contractors be bonded.

The developer can also negotiate directly with key subcontractors with whom she has good relationships. In such situations, the developer might negotiate a price with the subcontractors and then ask various general contractors for a bid, requiring a particular subcontracted job to be performed by a specified subcontractor. The general contractor is thus relieved of the difficulty of finding a subcontractor to perform the particular job. The general contractor will be willing to submit a bid only if he respects the particular subcontractors' work. As with many aspects of the process, no hard and fast rules exist, and so developers devise processes that best serve their needs.

Fast-Track Construction

During periods when interest rates are inordinately high or when the project must be completed rapidly to satisfy a tenant who is willing to pay for speed, a developer may find it beneficial to engage in *fast-track construction*. The idea is to have as many steps as possible underway at the same time. One possibility is to start excavation as soon as the architect has completed the general layout and to start building the structure before the interior design has been completed. Fast-track construction involves the developer in negotiating a cost-plus contract. When it works, fast-track construction can help the developer beat competitors to the marketplace and reduce interest costs. When coordination of activities is weak, however, the results can be disastrous. Another problem with fast-track projects is the need to determine how to adjust the contract price to reflect the final "for construction" plans and specifications. The contractor's leverage increases greatly if work begins before the contractor and developer agree on the final price.

A classic illustration of how fast-track construction can get out of control concerns a retail development south of Mexico City. Because interest rates are periodically high in Mexico, fast-track construction has not been uncommon there; however, the volcanic subsurface soils in some areas can pose serious problems for construction. In this development, with the project half finished, the architect realized that it would be difficult to complete the structure according to the original plans and within the original budget. The foundation work specified by the architect had been done before all the building plans were completed, yet the foundation now built would not support the optimal structure. The architect was not sure how best to remedy the problem. Though the developer could have brought a lawsuit against the architect, lawsuits are usually a poor recourse for problems encountered under the pressure of constructing a building on time. The high interest costs of the financing made it critical to accelerate the opening. Thus, the developer had to knock out the portion of the foundation that did not fit the new plan (which he decided to complete with a second architect). The additional cost placed considerable stress on the construction financing.

Bonding

Bonding is a guarantee of completion and/or payment. The city might require developers to provide a bond to prove that they have the capacity to complete the infrastructure. The developer might ask the contracting firm to provide a bond to prove that the general contractor has the wherewithal to complete the job. Bonds enable the developer or general contractor to ask a surety company to stand behind a nonperforming firm in a lawsuit. When issuing a bond, a *surety company* examines the credibility of the individuals or institutions to be bonded. The assessment covers both their capacity to do the work and their financial standing. Bonds are the most common form of guarantee, although alternatives such as a letter of credit or escrowed assets can be used to accomplish the same purpose.

During stage four, a developer might want the general contractor to be bonded if the developer fears that the contractor might not be able to perform or cannot muster the financial resources to pay a judgment in the event of a lawsuit. Federal, state, and local government contracts often require the general contractor to be bonded. Often government agencies do not have the personnel to monitor construction yet want to ensure that taxpayers' dollars will not be lost.

Bonding entails several considerations. Payment bonds and completion bonds (also called performance bonds), for example, differ markedly. A payment bond ensures that the surety (insuring company) will pay all valid claims for work performed and materials supplied by the contractor. Thus, a payment bond covers any successful claims for mechanic's liens.[3] A completion bond ensures that the project will be completed, notwithstanding the default or bankruptcy of the contractor. It covers whatever it takes to finish the job, regardless of the contractor's claims against the developer. When only a payment bond is in place, if the developer secures a judgment against the general contractor in a lawsuit, the surety on the payment bond is liable for that judgment. In this situation, the surety company can use all the defenses available to the general contractor. If the developer has caused part of the problem, he might not be able to collect on the bond.

Lenders and investors clearly have less risk with a completion bond; unfortunately, completion bonds are considerably more expensive. Bonding thus provides some, albeit not complete, protection. Regardless of the type of bond, most developers believe that when they are forced to call on a bonding agent, they will, even in the best case, lose some money because of the time lost.

Construction Supervision

Another major decision in design and construction is whether construction should be supervised by the architect, an outside engineering firm, or a member of the in-house development team. Whatever the choice, someone representing the developer should regularly inspect the construction work and certify its compliance with design specifications and the construction contracts. Construction lenders are vitally concerned with the quality of this work, because they will be substantiating draws made under the construction loan agreement as construction progresses. Most lenders hire their own inspectors to verify the percentage of completion of the project. Likewise, architects want to be sure their ideas are properly translated into constructed space, and the general contractor wants to get paid. Consequently, provision for construction supervision is part of several of the contracts negotiated in stage four and signed in stage five.

DECISIONS ABOUT MAJOR TENANTS

Since stage one, the developer has had an idea of the primary tenant and/or tenant mix anticipated for the project. In a for-sale project, the developer had some idea of the end customer. That idea was refined in stage two and documented further in stage three. In stage four, the developer should make the final decision about how much space to allocate to major tenants and when to sign them. Applying sensitivity analysis to the pro forma numbers from the feasibility study can help the developer make this decision.

Pacific Station, in downtown Encinitas, California, is a mixed-use development anchored by a Whole Foods grocery store. The project also includes a restaurant, several small shops, 47 residential condominiums, 10,000 square feet of office space, and underground parking on a 1.4-acre site.

Large tenants know their power and usually drive a hard bargain. The earlier in the development process that they sign, the greater their power. Thus, the greater the number of major space users (particularly those with prominent names or well-recognized creditworthiness) that the developer signs early, the less the net rent (rent after consideration of concessions). Still, large tenants draw other tenants, especially in retail projects. Signing the anchors is usually the key to drawing smaller tenants and convincing lenders of the project's long-term viability. From the developer's standpoint, the more space that major tenants prelease, the lower the expected average rent per square foot upon completion—but also the lower the risk of NOI falling below expectations.

In regional malls, it is not uncommon for developers to nearly give away space to the top anchor tenants and earn most their return from smaller tenants. This practice capitalizes on the advertising and name recognition of the major tenants that draw customers to the mall and thus provide the smaller tenants' traffic. The critical decision is the percentage of space to allocate to major tenants. On the one hand, it is usually safer to reserve more space for major tenants. On the other hand, it is more lucrative to recruit a large share of smaller tenants

if they "stay and pay." The "right anchor" changes rather quickly in retailing and depends on the type of center and its location as well. Nordstrom, the high-end department store, has been a strong draw for certain types of large shopping malls; in the case of a neighborhood center, a Whole Foods Market has been particularly attractive.

In addition to deciding what proportion of space to allocate to major tenants (and all gradations between major and minor tenants), developers need to decide when to sign tenants. (Lenders' preleasing requirements often reduce the developer's flexibility in this regard.) Tenants signed early in the process commit to something they cannot see as well as to a possibly uncertain future opening date. To induce tenants to make an early commitment, developers may offer one or more concessions, perhaps a rent concession or a choice location.

After making decisions about the advance signing of tenants and the number of name tenants, the developer specifies the general conditions desired in other leases. What is involved is not just rent per square foot, which varies with location, the amount of space required, and other considerations. The developer also decides who pays what portion of which operating costs, how large tenant improvement allowances should be, and who provides what services. For example, who pays for carpeting and other interior features? If the developer pays, the rent is typically set higher to reimburse her for the additional costs incurred. Often developers give tenants a certain improvement allowance; tenants then pay whatever additional amount is necessary for upgraded fixtures beyond the amount specified in the lease. From a lender's perspective, tenant allowances are reasonable because money spent on permanent interior improvements creates additional value and collateral for the first lien on the project. Given that the developer typically negotiates the loan first, it is often easier to include in those negotiations a certain tenant allowance and then pass it along to tenants. The alternative is for tenants to borrow the necessary funds. Smaller tenants frequently find it difficult to finance improvements because their lenders cannot consider the fixed improvements as collateral.

Ongoing operating guidelines are also important. What services will the landlord provide? How often will the bathrooms be cleaned? How fast will the elevators travel? What kind of security will be provided? In many projects, particularly shopping centers, tenants also have obligations. What are the minimum hours and days of operation? How much cooperation is necessary for joint promotions? All these items are negotiated before the execution of leases to ensure that the total marketing effort for the project matches the expectations reflected in the other contracts being negotiated. Although the landlord would like higher rents with more expenses passed on to tenants and fewer allowances, the market may not tolerate such terms. Furthermore, although the landlord may hope to pass escalations in operating expenses through to tenants, tenants hope for just the opposite.

At this point, the developer should also decide whether leasing is to be handled by in-house staff or outside brokers. For some types of projects and some locations, it is preferable to use outside leasing agents, at least in part. In other cases, such as leasing (or sale) of retirement housing, the product may be so unusual and operations so complex that the developer often would do well to have the needed talent on staff, where he can monitor work more closely.

The developer is accountable for all these decisions and for ensuring that the corresponding documents are properly drafted. If the developer concludes that the numbers in the feasibility study cannot be met, stage four is a good time to abandon the project.

STAGE FIVE: COMMITMENT—SIGNING CONTRACTS AND INITIATING CONSTRUCTION

Several of the contracts negotiated during stage four are contingent on other contracts. It is common for the permanent lender to be unwilling to commit until certain major tenants have signed lease agreements. The construction lender's agreement is often contingent on a permanent loan takeout. The developer does not want to commit to a contractor until he has the funds available to pay for construction, and major tenants do not want to sign a contract until they are sure the developer has sufficient money and staff to complete the project.

Hence, many of the parties examine contracts in which they are not direct participants but that are necessary for them to realize their own objectives. It is often necessary to execute different contracts simultaneously. Regardless of whether the contracts are executed sequentially or simultaneously, negotiations on most of the contracts are fairly complete before other contracts are signed.

In stage five, the contracts are executed. If outside investors are involved, agreements documenting the formation of partnerships or other relationships typically are signed and filed with governmental jurisdictions at this stage. To complete the financial arrangements, the permanent loan commitment is signed and the fee paid; similarly, the construction loan agreement is signed and that origination fee paid. The developer signs the contract with the general contractor, and the general contractor signs a series of contracts with the subcontractors.

The local government is also involved. If possible, permits were obtained in stage three or at least early in stage four, but negotiations in stage four often cause changes that require renegotiation with the local government. For larger projects (and increasingly for smaller projects), local governments require the inclusion of impact fees or major off-site improvements before approving a development. These agreements are also finalized in stage four and signed in stage five.

The preleased space requires a formally executed lease, with memoranda of some (usually major) leases recorded. If an outside leasing agent or sales agent is used, a listing agreement or at least a memorandum of understanding may be necessary. Such a memorandum describes the type of space to be leased or sold and the conditions under which the transaction is to occur.

To close the construction loan, the developer closes on the option to buy the land or pays off any land loan if the land has already been purchased. This step is necessary to ensure that the construction lender's loan will be a first lien on the property.

On the administrative side, insurance for the construction period—liability, fire, and extended coverage—is put in force. An update of title insurance may be needed.

At this time, the developer switches to a more formal accounting system. Up to this point, he has probably simply aggregated all the costs associated with the project, but now a formal budget and cash controls are necessary.

The budget comes from the feasibility analysis (as amended by the negotiations in stage four). When it receives the construction lender's blessing, it becomes part of the procedure for drawing down funds as construction proceeds. It is also the basis of the contract with the general contractor.

Most important, the developer should now institute some type of control mechanism for the physical development, either by directing the architect to perform a certain amount of supervision or by employing an on-site construction manager. The general contractor also uses some type of formal control process. Common methods are the program

evaluation and review technique (PERT) and the critical path method (CPM).

SUMMARY

Developers use the feasibility study done in stage three as a management tool during stages four and five. Once the project is deemed feasible, the development team can move toward formalizing all the relationships necessary to implement the plan. During stage four, detailed relationships are negotiated, possibly leading to some changes in the plan. In stage five, the contracts negotiated in stage four are executed. Developers should be particularly careful to ensure that (1) the overall project remains feasible after all the contracts are negotiated; and (2) none of the participants has lost level two feasibility through the contract negotiations. By this point, developers have accumulated a significant amount of uncovered overhead. Nonetheless, failure to stop when the signals indicate stopping in stages four and five can lead to worse financial results in stages six, seven, and eight.

TERMS

- Bonding
- CERCLA
- Clean Air Act
- Clean Water Act
- Commitment letter
- Construction loan
- Ecosystems
- EPA
- Fast-track construction
- Hazardous waste
- Mezzanine financing
- Permanent loan
- Prime rate
- Superfund
- Surety company
- Takeout
- Vested right
- Wetlands mitigation

REVIEW QUESTIONS

14.1 Broadly describe how contracts help control risk.

14.2 What are some financing options for developers who do not have permanent financing committed before construction begins?

14.3 What is the difference between the risks taken by a construction lender and those taken by a permanent lender?

14.4 What is mezzanine financing, and why is it usually considered expensive money?

14.5 What are some types of equity investment vehicles?

14.6 Describe the contract that a developer signs with an architect and some of the issues that should be negotiated.

14.7 What are two primary ways in which a developer hires a general contractor?

14.8 How do allowance items in a construction contract allocate risk?

14.9 What occurs in stage five? Why does stage five depend so heavily on decisions made in stage four?

NOTES

1   Chester Karrass, *The Negotiating Game* (New York: Thomas Cromwell Company, 1970), p. 37.

2   Readers should use the material in this chapter and the financial logic developed in chapters 7 through 9 as bases for exploring professional real estate journals (such as *Real Estate Review*, *Real Estate Finance*, *Real Estate Finance Journal*, and *National Real Estate Investor*) for new ideas that can be modified to fit a proposed development.

3   A mechanic's lien on property comes about when a subcontractor claims to have been unpaid. Lenders find such liens troublesome because they often take effect as of the first day that the subcontractor furnished labor but appear in the title (the legal recorded history of ownership) only when filed. To avoid such potential clouds on a title, some lenders use title companies as disbursing agents, particularly in states that have especially strong statutes covering mechanic's liens.

Chapter 15

Stage Six: Construction

During the construction phase, managing time becomes even more crucial. The developer is more exposed to multiple uncertainties, most of them negative and potentially expensive. Unlike earlier stages of development, the developer is now fully committed to the project—with cash, guarantees, and human resources. Once the general contract has been executed and construction begins, it is not easy to stop or make major modifications without incurring significant financial consequences. Even if developers have arranged nonrecourse financing and are receiving substantial early development fees, their reputations—and usually a lot more—are on the line.

Once the agreements are signed and construction begins, the developer's focus shifts toward project management. The crucial items to be controlled are time, quality, and budget. It is the developer's responsibility to ensure that all players perform their jobs on time, that they deliver the quality of work specified in the contracts, and that all soft costs such as ongoing marketing are continuously monitored. The contracts negotiated in stage four and signed in stage five have created binding obligations. However, even with good planning and congruent binding obligations, the unexpected will happen, and the developer will need to respond. The feasibility study remains the key management tool, enabling the developer to quickly evaluate potential reactions to changing market conditions. This chapter discusses

- The continuing and now much more intense interaction among major players;
- Building the structure;
- Drawing down the construction loan;
- Leasing and building out the tenant space;
- Landscaping and exterior construction;
- Problems that might arise during construction;
- Completion and formal opening; and
- Risk control techniques during these stages.

Chapter 16 continues the examination of stages six and seven, but with a focus on the marketing activities that run in parallel with the physical construction.

STARTING CONSTRUCTION

In stage six, the developer (along with the other players now formally committed to the project) takes the major financial leap and begins construction.

Making life exciting is the high degree of uncertainty that necessarily remains part of the process in even the most exhaustively planned and fully contracted developments. Unknowns abound—from unexpected subsoil conditions to labor unrest. Markets can change rapidly. Even the most trusted partner can fail to perform as the result of an accident, major health issues, or divorce. The developer is ultimately responsible for overcoming whatever problems arise.

The Major Players during Construction

By carefully selecting a team of appropriately experienced professionals and by establishing formal and formally coordinated relationships during stages four and five, the developer is better able to manage the working relationship among the design, construction, marketing, financial, operations, and public sector players during stage six. Coordinating the players throughout the construction process is especially important in complex multiphase and mixed-use developments, which often involve multiple designers and builders, many users, and several opportunities for the general public to express its opinion and have an impact on the process. The developer—subject to the approval rights of lenders, investors, and tenants—is the one responsible for making the final decisions when tough judgments are needed.

During construction, several of the primary players are responsible for coordination and collaboration within their functions. For example, the architect will most likely work with her own team of design professionals, which could include a structural engineer, a mechanical engineer, a lighting designer, an acoustical consultant, an interior design professional, and others. The *general contractor* will coordinate a team of building professionals (which could involve negotiations with labor unions), materials suppliers, equipment rental companies, and insurers. Each team also works with public sector professionals—municipal inspectors, health inspectors, life safety inspectors—who have an interest in the development.

Developers can provide on-site management in several ways. In some instances, the architect who designed the project examines the work at various stages and certifies that it has been performed according to plans and specifications. But inspection services are not the same as project management. Thus the developer usually has on staff a *project manager*. This person is typically someone with an architectural, engineering, or construction background who is regularly on site and, among other things, monitors the general contractor's performance throughout the process. On larger projects, he is on site full time and is responsible for dealing with the general contractor's team, the design team, and the array of public sector officials involved. As problems occur, somebody should be available to make decisions quickly. Either the developer or some member of the staff should be there to work with the general contractor.

Project Manager

An effective project manager should be able to maintain a sense of cooperation and mutual achievement among the members of the development team as the inevitable problems and conflicts are resolved. Here is an example of how those responsibilities may be discharged: The contractor reports to the project manager, who is responsible for maintaining the project's schedule and on-site decisions that lie within his delegated authority. He ensures that all parties are kept current on relevant issues, including attainment of critical milestones, material deliveries, and work completion commensurate with the contractor's invoices. He has operating responsibility for the project budget and maintains communication with the developer's finance department.

Construction lenders are naturally interested in the arrangements for supervision and oversight of project construction. They require periodic sign-offs, usually once a month, by the architect or the project manager when the contractor asks for money and the developer requisitions a draw on the construction loan. Construction lenders (and occasionally institutional partners and permanent lenders) also inspect the construction work, but their presence

Harper Court is a mixed-use project located on a 3.18-acre site in the Hyde Park neighborhood of Chicago. It was initiated by the city of Chicago and the University of Chicago, with the objective of revitalizing a strategic commercial location. The project includes office and retail space, a hotel, and underground and structured parking. The project was 82 percent preleased when construction began.

reinforces rather than replaces the more technical reviews.

Marketing Manager

Marketing continues and often accelerates during stage six. Even when all the space is preleased or the building has a single tenant, marketing is an ongoing activity, as tenant buildout must meet the client's contractual expectations. Simultaneously with the initiation of construction, the marketing strategy is implemented in full force. As detailed in the next chapter, this usually involves advertising, coordination of the sales force (which is responsible for meeting with prospects and selling or leasing space), and planning for site visits by prospects.

Among the responsibilities of sales and leasing managers is providing feedback to the rest of the development team that they have gathered by interacting with potential end users. As space is leased or sold, it often becomes clear that certain aspects of the product fare better in the marketplace than others. Ideally, the original overall design offers enough flexibility that interior configurations, color schemes, and other features can be changed during the development process to suit the market as tenants' preferences are expressed.

Financial Officer

The development team's financial officer manages the project's budget, ensuring timely payment of bills and preparing loan draws. He also manages the relationships with the construction lender, the permanent lender, and any outside investors. At the outset of the project, the financial officer will have ensured that the chart of accounts and accounting system of the general contractor are compatible with those of the developer and the lender. The project manager should ensure that the invoices properly represent the on-site work in place and are reported so as to suit the financial officer's needs.

Financial officers should also make sure that the insurance coverage is exactly what is required and that the *marketing manager* stays within budget. Whenever feedback from the marketing staff or the architect suggests changes, an estimate of the cost of the suggested alternative is made. The financial officer then determines whether the increment in value of the change justifies the additional cost and whether the lender and/or the equity investor can be convinced to increase their financial commitment to the project to cover any additional costs.

Property Manager

The property manager, who—ideally—participated during the design stages, should also be involved during construction. As the marketing representative suggests changes and the *construction manager* responds with alternatives, the property manager should ensure that the proposed changes do not compromise the building's long-term manageability. When financing becomes tight, short-term decisions to solve financing problems—often referred to as "value engineering"—can cause long-term trouble (see chapter 17).

The future property manager, or some other member of the development team, should be aware of the developer's relations with the various city regulatory bodies during construction. The orchestration of physical inspections by regulatory agencies as work proceeds (usually coordinated by the general contractor and the project manager) is only one aspect of managing government partners. Most development projects have several more points of contact—from shared policing of the construction site to the coordination of streetscape and city-imposed use restrictions.

Building the Structure

As noted earlier, the general contractor typically contracts with a variety of subcontractors to accomplish the physical work, buy materials, and provide the needed equipment. These efforts involve installing the building's major systems, including the electrical, plumbing, and HVAC systems. Subcontractors are also typically engaged for excavation, foundation and concrete work, framing, drywall, roofing, trim, painting, and other trades. Some developers carry out several or even all of these functions with in-house staff. Either way, coordination during stage six remains a constant challenge.

Subcontractors vary dramatically in size and sophistication. Some subcontractors for mechanical systems are large regional or even national firms with sophisticated management procedures and accounting controls. By contrast, a masonry subcontractor or the painter could be one man and his nephew with a few tools in the back of a pickup truck. The general contractor should choose the appropriate subcontractor for the job at hand, remembering that it is expensive to hire someone more skilled than necessary and imprudent as well as dangerous to hire someone less skilled than necessary. In high-rise construction, the structural components are more difficult and the systems more complex, requiring a more skilled and credentialed team than a low-rise project. The appropriate subcontractor should possess the time and resources to do the job when needed and be likely to remain financially solvent throughout the construction period.

Ideally, the subcontractors have earned the general contractor's trust based on reputation, past relations, and the possibility of future business. Depending on the relationship between the developer and the general contractor, the developer's in-house construction expertise, and the needs of the project, a developer may hire individual subcontractors directly, for a number of reasons: to secure a particularly skilled worker, to lock in a price, or to secure a slot in a busy subcontractor's schedule. Regardless, the developer is ultimately responsible and needs to know how the general contractor is handling the tradeoff between quality and cost in selecting subcontractors.

The general contractor's most important task is properly scheduling the various subcontractors' work and then making every effort to maintain that schedule. Although it is difficult to put on a roof before the walls are up, when the weather turns inclement it is also difficult to know exactly how long it will take to put the walls up. Because most construction is performed outdoors in uncertain weather conditions, even the most reliable subcontractors can fall behind schedule. If one falls behind, the next subcontractor may be committed to another job by the time the first one completes its task. Thus, four days of heavy rain can push work far more than four days behind schedule. The general contractor should be flexible enough and forceful enough to make certain that subcontractors adjust their other schedules as necessary. The general contractor should be experienced enough to understand the sequence of events for the specific type of structure and how he can work around delays so as to minimize the impact on the schedule's critical path.

Meetings and Scheduling

One way to reduce construction delays is to have a standard preconstruction meeting with the architect, project manager, general contractor, and subcontractor before a subcontractor starts work. In this meeting, every aspect of the new subcontractor's work is talked through: how to access the site, where to store materials, what areas to work in first, what to expect to be ready for this work, how to store materials, where trash goes, when and where material deliveries are made, and how to leave the area for the next subcontractor. By reaching an understanding about these aspects weeks before an entire crew and materials show up on-site, many coordination issues are resolved. Each subcontractor knows what is expected. Also, any confusion in the plans, the scope of work, or the general contractor's understanding will arise quickly, before time and money are wasted.

Most construction jobs require frequent and regular on-site meetings involving the project manager, contractor, subcontractors, and other personnel who have an interest in day-to-day progress. These meetings are the developer's first line of defense against construction problems. The frequency of the meetings is usually a function of the complexity of the job. The project manager may make critical decisions that entail changes to the schedule or allocation of funds, or take other measures to ensure that the work progresses smoothly. The developer ensures that all relevant personnel are informed about critical issues. The comparison of the project's progress against schedule and the costs incurred against budget are the most important standing agenda items. Any problems may draw in other staff members, depending on the nature of the issue.

Scheduling may be monitored using a number of formal techniques, such as Project Evaluation and Review Technique (PERT), Critical Path Method (CPM), Gantt charts, and other formal methods for statistical analysis and cost allocations. There are many software packages available to perform scheduling analyses for construction.

Drawing Down the Construction Loan

Lenders normally provide funds only as construction progress is demonstrated and after the developer and/or equity investor contribute funds. Similarly, the developer is typically not required to pay the general contractor before the work is performed. However, general contractors and subcontractors are reluctant—and often unable—to wait until the completion of all construction and final inspections before receiving any payments. In most construction contracts, the parties agree that the developer will pay for the work program as it progresses while retaining a set amount (*retainage*)—often 10 percent of the cost of construction—until the end of the job. Thus, for a $100,000 construction job with a provision for 10 percent retainage that is 20 percent complete, the general contractor has earned a $20,000 payment but would receive only $18,000, with the

developer (and in turn the lender) retaining $2,000 until completion. Only upon satisfactory completion does the general contractor (and through him the subcontractors) receive the amounts retained. "Satisfactory" means that all provisions of the agreement between owner and general contractor have been met and accepted by the architect or project manager, municipal inspectors, and the developer. Thus, retainage is a major risk control device that ensures completion in accordance with plans and specifications. It is also partial protection for the developer against default by the general contractor.

The paperwork involved in drawing funds from the construction lender typically follows a clearly delineated path. Periodically—typically every month—subcontractors submit invoices for work completed. The general contractor compiles invoices from all the subcontractors and, often with input from the architect and the project manager, examines the subcontracted work to ensure that the percentage of completed work claimed has in fact been completed according to the plans and specifications. If discrepancies arise, the general contractor works them out with the subcontractor(s) and eventually sends an invoice to the developer for the combined total of all subcontractors' *draw requests* plus the general contractor's fee and other eligible costs. The project manager (or the architect) verifies to the developer and the lenders that the total invoice submitted by the general contractor agrees with the contract between the general contractor and the developer, that the work has been completed, and that it meets plans and specifications. At this point, the approved invoices are sent to the developer's financial officer. The financial officer combines the invoice for construction costs (the hard costs) with various other "soft costs" associated with the development (insurance, property taxes, marketing costs, and general administrative overhead), and then submits a total figure to the construction lender as a draw request.

The loan agreement with the construction lender typically stipulates that the lender will provide funding as needed to cover the costs so long as the costs are within budget. The financial officer uses the budget that was originally defined in the feasibility study, refined during stage four, and contracted in stage five to produce a monthly draw request. It ties to that original budget, summarizing costs to date, the amount for the relevant period, and the remaining balance available for completion, typically for each item in the cost budget. (During stage four, the developer argues for as few categories as possible to achieve more flexibility in moving funds around while the lender favors more categories to increase control.)

The construction lender verifies that the request from the developer is in accordance with the loan agreement and that all appropriate participants (the architect or project manager, the general contractor, and the financial officer) have initialed the request. The lender might decide to personally inspect the construction to ensure that the project is proceeding as the draw request indicates. Finally, the construction lender verifies that the development appears to be on time and within budget for both hard and soft costs.

Assuming that all requirements are satisfied, the construction lender deposits funds in the developer's account for the total amount of the draw. The financial officer then writes a check to the general contractor, who in turn pays the various subcontractors. In this way, individual subcontractors can be paid for the work completed minus the amount for retainage. Disbursements for soft costs are made directly to the appropriate vendors and service providers by the financial officer.

One risk control device that lenders may use is to disburse funds only through title companies. In such cases, subcontractors exchange *lien waivers* for their appropriate draw checks. The title company can thus ensure that all subcontractors have acknowledged payment before funds are disbursed, thereby protecting the lender from *mechanic's liens* filed by unpaid subcontractors.

Mechanic's liens are liens on the property that arise when a contractor goes to court to seek help in collecting payment for construction work. To protect workers (considered to be at risk relative to big institutions), the law provides that mechanic's liens take effect when the work is done, not when the lien is filed. Thus, the lender could lose the coveted first-lien position to a previously unrecorded claim. Laws that apply to mechanic's liens vary significantly by state, so developers are well advised to engage legal counsel familiar with applicable local laws.

The length of time from the billing cutoff date (usually the last day of each month) until funds are disbursed to the subcontractors is important. If the elapsed time between performance of the work and payment for the work becomes too long, a significant burden is imposed on the subcontractors. For example, if a subcontractor submits a bill at the end of each month for $50,000, and that payment is received on the 15th of the following month, the subcontractor must finance its work for one and one-half months or, in this example, the amount of $75,000. This burden can be minimized by making payments more often, perhaps twice a month, or by speeding the approval and payment process so the waiting time is reduced to perhaps one week rather than 15 days. But the principle is the same: every contractor and subcontractor must be financially able to carry the cost of performing a portion of the work until the disbursement of funds.

Leasing and Building Out Tenant Space

Even with extensive preleasing, some space usually remains unleased at the initiation of construction; consequently marketing continues during construction. Ideally, on the day the project opens tenants will pay rent on every square foot of the building. To cover all possibilities, though, the pro forma contains a cost item for an operating deficit during the period from immediately after construction until the building is sufficiently leased and occupied to cover all operating expenses and debt service. If budgeted total costs include the cost of funding a deficit and the deficit does not materialize because the building is fully leased and occupied when it opens, then the budget item moves from the cost column and eventually adds to the profit on the development. A major goal of most developers is to capture this "leasing reserve."

In addition to an operating budget shortfall or lease-up reserve, the loan agreement might provide for floor and ceiling loan amounts. For example, the amount of the loan might be only *x* dollars until *y* percent of the building is leased, at which time the remaining amount of the loan will be funded. If such a provision appears in the permanent loan, the construction lender typically lends only the floor amount, which is the permanent or takeout lender's minimum commitment. Usually this scenario requires the developer to put up any funds beyond the floor loan that are needed before construction starts. This type of loan provision places pressure on the developer's marketing in stage six, as described in the following chapter.

Usually the developer covers the required equity up to the floor level before the lender begins advancing funds. If the construction lender funds the loan without that "potential additional equity," the pressure on marketing is greater during construction. If marketing does not generate leases or sales according to schedule, the developer will, at some point, have drawn down the floor amount of the loan. The developer may then have to provide funds out of his own equity for the balance of the project. As construction progresses, it is seldom practical to tell workers to stop and wait a month until more of the future space is leased and more loan proceeds become available. Construction needs to continue as scheduled, to avoid cost *escalation*.

In addition to overall leasing requirements, several other loan provisions affect construction. Office space leases usually cover such physical details as the location of interior walls, the number of electrical outlets and plumbing fixtures, and the type of carpeting. Thus, the leasing agent's negotiations directly influence both the construction crew's work and the amount that needs to be financed. To secure the right tenant—one that will attract other tenants—the leasing agent may need to offer a substantial buildout at the owner's expense. Although this may be a smart move, in that it increases expected value more than it increases costs, this expense must be financed during construction. If the developer has already used up any contingency in the loan agreement, then additional equity is needed. Developers can cover such funding shortfalls themselves or induce outside investors to cover them. However, once a project is in trouble, it is much harder and more expensive to secure additional funding.

Landscaping and Exterior Construction

The feasibility study for a project likely includes at least one line item in the budget for landscape architecture and design—an important component in marketing a project. Landscape elements help set the image for a project and create an environment that will appeal to future tenants. Creative landscaping distinguishes a project from the competition and therefore can accelerate leasing progress.

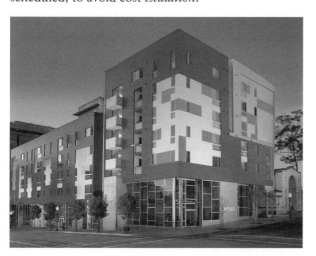

Cedar Gateway Apartments provides environmentally sustainable, affordable housing in downtown San Diego, California. The ribbon cutting was attended by members of the city council, the development team, residents, and others.

JIM DOYLE/APPLIED PHOTOGRAPHY

Landscaping covers a wide range of additions to the built environment. In a development of less expensive single-family houses, it might involve only spreading topsoil, seeding it, and planting a few shrubs. A major downtown mixed-use project might involve plazas, walkways, street furniture (such as benches, lighting, and signs), intensively planted areas, and even some works of art.

Landscape planning should begin early during site design, particularly if the site has features that should be preserved or protected during construction. For a variety of reasons, the installation of landscape elements typically is completed late in the construction process. From the perspective of design, landscape treatments can be used to respond to a different mix of tenants from that originally envisioned, adding an element of flexibility for the developer. Sometimes landscaping plans can be adjusted to mask design flaws that become evident during construction. From the perspective of operations, most installed landscaping requires maintenance, which can be a problem if appropriate maintenance personnel are not yet on staff. Furthermore, if installed too early in the construction process, landscape materials are likely vulnerable to damage by construction vehicles.

Potential Problems

Problems arise in any project, and interlinked problems are likely to plague most developers at some point during their career. The circumstances described in the following illustration all occurred on the same project.

Imagine the development of a tennis village designed to be one of the premier tennis facilities in the world. Located on a 200-acre site within an established resort, this "project within a project" was planned in multiple phases. The first phase covered the main clubhouse, the central tennis courts, a small hotel, and 50 townhouses. In subsequent phases, another 300 townhouses and more tennis courts will be added.

The financing negotiated for the project allows the developer, who is putting up $500,000, to borrow up to $24.5 million as needed. The developer's joint venture partner is a "deep-pocket" or well-capitalized equity investor and is personally guaranteeing the loan in return for 50 percent of the development profits. The $24.5 million initially available will cover the cost of the central courts, the 70-room hotel, the clubhouse, and the first 50 townhouses, and then become a revolving loan.

Under the arrangement, the developer will pay back part of the $24.5 million as he sells the first 50 townhouses. Assuming the units sell for $250,000 each, as projected in the feasibility study, 50 units will generate $12.5 million. This money will then be available for the developer to draw down again to continue building townhouses in subsequent phases. Accordingly, the project involves a certain amount of financing ($12 million) for the courts, hotel, and clubhouse. That financing will eventually be repaid from a permanent loan that will close with the expected transfer of the amenities to the property owners. The revolving portion of the construction financing enables the developer to continue building townhouses, so long as the first units sell. The logistics in the feasibility study show the developer realizing no profit from the first group of townhouses. They are priced to induce the first residents to buy into a novel concept. He does, however, receive a development fee on the first phase and expects to profit handsomely on subsequent phases as he increases the price but not the cost of the remaining 250 townhouse units. If the developer stays within the forecasted time and costs, which were incorporated in the loan document, the financing package will remain intact through multiple phases of development and produce substantial profits down the road. If marketing slips or construction is delayed, problems could arise.

The developer is now six months from completion of the clubhouse, the hotel, the stadium tennis courts, and the first 50 townhouses. Life is good; the joint venture partner is happy, and the return on investment looks huge. At the weekly project coordination meeting, the marketing staff reports that the two-bedroom units are sold out but that the one-bedroom units, which are essentially the same size but feature an interior balcony, are not selling at all.

The first 50 units were planned to include 25 two-bedroom units and 25 one-bedroom units, but now the marketing staff suggests changing most of the 25 one-bedroom units to two-bedroom units. The construction manager calculates that the additional walls and minimal additional electrical service needed for the change will require $450,000, or $18,000 per unit. The developer agrees to the change, planning to use the $625,000 allocated in the budget (and the loan agreement) for contingencies.

Then it rains—every day for two weeks—in what should have been the dry season. Because the subcontractors' other commitments are also backing up, rescheduling proves difficult and the project slips four weeks behind schedule. Time is critical: early buyers are looking forward to the tennis tournament scheduled for September, which will be carried on national TV and has been a major selling point. Moreover, the rescheduling costs some money. The subcontractors want incentive compensation to return promptly to the project, and their prompt return is essential to making the grand opening coincide with the tennis tournament. The interest meter will now run for a full additional month. The added expense will likely total $325,000. What to do?

The solution to the weather-related delay is for the developer to approach the construction lender and report, in an appropriately humble manner, that an act of God has wiped out the amount set aside for contingencies (the original $625,000 minus $450,000 for 25 conversions to two-bedroom units leaves only $175,000). The construction lender, who claimed to be a partner in the development process, should understand that events beyond the developer's control sometimes require a little more cash.

If the lender goes along with the request, however, he puts himself in a difficult position. The original financing provides a permanent takeout loan on the clubhouse, stadium tennis courts, and hotel for $12 million (predicated on completion of construction according to plans and specifications). If the cost overrun is allocated to these facilities, then the lender has loaned more than the agreed-upon $12 million, which is tied to his estimate of value for the improvements. What is the source of

payment for the additional funding? If the lender allocates the excess amount to the townhouses, he should believe that the sale price will be high enough to cover the loan. In other words, he must assume a little more risk or believe that the price can be higher than projected in the original feasibility study. He decides, based in part on the developer's charm, to allocate the excess to the townhouse units, believing that they can be sold at a somewhat higher price than specified in the feasibility study. These first two problems and their solution are rather common. What follows is less common.

Two weeks later, the marketing staff is highly upset. Architectural costs for this particular job were kept to a minimum by using the architect only through rough construction drawings. The in-house project manager (an engineer) finalized the site plans and has managed the process to date. As the job began, the general contractor noted a large quantity of rock at the end of the site where the first phase of townhouses was to be located. Working with the project manager, he determined that if the units were relocated slightly closer to the outlying tennis courts, which were in the center of each cluster of units, far less rock would have to be moved and costs could be kept to a minimum. The project manager approved the new location of the units, and the development team was pleased because a potential problem had been solved expeditiously with only a slight shift in design and no increase in site costs.

Regrettably, when the units were moved closer, the end units with the attractive bay windows no longer look out toward the mountains. Rather, they look into another bedroom window 12 feet away. According to the marketing staff, these units will not sell for any amount close to the projected price and will have to be rented instead. A developer cannot expect a limited price cut on a luxury item to clear the market when the item has a flaw that is obvious to even the most unsophisticated consumer. If the end units, eight of them in this first phase, are kept as rental rather than for-sale units and the $12.5 million townhouse construction loan for the townhouses is thus not fully paid back as planned, the developer will be short of cash as development continues. He might have to develop in smaller phases (fewer townhouses in each), which would be inefficient and raise construction costs. This is not a story a developer wants to tell a lender or partner who has guaranteed the loan.

The developer's troubles do not stop here. Three weeks before the scheduled grand opening, another deluge of rain sweeps through, and a second flaw in the redesign is discovered. With the units now located closer to the tennis courts, the stormwater runoff cannot be fully absorbed by the original drainage system, and the units on the lower side of the courts flood. The flood ruins the drywall and carpeting in ten units that had been scheduled to close in two weeks.

In addition to the costs of replacing the drywall and carpeting, the developer must find a solution to the drainage problem. Working with the in-house engineer and the general contractor, he identifies a solution that will cost $160,000 ($70,000 for new materials and other miscellaneous repairs, and $90,000 to install a new "Mediterranean" drainage system on the lower side of the tennis courts). Unlike the money involved in the no-view/no-sale units, the $160,000 for this repair is needed now. The end of the construction period is near, and not much leeway is left to shift expenditures between budget categories, even if the lender would permit it. The developer has already asked for and received more money for a problem that was an act of God and not his fault. What does he do now? If the developer shows weakness, the lender may "deem itself insecure" (a provision in most construction loans that allows foreclosure before default if the lender decides that there is no way for the developer to finish successfully). If the developer asks the joint venture partner for help, the partner will want to renegotiate the 50/50 split of the expected profits from subsequent phases of the development.

Assume the developer solves that problem. The project advances to the week before the scheduled grand opening. It is August in the Southwest, and the beautiful landscaping is brown. The flood was followed by two weeks of hot sun, and the lack of water during those two weeks was fatal. The landscape contractor assumed that the property manager would take responsibility for landscape maintenance. Somehow the property manager did not get the signal, and $100,000 worth of plants are dead. The high-end buyers may not go to closing with dead shrubs at their units. If the developer backs off the grand opening, he could lose existing presales; people who previously agreed to buy might decide they do not want to buy a unit in this development. Remember, everything is ultimately the developer's responsibility, and these are some examples of the kinds of problems that he may have to solve at stage six.

Problems that arise at this stage are typically interlinked ones. Suppose that, during the final stages of construction, a pipe on the 25th floor bursts, allowing water to seep through and damage key components of the fire alarm system. A fire inspection is scheduled for two days later, and tenants are moving in two days after that, but rewiring the alarm system will take longer than two days. Rescheduling the inspection will force a delay of at least two weeks even if the city inspector, whom the developer has been cultivating since stage three, bends over backward to be helpful. What does the developer tell tenants who plan to move in next week? Because it is "an act of God," he can attempt to work with the fire department to set up a "fire watch" to allow temporary occupancy. And he can authorize overtime work to correct the wiring and test the system. Finally, if the building is under a fire watch, he can request overtime inspection of the fire alarm system. The request may have to go from the developer to the fire department, from the contractor to the inspector, and from the tenant to the city manager. Should the developer encounter resistance, he might remind town officials that an operating company pays more taxes than a company forced to shut down due to an act of God.

With the tenants in place and paying rent, the permanent loan can be serviced. Typically, it is closed and the construction lender repaid during stage seven or the start of stage eight. In addition, a shift in the controlling equity interest might occur, from the developer to a new long-term equity investor. The new investor might have in-house management personnel, rely on outside property management companies, or hire the developer as the manager. In many cases, the developer stays on as a partner with the new investor. Even with this arrangement, a significant part of the risk shifts from the developer, who has now completed the development, to the long-term investor.

RISK CONTROL TECHNIQUES DURING CONSTRUCTION

Under pressure to keep construction and marketing on schedule while keeping costs within budget, developers use appropriate risk controls. As previously discussed, one of the first opportunities to avoid risk comes early in the process: stop the project at stage one, two, or three before much money has been committed. Other ways to control risk include hiring a competent team, experienced in the type of project being developed; investing in research to learn as much as possible about the market for the project; and transferring potential losses to other players through contracts or insurance.

Some techniques for avoiding risk are specific to stage six:

- Liability, fire, and extended insurance coverage are basic to controlling risks. For insurance to work, developers should be covered for what might happen, the insurance should be for the right amount and in force at the right time.
- By increasing the focus on critical events, software packages such as PERT and CPM are useful for managing time and thus controlling risk. They also link all participants via the internet so that project managers in the field can easily communicate with the architect in his office and the marketing team at a meeting.
- Good internal controls, particularly the accounting system, are critical during development. The closer the developer's financial officer or accountant is to the entire process, the less the risk of error, theft, and fraud.
- Architectural supervision and construction project management are obviously important risk control techniques. In addition to

In stage six, as construction began, Larry Short reconsidered tradeoffs in the quality of construction versus costs. The general contractor offered what he called "suggestions for value engineering." Short saw most of the suggestions as detail items that had been glossed over and underbid in the general contract. They included upgrades in such items as windows on the first level of the building and kitchen fixtures in the individual units. The general contractor's bid had assumed the minimum standards, but the market demanded a higher grade of finish. Reluctantly, Short

agreed to nearly $1 million in additional construction costs for these upgrades. The lender agreed to increase the loan amount accordingly because the LTV ratio was still low and preleasing of the units was very strong.

These last-minute changes made the construction schedule very tight, but the project was available for occupancy in time for the start of the fall semester, with the higher-quality construction complete. A few punch list items remained, but students were able to move in on time. *Continued on page 304*

supervising the general contractor, developers can require contractors to include warranties in their contracts for such things as structural integrity, which can be the basis of subsequent lawsuits. Furthermore, developers should check that subcontractors have the necessary licenses to perform the specified work. Unless the developer is one step ahead of a potential issue, the subcontractor with a problem could eventually become the developer's problem.

- Retainage (holding back cash to ensure completion of the work) helps ensure that work will be completed according to plans and specifications.

- The developer needs to ensure that building inspectors have agreed that final items were installed according to code.

- *Performance bonds* are another useful method of controlling construction risk. A surety company's guarantee of the completion or performance of a general contractor's contract provides deep-pocket support for the contractor's obligations. Still, a performance bond offers insurance only for contractor obligations that the developer can substantiate in court. Such guarantees do not eliminate risk related to timing. From the public sector's perspective, bonding a general contractor also reduces a city's risk when infrastructure is involved.

- Union relations are an important consideration in many areas of the country. Sensitivity to unions and to construction workers in general can only benefit a developer. On a high-rise project in certain cities, the construction process can be halted by one person—the worker who runs the construction elevator. If that person is a member of a different union than other workers and decides to strike, the other workers cannot get to their jobs, even if they are willing to cross a one-person picket line.

SUMMARY

Stage six, the construction phase, requires constant interplay among construction, marketing, financial,

government, and operating personnel. The developer's role shifts with the move to stage six: he becomes less a promoter and more a manager. Time becomes the critical risk element. It takes an extremely competent manager to successfully coordinate all the activities that unfold simultaneously during this stage.

Stage seven encompasses the activities associated with completion and the formal opening. It entails considerations involving the public sector, tenants, the interior layout, operations personnel, and the shift in financing to long-term investors. Stage seven is the end of the active phase of real estate development. It sets the stage for asset and property management, which is stage eight.

TERMS

- Construction manager
- Draw requests
- Escalation
- General contractor
- Lien waivers
- Marketing manager
- Mechanic's liens
- Performance bonds
- Project manager
- Retainage

REVIEW QUESTIONS

15.1 How does stage six differ from the first five stages?

15.2 What is the role of the developer in managing the construction process? How does it differ from the role of the project manager?

15.3 Why is appropriate scheduling particularly important for the project manager?

15.4 Describe the process of drawing down the construction loan.

15.5 Describe some of the risks inherent in stage six and some ways to avoid them.

Marketing, Sales, and Leasing

At stages six and seven, rental space is leased and for-sale units are sold to the target markets identified in the feasibility study. For both kinds of transactions, ongoing marketing activity during stage six further informs the developer's efforts and appropriate changes are made to the leasing or sales effort. Some of these changes may prompt physical alterations that require a change in construction. As explained in chapter 15, such alterations are far from painless.

Market research is used throughout stages one, two, and three to identify the project's potential users, their needs, and how much they are willing to pay for space. In stages four and five, decisions are made about the optimal paths to follow in the marketing effort and related contracts are negotiated and signed. This chapter covers the "blocking and tackling" of the ongoing marketing that occurs primarily during stage six. It reviews the marketing basics, which fall into two categories: the "soft" considerations such as planning and strategy, and the "hard" activities related to leasing and sales.

During stage six, any errors in the earlier work of refining the concept come home to roost. Furthermore, it is likely that the market has evolved and new competition is on the horizon. This means that despite all the rigorous planning in previous stages, the developer, as quarterback of the team, must remain flexible and react appropriately during construction. Just as the feasibility study continues to be a valuable management tool, adherence to the marketing concept is a valuable practice during the high stress of stage six.

The congruence of the market research and the marketing effort depends on at least four conditions:

- The market research correctly identified the target market, and the project concept is a valid response to that market.
- Construction is executed in a manner consistent with the recommendations of the market research.
- The marketing program is executed in a manner consistent with the findings of the market research.
- The market has not changed between the time of the initial market research study and the initiation of the marketing program.

Ideally, the marketing team has been engaged in the project from the beginning and has contributed to the creation and refinement of the project

CASE STUDY   Shortbread Lofts: Continuing Marketing and Market Research

Marketing of a student rental housing project differs a bit from that for other kinds of residential rentals. Just as resort developments have always tried to attract prominent first buyers, campus rentals aim to have the right Twitter connectors. On campus, Twitter connectors have large followings—some as many as 10,000—so both good and bad comments about where to live travel quickly.

The Shortbread marketing team planned to work cross-group communication in several ways. One was advertising on "campus carts"—electric vehicles that provide free late-night transportation for students who do not want to drive. The carts are financed with revenue from the advertising they carry. Shortbread Lofts paid $2,000 per month for ads on all four sides of one cart.

As Larry Short continued to study the market at stage six, he decided that demand would be significantly higher if the units were furnished and included more and better amenities than he originally proposed, in addition to the construction upgrades discussed in chapter 15. The lender agreed to increase the loan amount again, by another $1 million, to accommodate this adjustment to evolving market expectations.

The Shortbread Lofts website was a key marketing tool at this stage, and it continues to be a major resource for promoting and leasing the project, and keeping tenants informed. The website includes detailed floor plans of each unit type, photos of the property, and an online leasing application. It also provides a YouTube link to a three-minute virtual tour of the property and a detailed list of the features, functions, and benefits offered to residents, promoted as described in the following lists.

COMMUNITY FEATURES

- Rooftop garden terrace of 1,400 square feet with room to relax.
- All utilities included: electric, water, sewer, trash, recycling, high-speed wireless internet, cable TV. Write one check only.
- Gardening areas on the roof to practice your green thumb.
- State-of-the-art fitness center with stand-up tanning, boxing, free weights, full array of equipment, flat-screen TVs—open 24 hours.
- Doorman on duty every evening at the lobby entrance.
- Secured entrances to building, multiple security cameras, fully sprinklered concrete and steel structure.
- Wi-fi throughout building, including all apartments, rooftop, fitness center, and common areas—all free.
- Tech-friendly lobby area with Mac computers and printers, open 24 hours.
- Huge community flex room for group functions and fitness classes, as well as for a quiet study lounge before exams.
- On-site management office located near lobby entrance.
- Apply online, pay rent online, and request maintenance online. Add parents to your account for easy access.

APARTMENT UNIT FEATURES

- 42-inch flat-screen TV included in every apartment home.
- Individually keyed bedroom suites within each apartment are designed with sound insulation around each suite—no more roommate noise!
- Each bedroom has a private, full bath with either a large tub or an oversized 5-foot shower, and undermounted sink basin in vanity with granite top and storage drawers underneath.
- Choose to furnish or not:
  1. Unfurnished—bring all your own things!
  2. Furnished option—includes sofa, chair, coffee table, end table, and entertainment center with TV. Each bedroom has a queen-size bed with pillow-top mattress, personal mattress cover, desk, chair, double dresser, and nightstand.
- Full-size GE washer and dryer included in every apartment home.
- Ceiling fans with light in living room and every bedroom.
- Huge 8-foot-square, 9-pane living room window with dramatic views of downtown.
- Oversized closets extend up to 10.5-foot ceiling height, 7 to 9 feet wide—room to bring everything!
- Polished, high-shine, natural concrete floors throughout for easy-clean maintenance and low allergic response.
- Full kitchen with granite countertops and dining bar, GE high-end stainless-steel appliances including flat ceramic-top stove with self-cleaning oven, refrigerator with freezer drawer on bottom with sliding shelves, ebony wood cabinetry and shelving, microwave and dishwasher, and pendant lighting over bar.

Upgrades include granite countertops and stainless-steel appliances in kitchens.

Continued on page 333

concept. The team has developed themes that resonate with the target market and woven those themes into all aspects of the promotional program. For example, if the original concept is a multifamily project targeted to the psycho-demographic segment called "cultural creatives," then the project has an environmentally sensitive site plan, energy-saving features that go beyond the norm, and architecture that complements the site and appeals to this target market. The marketing program captures the environmental values in all of its collateral material: logo, brochures, advertising, and the marketing office. The sales staff has been trained to understand and promote these features. Advertising resources have been directed toward media most accessed by this target market.

The marketing team may be entirely or partially in-house, or may be a group of outside consultants retained for the project. Regardless of the arrangement, it is the responsibility of the developer to ensure that the marketing team understands the project concept and the target market. The developer also should ensure that the marketing team understands the promotional (soft) and the contractual (hard) challenges of marketing discussed in this chapter.

THE PROMOTIONAL (SOFT) SIDE OF MARKETING

If the developer did a good job designing the product for the target market, sales and leasing can be straightforward. The marketing team identifies and convinces potential users to purchase the product. They find and convince prospects that the subject development is superior to other available products. The target prospects may be narrowly defined, such as buyers for single-family homes, or broadly defined, such as tenants for a retail center and by extension the potential customers for the tenants' stores.

Timing is critical. The shorter the absorption period, the lower the time-related carrying costs. Furthermore, the earlier the marketing begins, the lower the chances that the market will evolve away from the features, functions, and benefits of the

Figure 16-1   **The Marketing Umbrella**

The Marketing Umbrella

Research | Strategy and Planning | Promotions | Sales

Source: Richard Burns.

given development. Marketing has the power to reduce these exposures.

This chapter uses marketing terminology that applies specifically to real estate, but the basic concepts can be found in any standard marketing textbook. The umbrella shown in figure 16-1 is a simple model for depicting the major components of real estate marketing. Research is learning about the market's audiences and competition for the project. Strategy and planning is developing the strategic course of action based on the development plan and market dynamics. Promotion is communicating to the target audiences with the appropriate messages and media to generate awareness, interest, and traffic. Sales is the transaction of the lease or sale. Research was discussed in previous chapters; this chapter focuses on strategy and planning, promotions, and sales.

Strategy and Planning: SWOT Analysis

The strategic marketing process is based on the information gathered through market research. It defines the project concept and provides background information on target markets. The strategic marketing plan begins with an analysis of the project's strengths, weaknesses, opportunities, and threats (SWOT). The SWOT analysis leads to the formation of the marketing vision—or theme—which encompasses the positioning of the property and the formulating of the marketing goals and objectives.

The SWOT analysis is a benchmarking process used to inventory all internal and external aspects of a project, both positive and negative. It identifies the internal strengths that can be incorporated into a positive presentation of the development as well as weaknesses that need to be overcome. The analysis identifies external opportunities and threats that are beyond the developer's control but can affect the success of the marketing program. All aspects of the analysis are viewed in the context of the target market.

Strengths

Strengths are internal attributes of the project that differentiate it from the competition. They include location, quality of the design and environment, pricing, amenities, and anything else that enables the project to be better than the competition. Knowing the project's strengths provides guidance for building a marketing program.

Weaknesses

Weaknesses are limitations of the project or property that have a negative impact on its marketability. They are the corresponding negative aspects of strengths, so they also include location, quality of the design and environment, pricing, amenities, and anything else that causes the project to be worse than the competition. Once weaknesses are identified, the marketing plan can address and mitigate them. Some weaknesses can be overcome through marketing. Others may require programmatic or product changes or price reductions.

Opportunities

Opportunities are situations or conditions that are external to the project. They can be global and omnipresent, or they can exist for a brief time. Among other things, they include economic and market conditions, demographic trends, and the financial climate. The marketing strategy should align opportunities with strengths.

Threats

Threats are conditions that are external to the project. Like opportunities, they vary in magnitude and longevity. Some can be mitigated through the marketing program. Others may be permanent. A major threat, such as a downturn in the economy, requires an adjustment to strategy. Smaller threats, such as the departure of a key tenant, may be a short-term marketing problem.

A well-conceived project responds to market demand (a market looking for a project) rather than the other way around (a project looking for a market). It is not impossible for a dynamic marketing program to facilitate the success of a bad project—and it is usually essential in workout situations. However, it is unwise and often fatal to initiate a project that does not have a previously identified market. Marketing is a component in the overall success of a project; it is not a panacea for poorly conceived or ill-timed projects.

The Marketing Vision

The marketing vision interprets the project concept for the public. Aspects of the marketing message include the project's physical qualities, environmental conditions, social dynamics, character, values, commitment to execution, and the quality of life and experience that will make the project different and special. These attributes are compiled into a vision upon which the marketing program will be based. A successful vision can capture the essence of a project in a single meaningful iconic image or statement that expresses location and experience to the target market. It becomes a benchmark for all marketing decisions.

The marketing program requires clear goals, objectives, and tactics. Goals identify measurable end results for the program. For an income project, one goal is often preleasing. Objectives assign specific quantities and matching numbers to time frames and target dates. For an income project, a goal could be to have 50 percent of the space preleased by a certain date. Tactics are distinct actions to take in order to realize goals and objectives. They designate who is given responsibility for the completion of objectives. For an income project, a tactic could be the engagement of a brokerage firm to prelease 80 percent of the property beginning at least two months prior to the completion of construction.

Positioning is the identification of measures to establish the project's place in the market and thereby create a competitive edge. Four approaches can be used to position the project: *product differentiation, repositioning, niche identification,* and *branding.* Although these strategies are not mutually exclusive, one usually dominates in determining the manner in which the project is packaged and presented.

- *Differentiation* is the most common positioning strategy. Differentiation is the promotion of project characteristics, as compared with other products in the market. For an office building, comparative characteristics that could be emphasized in positioning might be larger floor plates, more cutting-edge design, or superior location. Sometimes constraints can be used to differentiate a project. For example, if a project had to reach certain energy efficiency goals, that energy efficiency might be emphasized in a marketing program targeted to users for whom that is an appealing characteristic.

- *Repositioning* is the process of turning an existing product into something new or different. Repositioning can also result from rethinking how a property can maintain the same use and yet appeal to different markets. An example is an office building with large floor plates and employee service areas, such as a cafeteria and daycare facility, that has been vacated by a single corporate tenant. A developer could reposition the project by targeting the back-office requirements of other companies and promoting the on-site facilities that served the previous owner.

- *Niche identification* is the process of finding an underserved market segment. Niches are very specific types of buyers and users. Demographic changes running through Gen X and Gen Y cohorts have created a much richer and more fragmented market than in preceding generations. This has been reflected in the emergence of new retail formats, more open office configurations, and rental apartments that have smaller, more affordable units

as well as more communal amenities and more transit-friendly locations.

- *Project branding* creates an identity that speaks to target buyers. Branding establishes the value of the project, sets expectations about it, generates recognition of its name and the product type, and boosts its visibility. The most often cited definition of branding is "a promise." Great brands deliver products and services with a degree of consistency that meets customers' expectations with every experience. Branding for real estate requires common elements. For example, branded multifamily projects often use several elements to attract tenants. They use consistent identification material, such as signage, brochures, and logos, to create an association with other communities of the same brand. They offer the same package of physical amenities, such as pools, clubhouses, and other facilities, establishing an immediate expectation on the part of the renter. They offer a consistent level of property management services and a consistent leasing experience, providing an assurance of quality for the prospective tenant.

A strong example of a branded community is the award-winning Trilogy series by Shea Homes. Trilogy targets the new demographic of retiring baby boomers who want active resort-style living with a package of physical and service amenities designed for more engaged and active lifestyles. Physical amenities typically include state-of-the-art athletic and wellness facilities, and social programming includes continuing learning programs with local colleges and universities. In recognition of this market's desire to engage with the overall community, Trilogy is developing retirement communities within traditional master-planned communities. Age groups are integrated by pedestrian links but partly separated for certain recreation facilities. Trilogy offers developments in several states across the United States. Potential buyers familiar with the Shea product in one market can expect the same quality in other markets. For each community, Shea adapts the model to the locale where it is developed but maintains a consistency and continuity that makes the Trilogy brand always recognizable.

Commercial assets, such as major office buildings and shopping centers, require different marketing strategies. These business-to-business transactions typically involve corporate relocation decisions. Because lease transactions are an important part of the cost of doing business, the marketing and leasing responsibilities typically are delegated or assigned to an in-house or third-party group that specializes in the asset class. These specialists are familiar with the factors that influence the decisions of major tenants. They know the supply and demand dynamics of this market. They are experienced in negotiating complex, high-value, multiyear lease transactions.

In the office market, marketing strategies may involve leasing agents who specialize in representing either the landlord or the tenant. The tenant leasing agent is known as a tenant representative (or "tenant rep"). The landlord's leasing agent is responsible for regular communication with the tenant representatives. Leasing agents facilitate tours of the space, generate lease proposals (or respond to formal and sometimes extensive requests for proposals), and, with legal counsel, negotiate lease documents. Asset management staff also participate in the leasing process, either by establishing pre-approved minimum *lease terms* or by actively stepping into the direct negotiations.

Marketing strategies in the retail market are often more complex. A significant component of value in many retail developments derives from a tenant's sales volume (in the form of base, percentage rent, or a combination). In these properties, it is important that the owner and/or the major tenants develop a marketing program to attract shoppers so that tenant sales are maximized for the benefit of both tenants and landlord. Often a developer sets a lower rent for high-profile tenants who do extensive advertising because the customers they draw will also patronize the smaller tenants, who do far less direct advertising.

Regardless of the type and size of the property and the responsibility for ongoing marketing, the integrity of the revised pro forma is critical because it is used to estimate future rental rates. The pro forma includes all ongoing costs of marketing the space, including brokerage commissions, rental concessions, tenant allowances, space planning and design costs, moving allowances, and legal fees.

Risk Control Techniques during Marketing

Techniques that help to control risk are applied during every stage of the development process. The following are some of the techniques that are applied during the marketing phase:

- Preleasing and presales, to reduce the risk of initial high vacancies.
- Careful attention to the tenant mix. If tenants "fit" together or if one tenant draws others, problems with long-term vacancies are less likely to arise.
- For small tenants, lease guarantees or some type of letter of credit. Depending on the strength of the market, it may be possible to obtain high rent from a small tenant. Without some type of outside guarantee that the tenant can pay the rent, however, higher rents may bring no increase in value. Formal insurance for such tenants is relatively rare. Other forms of performance guarantee can range from the tenant designating a cosigner to the tenant completing a portion of the finish work, thereby enhancing its commitment to the space.
- Net leases, *expense stops*, and escalations. These are all important for long-term investors, and developers should structure leases with these possibilities in mind. When market conditions permit, developers should make sure that they are not the first or only entity to absorb all the pain in the event of rapid inflation in expenses.
- The operating agreement negotiated with tenants. By controlling how tenants relate to one another and to the building, developers can help ensure its long-term operating viability and minimize maintenance problems.

The Marketing Budget

The developer's budget necessarily includes a line item for marketing. Marketing cost estimates are not usually based on quantities and unit prices. They vary according to economic conditions at the location and time that the project is brought to market. A single number may be used in the due diligence and early feasibility stages, when details of the future market environment are unknown and the marketing expenditures represent a small portion of the budget. As the project progresses, the marketing budget is specified in greater detail, with additional line items added as the marketing program takes shape.

Three approaches to budgeting for marketing are common: fixed allocation budgeting, percentage budgeting, and zero-based budgeting:

- *Fixed allocation budgeting* is the assignment of an amount for marketing on the basis of company experience or project financial modeling. It may be based on past projects, formulas, or a discretionary decision. The numbers used do not reflect the specific market circumstances that will be examined later in the process. Allowances for the components of the marketing budget—for example, an estimated allowance of $200,000 for staffing the leasing center—are plugged in to arrive at a preliminary estimate of the total marketing budget.

- *Percentage budgeting.* For certain property types, there are established financial benchmarks—based on industry or company averages—for marketing budgets and their components. The percentage approach assumes that these industry or company averages are reasonable gauges of what it will cost to do the marketing. In early financial projections, industry averages may be useful for preparing a ballpark marketing budget. However, they can be misleading and may not be an accurate or appropriate gauge of the project's needs. In the early stages, the percentage approach may be applied to total sales revenues. As the marketing program is refined, the approach may be applied to the components of the marketing budget. An example would be a staffing allowance of 40 percent ($180,000) in a $450,000 marketing budget. Percentages and averages indicate what others are allocating to marketing activities in the aggregate, but they do not disclose the unique circumstances of the project's promotional requirements. Project size, local markets, economic conditions, and a host of other factors skew the percentages for each project.

- *Zero-based budgeting* assigns a cost to each line item or activity. It is the most reliable approach to preparing an accurate budget. It anticipates everything that needs to happen through the course of the marketing program. This budgeting process begins with a marketing plan that identifies all the activities necessary to achieve the marketing goals. As the development progresses, the description of each activity is expanded to include a list of specific actions. To ensure that no promising prospects go overlooked, a comprehensive checklist of activities appropriate for a wide range of products and markets is a good starting point.

The budget consists of both fixed and time-related expenses. Determination of the time-related expenses requires an estimate of the lease or sales period of the project (the absorption period). Market research can provide an estimated absorption rate, but achieving that rate may require a trade-off between marketing expenditures and timing—that is, spending more money may bring faster absorption. An example of a zero-based budget calculation could be two full-time sales personnel for $75,000 per year and two part-time sales personnel for $40,000 per year, for a total staffing cost of $230,000. The more distinctive the project, the more likely the developer will choose a zero-based budgeting approach.

It is difficult to accurately forecast the duration of the marketing and sales period. Because of the idiosyncrasies of a given market, fluctuating economic cycles, and a host of other conditions beyond the developer's control, marketing programs and budgets require a measure of flexibility. Budgets should include a contingency reserve if market conditions indicate the need for additional time or money to complete the program.

Whichever budgeting system is used, it is critically important that the productivity of marketing and sales activities be continuously measured in terms of leases produced or sales closed. Updated market research studies may be required in order to measure the effectiveness of the marketing program and to identify changes in the project's trade area. Feedback from the sales or leasing team and from prospects is essential. As the team develops a track record, its experience can be used to modify the original projections for the remainder of the sales or leasing effort.

Promotions

The promotional program is the mix of materials, activities, and tools used to reach the development's audiences. It is unique to every development and is driven by the strategy, the market, market conditions, and other factors. The itemization that follows may seem overly detailed to the untrained eye. However, attention to detail is important, so the developer is well served to at least consider each of these items. Common elements of the promotion program include

- Creation of an image, identity, and name;
- Establishment of marketing environments;
- Targeted advertising;
- Public relations; and
- Promotional events.

Image, Identity, and Naming

Real estate projects benefit from a well-conceived, memorable identity. An identity and image program typically includes a logo or logotype (the project name in a special typographic presentation) that presents an image that is consistent with the impression the developer is trying to convey. Naming is an important component of marketing. The name is the buyer's first introduction to the project, so it should conjure up a distinct impression. The following criteria should be considered when selecting a name:

- It should reflect the scale of the development.
- It should be meaningful and evocative, capturing the nature and character of the environment.
- It should engender an emotional reaction.
- It should be capable of being extended into a comprehensive naming system for related amenities, neighborhoods, streets, facilities, and features of the project.
- It should be distinctive, easy to recall, and not used elsewhere.
- It should reflect the vision for the development, implying its psycho-demographic target and lifestyle.
- It should be an element of the development story and a source for a compelling story in and of itself.

Marketing Environments

For many types of developments, a marketing or information center is a significant part of the promotional program. Such centers require space, presentations, and staff. They can range from simple displays in a designated space in a building or model home to elaborate freestanding buildings dedicated to controlling the visitors' experience. Most use interactive displays that enable potential buyers to explore the features of the project.

Every marketing facility, regardless of size or complexity, should present a calculated orchestration of the development story in a high-quality, imaginative presentation. For the prospect, the presentation should be an inviting experience. The story should advance in a logical sequence, building on the development's strengths and demonstrating its benefits to the audience. Displays and graphic sales aids can underscore the points stressed in the sales presentation. The design of each exhibit, model, and display; the message they convey; and their placement in the facility should help the story unfold with appropriate impact, helping the sales representative tell the story.

Targeted Advertising

Usually an outside advertising agency is responsible for writing advertising copy, producing a logo, preparing accompanying graphics, and—sometimes—creating the marketing budget. Larger developers may employ in-house marketing staffs, research staffs, and advertising professionals, who may work in conjunction with outside professionals.

MINH TRUONG

At North Post Oak Lofts, in Houston, Texas, the leasing center is warm and inviting, and reflects the character of the development. The project was designed to appeal to young professionals and families.

A basic principle of marketing is to place advertising where interested customers can find it. Communicating with an interested audience that is actively seeking information about a product is much more useful than attempting to capture the attention of people who have no initial interest in the product. The goal is to design and place advertisements that are powerful enough to induce responses in prospective buyers.

An important component of targeted advertising is determining the best mix of media. The target market itself suggests which media would be most productive. Newspaper advertising was once the medium of choice for real estate, regardless of product type. Today, the internet has overtaken print media as the primary channel for most real estate advertisers.

Websites are effective tools for marketing all classes of real estate. When designed for maximum marketing effectiveness, websites are a strong medium for offering substantive information. They provide a channel for prospective customers to obtain detailed price information, view floor plans, take virtual tours of available space, and find contact information. They can be updated easily to reflect product changes and sales conditions. The design of a site is critical: overly complex, tricky, or information-dense pages hinder legibility and fail to hold viewers. For larger developments, attention to

external blogs is important as certain target markets accept information more readily from outside sources.

If newspapers are used, the location of the advertisement in the paper is critical. Compared with newspapers, magazines and trade publications have longer life cycles and may deliver more highly targeted readers. The print quality of magazines is also much higher, especially if the magazines include full-color photographs. For upscale, particularly attractive developments, these factors can be compelling inducements. Local and statewide business magazines are natural choices for almost all types of income-producing properties. In many communities, some magazines survive almost exclusively on real estate–oriented advertising, particularly for residential developments in rapidly growing communities. Both residential and commercial developers may find opportunities in magazines targeted to area newcomers. Product-specific trade publications are another medium for advertising property developments, particularly in the commercial sector, where players are fewer and their interrelationships well established.

Radio and television can offer tremendous advertising impact, but typically at a high cost, particularly in major metropolitan markets. These media are especially useful for short-term promotion of a special event such as a grand opening. Many metropolitan areas have multiple radio stations, targeted to different profiles of listeners—and potential residential buyers. Cable television also offers creative possibilities for business-oriented developments.

Direct mail is the most highly targeted advertising medium and one of the most precise ways to communicate with target audiences. Numerous data sources provide demographically segmented mailing lists that make it possible to target audiences with highly customized messages. Careful selection and review of recipients helps to minimize wasted exposure. Most successful direct-mail campaigns use repeat mailings.

Printed or digital newsletters may be used to promote a development that requires dissemination of extensive information. Newsletters can be very effective in maintaining ongoing communications and connections with tenants and buyers. By focusing on issues of concern to customers, they play a role as a customer relations tool. They also enable developers to tell their story in their own way while subtly implying a third-party endorsement.

Finally, signage is an important part of any real estate promotions program. Real estate is about location, and the market for most projects exists within a relatively close radius of the property. Most of a project's prospects will pass by the property at some point. Creating awareness through on-site signage is highly effective and relatively inexpensive.

Public Relations

Targeted advertising should usually be reinforced by a coordinated public relations effort. Public relations is an untargeted promotion aimed at the public at large, and the best generator of positive public relations is the quality of the development itself. The public relations vehicle is often a press release that relates a compelling and newsworthy story about the development. Editors receive hundreds of such releases each day, so the message needs to be compelling enough to make editors want to run it.

Events

On-site events provide an excellent opportunity to promote a project and tell its development story. Ground-breaking ceremonies, topping-out parties, grand openings, tours for brokers, and open houses are events that can help potential clients get acquainted with the development. The most common on-site promotion is the grand opening (stage seven in the real estate development process).

Promotional events should be entertaining, but the overall focus should be on educating the public about the development and its story. In a well-executed event, the development environment can be enhanced with exhibits, tours, and presentations to maximize exposure.

Invitation lists for events before the opening should include prospective buyers or renters and those who are in a position to influence others in favor of the development. Invitees to grand openings should include government officials as well as representatives of the extended development team, investment principals, and potential prospects.

Sales and Leasing

The role of the broker or sales agent varies from project to project. Developers may use an outside brokerage company or their own in-house staff. The approach depends on the developer's capabilities, the property type, and market conditions.

When sales and leasing are handled in house, a developer has more control. Even with in-house sales teams, however, the extended brokerage community usually becomes involved in the sales process. Therefore, developers should maintain cooperative and productive relationships with outside brokers, including participating in the commission-sharing structure to provide appropriate incentives.

Successful brokers know about local market conditions and often have proprietary access to prospects. They are not readily excited by new products unless they are convinced that they can sell the products easily. They want assurance that developers will pay full commissions quickly. If a developer helps local agents build stronger relationships with their clients, the agents tend to become more enthusiastic about introducing their clients to the developer.

The Marketing and Sales Staff

Motivating the sales staff is an ongoing challenge. The real estate sales process is characterized by rejection and failure: attempted sales far surpass completed sales, and the number of prospects far surpasses the number of buyers. Many more selling days end in defeat than in victory, and most sales agents are compensated through commissions.

To be effective, an agent must fully understand the product. Most developers provide some type of orientation program for new agents. The need to educate salespeople in the specific skills needed to sell a particular project is less well understood. Continuing education enhances agents' professional skills, leading to more sales or leases for the developer. Continuing education also creates coherence within the organization, resulting in lower turnover of sales agents.

The profession of selling is built on the ability of salespeople to establish clear and compelling communication with prospects. Most often, sound communication is based on establishing as much personal rapport as possible with the prospect as soon as possible. Prospects who feel comfortable with a sales agent and are convinced that the agent is sincerely interested in their point of view are more likely to buy or lease a product.

One of the principal differences between commercial and residential real estate sales is the extent to which active prospecting takes place. In commercial developments, developer's representatives typically identify potential individual members of the target market and contact them directly to initiate a sale. Alternatively, developer's representatives may contact members of the brokerage community who enjoy exclusive leasing arrangements with prospective tenants.

The first potential set of prospects is the developer's current rent roll: tenants who may be thinking about expanding or relocating their facilities. Existing relationships with current tenants offer a great advantage to the developer who is not concerned about eroding occupancy in one building to increase it in another. When the same developer controls both existing and prospective leases, timing the shift is much easier.

Building the Sale

Once a salesperson has identified an interested prospect, the challenge shifts to making a successful sales presentation. The agent aims to identify the prospect's needs and convince her that the proffered product meets those needs, and that the value delivered is at least equal to the price. The best salespeople follow a planned sequence for the presentation that guarantees delivery of all needed information in a logical order as well as opportunities for ample feedback from the prospect. If the salesperson follows the sequence and delivers all the necessary information, the prospect will be more likely to buy the product.

Sixty London offers premium office space in a unique modern design. In 2013, the entire office component was preleased to Amazon. After signing that company, the developer was able to prelease the retail space as well.

Effective follow-up is essential for any sales transaction. Few sales are closed in the first meeting, and good salespeople work patiently with identified prospects. Given the effort and expense of creating a synergistic marketing and sales system, it makes sense to contact a nonresponsive prospect more than once. For a residential project, follow-up on presales efforts is intended to encourage return visits to the sales center. The agent should follow a schedule of e-mail and telephone contacts that is based on the number of days since the prospect's first visit to the sales center. For commercial properties, the same general idea holds, though with one major exception: the pace of follow-up should accelerate as the expiration date of the prospect's current lease approaches.

Reaching an agreement does not end the agent's follow-up responsibilities. One of the most important functions that a sales or leasing professional performs is holding the deal together between the signing and the move-in. After the tenant moves in, follow-up shifts to ascertaining that the space has been delivered in acceptable condition. It makes no sense to shepherd a prospect to an agreement only to have the deal fall apart. Likewise, it is of limited benefit to put a prospect into space the team has worked hard to create only to find the new tenant unhappy with some feature. The most efficient way to avoid such unfortunate circumstances is through systematic and sensitive follow-up by salespeople.

THE CONTRACTUAL (HARD) SIDE OF MARKETING

The end result of the marketing program is the legal document that binds the developer and buyer. These contracts produce the project's revenue stream. For for-sale projects, such as land in an industrial park, condominium units, or single-family homes, it is a one-step transaction: a purchase agreement sets up a closing at which title to the property is transferred from the developer to the buyer in exchange for the payment of an agreed amount. For investment properties, it is a two-step process: First, the income stream is established through leases between the developer and tenant. Then, that income stream is valued and sold at the optimum point in the development cycle through a purchase agreement between the developer and an investor.

The developer usually engages a transaction attorney to ensure that the business objectives for the project are accurately expressed through the sales contract or lease. The developer (rather than the buyer or tenant) usually offers the first draft of a document that contains his standard provisions. That document provides the platform for subsequent negotiations to close the deal. Deviations from the standard document are minimal for small transactions and may be more customized for major buyers or tenants.

The Leasing Transaction

In the classic definition of renowned researcher Frederick Case, the lease is an agreement "by means of which a property owner, the lessor, contracts to transfer to the tenant, the lessee, certain specified rights relating to the possession and use of a real property in return for which the lessee agrees to make certain payments."[1] The form and stream of payments creates the value of the real estate asset. It determines the net operating income stream that is capitalized to determine its value at the time of sale.

The nature of rental payments is determined by the market and the type of asset. Some leases are shorter term and have a fixed rent (flat rental); for example, leases for residential units are usually for

Infinity Tower | São Paulo, Brazil

Infinity Tower is an 18-floor, class A office building with ground floor retail in São Paulo, Brazil. In addition to its cutting-edge energy efficiency, which earned it LEED Gold certification, the building employed a leasing structure that is unusual in this region. Most office projects in Brazil are developed by pre-selling condominium-ownership offices to fund construction, and then leasing them to tenants, complicating the leasing process because tenants must negotiate with multiple owners. Infinity Tower was structured with a single owner, and units were pre-leased directly to tenants to fund construction. This strategy made the leasing process much easier for tenants and resulted in quick negotiations and lease-up. This streamlined leasing structure combined with the building's stylish design enabled the tower to attract multinational corporate tenants in high-end industries like law, luxury goods, finance, and information technology. More than half of the building was pre-leased to multinational companies before it was completed, and full lease-up was accomplished soon after completion.

a year. Commercial leases often have longer terms, sometimes up to 20 years, and may incorporate a variety of methods for increasing the rent over that period:

- A rental rate with agreed upon fixed increases at specific dates;
- A rental rate with increases linked to a reference value, such as the cost of living index; or
- A rental rate for retail spaces with a percentage participation in sales, usually above a specified *base rent*.

Commercial leases also have two kinds of mechanisms, sometimes called *escalation clauses*, for passing the risk of increases in operating expense through to lessees:

- Single, double, or *triple net leases*, in which the lessee agrees to pay directly for certain operating expenses such as property taxes, insurance, and maintenance; and
- Leases with expense stops, wherein the lessee agrees to pay for certain agreed-upon operating expenses above an agreed-upon level.

In the financial modeling during stages one through four, the developer has anticipated the form of lease. The financial model included assumptions for several items:

- Base rents and rent increases;
- Base operating expenses and operating expense increases, and the mechanism by which those increases are shared between lessor and lessee;
- Capital expenditures, such as major repairs (re-roofing, replacement of mechanical equipment, etc.); and
- Leasing and re-leasing costs, such as commissions and tenant improvements.

Financial modeling can become very complex when these assumptions are applied to each potential lease in a larger property. For example, a lease analysis might consider 50 or 60 tenant spaces in a single spreadsheet, using different combinations of location and size, anticipated lease terms, rent increases, leasing commissions, tenant improvements, renewal rates, expense recapture, and incentives. The product of this analysis is the developer's leasing strategy from feasibility through lease negotiations. Modeling software such as Argus enables the user to quickly calculate the expected outcome of various assumptions. Still, every situation differs. The developer must decide whether to use property- or transaction-specific spreadsheet models, or both.

For commercial buildings, owners use several definitions of space. Among them are the following:

- Total area: the total floor space of the building within the exterior walls.
- Gross leasable area or rentable area: the total floor area on which the tenants pay rent. In office buildings, this may include the tenant's share of service areas, lobbies, and hallways.
- Usable area: the private space that tenants can use to house their personnel, furniture, fixtures, and equipment.
- Common area: the area not designated for rental but available for use by all of the tenants and guests, such as lobbies, hallways, and restrooms.
- Load factor: in office buildings, the ratio of common area to rentable area.

All of these terms are carefully defined in the lease to accurately document the tenant's right to use and the obligation to pay for space and to determine common area charges.

Targeting the Tenant

Developers take different approaches to managing the leasing process. For example:

- A developer of a residential project may rely on in-house leasing staff or a team from an affiliated property management company. Alternatively, the developer may rely on an outside company.
- A developer of an industrial building or office project may rely on commercial brokers who have established relationships with potential tenants.
- A developer of a retail property may have direct relationships with tenants or tenant representatives from other projects.

The developer's relationship with a tenant may be a single transaction for a single project or, as is common in the retail sector, the developer may carry the relationship to multiple projects.

The leasing strategy is subject to other boundaries. The developer may be required by his financial sources to prelease a certain percentage of the project prior to receiving funding, to mitigate market risk. A self-financed developer may choose to defer leasing until the building is nearly completed in order to capture higher rental rates from a physical entity that prospective tenants can clearly see and understand. Some tenants exert considerable influence in the market. Large credit tenants may be able to obtain favorable terms by offering little default risk and committing to substantial blocks of space for long periods of time. For example, developers of regional malls have in some cases leased or sold sites at low values to anchor tenants in order to improve the rents they can obtain from smaller tenants.

Leases for retail projects often consist of two components: a "fixed" or "base" rent and a percentage rent. The percentage rent is paid if the tenant's sales exceed a certain amount, called the "breakpoint"; it is stated as a percentage of the excess sales. The base rent, breakpoint, and percentage rent are all stated on a per square foot basis. The breakpoint is further defined as natural or artificial. The natural breakpoint is the volume of annual sales per square foot that when multiplied by the figure for the percentage rent equals the base rent. Imagine a tenant has a base rent of $18 per square foot, a sales breakpoint of $300 per square foot, and a percentage rent of 6 percent. If the tenant has actual sales of $350 per square foot, the tenant's additional rent would be 6 percent of $50 per square foot, or an additional $3 per square foot, for a total rent of $21 per square foot. In this example, the natural breakpoint is $300 per square foot of sales—the level at which the base rent of $18 per square foot equals 6 percent of sales. The volume of sales per square foot and the associated percentages vary by type of store, retail center, and location.

Determining the Operating Expenses

Many projects include public areas that benefit the tenants but require ongoing maintenance and management. The costs of this work are often charged back to the tenants on the basis of their occupancy of the entire project, calculated as a percentage. Typical common area costs include maintenance for parking areas, lobbies, hallways and other public spaces, as well as central utility costs and promotion, administrative, and other operating expenses that cannot be billed by the provider directly to the tenant.

Depending on the lease terms, some or all of the operating expenses may be included in rents. In a gross lease, the lessor pays all operating expenses and bears all of the risk of increases in operating expenses. Net leases are a means of protecting lessors against increases in operating expenses:

- In a single net lease, the lessor passes property taxes through to the lessee.
- In a double net lease, the lessee pays for property tax and building insurance.
- In a triple net lease, the lessee pays all of the operating expenses and bears all of the risk of increases in those expenses.

Leases with expense reimbursement provisions, or expense stops, provide another way to allocate the risk of operating expense increases. In such arrangements, the lessor pays expenses up to a predetermined amount per square foot or pays expenses per square foot in a predefined lease year. In the latter case, for example, if a property has expenses of $10.00 per square foot and the lease provides for an expense stop of $8.50, the reimbursement or "additional rent" to the landlord would be $1.50.

The leasing effort involves other negotiations that allocate costs and rights between the landlord and tenant. Commercial leases, especially for new space, often have allowances for tenant improvements—the interior components of space necessary to make the space usable (such as partitions and lighting). The developer's pro forma identified the amount for these costs that the developer would pay, with the expectation that any excess would be paid by the tenant. In a lease, the agreed amount for the tenant improvement allowance depends on the attractiveness of the tenant, the strength of the market, and the tradeoffs against other lease terms.

Commercial leases also incorporate provisions regarding options to renew, cancellations, permitted uses and occupancy, parking, operating hours, security deposits, signage, subleasing, tenant alterations, insurance, and other contract considerations.

Hysan Place is a 40-story mixed-use office and retail complex in Hong Kong. The market-responsive design makes it possible to lease space for office or retail use, depending on market conditions. The building's high-end finishes respond to the demand for upscale retail space at this prime location, which commands some of the highest rents in the world.

| CASE STUDY | Irvine Tech Center: Completion |

For Wil Smith, the completion of ITC (stage seven) was the sale of the project in 2014 during the final entitlements process, before construction even began. Greenlaw was approached directly by a national multifamily builder that was ready to enter the market. The final step of a sale at this point required revisiting the feasibility and contract negotiation stages. The offer to purchase the project required an analysis of how the sales terms would affect Smith's return on investment, especially with a phased transaction (the potential buyer wanted to take down pieces of the site at different times).

The documentation required a return to the skill sets employed during the contract negotiation stage, and the execution entailed the same work as the commitment stage. As this case study shows, some projects are sold before construction even begins. For the purposes of the original developer, the development is considered "completed" at that point. In this case, the early sale was very profitable for both the developer and the development-period investor. ∎

Investment Property Sales Transactions

The sale of an investment property begins with the same financial tools that were used in the development of the property. Rents and operating expenses are projected over an investment period, taking into account the impact of rent and operating expense increases, lease rollovers, and capital expenditures. An investment package is assembled that includes the financial model and pertinent facts about the project. The project may be marketed directly to potential investors, presented to financial intermediaries, or promoted through a brokerage network. A confidentiality agreement may be involved, restricting the disclosure of any project data to anyone outside the prospective buyer's circle. The marketing channels are selected to be appropriate for the specific property with a focus on the product type, geographic area, and type of buyer being targeted. The marketing package may stipulate a price or it may call for bids to be received before a certain date.

The selection of a buyer may take different paths, depending on the developer, the investors, the type of property, and current market conditions. Negotiations may be initiated with a previously identified buyer and proceed directly to a sale. In other cases, multiple potential buyers may be identified and asked to submit bids. From these, the most promising bidders are selected and asked to submit a "best and final offer." Due diligence then occurs within a period negotiated in the purchase and sale agreement. If the property is sold through a bidding process, much of the due diligence may occur in a physical or virtual "data room" prior to bid submission.

The contract for sale follows the same considerations as the land acquisition contract, but from the other side of the table. It stipulates the price and manner of payment, include warranties and representations of the buyer and seller, and addresses administrative matters such as accruals to the date of closing, transfer of security deposits, estoppel certificates, and assignments.

For-Sale Property Transactions

For-sale properties include single-family homes, single and attached homes in common-area developments, condominiums, cooperatives, condominium offices, and build-to-suit commercial properties. The sales contracts contain the same provisions as investment properties, but residential transactions are often subject to additional legal and regulatory conditions.

There are two legal frameworks for the sale of residential properties: at the federal and state levels, sales are subject to antidiscrimination laws that govern the sale and financing of residential properties; and at the state level, laws govern the sale of

---

A New Model for Smart Density: D-Cube City, Seoul, South Korea

In South Korea's capital city, Seoul, D-Cube City represents a significant new model for urban renewal and smart density, as well as mixed-use, transit-oriented development. Located in a predominantly industrial zone near the Yeouido district, south of the Hangang River, the project site formerly held a large coal processing plant owned by the developer, Daesung Industrial Co. The former brownfield site, which is connected to the Sindorim subway station, now features a 42-story office and hotel tower; two 50-story residential towers; a hotel; a six-level, 800,000-square-foot leisure and cultural complex; 2,574 parking spaces; and more than six acres of public parks and plazas that connect to the adjacent Dorim River. Green roofs add to the usable public open space.

D-Cube City has emerged as Seoul's primary live/work/play destination. Transformation of the site into a mixed-use public district represents a milestone for land redevelopment in South Korea and acts as a catalyst for the continued growth and evolution of the area into a vibrant urban hub. The development has created more than 3,000 new jobs and draws an estimated 80,000 visitors daily. Land values in the general area have increased by an estimated 20 percent since the development was completed.

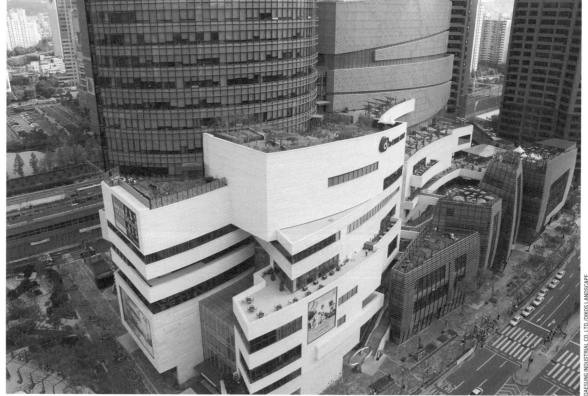

DAESUNG INDUSTRIAL CO. LTD./OIKOS LANDSCAPE

Organic building shapes and rooftop gardens evoke elements of traditional Korean landscape paintings.

subdivided property. Federal laws governing the sale of residential real estate include the following:

- The Federal Fair Housing Act, which prohibits discrimination against an individual on the basis of race, national origin, religion, sex, familial status, or handicap;
- The Americans with Disabilities Act, which addresses the removal of architectural barriers for certain classes of properties; and
- The Equal Credit Opportunity Act and the Home Mortgage Disclosure Act, which prohibit discriminatory lending practices.

Similar state legislation may reinforce or extend these federal regulations. State laws also govern the sale of subdivided residential properties. In addition to the conditions of approval that govern development standards, some states require public disclosure of certain aspects of the property. These aspects include site-specific elements such as access, utility availability, hazards or adverse environmental factors, use restrictions, and other information that enables buyers to make educated purchase decisions. States may also require disclosures regarding common area entities, including the provision of documents governing condominiums and homeowner associations. Some states set forth advertising criteria to prevent false or misleading claims.

STAGE SEVEN: COMPLETION AND FORMAL OPENING

There are many ways to open a project. If it is a single-tenant industrial building, the opening may be nothing more than turning over the keys upon the issuance of an occupancy permit. At the other extreme, a high-profile office building may have a completion party for the contractors, an opening party for public officials, and another opening celebration for occupants. In addition, the developer needs to train the operations personnel, connect utilities, begin on-site operations, and transition from the construction loan to the permanent loan.

Operations personnel are brought to the site before the grand opening. Their job is to make sure that tenants receive their spaces with the associated services specified in the lease agreements. The amount of time that the operations personnel spend on site before opening depends on their functions and on the project size and type. In a convention hotel, for example, some marketing staff may join the operations staff as much as two years before the opening.

During the construction phase, the contractor should complete all the interior finish work specified by tenants expected in the initial move-in stage. The marketing staff, working with the operations personnel, also handles activities before the opening—advertising, promotion, VIP parties, and the like. It is often good business for the developer to throw a party to thank those in the community who were involved in the project. Such an event can generate long-term goodwill. Before the party, the utilities need to be connected, meaning that the team needs to have met all obligations to the city.

SUMMARY

Physical construction and marketing, sales, and leasing are the key activities in stage six. Although each development's location is unique, the basic marketing concepts apply to all. This chapter contains details that will be more important for some developments than others. Still, it does not take long to periodically review the whole discussion, and missing a detail can be very painful in the fast-paced interactive world of stage six.

The developer is well advised to review those basics regularly, as the price of review is low and the cost of overlooking something is high. Many "soft," concept items require consideration, and hard items, such as legal contracts, are needed to enforce the soft concepts. All of this work happens in a time-challenged, interactive environment, which makes stage six the most exciting part of the development process.

TERMS

- Base rent
- Branding
- Product differentiation

- Escalation clause
- Expense stops
- Gross lease
- Lease terms
- Niche identification
- Repositioning
- Triple net leases

REVIEW QUESTIONS

16.1 Describe the marketing team's role at each stage of the development process.

16.2 What are the components of the SWOT analysis? What goals does it accomplish?

16.3 What are the three basic approaches to estimating a marketing budget?

16.4 How do hard and soft considerations interact in the marketing in stage six?

16.5 Describe the types of leases and what is included in each.

NOTE

1 Frederick Case, *Real Estate* (Boston: Allyn and Bacon, 1965), p. 275.

Chapter 17

Stage Eight: Property, Asset, and Portfolio Management

The value of an income-producing project derives from its expected long-term financial performance, which depends on the quality of ongoing property, asset, and portfolio management. From the beginning of the development process, the developer creates value by matching an idea to a site and guiding the process of constructing an attractive, efficient building. At the end of the development process, the property, asset, and portfolio management functions maintain and work to increase that value.

Depending on the type of ownership, management can operate at up to three levels of responsibility:

1. On-site property management: functions such as the provision of janitorial services and collection of rent;
2. *Asset management*: the execution of ownership responsibilities on behalf of the investment entity that owns the property, typically including major lease decisions as well as larger capital expenditures for major renovations; and

3. Portfolio management: the design and execution of major investment decisions across a group of investments.

Collectively, these three functions should operate in a coordinated fashion to deliver the cash flows anticipated in the feasibility study and to maintain the physical structure and site so as to protect and enhance the project's long-term profitability. The developer's final task is to ensure that all three functions are up and running as the property opens. The functions of the management triad (discussed later in this chapter) are interrelated and overlapping. Sometimes a single individual may perform two (or even all three) of the management functions. Still, the three functions are distinct.

This chapter discusses the following topics:

- The real estate management triad;
- The fundamentals of real estate management from the perspective of the development process;
- The transition from property development to asset management;

The authors would like to thank Roger Pratt of Prudential Real Estate for his contributions to this chapter.

- The creation and implementation of the *strategic plan*—the heart of this chapter;
- The *corporate real estate director*;
- The influence of the public sector in the management phase;
- Training for property, asset, and portfolio managers and for the corporate real estate director; and
- The globalization of portfolio management.

THE ENTERPRISE CONCEPT AND CONTINUING MANAGEMENT OF THE DEVELOPED ASSET

The enterprise concept, introduced in chapter 13, describes treating real estate as an ongoing business. At stage eight, the business management aspect becomes the primary focus. Residual value is maximized when the property functions well after opening (stage seven) and is expected to continue to perform well over its extended economic life (stage eight). Even a developer who does not plan for long-term ownership of a project should be conscious of the prospect for long-term profitability because that will determine his exit price.

King's Cross is a 67-acre regeneration project in central London that includes a mix of office, residential, retail, hotel, and other uses, totaling about 6 million square feet of development. Given the project's world-class location, the marketing strategy has focused on place rather than specific buildings. An extensive program of events makes Kings Cross a regional destination, drawing patrons to its shops and restaurants.

An example of the enterprise concept in action is the Showplace Square development in San Francisco's South of Market (SoMa) district. The development originated from a cluster of under-used industrial buildings when the initial developer Henry Adams saw the opportunity to satisfy a new need in the market. In the early 1980s, SoMa was a pioneering location; now it is a trendy area of design showrooms and home furnishing shops, and more recently, technology firms. For Showplace Square to survive both the twists and turns of market trends and the neighborhood's evolution has required considerable operations savvy on the part of Bill Poland, the long-term developer. A critical element for success has been treating Showplace Square as an operating business. To add life to the area and help create a sense of place, Poland has promoted trade shows and rented the vast facilities for weddings and other social functions in the evenings and on weekends. He continues to adapt to market trends and changes in the character of the neighborhood. In mid-2006, he sold a majority interest in Showplace Square's retail component and began developing condos and apartments on adjoining land in this now fashionable area. RREEF (the U.S. real estate subsidiary of Deutsche Bank) owns the high-quality retail asset in a fund managed for pension investors. The buildings in this location were far from "institution" quality when Adams had the vision that Poland made a reality.

THE REAL ESTATE MANAGEMENT TRIAD

Property management and ongoing marketing are at the heart of the traditional real estate investment model. However, with the emergence of large institutional investment vehicles, more sophisticated versions of these roles have emerged to fulfill fiduciary responsibilities to passive investors.

The Property Manager

The property management team is responsible for handling the day-to-day operation of the physical project and carrying out the directives of the owner. Broadly, its primary goal is to ensure a continuous cash flow for the owner by managing the property efficiently and at an appropriate level of quality for the tenants.

Professional property managers establish a *management plan* with an appropriate budget, then implement that plan. The property manager collects rents, maintains accounting records, and directs and performs routine building maintenance through on-staff personnel or outside contractors.

The composition of the property management and marketing team varies with the size and complexity of the property. Functions may be performed by staff or contracted for with third parties. The developer's job is to find the right combination of professionals for the particular development and to have them in place and performing as the project opens. The team may include many players:

- A senior property manager (also known as a general manager on projects that require large staff), who bears ultimate responsibility for operations, reporting, and team performance, with the exception of leasing.

- An assistant property manager, who functions as an adjunct for the senior property manager and is delegated duties in a large project that would be handled by the senior property manager in a small project.

- A lease administrator, who may have responsibility for new leases and who maintains lease compliance records.

- A purchasing manager, who is responsible for negotiating the acquisition of supplies for all of the properties under management.

- A chief engineer or maintenance manager, who ensures that the physical plant runs reliably and efficiently. He is responsible for preventive maintenance programs and refurbishment or replacement of equipment as needed.

- In a property management company, a construction manager who oversees major capital expenditures for tenant improvements. This work includes the preparation of design specifications and bids, the selection of contractors for construction projects larger than the maintenance staff can handle on a day-to-day basis, and contract administration, including oversight of draws, lien waivers, and compliance with drawings and specifications.

- A director of security, who hires and trains the security staff and bears responsibility for the security of occupants and for protection of real and personal property.

- A project accountant, who processes accounts payable and accounts receivable, and prepares balance sheets and income statements for asset management.

- A concierge, whose responsibilities can range from managing the staff of an information desk for a retail project to arranging theater tickets, making dinner reservations, and handling dry cleaning deliveries for a residential building. In smaller projects, a concierge may also be responsible for building security.

- A leasing team of licensed real estate sales agents who might be dedicated to a project or might handle multiple noncompetitive projects. The team's task is to identify prospective tenants and negotiate the terms and conditions of leases. Negotiations typically are closely coordinated with asset management staff; in some cases, they participate directly in negotiations.

- A marketing director or manager, who supports the leasing team by establishing the project's competitive brand and promoting it through media and on-site branding. In large retail centers, the role includes developing promotional events with tenants to increase the center's visibility and sales. By constantly monitoring the center's competitiveness within its market, the marketing director can effectively implement the strategic directives developed by the asset manager to satisfy the portfolio manager's objectives.

Although few projects require all of the positions enumerated here, it is useful for the developer to review the list to ensure that some combination of people is collectively accomplishing each of the necessary functions.

A number of certification programs exist for property management professionals. The best-known is that of the Institute of Real Estate Management, an affiliate of the National Association of Realtors, which offers two designations: certified property manager (CPM) and accredited residential manager (ARM).[1] The Building Owners and Managers Association International (BOMA) offers four professional management accreditations; the International Facilities Management Association offers another.[2] BOMA also publishes an array of statistics on office building operations similar to the analyses of apartment income and expenses produced by the Institute of Real Estate Management. The International Council of Shopping Centers generates statistics on retail real estate. These organizations seek to enhance professionalism in the field and to provide data that can be used in feasibility studies and long-term operating budgets.

The Asset Manager

When ownership of the real estate asset is held by an investment vehicle, that vehicle typically includes a number of properties and the asset manager may hire and supervise more than one property manager. The asset manager reviews the monthly financial statements for the asset against the budget and works with the property manager to identify market trends that may suggest changes to the property's operation. He is responsible for major decisions, such as expenditures that lie beyond the contractual authority of the property manager, larger leases, and changes to the operating plan. He provides guidance to enable the property manager to maximize the asset's value. He carries a fiduciary responsibility to the investors in the asset and is the de facto property owner.

The asset manager is usually an employee of the institution that created the investment vehicle that owns the property. He is typically located off site and is responsible for several properties. Depending on the organization of the institution, asset managers may specialize in a property type, a geographic location, or both (such as office buildings in New York City or apartments in the Southeast).

The asset manager has several responsibilities:

- Development and periodic updates of a long-term strategic plan for the asset including anticipated leasing, operating expenditures, capital expenditures, and a target liquidation date;
- Review, analysis, and approval of the annual operating budget for the asset submitted by the property manager;
- Delegation of authority to the property manager for local leasing and some operating decisions;
- Development of investor reports, audited financial statements, and income tax returns;
- Review and appeal of real estate taxes;
- Arrangement of property and liability insurance;
- Structuring and implementation of workout programs for distressed assets; and
- Completion of special studies that may be required by the portfolio manager.

The asset management team may include several kinds of professionals:

- The asset manager, who is the primary conduit between property management, the marketing team, and the portfolio management team, with full responsibility for all aspects of asset performance;
- A controller—usually supported by a staff of portfolio accountants—who consolidates reports of multiple projects for a single owner, investor, or fund and conducts performance analysis pursuant to a range of industry standards;
- A risk manager, who underwrites and administers general liability, property, umbrella, and other forms of insurance coverage to preserve the investment against physical damage and claims arising from operations; and

A Walgreens drugstore in Evanston, Illinois, uses the latest technologies to produce more energy than it consumes. Wind turbines in the parking lot produce some of the store's power.

- A financial analyst, who models prospective cash flows and analyzes the impact of asset management decisions and changes in market conditions on prospective rates of return.

The Portfolio Manager

In large institutions, portfolio managers are responsible for a fund or funds that acquire, manage, and dispose of real estate investments. They usually oversee the asset managers and the acquisitions team. A portfolio manager should have a deep understanding of the owner's investment objectives to use in evaluating asset management performance, analyzing the costs and benefits of prospective capital improvements recommended by asset management, and orchestrating acquisitions and dispositions of assets to maximize risk-adjusted portfolio returns.

Portfolio managers develop investment strategies on the basis of the risk parameters and return goals of the investors in a portfolio of properties. They oversee asset management, acquisitions, dispositions, and reinvestment decisions as well as supervising the reporting of financial performance to owners. To minimize risk in any one category, it is common for larger portfolios to diversify across product types, geography, industries, tenants, and capital events.

The portfolio management staff may include the following specialists:

- A portfolio manager, who manages the fund on behalf of multiple investors, defining the character of the portfolio and implementing the acquisitions, sales, and interim decisions about capital that drive performance;
- Economists and researchers, who identify market trends and investment opportunities along with associated risks, to facilitate the composition and maintenance of a portfolio that is consistent with the owner's objectives;
- Acquisition professionals, who are investment specialists charged with the task of acquiring property that is consistent with the risk-adjusted return and product requirements specified by the portfolio manager; and
- Disposition professionals, who are responsible for the sale of property, through either direct marketing or a brokerage group; their tasks are sometimes delegated to asset managers.

A variety of companies offer real estate investment management or advisory services. Some are subsidiaries of development companies; others are independent investment managers or subsidiaries of major financial institutions. Typically, the individuals who handle asset and portfolio management in investment management companies are educated in management, finance, or law. A large number of portfolio managers are members of the National Council of Real Estate Investment Fiduciaries (NCREIF), the Pension Real Estate Association (PREA), and/or the National Association of Real Estate Investment Managers (NAREIM).[3] Another professional organization, the Certified Commercial Investment Members (CCIM) Institute, focuses on asset management and certifies those who have successfully completed its training program.[4] The box on the following page highlights the major

---

Major Responsibilities of the Management Triad

Property Manager

- Tenant relations and retention
- Rent collection
- Control of operating expenses
- Financial reporting and record keeping
- Maintenance of property
- Planning capital expenditures
- Crisis management
- Security issues
- Public relations

Asset Manager

- Developing property strategic plan
- Analyzing whether to hold or sell the property
- Reviewing opportunities to reposition properties and to justify major expenditures

- Monitoring property performance
- Managing and evaluating the property manager by comparing property performance with peer properties in the particular submarket
- Assisting in tenant relations

Portfolio Manager

- Communicating with investors and setting portfolio goals and investment criteria
- Defining and implementing portfolio investment strategy
- Overseeing acquisitions, dispositions, asset management, and reinvestment decisions
- Accountable for portfolio performance
- Client reporting and cash management

---

responsibilities of the property manager, the asset manager, and the portfolio manager.

FUNDAMENTALS OF REAL ESTATE MANAGEMENT FROM THE DEVELOPMENT PERSPECTIVE

For the developer, detailed input from the property management team is important. This input should begin in the earliest states of the development process. The property manager lives with the daily reality of how tenants use their space and how to most efficiently serve their needs. He works with leases that specify the features, functions, and benefits that tenants expect from the building. The best managers bring local market knowledge of what tenants value. The developer bears the responsibility for designing a building that will enable lease obligations to be satisfied at a cost consistent with the pro forma.

The facility must have the appropriate spaces dedicated to building operation. For example, there must be facilities for equipment storage, trash storage and removal, and deliveries. These routine functions may occasionally be overlooked in the exuberance of the design process. For example, an apartment building in the Washington, D.C., area

was designed by a prominent architect without consideration for storage of janitorial supplies. An entire rental unit had to be taken off line and devoted to that need.

There is sometimes an inherent tension between the developer and the property manager. The property manager is motivated to make his job easier by recommending a "gold-plated" building that has the highest-quality, lowest-maintenance equipment and higher-level staffing in order to provide the best-quality service. The developer is motivated to develop a pro forma with the most favorable operating cost assumptions. This tension is heightened during the turnover period.

Sometimes during construction, there may be a need for design modifications to accommodate a major tenant. The property management team should be involved when any such changes are contemplated. To determine whether changes are cost-effective, the developer must estimate the initial cost and any incremental increase in operating expenses relating to those features.

For example, in a project under development, a lease is pending between a cinema operator and a shopping mall owner for interior space. Normally, such a cinema operation would be freestanding or would be accessed through a dedicated entrance. In this instance, however, no separate entrance or remaining outparcel is available. The leasing agent has considerable retail space that must be leased and is motivated to promote the lease as the cinema is expected to draw other tenants. The construction manager favors the change because construction for one large tenant is simpler and less expensive than for multiple tenants in the same space. The architect revises pedestrian flow through the mall hoping to benefit other tenants from the presence of theater patrons.

Should the developer approve the rearrangement? Not necessarily. The property management team's review of the revised leasing plan identifies shortcomings related to higher janitorial and security costs because the cinema will be open well beyond the normal operating hours of other mall tenants. From a quick revision of the numbers in the discounted cash flow model (originally part of the feasibility study), the developer sees that operating ramifications associated with the cinema will impair, rather than create, value. In this and similar situations, the feasibility study serves as a good tool for sensitivity analysis.

TRANSITIONING FROM DEVELOPMENT TO OPERATIONS

An astute developer plans carefully for the transition from development to ongoing operations. This is a period of potential overlapping responsibilities for operating management and construction costs. The general contractor faces the potential for callback work to correct construction deficiencies, and the developer faces the potential for operating losses if lease-up occurs more slowly than anticipated. The property manager is attempting to operate a building in which construction activities may still be underway. The developer's transition plan takes all of this into account. The developer works with the property manager to conduct several walk-through tours to make certain that all parties are satisfied with the quality of the work and to clarify any subsequent construction that may be required. As part of the transition, he turns over all operating manuals

and equipment warranties to the ongoing operations management staff.

An institutional buyer of an investment property develops an initial management plan to determine how the property management functions should be performed. It is based on a realistic assessment of the property's competitive position in the market and the owner's investment objectives. The details of the management plan need to be consistent with the ability to provide space over time and to provide the associated services necessary to compete effectively in the market. If the services are inconsistent with the market's desires, the project is unlikely to generate maximum net operating income over time.

The investor is concerned about good tenant relations, rent collection, operating expenses, releasing, maintenance schedules, energy conservation, security, personnel supervision, and other property and asset management functions. Security, for example, is a critical concern of many tenants, and the property design can dramatically affect it. Installing adequate exterior lighting and placing entranceways so they are clearly visible from the street are important considerations. Electronic card access systems, which add a greater sense of security, may reduce the need for guard services or electronic surveillance. Decisions made during the development process can affect the cost of insurance coverage. For instance, buildings that lack complete life safety systems typically incur higher insurance premiums.

Sometimes overlooked in the transition process is the original image conceived for the project. The success of a project lies in its social as well as its physical form: the developer's and the designer's vision both extend to how people will use the space. Unless that vision is transmitted to the property manager, the use of space can be compromised by the property manager's decisions. Signage, fencing, lighting, and other minor fixtures installed after development can erode the project's architectural statement. The operating plan must be crafted to maximize the leverage afforded by the project's architecture and operational possibilities.

If an income property is to be sold upon completion, its transfer to the asset management team is defined in the documents articulating the terms of sale. (If the property is held within the developer's organization, the transfer is defined by company policy.) The transfer may include several terms. The most basic is the transfer of legal title to the asset. Directly connected to that transfer is the condition of payment to the developer, which may range from payment at the time of transfer to a holdback for the completion of certain performance conditions, including lease-up or stabilized operation.

A project is usually considered stabilized when it is physically complete and its occupancy rate exceeds an operating breakeven point or some other level defined in the purchase and sale agreement. The length of the period required to stabilize varies with property type, market conditions, asset quality, and asset management. If the sales documents include performance conditions, the developer remains actively involved, working closely with the management group.

The documents in the transfer package vary with the size and complexity of the project but generally include the following:

- A brief narrative describing the status of the project at transfer and any major outstanding issues. All significant construction-related documents, including "as-built" plans and occupancy permits, should be included.
- A comparison of the pro forma with results to the date of turnover, together with an agreement on the responsibility for interim costs and expenses. All significant variances, both positive and negative, should be explained. Elements include the construction budget by line item, the length of the development period, the status of leasing and rental rates, and NOI and cash flow generated during the development period.

What Do Anchor Tenants Want? Bragging Rights

Let's face it. In addition to the hard economics of the lease, anchor tenants want bragging rights, personal attention, and perks. The CEO who signs a lease for office space wants to crow about the deal he got. He wants to tell his fellow CEOs around town about the rent, free rent, huge tenant improvement allowance, or equity extracted because *his* lease created all the value in the building. There will be a discussion of the showdown negotiation when the landlord caved at the last minute—or the terrific job the broker did getting the escalations capped, negotiating for landmark signage, or providing flexibility to expand or contract over time.

They Want Love and Affection

- A letter of credit from the landlord or a lender during construction of the building and tenant improvements
- A seat at the table during building design and development
- Branding of the building to enhance the tenant's business (signs, flags, sidewalk monuments, and so on)
- Expansion or rights of first offer as the anchor tenant
- Equity participation after a specified hurdle for the investors

They Want Red-Carpet Treatment

- The ability to use the building lobby for events so clients and investors think it is the tenant's building
- Attentive property manager and staff who are well dressed, on a first-name basis with key tenant personnel, and, above all, responsive to requests—basically similar to a hotel concierge

They Want Certain Building Amenities

- A gym, daycare, a café, a sundries shop, a shoeshine, priority parking, a car wash, a dry cleaner
- Tenant-appreciation and philanthropic events such as ice cream socials, stair-climbing challenges, food and toy drives, and so on

They Want Communication

- An open line of communication between principals, in which the building owner does not hide behind an asset manager or property manager
- Monthly or quarterly meetings (more frequent if necessary) to review what is good, what is not so good, and what is happening at the building
- Advance notice of any upcoming construction nearby, the availability of neighboring space, and any changes to operations that may affect employees
- Billing and operating expense information that is easy to understand and easy to access

Tenants should be treated as strategic partners and be provided with not just "quiet enjoyment" of their space, but complete enjoyment. The tenant-landlord relationship should not be adversarial; landlords should go out of their way to overdeliver on their obligations in the lease documents. Nearly all tenants pay their rent on time or in advance, so landlords should treat them in kind.

William McCall and David Richardson, McCall & Almy

Property Strategic Planning Process

Define and Analyze Property Problems and Opportunities
- Physical description of property
- Operating history
- Market conditions
- Property strengths and weaknesses compared with competition

Evaluate and Revise Objectives Based on Current Information
- Local market or competition
- Investor needs
- Tenant requirements
- Portfolio and other considerations

Consider Alternatives and Generate a Plan to Meet Objectives
- Review major decision points
  - ☐ Hold or sell?
  - ☐ Rehabilitate?
  - ☐ Change the use of the building?
  - ☐ Change the tenant mix?
  - ☐ Change the manager or leasing agent?
- Create a new pro forma for the property based on the plan

Implement the Plan
- Staffing
- Marketing program
- Operating budget
- Capital program

- The calculation of the overall cost of development and any outstanding items that remain to be completed.
- The calculation of the final proceeds due the developer.

DEVELOPING AN INITIAL STRATEGIC PLAN FOR THE PROPERTY

Investors vary in their strategies for acquiring property. Some investors conservatively target signature buildings in stable markets. Others try to time their investments to the bottom of the economic cycle and anticipate making their profits "on the buy." Some acquire distressed properties and use their workout skills to correct operational or financing problems. All of these actions represent the investor's portfolio-level strategic plan, usually articulated by the portfolio manager.

The implementation of the investment strategy falls to the asset manager, who prepares a project-level strategic plan. The box above summarizes the major elements of the real estate strategic planning process in the context of the *property life cycle*. Using appropriate research and documents from the transfer package, the asset management team defines the opportunities and challenges facing a property. This

analysis is not performed in a vacuum. Effective property and asset management draws from a wide variety of local experts in the course of formulating a plan.

The first step is to evaluate the existing objectives for the property and revise them as needed in response to current information. Variables that precipitate a revision of the original objectives include changes in local market competition, new tenant requirements, or evolving portfolio considerations in response to changing investors' needs.

With this information, asset and portfolio managers are in a position to examine the alternatives for the future of the property. The property management team needs to agree on the preferred direction for the property, which should be reflected in a new operating budget. Even though the budget numbers are only estimates predicated on multiple assumptions, these numbers provide a road map for the future direction that the asset management team takes for the project. In the absence of a clear, well-documented strategic plan, the project is unlikely to achieve its full potential.

Economic downturns, with their resulting layoffs, have highlighted the need for succession planning in any real estate enterprise, whether it be the operation of a shopping center or the key member

329

of the leadership of a multinational development company. As the global market becomes more institutionalized and complex, it is important to build a complete organization that is able to carry on in adverse circumstances.

IMPLEMENTING THE STRATEGIC PLAN

For the strategic plan to be realized, the resources devoted to its implementation must be commensurate with the objectives. For example, an established objective to increase occupancy in a shopping center from 65 percent to 90 percent in a year most likely requires a fully staffed and aggressive leasing team armed with a full complement of marketing tools. The four main elements in the implementation of a strategic plan are staffing, the marketing program, the operating budget, and the capital program.

On-Site Staffing

As discussed in the section on the enterprise concept, commercial real estate is at its core a service business. In a service business, the most important point of contact between the business and the customer is the front-line employee. In property management, front-line employees are the on-site management, rental, and maintenance personnel. The efforts of these employees often go unnoticed until there is a problem, when they usually bear the direct dissatisfaction of tenants. The effectiveness of on-site staff is a function of their initial training and of their ongoing supervision by the home office of the property management company.

Home Office Staffing

Property management companies can be organized on a line or staff basis. In the former, regional managers are responsible for all aspects of a project; in the latter, managers specialize by discipline and serve all projects. Those disciplines may include marketing, maintenance, purchasing, and other functions. Corporate property management is challenging because subordinates often are located in remote project sites and may see their direct supervisors only periodically.

Marketing and Leasing

The marketing program—designed both to attract new customers and to retain existing ones—is critical in implementing the strategy for a property. It involves making choices about personnel, advertising, promotional events, commission schedules, and other factors.

Ongoing marketing and leasing functions vary across property types. A small multifamily project may require little more than showing available apartments to prospective tenants. Larger multifamily assets might require the creation of collateral materials, signage, contracts with prospect referral firms, the development and placement of advertisements, coordination of cooperative advertising with local businesses, and the creation of corporate outreach programs targeted to areas that have traditionally provided residents for the community. A retail center may require an ongoing marketing program that promotes the center to the public through events, advertising, and community outreach efforts. In these instances, it is critical that the property management firm demonstrate its ability to track both the source and the quality of the prospects generated from its marketing efforts.

The rise of the internet and the use of search engines has transformed how real estate properties are marketed, particularly for those properties in which property owners interact directly with the consumer, such as apartment rentals. Over 90 percent of apartment renters now search for apartments online. The range of ways and services for accessing the online community runs from developing a proprietary website to outsourcing part or all of the online marketing activities. Still, print media is not dead, and many owners believe it is wise to use a variety of media services to find prospects. Such services may include print magazines and newspapers, as well as websites, search engines, smartphone apps, and social media. It is important to know both the costs—whether for paid advertising or "cost per click"—and expected returns of each of these services. This requires knowing the sources of renter traffic, so that the marketing budget can be adjusted periodically to reflect changing consumer behavior.

The marketing program must include a strategy for dealing with tenant turnover, which will be a focus once the property reaches stabilization. Turnover may be expensive in terms of costs to market the space and rent lost during vacant periods, but it may also offer an opportunity to raise rents for incoming tenants. Turnover can sometimes be minimized through good communication and a high level of customer service. It is important that the marketing team stay on top of any potential vacancies and be ready to remarket the space in a timely manner.

Operating Budget

Once the strategic plan is adopted, the property's annual operating budget is formalized. The operating budget is worked out by the major categories identified in the initial pro forma. It reflects the initial project pro forma, beginning with gross potential income and deducting vacancies to arrive at net income and then deducting operating expenses to arrive at NOI. The property management company refines those numbers by adding appropriate detail to each major category and providing the assumptions underlying each expense.

To develop the appropriate underlying assumptions for each line item, the property manager draws on experience as well as industry standards set by the various professional organizations. Although the details may vary according to asset class and company, the major operating expense categories typically include marketing and promotional costs, property management fees, maintenance and landscaping expenses (including salaries and supplies), and real estate taxes and insurance. The budget also includes capital expenditures. For an example of a budget showing line items for a particular project, see the Shortbread Lofts case study in chapter 13.

Learning from Downturns

What does it take to survive and thrive in a volatile economic environment in which real estate is integrated into the global economy more than ever? The strategy that a firm embraces depends on the investor's or developer's appetite for risk. But in order to reduce some of the undesired effects of volatility (such as bankruptcy, staff layoffs, and loss of clients' investments), it is helpful to consider some of the painful lessons learned from the Great Recession:

- A real estate development enterprise should look at its real estate exposure comprehensively as a portfolio rather than on a piecemeal basis. The portfolio risk exposure is different than the sum of the risk exposure of individual projects. The suitability of each investment should be considered from a portfolio perspective to avoid unintentional strategy drift.
- Portfolio reviews should be held regularly, with an eye to avoiding concentrations of positions and limiting the amount of riskier investments (such as land and pre-developed projects). It is useful to have some properties in the portfolio that help dampen portfolio volatility, such as property management services or stabilized core properties.* The overall capital structure of the enterprise is critical. In the past, the developer's objective might have been to borrow as much money as possible at the lowest rate on each project, but this strategy may result in a higher-than-desired risk profile at the enterprise level. Managers should determine the overall appropriate leverage level for the enterprise, and assess and monitor the use of recourse debt and off-balance-sheet exposure, as well as debt rates terms, covenants, and refinancing options. Stress tests of the portfolio for liquidity purposes should be conducted routinely.

- The firm's proprietary equity capital should be used judiciously in relation to its overall size, scale, and business plan. Additional equity capital should be raised as necessary to implement the firm's business plan and to maintain the desired leverage position of the enterprise.
- Portfolio managers should be aware of cycle risk and vintage year (the year in which capital is first invested) exposure of deals done at the peak of the cycle. To minimize unpleasant surprises, investments should be paced at a rate which ensures that documentation of equity and loan positions is done properly and that appropriate due diligence on partners, lenders, and other counterparties is accomplished.
- To establish and maintain trust, firms should communicate transparently and in a timely fashion with clients, partners, and counterparties.

Roger Pratt

* For an approach to portfolio management that aims to reduce overall volatility, see Roger Pratt, "A Beta Approach," *The Institutional Real Estate Letter, North America*, September 2011, pp. 37–42.

The process of creating a budget for a property is time-consuming but extremely important. To ensure that all potential revenues and expenses are accurately recognized, each revenue and expense line item from the property's chart of accounts should be carefully considered and detailed. Over- or under-estimating expenses or revenues can lead to inappropriate investment decisions. Typically, the operating budget is reviewed in detail and approved by the asset manager.

An examination of the details of the operating budget early in the development process can allow a developer to adjust the project as necessary to avoid serious construction errors. Although industry averages are a reasonable starting point, what matters in the final analysis is the cost of operating a particular property relative to what the market will pay for the features, functions, and benefits provided by that property. As the completed development is transferred to operating management, it is important to reexamine all assumptions so as to make well-informed decisions that take into account the most current market information.

In opaque emerging markets outside the United States, there may be no comparable projects to use as a guide, making the analysis more difficult. Such instances require creativity and applied research in order to estimate what a reasonable range of projections might look like.

Capital Program

The initial capital program often receives little attention, especially in the case of a new project, which usually requires few additional capital expenditures in its early years. In practice, however, most projects—even well-conceived new projects—require some additional capital input, either to remedy construction or design deficiencies not covered by warranties (such as inadequate drainage in a parking lot) or to meet expanded tenant requirements (such as demand for additional covered parking in an apartment project).

It is important to note that the upkeep of a commercial real estate building and its basic components is predictable, in the same way that a maintenance program for a new car is predictable. Accordingly, a ten-year schedule of capital expenditures should be created at the time that a property is transferred or acquired. Figure 17-1 is a graph of the repair and replacement schedule for three major components of

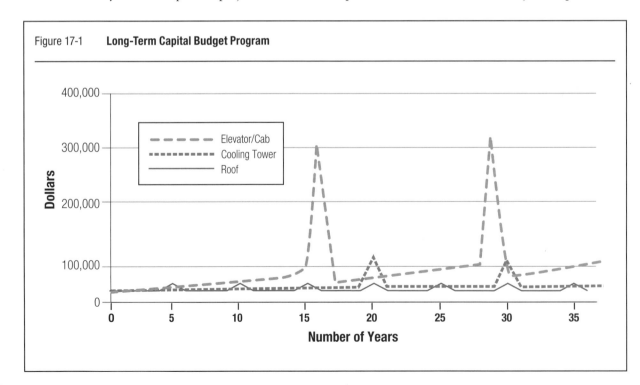

Figure 17-1   **Long-Term Capital Budget Program**

The certificate of occupancy was granted to the fully leased property only weeks before the scheduled move-in of students for the fall semester. Short was contemplating the final stage of the development process and trying to decide how best to capitalize on the option he had worked hard to preserve during the first seven stages. The NOI was well over $2 million and he had three choices: to sell the property, to hold and maintain the existing short-term loan, or to hold the property and refinance the loan. The capitalization rate on new apartments in attractive markets had dropped well below 5 percent, and long-term debt had gotten even more attractive. So he would either refinance the loan and hold the property for the long term or sell it. As of the publication of this book, Short was still pondering the decision. Most likely he will refinance the loan and hold the property. ■

Shortbread Lofts lobby.

an office property—the roof, the cooling tower, and the elevators. These capital projects are considered long-term building maintenance. Other projects involve tenant improvements related to re-leasing space as the initial terms of tenants' leases expire. Additional capital expenditures may arise as a result of changes in government regulations or market requirements. Life safety improvements, new security systems, energy management programs, and retrofits to provide improved access for people with disabilities are all examples of programs that have emerged in recent years but may not have been fully incorporated into developers' original pro formas. Although property and asset managers must be careful not to over-improve a facility, thereby draining a property's cash flow through excessive capital expenditures, they must maintain the property at the market standard if it is to have an extended useful life and compete effectively for tenants. Furthermore, scheduled preventive maintenance projects are usually less costly and less disruptive to tenants over the long run than crisis-driven emergency repairs.

Ongoing Planning

Strategic plans for a property should be reviewed at least annually and more frequently if circumstances dictate. Sometimes, as a result of changes in market conditions and tenants' requirements, a strategic

plan may become obsolete a short time after it is prepared. Ideally, asset and portfolio managers should look at the property with fresh eyes each year and ask themselves, "If we didn't already own this asset, would we acquire it again today? If not, why not?" By forcing the property to be "reacquired" each year, the asset management team invigorates the planning process and sloughs off the inertia so often endemic to the property management business. As Chuck Dannis, senior managing director of Dallas-based National Valuation Associates, notes, this exercise also helps the appraisers who value buildings in an institutional investor's portfolio on a regular basis.

Commercially available spreadsheet programs enable the asset manager to manage ongoing plans. They allow space-by-space assumptions for rent levels, rent increases, common area charges, operating expenses, and re-leasing costs. The asset manager uses these programs to update the projected financial performance of the project and facilitate decision making by the property management and portfolio management teams.

Property Management Contracts

A *property management contract* provides a framework for the relationship between the property management firm and the owner. It specifies which management services the owner pays for and which

A Standard Management Agreement

Article 1	Properties
Article 2	Commencement Date
Article 3	Manager's Responsibilities
Article 4	Insurance
Article 5	Financial Reporting and Record Keeping
Article 6	Owner's Right to Audit
Article 7	Bank Account
Article 8	Payment of Expenses
Article 9	Insufficient Gross Income
Article 10	Sale of a Property
Article 11	Cooperation
Article 12	Compensation
Article 13	Termination
Article 14	Subsidiaries and Affiliates
Article 15	Notices
Article 16	Nonassignables, etc.
Schedules	
A	Property Identification, Compensation Schedule, and Leasing Commission
B	Leasing Guidelines
C	Monthly Report Forms
C-1	Chart of Accounts
D	Reimbursable Employees
E	Subsidiaries and Affiliates
F	Insurance Certificate

the property management firm pays for. It determines who pays employees, who can authorize certain expenditures, who is responsible for keeping certain records, who is responsible for maintaining insurance coverage, and who handles advertising and promotion, as well as how the property management firm is compensated. The budget quantifies the management plan and ensures that the interests of owners and tenants are expressed consistently. Just as owners must be alert to general contractors' bids that do not include all essential items, they must scrutinize management plans and budgets to ensure the plans are comprehensive and the fee is sufficient to properly motivate the property management firm

to devote the resources necessary to accomplish the owner's objectives. When the capabilities of the property management firms are thoroughly scrutinized and the management contract negotiated and committed to paper, developers can be more certain that a qualified organization is ready to perform all specified services at the quoted price.

The responsibility for hiring the first property management firm may lie with the developer or the investor. The length of the management contract varies, but the progressively more common industry standard is to provide the owner with a right to terminate the contract without cause after 30 or 60 days' notice. The benefit to the owner is the ability to effect change quickly if performance is substandard and to ensure the constant attention of the property management firm. The elements of a standard management agreement are shown in the box on this page.

THE CORPORATE REAL ESTATE DIRECTOR

Real estate assets constitute a major portion of the balance sheets for many companies. For some, lease expenses represent a significant portion of operating costs. Access to the right space in the right location is often critical to a firm's competitiveness and its employees' quality of life. An attractive work environment is important for attracting and retaining employees, especially in tight labor markets.

Most major corporations have a real estate department headed by a senior executive who is responsible for the acquisition and maintenance of the spaces required by the corporation. Corporate real estate decisions vary with the type of company and its needs for serving its markets. In some cases, headquarters offices have moved to suburban locations to reduce costs. In others, companies have moved to larger cities to be more attractive to key employees.

Corporate real estate directors are involved in decisions about building capacity and layout from the perspective of the building user. They implement decisions to lease or buy space. They work with the firm's operating management team to create the best organization for the continuing management and monitoring of real estate assets. They also lead in creating a management information system for this purpose. They work to identify surplus or underused real property and seek ways to reuse those assets. They negotiate on the company's behalf in the lease or purchase of space. They initiate suggestions for alternative ways of owning or leasing real estate, such as the opportunity to create a joint venture if the company does not want to create its own development business but still wants to take advantage of its financial strength to reap the rewards of equity participation.

Many corporate real estate professionals are affiliated with organizations such as CoreNet Global and NAIOP.[5] Both of these professional organizations offer networking opportunities and educational programs.

THE INFLUENCE OF THE PUBLIC SECTOR ON MANAGEMENT OF REAL ESTATE

Chapters 7 and 8 detailed the role of the public sector in real estate development generally. Throughout the text, a recurring theme has been that the public sector plays a kind of partnership role in the development process. At stage eight, it is appropriate to look again at key issues relating to the public sector and ensure that the management triad continues to review a property's operations in light of evolving laws and regulations.

The real estate industry actively attempts to ensure that new legislation and regulations achieve the desired public purpose without creating undue hardships for the owners of real estate assets. Legislation that appears to target a specific public purpose may have the effect of creating unintended burdens that are less than desirable for real estate owners. Industry groups such as the National Multifamily Housing Council, the National Apartment Association, NAIOP, the International Council of Shopping Centers, the Real Estate Roundtable, and the Urban Land Institute seek to ensure that all interested parties understand the ramifications of the various rules adopted by local, state, and federal governments.

Over the years, federal legislation—such as the Americans with Disabilities Act (ADA) and Title IV of the Clean Air Act of 1990—has had an immediate and ongoing effect on both the methods and the costs associated with managing real estate projects. In its most general sense, as explained in chapter 7, the ADA prohibits discrimination against people with disabilities, with respect to employment, public services, and public accommodations operated by private businesses. Its intent is to provide such people with accommodations and access equal to, or similar to, those available to the general public. Title IV of the Clean Air Act of 1990 addresses the protection of atmospheric ozone and mandates the recycling, production phaseout, and elimination of ozone-depleting compounds. In addition, the act prohibits the release of chlorofluorocarbons into the atmosphere during the maintenance, servicing, and disposal of refrigeration equipment. These and other federal mandates are incorporated into the design criteria for all development projects.

Although sustainability objectives are not necessarily mandated by legislation, in recent years real estate firms around the world have expanded their use of such objectives. Sustainability is becoming ever more important to the real estate investment community worldwide. It is incorporated for consideration in most new institutional-quality real estate developments. Sustainability is increasingly becoming benchmarked or certified through such programs as the EPA's Energy Star Program; the U.S. Green Building Council, which oversees the LEED program; and the ULI Greenprint Center for Building Performance, which fulfills both benchmarking and reporting needs for energy performance and carbon emission monitoring.

Awareness has also increased of the health implications of microbial growth, or mold, especially for people with special sensitivity to certain types of mold. Restoration of damage caused by a leaky roof or failed waterline or drain now entails both a construction solution and a remediation solution, requiring that materials that present a risk of hosting mold are encapsulated and removed. It has become

77H: Mixed-Use Development Meets Neighborhood Needs

A mixed-use project reconnects the urban grid and brings a full-service grocery store to an underserved neighborhood of Washington, D.C. The project, called 77H, includes 300 rental apartment units on four levels, a 75,000-square-foot Walmart, 10,000 square feet of street-level retail, and 373 underground parking spaces. The project is in a downtown location, within walking distance of three subway stations, bus lines, and Union Station, one of the busiest train stations in the United States.

The development team, JBG Companies and the Bennett Group, overcame many design challenges. First, locating the Walmart on the second floor avoids a big-box character and enables the street level to be used for smaller, neighborhood-serving establishments. Access for deliveries is often unattractive, and the activity can be disruptive and noisy. But at 77H, all loading docks are located inside the building behind a solid door. All parking for residents and shoppers is underground with controlled access.

An innovative lease structure helped ensure the early financial success of the development. The agreement with Walmart required that a retail shell be delivered significantly earlier than the residential portions were completed. This meant that the retail component could be completed and ready for opening by the time the first residents moved in. It also meant that 30 percent of the project's net operating income, which comes from Walmart's lease, was in place well before residential lease-up was completed.

JBG AND THE BENNETT GROUP

more urgent to attend to these problems immediately, before mold can develop and affect air quality (typically within 48 hours of an event).

The impact of the public sector on the planning, design, feasibility analysis, and operation of real estate projects reinforces how important it is to involve both the asset manager and the property manager throughout the development process. Like other members of the development team, the asset and property managers should interact regularly with the public sector during the development process,

setting up the vital working relationship that of necessity exists during stage eight.

GLOBALIZATION AND REAL ESTATE PORTFOLIO MANAGEMENT

The real estate capital markets have changed dramatically in recent years. It is now relatively rare for the largest real estate enterprises to develop in a single country. The evolution of the Prudential Real Estate Investors (PREI) platform provides a snapshot of how the industry has evolved. In 1970, PREI launched the first perpetual commingled, private real estate institutional equity fund (called "PRISA") in the United States, and the need for institutional management of real estate portfolios was born. The strategy for PRISA in the early years was to acquire first-class stabilized "core" properties for all cash—meaning that the fund had no development exposure and limited reliance on the debt or mortgage markets. At the time, there was virtually no public real estate market anywhere (the REIT structure had been created but had not yet taken off, and there was no public debt market). Today PREI is one of the world's largest global real estate investors, with approximately $56 billion in assets under management, about 36 percent of them outside the United States. The platform embraces a wide variety of core, value-added, and opportunistic strategies (including development in partnership with entrepreneurial firms) as well as global real estate securities, mezzanine and senior debt, and a variety of niche strategies.

In the emerging markets of Latin America and Asia, the combination of accelerated economic growth, a movement of population to the cities, a growing consumer middle class, and greater world trade offers the opportunity to earn higher returns than in mature, stable, developed markets such as those in the United States, Western Europe, and Japan. PREI's experience in Latin America underscores this opportunity. Its first fund in Mexico was launched in 2002; the firm now has $3.9 billion in assets under management in the region, with funds focused on industrial distribution and light manufacturing, residential (single-family and rental aimed at the emerging middle class), and neighborhood shopping centers. Owing to the dearth of institutional-grade real estate, all of these funds have had a development focus. Similarly, Mexico did not have a public REIT market until 2011. By 2014, the Mexican real estate market, FIBRA, had eight companies listed, with a total market cap of approximately $18 billion.

The bottom line is that there is a greater need for real estate development in the emerging markets than in the developed markets, and there is comparatively little institutional-quality competition. That leaves an opening for new entrants from the developed world. That said, a pioneering development strategy is never without risk. Moreover, a real estate portfolio that includes both developed and emerging property exposure is clearly more complicated on many dimensions than a portfolio that focuses solely on the U.S. domestic market.

SUMMARY

As James A. Graaskamp urged, real estate assets should be viewed as more than just bricks and mortar. They should be recognized as dynamic business enterprises operating in an always-changing marketplace.

The triad of real estate management—property, asset, and portfolio management—exercises critical functions related to ensuring that the project reaches its maximum value. The importance of each of these disciplines throughout the life cycle of the asset is hard to overestimate. Ongoing training is critical to ensure that the property management team and its on-site personnel perform well in the increasingly competitive and demanding marketplace.

The role of asset and portfolio management in real estate continues to expand and evolve. Although asset management's fundamental involvement and interaction with property management remains a priority, portfolio management is assuming a much more active role in the development and acquisition of assets, the positioning of the project throughout its life cycle, and the timely disposition of the asset.

TERMS

- Asset management
- Corporate real estate director
- Enterprise concept
- Management plan
- Portfolio management
- Property life cycle
- Property management contract
- Property strategic plan

REVIEW QUESTIONS

17.1 Describe the differences between the property, asset, and portfolio management functions and how they are interrelated.

17.2 How does the property management team use a management plan?

17.3 Why is the involvement of property managers early in the development process important?

17.4 What are some potential problems facing asset managers, even in good markets?

17.5 What are the four main elements of a strategic plan? Discuss each one.

17.6 Why is it so important to create a realistic and accurate operating budget?

17.7 What issues does the property management contract spell out?

17.8 Why is real estate such an important asset to corporations?

NOTES

1 See www.irem.org.
2 See www.boma.org and www.ifma.org.
3 See www.ncreif.org, www.prea.org, and www.nareim.org.
4 See www.ccim.com.
5 See www.corenetglobal.org and www.naiop.org.

Chapter 18

Preparing for the Future

This book offers a basic framework for understanding the real estate development process. Decisions about the development of real property are critical not only to those who invest in those projects, but also to society at large. A large share of the nation's wealth is invested in real property, both residential and commercial. Moreover, the built environment has a major impact on almost everyone's life. The better today's development decisions, the better tomorrow's built environment will be.

The eight-stage model of the real estate development process discussed throughout this text is a flexible, strategic tool that enables developers to make better decisions today—to see the whole while focusing on the particular. The logic behind the model is clearly financial, but the motivation comes from the market for space. Development involves complex design, financial, political, and production tasks as well as many kinds of interpersonal relationships. Still, all the activity occurs in response to particular market segments and the consumers in those segments—consumers whose preferences are constantly changing. Because constructed space can

be expected to last for many decades, a long-term historical perspective is an important starting point in anticipating what society will demand over an extended period of time.

LEARNING FROM THE PAST

A complete understanding of the development process is impossible without a historical perspective. Lessons learned from studying history help developers, government agencies, and others involved in the development process to learn from mistakes of the past. Chapters 4 through 6 point out some of the mistakes made over the decades; it is smart for today's players to learn from those lessons and avoid making those same mistakes in the future.

Although learning from the past is something every professional tries to do, estimating what may be different in the future is more subjective and difficult. It is critically important not to "straight-line" a forecast, but that does not mean everyone will agree on how to draw the curves. Although it is not possible to predict a new political or economic event or its impact on the world, it is possible to look at current trends and predict reaction to and interaction among those trends. All investors do it implicitly, but the best do it explicitly as well. Making these judgments requires good data and good interpretive skills.

TRENDS AND ISSUES

The environment in which developers work is influenced by a nearly unlimited number of factors. Most are beyond the developer's control, but should be understood and the related possibilities integrated into plans. Beyond what typically is incorporated in well-publicized economic forecasts, this section discusses a few important factors that may influence real estate development and investment over time, including demographic shifts, technological innovations, natural phenomena, and changing tastes and preferences. The successful developer will correctly anticipate the impact of these ideas, and their evolution, on his projects.

Known Demographic Changes with Knowable Consequences

Demographics is a science that can predict certain trends with a fair degree of accuracy. Once these trends are understood, developers can hone their skill in converting the "knowable" cohorts of age, income, ethnicity, and so on into overall demand and the type of space that will be desired within a region during a certain period of time.

In the mid-20th century, one-third of the world's population lived in urban areas. Today, half of the world's population is urban.[1] This trend has broad implications for real estate development worldwide. Developers will need to provide suitable space for the world's growing urban population to live, work, and thrive.

In the United States, Gen Y (those born between 1979 and 1995) will shape much of the future, but the aging baby boom generation will continue to make its mark as well. Gen Y lives, works, and plays in different ways than previous generations, and

its impact is felt in most real estate sectors. Gen Y members are currently more urban and less suburban. They gravitate to walkable, mixed-use environments, not the homogenous cul-de-sac suburbs in which they grew up.[2] Their preference is one of the reasons that homeownership percentages began declining in 2005. Although some of the decline can be attributed to the Great Recession, it is also true that Gen Y is marrying later and at lower rates than previous generations, and therefore embarking on homeownership at lower rates than their parents. However, Gen Y members' longer-term aspirations show the same single-family bias as their parents.[3]

As baby boomers retire, they are doing so in different ways from previous generations. Some are moving from suburban family homes to urban multifamily homes in walkable, mixed-use settings. Others are downsizing in communities where they already live. Others are upsizing to make room for visits from children and grandchildren. The Great Recession eroded the wealth of many baby boomers, who in many cases now must work longer than planned or reduce their retirement goals in various ways. Despite that, they stand to benefit from one of the largest intergenerational transfers of wealth in history as they inherit assets from their parents, members of the industrious and creative Greatest Generation who themselves benefited from the financially conservative Silent Generation.

As these large cohorts age, the problem of caring for those with dementia will grow. The disease is already more costly than cancer or heart disease. In addition to severely straining family resources, the disease will increasingly affect the ability of governments to provide a safety net. Some obvious implications for real estate include the need for homes and services to accommodate those with dementia.

As income and wealth continue to become more stratified worldwide, eventually, a reaction to this long-running trend will occur. The ability to interpret these reactions and interactions from the perspective of demand for built space will separate the successful developers from the rest.

Micro Units: Trading Space for Place

Micro units are a housing type that is gaining favor among urban dwellers in high-cost markets who are willing to trade space for improved affordability and proximity to downtown neighborhoods. Micro units are typically about 350 square feet but can range from less than 250 to 500 square feet, depending on local building code requirements. They have no separate bedroom—sleeping and living spaces are combined—but they do have fully functional bathrooms and kitchens. Micro-unit communities place heavy emphasis on amenities outside the units, such as shared communal spaces that encourage socializing and foster a sense of community.

- The target market is predominantly young professional singles, under 30 years of age, earning less than $40,000, trending slightly more toward males than females. Other market segments include couples, single empty nesters, and temporary users. Singles living with roommates tend to be the most interested in making the switch from a traditional unit to a micro unit.

- Those living in micro units cite location as the top factor influencing their decision to move into the small units, followed by price, proximity to work/education institutions, proximity to neighborhood amenities, the ability to live alone, and proximity to transit.

- Those who are interested in switching to micro units rank access to a grocery store as their top priority for a neighborhood amenity, followed by restaurants and a gym. In terms of project amenities, a laundry room ranked highest, followed by assigned parking.

- Smaller and micro units outperform conventional units in the marketplace in terms of achieving higher occupancy rates and garnering significant rental rate premiums (rent per square foot).

- Despite the rising popularity of micro units, some developers are building in the flexibility to easily convert two side-by-side units into one larger unit if demand shifts back to more conventional models.

In San Francisco, Smartspace is a complex of 23 prefabricated micro units. Each unit includes full kitchens and fold-out beds in less than 300 square feet of space.

Environmental Concerns

Key elements of responsible development are protecting the environment and conserving natural resources. Increasingly ominous predictions from climate scientists suggest that adverse events related to climate change pose a growing risk to communities worldwide. As discussed in chapter 2, the world is becoming increasingly urban, and cities tend to lie in particularly vulnerable areas. From sea level rise to heat waves, from storm surges to drought, climate-related events threaten the built environment in ways that have serious consequences for the health and economic vitality of the world's population.

The effects of climate change on cities and developers are likely to increase in frequency and magnitude. Damage to life, property, and infrastructure from catastrophic weather is significant. Major storms such as Hurricane Katrina in New Orleans and Superstorm Sandy in New York and New Jersey caused combined property damage of more than $150 billion, in addition to untold injuries and thousands of deaths. Storms such as these are expected to become more frequent and widespread, and push farther up the East Coast. Eventually, this trend will significantly change coastlines, affecting beachfront property and resorts throughout the developed world. In the less developed world, climate change will bring more serious problems, including shrinking land for food production due to rising sea levels and desertification, along with less predictable patterns of rainfall, affecting crop viability and fresh water availability. Rapidly growing populations will compound such problems.

Arverne by the Sea is a master-planned community on the Rockaway Peninsula in the Queens borough of New York City. Rockaway was severely affected by Hurricane Sandy, but Arverne by the Sea suffered limited damage because it incorporates a variety of resilient design features.

Life Hub @ Daning is a retail-anchored, mixed-use development in the Zhabei district of Shanghai. The 2.7 million-square-foot project has transformed an underdeveloped, low-income community into a vibrant, amenity-rich neighborhood.

Conserving vital resources, including land, energy, and water, is part of sustainable development. In many states, new growth management regulations are emerging as a strategy for land conservation. Water is already in short supply in many parts of the world, including the southwestern and western United States, where scarcity may greatly influence where development will be allowed to occur in the future.

Globalization and Shifting Economies

Major corporations have become increasingly willing to outsource work to smaller firms across the country and throughout the world. At the same time, sensing the potential advantages of globalization, many nations have lowered trade barriers. Linking those trends is an ever-growing technological network that enables everything from working from home to just-in-time global sourcing and assembly. As these changes in how business is done play out across markets, space needs will change drastically, offering another opportunity for astute developers to find their niche. Of course, within this longer-term trend, there will be economic reactions against globalization as well as restrictions to deal with growing security concerns across the globe.

Although ups and downs will continue, China will likely strengthen its standing as an economic powerhouse. It is noteworthy that, of the 100 tallest buildings under construction at this writing, about 60 are in China—and many are in second-tier cities such as Shenyang, Wuhan, and Suzhou.[4]

Economic growth can bring populations out of poverty, but slums are a persistent reminder of the failings of urbanization for the poorest residents. The United Nations estimates that there are 200,000 slums and shantytowns in the world.[5] Some megacities of the developing world are home to gigantic slums. Mexico City has what is believed to be the world's largest, Neza-Chalco-Itza, with a population in the millions.[6] Other cities with massive slum populations include Karachi, Pakistan; Mumbai, India; and Cape Town, South Africa. Related economic and social shortcomings create additional concerns about global pandemics and mutating viruses, as well as terrorism by extremists. Reactions to these threats will play out in development patterns across the globe.

Doing More with Less

Governments in many parts of the world have overspent in recent years, with results ranging from reactionary cost-cutting to widespread political unrest. Southern European countries are heavily in debt, with very high levels of unemployment that are already leading to social unrest. Similar conditions exist in less publicized form in much of the world. In the United States, consumption is higher than production, with the government financing most of the deficit. Debt reduction will differentially affect cities that have a high percentage of government jobs—both defense and non-defense jobs.

At the government level, this overspending will mean fewer services of all kinds. Some of these cuts will affect real estate operations and land use decisions. For example, the declining crime rates that much of the United States has enjoyed for several decades may reverse (at least in perception) if budgets for police and social services are cut. This means that being in the right submarket—even within a prospering metropolitan statistical area (MSA)—will be important. As cities with significant budget issues, such as Detroit and Cleveland, become ever less capable of maintaining their infrastructure, business improvement districts (BIDs), homeowners associations (HOAs), and other quasi-government entities will have to pick up the slack with creative solutions. Public/private partnerships will need to be more resourceful than ever to provide the services and amenities that the public will continue to demand.

Municipalities are recognizing that sprawl is expensive, with higher costs for infrastructure and lower tax revenue yields per acre. Many municipalities are establishing policies to control sprawl, by densifying urban areas. Higher densities have many implications for developers, from overcoming stakeholder opposition to designing compact projects that appeal to the market.

Technology: Changing Real Estate Practice

It is difficult to predict truly new phenomena. For example, it would have been nearly impossible to predict the creation and penetration of Facebook or Twitter. Still, once such innovations occur, it is often possible to predict some of the trends they may spawn. It is a matter of looking at existing trends for "expectable" discontinuities. Reactions to trends, as well as interactions among trends, can be thought about rationally. Noted in the following subsections

are some of the technology-driven changes that are already happening. The developer's job is to evaluate how these trends will evolve and to anticipate consumer reactions.

Now that social media is such an integral part of most people's lives, it is a key element of most marketing efforts. Development projects are using social media to provide consumer feedback, encouraging management to operate at a higher level of service. Customer relationship management software can transmit information to potential tenants and buyers. Multifamily developments use social media—blogs, Twitter, YouTube, Facebook—to help build and maintain communities within their tenant base, enabling tenants to communicate constantly with management and with each other. Social media also plays a role in the approvals process, when it is used to dispense information about public meetings and facilitate discussions afterward, as well as facilitate media outreach at every phase of the development process.

Other technologies are also being integrated into the development process. Geographic information systems offer developers a range of functions for the planning stages, from fine-grained demographic data to visualizations of a neighborhood. Luis Belmonte, principal of Seven Hills Properties in San Francisco, comments on how technology has simplified what used to be a time-consuming and costly process: "I used to work site selection in three ways: driving the site and surrounding area, air photos, and a helicopter tour. Now I use Google Earth for everything except a final drive of the site." Belmonte describes executing a fairly significant rehab project without being physically present. The contractor's bid was authorized by e-mail. "His draw procedure consisted of sending me a cell phone video, off of which I paid him in 10 percent of completion increments. The first time I saw the job was to make the final payment."

There is another side to technology and its effects on development practice, as some argue that the ease of computer-assisted work can constrain the creative thought process. Technology expert Nicholas Carr notes, "Computer-aided design has helped architects to construct buildings with unusual shapes and materials, but when computers are brought into the design process too early, they can deaden the aesthetic sensitivity and conceptual insight that come from sketching and model-building. Working by hand, psychological studies have found, is better for unlocking designers' originality."[7]

Smaller, Smarter Spaces

Technology is changing not only the real estate development process, but also physical space. Developers continue to grapple with changes in tenant demand, driven by technology and a relentless pursuit of ways to cut costs. Cost-cutting is the impetus for much of today's office designs. As the Urban Land Institute's *Emerging Trends in Real Estate® 2013* found, "Whereas only a few years ago, office users placed a premium on scale and quality, today they want space that can 'provide efficiency' and 'encourage productivity.'"[8] Space that encourages better collaboration is also becoming more important. Even formerly status-conscious firms are cutting back on windowed offices and creating more open—and less space-consuming—environments for employees. With the advent of the "paperless office" and the shrinking of computer equipment, less space is needed for file storage and workers may make do with a smaller desk—or no desk at all. More and more often, people can work anywhere, and thus may work at home or at a coffee shop. But people still need social contact, and the sort of workplace situation that enables such contact.

Retailing has changed dramatically and will continue to evolve as more shopping is done online. Many retailers have downsized—in store size, number of stores, or both. Others have embraced a model that combines the best features of online and in-person shopping. For example, the home furnishings store Crate and Barrel allows customers to make a purchase online and then pick up the goods in a store of their choosing within hours of purchase. This enables the customer to save shipping costs and receive the order almost immediately, combining the best features of both digital and bricks-and-mortar shopping.

Today's shopper expects to be able to make use of all channels, from social media to price comparison apps, to in-store shopping. According to David Lobaugh of August Partners, which conducts market research for shopping malls, 71 percent of shoppers expect to view in-store inventory online, and 39 percent will not even visit a retail outlet if they cannot check items online first.[9]

Coupled with the changing retail environment, warehousing is going through a digital evolution. Warehouse space is being designed and located where it can meet the needs of online retailers. Manufacturers are doing everything they can to speed delivery times, and warehouses are evolving into flow-through facilities rather than storage facilities. Obsolete warehouses can present interesting opportunities. For years, those in desirable urban locations have been snapped up for loft apartments, offices, or retail space. Now some are being repurposed as data centers. No doubt other uses will emerge to meet changing needs.

Mobility: Driverless Cars, Transit, Smart Parking, and Active Transportation

How people get around will change with more efficient transit and with robotic vehicles and parking solutions on the horizon. Robotic vehicles may greatly improve the efficiency and safety of existing highways. They are also likely to change people's driving and car-ownership patterns. Robotic parking garages will change project designs: they require less space than traditional garages as cars can be stacked tighter and often no drive lanes are required.

"Transit-oriented development" has become a common term in the real estate lexicon. In coming years, the term "trail-oriented development" may also become common. Many communities are investing in bicycle and pedestrian infrastructure because they recognize that walking and biking are the least expensive forms of transportation. Gen Y has shown less propensity to own and drive cars than their parents, and more interest in transit, biking, and walking.

Walkable communities are gaining popularity. Every trip, whether by car or transit begins and ends

Global Challenges and Opportunities

The world is changing rapidly, bringing new challenges as well as opportunities. Some likely challenges include higher energy costs, scarcer clean water, unsustainable population growth, and ever more globalization. Here are some predictions, many of which have implications for real estate developers.

- *Energy is relatively cheap today but will cost more in the future.* The United States may become energy independent. The emerging economies of Asia will require more energy and face higher costs. With potential new natural gas sources, the United States may see energy costs stabilize and may become less dependent on unstable foreign sources. That could have important economic and political effects, and could even shift some manufacturing back to the country, changing transportation patterns and the locations of industrial portfolios. The Japanese can now extract gas from methane hydrate (sometimes called "flammable ice"), an advance that may have a similar impact. Pipeline and port facilities will need to be augmented to deal with such new realities.

- *Clean water will become scarcer.* In the United States, much of the subsidy and pricing system for water was designed to encourage the conversion of raw land to agricultural uses. In many western states, agricultural water is priced much lower than municipal water, leading to conflicts between urban and rural interests. Yet such conflicts are not nearly as severe as the political problems surrounding water rights for the rivers of Southeast Asia. Innovations in desalination could help alleviate some problems, but desalination itself can cause environmental damage.

- *Developing countries are seeing rapid population growth and face the threat of significant food shortages.* Egypt was a food exporter before the construction of the Aswan dam in the 1960s. By the 1990s, despite the expansion of cultivatable land and growing seasons made possible by the dam, Egypt had become a food importer. In recent years, caloric intake per capita has dropped for the bottom half of India's population.

These trends have created difficulties for those countries but could mean expanding markets for big producers such as Argentina and the United States.

- *Classic economics makes clear the potential benefits of globalization, but these benefits are not without costs.* At its worst, globalization can lead to pandemics as everything from drug-resistant tuberculosis to Ebola spreads with the increasingly mobile world population and the uneven quality of health care. International institutions and wealthy individuals can move in or out of domestic markets quickly with large investments. Consequently, it is now harder for any country to control its interest rates. Computer technology and global outsourcing have reduced middle-management jobs as well as skilled manufacturing jobs, making it hard to maintain a middle class in developed economies.

- *Immigrants will become more important in determining many aspects of global lifestyles.* In the United States, immigration is usually a positive factor for economic growth. The ability to smoothly assimilate migrants from all countries can have lifestyle implications for everything from the types of housing demanded to the types of amenities that cities need to provide to remain attractive places to live.

- *The pace of urbanization may reverse course in certain markets.* Throughout human history, people have migrated to cities for many reasons but, in part, for the safety they have provided. Crime in American cities has been declining since the early 1990s, encouraging further migration to urban places. However, any number of factors could reverse this trend.

- *Many trends are accelerating, provoking additional reactions and interactions.* Beyond the effects of global terrorism, radicalism and high levels of corruption in some countries are having pronounced impacts that could negatively affect the interactions of those countries with the rest of the world.

with walking, and walkability is a cornerstone of an efficient ground transportation system. What's more, walkable and bikeable communities foster social interaction, improve physical fitness, and likely increase real estate value.

Bike lanes are increasingly being added to urban and suburban streets. Bicycling is America's fastest-growing form of transportation, increasing more than 40 percent between 2009 and 2014—and more than 80 percent in so-called "bicycle-friendly" cities.

According to the Federal Highway Administration, in 2012, 11.4 percent of all trips were taken by bicycle or on foot, but only 2.1 percent of federal transportation funding went to bicycling and walking projects. Cities that have invested in bicycle and pedestrian infrastructure have seen enormous impacts from their investments. Portland, Oregon, for example, has seen a 200 percent increase in cycling since investing in a 300-mile network of bike trails, bike lanes, and bike boulevards. This system was built for about the same cost as one mile of four-lane urban freeway.

A growing number of developers have taken advantage of the growing interest in "active (human-powered) transportation" by building projects and communities centered on bike trails and cycling. In 2014, for example, 13 new multifamily projects were built along and oriented to the Midtown Greenway—a multilane, urban bikeway—in Minneapolis, Minnesota. Walking and biking will never eliminate the need for motor vehicles, but the growing popularity of non-motorized transportation means that bike trails and pedestrian paths are starting to reshape development in the same way that train stations and highways reshaped development in the past.

Green Buildings, Sustainable Development, and Resilience

Issues relating to climate change and energy costs are likely to continue to influence development in much of the world. With the search for solutions to both problems, sustainable development and green building have become more than fringe movements and now are in the mainstream in many countries. European and Australian developers were early adapters. Since the late 1990s, green building has grown into an accepted way of approaching design, construction, and management in the United States. The U.S. Green Building Council (USGBC), a leader in the field, has seen its membership swell as developers, designers, and manufacturers have jumped on the green bandwagon and as the number of buildings certified as "green" under its LEED rating system has increased rapidly.

Proponents of green building argue that it costs little or no more to go green—and even when initial costs of new buildings are higher, ample opportunities are available to achieve savings down the road, especially through reduced energy consumption. As more architects and contractors have become experienced in green development and a wider range of sustainable products, the potential added costs of building to green standards have gone down.

The Zuellig building is a multitenant office building in Makati City, the Philippines. The 33-story tower earned LEED Platinum certification.

The six-story, 45,000-square-foot Bullitt Center, in Seattle, has been referred to as the "world's greenest office building" thanks to its many environmentally friendly and energy-efficient features, including a rooftop photovoltaic array, rainwater collection, geothermal heat exchange, and composting toilets.

As the market has grown more aware of the benefits of high-performance buildings with their healthier indoor environments, lower energy costs, and benefits to the larger community, not being green is becoming a liability for new construction. Furthermore, some owners of older buildings, particularly in the office sector, are finding it necessary to undergo expensive environmental retrofitting to stay competitive with newly constructed LEED-certified buildings. Tenants want the savings from energy-efficient systems as well as good publicity for occupying environmentally friendly space.[10] In addition, tenants themselves can now be LEED-certified.

In the United States, the new urbanism movement that began in the 1980s and the closely related smart growth movement that began in the late 1990s started a dialogue on how to handle development pressures in ways that are environmentally sensitive, economically viable, community oriented, and sustainable. A convergence is taking place between green building, new urbanism, and smart growth today. This trend is leading to a more holistic approach that integrates building design and site planning with larger-scale neighborhood design and infrastructure, as evidenced by the LEED ND certification category for neighborhoods, and form-based codes, such as SmartCode, which focuses on building forms, positioning, and other elements that contribute to place making and walkability.

Place Making

Overlapping the move toward more sustainable development is the increasing focus on creating places that have a strong sense of identity and community or "place." The new urbanism movement has drawn people's attention to the fact that urban form, when executed well, is a key component of sophisticated place making and is essential for maximum pedestrian functionality and enjoyment. The places with the highest real estate values—such as central business districts—usually are urban in form. People travel great distances to see and to walk in the urban beauty of old European and some American cities. As an outgrowth of new urbanism, a trend toward replacing, or at least augmenting, traditional Euclidean zoning with form-based codes is gaining momentum. Savvy developers and local governments are recognizing that places offering a sustainable high quality of life—in the form of efficient transportation, pedestrian orientation, recreational and cultural amenities, high-performance offices and homes, and diverse, compact neighborhoods—are most likely to come out ahead in the long run. With sufficient density and nightlife vitality, this description approximates the description of a 24-hour city, which many surveys have indicated is the preferred investment environment for many real estate investors.

Health and the Built Environment

For many years, health and medical research has investigated various impacts of urbanization and environmental influences on people's health. Because a variety of factors influence health, establishing causation between physical spaces and community health is difficult. Still, as demand for accountability continues to rise, the relationship between the physical design of cities and the health of the people who live, work, and play in them is becoming better understood.

Since the early 2000s, initiatives by public sector and nonprofit advocates have pushed a number of initiatives to prioritize and develop solutions to address urban health problems. Examples include the U.S.-based Robert Wood Johnson Foundation's Healthy Communities program, the World Health Organization's Healthy Cities guidelines, and local assessments that measure the potential effects of a proposed policy, plan, or program on community health. These broadly scoped visions of healthier, more active communities have advocated and established principles for the integration of public health concerns in urban planning and development. The private sector has shown interest as well: incorporating health-related amenities is a growing trend in residential developments as well as in office and retail spaces.

In fact, programs related to incorporating health and wellness considerations in buildings

The High Line is a public park built on an abandoned freight-rail line elevated above the streets in lower Manhattan. It has become a popular walking trail and gathering place and has spurred redevelopment of many properties along its route.

Elements of Healthy Development

LOCATION AND COMMUNITY

- Compact land use and a mix of uses to facilitate walking as transportation mode
- Proximity to nature and attractive parks and playgrounds
- Programs that encourage activity and social interaction
- Ready access to healthy food, including grocery stores, farmers markets, and community gardens

TRANSPORTATION

- High-quality and reliable transit service
- Walkable streets that accommodate all types of users
- Bike trails and designated bike lanes

BUILDING DESIGN

- Green roofs
- Operable windows for ventilation
- Healthy building materials inside and out
- Views of nature and exposure to sunlight
- Centrally placed, inviting, and accessible stairways
- Universal design features

BUILDING AMENITIES

- Storage for bikes
- Workout spaces
- Lockers, bike racks, and places to shower

Designed by Michael Graves for returning soldiers with disabilities, the Wounded Warrior Home Project in Fort Belvoir, Virginia, provides housing with universal design features that enable residents to be self-sufficient. The project also serves as a design laboratory for creating homes for an aging population.

and communities are burgeoning. In 2014, the International Well Building Institute released the WELL Building Standard, which certifies projects that represent best practices in design and construction with evidence-based health and wellness interventions. This peer-reviewed program was developed in collaboration with the Green Building Certification Institute. Much like the LEED Green Building Rating System, the WELL Building Standard evaluates building typologies based on criteria that support human health, well-being, and comfort.

ETERNAL ISSUES FOR REAL ESTATE DEVELOPERS

Real estate development creates social and political issues that are debated in one form or another in most projects but are hard to completely resolve. Some are reviewed in this section.

Property Rights versus Public Interest

The entitlement process for any real estate project raises issues related to the respective rights of a property owner and the public interest. The specific manifestation may obscure the underlying issue, but it eventually comes down to what inherent rights are carried with property. The externalities of proposed development become more apparent and intense as land becomes scarcer.

The balance between public and private interests is not fixed. It is continually contested, sometimes all the way to the U.S. Supreme Court. In encounters with the regulatory and political community, a developer needs to be aware of the legal interpretation of issues relevant to the project and of the conditions that give rise to changes in the rules of the game.

Neighborhood Self-determination versus Regional Interests

Most neighborhoods value the status quo. Development brings change and change brings scrutiny, and often opposition. The stakes are higher when a neighborhood is asked to accept its share of regional infrastructure or affordable housing. Transportation is a good example. Orange County, California, soundly rejected the conversion of a

Guidelines for Tomorrow's Developers

Although the authors of this text do not necessarily agree on the probabilities of the possibilities enumerated in this chapter coming to pass, they do agree that one of a developer's most important jobs is to think about dealing with such changes. The object is to combine rigorous thought about the future with personal inspiration to produce guidance for the work as a developer. This is, of course, a very personal matter. Developers should create their own guidance based on facts, trends, anticipated reactions to those trends, and their personal ethics. As an example, here are 12 rules that the authors have assembled:

- *Rule 1.* Do business only with people who are pleasant. In fact, as you get older, add to that only people who are fun or interesting. After all, people are the critical resource.

- *Rule 2.* Measure personal success by a self-defined quality of life. Relying on others' definitions can make you the victim of the "reaction syndrome" and put you in the wrong circle of associates.

- *Rule 3.* Measure self-worth by what you can give away (which need not be monetary). It is incumbent on anyone who wants to have a meaningful life to contribute something to the neighborhood where he lives, if not to the region and the world.

- *Rule 4.* Strive to improve education, yours and others'. Continuing education is a must. Do not get locked into a narrow educational path. The best work is facilitated by a broad educational background.

- *Rule 5.* Try not to segment things into little boxes. Breakthroughs come at the interfaces. Continuing education should not all focus on the same field. Real estate development is an interdisciplinary activity, and the successful player needs an understanding of many aspects of life—sociological, psychological, architectural, and historical—as well as of business and politics.

- *Rule 6.* Be wary of textbook economists. In an information society, you can give information away and still have it. This fact does not fit well in traditional economic models.

- *Rule 7.* Think globally, act locally. Watch federal and international events for destabilizing activities, but make it happen in your world, which is probably your neighborhood or your city.

- *Rule 8.* Seek knowledge and eventually wisdom, not just information. There are already more newsletters in the real estate area than anyone could read regularly. Beyond that, an incredible array of facts and information is available through the internet. The challenge is to develop the conceptual framework that makes it possible to process this sea of information into knowledge, especially the knowledge needed to act decisively.

- *Rule 9.* Always fully segment markets. Do not get trapped into measuring the MSA exclusively when dealing with a world of neighborhoods. Remember that everyone lives not in one neighborhood but in a series of neighborhoods. One is the work environment, another is the social environment, and there can be many more, depending on the different facets of people's lives. In building space, a developer is satisfying the needs of people who function in neighborhoods that probably overlap. Consideration of the census tract is an easy first pass but it does not give the whole story.

- *Rule 10.* Remember that change is the only constant. This recognition will continue to force a search for spiritual certainty that will, in turn, have an impact on other aspects of life. Given that the critical resource is people, not capital, the search for meaning will become increasingly important.

- *Rule 11.* Do not fool yourself into believing that business school thinking based solely on manipulating available data is real thinking. Even the latest accounting rules are driven by looking in a rear-view mirror, and contemporary appraisal practices still ignore many of the big issues discussed in this chapter. No amount of getting it right in the present can make up for a major miss on future trends.

- *Rule 12.* Remember that you need partners—not suppliers, not customers, not acquisition targets, but partners. Partnerships should not be based solely on legal agreements but rather on reciprocally fair deals oriented toward mutual interests and maintained in an atmosphere of good will.

closed Marine air base to a commercial airport that would have served a broader region. Few, if any, philosophical or practical governmental models provide sufficient insight into the proper balance between local and regional needs.

Allocation of the Cost of Growth

Regional infrastructure, both physical and social, must be expanded or replaced to meet the requirements of growing populations. Many communities have adopted the position that growth must pay its own way—either in the form of direct funding by the developer or through public finance vehicles that rely on tax assessment on newly developed projects. Setting aside questions of equality of costs and benefits among users, there are also infrastructure needs beyond those which can be financed by new development. Finding the best funding sources remains a set of issues in search of satisfactory resolution.

Market Demand versus Good Planning

The desires of the marketplace, especially relating to density and transportation, do not always align with good planning. The best societal or aesthetic solution is often set aside in favor of more marketable and/or more politically acceptable solutions. One example is the tension between the automobile-dependent single-family house and denser urban housing models.

SUMMARY

This chapter touches on some of the factors that developers should consider as they think about upcoming development opportunities. It is helpful to read widely and talk regularly with many kinds of people. Urban Land Institute programs and publications are a good place to start. The annual *Emerging Trends* series provides up-to-date thinking on what is going on in the world that will affect real estate.

Although developers cannot continuously focus on broad societal trends, over the long run big-picture changes account for the largest differences between successful and less successful developments. As providers of space over time with associated services, developers should continuously respond to the changing needs and wants of consumers. Sensitivity to underlying shifts in preferred locations, commuting habits, customs and cultural orientation, and household characteristics is critical to effective decision making. The developer's first job is to anticipate what consumers will want from the built environment—one of the most exciting, challenging, and rewarding tasks in today's world.

Real estate development is an important endeavor that should be highly esteemed. It creates the built environment that serves society's needs for shelter, commerce, and the enjoyment of life.

Development leaves a permanent mark that reflects a culture and its values. Developers have a responsibility to their customers to respond to their needs and wants. And they have a responsibility to

their fellow citizens to be the best they can at their profession.

REVIEW QUESTIONS

18.1 How can looking at the past help us to think about the future?

18.2 How has the trend toward privatization of services affected developers?

18.3 How do the lifestyles of baby boomers and Gen Y differ? How are they influencing trends in real estate?

18.4 The authors offer advice to read as widely as possible and talk to as many kinds of people as possible. Why would it be beneficial to follow that advice? Are there any possible pitfalls?

18.5 The authors lay out some potential scenarios that may affect developers in the future. What others might occur? How would they affect cities, development, and the real estate profession?

NOTES

1   United Nations Human Settlements Programme, *State of the World's Cities 2010/2011: Bridging the Urban Divide* (Nairobi, Kenya: UN HABITAT, 2010), p. ix.

2   M. Leanne Lachman and Deborah L. Brett, *Generation Y: Shopping and Entertainment in the Digital Age* (Washington, D.C.; Urban Land Institute, 2013).

3   M. Leanne Lachman and Deborah L. Brett, *Generation Y: America's New Housing Wave* (Washington, D.C.; Urban Land Institute, 2013), p. 10.

4   Council on Tall Buildings and Urban Habitat, "Tallest Buildings Under Construction," skyscrapercenter.com.

5   United Nations Human Settlements Program, *State of the World's Cities 2010/2011: Bridging the Urban Divide* (Nairobi, Kenya: UN HABITAT, 2010).

6   Daniel Tovrov, "5 Biggest Slums in the World," *International Business Times*, December 9, 2011, www.ibtimes.com/5-biggest-slums-world-381338.

7   Nicholas Carr, "Automation Makes Us Dumb," *Wall Street Journal*, November 21, 2014.

8   *Emerging Trends in Real Estate® 2013* (Washington, D.C.: Urban Land Institute, 2013), p. 11.

9   Nellie Day, "A Lesson in Ingenuity," *Western Real Estate Business*, June 2014, volume 11, issue 10, p. 1.

10   *Emerging Trends in Real Estate® 2009* (Washington, D.C.: Urban Land Institute, 2009), p. 10.

Glossary

100 percent corner. The most desirable location for a particular use, taking into account street frontage, visibility, foot traffic, adjacent uses, and other locational elements.

Absorption period. The time between opening and either sell out or lease-up of a property.

Absorption schedule. The estimated schedule or rate at which properties for sale or lease can be leased or rented in a given locality; usually used when preparing a forecast of the sales or leasing rate to substantiate a development plan and to obtain financing.

Affordable housing. According to the U.S. Department of Housing and Urban Development, housing that does not cost more than 30 percent of a household's gross income. Sometimes used synonymously with subsidized housing, for which local, state, and federal programs exist to serve low- to moderate-income families by offering lower cash downpayments, eased loan-qualifying rules, below-market interest rates, or rent assistance. Subsidies depend on a variety of factors, including household size and disability status.

Agglomeration. Concentration of commercial activity within a given area, tending to have a synergistic effect by increasing diversity, specialization, and overall business activity. In the context of urban sprawl, an overlap of population and government jurisdictions.

AHERA (Asbestos Hazard Emergency Response Act). Legislation passed in 1986 that requires all public schools to be inspected for asbestos by certified inspectors and mandates the preparation of a management plan if the presence of asbestos is identified.

Amenity. Nonmonetary tangible or intangible benefit derived from real property (often offered to a lessee); typically swimming pools, parks, valets, and the like.

Americans with Disabilities Act of 1990 (ADA). A federal law that prohibits discrimination against people with disabilities in employment, public services and transportation, public accommodations and commercial facilities, and telecommunications.

Amortization. The periodic writing off of an asset over a specified term. Also the periodic repayment of debt over a specified time.

Anchor tenant. The major chain(s) or department store(s) in a shopping center, positioned to generate traffic for the smaller stores in the facility.

Appraisal. An opinion or estimate of value substantiated by various analyses.

Architect. Primarily a designer of buildings and supervisor of construction. All states require architects to be licensed under laws governing health, safety, and welfare.

Asset manager. A person who balances risk and reward in managing investment portfolios, including, but not limited to, real property and improvements. Asset managers either oversee property management or are responsible for it themselves.

Attached housing. Two or more dwelling units constructed with party walls (for example, townhouses, stacked flats).

Audit. In real estate development, the assessment of the credibility and reliability of real estate market data.

Availability payment. A means for a government entity to compensate a private contractor for work, often for public infrastructure.

Axial theory. A theory of land use development that suggests that land uses tend to develop in relation to time-cost functions of transportation axes that radiate from the central business district.

Balloon loan. A loan that does not fully amortize over the term and requires a lump-sum payment of remaining principal at maturity.

Basis point. One hundredth of one percent, used to express differences in interest rates.

Binding constraint. Legally enforceable limit on the allowable development on a given site.

Bonding. A guarantee of completion or performance, typically issued by an insurance company that will back up the bonded party in any lawsuit. In real estate, contractors, for example, are often bonded as assurance that they will complete the work.

Bottom-up approach. An approach to developing an analysis based on the most disaggregated data available.

Break-even ratio. In finance, the point at which total income is equal to total expenses.

Broker. A person who, for a commission, acts as the agent of another in the process of buying, selling, leasing, or managing property rights.

Brokerage. The business of a broker; includes all the functions necessary to market a seller's property and represent the seller's (principal's) best interests.

Brownfield. A site previously used for industrial or certain commercial uses and possibly contaminated from those uses, but developable upon cleanup.

Build to suit. Construction of land improvements according to a tenant's or purchaser's specifications.

Building efficiency ratio. The ratio of net leasable area to gross leasable area.

Building Owners and Managers Association International (BOMA). A trade association of owners and managers of apartment and office buildings.

Buildout. Construction of specific interior finishes to a tenant's specifications.

Business improvement district (BID). A public/private partnership in which the business owners in a district, through legislative approval, contribute funds through a special tax to the maintenance, development, and marketing of their commercial area.

Capital. Money or property invested in an asset for the creation of wealth; alternatively, the surplus of production over consumption.

Capital improvement projects. Investments in infrastructure such as roads, bridges, and ports.

Capital market. Financial marketplace in which savings (from individuals, companies, or pension funds) are aggregated by financial intermediaries and allocated to real investors.

Capitalization. The process of estimating value by discounting stabilized net operating income at an appropriate rate.

Capitalization rate (cap rate). The rate, expressed as a percentage, at which a future flow of income is converted into a present value figure.

Capture rate. Forecasted rate of absorption in a targeted market segment for a proposed project, based on an analysis of supply and demand.

Central business district (CBD). The center of commercial activity in a town or city; usually the largest and oldest concentration of such activity.

CERCLA (Comprehensive Environmental Response, Compensation, and Liability Act of 1980). Legislation adopted to provide partial funding for the cleanup of environmentally contaminated sites by requiring the party responsible for the contamination to undertake cleanup efforts or provide compensation for cleanup costs; also known as the Superfund law.

Codevelopment. Term that refers to the combined development of real estate by the private sector and government, where the public sector assumes risks or costs normally borne by private developers.

Commercial paper. Short-term negotiable financial instruments, usually unsecured, such as promissory notes, bank checks, bills, and acceptances.

Commercial real estate. Improved real estate held for the production of income through leases for commercial or business use (for example, office buildings, retail shops, and shopping centers).

Commitment letter. A written agreement by a lender to loan a specific amount of money at a specified interest rate within a particular period of time.

Community builder. One who engages in the platting and improvement of subdivisions.

Community development block grants (CDBGs). Federal grants received by cities that may be used for a variety of community development activities; based on a formula that considers population, extent of poverty, and housing overpopulation.

Community development corporations (CDCs). Entrepreneurial institutions combining public and private resources to aid in the development of socioeconomically disadvantaged areas.

Community Reinvestment Act (CRA). Legislation enacted in 1978 that directs federal agencies with supervisory authority over depository lenders to consider a lender's record in serving local credit needs when making decisions about the expansion plans of depository institutions.

Comparable property. Another property with which a subject property can be compared to reach an estimate of market value.

Compound interest. Earned interest that is immediately added to principal, thereafter also earning interest.

Comprehensive planning. Long-range planning by a local or regional government encompassing the entire area of a community and integrating all elements related to its physical development, such as housing, recreation, open space, and economic development.

Concentric zone theory. Urban development theory that holds that because mobility is paramount to community growth, land uses tend to be arranged in a series of concentric, circular zones around a city's central business district.

Concession. Discount given to prospective tenants to induce them to sign a lease, typically in the form of some free rent, cash for improvements furnished by the tenant, and so on.

Condominium. A form of joint ownership and control of property in which specified volumes of air space (for example, apartments) are owned individually while the common elements of the building (for example, outside walls) are owned jointly.

Construction lender. Entity or individual providing interim financing during the construction phase(s) of the real estate development process.

Construction loan. A loan made, usually by a commercial bank, to a builder to be used for the construction of improvements on real estate and typically running for six months to two years.

Contingent interest. A form of equity participation by lenders enabling them to receive an additional return if the income property securing the loan exceeds its projected profit or cash flow goals.

Convenience goods. Items typically purchased at the most convenient locations. They are usually not very expensive or long-lasting, and their purchase involves little deliberation. Convenience goods are distinguished from shopper goods in retail market studies.

Convertible loan. A loan in which the lender, in addition to receiving a stated interest rate, reserves the right to convert its debt on a project to equity and thereby participate in the profits.

Covenant. A restriction on real property that is binding, regardless of changes in ownership, because it is attached to the title. Used generally in covenants, conditions, and restrictions.

Covenants, conditions, and restrictions (CC&Rs). Limitations or restrictions placed on real estate (such as size of a building, character of landscaping, or color of house paint), usually decided by a homeowners association.

Critical path method (CPM). A network analysis method that visually displays the activities involved in completing a project and shows the relationship between the activities. This display can show how a delay in one activity will affect other activities.

Debt service. Periodic payments on a loan, with a portion of the payment for interest and the balance for repayment of principal.

Debt (service) coverage ratio. The ratio of the annual net operating income of a property to the annual debt service of the mortgage on the property.

Deed restrictions. Private form of land use regulation using covenants or conditions placed on the title to a property; for example, minimum lot sizes.

Delphi method. A project analysis tool in which a group of diverse experts is presented with a set of questions on a particular topic. The responses are then compared and more refined questions developed for the group. The ultimate goal is the development of a single, coherent response.

Demand deposits. Shorter-term deposits, such as checking accounts, that banks typically put into relatively short-term investments.

Demising wall. Wall that separates one tenant's space from another's and from the common areas.

Demographics. Information on population characteristics by location, including such aspects as age, employment, earnings, and expenditures.

Density. The level of concentration (high or low) of buildings, including their total volume, in a given area. Often expressed as a ratio, for example, dwelling units per acre or floor/area ratio.

Density bonus. A zoning tool that permits developers to build at a higher density in exchange for providing some benefit to the community.

Department of Housing and Urban Development (HUD). The cabinet-level federal department responsible for carrying out national housing programs, including Federal Housing Administration subsidies, home mortgage insurance, urban renewal, and urban planning assistance.

Detached housing. A freestanding dwelling unit, normally single-family, situated on its own lot.

Developer. One who prepares raw land for improvement by installing roads, utilities, and other necessary elements; also a builder (one who constructs improvements on real estate).

Development fee. Compensation paid to a developer in return for managing a development project on behalf of a client such as a corporation or public sector agency.

Development process. The process of taking a site from raw land (or an underused or outdated structure) to improved property.

Development team. The range of participants engaged by a developer, both public and private, to assist in the planning, design, construction, marketing, and management of a development project.

Discounted cash flow. Present value of monies to be received in the future; determined by multiplying projected cash flows by the discount factor.

Downzoning. A change in the zoning classification of property from a higher use to a lower use (for example, from commercial to residential).

Draw. The lender's release of construction loan funds in accordance with set procedures for providing portions of the total amount as each stage of construction is satisfactorily completed.

Due diligence. A forthright effort to investigate all reasonable considerations in a timely manner.

Econometrics. The application of statistical methods to the study of economic data and problems.

Ecosystem management. Management of the interrelationships among the biological members of a community and their environment.

Effective rent. Rental income after deductions for financial concessions such as no-rent periods during a lease term.

Eminent domain. The power of a public authority to condemn and take property for public use on payment of just compensation.

Enabling legislation. Legislation typically delegated to local government that specifies the police power the state is giving to the local government. Cities, counties, and other local governments undertake planning, zoning, and additional forms of development regulation according to state enabling statutes.

Enterprise concept. The idea that encouraging private enterprise will facilitate economic revitalization or other socioeconomic goals. Encourages owners to look at real estate as another type of private enterprise.

Entrepreneur. One who assumes all the risk and reward of a business venture.

Environmental scanning. The surveying of a variety of indicators in order to gauge the overall business, economic, social, political, or financial conditions that could affect a project's development.

Equity. That portion of an ownership interest in real property or other securities that is owned outright, that is, above amounts financed.

Equity kicker. A provision in the loan terms that guarantees the lender a percentage of the property's appreciation over some specified time or a percentage of income from the property or both.

Escalation clause. A provision in a lease that permits a landlord to pass through increases in real estate taxes and operating expenses to tenants, with each tenant paying its prorated share. Also a mortgage clause that allows the lender to increase the interest rate based on the terms of the note.

Estoppel letter. A written statement made by a tenant, lender, or other party establishing certain facts and conditions with regard to a piece of real estate.

Eurodollars. U.S. dollars deposited in European foreign banks and used as a medium of international credit.

Exactions. Fee or payment-in-kind required of a developer by a local jurisdiction for approval of development plans, in accordance with state and local legislation regarding the provision of public facilities and amenities.

Exclusionary zoning. Zoning practices such as large lot requirements and minimum housing sizes that serve to exclude from a community, intentionally or not, racial minorities and low-income persons.

Exurbs (exurban area). Communities located beyond older suburbs.

Fast-tracking. A method of project management in which construction of a project actually begins before all details are finalized.

Feasibility study. A combination of a market study and an economic study that provides the investor with knowledge of both the environment where the project exists and the expected returns from investment in it.

Federal Home Loan Mortgage Corporation (Freddie Mac). Subsidiary of the Federal Home Loan Bank System (FHLBS) established in 1970 to act as a secondary mortgage market for savings and loan associations that are members of the FHLBS.

Federal Housing Administration (FHA). Federal agency created by the 1934 National Housing Act that insures residential mortgages originated by private lenders on properties and borrowers meeting certain minimum standards and requirements.

Federal National Mortgage Association (Fannie Mae). A quasi-private corporation chartered by the federal government to function as a secondary market for residential mortgages.

Fee simple absolute. The most extensive interest in land recognized by law. Absolute ownership but subject to the limitations of police power, taxation, eminent domain, escheat, and private restrictions of record.

Fee simple determinable. Fee simple ownership that terminates on the occurrence (or failure to occur) of a stated condition. Also referred to as a "defeasible fee."

Festival marketplace. A specialty retail center incorporating aspects of old marketplaces, including significant public spaces and a variety of activities.

Financial Institutions Reform, Recovery, and Enforcement Act of 1989 (FIRREA). A comprehensive legislative act designed to overhaul the regulatory structure of the thrift industry.

FIRE (finance, insurance, real estate). An employment classification, used by the Department of Labor in analyses of the service industry.

Floodplain. Land adjacent to rivers and streams subject to overflow and flooding.

Floor amount. Initial portion of a floor-to-ceiling mortgage loan, advanced when certain conditions—for example, construction of core and shell—are met.

Floor/area ratio. The ratio of floor area to land area, expressed as a percentage or a decimal number, that is determined by dividing the total floor area of the building by the area of the lot; typically used as a formula to regulate building volume.

Floor load. The weight that the floor of a building is able to support if such weight is evenly distributed; measured in pounds per square foot.

Focus group. Market analysis tool in which a moderator presents a set of carefully prepared questions to a group, usually eight to 12 people, in order to collect detailed and specific information on consumer attitudes and preferences.

Foreclosure. The legal process by which a mortgagee, in case of a mortgagor's default, forces sale of the mortgaged property to provide funds to pay off the loan.

Formal feasibility. Formal demonstration through the use of quantitative, objective data that a proposed project is or is not viable.

Friable. Material able to be crushed or pulverized by hand pressure such that the particles become airborne; used to describe types of asbestos.

Garden apartments. Two- or three-story multifamily housing featuring low density, ample open space around buildings, and convenient on-site parking.

Garden city. Movement begun in late 19th-century Europe that sought to counter the rapid, unplanned growth of industrial cities by constructing self-contained planned communities emphasizing environmental reform, social reform, town planning, and regional planning.

General contractor. Person or firm that supervises a construction project under contract to the owner; also known as the "prime contractor."

General obligation bond. Municipal bond backed by the full faith and credit of the issuer as opposed to being backed by a particular project.

Geographic information system (GIS). An information system that enables users to work with data that are geographically referenced to the Earth, allowing them to add, store, edit, analyze, map, and present the data. GIS, also known as geographic information science, is frequently used to assist decision making for planning and real estate development.

Government National Mortgage Association (Ginnie Mae). Agency of the U.S. Department of Housing and Urban Development that operates as a participant in the secondary mortgage market, guaranteeing privately issued securities backed by pools of FHA or VA mortgages.

Gray Areas Program. Program launched by the Ford Foundation in 1960 to foster the revitalization and redevelopment of communities in minority areas.

Green building. The practice of designing and engineering more efficient buildings to conserve materials and resources such as water and energy and to reduce other negative environmental impacts and health consequences.

Greenbelt. Area of undeveloped, open space that serves as a buffer between developed areas.

Gross income multiplier. Rule-of-thumb calculation to estimate the value of residential property, derived by dividing the sale price of comparable properties by their gross annual or monthly rent.

Gross leasing activity. The sum of all leases signed during a given time period, including renewals and leases signed in new buildings.

Ground lease. A long-term lease on a parcel of land, separate from and exclusive of the improvements on the land.

Growth management. The public sector's control over the timing and location of real estate development by various means, including legislative and administrative.

Growth path. The area of a city where development, price appreciation, and user or tenant demand are the greatest.

Guaranteed investment contract (GIC). A written guarantee to an investor of a certain yield for a defined period of time.

Hard costs. In new construction, includes payments for land, labor, materials, improvements, and the contractor's fee.

High rise. Tall building or skyscraper, usually more than ten stories.

Highest and best use. The property use that, at a given time, is deemed likely to produce the greatest net return in the foreseeable future, whether or not such use is the current use of the property.

Homesteader. A person residing on public land and establishing a homestead for the purpose of acquiring legal title to the land.

HVAC system. A building system supplying heating, ventilation, and air conditioning.

Impact fee. Charge levied (on developers) by local governments to pay for the cost of providing public facilities necessitated by a given development.

Improvements. In real estate, any permanent structure affixed to land.

Income kicker. A provision in loan terms that guarantees the lender's receipt of a portion of gross income over an established minimum, for example, 10 percent of the first year's gross rent receipts.

Industrial park. A large tract of improved land used for a variety of light industrial and manufacturing uses. Users either purchase or lease individual sites.

Infill. The development of unused or abandoned land in a built-up area, especially as part of smart growth. Often, adequate infrastructure is already present, reducing potential costs.

Inflation risk. The risk that inflation will reduce the purchasing power of monies lent.

Infrastructure. Services and facilities provided by a municipality, including roads, highways, water, sewerage, emergency services, and parks and recreation; can also be provided by a private entity.

Institute of Real Estate Management (IREM). An affiliate of the National Association of Realtors® whose purpose is to promote professionalism in the field of property management.

Intelligent building. A building that incorporates technologically advanced features to facilitate communications, information processing, energy conservation, and tenant services.

Internal rate of return (IRR). The discount rate at which an investment has zero net present value (that is, the yield to the investor).

International Council of Shopping Centers (ICSC). An international trade association for owners, developers, and managers of shopping centers.

IPO (initial public offering). The first offering of stock in a previously privately held company.

Joint venture. An association of two or more firms or individuals to carry on a single business enterprise for profit.

Junk bond. Any bond (a long-term debt obligation of a corporation or a government) with a relatively low rating. The lower the rating, the more speculative or risky the investment. Returns can be much higher than for a less speculative investment, however. Bonds are rated by credit-rating companies, the best known being Standard & Poor's.

Land development. The process of preparing raw land through clearing, grading, installing utilities, and other activities, for the construction of improvements.

Land planner. Individual who specializes in the allocation of desired land uses in a particular site to maximize the site's value and utility, striving for efficient internal traffic circulation, well-placed uses and amenities, and adequate open space.

Leadership in Energy and Environmental Design (LEED). A system developed by the U.S. Green Building Council to provide standards for environmentally sustainable design. LEED certification consists of four levels (certified, silver, gold, and platinum) for buildings; a number of versions of the LEED system exist for specialized project types, including office buildings, retail spaces, and neighborhoods.

Lease. A contract that gives the lessor (the tenant) the right of possession for a period of time in return for paying rent to the lessee (the landlord).

Lease concession. A benefit to a tenant to induce him to enter into a lease; usually takes the form of one month or more of free rent.

Lease-up. Period during which a real estate rental property is marketed, leasing agreements are signed, and tenants begin to move in.

Leverage. The use of borrowed funds to finance a project.

Levered. With use of debt financing. Unlevered is before debt financing is taken into account.

LIBOR (London interbank offered rate). An interest rate frequently used as an index in adjustable mortgage loans; most often the interest rate on three- or six-month euro deposits.

Lien. The right to hold property as security until the debt that it secures is paid. A mortgage is one type of lien.

Limited partnership. A partnership that restricts the personal liability of the partners to the amount of their investment.

Linkage. Typically, a payment to a municipality for some needed development that is not necessarily profitable for a developer (say, low-income housing) in exchange for the right to develop more profitable, high-density buildings (say, commercial development).

Loan placement analysis. The decision by a lender to hold a loan or to sell the loan in the secondary market, or the decision not to make a loan if the lender is unwilling to hold it and no secondary market exists.

Loan-to-value (LTV) ratio. The relationship between the amount of a mortgage loan and the value of the real estate securing it; the loan amount divided by the market value.

Location quotient. Market analysis tool used to compare local workforce estimates with national averages, derived by taking the percentages of the workforce employed in each major industry group locally and dividing them by the percentages of the workforce employed in the industry groups nationally.

Low rise. A building usually with four or fewer stories, typically served by stairs rather than elevators.

Maquiladora. In Mexico, a manufacturing plant that temporarily imports capital goods duty free and then ships finished goods out of the country as exports. Most are located near the U.S. border.

Market niche. A particular subgroup of a market segment distinguishable from the rest of the segment by certain characteristics.

Market research. A study of the needs of a target market used to develop a product appropriate for that market.

Market study. An analysis of the general demand for a real estate product.

Marketability risk. The risk that a lender will be unable to sell a loan in a secondary market.

Marketability study. A study that determines the price or rent appropriate to market a project successfully.

Mechanic's lien. A claim that attaches to real estate to protect the right to compensation of one who performs labor or provides materials in connection with construction.

Mechanistic model. A forecast method that is based on research indicating generalized algorithms that can be applied to a given property type across all markets.

Metropolitan statistical area (MSA). An urban area containing multiple political jurisdictions grouped together for purposes of counting individuals by the Census Bureau.

Miniperm loan. A short-term loan (usually five years) meant to be an interim loan between a construction loan and a permanent loan. A miniperm loan is usually securitized like any other loan; the interest rate could be less onerous than a construction loan but not as favorable as a permanent loan.

标记

Miniwarehouse. A building, usually one story, subdivided into numerous small cubicles intended to be used as storage by families or small businesses.

Mixed-use development. A development, in one building or several buildings, that combines at least three significant revenue-producing uses that are physically and functionally integrated and developed in conformance with a coherent plan. A mixed-use development might include, for example, retail space on the ground floor, offices on the middle floors, and condominiums on the top floors, with a garage on the lower levels.

Monetary policy. The actions and procedures of the Federal Reserve System meant to control the availability of loanable funds.

Money market instruments. Investment tools such as U.S. Treasury bills and commercial paper used by money markets.

Money markets. Name given to financial markets for short-term investment instruments that mature in one year or less.

Mortgage. An instrument used in some states (rather than a deed of trust) to make real estate the security for a debt. A two-party instrument between a mortgagor (a borrower) and a mortgagee (a lender).

Mortgage-backed security. A type of bond or note that is based on pools of mortgage loans or collateralized by the cash flows from the principal and interest payments of a set of mortgage loans.

Mortgage banking. The process of originating real estate loans and then selling them to institutional lenders and other investors.

Mortgage loan constant. Percentage of the original loan balance represented by the constant periodic mortgage payment.

Move-up housing. Typically, larger, more expensive houses that homeowners buy as their incomes increase. First homes, or "starter homes," are generally modestly sized and priced.

Multifamily housing. Structures that house more than one family in separate units (apartments). Can be high rises, low rises, garden apartments, or townhouses.

National Association of Housing and Redevelopment Officials (NAHRO). Professional association of agencies and private officials involved in publicly assisted housing and community development activities.

National Association of Industrial and Office Properties (NAIOP). Trade association representing the interests of commercial real estate developers, owners, and managers.

National Association of Realtors (NAR). The largest real estate organization in the country and probably in the world. Members are entitled to use the designation "Realtor."

National Housing Act of 1968. Legislation that created several programs designed to encourage the production and rehabilitation of low-income housing.

Neighborhood. A segment of a city or town with common features that distinguish it from adjoining areas.

Neighborhood Reinvestment Corporation. A public, nonprofit corporation created by law in 1978 that uses congressional appropriations to encourage public/private partnerships in the interest of revitalizing older urban neighborhoods.

Net absorption. The change in square feet of occupied inventory over a specified period of time, including the addition or deletion of building stock during that period of time.

Net operating income (NOI). Cash flow from rental income on a property after operating expenses are deducted from gross income.

Net present income. The value of an income-producing property at a given discount rate, minus the original investment cost.

New urbanism. An urban design movement whose goal is to create and restore compact, diverse, and walkable mixed-use towns and cities. Emphasizes a discernible town center, public spaces, the placement of buildings close to the street, and the proximity of essential community features (housing, places of employment, schools, and services) to the town center. New urbanism tries to eliminate sprawl, reduce automobile traffic, and reinforce a sense of community.

Nominal group process. A decision-making technique used to set priorities for ideas generated by a group.

Nonrecourse loan. A loan that, in the event of default by the borrower, limits the lender to foreclosure of the mortgage and acquisition of the real estate; that is, the lender waives any personal liability by the borrower.

Not in my backyard (NIMBY). The tendency of some residents to oppose nearby development or land uses that they see as undesirable such as homeless shelters, wastewater treatment plants, and airports.

Office building. A building or area of a building leased to tenants for the conduct of business or practice of a profession, as distinguished from residential, commercial, or retail uses.

Open market operations. The buying and selling of government securities by the Federal Reserve System; a tool for controlling the availability of loanable funds.

Operating budget. A budget, usually prepared a year in advance, listing projected costs of maintenance and repair for a building.

Operating expense ratio. The ratio of operating expenses to either potential gross income or effective gross income.

Operating expenses. Expenses directly related to the operation and maintenance of a property, including real estate taxes, maintenance and repair, insurance, payroll and management fees, supplies, and utilities. Debt service on mortgages or depreciation is not included.

Opportunity cost. The return on capital invested in a particular asset compared with the return available from alternative uses of that capital.

Option. The right given by the owner of property (the optionor) to another (the optionee) to purchase or lease the property at a specific price within a set time.

Origination fee. A charge made by the lender at the inception of the loan to cover administrative costs.

Outlier forecast. A forecast in a group of projections that differs substantially from all others in the group as well as from the group average.

Participation loan. A mortgage wherein one or more lenders have a share in a mortgage with the lead or originating lender.

Passive investor. An investor who seeks no active role in construction or operation of a building but merely seeks to invest funds to earn a return. Institutional investors such as pension funds are typically passive investors.

Pass-through. Lease provision whereby certain costs flow through directly to the tenant rather than to the owner (for example, property tax increases on a long-term lease).

Pass-through certificate. An investment instrument in which the periodic debt service payments on a package of mortgage loans are paid out (passed through) to the investors owning the instrument.

Peer group. Those properties most directly comparable and competitive with a subject property.

Pension fund. An institution that holds assets to be used for the payment of pensions to corporate or government employees, union members, and other groups.

Permanent lender. A financial institution undertaking a long-term loan on real estate subject to specified conditions (for example, the construction of improvements).

PERT (program evaluation and review technique). A technique that provides project managers with a flowchart representing construction schedule times. Includes a critical path that indicates the activities that must be completed on time so as not to delay completion.

Planned unit development (PUD). Zoning classification created to accommodate master-planned developments that include mixed uses, varied housing types, or unconventional subdivision designs.

Points. An amount charged by the lender at the inception of a loan to increase the lender's effective yield. Each point equals 1 percent of the loan.

Police power. The right of government to regulate property to protect the health, safety, and general welfare of citizens.

Portfolio. A collection of varied investments held by an individual or firm. Real estate is often among those investments.

Preliminary drawings. Architectural renderings of a project showing definite project dimensions and volumes and including such items as exterior elevations, rentable square feet or salable units, parking, and the type of HVAC system.

Prepayment or callability risk. The risk that a borrower will pay off a loan before it has matured, thus depriving the lender of additional interest payments.

Present value. The current value of an income-producing asset, estimated by discounting all expected future cash flows over the holding period.

Prime rate. The lowest interest rate charged to the largest and strongest customers of a commercial bank for a short-term loan.

Pro forma. A financial statement that projects gross income, operating expenses, and net operating income for a future period based on a set of specific assumptions.

Profitability ratios. A set of single-period ratios that indicate the capacity of a project to produce income relative to the capital investment required to obtain that income.

Property life cycle. The three periods in the life of a building—the development period, the stabilization period, and the decline period.

Property manager. An individual or firm responsible for the operation of improved real estate. Management functions include leasing and maintenance supervision.

Psychographic profile. A detailed description of a group that goes beyond personal data, such as place of residence, to include more psychological aspects, such as interests and degrees of aspiration.

Purchasing power. The financial means (including credit) that people possess to purchase durable and nondurable goods.

Rational nexus. A reasonable connection between impact fees and improvements that will be made with those fees. Jurisdictions must be able to justify the fees they charge developers by showing that the fees will be spent on improvements related to the development. For example, a fee of $25 per square foot charged for a shopping center might not be justifiable if it is to be used for building an addition to the local elementary school. It might be justified, however, if it will be used to improve roads near the shopping center because of the additional traffic that the shopping center is likely to generate.

Real estate development. The process of converting undeveloped tracts of land into construction-ready parcels or components of the built environment.

Real estate investment trust (REIT). A tax-free ownership entity that provides liquidity and limited liability. Ownership is evidenced by shares of beneficial interest similar to shares of common stock.

Real estate mortgage investment conduit (REMIC). An issue of publicly traded debt securities backed by a fixed pool of mortgages that can be used as a pass-through entity for federal income tax purposes.

Realtor. A member of the National Association of Realtors. "Realtor" is also a generic term used to describe professionals involved in selling property.

Recourse loan. A loan offering no protection to the borrower against personal liability for the debt, thus putting at risk the borrower's personal assets in addition to any collateral securing the loan.

Redevelopment. The redesign or rehabilitation of existing properties.

Redlining. The practice of denying loans or insurance coverage to residents in a specific geographic area, usually low-income inner-city neighborhoods.

Reliability. The ability to remain consistent under repeated tests.

Rent control. Limitations imposed by state or local authorities on the amount of rent a landlord can charge in certain jurisdictions.

Repos. Short-term repurchase agreements between financial institutions.

Resolution Trust Corporation (RTC). A mixed-ownership government corporation created by Congress to manage failed thrift institutions and their holdings.

Retainage. A portion of the amount due under a construction contract that the owner withholds until the job is completed in accordance with plans and specifications; usually a percentage of the total contract price.

Revenue bonds. Bonds issued by municipalities and backed by specific fees or service charges.

Risk. The possibility that returns on an investment or loan will not be as high as expected.

Risk-free interest rate. A short-term, base interest rate calculated before various risk premiums are added; approximated by the rate on U.S. Treasury bills.

Rural Housing Services/Rural Development. Agency (formerly Farmers' Home Administration) of the Department of Agriculture that provides credit to farmers and nonfarm businesses in rural areas as well as guaranteeing and insuring certain loans.

Savings and loan (S&L) association. A type of savings institution that is the primary source of financing for one- to four-family homes. Most S&Ls are mutual (nonstock) institutions.

Secondary mortgage market. The market in which existing mortgages are bought and sold: conventional loans by Freddie Mac and Fannie Mae, FHA and VA loans by Fannie Mae, and special-assistance (HUD-regulated) loans by Ginnie Mae.

Sector theory. Land use development theory postulating that land uses tend to develop along transportation corridors outward from the city center, forming wedge-shaped sectors that follow the path of least resistance and lowest costs.

Securitization. The pooling of mortgages for securities offerings.

Security. Stocks or bonds.

Segmentation. The classification of a population group into segments for the purpose of identifying marketing subgroups.

Sensitivity analysis. A cost-benefit examination of the features and aspects of a real estate development project such as operating costs, amenities, management costs, and visual appeal, and the impact of adjustments to them on the value of the project.

Setback. The part of zoning regulations that restricts the location of a building to within a specified distance from the front line of the property or edge of the public street; thus, the structure must be set back a given number of feet.

Shopper goods. Items purchased after some degree of deliberation or shopping around. Generally, they are differentiated through brand identification, the retailer's image, or the ambience of the shopping area. Such purchases are made less often than other kinds of purchases, and the product is typically more durable and expensive than more frequently purchased products.

Shopping center. Integrated and self-contained shopping area, usually in the suburbs. Classified as neighborhood (30,000 to 100,000 square feet and providing convenience goods and personal services), community (100,000 to 500,000 square feet and providing a wider range of goods), regional (about 500,000 square feet with one or two department store anchors), and super regional (1 million plus square feet with three or more department store anchors).

Single-family housing. A dwelling unit, either attached or detached, designed for use by one family and with direct access to a street; does not share heating facilities or other essential building facilities with any other dwelling.

Single-point-in-time analyses. Analyses of market performance and various demand indicators such as construction levels, absorption, vacancy, and rent growth recorded at only one point in time.

Situs. The total environment in which a specific land use on a specific land parcel functions and with which it interacts at a specific time. More simply, location.

Smart growth. A movement that supports concentrating growth in urban centers to avoid urban sprawl and create sustainable design. Advocates compact, transit-oriented, walkable, bicycle-friendly land use, including mixed-use development with a range of affordable housing choices.

Societal marketing concept. The idea that a real estate project has an effect on more than just the users of the product and therefore must be marketed to the collective satisfaction of neighbors and regulators.

Soft costs. Outlays for interest, origination fees, appraisals, and other third-party charges associated with real estate development.

Special taxing districts. Districts established by local governments, in the form of assessment districts or public improvement districts, in which a special tax is levied on property owners to fund public improvements that will directly benefit those owners.

Stabilization. In appraisal, the use of one year's typical property income and expenses and annualized capital reserve expenditures to represent each year's income stream.

Steering. The illegal practice of directing prospective homebuyers or renters away from neighborhoods of racial or ethnic composition different from those of the buyers or renters.

Strip mall. A shopping center with a linear configuration, located on a highway or major street along which development has sprawled outward from a town or city center.

Subcontractor. An individual or company that performs a specific job for a construction project pursuant to an agreement with the general contractor.

Subdivision. Division of a parcel of land into building lots; can also include streets, parks, schools, utilities, and other public facilities.

Subdivision controls. Development restrictions placed on parcels in a recorded subdivision.

Submarket. A geographic area surrounding a site that will provide a substantial portion of the customers for a real estate project.

Subordination clause. Clause in which one party agrees, under certain conditions, to yield its priority to another mortgagee.

Subprime rate. A rate that is at least three points above the current prime rate for a bond of comparable maturity. Loans at subprime rates are costlier and higher risk, and are generally given by commercial banks to customers who have poor or insufficient credit.

Suburbanization. The movement of development to the suburbs created by the overflow effect of cities and by the automobile, which enabled greater access to these outer areas.

Surety company. A company that guarantees the performance or debt of another in case of default.

Sustainable development. In its most comprehensive form, a three-pronged approach to development that considers social needs, economic needs, and environmental protection; also, real estate development that meets the needs of the present without compromising the ability of future generations to meet their needs.

Syndication. The process of acquiring and combining equity investments from multiple sources (for example, syndicating units in a limited partnership).

Takeout commitment. The permanent loan commitment for a project to be constructed.

Takeout loan. The long-term financing that replaces or "takes out" the construction loan.

Taking. The acquisition or seizure of land without just compensation or the application of police power constraints so restrictive as to prevent any viable use of the land.

Tax increment financing (TIF). A type of special district financing in which tax revenues raised only from new development, as assessed by the net increase over the existing property tax base, are earmarked to fund capital improvements.

Taxation risk. The risk that changes in tax laws will adversely affect taxes on the interest of a loan or will undermine the value of the underlying loan collateral.

Temporary financing. Short-term financing, usually for land acquisition, preconstruction infrastructure, and construction of improvements.

Tenant. One who rents from another.

Tenant allowance. A cash payment made by the developer to a tenant (usually in an income property) to enable the tenant, rather than the developer, to complete the interior work for the leased premises.

Tenant mix. The combination of various types of tenants in a leased building.

Term or maturity risk premium. Risk premium charged by lenders to compensate for the opportunity costs of long-term loans.

Tilt-up construction. Concrete elements such as wall panels that are cast horizontally, adjacent to the building footprint, then tilted up to final vertical position when hardened.

Time-series analyses. Analyses of market performance and other measures of market cyclicity such as construction levels, absorption, vacancy, and rental growth recorded during periods of market expansion and contraction.

Time value of money. The idea that because money is assumed to earn interest, a dollar today is worth more than a dollar at some future date.

Title. Evidence of ownership of real property, often used synonymously with the term "ownership" to indicate a person's right to possess, use, and dispose of property.

Title company. A company that examines title to real estate, determines whether it is valid and whether any limitations on the title exist, and, for a premium, insures the validity of the title to the owner or lender.

Title I. FHA-insured property improvement or rehabilitation mortgage.

Top-down approach. An approach to analysis that is based on the use of aggregated data first.

Total marketing concept. The process of determining consumer desires, producing a product to match those desires, and persuading consumers to purchase or rent that product.

Townhouse. Single-family attached residence separated from another by party walls, usually on a narrow lot offering small front- and backyards.

Trade area. Geographic area from which a retail facility consistently draws most of its customers.

Traditional neighborhood design. An urban design approach stemming from the new urbanism and based on a compact grid that promotes higher-density, walkable development and intensified, compatible mixed uses.

Tranche. Multiple classes of tiered bond or security ownership interests issued by real estate mortgage investment conduits (REMICs).

Transfer package. Documentation compiled at the time a project is sold or transferred to an asset manager that attempts to measure objectively the project's standing in the marketplace in order to provide a benchmark for the asset manager's future performance.

Transferable development rights. A method of allowing landowners to sever development rights for a tract of land and sell those rights to develop, which then can be assigned to another tract of land to enable higher-density development. For example, the "sending area" may be farmland, ensuring that it will never be developed, and the "receiving area" may be an urban area with a strong demand for development, which can then benefit from the allowance of greater density.

Transit-oriented development. A mixed-use area designed to maximize access to public transportation, generally seeking to create high-density developments within a quarter mile of a mass transit stop.

Underwriters. Employees of mortgage lenders charged with making recommendations on loan approvals or disapprovals based on their knowledge of the applicant's creditworthiness and the quality or value of any collateral available to secure the loan.

Universal design. Concepts used to create buildings and environments that are accessible to all: aging people, people with disabilities, and those without disabilities.

Unlevered. See levered.

Urban development action grants (UDAGs). Program of grants begun in 1977 and administered through the Department of Housing and Urban Development for the revitalization of distressed urban areas; program has not been funded since the mid-1980s.

Urban economics. Economic concepts applied in the context of a particular urban area.

Urban renewal. The physical improvement and redevelopment of an area through government action or assistance.

Validity. Execution with proper legal authority.

Value. The worth or utility of a property; in appraisal, the price the market is willing to pay ("market value"). In finance, value is the result of direct capitalization or discounted cash flow analysis.

Value capture. With regard to the joint development of transportation facilities, the government purchase, management, or control of land adjacent to these developments that enables the public to share in the potential financial and community development benefits that would not otherwise be possible.

Variance. In general, the difference between expected results and actual results. Statistically, "variance" refers to the square of the standard deviation. Can be used as a measure of risk.

Venture capital. Funds available for early-stage, often high-risk investment in a profit-seeking enterprise.

Veterans Affairs (VA). A department of the federal government that administers the veteran benefit programs intended to help returning veterans transition to civilian life; formerly the Veterans Administration.

Warehouse. A building that is used for the storage of goods or merchandise and that can be occupied by the owner or leased to one or more tenants.

Workforce housing. Housing for working individuals or families making between 60 and 120 percent of the area median income in their MSA—individuals or families who generally do not qualify for housing subsidies yet cannot afford market-rate housing.

Workout. Negotiated arrangements between a lending institution and a developer unable to fulfill a loan agreement.

Writedown. A deliberate reduction in the book value of an asset, typically made because of changes in market conditions, deterioration of properties, loss of tenants, and the like.

Xeriscaping. Landscaping that thrives with little or no water.

Yield curve. The relationship between the yield on an instrument and the number of years until it matures or comes due.

Zone of transition. Neighborhoods surrounding the central business district of a city.

Zoning. Classification and regulation of land by local governments according to use categories (zones); often includes density designations as well.

Bibliography

PART 1 Introduction

REAL ESTATE DEVELOPMENT AND PLANNING BOOKS

Adams, David, and Steven Tiesdell. *Shaping Places: Urban Planning, Design, and Development.* London: Routledge, 2013.

Barras, Richard. *Building Cycles and Urban Development.* Oxford, U.K.: Blackwell, 2009.

Brown, Peter Hendee. *How Real Estate Developers Think: Design, Profits, and Community.* City in the Twenty-First Century Series. Philadelphia: University of Pennsylvania Press, 2015.

Calthorpe, Peter. *The Regional City: Planning for the End of Sprawl.* Washington, D.C.: Island Press, 2001.

Carmon, Naomi, and Susan S. Fainstein, eds. *Policy, Planning, and People Promoting Justice in Urban Development.* City in the Twenty-First Century Series. Philadelphia: University of Pennsylvania Press, 2013.

Cisneros, Henry. *Urban Real Estate Investment: A New Era of Opportunity.* Washington, D.C.: Urban Land Institute, 2015.

DeLisle, James R., and Elaine M. Worzala, eds. *Essays in Honor of James A. Graaskamp: Ten Years After.* Boston: Kluwer Academic Publishers, 2000.

Dewberry Companies. *Land Development Handbook Planning, Engineering, and Surveying*, 3rd ed. New York: McGraw-Hill, 2008.

Duany, Andrés, and Jeff Speck. *Smart Growth Manual.* New York: McGraw-Hill, 2010.

Fainstein, Susan S., and Scott Campbell. *Readings in Planning Theory.* Malden, Mass.: Wiley-Blackwell, 2012.

Garvin, Alexander. *The American City: What Works and What Doesn't*, 3rd ed. New York: McGraw-Hill Education, 2014.

———. *The Planning Game: Lessons from Great Cities.* New York: W. W. Norton & Company, 2013.

Gehl, Jan, Birgitte Svarre, and Karen Ann Steenhard. *How to Study Public Life.* Washington, D.C.: Island Press, 2013.

Goldsmith, Stephen A., and Lynn Elizabeth, eds. *What We See: Advancing the Observations of Jane Jacobs.* Oakland, Calif.: New Village Press, 2010.

Graaskamp, James A. *Fundamentals of Real Estate Development.* Washington, D.C.: Urban Land Institute, 1981.

Hewlet, Charlie, and Gadi Kaufmann. *Strategies for Real Estate Companies.* Washington, D.C.: Urban Land Institute, 2008.

Jacobs, Jane. *The Death and Life of Great American Cities*, 50th anniversary ed. New York: Modern Library, 2011.

Jacobus, Charles J. *Real Estate Principles*, 12th ed. Mason, Ohio: OnCourse Learning, 2013.

Jarchow, Stephen P., ed. *Graaskamp on Real Estate.* Washington, D.C.: Urban Land Institute, 1991.

Jerke, Dennis. *Urban Design and the Bottom Line: Optimizing the Return on Perception.* Washington, D.C.: Urban Land Institute, 2008.

Johnson, David E. *Fundamentals of Land Development: A Real World Guide to Profitable Large-Scale Development.* Hoboken, N.J.: Wiley, 2008.

Katz, Peter. *The New Urbanism: Towards an Architecture of Community.* New York: McGraw-Hill, 1994.

Lassar, Terry J., and Douglas R. Porter. *The Power of Ideas: Five People Who Changed the Urban Landscape.* Washington, D.C.: Urban Land Institute, 2005.

Leinberger, Christopher B. *The Option of Urbanism: Investing in a New American Dream.* Washington, D.C.: Island Press, 2008.

Levy, John M. *Contemporary Urban Planning*, 10th ed. Upper Saddle River, N.J.: Pearson Education, 2013.

Ling, David C., and Wayne R. Archer. *Real Estate Principles: A Value Approach*, 4th ed. Boston: McGraw-Hill/Irwin, 2013.

Mandelker, Daniel R. *Planning and Control of Land Development: Cases and Materials*, 8th ed. Newark, N.J.: LexisNexis, 2011.

McDonald, John F., and Daniel P. McMillen. *Urban Economics and Real Estate: Theory and Policy*, 2nd ed. Hoboken, N.J.: Wiley, 2011.

Moskowitz, Harvey S., Carl G. Lindbloom, and David Listokin. *The Complete Illustrated Book of Development Definitions*, 4th ed. New Brunswick, N.J.: Transaction Publishers, 2015.

Mumford, Lewis. *The City in History: Its Origins, Its Transformation, and Its Prospects.* New York: MFJ Books, 1961.

Nelson, Arthur C., and Robert Lang. *Megapolitan America: A New Vision for Understanding America's Metropolitan Geography.* Chicago: APA Planners Press, 2011.

Newman, Peter. *The End of Automobile Dependence: How Cities are Moving Beyond Car-Based Planning.* Washington, D.C.: Island Press, 2015.

Olsen, Joshua. *Better Places, Better Lives: A Biography of James Rouse.* Washington, D.C.: Urban Land Institute, 2004.

Palermo, Pier Carlo, and Davide Ponzini. *Place-Making and Urban Development: New Challenges for Contemporary Planning and Design.* London: Routledge, 2015.

Paumier, Cyril B. *Creating a Vibrant City Center: Urban Design and Regeneration Principles.* Washington, D.C.: Urban Land Institute, 2004.

Peiser, Richard. *Regenerating Older Suburbs.* Washington, D.C.: Urban Land Institute, 2007.

Peiser, Richard, and David Hamilton. *Professional Real Estate Development: The ULI Guide to the Business*, 3rd ed. Washington, D.C.: Urban Land Institute, 2012.

Riggs, Trisha. *Visionaries in Urban Development: 15 Years of the ULI J. C. Nichols Prize Winners.* Washington, D.C.: Urban Land Institute, 2014.

Rybczynski, Witold. *Makeshift Metropolis: Ideas About Cities.* New York: Scribner, 2010.

Scheer, Brenda Case. *The Evolution of Urban Form: Typology for Planners and Architects.* Chicago: APA Planners Press, 2010.

Schilling, Joseph, and Alan Mallach. *Cities in Transition: A Guide for Practicing Planners.* Chicago: APA Planners Press, 2012.

Seltzer, Ethan, and Armando Carbonell, eds. *Regional Planning in America: Practice and Prospect.* Cambridge, Mass.: Lincoln Institute of Land Policy, 2011.

Squires, Graham, and Erwin Heurkens. *International Approaches to Real Estate Development.* London: Routledge, 2015.

Stein, Jay M. *Classic Readings in Urban Planning*, 2nd ed. Chicago: APA Planners Press, 2004.

Toker, Umut. *Making Community Design Work: A Guide for Planners.* Chicago: APA Planners Press, 2012.

Wachter, Susan M., and Kimberly A. Zeuli. *Revitalizing American Cities.* City in the Twenty-First Century Series. Philadelphia: University of Pennsylvania Press, 2013.

SUSTAINABLE PLANNING AND DEVELOPMENT

Beatley, Timothy. *Biophilic Cities: Integrating Nature into Urban Design and Planning.* Washington, D.C.: Island Press, 2011.

———. *Blue Urbanism: Exploring Connections Between Cities and Oceans.* Washington, D.C.: Island Press/Center for Resource Economics, 2014.

———. *Planning for Coastal Resilience: Best Practices for Calamitous Times.* Washington, D.C.: Island Press, 2009.

Blakely, Edward J., and Armando Carbonell. *Resilient Coastal City Regions: Planning for Climate Change in the United States and Australia.* Cambridge, Mass.: Lincoln Institute of Land Policy, 2012.

Brown, Hillary. *Next Generation Infrastructure: Principles for Post-Industrial Public Works.* Washington, D.C.: Island Press, 2014.

Calthorpe, Peter. *The Next American Metropolis: Ecology, Community, and the American Dream.* New York: Princeton Architectural Press, 1995.

———. *Urbanism in the Age of Climate Change,* Washington, D.C.: Island Press, 2011.

Daniels, Tom. *The Environmental Planning Handbook for Sustainable Communities and Regions*, 2nd ed. Chicago: APA Planners Press, 2014.

Eraydın, Ayda, and Tuna Taşan-Kok. *Resilience Thinking in Urban Planning.* Dordrecht: Springer, 2013.

Gause, Jo Allen, et al. *Developing Sustainable Planned Communities.* Washington, D.C.: Urban Land Institute, 2007.

Gehl, Jan. *Cities for People.* Washington, D.C.: Island Press, 2010.

Godschalk, David R., and Emil E. Malizia. *Sustainable Development Projects: Integrated Design, Development, and Regulation.* Chicago: APA Planners Press, 2013.

Godschalk, David R., and David C. Rouse. *Sustaining Places: Best Practices for Comprehensive Plans.* Planning Advisory Service Report 578. Chicago: APA Planning Advisory Service, 2015.

Johnston, Sadhu Aufochs, Steven S. Nicholas, and Julia Parzen. *The Guide to Greening Cities.* Washington, D.C.: Island Press, 2013.

Leigh, Nancey Green, Nathanael Z. Hoclzcl, Benjamin R. Kraft, and C. Scott Dempwolf. *Sustainable Urban Industrial Development.* Planning Advisory Service Report 577. Chicago: APA Planning Advisory Service, 2014.

McMahon, Ed. *Conservation Communities: Creating Value with Nature, Open Space, and Agriculture.* Washington, D.C.: Urban Land Institute, 2014.

Montgomery, Carleton. *Regional Planning for a Sustainable America: How Creative Programs are Promoting Prosperity and Saving the Environment.* New Brunswick, N.J.: Rutgers University Press, 2011.

Pirani, Robert, and Laura Tolkoff. *Lessons from Sandy: Federal Policies to Build Climate-Resilient Coastal Regions.* Cambridge, Mass.: Lincoln Institute of Land Policy, 2014.

Porter, Douglas. *State and Local Financing and Incentives for Green Development.* Washington, D.C.: Urban Land Institute, 2011.

Rodin, Judith. *The Resilience Dividend: Being Strong in a World Where Things Go Wrong.* New York: PublicAffairs, 2014.

Tobias, Leanne. *Retrofitting Office Buildings to Be Green and Energy-Efficient: Optimizing Building Performance, Tenant Satisfaction, and Financial Return.* Washington, D.C.: Urban Land Institute, 2009.

Urban Land Institute. *After Sandy: Advancing Strategies for Long-Term Resilience and Adaptability.* Advisory Services Panel Report. Washington, D.C.: Urban Land Institute, 2013.

———. *Ten Principles for a Sustainable Approach to New Development: Towards Sustainable and Integrated Large-Scale Developments for a More Livable Hong Kong.* Washington, D.C.: Urban Land Institute, 2011.

———. *Ten Principles for Sustainable Development of Metro Manila's New Urban Core.* Washington, D.C.: Urban Land Institute, 2013.

Watson, Donald, and Michele Adams. *Design for Flooding: Architecture, Landscape, and Urban Design for Resilience to Flooding and Climate Change.* Hoboken, N.J.: John Wiley & Sons, 2011.

Wilbanks, Thomas J., and S. J. Fernandez. *Climate Change and Infrastructure, Urban Systems, and Vulnerabilities.* Washington, D.C.: Island Press, 2014.

Specialized Publications

Bohl, Charles. *Place Making and Town Center Development.* Washington, D.C.: Urban Land Institute, 2003.

Campoli, Julie. *Made for Walking: Density and Neighborhood Form.* Cambridge, Mass.: Lincoln Institute of Land Policy, 2012.

Campoli, Julie, and Alex S. MacLean. *Visualizing Density.* Cambridge, Mass.: Lincoln Institute of Land Policy, 2007.

Ewing, Reid. *Pedestrian- and Transit-Oriented Design.* Washington, D.C.: Urban Land Institute, 2013.

Ferguson, William J. *Keepers of the Castle: Real Estate Executives on Leadership and Management.* Washington, D.C.: Urban Land Institute, 2009.

Galatas, Roger, and James Barlow. *The Woodlands: The Inside Story of Creating a Better Hometown.* Washington, D.C.: Urban Land Institute, 2004.

Gause, Jo Allen, ed. *Great Planned Communities.* Washington, D.C.: Urban Land Institute, 2002.

Gibbs, Robert J. *Principles of Urban Retail Planning and Development.* Hoboken, N.J.: John Wiley & Sons, 2012.

Gupta, Prema Katari. *Creating Great Town Centers and Urban Villages.* Washington, D.C.: Urban Land Institute, 2008.

Haughey, Richard. *Getting Density Right: Tools for Creating Vibrant Compact Development.* Washington, D.C.: Urban Land Institute, 2008.

Jackson, Richard, and Stacy Sinclair. Designing Healthy Communities. San Francisco: Jossey-Bass, 2012.

Kramer, Anita. *Retail Development Handbook*, 2nd ed. Washington, D.C.: Urban Land Institute, 2008.

Kramer, Anita, Terry J. Lassar, Mark Federman, and Sara Hammerschmidt. *Building for Wellness: The Business Case.* Washington, D.C.: Urban Land Institute, 2014.

Larco, Nicolas, Kristin Kelsey, and Amanda West. *Site Design for Multifamily Housing: Creating Livable, Connected Neighborhoods.* Washington, D.C.: Island Press, 2014.

MacCleery, Rachel, Casey Peterson, and Julie D. Stern. *Shifting Suburbs: Reinventing Infrastructure for Compact Development.* Washington, D.C.: Urban Land Institute, 2012.

Schmitz, Adrienne, et al. *Multifamily Housing Development Handbook.* Washington, D.C.: Urban Land Institute, 2000.

Schmitz, Adrienne, et al. *Residential Development Handbook*, 2nd ed. Washington, D.C.: Urban Land Institute, 2004.

Schmitz, Adrienne, et al. *Resort Development Handbook*, 2nd ed. Washington, D.C.: Urban Land Institute, 2008.

Schmitz, Adrienne, and Jason Scully. *Creating Walkable Places: Compact Mixed-Use Solutions.* Washington, D.C.: Urban Land Institute, 2006.

Schwanke, Dean, et al. *Mixed-Use Development Handbook*, 2nd ed. Washington, D.C.: Urban Land Institute, 2003.

Urban Land Institute. *Building Healthy Places Toolkit: Strategies for Enhancing Health in the Built Environment.* Washington, D.C.: Urban Land Institute, 2015.

DEMOGRAPHIC INFORMATION

Demographic Data/Statistical Sources—Government

American Community Survey
U.S. Census Bureau
www.census.gov/acs

American Factfinder
U.S. Census Bureau
http://factfinder.census.gov

American Housing Survey
U.S. Census Bureau
www.census.gov/programs-surveys/ahs.html

Census State Data Centers
U.S. Census Bureau
https://www.census.gov/sdc/

County Business Patterns
U.S. Census Bureau
www.census.gov/econ/cbp/

Current Population Statistics
U.S. Census Bureau
www.census.gov/cps/

U.S. Bureau of Labor Statistics
http://stats.bls.gov

Demographic Data/Statistical Sources—Commercial

America's Top-Rated Cities: A Statistical Handbook. Amenia, N.Y.: Grey House Publishing, 2015. www.greyhouse.com/list_statistics.htm.

America's Top-Rated Smaller Cities: A Statistical Handbook. Amenia, N.Y.: Grey House Publishing, 2014/2015. www.greyhouse.com/list_statistics.htm.

Comparative Guide to American Suburbs. Millerton, N.Y.: Grey House Publishing, 2014. www.greyhouse.com/list_statistics.htm.

Environmental Systems Research Institute, Inc. (ESRI). www.esri.com.

Nielsen SiteReports. www.claritas.com/sitereports/Default.jsp.

Woods and Poole Economics. *Cedds: The Complete Economic and Demographic Data.* Washington, D.C.: Woods and Poole Economics. www.woodsandpoole.com.

Demographics

Lachman, M. Leanne. *Global Demographics and Real Estate: Shaping Real Estate's Future.* Washington, D.C.: Urban Land Institute, 2008.

Lachman, M. Leanne, and Deborah L. Brett. *Generation Y: Shopping and Entertainment in the Digital Age.* Washington, D.C.: Urban Land Institute, 2013.

McIlwain, John. *Housing in America: The Baby Boomers Turn 65.* Washington, D.C.: Urban Land Institute, 2012.

Nelson, Arthur C. *The New California Dream: How Demographic and Economic Trends May Shape the Housing Market.* Washington, D.C.: Urban Land Institute, 2011.

New Strategist. *The American Marketplace: Demographics and Spending Patterns.* Ithaca, N.Y.: New Strategist Publications, 2014.

PART 2 The History of Real Estate Development in the United States

THE COLONIAL PERIOD TO THE LATE 1800S

Boehm, Lisa Krissoff, and Steven H. Corey. *American Urban Form: A Representative History.* New York: Routledge, 2014.

Hartog, Hendrik. *Public Property and Private Law: The Corporation of the City of New York in American Law, 1730–1870.* Chapel Hill: University of North Carolina Press, 1983.

Hoyt, Homer. *One Hundred Years of Land Values in Chicago: The Relationship of the Growth of Chicago to the Rise in Its Land Values, 1830–1933.* Chicago: University of Chicago Press, 1933.

Jackson, Kenneth T. *Crabgrass Frontier: The Suburbanization of the United States.* New York: Oxford University Press, 1985.

Lubove, Roy. *The Progressives and the Slums: Tenement House Reform in New York City, 1890–1917.* Pittsburgh, Pa.: University of Pittsburgh Press, 1962.

Moehring, Eugene P. *Public Works and the Patterns of Urban Real Estate Growth in Manhattan, 1835–1894.* New York: Arno Press, 1981.

Reitano, Joanne. *The Restless City: A Short History of New York from Colonial Times to the Present*, 2nd ed. New York: Taylor & Francis, 2010.

Reps, John W. *The Making of Urban America: A History of City Planning in the United States.* Princeton, N.J.: Princeton University Press, 1965.

Robbins, Roy M. *Our Landed Heritage: The Public Domain, 1776–1936*, 2nd ed. Lincoln: University of Nebraska Press, 1976.

Sakolski, A. M. *The Great American Land Bubble: The Amazing Story of Land-Grabbing, Speculations, and Booms from Colonial Days to the Present Time.* New York: Harper, 1932.

Smith, Arthur D. Howden. *John Jacob Astor: Landlord of New York.* Philadelphia: Lippincott, 1929.

Warner, Sam Bass. *American Urban Form: A Representative History.* Cambridge, Mass.: MIT Press, 2012.

———. *Streetcar Suburbs: The Process of Growth in Boston, 1870–1900.* Cambridge, Mass.: Harvard University Press, 1962.

Weiss, Marc A. *The Rise of the Community Builders: The American Real Estate Industry and Urban Land Planning.* New York: Columbia University Press, 1987.

THE LATE 1800S TO WORLD WAR II

Blackford, Mausel G. *The Lost Dream: Businessmen and City Planning on the Pacific Coast, 1890–1920*. Columbus: Ohio State University Press, 1993.

Boehm, Lisa Krissoff, and Steven H. Corey. *American Urban Form: A Representative History*. New York: Routledge, 2014.

Community Builders Council. *Community Builders Handbook*. Washington, D.C.: Urban Land Institute, 1947.

El-Khoury, Rodolphe, and Edward Robbins. *Shaping the City: Studies in History, Theory, and Urban Design*. New York: Routledge, Taylor & Francis Group, 2013.

Eskew, Garnett Laidlaw. *Of Land and Men: The Birth and Growth of an Idea*. Washington, D.C.: Urban Land Institute, 1959.

Ewalt, Josephine Hedges. *A Business Reborn: The Savings and Loan Story, 1930–1960*. Chicago: American Savings and Loan Institute, 1962.

Fogelson, Robert M. *The Fragmented Metropolis: Los Angeles, 1880–1930*. Cambridge, Mass.: Harvard University Press, 1967.

Gibbs, Kenneth Turney. *Business Architectural Imagery in America, 1870–1930*. Ann Arbor, Mich.: UMI Research Press, 1984.

Hall, Peter. *Cities of Tomorrow: An Intellectual History of Urban Planning and Design Since 1880*. Hoboken, N.J.: Wiley Blackwell, 2014.

Howard, Ebenezer. *Garden Cities of Tomorrow*. London: Faber & Faber, 1945.

Hoyt, Homer. *The Structure and Growth of Residential Neighborhoods in American Cities*. Washington, D.C.: Federal Housing Administration, 1939.

Jackson, Kenneth T. *Crabgrass Frontier: The Suburbanization of the United States*. New York: Oxford University Press, 1985.

Kahn, Judd. *Imperial San Francisco: Politics and Planning in an American City, 1897–1906*. Lincoln: University of Nebraska Press, 1979.

Lotchin, Roger W. *Fortress California, 1910–1961: From Warfare to Welfare*. New York: Oxford University Press, 1992.

Reitano, Joanne. *The Restless City: A Short History of New York from Colonial Times to the Present*, 2nd ed. New York: Taylor & Francis, 2010.

Schactman, Tom. *Skyscraper Dreams: The Great Real Estate Dynasties of New York*. Boston: Little, Brown, 1991.

Schaffer, Daniel. *Garden Cities for America: The Radburn Experience*. Philadelphia: Temple University Press, 1982.

Stern, Robert A. M., Gregory Gilmartin, and Thomas Mellins. *New York, 1930: Architecture and Urbanism Between the Two World Wars*. New York: Rizzoli, 1987.

Teaford, Jon C. *The Unheralded Triumph: City Government in America, 1870–1900*. Baltimore: Johns Hopkins University Press, 1984.

Weiss, Marc A. "Density and Intervention: New York's Planning Traditions." In *The Landscape of Modernity: Essays on New York City, 1900-1940*. Edited by David Ward and Oliver Zunz. New York: Russell Sage Foundation, 1992.

———. "Richard T. Ely and the Contribution of Economic Research to National Housing Policy, 1920–1940." Urban Studies (February 1989): 115–26.

———. *The Rise of the Community Builders: The American Real Estate Industry and Urban Land Planning*. New York: Columbia University Press, 1987.

Wood, Edith Elmer. *Slums and Blighted Areas in the United States*. Public Works Administration, Housing Division Bulletin No. 1. Washington, D.C.: U.S. Government Printing Office, 1935.

Worley, William S. *J. C. Nichols and the Shaping of Kansas City: Innovation in Planned Residential Communities*. Columbia: University of Missouri Press, 1990.

Wright, Gwendolyn. *Moralism and the Model Home: Domestic Architecture and Cultural Conflict in Chicago, 1873–1913*. Chicago: University of Chicago Press, 1980.

POST–WORLD WAR II TO THE PRESENT

Besel, Karl, and Viviana Andreescu. *Back to the Future: New Urbanism and the Rise of Neotraditionalism in Urban Planning*. Lanham, Md.: University Press of America, 2013.

Bloom, Nicholas D. *Merchant of Illusion: James Rouse, America's Salesman of the Businessman's Utopia*. Columbus: Ohio State University Press, 2004.

Boehm, Lisa Krissoff, and Steven H. Corey. *American Urban Form: A Representative History*. New York: Routledge, 2014.

Breckenfeld, Gurney. *Columbia and the New Cities*. New York: Ives Washburn, 1971.

Caro, Robert A. *The Power Broker: Robert Moses and the Fall of New York*. New York: Random House, 1974.

Checkoway, Barry. *The Politics of Postwar Suburban Development*. Berkeley: University of California, Childhood and Government Project, 1977.

Cisneros, Henry G., ed. *Interwoven Destinies: Cities and the Nation*. New York: Norton, 1993.

Eichler, Ned. *The Merchant Builders*. Cambridge, Mass.: MIT Press, 1982.

———. *The Thrift Debacle*. Berkeley: University of California Press, 1989.

El-Khoury, Rodolphe, and Edward Robbins. *Shaping the City: Studies in History, Theory, and Urban Design*. New York: Routledge, Taylor & Francis Group, 2013.

Frieden, Bernard J., and Lynne B. Sagalyn. *Downtown, Inc.: How America Rebuilds Cities*. Cambridge, Mass.: MIT Press, 1989.

Garreau, Joel. *Edge City: Life on the New Frontier.* New York: Doubleday, 1992.

Gelfand, Mark I. *A Nation of Cities: The Federal Government and Urban America, 1933–1965.* New York: Oxford University Press, 1975.

Griffin, Nathaniel M. *Irvine: Genesis of a New Community.* Washington, D.C.: Urban Land Institute, 1974.

Hall, Peter. *Cities of Tomorrow: An Intellectual History of Urban Planning and Design Since 1880.* Hoboken, N.J.: Wiley Blackwell, 2014.

Hayden, Dolores. *Building Suburbia: Green Fields and Urban Growth, 1820–2000.* New York: Pantheon Books, 2003.

Jackson, Kenneth T. *Crabgrass Frontier: The Suburbanization of the United States.* New York: Oxford University Press, 1985.

Jacobs, Jane. *The Death and Life of Great American Cities.* New York: Random House, 1961.

Katz, Peter. *The New Urbanism: Toward an Architecture of Community.* New York: McGraw-Hill, 1994.

Kotkin, Joel. *The City: A Global History.* New York: Modern Library, 2006.

Reitano, Joanne. *The Restless City: A Short History of New York from Colonial Times to the Present*, 2nd ed. New York: Taylor & Francis, 2010.

Rybczynski, Witold. *Last Harvest: How a Cornfield Became New Daleville: Real Estate Development in America from George Washington to the Builders of the Twenty-first Century, and Why We Live in Houses Anyway.* New York: Scribner, 2007.

Sobel, Robert. *Trammell Crow, Master Builder: The Story of America's Largest Real Estate Empire.* New York: Wiley, 1989.

Teaford, Jon C. *The Rough Road to Renaissance: Urban Revitalization in America, 1940–1985.* Baltimore: Johns Hopkins University Press, 1990.

Weiner, Edward. *Urban Transportation Planning in the United States: History, Policy, and Practice*, 4th ed. New York: Springer, 2013.

Weiss, Marc A. "Marketing and Financing Homeownership: Mortgage Lending and Public Policy in the United States, 1918–1989." *Business and Economic History* (1989): 109–118.

———. "The Origins and Legacy of Urban Renewal." *Federal Housing Policy and Programs: Past and Present.* Edited by J. Paul Mitchell. New Brunswick, N.J.: Rutgers University Center for Urban Policy Research, 1985: 253–276.

———. *The Rise of the Community Builders: The American Real Estate Industry and Urban Land Planning.* New York: Columbia University Press, 1987.

Zeckendorf, William, and Edward McCreary. *The Autobiography of William Zeckendorf.* New York: Holt, Rinehart & Winston, 1970.

PART 3 The Public Interest

THE PUBLIC ROLES

Buckley, Michael E. *Practical Guide to Zoning and Land Use Law.* Eau Claire, Wis.: National Business Institute, Inc., 2013.

Dale, C. Gregory, Benjamin A. Herman, and Anne F. McBride. *The Planning Commissioners Guide.* Chicago: APA Planners Press, 2013.

Deems, Nyal D., N. Stevenson Jennette III, and Eric Damian Kelly. *A Practical Guide to Winning Land Use Approvals and Permits.* New Providence, N.J.: LexisNexis, 2014.

Forester, John. *Planning in the Face of Conflict: The Surprising Possibilities of Facilitative Leadership.* Chicago: APA Planners Press, 2013.

Garvin, Alexander. *The Planning Game: Lessons from Great Cities.* New York: W. W. Norton & Company, 2013.

Heller, Gregory L. *Ed Bacon: Planning, Politics, and the Building of Modern Philadelphia.* City in the Twenty-First Century Series. Philadelphia: University of Pennsylvania Press, 2013.

Juergensmeyer, Julian Conrad, and Thomas E. Roberts. *Land Use Planning and Development Regulation Law*, 3rd ed. St. Paul, Minn.: West, 2013.

Katz, Bruce, and Jennifer Bradley. *The Metropolitan Revolution: How Cities and Metros are Fixing Our Broken Politics and Fragile Economy.* Washington, D.C.: Brookings Institution Press, 2013.

Kmiec, Douglas W., and Katherine Kmiec Turner. *Zoning and Planning Deskbook.* New York: Thomson Reuters, 2014–2015 ed.

Mandelker, Daniel R. *Planning and Control of Land Development: Cases and Materials.* 8th ed. New Providence, N.J.: LexisNexis, 2011.

Nelson, Arthur C. *Foundations of Real Estate Development Financing A Guide to Public-Private Partnerships.* Washington, D.C.: Island Press/Center for Resource Economics, 2014.

Nelson, Arthur C., James C. Nicholas, and Julian C. Juergensmeyer. *Impact Fees: Principles and Practice of Proportionate-Share Development Fees.* Chicago: APA Planners Press, 2009.

Porter, Douglas R., and Suzanne Cartwright. *Breaking the Development Logjam.* Washington, D.C.: Urban Land Institute, 2006.

Ramesh, G., Vishnuprasad Nagadevara, and Gopal Naik. *Public Private Partnerships.* London: Routledge, 2010.

Sabol, Patrick and Robert Puentes. *Private Capital, Public Good: Drivers of Successful Infrastructure Public-Private Partnership.* Washington, D.C.: Brookings Institution, 2014.

Walker, Doug, and Tom Daniels. *The Planners Guide to CommunityViz: The Essential Tool for a New Generation of Planning.* Orton Family

Foundation Books. Chicago: APA Planners Press and the Orton Family, 2011.

World Bank Group. *How to Engage with the Private Sector in Public-Private Partnerships in Emerging Markets.* Washington, D.C.: World Bank, 2011.

AFFORDABLE HOUSING

Black, Jill. *The Financing & Economics of Affordable Housing Development: Incentives and Disincentives to Private-Sector Participation.* Toronto: Cities Centre, University of Toronto, 2012.

Downs, Anthony, ed. *Growth Management and Affordable Housing: Do They Conflict?* Washington, D.C.: Brookings Institution Press, 2004.

Gilmore, Dorcas R., and Diane M. Standaert. *Building Community Resilience Post-Disaster: A Guide for Affordable Housing and Community Economic Development Practitioners.* Chicago: ABA Forum on Affordable Housing and Community Development Law, 2013.

Harvard University, Joint Center for Housing Studies. *The State of the Nation's Housing.* Cambridge, Mass.: Harvard University, annual issues. www.jchs.harvard.edu.

Haughey, Richard M. *Best Practices in the Production of Affordable Housing.* Washington, D.C.: Urban Land Institute, 2005.

———. *The Business of Affordable Housing.* Washington, D.C.: Urban Land Institute, 2006.

———. *Developing Housing for the Workforce: A Toolkit.* Washington, D.C.: Urban Land Institute, 2007.

———. *Workforce Housing: Innovative Strategies and Best Practices.* Washington, D.C.: Urban Land Institute, 2006.

Iglesias, Tim, and Rochelle E. Lento. *The Legal Guide to Affordable Housing Development.* Cleveland, Ohio: American Bar Association, 2014.

Jakabovics, Andrew, Lynn M. Ross, Molly Simpson, and Michael Spotts. *Bending the Cost Curve: Solutions to Expand the Supply of Affordable Rentals.* Washington, D.C.: Urban Land Institute, 2014.

Massey, Douglas S. *Climbing Mount Laurel: The Struggle for Affordable Housing and Social Mobility in an American Suburb.* Princeton, N.J.: Princeton University Press, 2013.

Meck, Stuart, Rebecca Retzlaff, and James Schwab. *Regional Approaches to Affordable Housing.* Planning Advisory Service Report 513/514. Chicago: APA Planning Advisory Service, 2003.

Porter, Douglas R. *Inclusionary Zoning for Affordable Housing.* Washington, D.C.: Urban Land Institute, 2004.

Rosan, Richard. *Housing America's Workforce: Case Studies and Lessons from the Experts.* Washington, D.C.: Urban Land Institute, 2012.

Schmitz, Adrienne, et al. *Affordable Housing: Designing an American Asset.* Washington, D.C.: Urban Land Institute, 2005.

Tighe, J. Rosie, and Elizabeth J. Mueller. *The Affordable Housing Reader.* London: Routledge, 2013.

Urban Land Institute. *Best Practices: Workforce Housing Development.* Washington, D.C.: Urban Land Institute, 2009.

PART 4 Ideas

INCEPTION AND REFINEMENT OF AN IDEA

Krueger, Richard A., and Mary Anne Casey. *Focus Groups: A Practical Guide for Applied Research*, 5th ed. Thousand Oaks, Calif.: Sage, 2015.

Kwartler, Michael, and Gianni Longo. *Visioning and Visualization: People, Pixels, and Plans.* Cambridge, Mass.: Lincoln Institute of Land Policy, 2008.

Lennertz, Bill, and Aarin Lutzenhiser. *The Charrette Handbook.* Chicago: APA Planners Press, 2014.

Stout, Louis. *Collective Visioning: How Groups can Work Together for a Just and Sustainable Future.* San Francisco: Berrett-Koehler Publishers, 2011.

Walzer, Norman, and Gisele Hamm. *Community Visioning Programs: Processes and Outcomes.* Milton Park, Abingdon, Oxon, U.K.: Routledge, 2012.

MARKET RESEARCH

Brace, Ian. *Questionnaire Design: How to Plan, Structure, and Write Survey Material for Effective Market Research.* London: Kogan Page Limited, 2013.

Brett, Deborah L., and Adrienne Schmitz. *Real Estate Market Analysis.* Washington, D.C.: Urban Land Institute, 2009.

Brooks, Chris, and Sotiris Tsolacos. *Real Estate Modelling and Forecasting.* Cambridge, U.K.: Cambridge University Press, 2010.

Fanning, Stephen F. *Market Analysis for Real Estate: Concepts and Applications in Valuation and Highest and Best Use*, 2nd ed. Chicago: Appraisal Institute, 2014.

Graaskamp, James A. "Identification and Delineation of Real Estate Market Research." *Real Estate Issues* 10:1 (Spring/Summer 1985): 6–12.

Hague, Paul N., Nick Hague, and Carol-Ann Morgan. *Market Research in Practice: How to Get Greater Insight from Your Market.* London: Kogan Page, 2013.

Li, Ling Hin, Hui Sun, Ka-ho Kevin Kwong, and Tiffany Ka Yan Chung. *Alternative Real Estate Research.* London: Routledge, 2015.

Poynter, Ray, Navin Williams, and Sue York. *The Handbook of Mobile Market Research Tools and Techniques for Market Researchers.* Hoboken, N.J.: John Wiley & Sons, 2014.

PART 5 Financing the Project

Albert, Kevin K., Bob Brown, and Jessica H. Brennan. *Private Market Fundraising: World-Class Techniques for Raising Private Equity,*

Debt, Real Estate, and Infrastructure Funds. London: PEI Media Ltd., 2013.

Baker, H. Kent, and Peter Chinloy. *Private Real Estate Markets and Investments.* Oxford, U.K.; New York: Oxford University Press, 2014.

Brueggeman, William B., and Jeffrey D. Fisher. *Real Estate Finance and Investments*, 15th ed. Boston: McGraw-Hill, 2014.

Bruner, Robert F. *Case Studies in Finance: Managing for Corporate Value Creation*, 7th ed. London: McGraw-Hill, 2014.

Clauretie, Terrence M., and G. Stacy Sirmans. *Real Estate Finance: Theory and Practice*, 7th ed. Mason, Ohio: OnCourse Learning, 2014.

Collier, Nathan S., Courtland A. Collier, and Don A. Halperin. *Construction Funding: The Process of Real Estate Development, Appraisal, and Finance*, 4th ed. Hoboken, N.J.: John Wiley & Sons, 2008.

Downs, Anthony. *Real Estate and the Financial Crisis: How Turmoil in the Capital Markets Is Restructuring Real Estate Finance.* Washington, D.C.: Urban Land Institute, 2009.

Geltner, David M., Norman G. Miller, Jim Clayton, and Piet Eichholtz. *Commercial Real Estate Analysis and Investments*, 3rd ed. Mason, Ohio: OnCourse Learning, 2014.

Glickman, Edward A. *An Introduction to Real Estate Finance.* Waltham, Mass.: Academic Press, 2014.

Kolbe, Phillip T., Gaylon E. Greer, and Bennie D. Waller. *Investment Analysis for Real Estate Decisions.* La Crosse, Wis.: Dearborn, 2013.

———. *Real Estate Finance*, 3rd ed. La Crosse, Wis.: Dearborn, a Kaplan Real Estate Education Company, 2012.

Ling, David C., and Wayne R. Archer. *Real Estate Principles: A Value Approach*, 4th ed. Boston: McGraw-Hill/Irwin, 2013.

Linneman, Peter. *Real Estate Finance and Investments: Risks and Opportunities*, 3.1 ed. Philadelphia: Linneman Associates, 2013.

Long, Charles. *Finance for Real Estate Development.* Washington, D.C.: Urban Land Institute, 2011.

Lynn, David J. *The Investor's Guide to Commercial Real Estate.* Washington, D.C.: Urban Land Institute, 2014.

Nelson, Arthur C. *Foundations of Real Estate Development Financing: A Guide to Public-Private Partnerships.* Washington, D.C.: Island Press/Center for Resource Economics, 2014.

PwC and Urban Land Institute. *Emerging Trends in Real Estate.* Washington, DC: Urban Land Institute and PwC, annual issues.

PwC and Urban Land Institute. *Emerging Trends in Real Estate: Asia Pacific.* Washington, D.C.: Urban Land Institute and PwC, annual issues.

PwC and Urban Land Institute. *Emerging Trends in Real Estate: Europe.* Washington, D.C.: Urban Land Institute and PwC, annual issues.

Rauf, Natalie H., et al. *Commercial Real Estate Finance Strategies: Leading Lawyers on Navigating the Changing Real Estate Market and Negotiating the Best Financing Outcomes.* Boston: Aspatore, 2013.

Sirota, David, and Doris Barrell. *Essentials of Real Estate Finance*, 13th ed. Chicago: Dearborn Real Estate Education, 2012.

Tiwari, Piyush, and Michael White. *Real Estate Finance in the New Economy.* Oxford, U.K.: Wiley Blackwell, 2014.

PART 6 Proving the Concept

REAL ESTATE MARKET AND FEASIBILITY STUDIES

Appraisal Institute. *The Appraisal of Real Estate*, 14th ed. Chicago: Appraisal Institute, 2013.

Baum, Andrew E., Nick Nunnington, and David Mackmin. *The Income Approach to Property Valuation.* London: Estates Gazette, 2011.

Betts, Richard M., and Silas J. Ely. *Basic Real Estate Appraisal: Principles & Procedures*, 8th ed. Mason, Ohio: Cengage Learning, 2013.

Brett, Deborah L., and Adrienne Schmitz. *Real Estate Market Analysis: Methods and Case Studies.* Washington, D.C.: Urban Land Institute, 2009.

Brooks, Chris, and Sotiris Tsolacos. *Real Estate Modelling and Forecasting.* Cambridge, U.K.: Cambridge University Press, 2010.

Building Owners and Managers Association. *Experience Exchange Report.* Washington, D.C.: Building Owners and Managers Association, 2014 (updated annually).

DeLisle, James, ed. *Appraisal, Market Analysis, and Public Policy in Real Estate: Essays in Honor of James A. Graaskamp.* Boston: Kluwer Academic Publishers, 1994.

Fanning, Stephen F. *Market Analysis for Real Estate: Concepts and Applications in Valuation and Highest and Best Use*, 2nd ed. Chicago: Appraisal Institute, 2014.

Geltner, David M., and Norman G. Miller. *Commercial Real Estate Analysis and Investments*, 3rd ed. Mason, Ohio: OnCourse Learning, 2014.

Graaskamp, James. *A Guide to Feasibility Analysis.* Chicago: Appraisal Institute, 1970.

Kolbe, Phillip T., Gaylon E. Greer, and Bennie D. Waller. *Investment Analysis for Real Estate Decisions*, 8th ed. La Crosse, Wis.: Dearborn, 2013.

Kulwin, Michael. *Feasibility Studies in Construction Projects: Practice and Procedure.* New York: Routledge 2014.

Manganelli, Benedetto. *Real Estate Investing: Market Analysis, Valuation Techniques, and Risk Management.* Cham, Switzerland: Springer International Publishing AG, 2014.

National Apartment Association. *Survey of Income & Expenses.* Arlington, Va.: National Apartment Association, 2014 (updated annually).

Peiser, Richard B., and David Hamilton. *Professional Real Estate Development: The ULI Guide to the Business*, 3rd ed. Washington, D.C.: Urban Land Institute, 2012.

Rattermann, Mark. *The Student Handbook to the Appraisal of Real Estate*, 14th ed. Chicago: Appraisal Institute, 2014.

Roddewig, Richard J. *Valuing Contaminated Properties: An Appraisal Institute Anthology.* Volume II. Chicago: Institute of Real Estate Management, 2014.

Sorenson, Richard C. *Appraising the Appraisal: The Art of Appraisal Review*, 2nd ed. Chicago: Institute of Real Estate Management, 2010.

Wyatt, Peter. *Property Valuation*, 2nd ed. Chichester, West Sussex: Wiley-Blackwell, 2013.

PART 7 Making It Happen

CONTRACT NEGOTIATION AND FORMAL COMMITMENT

American Institute of Architects. *AIA Contract Documents.* Washington, D.C.: American Institute of Architects (updated regularly).

Bockrath, Joseph T., and Fredric L. Plotnick. *Contracts and the Legal Environment for Engineers & Architects*, 7th ed. New York: McGraw-Hill, 2010.

Chappell, David. *Construction Contracts: Questions and Answers*, 3rd ed. New York: Routlege, 2015.

Cook, Charles W. *Successful Contract Administration: For Constructors and Design Professionals.* Abingdon, Oxon; New York: Routledge, 2014.

Friedman, Milton R., and James Charles Smith. *Friedman on Contracts and Conveyances of Real Property.* Real Property Law Library. New York: Practising Law Institute, 2014 (updated continually).

Frier, Bruce W., and James J. White. *The Modern Law of Contracts*, 3rd ed. St. Paul, Minn.: Thomson/West, 2012.

Hinze, Jimmie. *Construction Contracts*, 3rd ed. New York: McGraw-Hill, 2011.

Hughes, William, J. R. Murdoch, and Ronan Champion. *Construction Contracts: Law and Management*, Abingdon, Oxon, U.K.; New York: Routledge, 2015.

Senn, Mark A., ed. *Commercial Real Estate Transactions*, 4th ed. New York: Wolters Kluwer Law & Business, 2014.

Sweet, Jonathan J. *Sweet on Construction Industry Contracts: Major AIA Documents*, 6th ed. New York: Wolters Kluwer, 2014.

CONSTRUCTION, COMPLETION, AND FORMAL OPENING

De Marco, Alberto. *Project Management for Facility Constructions a Guide for Engineers and Architects.* Heidelberg, N.Y.: Springer, 2011.

Allen, Edward, and Joseph Iano. *Fundamentals of Building Construction: Materials and Methods*, 6th ed. Hoboken, N.J.: Wiley, 2014.

Ching, Francis D. K. *Building Construction Illustrated*, 5th ed. Hoboken, N.J.: Wiley, 2014.

Construction Specifications Institute. *The CSI Sustainable Design and Construction Practice Guide.* Hoboken, N.J.: Wiley, 2013.

Depico, Wayne J. *Project Control Integrating Cost and Schedule in Construction.* Hoboken, N.J.: Wiley, 2013.

Fisk, Edward R., and Wayne R. Reynolds. *Construction Project Administration*, 10th ed. Upper Saddle River, N.J.: Prentice Hall, 2014.

Halpin, Daniel W., and Bolivar A. Senior. *Construction Management*, 4th ed. Hoboken, N.J.: Wiley, 2012.

Harris, Cyril M. *Dictionary of Architecture and Construction*, 4th ed. New York: McGraw-Hill, 2006.

Harris, Frank, Ronald McCaffer, and Francis Edum-Fotwe. *Modern Construction Management*, 7th ed. Chichester, West Sussex, U.K.: Wiley Blackwell, 2013.

Kerzner, Harold. *Project Management: A Systems Approach to Planning, Scheduling, and Controlling*, 11th ed. New York: Wiley, 2013.

Lambeck, Richard, and John Eschemuller. *Urban Construction Project Management.* New York: McGraw-Hill, 2009.

Levy, Sidney M. *Project Management in Construction*, 6th ed. New York: McGraw-Hill, 2012.

Pierce, David R. *Project Scheduling and Management for Construction*, 4th ed. Kingston, Mass.: R. S. Means, 2013.

Ritz, George J., and Sidney M. Levy. *Total Construction Project Management*, 2nd ed. New York: McGraw-Hill, 2013.

Rosen, Harold J. *Construction Specifications Writing: Principles and Procedures*, 6th ed. Hoboken, N.J.: Wiley, 2010.

R.S. Means Company. *Building Construction Cost Data.* Norwell, Mass.: RSMeans, 2015 (published annually).

———. *Electric Cost Data.* Norwell, Mass.: RSMeans, 2015 (published annually).

———. *Square Foot Costs.* Norwell, Mass.: RSMeans, 2015 (published annually).

———. *Means Illustrated Construction Dictionary.* Student edition. Hoboken, N.J.: Wiley, 2012.

Schaufelberger, John, and Ken-Yu Lin. *Construction Project Safety.* Hoboken, N.J.: John Wiley & Sons, Inc., 2014.

ASSET AND PROPERTY MANAGEMENT

Alexander, Alan A., and Richard F. Muhlebach. *Managing and Leasing Commercial Properties.* Chicago: Institute of Real Estate Management, 2007.

Baiamonte, Lawrence W. *Troubled Properties: A Practical Guide for Turning Around Troubled Assets.* Chicago: Institute of Real Estate Management, 2011.

Carretta, Alessandro. *Asset Pricing, Real Estate and Public Finance over the Crisis.* Houndmills, Basingstoke, Hampshire, U.K.; New York: Palgrave Macmillan, 2013.

Gibson, Roger C., and Christopher J. Sidoni. *Asset Allocation*, 5th ed. New York: McGraw-Hill Education, 2013.

Haynes, Barry P., and Nick Nunnington. *Corporate Real Estate Asset Management: Strategy and Implementation.* Amsterdam: EG Books, 2010.

Institute of Real Estate Management. *Field Guide for Practical Apartment Management.* Chicago: Institute of Real Estate Management, 2015.

———. *Income/Expense Analysis.* Chicago: Institute of Real Estate Management, 2014 (updated annually).

———. *Glossary of Real Estate Management Terms.* Chicago: Institute of Real Estate Management, 2003.

———. *Principles of Real Estate Management*, 16th ed. Chicago: Institute of Real Estate Management, 2011.

Muhlebach, Richard F., and Alan A. Alexander. *Business Strategies for Real Estate Management Companies*, 3rd ed. Chicago: Institute of Real Estate Management, 2014.

Prassas, Fred. *Investment Real Estate: Finance & Asset Management.* Chicago: Institute of Real Estate Management, 2013.

Scarrett, Douglas. *Property Asset Management*, 3rd ed. New York: Routledge, 2011.

Smith, Dana K., and Michael Tardif. *Building Information Modeling: A Strategic Implementation Guide for Architects, Engineers, Constructors, and Real Estate Asset Managers.* Hoboken, N.J.: Wiley, 2009.

SALES AND MARKETING MANAGEMENT

Grabel, Gary. *Wealth Opportunities in Commercial Real Estate: Management, Financing and Marketing of Investment Properties.* Hoboken, N.J.: Wiley, 2012.

Grover, Chris. *Sales and Marketing 101 for Real Estate Professionals.* La Cross, Wis.: Dearborn Real Estate Education, 2012.

Romer, Adam Von and Patricia O'Connor. *Getting Started in Commercial Real Estate Ten Step Program to Success!* Fort Lauderdale, Fla.: The Veritas Real Estate Group, Inc., 2013.

Scott, David M. *The New Rules of Marketing & PR: How to Use Social Media, Online Video, Mobile Applications, Blogs, News Releases, & Viral Marketing to Reach Buyers Directly.* Hoboken, N.J.: Wiley, 2013.

Sirgy, M. Joseph. *Real Estate Marketing: Strategy, Personal Selling, Negotiation, Management, and Ethics.* Hoboken, N.J.: Taylor and Francis, 2014.

Young, Antony, and Lucy Aitken. *Profitable Marketing Communications: A Guide to Marketing Return on Investment.* Philadelphia: Kogan Page, 2007.

THE FUTURE

Baumohl, Bernard. *The Secrets of Economic Indicators: Hidden Clues to Future Economic Trends and Investment Opportunities*, 3rd ed. Upper Saddle River, N.J.: FT Press, 2013.

Bazzanella, Liliana. *The Future of Cities and Regions: Simulation, Scenario and Visioning, Governance and Scale.* Dordrecht: Springer, 2012.

Benton-Short, Lisa. *Cities of North America: Contemporary Challenges in U.S. and Canadian Cities.* Lanham, Md.: Rowman & Littlefield, 2014.

Cisneros, Henry. *Urban Real Estate Investment: A New Era of Opportunity.* Washington, D.C.: Urban Land Institute, 2015.

Conventz, Sven, and Alain Thierstein. *Airports, Cities, and Regions.* Abingdon, Oxon, U.K.: Routledge, 2015.

Cowen, Scott S., and Betsy Seifter. *The Inevitable City: The Resurgence of New Orleans and the Future of Urban America.* New York: Palgrave Macmillan, 2014.

Dent, Harry S. *The Demographic Cliff: How to Survive and Prosper During the Great Deflation of 2014–2019.* New York: Portfolio/Pengiun, 2014.

Haas, Tigran. *Sustainable Urbanism and Beyond: Rethinking Cities for the Future.* New York: Rizzoli, 2012.

Kraas, Frauke. *Megacities: Our Global Urban Future.* Dordrecht: Springer, 2014.

Krause, Linda. *Sustaining Cities: Urban Policies, Practices, and Perceptions.* New Brunswick, N.J.: Rutgers University Press, 2013.

Listokin, David. "Housing Rehabilitation and American Cities." *Housing Policy in the New Millennium*, Conference Proceedings. Washington, D.C.: U.S. Department of Housing and Urban Development, 2013.

Lucy, William H. *Foreclosing the Dream: How America's Housing Crisis Is Reshaping Our Cities and Suburbs.* Chicago: APA Planners Press, 2010.

ORGANIZATIONS

General Real Estate and Planning

American Institute of Architects
www.aia.org

American Planning Association
www.planning.org

American Society of Landscape Architects
hwww.asla.org

Building Owners and Managers Association
www.boma.org

Commercial Investment Real Estate Institute
www.ccim.com

Commercial Real Estate Women
www.crewnetwork.org

Congress for the New Urbanism
www.cnu.org

CoreNet Global
www.corenetglobal.com

Counselors of Real Estate
www.cre.org

Design-Build Institute of America
www.dbia.org

Institute of Real Estate Management
www.irem.org

International Downtown Association
www.ida-downtown.org

International Real Estate Federation
www.fiabci-usa.com

Lincoln Institute of Land Policy
www.lincolninst.edu

National Association of Realtors
www.nar.org

National Council for Public-Private Partnerships
www.ncppp.org

National League of Cities
www.nlc.org

National Trust for Historic Preservation
www.nthp.org

Real Estate Board of New York
www.rebny.com

Real Estate Educators Association
www.reea.org

Real Estate Research Institute
www.reri.org

Real Estate Roundtable
www.rer.org

Royal Institution of Chartered Surveyors
www.rics.org

Affordable Housing

Affordable Housing Tax Credit Coalition
www.taxcreditcoalition.org

Center for Community Change
www.communitychange.org

Council of Large Public Housing Agencies
www.clpha.org

Council of State Community Development Agencies
http://coscda.org

The Enterprise Foundation
www.enterprisefoundation.net

Fannie Mae
www.fanniemae.com

Freddie Mac
www.freddiemac.com

Habitat for Humanity
www.habitat.org

Housing Partnership Network
www.housingpartnership.net

J. Ronald Terwilliger Foundation for Housing America's Families
www.jrthousing.org

Local Initiatives Support Corporation
www.lisc.org

National Affordable Housing Management Association
www.nahma.org

National Alliance to End Homelessness
www.endhomelessness.org

National Association of Home Builders
www.nahb.org

National Association of Housing and Redevelopment Officials
www.nahro.org

National Association of Local Housing Finance Agencies
www.nalhfa.org

National Coalition for the Homeless
www.nationalhomeless.org

National Council for State Housing Agencies
www.ncsha.org

National Housing Conference + Center for Housing Policy
www.nhc.org

National Housing Law Project
www.nhlp.org

National Housing Trust
www.nhtinc.org

National Low-Income Housing Coalition
www.nlihc.org

NeighborWorks America
www.nw.org

ULI Terwilliger Center for Housing
www.uli.org/research/centers-initiatives/
terwilliger-center-for-housing

U.S. Conference of Mayors
www.usmayors.org

U.S. Department of Housing and Urban Development
www.hud.gov

Urban Institute
www.urbaninstitute.org

Urban Land Institute
www.uli.org

Specialized

American Bankers Association
www.aba.com

American Hotel and Lodging Association
www.ahma.com

American Industrial Real Estate Association
www.airea.com

American Resort Development Association
www.arda.org

American Seniors Housing Association
www.seniorshousing.org

Appraisal Institute
www.appraisalinstitute.org

Association of Foreign Investors in Real Estate
www.afire.org

Construction Financial Management Association
www.cfma.org

International Council of Shopping Centers
www.icsc.org

Manufactured Housing Institute
www.manufacturedhousing.org

Mortgage Bankers Association of America
www.mbaa.org

National Apartment Association
www.naahq.org

National Association of Counties
www.naco.org

National Association of Home Builders
www.nahb.com

National Association of Industrial and Office Parks
www.naiop.org

National Association of Real Estate Investment Managers
www.nareim.org

National Association of Real Estate Investment Trusts
www.nareit.com

National Council of Real Estate Investment Fiduciaries
www.ncreif.com

National League of Cities
www.nlc.org

National Multifamily Housing Council
https://nmhc.org

Pension Real Estate Association
www.prea.org

Society of Industrial and Office Realtors
www.sior.com

PERIODICALS

Journals and Magazines: General Real Estate and Planning

American City and County
www.americancityandcounty.com

Architectural Record
www.archrecord.construction.com

Architecture
www.architecturemag.com

Builder
www.builderonline.com

Building Design & Construction
www.bdcmag.com

Buildings
www.buildings.com

Commercial Investment Real Estate
www.ccim.com/magazine

Commercial Property Executive
www.cpexecutive.com

Design Cost Data
www.dcd.com

Economic Development Quarterly
http://edq.sagepub.com

Engineering News-Record (ENR)
www.enr.com

Estates Gazette
www.estatesgazette.com

Globe St.com
www.globest.com

Governing
www.governing.com

Institutional Real Estate Inc.
www.irei.com

JAPA: Journal of the American Planning Association
https://www.planning.org/japa

Journal of Property Investment & Finance
www.emeraldinsight.com/journal/jpif

Journal of Property Management
www.irem.org/JPM

Journal of Real Estate Finance and Economics
http://link.springer.com/journal/11146

Journal of Real Estate Literature
www.aresnet.org/pages/page_content/primary_publications_
journal-of-real-estate-literature.aspx

Journal of Real Estate Portfolio Management
www.aresnet.org/pages/page_content/primary_publications_
journal-of-real-estate-portfolio-management.aspx

Journal of Real Estate Practice and Education
www.aresnet.org/pages/page_content/primary_publications_
journal-of-real-estate-practice-and-education.aspx

Journal of Real Estate Research
www.aresnet.org/pages/page_content/primary_publications_
journal-of-real-estate-research.aspx

Journal of Sustainable Real Estate
www.aresnet.org/pages/page_content/primary_publications_
journal-of-sustainable-real-estate.aspx

National Real Estate Investor (NREI)
www.nreionline.com

New Urban News
bettercities.net

Planning
www.planning.org/planning

Practical Real Estate Lawyer
www.ali-cle.org/index.cfm?fuseaction=publications.
periodical&pub=PREL

Professional Builder
www.probuilder.com

Property Week
www.propertyweek.com

Real Estate Forum
www.globest.com/realestateforum/

Real Estate Weekly
www.rew-online.com

Urban Affairs Review
http://uar.sagepub.com/

Urban Land
http://urbanland.uli.org

Journals and Magazines: Specialized

Chain Store Age
www.chainstoreage.com

Development
www.naiop.org/en/magazine.aspx

Developments
www.arda.org

Hotel Business
www.hotelbusiness.com

Hotels
www.hotelsmag.com

Inside Self-Storage
www.insideselfstorage.com

Multifamily Executive
www.multifamilyexecutive.com

Multi-Housing News
www.multihousingnews.com

Parking
http://weareparking.org/?page=Parking_Magazine

Parking Professional
www.parking.org/publications/the-parking-professional-
magazine.aspx

Shopping Center Business
www.shoppingcenterbusiness.com

Shopping Centers Today
www.icsc.org/sct/sct-usa/

Value Retail News
www.valueretailnews.com

Units
http://units.naahq.org

Index